A

COMMENTARY

on the

NEW TESTAMENT

by Robert Hawker

Volume One
The Gospels

Solid Ground Christian Books
Birmingham, Alabama USA

Solid Ground Christian Books
2090 Columbiana Rd. Suite 2000
Birmingham AL 35216
205-443-0311
sgcb@charter.net
http://solid-ground-books.com

The Poor Man's New Testament Commentary: Volume One
by Robert Hawker (1753-1827)

Taken from the 1815 edition by Sherwood, Neely and Jones of London

ISBN – 1-932474-36-6

Acknowledgements

This reprint of Robert Hawker's *Poor Man's Commentary* has been accomplished, in God's good providence, by the assistance of many in the United States and England, who desire to see this excellent work made available to the public again. We wish to acknowledge and express thanks to them for their work and generosity. Mr. Jeremy Roe, Ossett, West Yorkshire, England, allowed us to use his set of Hawker's commentary for the reprint. And the following churches provided funds for the layout and printing costs.

Bethel Baptist Church
Spring Lake, North Carolina
Rupert Rivenbark, Pastor

Sovereign Grace Baptist Church
The Dalles, Oregon
Norm Wells, Pastor

Grace Baptist Church of Danville
Danville, Kentucky
Don Fortner, Pastor

The Poor Man's Commentary may be obtained in Great Britain through

CBO Publications
21 Queen Street
Ossett
West Yorkshire
WF5 8AS
www.christianbookshopossett.co.uk

Foreword

I have long cherished my nine-volume set of Robert Hawker's *Poor Man's Commentary on the Old and New Testaments*, not so much for its exegetical expertise as for its heartwarming, devotional character. Hawker's six volumes on the Old Testament and three on the New Testament, which contain the entire text of the Authorized Version of the Scriptures, are highly informative on certain texts but make little or no comment on other texts. Obviously, Hawker did not aim for the exegetical acuity of John Calvin, the homiletical breadth of Matthew Henry, or the pastoral succinctness of Matthew Poole. Rather, his purpose was to edify believers by providing spiritual and experiential comments on each section of Scripture. Consequently, these volumes are most profitable as a daily devotional rather than as a regular commentary. The prayerful "reflections" section that follows Hawker's comments on each chapter of Scripture marvelously enhance this devotional character. They alone are worth the purchase of these volumes. Here is one sample to whet your appetite. Reflecting on John 18, Hawker writes:

> Oh! Gethsemane! Sacred, hallowed spot! Did Jesus oft-times resort thither with his disciples? And wilt thou now, O LORD, by thy sweet Spirit, aid my meditations, that I may take the wing of faith and often traverse over the solemn ground? It was a garden in which the first Adam began to break through the fence of God's holy plantation. And in a garden the second Adam, so called, shall begin the soul-travail of sorrow, to do away the effects of it. And, oh! What humiliation, what agonies, what conflicts in the arduous work? Oh! How vast the glory, when smiting to the earth his enemies, the LORD JESUS proved his GODHEAD by the breath of his mouth! Sweetly do I see thee, LORD, by faith, going forth a willing sacrifice. Lo! I come! said JESUS. So come, LORD, now, by grace!
>
> Hail, thou King of Zion, for thou hast here most blessedly borne testimony to this glorious truth. Then as a King do thou reign and rule over thy Church, thy people, both in heaven and earth. And let my soul continually discover the goings of my GOD and King, in his sanctuary. Surely, dear LORD, it is thine, both by nature, providence, grace, and glory, to maintain and order, to regulate and appoint, to establish and confirm thy royal laws, and the government of thy kingdom, in the hearts and minds of all thy people, whom thou hast made willing in the day of thy power! Reign thou, and rule in me, the LORD of life and glory! Amen.

Hawker's devotional commentary is so named because it was originally published in small "penny" portions to be affordable to the poor. The New Testament portions were gathered and published in four volumes in 1815 and 1816 by W. Stratford of London. A few years before he died, Hawker completed a new edition, titled *The Poor Man's Commentary on the New Testament: A new edition, corrected, with final amendments of the author*, 4 vols. (London: Printed for Sherwood, Gilbert, and Piper by B. M'Millan, 1823-26). By 1850, several improved editions had been published in three volumes. Though Hawker's other writings were reprinted in the twentieth century, his commentary was not. We are grateful that Solid Ground Christian Books is making this edifying work available again. We commend it for private and family worship.

Hawker was a prolific author and Calvinist preacher in the Church of England who, like Samuel Rutherford, became known for his love for Christ. That love is abundant on nearly every page of his comments as well as throughout his reflections. Hawker excels in Christ-centered, experiential divinity. He was taught by the Spirit how to find Christ in the Scriptures, as well as how to present Him to hungry sinners in search of daily communion with a personal Redeemer. For the genuine Christian, here is devotional writing at its best: it is always warmly Christ-centered, eminently practical, personally searching.

The only definitive biography of Hawker is by John Williams, who sat under Hawker's ministry before becoming pastor of Stroud, Gloucestershire. That biography is in the preface to volume 1 of Hawker's *Works* and was first published in 1831. Of Hawker's writings, Williams notes, "His remarks exhibit a great warmth of affection, a lively energy of expression, a graceful flow of language, and an affluent store of scriptural sentiments. There is a lovely simplicity in his sublimest thoughts, and in his humblest themes a becoming dignity."

Robert Hawker was born to God-fearing parents April 13, 1753, at Exeter, England. His father, a reputable surgeon, and his young sister died when he was an infant. He was raised by his mother with the help of two aunts, one of whom taught him to memorize numerous portions of Scripture before he went to school. The memorized Scripture served him well throughout his long ministry and convinced him that the early education of all children should be centered on the Word of God. Out of this conviction, Hawker compiled *The Child's First and Second Books*, consisting of simple lessons or illustrations from Scripture.

As a child, Hawker attended Exeter's grammar school, where he learned Greek and Latin. His mother, who wanted her son to be a physician like his father, had him study surgery and medicine under Dr. White, a surgeon from Plymouth.

At the age of eighteen, Hawker married Anne Rains. They had eight children. Hawker pursued further training in the hospitals of London prior to spending three years as assistant surgeon in the royal marines. Against this background, he would later write *Zion's Warrior, or the Christian Soldier's Manual*, in which he described the spiritual dimensions of the duties and occupations of the military life.

While in the marines, Hawker had numerous religious impressions and decided to pursue the ministry. He entered Oxford University as a member of Magdalen Hall in 1778. He took holy orders and became curate of St. Martin for three months prior to becoming curate to John Bedford, vicar of Charles, near Plymouth. Upon Bedford's death in 1784, Hawker became vicar of Charles, where he enjoyed the love and respect of his congregation for the next forty-three years. He was buried on his seventy-fourth birthday, Good Friday, 1827.

In his early years as pastor of Charles, Hawker corrected his erroneous views on the doctrines of grace. He abandoned his former convictions that a sinner's salvation depended upon an act of free will and embraced the Calvinistic doctrines of salvation by Christ alone, through grace alone.

Hawker reached out to people beyond Charles through his prolific writing and a variety of religious activities. In 1792 he was awarded a doctorate of divinity by Edinburgh University for his *Sermons on the Divinity of Christ*. In 1797 he accepted the deputy-chaplaincy of the garrison at Plymouth. In 1802 he founded The Great Western Society for Dispersing Religious Tracts among the Poor. In 1813 he established the Corpus Christi Society, which aimed to provide spiritual and financial relief to "the body of Christ."

Meanwhile, Hawker increased in fame and popularity as a powerful "high Calvinist" preacher. He rejected indiscriminate gospel offers and invitations on theological grounds, yet was remarkably winsome in preaching Christ to all. He believed in "holding up" Christ to all rather than offering him to all. For many years, he annually visited London where he preached to crowds in some of the city's most renowned pulpits and was much used for the conversion of sinners and the edification of saints.

Hawker's major writings are included in his ten volumes of works except for *The Poor Man's Commentary on the Old and New*

Testaments. Other principal books not yet mentioned include *The Poor Man's Morning and Evening Portion*, which became his most popular work; *Sermons on the Divinity and Operations of the Holy Spirit*; *Paraclesis, or Consolations for a Dying Hour*; *Zion's Pilgrim*; *The Sailor Pilgrim*; *Visits to and from Jesus upon the most interesting occasions*; *Lectures on the Person, Godhead, and Ministry of the Holy Ghost*; *The Poor Man's Concordance and Dictionary to the Sacred Scriptures*; *Catechisms and Books for the Use of Children*. His works contain nearly a hundred articles on various subjects, two volumes of sermons, and a volume of expositions of "Scripture extracts."

Hawker lived and died by the doctrines of free grace. On the day after his seventieth birthday, he wrote:

> From the first dawn of the day-spring which from on high visited me, when the Lord was pleased to bring me into acquaintance with myself, and to make me know the plague of my own heart, I have been unlearning what I had before been studying with so much care—how to recommend myself by human merit to divine favour. But when the Lord in mercy took me under his pupilage, he inverted this order of teaching. I was then led to see more of his ways, and to think less of my own. And from that hour of matriculation in his school to the present, I have been learning to get daily out of love with myself, and in love with Christ. And so it hath proved, that in the exact ratio in which I have advanced in the knowledge and love of the Lord, and in the ways of grace, I have been going back in my estimation of all creature excellency and creature attainments.

As a daily devotional or in family worship, let these volumes of Hawker bring the Word of God close to your conscience. Above all, pray for the Spirit to apply his writing to you, so that Christ may increase in you and self may decrease (John 3:30). That, after all, was Hawker's great goal.

Joel R. Beeke
Puritan Reformed Theological Seminary
Grand Rapids, Michigan

A
COMMENTARY

ON THE

NEW TESTAMENT.

THE GOSPEL ACCORDING TO

SAINT MATTHEW.

GENERAL OBSERVATIONS ON THE GOSPEL ACCORDING TO ST. MATTHEW.

ONE general observation will meet the Reader, at his entrance, on all the *four* Books of the Evangelists : namely, that they are directed to one and the same interesting subject. They form a corresponding harmony and agreement, in giving the history of the blessed JESUS. And they form therefore, when taken together, the whole of those inspired records, which GOD the HOLY GHOST hath thought proper to give to the Church, concerning the Person, Life, Ministry, Miracles, Discourses, Death, Resurrection, Ascension, and unchanging Priesthood of the Almighty SAVIOR of the world, *whom truely to know is life eternal.*

The word Gospel is borrowed from the Saxons, the early inhabitants of this island. They were accustomed to call our holy faith by this name. And hence, it is probable, that it hath been ever since distinguished by this title. But perhaps it was not always pronounced, as we are now accustomed to do, by the name *Gospel;* but rather *God's-spell,* meaning *God's blessing.* And surely, it is in the highest and fullest sense of the word, the greatest blessing which ever the LORD JEHOVAH bestowed upon mankind, in the gospel of salvation, by GOD's dear SON.

In the present acceptation of the word Gospel, is meant *glad tidings; great joy to all people.* And in this sense also it must be allowed, that CHRIST and his salvation is the most joyful tidings which were ever proclaimed to sinful, dying men. So much so, that one of the Prophets declared the very feet of them who were sent to preach it, were beau-

tiful. Isaiah lii. 7. Nay, angels themselves, as if earnest to
become the first heralds of such blissful tidings to a lost world,
hastened to come down upon the earth the moment the news
brake out in heaven, and in a multitude together sung the
song of redemption : *Glory* (said they) *to* GOD *in the highest,
and on earth peace; good will toward men.* Luke ii. 10—14.

The Gospel, according to St. *Matthew*, opens with the
genealogy of the LORD JESUS CHRIST, in the time of *Joseph*
his reputed father; as that of the Evangelist *Luke*, traces the
pedigree in the line of the Virgin *Mary*. And *Matthew*,
carries on the history of CHRIST through the whole of our
LORD'S continuance upon earth; including a period of about
three and thirty years and half. But the exercise of CHRIST'S
ministry did not exceed *three years and half.* Luke iii. 23.

The name of *Matthew*, or *Matthai*, signifies a *gift*, or a
thing *given*. And this was not an unsuitable name for this
Evangelist, for he might be truly said to be given to CHRIST.
And thus the LORD JESUS speaks of his people, to whom he
manifested his FATHER'S name, that they were the men whom
he had *given* him out of the world. Of such, JESUS said,
that all whom the FATHER had *given* him, must *come to him;
and him that came, he would in no wise cast out.* John xvii.
6, 9, compared with John vi. 37. But besides this name of
Matthew, he was also called *Levi.* Luke v. 27. And this
double name seems to decide, that though a *publican* by office,
yet was *Matthew* a *Jew* by birth. For it was common with
the children of Israel to give two names to their children;
but not so generally with other nations. The history of *Matthew*, and his wonderful conversion, will meet the Reader in
its proper place. I only here detain him in those general observations, to remark, that as a Son of *Abraham*, his engaging
in the odious calling of a tax-gatherer for the *Romans*, which
they called a *Publican*, and which the children of Israel considered as oppressive, must have been the more intolerable to
them when performed by any of the seed of *Abraham*.

The Gospel of *Matthew*, is supposed by *some*, to have
been written as early as within *eight* years after our LORD'S
ascension. But *others* place it at a later period, even to *fifteen*
years. However, in either case, supposing the latest of the
two, it may serve to teach us how graciously GOD the HOLY
GHOST watched over the Church, that before that generation
was passed away; among whom the wonderful actions of the
LORD JESUS had been wrought; the records were made for the
benefit of all succeeding ages of the Church, to the consummation of all things.

I shall make no further observations in a way of preliminary
to the Gospel of St. *Matthew*, but proceed with the Reader to
the perusal of the Gospel itself: praying only, that the same

gracious LORD who called *Matthew* from the receipt of custom, may, by the ministry of his writings, call many *from darkness to light, and from the power of Sin and Satan to the living* GOD. And, if the LORD will condescend to make this *Poor Man's Commentary* upon it useful to the blessed purpose, that both Reader and Writer may find the unction of the HOLY GHOST upon it, as they prosecute the delightful subject: may they be enabled to invite the LORD JESUS to their houses and hearts, as this Evangelist did; and call many Publicans and Sinners to sit down to the holy feast with JESUS and his disciples; that many, many may be the partakers of *this glorious Gospel of the ever blessed God.*

CHAP. I.

CONTENTS.

The Gospel opens with the relation of the genealogy of CHRIST *after the flesh. We have an account of the miraculous conception:* CHRIST'S *birth and name.*

THE book of the generation of Jesus Christ, the son of David, the son of Abraham.

There is somewhat very striking and particular in this opening of the Gospel. The Old Testament begins with the account of the Creation. The New Testament begins with the account of Him, by whom all things were created. Heb. i. 1, 2. The great design of this pedigree concerning CHRIST after the flesh, is to prove CHRIST'S lineal descent from *Abraham.* For unless this be proved, the evidence that CHRIST is the promised seed, would be wanting. *For to Abraham and his seed were the promises made. He saith not to seeds as of many, but as of one, and to thy seed which is* CHRIST. Compare Gal. iii. 16. with Gen. xii. 3. and Gen. xxii. 18. Hence, therefore, the importance of this pedigree is evident. And the correctness of the one here given, is striking. I beg the Reader to observe it with a suitableness equal to its consequence. Perhaps it were a thing impossible in any other instance, but in the genealogy of CHRIST, to find among all the pedigrees of the Jews, from the days of our LORD to this hour, a correct genealogy of any one house, or tribe, or family, even for *fourteen* generations together: whereas in this of CHRIST, we have *three times fourteen.* What can more decidedly manifest the over-ruling providence and watchfulness of GOD!

2 Abraham begat Isaac; and Isaac begat Jacob; and Jacob begat Judas and his brethren;

3 And Judas begat Phares and Zara of Thamar; and Pharez begat Esrom; and Esrom begat Aram;

4 And Aram begat Aminadab; and Aminadab begat Naasson; and Naasson begat Salmon;

5 And Salmon begat Booz of Rachab; and Booz begat Obed of Ruth; and Obed begat Jesse;

6 And Jesse begat David the king; and David the king begat Solomon of her *that had been the wife* of Urias;

7 And Solomon begat Roboam; and Roboam begat Abia; and Abia begat Asa;

8 And Asa begat Josaphat; and Josaphat begat Joram; and Joram begat Ozias;

9 And Ozias begat Joatham; and Joatham begat Achaz; and Achaz begat Ezekias;

10 And Ezekias begat Manasses; and Manasses begat Amon; and Amon begat Josias;

11 And Josias begat Jechonias and his brethren, about the time they were carried away to Babylon:

12 And after they were brought to Babylon, Jechonias begat Salathiel; and Salathiel begat Zorobabel;

13 And Zorobabel begat Abiud; and Abiud begat Eliakim; and Eliakim begat Azor;

14 And Azor begat Sadoc; and Sadoc begat Achim; and Achim begat Eliud;

15 And Eliud begat Eleazar; and Eleazar begat Matthan; and Matthan begat Jacob;

16 And Jacob begat Joseph the husband of Mary, of whom was born Jesus, who is called Christ.

There would be nothing particularly necessary for me to detain the Reader with in going over this pedigree of names, more than to mark the correctness, if the mere pedigree was all. But there is somewhat more worth noticing in this genealogy: and I venture to believe, that God the HOLY GHOST did intend that the Church should make other observations upon the record here given, and therefore I beg to point them out as they strike me.

In the *first* place, I desire the Reader not to overlook the pointed reference in every name here mentioned to the LORD JESUS CHRIST. *Abraham* had many sons beside *Isaac*, but none are noticed but him.

And the reason is plain. The promise in the charter of grace was, *in Isaac shall thy seed be called.* And hence to all the other Sons of *Abraham;* the *Ishmaels,* and the *Esaus,* of every generation, there is no respect. Amos iii. 2.

Secondly, In this pedigree we find many of the characters whose lives gave evident proof, that though by *nature* they were in the ancestry of CHRIST, yet in *grace* they had no relation to him. Not to enter into many particular proofs, it may be observed, that *Roboam,* (or *Rehoboam,) Abia,* and *Jechonias,* are marked in Scripture under peculiar tokens of divine displeasure. 1 Kings xii. 15. 1 Kings xv. 3. 2 Kings xxiv. 9. Jerem. xxii. 24, &c. Now the Reader ought to make due remarks upon these circumstances, in proof that grace is not hereditary. It descends not from father to son. Yea, on the contrary we are told, that *they which are sons of* GOD, *are born not of blood, nor of the will of the flesh, nor of the will of man, but of* GOD. John i. 12, 13. And what a sweet thought to a child of GOD is the consideration, that from our union with CHRIST, as it was with the LORD JESUS when upon earth; so will it be with his people in heaven: *Whosoever* (said JESUS) *shall do the will of my* FATHER *which is in heaven, the same is my brother, and sister, and mother!* Matt. xii. 50.

Thirdly. It is remarkable in this pedigree of the LORD JESUS, that there are *four* names recorded in the female line; and *three* of them, in point of moral characters, are spoken of as exceptionable. *Thamar* is she with whom *Judah* committed incest. Gen. xxxviii. 13. to the end. *Rachab* (or *Rahab)* the harlot. Joshua ii. 1. Heb. xi. 31. James ii. 25. And *Bathsheba,* with whom *David* committed adultery. 2 Sam. xi. 3, 4. Let the Reader pause over this view. We know that CHRIST was made *sin for us, who knew no sin.* And he was also made *a curse for us.* And he was made *in the likeness of sinful flesh.* See 2 Cor. v. 21. Gal. iii. 13. Rom. viii. 3. All these things are explained to us in the causes and reasons for the wonderful appointment. But was it needful also, that his holy, spotless nature should come through such channels of sin, and uncleanness? Was it absolutely necessary that He who was separate from sinners, and made higher than the heavens, should be thus manifested to his Church by such ancestry? Reader! ponder well the subject! And do not overlook in it the unequalled humility of the SON of GOD!

Fourthly. I beg to detain the Reader with one observation more on this pedigree of JESUS. We find *Rahab* and *Ruth,* in this genealogy of CHRIST. Now both these women were Gentiles. *Rahab,* of *Jericho;* and *Ruth,* of *Moab.* And yet are here incorporated with Israel, and from this union after the flesh CHRIST came. Was this to shew, that though with Israel was deposited the promises, yet the Church of JESUS should be made of both Jew and Gentile? And, as in after ages, when redemption-work was finished, and the middle wall of partition taken down, both should be brought into one fold; yet before all this, yea, before the coming of CHRIST, the alliance of JESUS with his *Gentile* Church, as well as with the *Jewish,* should be shewn and proved by such an union as CHRIST after the flesh, arising out of both? Reader! ponder this well also, for it is blessed. See Isaiah xlix. 6. Gal. iii. 28.

17 So all the generations from Abraham to David *are* fourteen generations; and from David until the carrying away into Babylon *are* fourteen generations; and from the carrying away into Babylon unto Christ *are* fourteen generations.

I think it more than probable, that the HOLY GHOST had some object in view in the division made of the three equal proportions of *fourteen* generations, in this genealogy of CHRIST. But though I am inclined to this opinion, yet I am free to confess I cannot explain it. But surely GOD the SPIRIT must have watched over those records with peculiar regard, or they could not but have been lost during the wars of *Canaan*, and the captivity in *Babylon*, which followed. And the correctness of this genealogy by *Matthew*, is striking. For the *Targum* is in perfect correspondence with it, only with this difference, and which is yet worthy of more particular regard, for that difference; namely, that while both the *Targum*, and *Matthew*, make the number of the generations from *Zorobabel fourteen*: the *Targum* call the last *Anani*, saying at the same time, " this is the King Messiah, who is to be revealed." And this is worthy of the greater attention, in that as the *Targum* is supposed to have began in the days of *Ezra*; therefore the *Messiah*, according to their own tradition, must have been long since. So that here is an additional evidence, (if it were needed,) to all *the cloud of witnesses* with which we are encompassed, *to the truth as it is in* JESUS.

18 ¶ Now the birth of Jesus Christ was on this wise: When as his mother Mary was espoused to Joseph, before they came together, she was found with child of the Holy Ghost.

. The subject of the miraculous conception, here intimated, being in itself so highly momentous, I would beg the Reader to attend to it with an affection equal to its vast importance. For this once admitted, brings up after it the glorious doctrine of the Atonement, with all the blessings connected with redemption. Let us consider therefore the subject particularly.

The expression here used respecting the miraculous conception, is most striking indeed. The birth of JESUS CHRIST was on this wise: *Mary was found with child of the* HOLY GHOST. And the parallel passage in *Luke*, is to the same amount. *The* HOLY GHOST *shall come upon thee, and the power of the Highest shall overshadow thee.* Luke i. 35. Hence it must undeniably follow, that the conception was without the intervention of an human father, and wrought by the express work of GOD the HOLY GHOST. And, as if to confirm this still more, the Angel further declared, that what was conceived in the womb of the Virgin Mary, was of the HOLY GHOST. Verse 20. So much then in proof of the agency of GOD the HOLY GHOST.

Let us next enquire, what Scripture speaketh further of divine agency on this wonderful subject. That GOD the FATHER had an hand in this great work, is as plainly declared by CHRIST himself,

under the spirit of prophecy. For, speaking to the FATHER of the
inefficacy in all sacrifices to take away sin, and making a voluntary
offer of himself, JESUS saith, *A body hast thou prepared me.* Compare
Psm. xl. 6. with Heb. x. 5. And elsewhere, speaking still in the
spirit of prophecy, CHRIST saith, *Thou hast covered me in my mother's womb. I am fearfully and wonderfully made: when I was made
in secret, and curiously wrought on the lowest parts of the earth;* that
is, the dark chamber of his mother's womb. Psm. cxxxix. 13, 14, 15.

Hence, therefore, in the agency of GOD the FATHER, which is
here most plainly shewn, added to what we before noticed of the work
of GOD the HOLY GHOST, every thing most decidedly proves, that the
conception was wholly miraculous.

Let us next call into our view what the Scriptures relate concerning *Mary.* That she was what the Jews called *Almah,* that is, a
pure virgin, will never be questioned by those who believe the word
of GOD. And therefore I shall not think it at all necessary to dwell
upon it. But, what I wish chiefly to have impressed upon the Reader's
mind, respecting the part *Mary* bore in the miraculous conception, is
this, that no taint of our corrupt nature was taken into the act. The
promise at the fall was, *the seed of the woman* should bruise the
serpent's head. And therefore CHRIST, to fulfil this promise, must
be of *the seed of the woman.* By his incarnation in her womb, he
fully proved this. But then this incarnation being without an human
father, and accomplished wholly by the work of both GOD the FATHER
and GOD the HOLY GHOST; the mere act of conception was all which
Mary bore in the great deed. And as this conception was not by
generation, in the ordinary way, so there was nothing in it that could
pollute or defile. The angel's message to Joseph, most clearly shews
this: *fear not,* said he, *to take unto thee Mary thy wife, for that
which is conceived in her is of the* HOLY GHOST.

And I desire the Reader to consider the subject yet further, for
it is a point never to be lost sight of on this occasion. CHRIST is no
where said in the scripture to be *begotten* of a woman, but *made* of
a woman. GOD sent forth his SON, *made* of a woman. Gal. iv. 4.
And who was the maker but GOD the FATHER? *A body hast thou
prepared me.* And who wrought upon the body of the Virgin *Mary*
but GOD the HOLY GHOST? *The* HOLY GHOST *shall come upon thee,
and the power of the Highest shall overshadow thee.* Now mark
what follows. *Therefore also that* HOLY THING *which shall be born
of thee, shall be called the* SON *of* GOD. So that it was not *man
generating,* but GOD the HOLY GHOST *overshadowing.* Had Mary's
conception been by the act of generation by man, no doubt but the
same taint of sin must have followed, as follows all the generations
of our race. Then, (as *David* said of his mother, and we may all say
of ours,) *in sin did my mother conceive me.* Psm. li. 5. But the Virgin's
womb became only the sacred chamber of formation; whereas CHRIST
saith, he was *fearfully and wonderfully made.* And her conception
was of that pure and *holy Thing* as the angel called CHRIST, being
wrought by the HOLY GHOST, which was *holy, harmless, undefiled;
separate from sinners, and made higher than the heavens.* And hence
was fulfilled that which the Prophet was appointed to foretell. *The
LORD hath created a new thing in the earth, a woman shall compass a*

man. Jerem. xxxi. 22. Hence CHRIST also is called *the second man, the* LORD *from heaven.* 1 Cor. xv. 47.

If I have succeeded in stating the scripture account of this most sublime subject, in terms sufficiently plain to be understood by the Reader of my *Poor Man's Commentary;* I shall hope, under divine teaching, that the Reader will not only henceforth be led to form proper and just apprehensions of the miraculous conception; but also be taught to connect with it the great and glorious doctrine of the atonement, which immediately follows. For wherefore was this miraculous conception of *Mary,* and this holy incarnation of CHRIST, but for the express purpose to make his soul an offering for sin? And wherefore this offering for sin, but *to do away sin by the sacrifice of himself?* And now the LORD JESUS CHRIST, having by that one offering of himself, once offered, *finished transgression, made an end of sin, made reconciliation for iniquity, and brought in an everlasting righteousness:* this righteousness is *to all, and upon all that believe:* for by that *one offering of himself once offered, he hath perfected for ever them that are sanctified.* See Dan. ix. 24. Rom. iii. 21, 22. Heb. x. 14.

19 Then Joseph her husband, being a just *man,* and not willing to make her a public example, was minded to put her away privily.

For the better apprehension of what is here said, it should be remembered, that it was the custom among the Jews to betroth, or make engagements for future marriages, before that any intention was formed of the time when the nuptials were to be consummated. Sometimes those betrothings were made years before the parties came together. Yea, Jewish parents sometimes contracted for their children, before the young persons had any knowledge of, and much less a predilection for, each other. Hence, in case afterwards matters arose of difference, there was a law made for disannulling. See Deut. xxii. 23, 24, and Deut. xxiv. 1, &c. Such was the case of *Joseph* and *Mary.* They were but betrothed to each other, though Mary is here called his wife. So that the miraculous conception took place before that they came together. Joseph is here represented as deliberating how to act on the occasion. And it must be confessed, that it affords an amiable picture of his mind.

20 But while he thought on these things, behold, the angel of the LORD appeared unto him in a dream, saying, Joseph, thou son of David, fear not to take unto thee Mary thy wife: for that which is conceived in her is of the Holy Ghost.

21 ¶ And she shall bring forth a son, and thou shalt call his name JESUS: for he shall save his people from their sins.

It is very probable that this was the same angel which announced to *Mary* the first tidings of her miraculous impregnation. And the

Church hath found cause to bless the LORD for his ministry. For without it we should not have had ability to have formed suitable and becoming conceptions, equal to what, under grace, we are now enabled to do, of an event in which we are so highly concerned. See Luke i. 26, &c.

I detain the Reader at this scripture, while observing the name of our adorable LORD, and the reason assigned by the angel, wherefore He is called JESUS, just to remark, what a precious name it hath been in all ages of the Church; it still is, and will be through all eternity. It is the same name, in point of significancy, as that of *Joshua*, or *Hoshea*, both meaning a Savior. One of the old writers hath made a very sweet and comprehensive sense of it, when he said, " In the name of JESUS, the whole of the Gospel is hid: for it is the light, the food, the medicine, yea, the very life of the soul." And if the Reader also makes his full remark upon the angel's words, he will say the same. *Thou shalt call his name* JESUS! Wherefore? It is immediately answered. *For he shall save his people from their sins.* Now observe the beauty and blessedness of those expressions. JESUS had a people then, even before his incarnation. And it was known, that this people would be sinners. And a provision was therefore made, in the grace of GOD, for their recovery, even before they had a being. And the very office of JESUS, is to save them from their sins. Yea, the very reason why he is called JESUS, is on this account. Precious LORD JESUS! I would say, Oh give thy people grace to see thee, and to know thee, in this most blessed name, and never to hear this sweet name, or to call upon thee by it, without connecting with it the angel's words. *Thou shalt call his name* JESUS; *for he shall save his people from their sins.* See Gen. xxii. 8—18. Psm. lxxii. 17. Isaiah vii. 14. Jerem. xxiii. 6. Dan. ix. 24. Acts iv. 12. Heb. vii. 25.

22 Now all this was done, that it might be fulfilled which was spoken of the Lord, by the prophet, saying,

23 Behold, a Virgin shall be with child, and shall bring forth a son, and they shall call his name Emmanuel; which being interpreted is, God with us.

It is always blessed when we are enabled by the Spirit's teaching, to find out the beautiful correspondence between one scripture and another, upon the same subject; for then we behold how one explains the other. Thus, as in this instance. The Prophet *Isaiah*, more than seven hundred years before the coming of CHRIST, declared the miraculous impregnation of a virgin: and at the same time told what the name of the son she should conceive and bring forth, should be called, in proof of the mysterious union of his nature, of GOD and man, in one person. See Isaiah vii. 14. Now here the event is accomplished, and the Evangelist refers back to that scripture in proof. Think, Reader, of the wonderful correspondence! Who but GOD could have foretold? What power less than GOD, could have brought it to pass? And I beg the Reader to remark yet further; every thing in the prediction was mysterious. That a virgin should conceive; and that a virgin should bring forth a son. For the mysterious part was that she continued in both still a virgin. For there would have been nothing mysterious or uncommon, that a virgin should conceive, if the ordinary means for conception had been used. But the very prophecy implied what the fact proved, that it was without human means the virgin conceived; and when she brought forth her son, still she remained a virgin. And hence the grand infinite importance of the whole design; to accomplish redemption. And here I beg the Reader to ponder well the subject, and then let him with me humbly enquire, (for I do not presume to speak decidedly upon the subject) was not all this preached by the Hᴏʟʏ Gʜᴏsᴛ to the Church, in that law of Moses: *Whatsoever openeth the womb among the children of Israel, both of man and beast, it is mine.* Exod. xiii. 2. I humbly ask this question; was not this preaching Cʜʀɪsᴛ, at every birth of the first-born? And was not this law enjoined wholly on Cʜʀɪsᴛ's account? See then, Reader, if so, how Jᴇʜᴏᴠᴀʜ had an eye all along to this one great and glorious event. And then think, how precious the event of Cʜʀɪsᴛ's incarnation ought to be in our eye! But I beg to make one observation more on this interesting passage.—Though the Lᴏʀᴅ commanded the first-born, both of man and beast, to be sanctified to him, as a type of Jᴇsᴜs; yet, strictly and properly speaking, the opening of the womb at the birth cannot be called the *first* opening, either in man or beast. This must have taken place before. But, in the instance of Cʜʀɪsᴛ, and him *only*, it was strictly and properly so. He, and he alone, opened the womb. So that here, as in all other points, Jᴇsᴜs must have the pre-eminence. The types of Him could come no nearer in resemblance, than what is said of them. But Cʜʀɪsᴛ, miraculously conceived and miraculously born, truly and properly, in both acts, conception and birth, opened the womb of the virgin; as in the great work of redemption afterwards by his resurrection, he opened the womb of the earth. So that it was Cʜʀɪsᴛ, and Cʜʀɪsᴛ only, of whom Jᴇʜᴏᴠᴀʜ spake in all those scriptures, which declared, that *whatsoever opened the womb*, should be *sanctified to the* Lᴏʀᴅ. Hence He, and He only, became the true Nazarite to Gᴏᴅ. Oh! what beauties are there in the scriptures of our Gᴏᴅ! And what sweet, soul satisfying evidences do they bring with them, at the same time of the truth of our most holy faith. Reader! I pray you to be very cheery of them, in the present day of rebuke and blasphemy; and beg of Gᴏᴅ the Hᴏʟʏ Gʜᴏsᴛ, to enable you to bind them as frontlets between your eyes. They are always precious to a believer. And they will be eminently so, if I greatly mistake not, to the rising generation, in proportion as those glorious truths, in this land, will be less and less regarded. See John xvii. 19. Luke i. 35. Levit. xxvii. 26. Numb. iii. 13. Luke ii. 23, &c. Luke xviii. 8.

24 ¶ Then Joseph being raised from sleep did as the angel of the Lord had bidden him, and took unto him his wife:

25 And knew her not till she had brought forth
her first-born son: and he called his name JESUS.

There is a great sweetness and modesty in the original word, for
knowing her not. And the chastity of scripture language, is ever
to be admired and esteemed. How much it teacheth a chastity
of conversation among the people of GOD; even, when necessity at
any time constrains us to speak of what relates to the present infirmities of our poor fallen nature.—When it is said, that *Mary* continued in the single state *unto the birth of Christ;* it saith no more
than what the prophecy declared. A virgin was to conceive, and a
virgin bring forth a son. This was literally accomplished. So that
no question should arise concerning the chastity of the virgin, until
the birth of CHRIST was accomplished. Very much hath been both
said and written, in respect to the cohabitation of *Mary* with *Joseph,*
after the birth of CHRIST. But the scriptures are wholly silent upon
the subject. And therefore it becomes the Church of GOD to be silent
also. Whether Mary did, or did not, continue in a single state, is
no article of faith. All the after events of her life were to herself,
and not to the Church. And it should seem, from the words of
the LORD JESUS to her, at the marriage feast in *Cana* of *Galilee,*
as if the LORD would discourage his people from ascribing unsuitable honors to the virgin. Though she was declared by the angel
to be highly favored and blessed among women, in being singled
out for the high honor in the miraculous conception; yet, in all other
points, *Mary* stood upon the same footing with every child of GOD
in the Covenant. And that *Mary* herself considered it as such, and
looked for salvation, as all others of the redeemed do, in and by
CHRIST, is evident from the song she sung upon the occasion: Mary
said, *My soul doth magnify the* LORD, *and my spirit hath rejoiced in*
GOD *my* SAVIOR. Luke i. 46, 47, &c.

REFLECTIONS.

PAUSE, Reader! at this opening of the Gospel of JESUS CHRIST,
the SON of GOD; and while beholding the relation of the pedigree of
CHRIST, after the flesh, who was made *not after the genealogy of a
carnal commandment, but after the power of an endless life;* well may
we both cry out, with the astonishment of the Prophet, *Who shall
declare his generation?* Oh! for grace to discover the wonderful relationship between CHRIST and his people; and to exult with the
Church, in the glorious truth: *Unto us a child is born: unto us a son
is given: and the government shall be upon his shoulder: and he shall
be called Wonderful, Counsellor; the Mighty* GOD; *the Everlasting
Father, the Prince of Peace!*

And, Reader! as we have both such abundant cause, so let us seek
from the LORD all suited grace, to bless him for the discovery here
made; how the human nature of CHRIST was produced, by the body
which GOD the FATHER prepared him; and by the overshadowing
power of GOD the HOLY GHOST, by which he was conceived in the
womb of the virgin. Let us both bless GOD for the gracious re-

velations of this stupendous event; whereby the necessity of atonement, and the infinite importance of it, is most fully shewn. And oh! thou dear LORD JESUS; never, never, may any of the children lose sight of thine infinite condescension, who, though in the form of GOD, and with whom it was no robbery to be equal with GOD: yet didst thou make thyself of no reputation, and took upon thee the form of a servant, and was found in fashion as a man, and didst humble thyself even to the death of the cross!

LORD JESUS! give us to know thee, to love thee, to delight in thee, by every endearing name, and office, and character, in which thou standest revealed to thy people. Thou art indeed Emmanuel; GOD with us; GOD in us; GOD for us! Thou art JEHOVAH our righteousness. Thou art indeed JESUS, for in that sweet name is comprehended every other. And what endears it yet more to our hearts, thou hast commanded us to call thee so. For in this blessed scripture it is said, *Thou shalt call his name* JESUS; *for he shall save his people from their sins.* Amen.

CHAP. II.

CONTENTS.

We have here related to us the birth of CHRIST; *the visit of the Wise Men from the East, led by a star to worship him; the consternation induced in the minds of* Herod, *and the whole city of Jerusalem, at the event of* CHRIST's *birth; the ministry of an angel to Joseph, and the flight of Joseph, with his family, into Egypt.*

NOW when Jesus was born in Bethlehem of Judea, in the days of Herod the king, behold, there came wise men from the east to Jerusalem,

I detain the Reader at the very entrance on this Chapter, to remark several very interesting particulars in this short, but sweet account of the birth of the LORD JESUS after the flesh. *Bethlehem,* which signifies the *house of bread,* had been expressly declared by one of the Prophets to be the place which should be rendered sacred to this great event. Micah. v. 2. And what place so proper to give birth to JESUS, who is himself *the bread of life and the living bread?* John vi. 41 to 58. And as our misery and leanness arose from originally leaving this *Bethlehem,* as was typified. Ruth i. to 6. So the LORD JESUS CHRIST begins his salvation at the very spot where our ruin began. Moreover, the humbleness of the place became most highly suited for the humble SAVIOR to make his first appearance, in substance of our flesh.. For this *Bethlehem* was about five or six miles from Jerusalem, and a little city in *Judah.* Joshua xvii. 7. There was another *Bethlehem* in *Zebulon.* Joshua xix. 5. But as our LORD sprang out of *Judah,* so from *Judah,* in the midst of the tribes, he will arise. It was said of him, that he should *grow out of his place.* Zech. vi. 12. And here it is. I should not forget also to observe, that some have called *Bethlehem, the house of flesh;* for *Lechem* may be so rendered. And if so, the beauty of the expression is doubled. CHRIST calls his body *the flesh, which he will give for the life of the world.* And both *John* and *Paul,* use the same. John i. 14. 1 Tim. iii. 16. Reader! shall not you, and I, join the disciples' prayer! LORD! *evermore give us this bread!* 2 Sam. xxiii. 15. Luke ii. 4. to 20. Haggai ii. 7—9. Malachi iii. 1. John vi. 51 to 57.

2 Saying, Where is he that is born King of the Jews? for we have seen his star in the east, and are come to worship him.

I should be led to conceive, that this visit of the Wise Men was not immediately on the birth of CHRIST, but perhaps a considerable time after. Some have thought nearly *two years.* For as the flight into Egypt could not have been so immediately on the birth, we may reasonably infer, that the over-ruling providence of the LORD, did, in this instance, as in that of *Moses,* conceal the wonderful event to the most suited time for discovery. Exod. ii. 2. I mention this the rather, because it is no uncommon thing to behold representations of the virgin, and an infant, in pictures, by way of setting forth the nativity. Alas! how senseless and unbecoming are all such things in relation to the solemn subjects of holy scripture! And how much they degrade what they mean to embellish!—In relation to those wise men, we are wholly at conjecture who they were, or from whence, (more than from the East,) they came. Some have thought that they were men who practised magic, like *Balaam.* And it is remarkable, that this man prophesied of *a star which should come out of Jacob.* Numb. xxiv. 17. And JESUS himself is called *the bright and morning star.* Rev. xxii. 16. But be this as it may, certain it is that an angel from heaven proclaimed to the *Jewish* shepherds the birth of CHRIST. And why should it be thought incredible, that the same glorious intelligence was communicated to *Gentile* philosophers by the ministry of a star? Reader! let us both pause over this account of the wise men. Did they come from the East, over vast regions, to hail the SAVIOR? And shall not we feel constrained to welcome his approach? Did the LORD hang out in the heavens a light so direct to point to JESUS? And shall not you and I hope, that he will send out his light and his truth to guide us unto JESUS? Surely the grace shewn to those Gentiles ought to encourage us!

3 When Herod the king had heard *these things,* he was troubled, and all Jerusalem with him.

That *Herod* should be troubled at this intelligence was natural enough; and from the character which follows in this chapter of this unfeeling man, it is easy enough to discover the cause of his trouble. But that all Jerusalem should be troubled, which one might have thought would have shouted aloud for joy at the account; how strange is this representation. Zech. ii. 10, 11. But, Reader! such is the reception JESUS meets with from even his own people, until by his grace and Holy Spirit he shews them who he is, and how much they need him. Read Isaiah liii. 1, 2, 3. John i. 10, 11, 12, 13.

4 And when he had gathered all the chief priests and scribes of the people together, he demanded of them where Christ should be born !

Herod, it should seem by this question, was no stranger to the prophecies of scripture, and had heard how *Israel* expected a king, that should arise to deliver them from bondage. And though the children of *Israel*, no more than *Herod*, had the most distant idea that this deliverance was of a *spiritual* nature; yet it proves how general the expectation was at this time of the coming Savior. The dying *Jacob* had said, that *the sceptre should not depart from Judah, nor a lawgiver from between his feet, until the Shiloh should come.* Gen. xlix. 10. And now the intelligence is brought, and by wise men also, from the East, that the sovereign stranger is arrived. *Daniel* also had in his day mentioned the *time*. And from all calculations the time was fulfilled. Dan. ix. 24. to the end. Add to these, *Herod* knew, that he was by birth an *Edomite*, and a stranger, and therefore by the laws of Israel could not reign by just right. Deut. xvii. 15. See Psm. ii. 1—6. Acts iv. 27, 28. John xviii. 37.

5 And they said unto him, In Bethlehem of Judea: for thus it is written by the prophet,

6 And thou Bethlehem, *in* the land of Juda, art not the least among the princes of Juda: for out of thee shall come a Governor, that shall rule my people Israel.

It is very blessed to behold, how the LORD is causing both Jews and Gentiles to minister unto his dear Son. Let the Reader turn to the 60th chapter of the prophecy of Isaiah, and observe how the LORD declared the Church's glory in CHRIST; and compare what is there said with those Eastern sages worshipping CHRIST; and the Jewish chief priests and scribes bringing forward the prophecies of their scriptures concerning Him, whom afterwards they despised; and what testimonies by the way they become to *the truth as it is in JESUS!* If the Reader compares the passage from *Micah* with what is here said by the chief priests and scribes, he will perceive, that the quotation is not correct. But the difference is not great. And let it be remembered that it is not *Matthew* which quotes the passage from the Prophet, but the chief priests and scribes.

7 Then Herod, when he had privily called the wise men, enquired of them diligently what time the star appeared.

8 And he sent them to Bethlehem, and said, Go, and search diligently for the young child;

and when ye have found *him*, bring me word
again, that I may come and worship him also.

I would beg the Reader to pause over those verses, for several interesting circumstances of improvement arise from them. What an
awful picture is here drawn of the human heart, in the character of
Herod! He was now an old man; had long reigned; and this young
prince just born, supposing all that Herod might suppose of an
earthly monarchy could not, in the nature of things, hastily arise
to oppose him. And yet with what deep artifice and hypocrisy did
he cover over the cruel design he had formed of murdering the new-
born stranger. Look at the chief priests and scribes also. Though
they saw, as well as *Herod*, with what earnestness and labor the wise
men from the East had come, a vast journey to worship the king of
the Jews; yet they who were Jews, felt no concern about the glorious
æra of his birth; though their Prophets had so plainly declared both
the *place* and the *time* of his coming. The wise men were told where
they might find CHRIST; but none of the priests or scribes, it should
seem, went with them to see him. But, Reader! do not fail to remark
a circumstance yet more interesting than either; surely, it must have
been the LORD, by his providence, over-ruling things, that so JESUS
might remain in safety, until a more convenient season for his flight
into Egypt should arrive.

9 When they had heard the king, they departed; and, lo, the star which they saw in the east
went before them, till it came and stood over
where the young child was.

10 When they saw the star, they rejoiced with
exceeding great joy.

It appears that *Herod* had so disguised his intentions, that the wise
men had no consciousness of it. So is it in common life. But the
LORD readeth the heart. What a wonderful ministry was this star!
Evidently it must have had a particular motion, and different from
the ordinary course of the stars. For the star which had been first
seen by them in the East, now appeared to them in those Western
heavens. And it was not confined to the ministry of the night, for now
it appeared by day. And very low it must have shone, for it even
pointed to an house; *for it went before them until it came and stood
over where the young child was!* Reader! do not fail to observe the
grace of GOD in this providence. He who hung out this star, did not
hang it out in vain. The same GOD who led Israel by the cloud, led
those wise men by a star. And while hanging a light *without*,
gave the proper apprehension of the meaning *within*. And the effect
was, as might be supposed, *when they saw the star they rejoiced with
exceeding great joy!* And is it not so with his people, whom he
guides to JESUS now? The *day dawn*, and the *day star*, when first
shining in the heart, and pointing to CHRIST, calls forth the anxious
enquiry after CHRIST. And when darkness at any time intervenes,
how blessed is it again after such obscurity, and doubt, and mis-

giving, to have new discoveries of Christ; and in so clear and open a manner, leading to Christ, which, like this star, points to his very person, to shew where. he is!

11 ¶ And when they were come into the house, they saw the young child with Mary his mother, and fell down, and worshipped him: and when they had opened their treasures, they presented unto him gifts; gold, and frankincense, and myrrh.

I beg the Reader to remark with me, that the Wise Men saw not Joseph. For as Joseph was not the real but only the reputed father, his presence was not necessary; perhaps it might have been improper. But must not the same power which hung out the star, and directed the minds of these men to interpret the meaning of it, have influenced them also to worship Christ. For otherwise, how ill did the poverty of Christ's appearance correspond to the greatness of his dignity. It hath been supposed, that the gifts they presented of *gold*, and *frankincense*, and *myrrh*, had some significancy. Perhaps they might. But the Holy Ghost is silent upon this subject. Instead, therefore, of conjecture, I would refer the Reader to those scriptures. Song v. 11. Song i. 13. Song iv. 14. Psalm lxxii. 10 to 15. 1 Kings x. 2.

12 And being warned of God in a dream, that they should not return to Herod, they departed into their own country another way.

I stay not to enquire further concerning the divine intimation to those men, but just to remark, how the Lord was watching over the whole of this most interesting event, in relation to Christ. But we cannot but be led to hope, that these Wise Men, who came so far to worship the Lord Jesus, and was so evidently guided in their enquiry after him, were brought by the same Almighty teaching, into a saving acquaintance with him. The man of *Æthiopia*, we read of in the after age of the church, was so blessed. Acts viii. 27 to 39. And it is probable, that the Lord had an eye of grace on those men. But it is remarkable, that there is no further account of them in the word of God. Oh! what unknown, unnumbered multitudes from the East and the West, will arise to the triumphs of the Lord Jesus, when he comes to make up his jewels! Luke xiii. 29. 2 Thess. i. 10.

13 And when they were departed, behold, the angel of the Lord appeareth to Joseph in a dream, saying, Arise, and take the young child and his mother, and flee into Egypt, and be thou there until I bring thee word: for Herod will seek the young child to destroy him.

What an interesting subject the flight of Jesus into Egypt furnisheth! What! must the Son of God flee for safety? Yes! What
a sweet lesson then doth it teach his people, in all their exercises.
But wherefore Egypt? Here it was the church was first formed into a
Church. Exod. iv. 22. And here then the Great Head of the Church
shall go. The Prophet *Hosea* ages before had been taught to prophesy
to the church, that *out of Egypt would* God *call his Son.* Hosea xi. 1.
Let not the Reader take offence with the carnal world, at this humiliation of the Son of God. *It behoved him in all points to be like unto
his brethren.* Sweet thought to my poor soul! Rev. xii. 4. Isaiah
xix. 18. to *end.*

14 ¶ When he arose, he took the young child
and his mother by night, and departed into Egypt:

15 And was there until the death of Herod: that
it might be fulfilled which was spoken of the Lord
by the prophet, saying, Out of Egypt have I called
my son.

It is worthy observation, here all along mention is made of the
young child and his mother, without the least intimation of any relationship to *Joseph.* It appears from the history of those times, that
Herod himself survived but a little space Christ's departure into
Egypt. What a beautiful observation the Psalmist makes of the
shortness and transiency of all such characters. *For yet a little while,
and the wicked shall not be; thou shalt diligently consider his place,
and it shall not be.* Psm. xxxvii. 10.

16 Then Herod, when he saw that he was
mocked of the wise men, was exceeding wroth,
and sent forth, and slew all the children that were
in Bethlehem, and in all the coasts thereof, from
two years old and under, according to the time
which he had diligently enquired of the wise men.

17 Then was fulfilled that which was spoken by
Jeremy, the prophet, saying,

18 In Rama was there a voice heard, lamentation, and weeping, and great mourning, Rachel
weeping *for* her children, and would not be comforted, because they are not.

Here is opened the mystery of iniquity, which lay brooding in the
heart of *Herod,* all the while he put on the apparent regard he proposed to shew to the new born King. But, can the imagination form
an idea so horrid, as that of the destruction of such a number of little
harmless children, in order to be sure of the One? Alas! what is the
human heart, in a state of unrenewed nature! But, Reader, be not

offended. Your heart, my heart, every man's heart by nature is the
same. And we read this account of *Herod* to little profit, if we do
not see in him the portrait of every son and daughter of Adam, by the
fall. For there can be no difference in the same nature, but what sovereign grace hath wrought. What one man's nature hath done,
every man's nature is capable of doing; yea, and would do, if the
same corresponding causes, temptations, and opportunities, led to it,
and grace did not restrain. Oh! who shall calculate, who shall tell,
to what a desperate state of wickedness the whole nature of man is
fallen, by the original apostacy of our first father? Reader! do you
believe this? I do from my very heart. And I bless God the Holy
Ghost for the merciful discovery. For never should I have known
the want of salvation, neither rightly valued that salvation, but for
this divine teaching. Never should I have loved thee, or wouldest
thou have been so endeared to my soul, blessed, precious Lord Jesus,
as thou now art, had not God the Holy Ghost, as thou didst promise
concerning him, *convinced me of sin, of righteousness, and of judgment.* John xvi. 8—11. Jerem. xvii. 9. 2 Kings viii. 11, 12, 13.

Concerning the murder of those babes: if the Reader will turn to
Jerem. xxxi. from the 15th verse to the end; he will, I think, behold
the sweet consolation that is there pointed out in Christ, as the everlasting remedy to this, and all other bereaving providences. And in
relation to the infants themselves; they were only removed from the
evil to come. Had they lived to old age, they would have lived to
have seen the siege and destruction of Jerusalem, which the Lord
Jesus so mournfully foretold; Matt. xxiv. Mark xiii. Luke xxi.
when they would have said; *blessed are the barren and the wombs
that never bare, and the paps which never gave suck.* If those sweet
babes who died *for* Christ, died also *in* Christ, were they not such as
John heard a voice from heaven concerning, saying, *blessed are the
dead which die in the* Lord, Rev. xiv. 13. And is it not said, *precious in the sight of the* Lord *is the death of his saints.* Psal. cxvi. 15.
And may we not without violence to the words suppose, that these
little ones of Christ's fold, were among that holy army John saw on
Mount *Zion*, when he said, *I looked, and lo, a Lamb stood on the
Mount Zion, and with him an hundred and forty and four thousand,
having his* Father's *name written in their foreheads.* See Rev. xiv.
1—5. See also 1 Thess. iv. 13. to the end.

19 But when Herod was dead, behold, an angel of the Lord appeareth in a dream to Joseph in Egypt,

Reader! pause over this verse, and contemplate the awful death
of this man. Ah Herod! is this the termination of all thy grandeur?
Hast thou so shortly after followed thy murdered subjects to the
grave? If the Reader would see a striking representation of such an
end as this of *Herod's,* he may find it, Isaiah xiv. 4—20. I cannot
refrain from quoting what *Eusebius* hath related in his Ecclesiastical
History (and which he had from *Josephus*) concerning the dreadful
close of Herod's life. He saith " that a burning fever seized him,
with an intolerable itching over his whole body. He was visited

with grievous wounds, which putrified, and bred worms. So that his whole body became so horridly offensive, that none could approach him. And such was his unbounded rage, as to be the dread of every one. Finding death drawing nigh, he attempted to destroy himself, but was prevented. At length he expired in agonies."

It is worthy remark, that three, out of the four *Herods* we read of in the New Testament were such awful characters. This was the *first*. The second is but just mentioned by the name of *Philip.* Mark vi. 17. The *third* was He who caused the beheading of John the Baptist. Matt. xiv. 1, 2. And the *fourth* was eaten by worms before his death. Acts xii. Reader! doth the Lord manifest to his dear children in poor circumstances, his contempt of riches, by bestowing them so often upon the most worthless of men? Oh! for grace to bless him for a sanctified use of humble poverty. 1 Cor. i. 26, 27.

20 Saying, Arise, and take the young child and his mother, and go into the land of Israel: for they are dead which sought the young child's life.

21 And he arose, and took the young child and his mother, and came into the land of Israel.

22 But when he heard that Archelaus did reign in Judea in the room of his father Herod, he was afraid to go thither: notwithstanding, being warned of God in a dream, he turned aside into the parts of Galilee:

23 And he came and dwelt in a city called Nazareth: that it might be fulfilled which was spoken by the prophets, He shall be called a Nazarene.

The most interesting of all subjects, is to eye Christ as the Great *Nazarene.* Few have ever considered the importance of the name; and yet there is none, by which the Lord Jesus is distinguished in his holy scriptures, more personally directed by way of emphasis, than this. For my part, so very highly significant is it in my view, that I venture to believe that all we read of in the word of God of the *Nazarites,* and the particularity of their order, had no one object whatever, but to point to Christ; and He, and he alone, is the One, and only One *Nazarite* to God. If the Reader will first turn to the following scriptures, and carefully read them, I will venture to offer him my view upon the subject. Numb. vi. 2—21. Judges xiii. 5. to the end. Lament. iv. 7. Amos ii. 11, 12.

The name of *Nazarite*, is evidently taken from *Netzar* the branch; and this is well known to be the name of the Lord Jesus Christ. The Patriarch Jacob had pointed to Christ, in that prophecy concerning Joseph the *Nazarite*: He *separated* from his brethren. Gen. xlix. 26. So that the whole concerning the law of separation, had a direct reference to JESUS. In CHRIST therefore, being called JESUS *of Nazareth,* this must have been wholly upon this account: for CHRIST was born in *Bethlehem,* and not in *Nazareth.* And it should seem to have been nothing less than the overruling power of GOD, which could have so universally procured this name to CHRIST, when there were no causes but the LORD JESUS dwelling there which could have led to the idea. I have in my *Poor Man's Concordance* more fully dwelt upon this subject; so that I shall not in this place enlarge. I will only beg before I dismiss it to observe, that this name was made use of in a manner, and way particularly striking. The *Devils* used it. Mark i. 24. The *Apostles* used it while JESUS was upon earth. John i. 45. And again after our LORD's resurrection. Acts ii. 22. Acts iv. 10. The *band of armed men* which came to apprehend CHRIST used it. John xviii. 5. *Pilate* used it in his inscription on the cross. John xix. 19. The *servant maid* at the hall of Pilate used it. Matt. xxvi. 71. The *Angels* at the tomb used it. Mark xvi. 6. Yea *the* LORD *himself* from heaven used it. Acts xxii. 8. And if all these were intended (as I venture to believe they were) purposely to point to CHRIST as the true *Nazarite* to GOD, yea the only One; surely there is much blessedness in the view; and we see sufficient cause wherefore it was that JESUS came and dwelt in the city of Nazareth that he might be called *a Nazarene.*

REFLECTIONS.

READER! let you and I ponder well the sweet and interesting record here given of the birth of CHRIST. If angels, who needed no redemption, praised GOD at his birth, with what holy rapture and joy ought our songs to go forth in thanksgivings for the same. Behold! with what unequalled humbleness the SON of GOD, as man, when he came and tabernacled in our flesh, manifested himself to the church. But behold! how GOD the FATHER honoured his nativity, in not only sending wise men from the east to worship him, but in causing a star to point to the SAVIOUR. Was not this indeed sweetly fulfilling that blessed scripture; *the Gentiles shall come to thy light, and kings to the brightness of thy rising.* But did the LORD GOD, in order that his blessed SON should be known, grant such a starry influence to the wise men; and will he withold the light of his grace from the hearts of his people? Will he not reveal CHRIST in all his glory, and suitableness, and all sufficiency, that, like them, we may fall down and worship him, and present him more than gold, and frankincense, and myrrh, even those graces of his Holy Spirit which are his own?

And was it needful that the LORD of life and glory should go down into *Egypt,* that what the Prophet had said of calling GOD's dear SON out of Egypt might be fulfilled? Surely then, LORD, it must be needful to call all thy sons from the Egypt of this world; for all by nature are in that house of bondage, before that an act of sovereign grace hath called them out. Was JESUS, the holy, harmless, undefiled LORD JESUS, here also, as in a thousand other instances, the forerunner and glorious Head of his redeemed? Oh for grace to follow the LAMB whithersoever he goeth!

But Oh! thou true and only real Nazarite of God! Precious JESUS, thou art indeed the Branch, the Plant of Renown, the Spiritual Joseph of thy people, whose branches run over the wall. Blessings be on the Head of Him, and on the Crown of the Head of Him that was the *Netzar*, the Separate, from thy brethren! Methinks I hear my LORD again say, as he did once in the days of his flesh: *for their sakes I sanctify myself!* Ever precious, and dear name, JESUS CHRIST *of Nazareth!* Thou art thy church's *Nazarene!*

CHAP. III.

CONTENTS.

This Chapter opens with an account of the ministry of John the Baptist. The description of his office and ministry. The Chapter closeth with an account of his baptizing the LORD JESUS CHRIST, *and the glorious manifestations on the occasion.*

IN those days came John the Baptist, preaching in the wilderness of Judea,

2 And saying, Repent ye: for the kingdom of heaven is at hand.

3 For this is he that was spoken of by the prophet Esaias, saying, The voice of one crying in the wilderness, Prepare ye the way of the Lord, make his paths straight.

4 And the same John had his raiment of camel's hair, and a leathern girdle about his loins; and his meat was locusts and wild honey.

I include the whole of these verses into one view, for the better apprehension, and of connecting together what is recorded of John the Baptist. And first let us pause and consider the person and character of this illustrious man. His birth, though not miraculous, was attended with such remarkable circumstances, as intimated a more than ordinary purpose intended from his ministry. As the herald and harbinger of the LORD JESUS CHRIST, the Prophets *Isaiah* and *Malachi* foretold of his coming. Isaiah xl. 3. Malachi iii. 1. And his birth was not only announced by the ministry of an angel, but it was declared of him by the same heavenly messenger, that *he should be filled with the* HOLY GHOST *even from his mother's womb.* Luke i. 13—17. And the LORD JESUS himself declared concerning him, that *among them that are born of women, there had not risen a greater than John the Baptist.* Matt. xi. 11. Now before the Reader goes a step further in the account of John, let him pause, and ponder over the precious testimony which this wonderful man, this greatest of men born of women, gave of his Almighty LORD and Master. For when the Jews upon John's appearing, sent to ask him who he was, and the object of his mission; he declared himself to be unworthy of the office of even unloosening the very latchets of CHRIST's shoes. *I am* (said John) *the voice of one crying in the wilderness, prepare ye the way of the* LORD. John i. 19—36. And what is a voice? It is a non-entity, a mere sound, light as air, and so short in its being and existence, if it can be called by such a name, that when it hath performed its office, it dies away in the air, is dissolved, and is known no more. Such said John am I, when considered in any comparative view with my LORD and Master. Reader! are you a believer in the GODHEAD of CHRIST? Oh! think what a precious testimony this is to that glorious doctrine of our holy faith! And should a reader of the *Arian* or *Socinian* heresy but glance the same; oh that the LORD the HOLY GHOST may graciously carry conviction to his very soul of the blessed truth, and bring him upon his knees with *Thomas;* crying out *My* LORD *and My* GOD!

The next thing to be noticed in the account of John, is of his office and ministry. He came preaching and baptizing. Baptizing was altogether a new rite in the church, and probably John was called the Baptist on this account, for he was the first who used it. But both his preaching the doctrine of repentance, and the use of baptism, were evidently intended only as preparatory to the coming of CHRIST: for no efficacy did John pretend to convey by his *preaching* the doctrine of *repentance :* for to CHRIST is reserved the power of communicating the grace of repentance in the heart: for it is said, that *he was exalted as a Prince and a Savior for to give repentance to Israel and forgiveness of sins.* Acts v: 31. And John no less drew a line of everlasting distinction between his water ordinance, and the unction of the HOLY SPIRIT. I indeed *baptize you* (said he) *with water; but He shall baptize you with the* HOLY GHOST *and with fire.* Matt. iii. 11.

I pass over all notice of the endless disputes which have taken place in the church of CHRIST on the subject of baptism. The warmest advocates for immersion, who are themselves partakers of the baptism of the SPIRIT, will be free to confess that the *outward* sign, void of the *inward* effect, is nothing worth. And they who contend for infant baptism, if they know any thing of the LORD, must as readily allow, that nothing short of the regeneration of the heart, can be profitable before GOD. Here then let it rest. It is awful to behold thousands who have been baptized in their infancy by water only, and who, in riper years, live and die as complete infidels as those who never heard of CHRIST. And it is equally awful to behold numbers who have been immersed in riper years; and yet, by their after conduct, as fully proved that they never were baptized by the HOLY GHOST. Oh! LORD! grant to my soul the continual baptisms and *renewings of the* HOLY GHOST, *to be shed upon me abundantly, through* JESUS CHRIST *our* LORD. Titus iii. 5, 6.

The poor food, and the austere dress and manners of the Baptist, are particularly noticed by the Evangelist. His raiment perhaps, was somewhat in conformity to antient times. See 2 Kings i. 8. Zech. xiii. 4. The Locusts were among the clean beasts allowed for food. Levit. ii. 22. Reader! It is our happiness under the gospel to remember that *meat commendeth us not to* GOD. *The Kingdom of* GOD *is not meat and drink, but righteousness and peace, and joy in the* HOLY GHOST. Rom. xiv. throughout. 1 Tim. iv. 1—5. Titus i. 15.

5 Then went out to him Jerusalem, and all
Judea, and all the region round about Jordan,

6 And were baptized of him in Jordan, confessing their sins.

The wilderness of Judæa John preached in, is not to be considered
by us as what we should now call a wilderness, that is a solitary place,
for there were both towns and villages in it. The multitude thronging
to him is not to be wondered at, when we consider how long an interval, even of 350 years, had taken place in the church, from the
days of *Malachi*, the last Prophet.

7 ¶ But when he saw many of the Pharisees
and Sadducees come to his baptism, he said unto
them, O generation of vipers, who hath warned
you to flee from the wrath to come?

8 Bring forth therefore fruits meet for repentance;

9 And think not to say within yourselves, We
have Abraham to *our* father: for I say unto you,
that God is able of these stones to raise up children
unto Abraham.

10 And now also the ax is laid unto the root of
the trees: therefore every tree which bringeth not
forth good fruit is hewn down, and cast into the
fire.

11 I indeed baptize you with water unto repentance: but he that cometh after me is mightier
than I, whose shoes I am not worthy to bear: he
shall baptize you with the Holy Ghost, and *with*
fire:

12 Whose fan *is* in his hand, and he will thoroughly purge his floor, and gather his wheat into
the garner; but he will burn up the chaff with
unquenchable fire.

The *Pharisees* were a sect who prided themselves upon a more than
ordinary sanctity of life and manners. The Evangelist *Luke* hath
drawn the portrait of one, which may serve as a sample of all. Luke
xviii. 9—14. And their general character our LORD himself hath
most strikingly marked in a whole chapter. Matt. xxiii. The *Sadducees*, in their very name, which implied *righteousness*, from *Sedek*,
were of that class who justified themselves before GOD. What

unceasing persecutions our dear LORD sustained from both these characters I need not enumerate, for the history of the life of JESUS is full
of them. But what a name did the Baptist give them; *O generation*
of Vipers! A name which can belong only to the seed of the Serpent.
And I pray the Reader, once for all, to observe this feature of character as uniformly given to the reprobate, and to them only, throughout the whole Bible. See Matt. xxiii. 33. Rev. xii. 9. John
viii. 44. The children of the Kingdom are never once in all the
word of GOD called by such a name. See Note on Ephes. ii. 3. I
pray the Reader to weigh this consideration well, for it is highly important. And I pray the Reader to remark yet further with me,
that (as far as my memory chargeth me) we do not find a single
Pharisee or *Sadducee* who saw CHRIST in the days of his flesh, (*Nico-*
demus excepted,) ever savingly converted. *Paul* was a Pharisee indeed, and of the highest order in point of high, self exalting notions:
but then *Paul* lived not in the days of CHRIST's flesh, so as to know
CHRIST; and saw nothing of JESUS, until he saw him in his glory in
his way to *Damascus.* It furnisheth out a solemn consideration this,
that not one (*Nicodemus* excepted) of those sects in the days of CHRIST,
and who assumed a greater degree of holiness than others, was savingly
converted!

The children of *Abraham,* according to the Covenant made with
Abraham, were those of grace, and not counted after nature. The
one decisive feature of this family is; *if ye be* CHRIST's, *then ye are*
Abraham's seed, and heirs according to the promise. Gal. iii. 29. So
hath it been in all ages. So was it then. So is it now. And such
will it be for ever. The *Ishmaels,* and the sons of *Keturah ;* the
Esaus, and the whole troop of natural descendants from Abraham :
these, as the HOLY GHOST hath said by *Paul, which are the children*
of the flesh ; these are not the children of GOD ; *but the children of the*
promise are counted for the seed. In Isaac shall thy seed be called!
Reader! think what a blessed thing it is to be able to say, as Paul
did, *Now we brethren, as Isaac was, are the children of promise.*
Rom. ix. 7, 8. Gal. iv. 28.

13 ¶ Then cometh Jesus from Galilee to Jordan unto John, to be baptized of him.

Here we have, at this verse, the introduction of the LORD of life
and glory, in his public entrance upon his divine office, as the
GOD-Man Mediator. *Luke* in his relation of this wonderful event,
tells the Church, that at this time, JESUS himself began to be about
thirty years of age. Luke iii. 23. Hence we learn that the SON of
GOD waited the appointed time for the being manifested unto Israel.
But let not the Reader suppose, that the long interval from his birth,
to this public entrance upon his ministry, was spent without an
eye to the redemption-work he became incarnate to perform. No
doubt every act, and every incident, in the life of CHRIST, had respect
to the great object for which he came. The poverty of his birth, the
humbleness of his calling, as a carpenter, the meanness of his companions, to one who from all eternity had lain in the bosom of the
FATHER; no doubt, some great and special ends were intended
from the whole. That sweet and precious scripture answers every

enquiry, though it enters not into the full investigation of the cause: *Wherefore in all things it behoved him to be made like unto his brethren.* Heb. ii. 17. Precious JESUS! how ought such views to endear thee to thy people!

14 But John forbad him, saying, I have need to be baptized of thee, and comest thou to me?

15 And Jesus answering said unto him, Suffer *it to be so* now: for thus it becometh us to fulfil all righteousness. Then he suffered him.

It should seem from the modesty of John in first declining this office, that he had some consciousness concerning the Person of CHRIST. The relation John gives of himself, John i. 26—34, was that he knew him not, but only that he should be made manifest to Israel. But at this transaction of CHRIST's baptism, the knowledge of his person and character was to be more strikingly given to John. I beg the Reader to remark what John saith: *I have need to be baptized of thee.* Yes! though John was filled with the HOLY GHOST, even from his mother's womb, Luke i. 15, yet the work of GOD the SPIRIT upon the child of GOD, doth not supersede the necessity of the work of GOD the SON. All the office-work of each glorious person of the GODHEAD becomes essential in the covenant of redemption. And the baptism of the LORD JESUS is not water baptism; for it is expressly said, that JESUS baptized none. John iv. 2. Acts i. 5.

The importance of CHRIST's baptism is evident from what the LORD saith: *thus it becometh us to fulfil all righteousness.* But who shall take upon him to explain all that is contained in this expression? It is most certain, that here, at this solemn transaction of CHRIST's baptism, he openly entered upon his office, and therefore it should seem the whole persons of the GODHEAD would publickly give the commission. The SON of GOD, all along in the Old Testament dispensation, had been set up and made known to the church as the *Messiah,* or anointed; and now therefore in the New, he shall have the public seal to the same. If the Reader will consult and compare a few scriptures on this point, they do, in my view, beautifully elucidate and explain each other. Isaiah xlviii. 16, 17. Isaiah lxi. 1. with Luke iv. 18. Acts x. 37, 38.

16 And Jesus, when he was baptized, went up straightway out of the water: and, lo, the heavens were opened unto him, and he saw the Spirit of God descending like a dove, and lighting upon him:

17 And lo, a voice from heaven, saying, This is my beloved Son, in whom I am well pleased.

Here is every thing that is solemn, sublime, and glorious to be contemplated in this transaction: but of the scene itself, we can only behold with the most profound reverence and holy awe, without attempting to be wise above what is written. We behold the testimony of that glorious doctrine which is the foundation of our holy faith : that *there are Three which bear record in heaven; the* FATHER, *the* WORD, *and the* HOLY GHOST, *and these Three are One.* 1 John i. 7. And here they distinctly manifested themselves at the baptism of the LORD JESUS. Here is the FATHER, by a voice from heaven, manifesting himself. Here is GOD the SON, incarnate in the Water. And here is GOD the HOLY GHOST, manifesting his person in the likeness of a Dove, hovering over the person of CHRIST. What can be more conclusive and satisfactory, in proof of this precious doctrine of our most holy faith? In addition to the testimony this scripture brings, of the personality of the HOLY THREE in ONE, let not the Reader overlook the testimony it also brings of their perfect approbation of redemption-work. JEHOVAH is not only well pleased *with* CHRIST ; but *in* CHRIST : all that are *in* CHRIST. CHRIST and his members : CHRIST and his church. And the whole persons of the GODHEAD, take the same delight and complacency together. For it is said, GOD *was in* CHRIST *reconciling the world to himself.* 2 Cor. v. 19. that is, the whole three persons, constituting the One Eternal, undivided JEHOVAH, were in CHRIST. GOD the FATHER was, and is, in CHRIST : for so saith the LORD JESUS. *Believest thou not that I am in the* FATHER, *and the* FATHER *in me? Believe me, that I am in the* FATHER, *and the* FATHER *in me.* John xiv. 10, 11. GOD the SON was, and is, in CHRIST. For GOD the SON, in his own eternal power and GODHEAD, had his Almighty hand in the work and purposes of redemption, as much as the person of GOD the FATHER, or GOD the HOLY GHOST. Neither could there have been any access to the Person of GOD the SON, as GOD, more than to the person of the FATHER, or the person of the HOLY GHOST, without CHRIST, as the God-Man-Mediator. The SON of GOD doth not lose the glory and perfection of his essential divinity, because of his infinite condescension, in assuming our nature for the purpose of redemption. And it is most exceedingly necessary, that in contemplating the great object of faith, true believers in CHRIST should everlastingly keep in view the GODHEAD of the SON of GOD, as one of the glorious persons constituting JEHOVAH; while we keep no less in view, that the SON of GOD, in his twofold nature, of GOD, and Man, in one person, becomes the CHRIST of GOD, *in* whom, and *through* whom, and *by* whom, we have access to JEHOVAH: FATHER, SON, and HOLY GHOST, in grace here, and glory for ever. In like manner GOD the HOLY GHOST was, and is, in CHRIST. Not simply in his anointings, and endowments, without measure, given to CHRIST, in the qualifying him for the vast undertaking he came to perform; but as One of the glorious persons of the GODHEAD, was, and is in CHRIST, reconciling the world to himself, in common with the FATHER, and the SON. So that, as JEHOVAH, in his three-fold character of person ; FATHER, SON, and HOLY GHOST, were all alike concerned in the indignity shewn by the fall of man ; so all alike were concerned in the recovery, by the glorious undertaking, and accomplishment of salvation by CHRIST JESUS. Such are the scriptural views of this most sublime subject. Before we desire further information, let it be considered, that it is proposed to us as an article of faith, and not for our full investigation. Perhaps it is impossible, in the present imperfect state of being, to know more. The LORD be praised for what he hath thought proper to reveal. And with this measure of knowledge, may the LORD give grace to both Writer, and Reader, of this Poor Man's Commentary, to be thankful.

I will only detain the Reader with a short observation more upon those verses, just to notice the descent of the HOLY GHOST, which both the LORD JESUS, and his servant John, saw in the form of a dove. Some visible appearance, to make it personal, was thought necessary. I presume not to say wherefore it was necessary, but only humbly propose the enquiry. Was it because in after ages heresies would spring up in the church, in denying the personality of GOD the SPIRIT? And was the LORD pleased, by way of giving his assurance to the glorious truth in the minds of his people, thus to assume a personal appearance? Let the Reader remember, I do not presume to determine the point: I only humbly ask the question. But whether I am right or not, certain it is, that both JESUS, and John, saw *the* SPIRIT *of* GOD *descending like a dove, and lighting upon him.* John i. 32—34. Like a dove, I apprehend means as a dove lighting down, or hovering over. There is a great beauty in this scripture. The appearance of the HOLY GHOST shall not be in the form of a man: for this was specially belonging to the SON of GOD; but of a dove. And a dove was, of all the other creatures of GOD, the most suited, both to represent that glorious person, who thus descended, and abode upon CHRIST, and CHRIST himself. For, not to notice the meekness and gentleness of the dove, and the loving affections of its nature; it is worth remarking, that the dove hath no gall, neither talons. Sweet emblems of manifesting the frame of GOD the HOLY GHOST himself, when anointing JESUS in our nature, to the blessed offices he hath communicated to our nature! And sweet emblem, no less to shew, how JESUS should manifest to his people the tenderness and love of his heart, as doves do to each other. Reader! recollect what the Evangelist records of the LORD JESUS immediately after this descent of the HOLY GHOST, and never lose sight of it through life. *The Spirit of the* LORD *is upon me,* (said that sweet SAVIOR) *because he hath anointed me to preach the gospel to the poor: he hath sent me to heal the broken hearted; to preach deliverance to the captives, and recovering of sight to the blind, to set at liberty them that are bruised; to preach the acceptable year of the* LORD. Luke iv. 18, 19.

REFLECTIONS.

WELCOME, John the Baptist, thou faithful herald of thy LORD! As the star of the morning becomes the sure pledge of day; so thy coming plainly foretold the LORD of his temple was at hand. But thrice welcome, yea, everlastingly and eternally welcome, thou glorious Sun of Righteousness, precious LORD JESUS, art thou in thy arising, with healing in thy wings, to all thy people. Oh! do thou, LORD, thou great baptizer with the HOLY GHOST, bring my soul, and the souls of all thy redeemed, under the continual and unceasing baptisms of thy Spirit: fill our hearts, fill our houses, fill thy church, thy whole people, with grace!

And from this blessed unction given to the souls of thy people, grant, LORD, to every one, grace, *according to the measure of the gift of* CHRIST; that we may bless and adore the HOLY THREE in ONE, who bear record in heaven; for the record given in this chapter, to the LORD JESUS CHRIST, on his entering upon his public ministry, at his holy baptism. And may the LORD mercifully grant, that the whole church of GOD, through divine teaching, may be enabled to keep in unceasing remembrance, the FATHER'S testimony to his dear SON. And while my soul, and the souls of all his redeemed, are thus continually hearing, and receiving, the precious assurance of GOD's being well pleased with his dear SON, for his redeeming love to his church, and his finished salvation for his people; oh, for grace to love Him, whom JEHOVAH, in all the persons of the GODHEAD, loves; and to delight in Him, in whom JEHOVAH delighteth. Precious LORD JESUS! I would say, *Whom have I in heaven but thee; and there is none upon earth my soul desireth but thee. My flesh and my heart faileth: but thou art the strength of my heart, and my portion for ever.*

CHAP. IV.

CONTENTS.

CHRIST'S *temptations. The call of his Apostles. His Preaching and Miracles.*

THEN was Jesus led up of the Spirit into the wilderness to be tempted of the devil.

I detain the Reader at this verse but for the moment, to observe, that there is a peculiar emphasis in the word *then*. When JESUS had thus received the anointings for his ministry, *then* more eminently the powers of darkness made a more furious attack upon him. Reader! as it was with the glorious Head, so is it with his members. The devil certainly doth not know GOD's children until they are awakened and regenerated by the HOLY GHOST. But no sooner is a work of grace wrought in their hearts, but all hell is up in arms.

2 And when he had fasted forty days and forty nights, he was afterward an hungred.

It is remarkable in the Old Testament Scripture, of those that were types of CHRIST, concerning fasting, that they observed such seasons: *Moses*, Exod. xxxiv. 28. and *Elijah*, 1 Kings xix. 8. What a sweet thought is it, that the LORD JESUS was in all points as his people are, yet without sin! Precious LORD! was it not intended to prompt thy redeemed to come to thee with more confidence from fellow feeling?

3 And when the tempter came to him, he said, If thou be the Son of God, command that these stones be made bread.

4 But he answered and said, It is written, Man shall not live by bread alone, but by every word that proceedeth out of the mouth of God.

5 Then the devil taketh him up into the holy city, and setteth him on a pinnacle of the temple,

6 And saith unto him, If thou be the Son of God, cast thyself down: for it is written, He shall give his angels charge concerning thee: and in *their* hands they shall bear thee up, lest at any time thou dash thy foot against a stone.

7 Jesus said unto him, It is written again, Thou shalt not tempt the Lord thy God.

8 Again, the devil taketh him up into an exceeding high mountain, and sheweth him all the kingdoms of the world, and the glory of them;

9 And saith unto him, All these things will I give thee, if thou wilt fall down and worship me.

10 Then saith Jesus unto him, Get thee hence, Satan: for it is written, Thou shalt worship the Lord thy God, and him only shalt thou serve.

11 Then the devil leaveth him, and, behold, angels came and ministered unto him.

The subject of CHRIST's temptations, is a subject attended with much difficulty thoroughly to explain. One of the great causes for which the SON of GOD was manifested, was, that *he might destroy the works of the Devil.* 1 John iii. 8. And if we take the whole purport of scripture on this point, one mass of particulars, we shall be led to conclude, that the quarrel between CHRIST and the devil was *personal.* Jude 6. Rev. xii. 7, 8, 9. Now when CHRIST came upon earth, the conflict was with this accursed enemy. Hence CHRIST combated personally with Satan, when he began his temptations, and afterwards at the cross. Heb. ii. 14. He doth this also, when in his people he enables his redeemed to resist him, and at length brings Satan under their feet. James iv. 7. Rom. xvi. 20. And there is another triumph, scripture seems to intimate, which the SON of GOD will have over Satan, before the day of judgment; namely, when Satan is to be shut up, and restrained from his cursed temptations over the LORD's people. Rev. xx. 1, 2, 3. And, lastly, at the great day of all, then the devil will be brought forth for final judgment, and eternal punishment, before the whole world. Rev. xx. 10, &c.

I do not think it necessary to go minutely over the several temptations with which the devil assaulted CHRIST. The whole was necessary, no doubt, that CHRIST should fulfil all righteousness. But it was necessary also, on the account of his redeemed. *For in that he himself hath suffered, being tempted, he is able to succour them that are tempted.* Heb. ii. 18. Few have taken into their soul's comfort the whole blessedness of this account of JESUS. It is not meant simply to say, that as GOD, and as man, in one person, he knoweth what temptations are; but it is meant to say, that from his personal knowledge of them, and his own exercises in those seasons, he knoweth both what his people feel under temptations, and how to administer the very succour which will exactly suit their case and circumstances. And nothing can give equal relief as this assurance to every tempted Child of GOD?

Moreover, it should be added, that in those temptations, wherewith JESUS was assaulted, the believer ought to draw comfort, if at any time his exercises are the same. In those temptations in the wilderness CHRIST was assaulted with the sin of distrust; unbelief; to worship the devil; and to self-murder. And if the tempter thus dared to attack the LORD of life and glory, is it a wonder that he should his members? Oh! for grace upon all occasions, when assaulted with the fiery darts of Satan, to look unto JESUS, and to take the shield of faith, and the sword of the Spirit, which is the word of GOD. JESUS will make all his redeemed more than conquerors, through his grace enabling them. And in due season, that song will be heard by every redeemed soul which John heard; *Now is come salvation and strength, and the kingdom of our* GOD, *and the power of his* CHRIST: *for the accuser of our brethren is cast down, which accused them before our* GOD *day and night.* Rev. xii. 10. And as in the instance of the glorious Head, so all his members, when temptations cease, the ministering services of angels are enjoyed. Heb. i. 14.

12 ¶ Now when Jesus had heard that John was cast into prison, he departed into Galilee;

13 And leaving Nazareth, he came and dwelt in Capernaum, which is upon the sea coast, in the borders of Zabulon and Nephthalim:

14 That it might be fulfilled which was spoken by Esaias the prophet, saying,

15 The land of Zabulon, and the land of Nephthalim, *by* the way of the sea, beyond Jordan, Galilee of the Gentiles;

16 The people which sat in darkness saw great light; and to them which sat in the region and shadow of death light is sprung up.

These are sweet views of JESUS, in his humbleness of character! And what a blessed testimony they become in proof of his mission. Isa. ix. 1, 2.

17 ¶ From that time Jesus began to preach, and to say, Repent: for the kingdom of heaven is at hand.

It is observable that *Mark* records the same words of CHRIST's Sermon!

18 ¶ And Jesus, walking by the sea of Galilee, saw two brethren, Simon called Peter, and Andrew his brother, casting a net into the sea: for they were fishers.

19 And he saith unto them, Follow me, and I will make you fishers of men.

20 And they straightway left *their* nets, and followed him.

21 And going on from thence, he saw other two brethren, James *the son* of Zebedee, and John his brother, in a ship with Zebedee their father, mending their nets; and he called them.

22 And they immediately left the ship and their father, and followed him.

I pray the Reader not to overlook the sovereignty of the LORD's call. What a marvellous light, and what a marvellous power must have accompanied his words! And I pray the Reader to keep also in remembrance, what the HOLY GHOST hath said of those effectual calls of grace, by his servants. Rom. viii. 29, 30. 2 Tim, i. 9. 2 Peter i. 10.

23 And Jesus went about all Galilee, teaching in their synagogues, and preaching the gospel of the kingdom, and healing all manner of sickness, and all manner of disease among the people.

24 And his fame went throughout all Syria: and they brought unto him all sick people that were taken with divers diseases and torments, and those which were possessed with devils, and those which were lunatick, and those that had the palsy: and he healed them.

25 And there followed him great multitudes of people from Galilee, and *from* Decapolis, and *from* Jerusalem, and *from* Judea, and *from* beyond Jordan.

What a lovely picture is here drawn of the SON of GOD! Behold him thus going about preaching the kingdom, and healing every where. And, Reader! do not fail to connect with this view, that he is still the same, JESUS CHRIST, *yesterday, and to day, and for ever!* What diseases of his people doth he not know? And what sicknesses are there, that JESUS cannot cure? Read, I beseech you, what was said of him ages before his birth. Isa. lxiii. 7, 8, 9. Call to mind what is said of him in the days of his flesh. John xiii. 1. And follow him by faith to glory. Rev. vii. 17. and behold him feeding the church, where all tears are wiped away from all faces. And then ask, will he forget you; Oh, ye of little faith! Precious LORD JESUS! wherefore was it that *it behoved thee to be made like unto thy brethren?* Was it not that *thou mightest be both a merciful and a faithful High Priest in things pertaining to* GOD? And art thou not all this, and more, that thy redeemed might *come at all times boldly unto thy throne of grace, and obtain mercy, and find grace to help in all times of need?*

REFLECTIONS.

READER! let you and I pause over the view of CHRIST's temptations, and ponder well the wonderful subject. And was it needful that CHRIST should be thus exercised? Yes! The HOLY GHOST has said; *that in all things it behoveth him to be made like unto his brethren. Forasmuch as the Children are partakers of flesh and blood, he also himself likewise took part of the same.* The destruction of the devil was folded up in this. And the deliverance of his people from the power of hell was accomplished in the same. Hence therefore, in the victory of CHRIST in his seasons of temptations, the children of CHRIST discover their victory in their seasons and temptations in and by Him. And during the exercise, they know how JESUS, from fellow-feeling can, and will, minister to them every suited relief. *For in that he himself hath suffered being tempted, he is able to succour them that are tempted.* The issue therefore is never doubtful. The children may be tempted, as JESUS was, to unbelief, to a distrust of GOD, yea, to self-murder. Perhaps there never was a child of GOD but what, more or less, hath been so tempted. Yea, it should seem to be a sweet testimony of our fellowship with JESUS, as members with the Head. *Blessed is the man,* saith the HOLY GHOST by *James, that endureth temptation.* But the issue is never doubtful. As CHRIST overcame every assault of Satan, so CHRIST's redeemed must also in him. Reader! let you and I carry all our trials and temptations to JESUS. He knows them all before. But by our taking them to Him, we testify that we are looking wholly for strength from Him, and engaging CHRIST on our behalf. And, oh! the blessedness of having JESUS for our strength. The devil will leave us as he did Him, and the LORD of angels himself will come and minister every suited relief to our necessity!

Behold Reader! on the close of this chapter, how He, who in the opening of it, is said to have been assaulted by hell, is here manifesting forth his sovereignty as God. Oh! that that dear LORD, who thus in the days of his flesh, went about preaching his gospel, and healing the bodies of the deceased, would now, in the day of his Almighty power, come forth in a preached gospel, and heal the souls of his redeemed. Precious LORD JESUS! behold the diseased state of thy church, and in compassion to Zion take the glorious cause into thine own Almighty hand. And as then, so now, LORD, cause the multitudes of thy people to come to thy standard, until thou shalt have brought all thy blood-bought children home to thy church, and all the blessed purposes of thy temptations and ministry be abundantly answered in the salvation of thy chosen. Amen.

CHAP. V.

CONTENTS.

We have in this Chapter, and the two which follow, our LORD's sermon on the Mount. A great variety of beauties is contained in it.

A ND seeing the multitudes, he went up into a mountain : and when he was set, his disciples came unto him :

2 And he opened his mouth, and taught them, saying,

We have a beautiful view of our dear LORD opening his commission as the Great Prophet of his church and people. The law had been given from the Mount, therefore JESUS will here also deliver his Gospel. But there were bounds set, when the law was given, which the people were not to pass. Not so with JESUS and his Gospel. JESUS saith, *Come ye near unto me and hear ye this.* I pray the Reader to turn to the sweet scripture, Isaiah xlviii. 16, 17. Oh! how blessed must it have been to have sat at JESUS' feet on this occasion, and to have heard the gracious words which proceeded out of his mouth? Let the poor man learn how sweetly his LORD hath consecrated places for the manifestation of himself. JESUS preached on the mountain; from a ship; in the fields; every where and every place is sacred which the LORD makes holy. Moses found CHRIST first at the *Bush.* Exod. iii. 2. And Jacob, ages before, at *Bethel*, Gen. 28. 10—22. And why may not the Reader of this Poor Man's Commentary have gracious manifestations of the LORD JESUS at his labor, in his work, at home, or abroad; in the house of GOD, or in his own house. John xiv. 23. Isaiah ii. 3—5. Micah iv. 1, 2, &c. Heb. i. 1. Prov. viii. 1, &c.

3 ¶ Blessed *are* the poor in spirit : for theirs is the kingdom of heaven.

4 Blessed *are* they that mourn : for they shall be comforted.

5 Blessed *are* the meek : for they shall inherit the earth.

6 Blessed _are_ they which do hunger and thirst after righteousness: for they shall be filled.

7 Blessed _are_ the merciful: for they shall obtain mercy.

8 Blessed _are_ the pure in heart: for they shall see God.

9 Blessed _are_ the peace-makers: for they shall be called the children of God.

10 Blessed are they which are persecuted for righteousness' sake: for their's is the kingdom of heaven.

11 Blessed are ye, when _men_ shall revile you, and persecute _you_, and shall say all manner of evil against you falsely, for my sake.

12 Rejoice, and be exceeding glad: for great _is_ your reward in heaven: for so persecuted they the prophets which were before you.

We have here the opening of our LORD's Sermon, and a most blessed sermon it is! Let the Reader observe how JESUS opens it in pronouncing blessings. JESUS himself is the great comprehensive blessing of all blessings, and the blessedness of his people. It is worthy remark that the Old Testament ended, yea in the very last word of it, with the LORD's threatenings of a _Curse_. Malachi iv. 6. The first word of CHRIST's Gospel is _Blessing_. CHRIST himself is the WORD, the Uncreated Word, and the Blessing. John i. 1. How truly delightful is it to look at the Old Testament through the New, and to view the Law by the Gospel.

If the Reader looks attentively to this opening of our LORD's sermon, he will find no less than _eight_ distinct characters JESUS speaks of as _blessed;_ namely, poor in spirit; they that mourn; the meek; they who hunger and thirst after righteousness; the merciful; the pure in heart; the peace-makers; and the persecuted (and falsely reviled) for righteousness' sake. Now the question instantly ariseth; where are these characters to be found? Not in themselves it must be immediately confessed; for when the LORD looked down from heaven upon the children of men, to see if there were any that would understand and seek after GOD, we are told from the Word of GOD, that the result of that enquiry was, that there was none that did good, no not one. Psm. xiv. 1—3. Rom. iii. 10, &c. Hence therefore when the LORD came himself from heaven, and came, as he himself saith, _to seek and save that which was lost_, could JESUS mean, in coming, not to call the righteous but sinners to repentance, that he should find such characters as he hath here declared to be blessed. Oh! how plain, how very plain is it, that the persons here spoken of are the redeemed given by the FATHER, made blessed in the righteousness of the Son, and regenerated and sanctified by the Holy Ghost. Reader! If we read the precious words of Jesus in this true gospel sense, we shall, under divine teaching, discover that all such as are here spoken of, are blessed in Jesus indeed. The first feature of character the Lord takes notice of them is, that they are *poor in spirit*, not poor in pocket; for outward circumstances, either in poverty or riches, have nothing to do with inward grace. Many that are poor in worldly things, are *rich in faith, and heirs of the kingdom*. And many it is to be feared, by what we behold in the world, are poor in this life, and will be poor to all eternity in the life to come. But *the poor in spirit*, means poor in soul concerns. They know, through the Lord's teaching, their *spiritual* poverty, their lost, their undone estate before God. They are conscious they owe ten thousand talents, and have nothing to pay. Ruined in Adam, they view their lost estate, and are convinced that there can be no salvation but in Christ. Such Jesus declares to be blessed, for theirs is the kingdom of heaven. They were chosen in Christ, and are thus training for the everlasting enjoyment of Christ, to all eternity.

The Lord next describes them (for they are all one and the same persons, all that he hath here declared to be blessed :) as *mourners*. *Blessed are they that mourn, for they shall be comforted.* And this mark of grace follows the former. The eye of the soul is no sooner opened to see his state of poverty and wretchedness before God, but the heart melts at the view of it. Sin; in-dwelling, in-bred sin, opens a constant spring of sorrow. Like Paul they cry out, *Oh! wretched man that I am! who shall deliver me from this body of death?* And never, until Jesus is opened to their view, in all the glories of his person, blood, and righteousness: yea, until by the Holy Ghost, Christ is brought personally home, and applied to the heart, and formed in the heart the hope of glory, can any comfort be found. And even to the close of life, the conscious sense of the remains of in-dwelling corruption, tends, under grace, to keep open an unceasing spring of our repentance towards God, while the soul is supported in the assured interest in Christ; by which, Christ is more and more endeared to the heart, to be more in love with him, and more out of love with themselves, until grace is finished in everlasting glory. It is such holy mourners, the Lord Jesus saith, shall be comforted. All the persons of the Godhead do now comfort them: the word of God is their comfort: ordinances are their comfort: the promises are their comfort: all the discoveries of pardoning love, grace, mercy, refreshments, manifestations of divine love, providences; all and every tendency of the Lord towards them are full of comfort: and, at length, when they come to drop the body in the grave, they will be indeed comforted, for they will be introduced unto the general assembly of the first-born, and dwell for ever in the joy of their Lord. Isaiah lxi. 1. James ii. 5.

In like manner, the whole of the features of character, which follow, if construed with an eye to the whole tenor of Christ's gospel, plainly shew forth whom the Lord Jesus had in view. *Blessed are the meek:* not the meekness of suppressed anger induced by the rigid constraints of philosophy; but the meekness induced by the fruits of the Spirit of God. Had Christ meant the mere moral virtue of meekness, such as it is called of the Stoic; who so much esteemed as the *Romans* and the *Lacedemonians* of old? But yet they perished in their heathenism and sins. The meekness the SON of GOD pronounced blessed, is the meekness inwrought in the soul, by the gracious influence of GOD the HOLY GHOST. It is learnt *of* JESUS. Matt. xi. 29. It is wholly *from* JESUS. John xv. 4, 5. And it is his regenerated members of whom he saith, the LORD will *beautify the meek with salvation.* Psalm cxlix. 4. This meekness of the LORD's own creating in the soul is of great price. 1 Peter iv. 3.

So again, the blessedness pronounced on them *who hunger and thirst after righteousness.* It were a weakness of judgment indeed, to suppose, that the righteousness such souls most earnestly desire, is the righteousness of mere moral honesty and justice between man and man in life. These things the laws among men enforce, and the Scribes and Pharisees of our LORD's days, prided themselves upon them. Surely no one who reads his Bible can for a moment, if he thinks rightly, suppose that the SON of GOD came upon earth to preach what even unenlightened heathens had always insisted upon. This would be indeed to run back to the law of Moses, instead of preaching the Gospel of CHRIST. But the righteousness the SON of GOD had in view, when declaring these souls blessed which hungered and thirsted for it, was his own complete righteousness, which alone can justify a poor sinner in the sight of GOD. So that in the hungering for it, the soul gave evident proofs that he had no righteousness of his own to appear in before GOD, and therefore earnestly longed to be cloathed with CHRIST's robe of righteousness, and garment of salvation. And graciously the LORD JESUS here declares all such shall not hunger in vain. He who excites the hunger in the soul, is He who also satisfieth it. And hence the promises and the performance. Psalm cxxxii. 9—16. Isaiah lxi. 1, 2, 3, 10, 11.

I must not trespass in my *Poor Man's Commentary,* to explain to the full on gospel principles the whole of the characters which the LORD JESUS hath here drawn, but were it not for enlarging, I might otherwise shew how beautiful a correspondence they all bear to each other. *Blessed are the merciful.* Not merely kindness to the bodies of men, no nor to the souls of men only. These are the *fruits* and *effects* of the mercifulness the LORD JESUS speaks of, and not the thing itself. But the mercifulness JESUS pronounceth blessed, is that mercy of soul inwrought by the regenerating influence of the HOLY GHOST, and from an union with CHRIST, the mercy of mercies. And from this source within, this union and communion with CHRIST, all the gracious acts will flow forth in mercy to others, and which the blessed souls themselves are receiving from their glorious merciful Head.

Blessed are the pure in heart; made so by regenerating grace; for by nature *the heart is deceitful above all things, and desperately wicked.* Jerem. xvii. 9. Hence the LORD promiseth his people *to take away the heart of stone, and give them an heart of flesh.* Ezek. xxxvi. 25, 26. The people that are blessed are those whose hearts the LORD hath changed, who are indeed holy and pure in the cleansing and justifying purity and holiness of the LORD, their righteousness; but who feel conscious of the remains of indwelling corruption under which they groan. They see GOD in CHRIST in all the blessedness of salvation here in the life that now is, and they shall see him in the complete enjoyment of him in the life of glory that is to come.

The *peace-makers* are said to be *blessed*. But of whom doth CHRIST speak ? Not simply peace-makers between man and man in the strifes of the world, for *there is no peace saith my* GOD *to the wicked*. Neither can it mean a man making his own peace with God, for that is impossible. CHRIST is the alone peace-maker, in making *our peace in the blood of his cross*. But the peace-makers here said to be blessed, shall be called the children of GOD. They are proved to be so by adoption and grace. And that *peace of* GOD *which ruleth in their hearts*, will manifest itself in acts of peace *among them which make peace*.

And the blessedness to those who are *persecuted for righteousness' sake*, and *reviled falsely* for CHRIST'S sake, very plainly refer not to the mere act of *persecution* or *reviling*, but when those acts of cruelty are shewn to the followers of the LORD Jesus on *his account*, and for their attachment *to him*. Then, and then only, is it said by the LORD to be blessed.

I have studied as much brevity as possible in my illustration of those characters, that I might not unnecessarily swell the pages of the Poor Man's Commentary. But I hope enough hath been said in proof that our LORD's expressions are wholly to be considered on Gospel principles, and that the blessedness he pronounceth is the privilege of his redeemed in him.

13 ¶ Ye are the salt of the earth : but if the salt have lost his savour, wherewith shall it be salted ? it is thenceforth good for nothing, but to be cast out, and to be trodden under foot of men.

14 Ye are the light of the world. A city that is set on an hill cannot be hid.

15 Neither do men light a candle, and put it under a bushel, but on a candlestick ; and it giveth light unto all that are in the house.

16 Let your light so shine before men, that they may see your good works, and glorify your Father which is in heaven.

Well may the LORD's people rejoice, convinced of their interest in him. Luke x. 20. Philip. iii. 3. But with respect to the reward the LORD speaks of, let not the Reader for a moment overlook the cause. It is all of grace, not of debt. All on CHRIST's account, not their own. Ephes. ii. 8, 9. Rom. xi. 6. And blessed is the example of the Prophets in this particular. Heb. xi. 33. to the end. James v. 10, 11. The figures of *salt* and *light* are very expressive. CHRIST is the salt of the covenant. Levit. ii. 13. Numb. xviii. 19. with Mark ix. 49. CHRIST is the light of the world. John i. 4. And hence by so much as there is of CHRIST in his redeemed, by so much salt and light is there in the world. And well is it for the world that CHRIST's seed are in the earth. For without this salt the whole otherwise would be in a state of putrefaction ; and without this light the whole would be in a state of darkness. Oh! the blessedness of such a state of the church. *Such honor have all his Saints!* Philip. ii. 15.

17 Think not that I am come to destroy the law, or the prophets: I am not come to destroy, but to fulfil.

18 For verily I say unto you, Till heaven and earth pass, one jot or one tittle shall in no wise pass from the law, till all be fulfilled.

In this passage, we meet with the word *Amen,* or *Verily,* for the first time, and therefore, once for all, I beg to observe upon it, that it is of the highest import when used by CHRIST. It is indeed one of his precious names. JESUS therefore, in the use of it, puts his name to what he delivers. See Isaiah lxv. 16. Rev. iii. 14. I must refer the Reader, for the sake of shortness, to my *Poor Man's Concordance* for the full explanation of it; he will find it under the article *Amen* in that little work.

Reader! do not fail to remark what the LORD JESUS here saith of the law, for most blessed it is to behold him as our law-surety, and our law-fulfiller. For as such he becomes the LORD our Righteousness, and is *the end of the law for righteousness to every one that believeth.* Rom. x. 4.

19 Whosoever therefore shall break one of these least commandments, and shall teach men so, he shall be called the least in the kingdom of heaven: but whosoever shall do and teach *them,* the same shall be called great in the kingdom of heaven.

20 For I say unto you, That except your righteousness shall exceed *the righteousness* of the scribes and pharisees, ye shall in no case enter into the kingdom of heaven.

These are very strong expressions of CHRIST, in proof that nothing short of a whole and complete obedience to the law, can justify a soul before GOD. And hence the presumption of the Scribes and Pharisees. Oh! the folly of the Pharisees of the present hour! Oh! the blessedness of being found, as Paul was, in CHRIST's righteousness! Philip. iii. 8, 9.

21 ¶ Ye have heard that it was said by them of old time, Thou shalt not kill; and whosoever shall kill shall be in danger of the judgment:

22 But I say unto you, That whosoever is angry with his brother without a cause shall be in danger of the judgment: and whosoever shall say to his

brother, Raca, shall be in danger of the council :
but whosoever shall say, Thou fool, shall be in
danger of hell fire.

No doubt the Reader would wish to have a clear apprehension of
the words *Raca* and *Fool.* The most acceptable service on these
verses I can offer, will be to explain them. *Raca*, was a word used
by the Jews to imply the utmost abhorrence, as if a man was spit
upon, which was a mark of the greatest contempt among that people.
For a man to call another *Raca*, was to call him a graceless
wretch. But the word *Fool*, in the sense here intended, was, if possible, worse; for it implied one predestinated to everlasting misery ;
meaning a child of hell. Matt. 23—33. Jude 4. Nothing can be
more proper than to have a just conception of those terms, and of
the sense in which our LORD meant them. The word *fool*, when
meaning a person dull or slow of understanding, totally differs from
the word *fool* as here referred to by CHRIST. The LORD himself
called his disciples fools in this sense, for their dulness of apprehension.
Luke xxiv. 25. And both Paul and James, his Apostles, did the
same upon similar occasions. 1 Cor. xv. 36. Gal. iii. 1. James ii. 20.
But the folly which implies a state of reprobation, is totally different
from this weakness of the mind. Isaiah speaks of it, chapter xxvii.
11. *For it is a people of no understanding*, meaning, to whom no
grace is given. Not children of the kingdom, but the children of the
wicked one ; *therefore he that made them* (saith the Prophet) *will not
have mercy upon them, and he that formed them will shew them no favour.* In this sense, for any man to decide upon another, and say,
thou fool ! thou child of hell ! is to endanger his own state before
GOD. The LORD JESUS, who knows the heart, and knows them that
are his, might truly, as he did, tell some in his day, that they were
of the generation of vipers, and who could not escape the damnation of hell. But none but the Great Searcher of Hearts can be qualified or authorized to do so. And it should seem that *Moses* incurred
the displeasure of the LORD, for calling the LORD's people *Rebels,*
(which is a similar word to that of fool in this place,) at the waters of
Meribah. Numb. xx. 10. I beg to refer the Reader to my *Poor
Man's Concordance*, under the words *Rebel* and *Rebels.*

23 Therefore if thou bring thy gift to the altar,
and there rememberest that thy brother hath ought
against thee ;

24 Leave there thy gift before the altar, and go
thy way ; first be reconciled to thy brother, and
then come and offer thy gift.

CHRIST is our New Testament Altar, neither have we any other.
It is painful to hear men call the communion table *Altar*, a name
which belongs only to JESUS. But seen in this point of view, when
drawing nigh at any time to JESUS, and recollecting some offence
given to our brother, how truly doth this correspond to the union
and harmony subsisting between CHRIST and his members, to come to

Him as the Head, and to bring with us, by faith, the whole body in our arms to the LORD. John xvii. 21. 1 Cor. xii. 25, 26, 27. For the members are to have the same care one for another, as one member of the body hath for its fellow member.

25 Agree with thine adversary quickly, while thou art in the way with him ; lest at any time the adversary deliver thee to the judge, and the judge deliver thee to the officer, and thou be cast into prison.

26 Verily I say unto thee, Thou shalt by no means come out thence, till thou hast paid the uttermost farthing.

These are sweet verses if referred to that lawsuit we all have, by reason of sin and transgression, with GOD. An adversary doth not always mean the evil spirit. It is indeed one of his names. 1 Pet. v. 8. But the LORD saith *I will be an adversary to thine adversaries.* Exod. xxiii. 22. And the Lord is represented as an adversary to his people in the day of their sorrow. Lament. ii. 4. In this sense JEHO-VAH hath a controversy and a lawsuit with his people by reason of sin, and the LORD JESUS recommends his church in these verses, to make up the breach quickly while we are in the way, that is, JESUS himself is the way, and the only way of reconciliation. Reader! what a refreshing thought! CHRIST is our peace. Micah v. 5. GOD *was in* CHRIST *reconciling the world unto himself.* 2 Cor. v. 19. And *now there is no condemnation to them that are in* CHRIST JESUS. Rom. viii. 1. But to those who live and die in the natural enmity of their mind, CHRIST becomes the judge, to whom the ungodly are delivered. John v. 22. Angels are the officers of judgment. Matt. xiii. 41, 42. And the prison is explained to us in the Scriptures as Hell, where they will be cast and remain for ever. 2 Pet. ii. 4. Rev. xx. 15.

27 Ye have heard that it was said by them of old time, Thou shalt not commit adultery.

28 But I say unto you, That whosoever looketh on a woman, to lust after her, hath committed adultery with her already in his heart.

29 And if thy right eye offend thee, pluck it out, and cast it from thee : for it is profitable for thee that one of thy members should perish, and not *that* thy whole body should be cast into hell.

30 And if thy right hand offend thee, cut it off, and cast *it* from thee : for it is profitable for thee that one of thy members should perish, and not that thy whole body should be cast into hell.

Reader! do not fail to observe the spiritual nature of the law of GOD. It is not limited to actions, but includes thoughts. The heart is the forge where all actions are worked. And whether they be brought forth into actual deeds or not, in the eye of the LORD the intention is the same. Surely the whole earth is at once brought in guilty before GOD. It is the grossest mistake in the world for any man to take shelter from guilt, in a supposed exemption from this or that particular sin. The heart sin, the nature sin, the mother sin, it is this which gives birth to all. And that it doth not break out in all men alike, is not from any difference in nature, for all are the same, but from certain restraints, particularly the restraints of grace. Read what the LORD said to *Abimelech* on this subject, which may serve to explain the cause to every man. Gen. xx. 6.

31 It hath been said, Whosoever shall put away his wife, let him give her a writing of divorcement:

32 But I say unto you, That whosoever shall put away his wife, saving for the cause of fornication, causeth her to commit adultery: and whosoever shall marry her that is divorced committeth adultery.

The law made a provision for the putting away a wife in cases of adultery, Deut. 24. i. &c. But the LORD JESUS saith that this was permitted only in consequence of the hardness of their hearts; for from the beginning of the creation of GOD it was not so. Mark x. 5, 6, 7, &c. And what a sweet thought is it to the souls of GOD's people married to JESUS, that notwithstanding all their adultery and spiritual fornication, our gracious Husband never put his wife away. See those blessed Scriptures in confirmation. Isaiah liv. 5, &c. Jerem. iii. 1. Hosea ii. 19. 20. And though the LORD in several scriptures speaks of the justice of the deed, Jerem. iii. 8. Hosea ii. 2. yet the LORD demands where is the bill of divorce, and to which of his creditors did he sell her. Isaiah l. 1. So that there never was a divorce, for the LORD GOD of Israel saith, that *he hateth putting away.* Malachi ii. 14—16. Hosea ii. 7.

33 Again, ye have heard that it hath been said by them of old time, Thou shalt not forsware thyself, but shalt perform unto the Lord thine oaths:

34 But I say unto you, Swear not at all; neither by heaven: for it is God's throne:

35 Nor by the earth; for it is his footstool; neither by Jerusalem; for it is the city of the great King.

36 Neither shalt thou swear by thy head, because thou canst not make one hair white or black.

37 But let your communication be, Yea, yea; Nay, nay: for whatsoever is more than these cometh of evil.

What a beautiful train of thoughts arise from those words of JESUS. Not only the prohibition of the LORD to what is so highly unsuitable and offensive in oaths and the like, but the injunction to a simple confirmation of the Yea and Nay among the followers of Him whose name is Amen.

38 Ye have heard that it hath been said, An eye for an eye, and a tooth for a tooth:

39 But I say unto you, That ye resist not the evil: but whosoever shall smite thee on the right cheek, turn to him the other also.

40 And if any man will sue thee at the law, and take away thy coat, let him have *thy* cloke also.

41 And whosoever shall compel thee to go a mile, go with him twain.

42 Give to him that asketh thee, and from him that would borrow of thee turn not thou away.

Who can read the justice and equity of that strict law, which enjoins an eye for an eye and a tooth for a tooth, without having his mind directed to the contemplation of CHRIST as our surety. In him this law was literally fulfilled, when *he who knew no sin became sin for us, that we might be made the righteousness of* GOD *in him.* Oh! how blessed so to contemplate CHRIST. 2 Cor. v. 21.

43 Ye have heard that it hath been said, Thou shalt love thy neighbour, and hate thine enemy.

44 But I say unto you, Love your enemies, bless them that curse you, do good to them that hate you, and pray for them which despitefully use you, and persecute you;

45 That ye may be the children of your Father which is in heaven: for he maketh his sun to rise on the evil and on the good, and sendeth rain on the just and on the unjust.

46 For if ye love them which love you, what reward have ye? do not even the publicans the same?

47 And if ye salute your brethren only, what do ye more *than others?* do not even the publicans so?

48 Be ye therefore perfect, even as your Father which is in heaven is perfect.

Was there ever such a refinement of the most perfect law of the LORD as is here drawn? And where shall we look for the fulfilment of it but in the LORD JESUS himself? He indeed, and He only, observed it in the fullest extent of it. And therefore the close of the chapter is express to the purpose with an eye to him. *Be ye perfect ;* that is, in the perfection of JESUS, for there is no other way of finding perfection but in him. What men talk of respecting sincerity for perfection, is a fancy formed no where but in their own brain. But as the members of the body partake in all that belongs to the head, so the members of CHRIST's body are considered perfect in him. And when JESUS saith be ye perfect, he wills what he commands; his biddings are enablings. Be ye perfect in me. Hence the answer by the Prophet; *Surely in the* LORD *have I righteousness and strength :* Or as the apostle renders it, *perfect in* CHRIST JESUS. Isaiah xlv. 24, 25. Coloss. i. 28. 1 Cor. i. 30.

REFLECTIONS.

HAIL! thou Almighty Prophet of thy people, blessed LORD JESUS! We praise thee for thy gracious proclamation in the Mount. Oh! grant thy people to be poor in spirit, rich in faith, and heirs of the kingdom. Holy mourners we shall be when the LORD hath convinced us of sin, of righteousness, and of judgment. And Oh! for that meekness in JESUS, that hungering and thirsting for JESUS and his righteousness, as those who are conscious that they have neither in themselves, and seek all in the LORD. Defer not, O our GOD, to induce all those graces of thy Spirit in the hearts of all thy redeemed, that *mercy* they may learn from thee, *purity of heart* find in thee, and as children of GOD, may walk in peace and love, as CHRIST also hath loved us, and given himself for us an offering and a sacrifice to GOD for a sweet smelling savor. And to all the persecutions and revilings of life, be looking stedfastly to JESUS, *who for the joy that was set before him endured the cross, despised the shame, and is set down on the right hand of the Majesty on high !* And grant dearest LORD, while learning under the influences of thy Holy Spirit, to mortify the deeds of the body that we may live. Oh! for grace to be living out of ourselves upon thee and thy fulness, and never to lose sight for a moment that thou art in our stead and law-room all that is here enjoined, and hast both magnified the law and made it honorable, and fulfilled the whole for us and our salvation. Yea! blessed JESUS! thou art the LORD our righteousness, and all thy people are righteous in thee. Amen.

C H A P. VI.

CONTENTS.

This Chapter is a continuation of the former. Most blessedly the LORD
JESUS *prosecutes the subject of his Sermon through the whole of it.*

TAKE heed that ye do not your alms before
men, to be seen of them : otherwise ye have
no reward of your Father which is in heaven.

2 Therefore when thou doest *thine* alms, do not
sound a trumpet before thee, as the hypocrites do
in the synagogues and in the streets, that they
may have glory of men. Verily I say unto you,
They have their reward.

3 But when thou doest alms, let not thy left hand
know what thy right hand doeth :

4 That thine alms may be in secret : and thy
Father which seeth in secret himself shall reward
thee openly.

The LORD JESUS is here giving instructions concerning the gift
of *alms.* And his directions are so plain that they need no comment.
Alms-giving, when given with an eye to the divine glory, and the
real love of men, is the gift of the heart, therefore there needs no
lookers on. What flows *from* GOD will tend *to* GOD. JESUS is then
in all, and a respect to him is the aim of all.

5 ¶ And when thou prayest, thou shalt not be
as the hypocrites *are :* for they love to pray standing the synagogues and in the corners of the streets,
that they may be seen of men. Verily I say unto
you, They have their reward.

6 But thou, when thou prayest, enter in thy
closet, and when thou hast shut thy door, pray to
thy Father which is in secret; and thy Father
which seeth in secret shall reward thee openly.

7 But when ye pray, use not vain repetitions,
as the heathen *do :* for they think that they shall
be heard for their much speaking.

8 Be not ye therefore like unto them : for your
Father knoweth what things ye have need of, before ye ask him.

Here the LORD speaks of *prayer*, and which is yet more express in reference to the LORD. Secret it must be between GOD and the soul, even in the public congregation, for what indeed is prayer but immediate communion, in which the only parties are JEHOVAH and his people. No lookers-on, no standers-by, can be supposed to interrupt the conference. But alas! how little understood by the great mass of what the world calls worshippers! Strictly and properly speaking, there can be no prayer, where there is no acquaintance. And until the Child of GOD is brought into an acquaintance with GOD in CHRIST, however he may offer a multitude of words, the heart is not interested, and consequently there is no prayer. But when we have received the spirit of adoption, and the new born child of GOD is brought forth into the spiritual life, instantly the cry of the soul is, Abba, Father! Reader! if the LORD the HOLY GHOST hath awakened your soul, regenerated your nature, and brought you into an heartfelt acquaintance with GOD in CHRIST, your own feelings, under divine teaching, will form the best comment on those precious words of JESUS; for you then know all that the LORD hath here said of secret communion with your Father. But otherwise, in secret or in public, you are a stranger to real prayer. Every graceless person is a prayerless person.

9 After this manner therefore pray ye : Our Father which art in heaven, Hallowed be thy name.

10 Thy kingdom come. Thy will be done in earth, as *it is* in heaven.

11 Give us this day our daily bread.

12 And forgive us our debts, as we forgive our debtors.

13 And lead us not into temptation, but deliver us from evil: For thine is the kingdom, and the power, and the glory, for ever. Amen.

We have here the pattern of prayer, which the LORD JESUS himself hath given. It were to hold up a small taper to the sun, to attempt an explanation of it, so plain, so evident, and so suited to every capacity. I only desire for myself, and every one whom GOD the HOLY GHOST directs in the use of it, that the sweet spiritual sense of it, by his most gracious power, was incorporated in our very heart, for then we should enter into the spiritual enjoyment of it, whenever we thus approach the throne. JEHOVAH in his threefold character of person, is indeed our FATHER, as JESUS taught, for he said in the moment of his departure, when redemption-work was finished, *I ascend to my Father and your Father, to my* GOD *and your* GOD. John xx. 17. And as we adore him on his throne in heaven, so we pray that his name may be hallowed on earth, and his kingdom of grace be established here among all his redeemed, as his kingdom of glory is, and will be, established above to all eternity. And the bread we pray for in the daily supply, is not simply the bread of the body which perisheth with using, but the bread of the soul, and which endureth to everlasting life, even JESUS himself, the living bread, *of which whosoever eateth shall live for ever.* As CHRIST is the gift of GOD, so the cry of the hungry soul is, LORD! *evermore give us this bread!* The pardon of sins the renewed soul needs daily, hourly, as he needs the bread of life. And therefore the petition comes in very sweet for forgiveness to our sins, as we delight to forgive the trespasses of others. And as the LORD alone can keep his people in the hour, and from the power of temptation, so JESUS hath graciously taught us to pray that the LORD would keep us from the evil one who goeth about as a roving lion, seeking whom he may devour. And most blessed is the concluding part, in ascribing all glory to the LORD. *For of him, and through him, and to him, are all things, to whom be glory for ever.* Rom. xi. 35. JESUS puts his name to the whole. *Amen.* And unless JESUS doth so, our Amen is nothing. It were to be devoutly wished, that every individual, in every congregation, would consider this when the Amen is pronounced. It should be done with the greatest reverence and solemnity, and with an eye to CHRIST. For it is not simply saying, as some have interpreted the word Amen, so be it, or be it so; thereby giving our confirmation to what hath been spoken. But it is calling upon the LORD JESUS by one of his names, even the *Amen,* to confirm it. We should feel the striking nature of the expression, if at the end of sermons, or prayers, or in any other part of our ordinances, we were solemnly to close all with saying JESUS. But yet in fact we do this when we say *Amen.* For this is as truly the name of the LORD JESUS as any other. May the LORD give both to Writer and Reader a right understanding in all things!

14 ¶ For if ye forgive men their trespasses, your heavenly Father will also forgive you.

15 But if ye forgive not men their trespasses, neither will your Father forgive your trespasses.

We must not suppose from those expressions at the close of the LORD's prayer, as if the condition of our forgiveness was suspended upon our forgiving of others. Our glorious LORD could not be supposed to mean this, because our pardon and acceptance with GOD is wholly on CHRIST's account. But it is meant as a blessed evidence of grace. Paul, his servant, marks the feature of a renewed heart as a precious token of JESUS's love reigning there; *be ye kind* (saith he) *one to another, tender-hearted, forgiving one another, even as* GOD *for* CHRIST's *sake hath forgiven you.* Ephes. iv. 32.

16 ¶ Moreover when ye fast, be not, as the hypocrites, of a sad countenance: for they disfigure their faces, that they may appear unto men to fast. Verily I say unto you, They have their reward.

17 But thou, when thou fastest, anoint thine head, and wash thy face;

18 That thou appear not unto men to fast, but unto thy Father which *is* in secret: and thy Father, which seeth in secret, shall reward thee openly.

We have our LORD's direction in these verses concerning the proper observance of *Fasts.* In which JESUS doth not condemn seasons of humbling the soul, but he reproves the Pharisaical method of pretending to mortify the body. Perhaps nothing in the Church of CHRIST hath opened to greater evil under the cloak of religion, than *Fasts* and *pretended Fasts.* It was the reproach those Pharisees of our LORD's days presumed to throw upon the SON of GOD himself and his disciples, that they observed them not. *Why* (say they) *do the disciples of John fast often, and make prayers, and likewise the disciples of the Pharisees, but thine eat and drink?* Luke v. 33. How little do they know the true spirit of the Gospel of CHRIST, who consider an abstinence from food as a real fast of the soul towards GOD! *Fasts* and *Festivals,* the former to mortify, and the latter to gratify the body, what are these things in the view of the LORD? *The kingdom of* GOD *is not meat and drink, but righteousness and peace, and joy in 'the* HOLY GHOST. Rom. xiv. 17. And we may say upon all those things as the Apostle doth upon another occasion; *for meat commendeth us not to* GOD, *for neither if we eat are we the better, neither if we eat not are we the worse.* 1 Cor. viii. 8. It is astonishing to behold, what the pride and corruption of our poor fallen nature prompts us to do, in substituting any thing in the place of real vital godliness. Oh! what would we give or suffer, in respect to the body, to atone for the sin of the soul? And the reason is obvious, could men but see it. For it tends to gratify the pride of our unhumbled nature. Any thing but CHRIST. To rely wholly upon the person, and finished salvation of the LORD JESUS, who but those taught by the Spirit of JESUS can fully do it? But those things which the Apostle saith, *have indeed a shew of wisdom in will, worship, and humility, and neglecting the body:* Oh! how much they tend to lead the heart *from* CHRIST, instead of directing *to* CHRIST. Coloss. ii. 16, to the end.

19 Lay not up for yourselves treasures upon earth, where moth and rust doth corrupt, and where thieves break through and steal:

20 But lay up for yourselves treasures in heaven, where neither moth nor rust doth corrupt, and where thieves do not break through nor steal:

21 For where your treasure is, there will your heart be also.

22 The light of the body is the eye: if therefore

H 2

thine eye be single, thy whole body shall be full
of light.

23 But if thine eye be evil, thy whole body
shall be full of darkness. If therefore the light
that is in thee be darkness, how great *is* that
darkness !

24 ¶ No man can serve two masters : for either
he will hate the one, and love the other; or else
he will hold to the one, and despise the other. Ye
cannot serve God and mammon.

These directions of our LORD are so very plain that they need no
comment. I detain the Reader, however, just to ask the question,
not to decide upon that verse: *if therefore the light that is in thee be
darkness, how great is that darkness?* Doth not JESUS allude to that
kind of head-knowledge, void of heart-influence, which devils and
some men possess; whereby they have a clear apprehension of the
great truths of GOD, but no affection towards them. Such was that
of *Balaam.* Numb. xxiv. 3, 4. His eyes (he saith himself) were
opened, but no regeneration of heart. He knew the LORD, but felt
no love towards him. The devils in the days of our LORD gave the
same testimony. *We know thee who thou art, the* HOLY ONE *of* GOD !
Luke iv. 33, 34. But *Balaam,* in the midst of this knowledge, hired
himself out to curse the people of GOD. And devils remain devils
with the full conviction of the GODHEAD of CHRIST, and his great
salvation upon them. Reader ! think what an awful state, to have
an historical head-knowledge of the LORD JESUS only; void of a
life-giving, soul-renewing grace, from the Spirit of CHRIST ! And
what increased sorrows will this very knowledge induce in another
world ?

25 Therefore I say unto you, Take no thought
for your life, what ye shall eat, or what ye shall
drink; nor yet for your body, what ye shall put
on. Is not the life more than meat, and the body
than raiment ?

26 Behold the fowls of the air: for they sow
not, neither do they reap, nor gather into barns ;
yet your heavenly Father feedeth them. Are ye
not much better than they ?

27 Which of you by taking thought can add
one cubit unto his stature ?

28 And why take ye thought for raiment : Consider the lilies of the field, how they grow; they
toil not, neither do they spin:

29 And yet I say unto you, That even Solomon in all his glory was not arrayed like one of these.

30 Wherefore, if God so clothe the grass of the field, which to-day is, and to-morrow is cast into the oven, *shall he* not much more *clothe* you, O ye of little faith?

31 Therefore take no thought, saying, What shall we eat? or, What shall we drink: or, Wherewithal shall we be clothed?

32 (For after all these things do the Gentiles seek:) for your heavenly Father knoweth that ye have need of all these things.

33 But seek ye first the kingdom of God, and his righteousness; and all these things shall be added unto you.

34 Take therefore no thought for the morrow: for the morrow shall take thought for the things of itself.. Sufficient unto the day *is* the evil thereof.

Who can add to the beauties, as well as doctrines of those *blessed* words of JESUS, by any attempted illustration. I have often read the contents of those sweet verses, and always I hope with increasing delight. Oh! who considers the eternal love of GOD, in CHRIST, to his church and people, can pause a moment with any doubt of his everlasting watchfulness and care in all the departments of nature, providence, grace, and glory. Chosen in CHRIST, blessed in CHRIST, preserved in CHRIST, and called! Ephes. i. 3—5. 2 Tim. i. 9. Jude 1. And in his providential mercies, how constant and unremitting, Isaiah xxvii. 3. Job. xxxvi. 7. how tender, Isaiah lxvi. 13. Zech. ii. 8. Isaiah xxxi. 5. how new and seasonable, Lament. iii. 25. and how sure and everlasting. Isaiah liv. 10. If I detain the Reader one moment longer over these verses I hope he will pardon me. I beg him to observe, if he hath not before, the very great beauty in the images here made use of to express the love contained in those expressions of JESUS. *Behold the fowls of the air!* Not the fowls of the barn, not the poultry, fed daily by some appointed hand, but the fowls of the air, who have neither store-house nor barn, and whose lodging of to night may be taken away before the morrow, and they are obliged to seek a new one. Behold the *lilies of the field!* Not the cultivated and watered plants of the garden, but the lilies of the field, exposed to be trodden down by the feet of the ox or the ass, and plucked up by every traveller. And doth JESUS give beauty to those, and which perhaps hath no eye but his to see their beauty? Doth JESUS watch them and water them, and cause his sun to shine upon them? Oh! then, ye redeemed of the LORD, ye that are the purchase of his blood, yea, if possible, more than even this; part of himself and *members of his body, of his flesh, and of his bones;* can he forget you, overlook you, yea, overlook and forget himself! Precious LORD JESUS! I would say, both for myself and every one of thy children, give us all grace to leave all our concerns with thee, and anxious only to be found of thy kingdom, regenerated by thy HOLY SPIRIT, adopted into the family of CHRIST and GOD, and justified in thy all-sufficient righteousness, we may take no thought for the morrow, knowing that *whether we live we live to the* LORD, or whether we die we die to the LORD, *so that living or dying we are the* LORD's.

REFLECTIONS.

READER! Pause over this part of our REDEEMER's sermon, as over the preceding portion of it, and let us both look up for grace in the teaching of GOD the HOLY GHOST, to gather the many precious instructions it contains. JESUS presupposeth that his redeemed give alms according to the ability he hath given them. And if you and I have received of the *upper* springs of the LORD's grace, shall we not be ready to give, and glad to distribute of the *nether* springs of the LORD's bounty? Not dear LORD to be seen of men, no! nor with the most distant view to recommend ourselves to thee. All we have is thine, and of thine own do we give thee, in imparting of what we have to refresh the bowels of our poorer brethren. Oh! for grace that all may be done *from* thee, and *for* thee, and from love *to* thee.

And in our approaches to thy throne in prayer, oh! grant that all may be in and through the LORD OUR RIGHTEOUSNESS. For if LORD we have found peace in the blood of thy cross, our access to the Father will be by one Spirit through thee. Not to be seen of men, but graciously accepted of GOD *in* CHRIST, *through* CHRIST, and both in the words and works of CHRIST.

In the abstinence of the body, and in the humblings of the soul, in dying daily to the world, and crucifying the flesh with its affections and lusts, oh! for grace *from* CHRIST to be walking daily *with* CHRIST, casting all our care upon him who careth for us. And while seeking, above all things, the kingdom of GOD and his righteousness, may we be for ever on the look-out for *the glorious appearing of the great* GOD *and our* SAVIOR JESUS CHRIST. Even so LORD prepare us for thy coming! Amen.

CHAP. VII.

CONTENTS.

The LORD JESUS *in this Chapter concludes his Sermon on the Mount, and a very blessed close he makes of it, in comparing the wise hearers of it to those who build on the Rock, and the foolish to those who build on the Sand.*

JUDGE not, that ye be not judged.

2 For with what judgment ye judge, ye shall be judged; and with what measure ye mete, it shall be measured to you again.

3 And why beholdest thou the mote that is in thy brother's eye, but considerest not the beam that is in thine own eye?

4 Or how wilt thou say to thy brother, Let me pull out the mote out of thine eye; and behold, a beam *is* in thine own eye?

5 Thou hypocrite, first cast out the beam out of thine own eye; and then shalt thou see clearly to cast out the mote out of thy brother's eye.

6 ¶ Give not that which is holy unto the dogs, neither cast ye your pearls before swine, lest they trample them under their feet, and turn again and rend you.

7 ¶ Ask, and it shall be given you; seek, and ye shall find; knock, and it shall be opened unto you.

8 For every one that asketh receiveth: and he that seeketh findeth; and to him that knocketh it shall be opened.

9 Or what man is there of you, whom if his son ask bread, will he give him a stone.

10 Or if he ask a fish, will he give him a serpent?

11 If ye then being evil, know how to give good gifts unto your children; how much more shall your Father which is in Heaven give good things to them that ask him?

I pass over the several most blessed things which the LORD JESUS here treats of, as being in themselves so plain, and by Him so beauti-fully expressed, as to render all explanation unnecessary. But I detain the Reader at the close of the passage, to beg his special and particular attention to that unequalled argument the LORD JESUS condescends to make use of, in representing the great predisposing grace of our heavenly Father to bless his children, under the figure of the solicitude of an earthly parent. It is as if JESUS had said; Is a poor worm of the earth, one of the fallen sinful sons of Adam, so prompt to listen to the cries of his children because he is a father, as to give them the best things the moment they ask them; think then how earnest the Great Father of mercies must be to give his Holy Spirit to his children, and who hath already given the greatest of all blessings, and unasked as it was, when giving them his only begotten Son. John xiv. 16, 17.

12 Therefore all things whatsoever ye would that men should do to you, do ye even so to them: for this is the law and the prophets.

This golden rule needs no comment. Oh! that all the followers of the LORD JESUS made it their rule with all men. It is said of one of the heathen emperors, *Alexander Severus,* that he was so great an admirer of this maxim, that he caused it to be written for public use, and often mentioned it in honor of CHRIST and the Christian religion. What a reproach to Christians who act not up to it!

13 ¶ Enter ye in at the straight gate: for wide *is* the gate, and broad *is* the way, that leadeth to destruction, and many there be which go in thereat:

14 Because strait *is* the gate and narrow *is* the way, which leadeth unto life, and few there be that find it.

15 Beware of false prophets, which come to you in sheep's clothing, but inwardly they are ravening wolves.

16 Ye shall know them by their fruits, do men gather grapes of thorns, or figs of thistles?

17 Even so every good tree bringeth forth good fruit; but a corrupt tree bringeth forth evil fruit.

18 A good tree cannot bring forth evil fruit, neither *can* a corrupt tree bring forth good fruit.

19 Every tree that bringeth not forth good fruit is hewn down and cast into the fire.

20 Wherefore by their fruits ye shall know them.

21 ¶ Not every one that saith unto me, Lord, Lord, shall enter into the kingdom of heaven: but he that doeth the will of my Father which is in heaven.

22 Many will say to me in that day, Lord, Lord, have we not prophesied in thy name? and in thy name have cast out devils: and in thy name done many wonderful works?

23 And then will I profess unto them, I never knew you: depart from me ye that work iniquity.

Nothing can be more interesting than what the LORD JESUS hath here said. And no form of words can be more decisive to mark the godly man from the hypocrite. I only detain the Reader to observe, how very awful those words of CHRIST are concerning false Teachers, in the great day of account. Preaching or prophesying in the name of CHRIST, and doing even miracles in the name of CHRIST, these are no proofs of the regeneration of the preacher's own heart. And very awful will it be then found; if there be no union with CHRIST here, there can be no communion with CHRIST to all eternity. And observe, that the LORD JESUS doth not say that this will be the portion of a few, but many! Oh! for grace to be found among the blessed few who have CHRIST formed in their hearts, *the hope of glory!*

24 Therefore whosoever heareth these sayings of mine, and doeth them, I will liken him unto a wise man, which built his house upon a rock;

25 And the rain descended, and the floods came, and the winds blew, and beat upon that house; and it fell not: for it was founded upon a rock.

26 And every one that heareth these sayings of mine, and doeth them not, shall be likened unto a foolish man, which built his house upon the sand:

27 And the rain descended, and the floods came, and the winds blew, and beat upon that house; and it fell, and great was the fall of it.

28 And it came to pass when Jesus had ended these sayings, the people were astonished at his doctrine:

29 For he taught them as *one* having authority, and not as the scribes.

Here the LORD closeth his discourse, and plainly sheweth whose are his from the men of the world. CHRIST is the Rock of Ages. The Precious Corner Stone JEHOVAH hath laid in Zion. And all that believe in him shall never perish, but have everlasting life. While on the contrary, those who build on the sand of their own attainments, when the storms of life come upon them, sink under the unequal pressure, and are buried in the everlasting ruins of their own confusion, and shall never come to the habitations of the blessed. The close of the LORD's sermon was, as might be expected. They were astonished at his doctrine. He spake as never man spake, and his word was with power.

REFLECTIONS.

READER! having gone over the whole of this blessed Sermon of CHRIST, let us sum up the contents, and beg of GOD the HOLY GHOST to write all the gracious truths contained in it in our hearts. And while we hear the LORD giving to his Church the whole Gospel of Salvation, oh! what a blessed consideration is it, that JESUS himself hath fulfilled all, and is all to his redeemed. Never may the Church of JESUS forget this, but receive CHRIST as the Father's gift, and the complete salvation of JEHOVAH to the end of the earth!.

Precious, blessed LORD JESUS! so may my soul hear these sayings of thine, and embrace them, that building upon thee as the foundation, the superstructure, and the whole, both of Law and the Prophets, when the LORD shall arise to shake terribly the earth, I may be found firm on the rock, *against which the gates of hell shall never prevail.* Despised as thou hast been, and still art, by Jews and false Christians, and a stone of stumbling and rock of offence; yet to me be thou more precious than the mountains of spices. In thy person, work and offices; in thy character and relations; in thy complete righteousness and salvation; be thou my LORD, my hope, and everlasting portion. LORD grant that I may never build on the sandy performance of any thing of my own, or mix up with thy complete work the hay and the stubble of any legal righteousness, which can stand no wind of the day of GOD's wrath; but be thou the all in all, of all grace here, and of glory for ever. Amen.

CHAP. VIII.

CONTENTS.

We have here the LORD JESUS *confirming his word by miracles.* JESUS *cleanseth a Leper, healeth the Centurion's servant, the mother-in-law of Peter, with many others; stilleth the waves of the sea, casteth out devils from two poor creatures, and permitteth them to enter into the swine.*

WHEN he was come down from the mountain, great multitudes followed him.

2 ¶ And behold, there came a leper and worshipped him, saying, Lord, if thou wilt, thou canst make me clean.

3 And Jesus put forth *his* hand, and touched him, saying, I will; Be thou clean, and immediately his leprosy was cleansed.

4 And Jesus saith unto him, See thou tell no man : but go thy way, shew thyself to the priest, and offer the gift that Moses commanded for a testimony unto them.

Though this act of cleansing the Leper is by *Matthew* recorded as the first of CHRIST's miracles, yet we have no authority so to conclude, for *John* records the first miracle to have been at the marriage feast. John ii. 14. And Mark and Luke do not place it in the same order. Mark i. 40. Luke v. 12. And some have thought that

this man was *Simon* the Leper. Matt. xxvi. 6. But the chief points
to be regarded in the history of this man's cleansing will be more to
our purpose to attend to. The leprosy was a disease so peculiar, that
it was always considered as a mark of divine displeasure on those who
were visited by it. Hence *Miriam*, the sister of *Aaron* was smitten
by it. Numbers xii. 10, &c. *Gehazi* the servant of *Elisha*. 2 Kings v.
27. *Uzziah* the king of Judah. 2 Chron. xxvi. 19, &c. And as the
disease was considered as coming from the LORD in judgment, so it
was deemed unlawful by the Jews in any to attempt to heal it. This
was the LORD's sole prerogative. 2 Kings v. 7. Add to these, the
unhappy persons afflicted by it were shut out, and precluded all civil
and religious communion.

Now what the leprosy is to the body, such is sin to the soul.
None but GOD can pardon the sinner, and nothing but the blood of
CHRIST can cleanse the sinner. So that the whole of our nature, by
reason of sin, is leprosy before GOD. The representation of this cleansing was set forth under the Law. Levit. xiv. But it is the Gospel
of CHRIST, which gives us the only possible cure in the person,
work, and righteousness of GOD our SAVIOR. Ezek. xxxvi. 25, &c.
1 John i. 7.

This poor creature, which came to JESUS, is the representative of
every poor sinner, when convinced of the leprosy of sin, from the
teaching of GOD the HOLY GHOST. Such an one is convinced of
CHRIST's ability, because GOD the SPIRIT hath taught him who CHRIST
is, and what CHRIST is able to perform. But it appears, that this
man's faith was but slender; for though he had no doubt of CHRIST's
ability, yet he had doubts whether the SON of GOD would exercise it
towards him. LORD, *(said he) if thou wilt, thou canst make me clean!*
I beg the Reader to remark this weakness of faith. Perhaps my
Reader knows somewhat of the same in his own experience. And if
so, may the LORD put a cry into his heart, that he may say with
the Apostles, LORD! *increase our faith!* But when he hath done this,
let him look unto JESUS, in his tenderness to this poor man, and observe, that the weakness of his faith, did not restrain CHRIST's mercy
and power.—For we are told, JESUS *put forth his hand and touched
him, saying, I will, be thou clean: and immediately his leprosy was
cleansed.* I beg the Reader to observe with me, not only the gracious
act of CHRIST's healing him, but touching him also in doing it.
Touching a leper! Yes! JESUS, though made in the likeness of sinful
flesh, contracted none of our pollutions when taking our flesh. His
unspotted purity could not be defiled by an union with our nature. The sun shines, and imparts all its warmings, healings, life-
giving properties, but yet contracts no defilement from the dung-hill
objects to which it communicates those blessings. And JESUS sheds
his blissful, sin-withering, soul-cleansing influence, without being
tainted with the maladies of defiled churches, and defiled souls, into
which he shines, and on which he ariseth, as *the Sun of righteousness, with healing in his wings.* Malachi iv. 2.

The precept which the LORD gave him, to tell no man of his cure,
seems to have been intended, not with a view to conceal the knowledge of the mercy he had received from the world; but only that
he should first make it known to the priest, as had been enjoined by
the law. Our first acknowledgments for all mercies, and especially

for Spiritual mercies, in the salvation of our souls by the LORD JESUS CHRIST, are due to the LORD. JESUS, our Almighty High Priest, the Author and Giver, of our blessings, is first to be eyed and acknowledged in our blessings. But when this is done, it is a suited frame of mind to call upon the whole world to the contemplation of the divine goodness towards us. *O come hither and hearken, all ye that fear* GOD, *and I will tell you what he hath done for my soul.* Psal. lxvi. 16.

5 ¶ And when Jesus was entered into Capernaum, there came unto him a centurion, beseeching him,

6 And saying, Lord, my servant lieth at home sick of the palsy, grievously tormented.

7 And Jesus saith unto him, I will come and heal him.

8 The centurion answered and said, Lord, I am not worthy that thou shouldest come under my roof: but speak the word only, and my servant shall be healed.

9 For I am a man under authority, having soldiers under me; and I say to this *man*, Go, and he goeth; and to another, Come, and he cometh: and to my servant, Do this, and he doeth *it*.

10 When Jesus heard *it*, he marvelled, and said to them that followed, Verily I say unto you, I have not found so great faith, no, not in Israel.

11 And I say unto you, That many shall come from the east and west, and shall sit down with Abraham, and Isaac, and Jacob, in the kingdom of heaven.

12 But the children of the kingdom shall be cast out into outer darkness: there shall be weeping and gnashing of teeth.

13 And Jesus said unto the centurion, Go thy way; and as thou hast believed, *so* be it done unto thee. And his servant was healed in the selfsame hour.

We have here another of CHRIST's miracles. *Capernaum* was a city of *Galilee,* not far from *Nazareth.* A *centurion* was an officer among the Romans. This man had a servant sick of the palsy.

Luke, in his account of this case, saith, that the servant was dear unto his master. Luke vii. 2, &c. Be that as it may, it appears that the centurion, though a Gentile, had such views of Christ, as none but the Lord could have given him. Reader! what a precious thought it is to us poor Gentiles, that in Christ Jesus *there is neither Jew nor Greek; bond nor free; for we are all one. And if we be Christ's, then are we Abraham's seed, and heirs according to the promise.* Gal. iii. 28, 29. If I detain the Reader a moment longer in the contemplation of this miracle of Jesus, it shall be to observe two or three of the striking features in this man's faith. Such was his apprehension of Christ's power, that he said it was unnecessary for Jesus to come to see the patient; for his word only would heal. What could manifest his belief of the Godhead of Christ more than this? And his sense of his own unworthiness, became another testimony what views he had of Jesus. There is a great beauty, as well as strong reasoning, the centurion made use of, respecting the exertion of Christ's power. As the soldiers under his command, must go, or come, at his pleasure; so the whole army of diseases, he knew, were under the controul of Christ. Think, Reader! what faith there must have been in this Gentile? Do not overlook the 11th verse in this passage! But if such was the faith of the centurion, what grace doth the whole manifest of the person of Jesus, the great Author, and Giver of faith, from whom every portion of it the centurion had received? Oh! thou dear Lord, do thou increase our faith!

14 ¶ And when Jesus was come into Peter's house, he saw his wife's mother laid, and sick of a fever.

15 And he touched her hand, and the fever left her: and she arose, and ministered unto them.

16 ¶ When the even was come, they brought unto him many that were possessed with devils: and he cast out the spirits with *his* word, and healed all that were sick :

17 That it might be fulfilled which was spoken by Esaias the prophet, saying, Himself took our infirmities, and bare our sicknesses.

What a beautiful representation is here made, in a short compass, of the lovely, and all-loving Jesus! With a word only the Lord healed! Think of his sovereignty: think of his grace. And let not the Reader overlook what is said of his taking our infirmities, and bearing our sicknesses. Mark, I pray you, it is said, that *Himself did it.* Jesus Christ personally did this. It is the Person of Christ, as God-man, in this instance, we are everlastingly to keep in view. Not the person of the Father, neither the person of the Holy Ghost, for neither of those glorious persons took our nature: but the person of Jesus, God-Man-Mediator. And I very earnestly desire the Reader to pause a moment over the wonderful relation. *Himself took our infirmities, and bare our sicknesses.* In himself, there was no possibility of his becoming sick; for sickness is the sole effect of sin; and as there was no taint of sin in his holy nature, there could be no sickness, which is the sole consequence of sin: yet, as by imputation he bore our sins; so by sympathy he bore our sicknesses. Yea, in this sense, he knew and felt more what sin, and the sorrows of sin and sickness are, than the sinners themselves for whom he bore them. For as Jesus sustained the persons of his redeemed; so he sustained their sorrows. He that felt the whole weight and burden of their sins, and the divine wrath as their surety, must have known more, and felt more, both of the bitterness of sin itself, and all the dire effects of it, than the whole body of sinners themselves. And if, as it is said, the righteous soul of *Lot* was vexed with *the filthy conversation of the wicked, day by day,* (2 Peter ii. 7.) what must have been the feelings of the LORD JESUS, during his whole life upon earth, in beholding the sins of his redeemed, and which he himself bore; and for which he gave himself a ransom. Reader! do not dismiss this view of the passage, before that you have first considered what a most blessed opening it gives us of the person of our LORD. And let me add, that of all the arguments under the grace of the HOLY GHOST, to restrain from the commission of sin in the LORD's people, this is the highest and the best. Oh! what a sad return for such unequalled love! A child of GOD might well say with Joseph, when tempted, *how can I do this great wickedness, and sin against* GOD. Gen. xxxix. 9. Rom. viii. 13.

18 ¶ Now when Jesus saw great multitudes about him, he gave commandments to depart unto the other side.

19 And a certain scribe came, and said unto him, Master, I will follow thee whithersoever thou goest.

20 And Jesus saith unto him, The foxes have holes, and the birds of the air *have* nests; but the Son of man hath not where to lay *his* head.

21 And another of his disciples said unto him, Lord, suffer me first to go and bury my father.

22 But Jesus said unto him, Follow me; and let the dead bury their dead.

As this is the first place in the Gospel we meet with the phrase Son *of* MAN, in reference to the person of CHRIST; and especially as it is a phrase the LORD JESUS was pleased frequently to make use of, and delighted in; I beg the Reader not to pass it by hastily. I do not presume to speak decidedly upon it, but yet I would humbly ask, Did not the Son of GOD take pleasure in shewing thereby his wonderful condescension, and his wonderful love to our nature? Think, Reader! what an endearment of character it is in JESUS. You and I might well exceed *Solomon's* surprize. He thought it a matter, as well he might, of infinite surprize, that the LORD should condescend to dwell by his gracious presence in the temple. But had *Solomon* lived to see, as you and I have done, GOD tabernacling in substance of our flesh, what would he then have said! Precious JESUS, dwell in me, and reign and rule in me, and be my GOD, and cause me to be thy servant! Amidst this great multitude, and amidst the forwardness of one, and the backwardness of another, how few truly followed CHRIST? The dead in trespasses and sins, do indeed bury their dead; for to be carnally minded is death. And all that are Christless and unregenerate, are dead while they live. 1 Tim. v. 6.

23 ¶ And when he was entered into a ship, his disciples followed him.

24 And, behold, there arose a great tempest in the sea, insomuch that the ship was covered with the waves; but he was asleep.

25 And his disciples came to *him*, and awoke him, saying, Lord, save us: we perish.

26 And he saith unto them, Why are ye fearful, O ye of little faith? Then he arose, and rebuked the winds and the sea, and there was a great calm.

27 But the men marvelled, saying, What manner of man is this, that even the winds and the sea obey him?

What a beautiful representation is here given of the two-fold nature of CHRIST. Behold the man, in his human nature, sleeping! Behold the GODHEAD, in his divine nature, rebuking the winds and sea. Let the infidel look at this, and ask himself, who but the Creator could thus command the mighty waters? Let not the child of GOD overlook the sweet consolation the passage brings with it, to hush all the winds and storms of life. JESUS may, to your view, be inattentive, as though he heard not, when the ship of life in which you are embarked is filling with waves, and when in the distress of your soul you are crying out, LORD, save, or I perish. But, remember, GOD incarnate is with you in the vessel, and he will bear the whole up until the time of deliverance. Then will he do by you, as he did in this instance with his disciples, arise, and rebuke both winds and sea, and there shall be a great calm. Storms of fear, and storms of temptation, must all subside at the command of JESUS.

28 ¶ And when he was come to the other side into the country of the Gergesenes, there met him two possessed with devils, coming out of the tombs, exceeding fierce, so that no man might pass by that way.

29 And, behold, they cried out, saying, What have we to do with thee, Jesus, thou Son of God? art thou come hither to torment us before the time?

30 And there was a good way off from them an herd of many swine feeding.

31 So the devils besought him, saying, If thou cast us out, suffer us to go away into the herd of swine.

32 And he said unto them, Go. And when they were come out, they went into the herd of swine: and behold, the whole herd of swine ran violently down a steep place into the sea, and perished in the waters.

33 And they that kept them fled, and went their ways into the city, and told every thing, and what was befallen to the possessed of the devils,

34 And, behold, the whole city came out to meet Jesus: and when they saw him, they besought *him* that he would depart out of their coasts.

We meet with the relation of this miracle, and somewhat more particularly enlarged, in the fifth Chapter of Mark's Gospel. I refer the Reader therefore to that part of my Commentary, for my observations upon it. I only detain the Reader for the moment, to observe, that the place, though mentioned differently, is one and the same. *Matthew* here calls it the country of the *Gergesenes*. *Mark* and *Luke* call it the country of the *Gadarenes*. But as it was on the lake of *Tiberias*, right over against *Galilee*, it is but one and the same. It was called in the days of *Joshua*, and indeed long before, the country of the *Girgashites*. Gen. xv. 21. Deut. vii. 1. Joshua iii. 10. The Syriac version gave it the name of *Gadarenes: Gergesa* and *Gadara*, was the same city.

REFLECTIONS.

READER! let you and I look on, and behold the wonders of our wonder-working GOD. See the leprous man cleansed; the paralytic healed; the raging fever subdued; yea, the winds, sea, and devils, in a moment brought under the word of our JESUS. But let us not stop here. He that cleansed the poor leper in his body, can and will cleanse all the leprosy of soul in his people. He that gave strength to the palsy of nature, can and will make the crippled in soul to leap as an hart; and all the feverish lusts of his redeemed, JESUS will subdue! Oh! thou gracious GOD of our salvation! no storms of hell,

nor storms of indwelling corruption, nor storms of the world, shall
drown thy people! JESUS, though for a while may appear to our
impatient minds as inattentive, but he hath said, *For the sighing of
the poor, and the oppression of the needy, now will I arise, saith* GOD!
And oh! with what tenderness and fellow-feeling, the LORD JESUS
enters into all the concerns of his redeemed. Truly LORD, it may
be said of thee, thou dost thyself take our infirmities, and bare our
sicknesses! Oh! vouchsafe thy continual presence with us! and
never, never LORD, do thou depart out of our coasts!

C H A P. IX.

CONTENTS.

The LORD JESUS *is here represented in the exercise of his ministry;
working miracles, and going about through all the cities and villages,
preaching his gospel, and healing every disease of the people.*

AND he entered into a ship, and passed over,
and came into his own city.

2 ¶ And, behold, they brought to him a man
sick of the palsy, lying on a bed: and Jesus seeing
their faith, said unto the sick of the palsy; Son, be
of good cheer; thy sins be forgiven thee.

3 And, behold, certain of the scribes said within
themselves, This *man* blasphemeth.

4 And Jesus knowing their thoughts said,
Wherefore think ye evil in your hearts?

5 For whether is easier, to say, *Thy* sins be
forgiven thee; or to say, Arise, and walk?

6 But that ye may know that the Son of man
hath power on earth to forgive sins, (then saith he
to the sick of the palsy,) Arise, take up thy bed,
and go unto thine house.

7 And he arose, and departed to his house.

8 But when the multitude saw *it*, they marvelled,
and glorified God, which had given such power
unto men.

In the relation of this miracle by Mark, he names *Capernaum* as
the place where it was wrought; so that this may serve to teach us,
that when CHRIST's own city is spoken of, it means *Capernaum*, and
not *Bethlehem*, where CHRIST was born. This miracle is among the
many, one of the highest in confirmation both of his GODHEAD, and
of his mission as the Messiah. The Prophet had said, *Behold,*

your GOD *shall come and save you;* and *then shall the lame man leap as an hart.* Isaiah xxxv. 4, 5, 6. Observe, the *first* act in proof of CHRIST's eternal power and GODHEAD which he manifested towards this man with the palsy, was to pardon his sins. The reasoning of the Scribes was well founded *in truth,* though formed by them *in malice,* that none but GOD himself can forgive sins. And the LORD JESUS, by the exercise of this authority, and in the cure of the body, which immediately followed, proved that he was GOD. The *second* act in proof of his GODHEAD was, that JESUS *knew their thoughts,* and acted upon that knowledge, by telling them what they thought. This also is the sole prerogative of GODHEAD; and this CHRIST exercised. Jerem. xvii. 10. Rev. ii. 23. And the evidence the LORD JESUS immediately gave of his person and power in the cure of the palsy, confirmed the whole beyond a doubt. When the Reader hath duly considered these grand things in this miracle, I would beg to call his attention to other considerations, which arise out of it. In this miracle the LORD JESUS seems to demand attention to his character as Messiah; for he calls himself *the* SON *of Man.* It was to be among the features of Him that was to come to be known under this character. Hence when John sent his disciples to ask JESUS whether he was the very person that should come, or were they to look for another, the LORD JESUS referred to those testimonies, in proof that he was the very SON of Man. Compare Isaiah lxi. 1. with Matt. ii. 2—6. And hence JESUS also, in his discourse with the Jews, when they attacked him for healing the man on the sabbath day, declared that all authority was given to him to execute judgment, because he was *the* SON *of Man.* So that over and above his own personal power and GODHEAD, in the essence of JEHOVAH, he here acted in his mediator-character, and thereby manifested who he was, and the great object for which he came. I pray the Reader, in order that he may have a clear apprehension of this subject, and to distinguish between the SON of GOD's person, as one of the persons in the GODHEAD, and his office-character, as mediator, GOD and Man in one person, that he will turn to those scriptures in proof before he goes further, John v. 17. to the end. John xvii. 2, 3. Matt. xxvi. 62—65. There is one point more in this miracle, which merits our earnest attention; namely, the tenderness and compassion of JESUS, which unasked, pardoned the sin of the soul, while healing the disease of the body. Well might the astonished beholders, in the contemplation of this miracle, express their thankfulness to GOD. But how is it, that under such impressions, no saving conviction of CHRIST is said to have been wrought upon their hearts? The Reader will find an answer to this, and similar questions of the like nature, Isaiah vi. 9, 10. Matt. xiii. 14. Mark iv. 12. Luke viii. 10. John xii. 40. Acts xxvii. 26. Rom. xi. 8. For other observations on this miracle, I refer the Reader to Mark ii. 2—12.

9 ¶ And as Jesus passed forth from thence, he saw a man, named Matthew, sitting at the receipt of custom : and he saith unto him, Follow me. And he arose, and followed him.

10 ¶ And it came to pass, as Jesus sat at meat in the house, behold, many publicans and sinners came and sat down with him and his disciples.

11 And when the Pharisees saw *it*, they said unto his disciples, Why eateth your Master with publicans and sinners ?

12 But when Jesus heard *that*, he said unto them, They that be whole need not a physician, but they that are sick.

13 But go ye and learn what *that* meaneth, I will have mercy, and not sacrifice : for I am not come to call the righteous, but sinners to repentance.

The call of *Matthew* is most interesting, and serves to mark the distinguishing grace of GOD. His name from *Mattan*, a *gift*, seems suited to one who received the free gift of the LORD. Here was no preparation, no enquiry after CHRIST; no waiting at ordinances, yea, not so much as a conscious sense in the heart of *Matthew*, of his want of salvation. He was sitting in his gainful office of a *Publican*, or tax-gatherer : an office odious to all the people of Israel, and when exercised by a descendant of Israel, yet more hateful. Such was *Matthew*; and so employed, when the LORD JESUS passed by, and called him from a tax-gatherer, to be an Apostle and Evangelist. Oh! what grace was here? How truly was that scripture fulfilled, *I am found of them that sought me not.* Isaiah lxv. 1. What an astonishing instance of mercy was this. How very powerful must have been the call! How gracious on the part of JESUS! How surprizing to the heart of *Matthew ?* And observe the instant effects. No sooner doth JESUS call, but *Matthew* obeys. And as JESUS opened *Matthew's* heart to receive him, *Matthew* opens his house to welcome JESUS. Neither is this all. For as this one Publican had found mercy from the LORD, *Matthew* invited other Publicans to come and find mercy also. There is enough in CHRIST for all. What a lovely view to behold the Great Redeemer, encircled at *Matthew's* table, with *Publicans* and Sinners! The murmuring of the *Pharisees* is just as might be expected, and such as hath marked *Pharisees* in all ages. But what a lovely answer the LORD gave to the charge. The very character of CHRIST, as the Physician of the Soul, naturally led him to haunts of sickness, for the exercise of his profession. And by referring them to that memorable passage in the prophet Hosea vi. 6. JESUS took the words as applicable to himself in confirmation of his office : JEHOVAH Rophe, *I am the* LORD *that healeth thee.* Exod. xv. 26.

14 Then came to him the disciples of John, saying, Why do we and the Pharisees fast oft, but thy disciples fast not?

15 And Jesus said unto them, Can the children of the bridechamber mourn, as long as the bridegroom is with them? but the days will come, when the bridegroom shall be taken from them, and then shall they fast.

16 No man putteth a piece of new cloth unto an old garment, for that which is put in to fill it up taketh from the garment, and the rent is made worse.

17 Neither do men put new wine into old bottles: else the bottles break, and the wine runneth out, and the bottles perish; but they put new wine into new bottles, and both are preserved.

It is wonderful to see how fond men have been in all ages to substitute any thing, and every thing, in the room of real godliness, and a change of heart. Fasting and alms-giving, and services, however costly, shall be set up, provided they may find pardon to the sins of nature. But all these are not regeneration. It is the old nature still. It is still the old creature, only dressed up in a new form: not transformed in the renewing of the heart. JESUS makes use of two beautiful similitudes to shew the folly of it. The new cloth put into the old garment; and the new wine into old bottles: neither of which can receive into union what is altogether the reverse of themselves. The strength of the new cloth will only tend to rend the old; and the old dried skins of bottles must burst if new fermenting wine is put into them. In like manner, the new robe of JESUS's righteousness cannot be joined to patch up our filthy rags: neither can the new wine of the Gospel be received into the old unrenewed skin of nature. But when the HOLY GHOST hath by regeneration made all things new, and CHRIST's righteousness is received as the new robe of salvation; and the blood of CHRIST as the wine that maketh glad the heart of man; both then are preserved and blessed. Judges ix. 13. Psm. civ. 15. Isaiah lxi. 10. See Mark ii. 18, &c.

18 While he spake these things unto them, behold, there came a certain ruler, and worshipped him, saying, My daughter is even now dead: but come and lay thy hand upon her, and she shall live.

19 And Jesus arose, and followed him, and so did his disciples.

20 ¶ And, behold, a woman, which was diseased with an issue of blood twelve years, came behind him, and touched the hem of his garment:

21 For she said within herself, If I may but touch his garment, I shall be whole.

22 But Jesus turned him about, and when he saw her, he said, Daughter, be of good comfort; thy faith hath made thee whole. And the woman was made whole from that hour.

23 And when Jesus came into the ruler's house, and saw the minstrels and the people making a noise,

24 He said unto them, Give place: for the maid is not dead, but sleepeth. And they laughed him to scorn.

25 But when the people were put forth, he went in, and took her by the hand, and the maid arose.

26 And the fame hereof went abroad into all that land.

We have here two most interesting miracles of the LORD JESUS; and they are blended into one view, because the one runs into the other, and both serve mutually to illustrate the glory of JESUS. The importunity of the poor man, that JESUS should hasten to his child, and the interruption which took place from the woman in detaining CHRIST for her cure, are finely worked up, both to heighten the miracle, to exercise the faith of the patient, and to manifest the sovereignty of the LORD. What an interruption was this woman's stopping CHRIST to the ardor of the ruler. How he must have felt! How his fears must have increased; lest, according to his views, CHRIST should come too late. And *Mark*, in the relation of this miracle adds to *Matthew's* account, that *while JESUS was speaking with this woman, there came certain from the ruler's house which said, thy daughter is dead, why troublest thou the master?* Mark v. 35. And *Luke* in like manner, Luke viii. 49. Let the children of GOD in their exercises of faith, while at any time the LORD is suspending his gracious answers to prayer, or bringing them into difficulties, or under all their dead and dying frames, think of this! Remember, it is one thing to feel and know our own totally lost and helpless state; and another to have lively faith in the LORD JESUS-CHRIST. For it is not what we are, but what CHRIST is. And it is good *to have the sentence of death in ourselves, that we may not trust in ourselves, but in him that raiseth the dead.* Oh! the blessedness of entering into the full enjoyment of those sublime truths of JESUS, when he saith, *I am the resurrection and the life; he that believeth in me though he were dead, yet shall he live; and he that liveth and believeth in me shall never die.* 2 Cor. i. 9. John xi. 25, 26.

The account of this woman, is uncommonly interesting. *Mark,* and *Luke,* add to the account of her *twelve years* labouring under this disease, that she had spent all her living upon physicians, and had

suffered many things of many of them, and was nothing better, but
rather worse. What a striking representation of the sinner, who is
seeking relief to his sin-sick soul, in any thing short of CHRIST!
Such it is, and such it must be, in every case, and circumstance of
spiritual malady. None but JESUS can cure. *Twelve years, or eighteen
years,* as the woman in the synagogue, (Luke xiii. 11.) or *eight and
thirty years,* as the man at the Pool of Bethsaida, (John v. 5.) are
all the same, until CHRIST is found! Oh! that every poor sinner, crippled by sin, was made sensible of this: that instead of looking to
Physicians of no value; in tears, and attempted reforms in their own
strength, might, like this woman, be led to CHRIST. Job xiii. 4. We
never can sufficiently admire the faith of this woman; neither can we
sufficiently bless Him, who gave her such strong faith; for she said
of CHRIST, *if I may but touch his garment I shall be whole.* Reader!
let us not hastily pass away from the view of such illustrious faith, in
this daughter of faithful Abraham, without first crying out with the
Apostles, LORD! *increase our faith!* I must beg the Reader also to
notice the humbleness of the woman, in the midst of such exalted faith;
she came behind CHRIST! The greatest faith is always blended with the
greatest humility. Never will a soul lay lower *before* GOD, than when
that soul is entering into the sweetest communion *with* GOD. The
higher views we have of the LORD's grace, the humbler views shall
we have of our own understandings. Gen. xviii. 27. Ezra ix. 56.
And I must beg the Reader also in noticing this woman's humbleness,
in coming *behind* CHRIST, to remark; that our approaches to JESUS,
in every direction, behind, or before, is the same. *The lamb is in
the midst of the throne.* Rev. vii. 17. Hence JESUS is acceptable, all
around, and in every direction. *They shall come from the east, and
from the west, and from the north, and from the south. They shall
come that are ready to perish.* Isaiah xxvii. 13. So that any poor
sensible sinner, who, like this woman, hath been spending all in pursuits after healing, and found none, because never looking wholly to
JESUS; but now being led by the HOLY GHOST to CHRIST; though
blushing to come *before* CHRIST in the sight of any fellow creatures,
from consciousness of disease, shall come *behind* CHRIST; the touch
of faith, the trust *in* CHRIST, will find virtue *from* CHRIST; and, like
her, the sinner be made perfectly whole.

  We must not dismiss our review of this miracle before that we have
also considered the grace and favor manifested by the LORD JESUS to
this woman; for this is the chief point in the miracle. JESUS, which
had, unknown to her, given her this lively faith to believe in him, as
instantly gave his blessing to that faith. And however unnoticed,
as she might suppose herself to have been, JESUS gave her to understand, that he both knew her complaint, and the cure he had
wrought for her. Reader! what a precious consideration it is, that however unknown our cases are to men, they are all well known to our
GOD. In the greatest throng, as well as in the secret place, JESUS
sees all, knows all, and both appoints, and will sanctify, all and
every individual case and exercise of his people We never can
sufficiently admire the abundant tenderness the LORD JESUS manifested
upon this occasion, to this poor woman. She wished the cure to be
in secret: but no! JESUS will have her faith in him made public.
His grace to poor sinners shall be proclaimed thereby; and her trust

in him shall make her history illustrious through endless generations. Both *Mark* and *Luke* relate this miracle with more particulars than *Matthew;* for they observe, that when the woman touched CHRIST's garment, JESUS, immediately knowing in himself what was done, and that healing virtue was gone out of him, (Reader! mark that, in testimony of his GODHEAD,) turned himself about, and said, *who touched me?* And when all denied, his unconscious disciples wondered how JESUS should make such an enquiry, while such a multitude were thronging and pressing him. But He, who knew all that had passed, while looking round to eye her, (as he did in after days look on Peter, Luke xxii. 61.) by his grace in her heart, inclined her to come and look on him. And oh! what a precious interview then took place, which neither of the Evangelists could relate; the love, and joy, and thankfulness to JESUS, in the consciousness of her cure, and the delight in the heart of JESUS in beholding the blessed effects of his salvation. Such, Reader! is now the case in every recovered sinner! And such will be the case of the whole Church of GOD, in every individual instance, *when the ransomed of the* LORD *shall return to Zion with songs and everlasting joy upon their heads, they shall obtain joy and gladness, and sorrow and sighing shall flee away.* Isaiah xxxv. 10.

It is high time to follow JESUS to the Ruler's house. Here death had taken place, and according to all human calculations, all hope was over. But not so with Him who came to be the life and light of men. As the LORD JESUS quickeneth the dead in trespasses and sins, so he was pleased in several instances to manifest the sovereignty of his power, in raising from the dead many of the bodies of his people. Matt. xi. 5. Oh! with what ease can JESUS now raise up our dead, and dying affections! Never should a soul despair that reads this miracle. Neither when the enemy, or graceless friends would tempt one to give it over, saying, in words like those who came to the ruler, *thy daughter is dead, trouble not the Master;* even then, when hope seems hopeless: oh! what cannot JESUS accomplish? And while he saith, be not afraid, only believe, may my soul say with one of old; *Though he slay me, yet will I trust in him!* Job xiii. 15.

27 And when Jesus departed thence, two blind men followed him, crying, and saying, *Thou* son of David, have mercy on us.

28 And when he was come into the house, the blind men came to him: and Jesus saith unto them, Believe ye that I am able to do this? They said unto him, Yea, Lord.

29 Then touched he their eyes, saying, According to your faith be it unto you.

30 And their eyes were opened; and Jesus straightly charged them, saying, See *that* no man know it.

31 But they, when they were departed, spread abroad his fame in all that country.

Concerning this miracle, I beg the Reader particularly to observe, that the cry of those men was evidently the cry of faith: for the name by which they distinguished Cʜʀɪsᴛ, *Thou* Sᴏɴ *of David!* was. the known character in which the Jews were taught to expect Cʜʀɪsᴛ. And the opening of the blind eyes was to be a token of his mission. Isaiah xxxv. 5. xlii. 7. lxi. 1.

32 ¶ As they went out, behold, they brought to him a dumb man possessed with a devil.

33 And when the devil was cast out, the dumb spake : and the multitudes marvelled, saying, It was never so seen in Israel.

34 But the Pharisees said, He casteth out devils through the prince of the devils.

Let the Reader, as he beholds the succession of miracles, and remarks the woeful effects of sin, from whence all the maladies of the world are derived, contemplate the glory and loveliness of Him who came *to do away sin by the sacrifice of himself?* Oh! the awful estate of being possessed with an evil spirit! Such are everlastingly dumb to proclaim the praises of Gᴏᴅ. Well is it for us that *the Son of* Gᴏᴅ *was manifested that he might destroy the works of the devil.* 1 John iii. 8.

35 And Jesus went about all the cities and villages, teaching in their synagogues, and preaching the gospel of the kingdom, and healing every sickness and every disease among the people.

36 But when he saw the multitudes, he was moved with compassion on them, because they fainted, and were scattered abroad, as sheep having no shepherd.

37 Then saith he unto his disciples, The harvest truly *is* plenteous, but the labourers *are* few;

38 Pray ye therefore the Lord of the harvest, that he will send forth labourers into his harvest.

What an interesting sight must it have been to have seen Jᴇsᴜs thus engaged, preaching the doctrines of grace, and confirming the word with ministering to all the wants of nature. And I beg the Reader not to overlook what is said of Jᴇsᴜs on those occasions : he was *moved with compassion,* that is, the compassions of Jᴇsᴜs were the compassions of Gᴏᴅ-Man, the divine and human nature blended. It is most essential to the proper apprehension of Jᴇsᴜs's feelings of our infirmities, always to keep this in view. For the LORD JESUS, having the same human nature as we have, hath the same affections, the same feelings as we have. And therefore, though the infinite perfections of his divine nature, give all that dignity and power which make his mercies *divine*, yet from his human nature being united to the GODHEAD, his compassions are no less *human* mercies also. Oh! the blessedness of such views of JESUS. See Heb. iv. 15, 16. The similitudes of a shepherd, and harvest, are too plain to need a comment. But as CHRIST alone is the shepherd of his flock, and the LORD of the harvest, the only One who can authorize to the ministry in the labors of it; we are to pray, but it is the LORD who must send suited servants to the harvest.

REFLECTIONS.

READER! behold your GOD and SAVIOR in this Chapter. See how he manifests who he is by what he wrought. As GOD! he pardons sin, as in the instance of the Paralytic! He reads the thoughts and reasonings of men's hearts, as in the case of the Scribes. He cures the souls, gives health to the bodies, raiseth the dead, casts out devils, and as man, yea the GOD-Man CHRIST JESUS, he is moved with compassion, and his bowels yearn over the lost estate and misery of our poor, ruined, and diseased nature. Oh! who that had seen his grace to *Matthew;* to the woman with the bloody issue; to the ruler of the synagogue, and his dead child; to the blind and the dumb; but must have said with the Prophet, *behold your* GOD *is come to save you!* And who that had seen him, at the table of *Matthew*, encircled with Publicans and Sinners, but must have said, was ever grace like this, in the unequalled condescension of the SON of GOD!

Oh! blessed LORD JESUS! do thou now still regard thy people, still behold them in all the miseries and sorrows of a state of nature and sin, in their palsied, blind, dumb, dead, and dying circumstances. Oh! thou Great Shepherd of thy blood-bought flock! Exalted as thou now art, at the right hand of the Majesty on high, send forth thine under pastors in thy fold, and let thine heritage be no longer scattered. Yea! dearest LORD JESUS! come thyself and visit them as thou hast said with thy great salvation, and bring them home to thy fold in heaven, from all places whither they are now scattered *in the dark and cloudy day!* Amen.

CHAP. X.

CONTENTS.

In this Chapter we have the call of the Apostles, and CHRIST'*s mission given to them, to work miracles, and preach the Gospel.*

AND when he had called unto *him* his twelve disciples, he gave them power *against* unclean spirits, to cast them out, and to heal all manner of sickness and all manner of disease.

We have here the LORD JESUS calling his Apostles. Their number *twelve*. Perhaps in allusion to the twelve tribes of Israel. The Church is represented by twelve stars. Rev. xii. 1. And the twelve foundations of the New Jerusalem are not without the same signification. Rev. xxi. 12—14. Yea, JESUS speaks of them, as sitting upon thrones to judge *the twelve tribes of Israel.* Luke xxii. 30. The call of every disciple of CHRIST is the same. The HOLY GHOST, by *Peter,* shews that the election of the church is discoverable by it. 2 Pet. i. 10. For if he hath *saved* us, he will *call* us. 2 Tim. i. 9. And whom he *called,* them he also *justified.* Rom. viii. 30. Oh! how truly evident this is, in the life of every believer. And in his ministers who are sent by him (and those unsent by *him* have no authority at all), how sure the spiritual effects which follow. JESUS's word, by them, works over unclean spirits; and all soul diseases, and sicknesses, in JESUS's name and power are healed.

2 Now the names of the twelve apostles are these; The first, Simon, who is called Peter, and Andrew his brother.; James *the son* of Zebedee, and John his brother;

3 Philip, and Bartholomew; Thomas, and Matthew the publican; James *the son* of Alpheus, and Lebbeus, whose surname was Thaddeus;

4 Simon the Canaanite, and Judas Iscariot, who also betrayed him.

I do not think it necessary to dwell upon the names of the Apostles, having, in my *Poor Man's Concordance,* already noticed each particular. But shall only briefly observe in this place, how blessed were those holy men, whose names were first written in the book of life: all excepting the traitor *Judas;* and his place was also marked from all eternity. Acts i. 25. John xvii. 12.

5 These twelve Jesus sent forth, and commanded them, saying, Go not into the way of the Gentiles, and into *any* city of the Samaritans, enter ye not.

6 But go rather to the lost sheep of the house of Israel.

7 And as ye go, preach, saying, The kingdom of heaven is at hand.

8 Heal the sick, cleanse the lepers, raise the dead, cast out devils: freely ye have received, freely give.

9 Provide neither gold, nor silver, nor brass in your purses,

10 Nor scrip for *your* journey, neither two coats, neither shoes, nor yet staves: for the workman is worthy of his meat.

11 And into whatsoever city or town ye shall enter, enquire who in it is worthy; and there abide till ye go thence.

12 And when ye come into an house, salute it.

13 And if the house be worthy, let your peace come upon it: but if it be not worthy, let your peace return to you.

14 And whosoever shall not receive you, nor hear your words, when ye depart out of that house or city, shake off the dust of your feet.

15 Verily I say unto you, it shall be more tolerable for the land of Sodom and Gomorrha in the day of judgment, than for that city.

We have in these verses, the Apostles' commission, where they were to preach, and what their preaching was to consist of; namely, of the near approach of Christ's kingdom; that is, Christ's Person and Christ's Salvation. The kingdom of grace distinguished from the law, and the kingdom of glory to which that grace led. John i. 17. And what a beautiful view is here afforded of those holy men going forth with their lives in their hands to preach Jesus. No gold, no silver, no money in their purse! And the awful consequence to those who rejected their preaching is read to us most solemnly, in that, *Sodom* and *Gomorrah* will find more favor at the last day!

16 Behold, I send you forth as sheep in the midst of wolves; be ye therefore wise as serpents, and harmless as doves.

17 But beware of men: for they will deliver you up to the councils, and they will scourge you in their synagogues;

18 And ye shall be brought before governors and kings for my sake, for a testimony against them and the Gentiles.

19 But when they deliver you up, take no thought how or what ye shall speak: for it shall be given you in that same hour what ye shall speak,

20 For it is not ye that speak, but the Spirit of your Father which speaketh in you.

21 And the brother shall deliver up the brother to death, and the father the child: and the children shall rise up against *their* parents, and cause them to be put to death.

22 And ye shall be hated of all *men* for my name's sake: but he that endureth to the end shall be saved.

23 But when they persecute you in this city, flee ye into another: for verily I say unto you, Ye shall not have gone over the cities of Israel, till the Son of man be come.

24 The disciple is not above *his* master, nor the servant above his lord.

25 It is enough for the disciple that he be as his master, and the servant as his lord. If they have called the master of the house Beelzebub, how much more *shall they call* them of his household?

26 Fear them not therefore: for there is nothing covered, that shall not be revealed: and hid, that shall not be known.

27 What I tell you in darkness, *that* speak ye in light: and what ye hear in the ear *that* preach ye upon the housetops.

28 And fear not them which kill the body, but are not able to kill the soul: but rather fear him which is able to destroy both soul and body in hell.

29 Are not two sparrows sold for a farthing? and one of them shall not fall on the ground without your Father.

30 But the very hairs of your head are all numbered.

31 Fear ye not therefore, ye are of more value than many sparrows.

32 Whosoever therefore shall confess me before men, him will I confess also before my Father which is in heaven.

33 But whosoever shall deny me before men, him will I also deny before my Father which is in heaven.

34 Think not that I am come to send peace on earth: I came not to send peace, but a sword.

35 For I am come to set a man at variance against his father, and the daughter against her mother, and the daughter-in-law against her mother-in-law.

36 And a man's foes *shall be* they of his own household.

37 He that loveth father or mother more than me is not worthy of me: and he that loveth son or daughter more than me is not worthy of me.

38 And he that taketh not his cross, and followeth after me, is not worthy of me.

39 He that findeth his life shall lose it: and he that loseth his life for my sake shall find it.

40 He that receiveth you receiveth me, and he that receiveth me receiveth him that sent me.

41 He that receiveth a prophet in the name of a prophet shall receive a prophet's reward; and he that receiveth a righteous man in the name of a righteous man shall receive a righteous man's reward.

42 And whosoever shall give to drink unto one of these little ones a cup of cold *water* only, in the name of a disciple, verily I say unto you, he shall in no wise lose his reward.

Our LORD's own words are so plain, so beautiful, and so expressive, that they would suffer rather by the attempt of a paraphrase, and cannot need a comment. I would only beg to observe upon them, that though they had a special reference to the first, and immediate disciples of JESUS, yet certainly JESUS had an eye to all his Apostles; that is, all sent forth by the HOLY GHOST to preach his Gospel to the end of time. Persecutions, and the offence of the cross, are never to cease. Were they to do so, we should lose one of the evidences of the Gospel. And as JESUS hath promised his unceasing presence with his people, so in an eminent manner with his sent servants. And what can express his attention more than in what the LORD hath closed the chapter with; that the smallest gift done in the name of CHRIST, is, in his eye, done to himself.

REFLECTIONS.

LET all the followers of the LORD JESUS, and especially his Ministers, behold in the commission here given by him to his Apostles, the love of his heart, and the interest he takes in all that concerns them. And let not our view of the unfaithfulness of hirelings in any age of the Church, give the smallest distress to true Pastors. JESUS chose a *Judas* to mingle with his faithful Apostles, though he knew that he was a devil when he chose him. But though he went in and out with the disciples, yet had he no part nor lot in the matter; and when he died, he went, as it is said, *to his own place.* Tares with the wheat, goats with the sheep, are nevertheless as distinguishable and separate as though they had never come together. *The* LORD *knoweth them that are his.* In the end, an everlasting separation will take place.

In the mean time, the persecution, hatred, and frowns of every enemy, shall minister rather to the Redeemer's glory, than to the smallest injury of the Redeemer's cause. And it never should be forgotten, that JESUS is *with his people always to the end of the world.* JESUS, therefore, looks on, knows all, sanctifies all, and blesseth all to his people's good! And JESUS speaks as in this chapter, to drive away all fear from the heart of his redeemed. *To him that overcometh, will I grant to sit with me in my throne, even as I also overcame, and am sat down with my Father in his throne.*

CHAP. XI.

CONTENTS.

We have in this Chapter the Message of John the Baptist to CHRIST, *and the* LORD's *answer. Towards the close of it,* JESUS *upbraids the cities around him for their hardness of heart, and unbelief, and thanks his Father for revealing his truths to his people.*

AND it came to pass, when Jesus had made an end of commanding his twelve disciples, he departed thence to teach and to preach in their cities.

2 ¶ Now when John had heard in the prison the works of Christ, he sent two of his disciples,

3 And said unto him, Art thou he that should come, or do we look for another?

4 Jesus answered and said unto them, Go and shew John again those things which ye do hear and see:

5 The blind receive their sight, and the lame walk, the lepers are cleansed, and the deaf hear,

the dead are raised up, and the poor have the gospel preached to them.

6 And blessed is *he*, whosoever shall not be offended in me.

When the LORD JESUS had finished his charge to his disciples, and was about to depart on his own personal ministry, he received a message from *John the Baptist*. We have noticed somewhat of this wonderful man, chap. iii. to which I refer. *John* was now in prison, for honestly telling *Herod*, that his intention of taking his brother *Philip's* wife, was unlawful. Matt. xiv. 4. *John* had given the most ample testimony to the Redeemer's person and character, and that not from human authority, but divine. John i. 30—34. He now sends his disciples to JESUS for their conviction also. I cannot for a moment conceive, that *John* himself had any doubts concerning CHRIST, though some writers have ventured to think so. Let the Reader turn to the Sermon *John* preached to the Jews, and judge for himself. John iii. 27, to the end. Our LORD's answer to *John's* disciples is very striking. I beg the Reader to turn to those Scriptures which speak of the Messiah in the Old Testament, and compare them with the life and ministry of JESUS in the New, and he will at once discover the beautiful correspondence. Gen. iii. 15. xxii. 17. xlix. 10. Isaiah xxxv. 4, 5, 6. lxi. 1. viii. 14, 15. Rom. ix. 33. 1 Pet. ii. 7, 8. And when the Reader hath duly pondered those blessed scriptures in proof, I will detain him but for the moment to observe, what a gracious testimony the LORD himself hath provided for his poor, doubting, fearful disciples, who, in the absence of higher evidences, can still say they love his name, amidst all their weaknesses and undeservings. John xxi. 17.

7 ¶ And as they departed, Jesus began to say unto the multitudes concerning John, What went ye out into the wilderness to see? A reed shaken with the wind?

8 But what went ye out for to see? A man clothed in soft raiment? behold, they that wear soft *clothing* are in kings' houses.

9 But what went ye out for to see? A prophet? yea, I say unto you, and more than a prophet.

10 For this is *he*, of whom it is written, Behold, I send my messenger before thy face, which shall prepare thy way before thee.

11 Verily I say unto you, Among them that are born of women there hath not risen a greater than John the Baptist: notwithstanding he that is least in the kingdom of heaven is greater than he.

12 And from the days of John the Baptist until now the kingdom of heaven suffereth violence, and the violent take it by force.

13 For all the prophets and the law prophesied until John.

14 And if ye will receive *it*, this is Elias, which was for to come.

15 He that hath ears to hear, let him hear.

The last words in this passage of our LORD's discourse, implies somewhat contained in it which requires deep attention. In this view I conceive the 10th verse to be the most weighty. If the Reader will turn to the Scripture which the LORD JESUS quotes from his servant, the Prophet Malachi, (Chap. iii. 1.) he will discover a very striking difference in the manner in which JESUS useth the words, from what they are there. In the words of the Prophet, it is JEHOVAH the LORD of Hosts speaking to the Church concerning John: He shall prepare the way before *me*. But here, as the LORD of his temple, CHRIST is spoken *to* on the same subject; and now the words are, behold I send my messenger before *thy* face, which shall prepare *thy* way before *thee*. What a decisive proof of the Oneness in the divine nature, in the *me* and *thee*; JEHOVAH's *way*, and CHRIST the Mediator's *way* is one and the same. And what can be more full in point to the GODHEAD of CHRIST? And hence it must undeniably follow, that the way of both, being one and the same; He, who is the LORD of his temple, and the Angel of the covenant, is One, with the other Persons of JEHOVAH, in nature, in essence, in way, will, and work; in property, honor, and worship; and in all the divine attributes, perfections, and glory! Hail! thou Almighty JESUS, whom all thy people delight in! Oh! for ears to hear what the SPIRIT saith concerning thee to the Churches! See Chapter iii. and Commentary throughout.

If I detain the Reader a moment longer on this discourse of JESUS, it shall only be to make a short observation on that passage in it, in which the LORD speaks of *the kingdom of heaven suffering violence, and the violent taking it by force.* There can be no doubt concerning what is meant by *the kingdom of heaven*, for the whole tenor of scripture refers this to *the kingdom of grace* upon all occasions, when speaking of the things of this life. But the violence this kingdom is said to suffer, and the being taken by force, these are terms not so clearly to be understood. The whole tide of Commentators, as far as I have seen, are all running in one, and the same opinion, that the words have reference to John's preaching, and the effects wrought upon the minds of the multitude thereby which flocked to his baptism. But I am free to confess, none of them satisfy my mind upon this subject. John's preaching of repentance can hardly be supposed to imply a violence done to CHRIST's kingdom, neither did it produce such an holy earnestness as might carry the expression of *the violent taking it by force.* See the parallel passage. Luke xvi. 16. I do not presume to speak decidedly on this, or any other portion of the word of GOD, which may be considered in the least of doubtful meaning; but I am rather inclined to think, the violence CHRIST's kingdom is said to have sustained by John's preaching, refers more to the opposition made *against it* by the powers of darkness, than to the conciliating the minds of men, *to it* by his outward ministry. John's chief scope of preaching was, as the herald of CHRIST, to testify of his approach, and that now it was very near. The hellish malice of the enemy is thereby the more excited, in proportion as Satan knew his kingdom was now tottering in the centre. See Malachi iv. 1. And as John called the great mass of *Pharisees* and *Sadducees*, which came to his baptism, *a generation of Vipers*, (See the Commentary on Matt. iii. 7.) it might be said the kingdom suffered violence from them, but cannot be conceived, that these were among the violent said to take the kingdom by force. But I leave the Reader to his own thoughts on the passage, under divine teaching, without adding aught more upon it.

16 But whereunto shall I liken this generation? It is like unto children sitting in the markets, and calling unto their fellows,

17 And saying, We have piped unto you, and ye have not danced; we have mourned unto you, and ye have not lamented.

18 For John came neither eating nor drinking, and they say, He hath a devil.

19 The Son of man came eating and drinking, and they say, Behold a man gluttonous, and a wine-bibber, a friend of publicans and sinners. But wisdom is justified of her children.

How just the statement JESUS hath here made, of the inefficacy both of law and gospel, unaccompanied with the grace of GOD. The waywardness of children is a striking figure in proof. For neither the melody of salvation by CHRIST, nor the awful threatenings by the law of Moses, have the least influence on the ungenerate heart. Reader! think of the infinite importance of the work of GOD the HOLY GHOST in conversion!

20 ¶ Then began he to upbraid the cities, wherein most of his mighty works were done, because they repented not?

21 Woe unto thee, Chorazin! woe unto thee, Bethsaida! for if the mighty works, which were done in you, had been done in Tyre and Sidon, they would have repented long ago in sackcloth and ashes.

22 But I say unto you, It shall be more tolerable for Tyre and Sidon at the day of judgment, than for you.

23 And thou, Capernaum, which art exalted unto heaven, shalt be brought down to hell: for if the mighty works, which have been done in thee, had been done in Sodom, it would have remained until this day.

24 But I say unto you, That it shall be more tolerable for the land of Sodom in the day of judgment, than for thee.

Reader! in the view of *Chorazin* and *Bethsaida*, and the awful woe pronounced upon those cities, which had been favoured with such high privileges, and regarded them not, think what will be the final condemnation of *Great Britain* in this particular? Would Jesus find faith, real saving faith, were he now to come among us? It is an awful thought! Luke xviii. 8. Matt. vii. 22, 23. Heb. ii. 3.

25 ¶ At that time Jesus answered and said, I thank thee, O Father, Lord of heaven and earth, because thou hast hid these things from the wise and prudent, and hast revealed them unto babes.

26 Even so, Father: for so it seemed good in thy sight.

27 All things are delivered unto me of my Father: and no man knoweth the Son, but the Father; neither knoweth any man the Father, save the Son, and *he* to whomsoever the Son will reveal *him*.

28 Come unto me, all *ye* that labour and are heavy laden, and I will give you rest.

29 Take my yoke upon you, and learn of me; for I am meek and lowly in heart: and ye shall find rest unto your souls.

30 For my yoke is easy, and my burden is light.

If I were to enter into the full Paraphrase and Comment upon this most sublime address of Christ to the Father, and the discourse connected with it to his people, it would swell many pages. The contracted nature of this work will not allow me. I must beg, however, the Reader not to pass it over, until that he hath first remarked with me, how the Lord Jesus thanks his Father for the *distinguishing grace* bestowed upon his people; that while hiding the wonders of re-demption from *the wise in their own eyes, and prudent in their own sight,* (Isaiah v. 21.) the LORD reveals his mercy unto the humble and the lowly. And I beg the Reader to observe further, the cause which JESUS assigns; namely, GOD's own appointment. To all the bold and presumptuous reasonings of the human mind, which have been or may be hereafter brought forward, against the exercise of JEHOVAH's sovereignty, the answer is direct. *Shall not the Judge of all the earth do right?* Surely the LORD is not called upon to give ac-count of the motives of his holy will and pleasure, to any of his creatures. One thing we know, namely, that *his counsel and purpose must stand, and he will do all his pleasure;* and that all He doeth is right. His conduct towards his creatures, is by an unerring standard. His mercy is not moved by any good in us, neither is it kept back by our undeservings; for neither our merit, nor our misery, can be said to have had any hand in disposing the purposes of His sovereign will towards us. That the LORD hath taken occa-sion from our misery, to magnify the abounding riches of his mercy, is true; but then his mercy was before our misery, and his own ever-lasting love the sole cause of our blessedness in CHRIST, therefore our LORD's own words are most blessed in point: *Even so Father! for so it seemed good in thy sight!*

I must beg to detain the Reader with a short remark more upon those very blessed words of JESUS, (for very blessed they are in my view) in which the LORD hath said, that the knowledge of the per-sons of the GODHEAD is *wholly in themselves;* and that none can know the SON but the FATHER; neither can any know the FATHER save the SON, and *he to whomsoever the Son will reveal him.* If those words of the LORD JESUS, were but duly attended to by those who call themselves Christians, after CHRIST, and consequently profess to believe, that what CHRIST hath said is true, (I mean such as deny his eternal power and GODHEAD, of every class and description,) could they, consistently with their own creed, presume to so daring an act of impiety, when JESUS himself hath said, that *no man knoweth the Son but the* FATHER? They it seems, in direct defiance of this scripture, declare *they know* the SON; and with an uncovered front, which makes one tremble at their blasphemy, advance further, and say that He is *not* One with the FATHER, over all GOD blessed for ever! Reader! do not fail to keep in remembrance those blessed words of JESUS, which so plainly, and so fully declare, that none can know the SON but the FATHER; than which there cannot be a more decisive testimony, that CHRIST is GOD.

But when the Reader hath duly pondered this unanswerable testi-mony of JESUS, to the certainty of his GODHEAD, I crave his indul-gence to dwell a little longer on this precious passage. If the reve-lation, both of the FATHER and of the SON (for both are One) be made, and is made, by JESUS concerning the FATHER, and by the FA-THER concerning the SON, oh! think how blessed it must be, when the LORD gives to any poor sinner a spirit of wisdom and revela-tion in this divine knowledge. I beg the Reader not to shut the book until he hath, in regular order, turned to those scriptures in blessed confirmation of this most unquestionable truth. And *first,* ac-cording to the order of those words, *No man knoweth the* SON *but the*

FATHER. See CHRIST's testimony to Peter. Matt. xvi. 13—17. See Paul's testimony also, concerning himself on this grand point. Gal. i. 11—16. Paul was called from the error of his way by CHRIST from heaven. So that, as he saith, *he never received the Gospel from man neither was taught it by man, but by* JESUS CHRIST. A plain and decided testimony that he knew CHRIST to be GOD. And the same Apostle saith, that it was GOD the FATHER that revealed his SON to him. Add to these, JESUS himself saith, *No man can come to me, except the* FATHER *which hath sent me, draw him.* John vi. 44. So much for the revelation of the SON by the FATHER, and of which Paul was so well convinced, agreeably to what our LORD hath said in this scripture, that none can know the SON but the FATHER and by his revelation of him, that the Apostle expressly prays for the Church at *Ephesus,* that *the Father would give unto them a spirit of wisdom and revelation in the knowledge of him.* I beg the Reader to read the whole passage Ephesians i. 15, to the end. Now then, in like manner, let the Reader consult those scriptures, which equally prove that the knowledge of the FATHER is only with the SON, and his redeemed, to whom the LORD JESUS reveals him. And here in proof, read John i. 18; then turn to John vi. 46; then John x. 15; and lastly, to mention no more, John xiv. 9, 10. Oh! the preciousness and blessedness of these things! Reader! may not you and I (if so be the LORD JESUS hath mercifully given us a spiritual knowledge herein,) may we not take to ourselves what JESUS said to Peter; and consider the same blessedness as ours also: for *flesh and blood hath not revealed it unto us, but our* GOD *and* FATHER *which is in heaven.* See also Luke x. 23, 24. John xvi. 13, 14, 15. 2 Cor. iv. 6.

I must not trespass further by enlarging on the many other blessed things contained in the close of this Chapter. But otherwise what a subject might be opened concerning the *All things* JESUS saith, as Mediator, are delivered unto him by his FATHER? (see the Commentary on Luke 10—22.) and of JESUS's invitation to the weary and heavy laden to come to him, and to find rest unto their souls? But I beg the Reader to consult some of the numberless scriptures on these glorious truths of our GOD: and may the HOLY GHOST open their beauties and saving influences to his soul! Psalm cxvi. 6. Isaiah xxviii. 12. Hebrews iv. 9.

REFLECTIONS.

WILL any send my soul to question, whether JESUS be indeed He that should come: or can there be a possibility of cause to look for another? Oh! no. He is the altogether lovely: and the chiefest and the fairest among ten thousand. Now, even now, as well as in the days of his flesh, the spiritually blind, are receiving from him their sight: the lame in soul, JESUS makes to leap as an hart; leprous sinners are cleansed in the fountain of his blood; the deaf hear the words of the book; the dead in trespasses and sins are raised; and the poor in spirit, hear and know the joyful sound, and through grace walk in the light of GOD's countenance. And can there be another JESUS: another Gospel which we have not received? Oh! thou dear LORD! blessed for ever blessed be thou for having said, *blessed is he whosoever shall not be offended in me!*

Lord! grant if it be thy blessed will, that it never may be the condemnation of our land like *Chorazin* and *Bethsaida!* Great Gospel privileges we have indeed; but what must follow if we neglect, or reject *such great salvation?*

Reader! let you and I listen to the sweet and gracious invitation, which Jesus gives to the weary in sin, and to the heavy laden under the burthen of it. Oh! for grace to learn of thee, thou meek and lovely Savior! Thou art indeed, both a rest and resting place, for thy people. In thee, my soul would rest from sin, and rest to God. Thou art both a shelter from the wind, and a covert from the tempest. Thou art my hiding place, thou wilt preserve me from trouble. Thou wilt compass me about with songs of deliverance. Haste, haste my soul, to thy rest, thy Jesus; for *the* Lord *hath dealt bountifully by thee!*

CHAP. XII.

CONTENTS.

We have our Lord *represented to us in this Chapter going on with his ministry. The sin against the* Holy Ghost *is here spoken of.*

AT that time Jesus went on the sabbath-day through the corn; and his disciples were an hungered, and began to pluck the ears of corn, and to eat.

2 But when the Pharisees saw *it,* they said unto him, Behold, thy disciples do that which is not lawful to do upon the sabbath-day.

3 But he said unto them, Have ye not read what David did, when he was an hungered, and they that were with him;

4 How he entered into the house of God, and did eat the shew-bread, which was not lawful for him to eat, neither for them which were with him, but only for the priests?

5 Or have ye not read in the law, how that on the sabbath-days the priests in the temple profane the sabbath, and are blameless?

6 But I say unto you, That in this place is *one* greater than the temple.

7 But if ye had known what *this* meaneth, I will have mercy, and not sacrifice, ye would not have condemned the guiltless.

8. For the Son of man is Lord even of the sabbath-day.

I do not think it necessary to swell my *Poor Man's Commentary*,
with making observations on whatever is plain and obvious. Our
LORD, who is both the original institutor, and LORD of the Sabbath,
hath clearly shown, how mercy is to supersede mere works of sacrifice.
But if the Jews were so tenacious of the ordinary sanctity of the sabbath, as to prohibit every thing but what was indispensible; what
would those men have said, had they lived in the present hour, when
reverence both for the sabbath, and the LORD of the Sabbath, is so
generally set aside. Ye people of GOD, in whose hearts the fear of
the LORD is! see to it that ye stand up, as *Moses* did in the gap, to
turn away the LORD's wrath from what may be generally expected;
the LORD avenging the breach of his sabbaths. JESUS! be thou the
very sabbath of my soul! See Mark ii. 23.

9 ¶ And when he was departed thence, he went
into their synagogue :

10 And, behold, there was a man which had *his*
hand withered. And they asked him, saying, Is it
lawful to heal on the sabbath-days? that they
might accuse him.

11 And he said unto them, What man shall
there be among you that shall have one sheep, and
if he fall into a pit on the sabbath-day, will he not
lay hold on it and lift *it* out?

12 How much then is a man better than a
sheep? Wherefore it is lawful to do well on the
sabbath-days.

13 Then saith he to the man, Stretch forth
thine hand ; and he stretched *it* forth, and it was
restored whole, like as the other,

Here was an immediate opportunity for CHRIST to prove himself LORD of the Sabbath, in healing this diseased man. The case
is simply, but earnestly related : and the effect as might have been
expected. But what I would have the Reader particularly to regard
in this case, is the spiritual sense of it. This man with a sinew shrunk
hand, was not in idleness at his own house, but in the synagogue.
He was waiting in the way of ordinances. It is good to be found
waiting on the LORD, and in the way of the LORD's own appointing.
He seemed unconscious of the mercy the LORD intended for him :
neither is it said, that he knew JESUS, much less that he made any
application to JESUS. Preventing mercies, are sweet mercies. *I was
found of them*, saith the LORD, *that sought we not.* Isaiah lxv. 1.
No doubt, JESUS knew this poor man was in the synagogue. And

He, of whom it is said, that *he must needs go* through Samaria, because there was a poor sinner who needed his mercies there, probably went to this Synagogue on purpose to manifest his grace to this man, with his withered hand, who needed him no less. John iv. 4. But what I would more particularly beg the Reader to notice, in the features of this miracle of CHRIST; is the precept of JESUS to the man : *Stretch forth thine hand!* I beg once for all to remark, that CHRIST's biddings are enablings. Unless the LORD JESUS had accompanied his command with power; and while bidding the sinner's shrunk hand to be stretched forth, he had communicated ability to obey, no blessing would have followed. It is truly blessed to eye this in every minute circumstance of life. Hence Paul was commissioned to direct the Philippians, *to work out their own salvation with fear and trembling :* because that the LORD himself would *work in them both to will and to do of his good pleasure.* Philip. ii. 12, 13. And hence the same Apostle adds, in the same Epistle, *I can do nothing of myself, but I can do all things through* CHRIST *who strengtheneth me.* Philip. iv. 13. It is truly blessed, to be enabled through grace, to have the lowest opinion of ourselves, that our views of JESUS, may be the more exalted ; and to be sensible of our nothingness, that the LORD may have all the glory !

14 Then the Pharisees went out, and held a council against him, how they might destroy him.

15 But when Jesus knew *it,* he withdrew himself from thence : and great multitudes followed him, and he healed them all ;

16 And charged them that they should not make him known ;

17 That it might be fulfilled which was spoken by Esaias the prophet, saying,

18 Behold, my servant, whom I have chosen; my beloved, in whom my soul is well pleased : I will put my spirit upon him, and he shall shew judgment to the Gentiles.

19 He shall not strive, nor cry; neither shall any man hear his voice in the streets.

20 A bruised reed shall he not break, and smoking flax shall he not quench, till he send forth judgment unto victory.

21 And in his name shall the Gentiles trust.

' It is striking to observe that those very scrupulous persons who professed so high a regard for the LORD's day, yet scrupled not to consult on that day, how they might destroy the LORD of life and glory.—Reader! did you ever notice any of the Pharisees of the present hour, (for they are the same in all ages). Oh! what vast regard they would have you suppose they have for the morality of the Gospel! But the Lord Jesus, who reads under this covering the heart of such men, tells us that notwithstanding all this, they should receive the ¹greater damnation. Matt. xxiii. 14. Now observe this was not for any immoralities, or for the neglect of prayers, and the like; for they were rigid to an excess in duties as they called them. But it was for setting up a righteousness of their own, against the righteousness of the Lord Jesus Christ. *Beware ye* (saith Jesus) *of the leaven of the Pharisees, which is hypocrisy!* Luke xii. 1.

But let us turn from the disgusting views of such characters, to contemplate the beautiful picture the Prophet *Esaias* hath drawn of Jesus, and which the Evangelist copies in this scripture from the original. See Isaiah xlii. 1—4. The Prophet introduceth Jehovah the Father as calling upon the Church to behold him; and as commending his person, in his gracious office as the Church's husband, and the Mediator, and as One in whom his soul delighteth. Nothing can be more blessed than what God the Father saith of him. And when his redeemed can answer to God the Father's approbation of him, as his servant; in their approbation of him as their surety, head, and Saviour, the subject is blessed indeed, *I will put my spirit in him,* saith Jehovah. I will put my soul and body in his Almighty hands, saith the poor awakened sinner. *He shall shew judgment to the Gentiles,* saith God. He hath shewn both judgment and mercy to me, saith the poor Gentile, whom grace hath recovered from sin and destruction. *He shall be a meek, a tender hearted Savior,* saith the Father, so that even *the bruised reed he shall not break, and the smoking flax* of his people's weaknesses, *he shall not quench,* Jesus is all this and more, saith the poor sinner; for *he hath remembered me in my low estate, for his mercy endureth for ever!* Oh! the unknown, the unnumbered mercies in the bowels of Jesus, which he bears to all his redeemed; and by which he manifests his grace to them, *otherwise than he doth to the world.* John xiv. 21, 22.

I detain the Reader for the moment, just to observe on the word *judgment,* in this passage, that though in the first view of it, there might be thought somewhat harsh in it, but it is not so. Bringing forth *judgment to the Gentiles, and unto victory,* implies, that Jesus will compleat the work of his free grace for his redeemed, in a way of judgment so wise, and excellent, that it shall commend his administration for the deed, while every thing of tenderness shall mark his features of character; so that the *bruised reed* and the *smoking flax,* which are in his way, he will not tread upon nor injure.

22 ¶ Then was brought unto him one possessed with a devil, blind, and dumb: and he healed him, insomuch that the blind and dumb both spake and saw.

23 And all the people were amazed, and said, Is not this the son of David?

Let the Reader always connect with the view of the miracles of JESUS, his compassion to the soul, while healing the body. It is the blind and dumb in spirit, JESUS came to deliver.

24 But when the Pharisees heard *it*, they said, This *fellow* doth not cast out devils, but by Belzebub the prince of the devils.

25 And Jesus knew their thoughts, and said unto them, Every kingdom divided against itself is brought to desolation; and every city or house divided against itself shall not stand:

26 And if Satan cast out Satan, he is divided against himself; how shall then his kingdom stand?

27 And if I by Beelzebub cast out devils, by whom do your children cast *them* out? therefore they shall be your judges.

28 But if I cast out devils by the Spirit of God, then the kingdom of God is come unto you.

29 Or else, how can one enter into a strong man's house, and spoil his goods, except he first bind the strong man? and then he will spoil his house.

30 He that is not with me is against me; and he that gathereth not with me scattereth abroad.

I pray the Reader to observe in these verses, several weighty things. *First:* the testimony here given to CHRIST's GODHEAD. JESUS *knew their thoughts.* A thing impossible had he not been GOD. *All the Churches shall know that I am he which searcheth the reins and hearts.* Rev. ii. 23. *Secondly.*—Observe the several persons of the GODHEAD mentioned in the casting out of devils. JESUS saith, if I by the SPIRIT of GOD cast them out. I; that is, GOD the SON, The SPIRIT; that is, GOD the HOLY GHOST. And GOD; that is, GOD the FATHER. *Thirdly.*—When JESUS, in answer to the blasphemy of the Pharisees, who ascribed his work of casting out devils to the power of *Beelzebub,* saith, *by whom do your children cast them out?* he did not admit the thing, as if any, in reality, had cast out devils among them, for it was impossible: but the LORD took occasion to reprove them on their own principles. Magic was an old practice. Exodus vii. 11. Numbers xxiv. 1. And even after CHRIST's return to glory, we read of exorcists. Acts xix. 13—17. But the dispossessing devils, was the prerogative of JESUS only. 1 John iii. 8.

But when the Reader hath paid all due notice to these things, I would beg his attention yet a little further, to what the LORD JESUS hath here said, of the kingdom of Satan. It is a point rightly to apprehend, of great importance, in the doctrines of the Gospel; and no child of GOD should be ignorant of it.

That Satan hath set up, and maintained an empire of sin, in the very heart of man, is a truth too certain to be questioned, and the awful effects of it, too well known to be denied. Holy Scripture, gives many sad relations of it. In fact, it was the setting up this kingdom against GOD and his CHRIST, for which the devil and his angels are said to have been cast out of heaven, and to have left their own habitation. Rev. xii. 7—12. Jude 6. At his expulsion from heaven, he seduced our first parents, and in them involved the whole of their posterity in the fall. And from that hour to the present, it is *he which worketh in the children of disobedience.* Hence the several names by which he is known: *the Great Dragon; that old Serpent, the Devil, and Satan, which deceiveth the whole world; the strong man armed; the Prince of the power of the air; the God of this world;* and whose vassals are led *captive by him at his will.* Rev. xii. 7, &c. Ephes. ii. 2. 2 Cor. iv. 4. 2 Timothy ii. 26.

Now the whole purpose and design of the Gospel is directed to overthrow this kingdom of Satan, and to introduce and restore perfect order, among all the works of GOD. Hence it is said, that for this purpose, *the* SON *of* GOD *was manifested that he might destroy the works of the devil.* 1 John iii. 8. And hence we find the LORD JESUS entering upon this service, immediately on his entrance into his ministry. *First,* by his own personal conquest over him on the cross. Heb. ii. 14, 15. Coloss. ii. 15. *Secondly,* at the conversion of his members; when, as in the scripture, the stronger than the strong man armed, even CHRIST, cometh upon him, destroyeth all his armor, and divideth the spoils. In every single instance of the saving conversion of a soul to GOD, this may be said to have been wrought, when that soul is *translated from the kingdom of darkness, into the kingdom of* GOD's *dear* SON. John xii. 31. John xiv. 30. John xvi. 7—11. 1 John ii. 13, 14. 1 John iv. 4. And a compleat victory is promised to the Church in the end. 1 Cor. x. 13. Rom. xvi. 22. *Thirdly,* there is a promise also of another triumph of JESUS, when a more signal display of victory will be shewn, in the LORD JESUS setting up a kingdom in the earth, before the day of judgment, and when Satan's power will be shut up and restrained. Rev. xx. 1—7. And, finally, at the universal judgment, the total and everlasting destruction of Satan's kingdom will take place. See Rev. xx, 10, &c. Such are the views scripture holds forth of these momentous truths!

31 Wherefore I say unto you, All manner of sin and blasphemy shall be forgiven unto men: but the blasphemy *against* the *Holy* Ghost shall not be forgiven unto men.

32 And whosoever speaketh a word against the Son of man, it shall be forgiven him: but whosoever speaketh against the Holy Ghost, it shall not be forgiven him, neither in this world, neither in the *world* to come.

33 Either make the tree good, and his fruit

good ; or else make the tree corrupt, and his fruit
corrupt: for the tree is known by *his* fruit.

I must postpone the observations on this passage to my Commentary on the similar one, Mark iii. 28, to which therefore I refer.

34 O generation of vipers, how can ye, being
evil, speak good things? for out of the abundance
of the heart the mouth speaketh.

I would beg the Reader to pause over this verse; and to collect the
sense of our LORD's expression, in calling those men whom he had in
view, *generation of vipers*. It is a very solemn consideration, but
therefore the more to be regarded, that throughout the whole word of
GOD, this generation is spoken of, in one and the same uniform
character. Indeed, the seed of the woman, and the seed of the serpent, are expressly marked and defined, from the first moment in which
the LORD declared, he would put enmity in the seed, to each other.
Genesis iii. 15. Hence those strong expressions of CHRIST: *Ye are
of your father the devil, and the lusts of your father ye will do.* John
viii. 44. And hence, as in this verse, JESUS speaks of it as a
thing impossible, that they should do otherwise than what is evil.
How can ye being evil speak good things? Ye believe not (said JESUS),
because ye are not of my sheep. John x. 26. And elsewhere, he calls
them, *serpents and a generation of vipers*, which cannot escape *the damnation of hell!* Matt. xxiii. 33. See Matt. xiii. 38. Matt. xxv. 33.
And in like manner, his servants the Apostles adopt the same language.
Paul called *Elymas* the sorcerer, *child of the devil.* Acts xiii. 10.
And *Peter* speaking of the same race, calls them *cursed children*; and
as *brute beasts made to be taken and destroyed.* 2 Peter ii. 12—14.
And *John* if possible, yet more strongly defines the stock; for when
speaking of *Cain's* murdering his brother, he asketh the question by
way of answering it. *And wherefore* (said he) *did Cain slay his brother? Because he was of that wicked one.* 1 John iii. 12. See those
scriptures in further confirmation. Gal. iii. 16—29. 1 John iii. 8, 9.

35 A good man out of the good treasure of the
heart bringeth forth good things: and an evil man
out of the evil treasure bringeth forth evil things.

I pause over this verse, by way of observing, once for all, the scriptural sense of a *good man.* The word of GOD hath expressly said,
that *there is none good, no not one.* Psm. xiv. 3. Rom. iii. 10.
Eccles. vii. 20. Proverbs xxiv. 16. Rom. v. throughout. Hence
therefore, as the word of GOD, cannot but be in perfect agreement
with itself, in every part; it is evident, that by *a good man*, is meant
one that is regenerated and born again ; one that is renewed in the spirit
of his mind, and justified in CHRIST JESUS. Paul speaks of such.
1 Cor. v. 11. So that this man differs from the natural man, yea,
from what he himself once was, before this sovereign act of grace
had passed upon his mind ; and therefore now, out of the good treasure of his heart, in CHRIST; and from the graces of his Holy Spirit

planted there, he brings forth the sweet and precious fruits in life and conversation, of the person, work, and righteousness of JESUS. Philip. i. 27. Psalm lxvi. 16.

36 But I say unto you, That every idle word that men shall speak, they shall give account thereof in the day of judgment.

37 For by thy words thou shalt be justified, and by thy words thou shalt be condemned.

As words as well as actions, yea thoughts, which are the womb of both, plainly manifest the state of the heart, whether renewed by grace, or remaining in the old state of unrenewed nature; the idle sinful discourse of the unawakened sinner, (for it is to such our LORD is here speaking,) daily testify the state in which he is; and who is already prejudged by his conversation; just as in like manner the lips of the gracious manifest that they are born to GOD, to whom there is no condemnation. Rom. viii. 1. Song iv. 11. Malachi iii. 16, 17, 18. I beg the Reader not to lose sight of this passage as referring to the unregenerate sinner living and dying out of CHRIST.

38 ¶ Then certain of the scribes and of the Pharisees answered, saying, Master, we would see a sign from thee.

39 But he answered and said unto them, An evil and adulterous generation seeketh after a sign; and there shall no sign be given to it, but the sign of the prophet Jonas:

40 For as Jonas was three days and three nights in the whale's belly: so shall the Son of man be three days and three nights in the heart of the earth.

41 The men of Nineveh shall rise in judgment with this generation, and shall condemn it; because they repented at the preaching of Jonas; and, behold, a greater than Jonas is here.

42 The queen of the south shall rise up in the judgment with this generation, and shall condemn it: for she came from the uttermost parts of the earth to hear the wisdom of Solomon; and, behold, a greater than Solomon is here.

43 When the unclean spirit is gone out of a man,

he walketh through dry places, seeking rest, and findeth none.

44 Then he saith, I will return into my house from whence I came out; and when he is come, he findeth *it* empty, swept, and garnished.

45 Then goeth he, and taketh with himself seven other spirits more wicked than himself, and they enter in and dwell there: and the last *state* of that man is worse than the first. Even so shall it be also unto this wicked generation.

I pass over all the several subjects contained in this passage of JESUS, from making any observations upon them, being in themselves self-evident; in order to call the Reader's attention to one here spoken of, which may not perhaps at first be so immediately plain and obvious. I mean, respecting the unclean spirit in his departure and return. The unclean spirit, no doubt, means the devil. And when men, under the cursed influences of the devil, are living in the open and notorious vices of profaneness, drunkenness, dishonesty, sabbath-breaking and the like, they may be said to have an *unclean spirit*. But if any outward reform takes place in such characters, and we behold a change wrought upon them, so that they are more decent in life and conversation, the devil may be said to have gone out from them, under the character of an *unclean spirit*. But if there be no saving change wrought in the soul by the regenerating power of the HOLY GHOST: if the devil be *gone out* of his own accord, and not *driven out* by the *stronger* man, he, even JESUS (see verse 29); this man's heart is still as much as ever under Satan's government; for he calls it *his house*, and saith *he will* return to it; yea, and he doth return to it, if so be there be no saving change wrought upon the man's heart by grace. So that, though he goes out an *unclean* devil, yet he comes back only somewhat cleaner, but still a devil; and reigns, and rules in his house, of the man's heart, as much as before. Yea, our LORD saith, that the last state of this man is worse than the first. For if, while under the same awful influence of an unrenewed, ungenerated heart, the man is prompted to put on the appearance of an outside sanctity; and covers over the uncleanness that is *within*, with a seeming zeal for religion *without*: these, are like the seven other spirits of the devil, more wicked than the former, because more desperately deceiving, both himself and the world; and of consequence, the end is more dreadful. And who shall calculate the numbers there are living under this most wretched of all delusions? Who shall say, the many, who go out of life well pleased with this whitening sepulchre-reform; in whose heart, no saving change hath been wrought; nor any acquaintance made with the person, work, or grace of GOD the HOLY GHOST. John iii. 3—9. Acts xix. 2. Reader! see to it that no change satisfies your mind, but that which is wrought by the HOLY GHOST and CHRIST, *formed in your heart the life of glory.* Romans viii. 9—17. 2 Cor. v. 17.

46 ¶ While he yet talked to the people, behold, *his* mother and his brethren stood without, desiring to speak with him.

47 Then one said unto him, Behold, thy mother and thy brethren stand without, desiring to speak with thee.

48 But he answered and said unto him that told him, Who is my mother? and who are my brethren?

49 And he stretched forth his hand toward his disciples, and said, Behold my mother and my brethren!

50 For whosoever shall do the will of my Father which is in heaven, the same is my brother, and sister, and mother.

It is a matter of no small importance in the faith of every child of GOD, to have right apprehensions of our LORD's relations after the flesh. As *Joseph* was only the reputed father of CHRIST (and not in reality), very plain it is, that on this side JESUS had none. And whether the Virgin *Mary* had, or had not children after the birth of CHRIST, it is of no moment to enquire, for it forms no article of faith: neither is it in the least connected with the present question. That *Mary* was a pure Virgin, at the time of her conception; that she continued so, to the birth of CHRIST; and that her conception, was altogether miraculous, by the HOLY GHOST, and without the intervention of an human father: these are the grand and the only points essential to be proved; and these are all most fully proved and ascertained in the scriptures. And hence it will follow, that any further relationship after the flesh, CHRIST had none. But his bretheren are the members of this *mystical* body, and not his *personal* body. CHRIST and his seed, are spoken of as one. He the head, and they the members; and concerning whom JEHOVAH saith, *I will pour my spirit upon thy seed, and my blessing upon thine offspring.* Isaiah xliv. 3. Isaiah lix. 21. In that holy portion of human nature which constituted CHRIST's body, underived from man, and given of GOD, from all the persons of the GODHEAD: (see in proof, Psalms xl. 6. Hebrews x. 5. Psalms cxxxix. 13—16. Heb. ii. 14—16. Luke i. 35. and Commentary on Matt. i. 18.) was formed the holy seed of all his members. And as it is said of *Levi*, that he was in the loins of his father, when *Melchisedec* met him, Heb. vii. 10; so must it be said of the seed of CHRIST: they were in CHRIST; chosen in CHRIST; blessed in CHRIST; yea, beheld in CHRIST, *before the world began.* Ephes. i. 3, 4, 5. Isaiah viii. 18. Heb. ii. 11. So that when the LORD JESUS, in answer to the person, speaking to him of his relations, as stated in this Chapter, stretched forth his hand towards his disciples, and pointing to certain among the throng, and said, *behold my Mother and my Brethren!* these were CHRIST's

relations both in nature and grace. And if the Reader will turn to
the following scriptures in proof, they will serve to throw great
light upon the subject. As the everlasting *Father,* Isaiah ix. 6.
Brother, John xx. 17. *Husband,* Isaiah liv. 5. *Friend,* John xv.
15. See the Poor Man's Commentary also on Chapter i. verse 22—25.

REFLECTIONS.

HAIL thou glorious LORD of the Sabbath! Do thou blessed JESUS,
manifest to my soul, and in my soul, that thou art both LORD of
the Sabbath and of my heart; by reigning there, and ruling there,
and giving me to eat of the shew-bread of thy body, which is the
bread of life, that I may have eternal life abiding in me. And do
thou by me, O LORD, as thou didst to the poor man in the Synagogue, to all the withered affections of my poor nature; both bid
me, and enable me, to stretch forth the hand of faith, and lay hold
of eternal life in thee!

And oh! Almighty Father! in thy gracious office-work in covenant mercies, give me to hear thy sweet proclamation of thy servant
whom thou hast chosen, and in whom, as the Church's Head and
Surety, thou art well pleased, and hast delighted. Oh! for the teachings of GOD the HOLY GHOST, to know JEHOVAH's chosen and JEHO-
VAH's beloved, as my beloved, a meek SAVIOR, a tender hearted
SAVIOR, a well qualified and powerful SAVIOR; who though so gentle
as not to break the bruised reed, nor quench the smoking flax, yet so
mighty as to send forth judgment unto victory, and in whose name
the Gentiles shall trust.

And no less Almighty SPIRIT, do thou so teach, and guide me into
all truth, that out of the good treasure by regeneration, and the daily
renewings of thy grace which thou hast put into my heart, I may
bring forth good things, while the generation of vipers, by their evil
things, manifest the seed from whence they spring. Yea! LORD give
me to see and know, by heartfelt experience, from thy sovereign
work there wrought, that I am of the mystical relationship of
CHRIST, and among the number whom JESUS will own as his brother,
and sister, and mother.

CHAP. XIII.

CONTENTS.

The LORD JESUS *is here instructing his diciples in Parables. Towards the close of the Chapter, the* LORD *assigns his reasons for this
mode of teaching.*

THE same day went Jesus out of the house,
and sat by the sea side.

2 And great multitudes were gathered together
unto him, so that he went into a ship, and sat;
and the whole multitude stood on the shore.

I detain the Reader on the very entrance of this Chapter, to remark several interesting things which ought to be noticed. First, observe the unwearied ministry of the LORD. It was *the same day* in which he had before preached, as in the foregoing Chapter. Oh! what a call on all his *sent* servants in the ministry, to be alive to the work of the Sanctuary! John ix. 4. 2 Tim. iv. 1, 2. The *place* of CHRIST's preaching. Not the synagogue, but the sea-side. Teaching us that all places are sanctified when the HOLY GHOST makes them so. And the *multitudes* which attended CHRIST's ministry, serve to shew how eager the people were to hear this divine preacher, *who spake as never man spake.* John vii. 46.

3 ¶ And he spake many things unto them in parables, saying, Behold, a sower went forth to sow;

4 And when he sowed, some *seeds* fell by the way side, and the fowls came and devoured them up:

5 Some fell upon stony places, where they had not much earth; and forthwith they sprung up, because they had no deepness of earth:

6 And when the sun was up, they were scorched; and because they had no root, they withered away.

7 And some fell among thorns; and the thorns sprung up, and choked them:

8 But other fell into good ground, and brought forth fruit, some an hundredfold, some sixtyfold, some thirtyfold.

9 Who hath ears to hear, let him hear.

10 And the disciples came, and said unto him, Why speakest thou unto them in parables?

11 He answered and said unto them, Because it is given unto you to know the mysteries of the kingdom of heaven, but to them it is not given.

12 For whosoever hath, to him shall be given, and he shall have more abundance: but whosoever hath not, from him shall be taken away even that he hath.

13 Therefore speak I to them in parables: because they seeing see not; and hearing they hear not, neither do they understand.

14 And in them is fulfilled the prophecy of

Esaias, which saith, By hearing ye shall hear, and shall not understand; and seeing ye shall see, and shall not perceive:

15 For this people's heart is waxed gross, and *their* ears are dull of hearing, and their eyes they have closed; lest at any time they should see with *their* eyes, and hear with *their* ears, and should understand with *their* heart, and should be converted, and I should heal them.

16 But blessed *are* your eyes, for they see; and your ears, for they hear.

17 For verily I say unto you, That many prophets and righteous *men* have desired to see *those things* which ye see, and have not seen *them;* and to hear *those things* which ye hear, and have not heard *them.*

18 Hear ye therefore the parable of the sower.

19 When any one heareth the word of the kingdom, and understandeth *it* not, then cometh the wicked *one,* and catcheth away that which was sown in his heart. This is he which received seed by the way side.

20 But he that received the seed into stony places, the same is he that heareth the word, and anon with joy receiveth it;

21 Yet hath he not root in himself, but dureth for a while: for when tribulation or persecution ariseth because of the word, by and by he is offended.

22 He also that received seed among the thorns is he that heareth the word; and the care of this world, and the deceitfulness of riches, choke the word, and he becometh unfruitful.

23 But he that received seed into the good ground is he that heareth the word, and understandeth *it;* which also beareth fruit, and bringeth forth, some an hundred-fold, some sixty, some thirty.

Very happily for the LORD's people, JESUS hath not left this parable of the sower to our interpretation, but hath given it himself, and which therefore supersedes all the labors of his servants. And so plain and clear is our LORD's explanation of it, that a little child, under grace, may understand it. I detain not the Reader to add to what JESUS hath here said, but only to observe upon it what a beautiful vein of instruction runs through the whole of it. When the LORD JESUS compares himself to a Sower, and the seed he soweth to the Gospel of his kingdom, we enter at once into the blessedness of apprehension concerning the whole purport of salvation. But when JESUS speaks of the devil, under the figure of the fowls of the air, catching away that which was sown in the heart, it should be remembered, that it is the ministry of the word, and not the grace of the LORD JESUS that is thus rendered unprofitable. The heart is sometimes put for the memory; as in the instance of *Mary*. And she kept all these sayings *in her heart*; that is, in her memory. Luke ii. 51. So that by the devil's catching away the word from them that understand it not, (See also what is meant in scripture of the want of understanding. Job. xxviii. 28.) means not that he taketh away what was sown of grace in the heart, for grace implanted by the LORD can never be taken away; but that he causeth the *graceless* hearers to forget what they heard. In them, as well as all others of the unprofitable hearers, as children *not* of the kingdom, is fulfilled that striking prophecy of *Isaiah*, which, from its vast importance, is quoted no less than six times in the New Testament; namely, in this Chapter, verses 14, 15. Mark iv. 12. Luke viii. 10. John xii. 40. Acts xxviii. 26. Rom. xi. 8. In like manner, concerning the Sun arising on the Stony-ground hearers, we are not to suppose that our LORD meant the Sun of righteousness, for He ariseth not to scorch, but to warm, and with healing in his wings. But by the sun being up, is meant the sun of persecution, the drying, scorching heat of what the Church complained of, Song i. 6. the anger of men. The persons here spoken of were never rooted in CHRIST, and therefore no dews of heaven to water them; and moreover the seed is said not to have fallen *into* the ground, but *upon* stony ground. And those men who, from hence, have argued of the possibility of falling *from* grace, should first have observed, that they never were *in* grace. It is impossible to lose *that* we never had. An union *with* CHRIST, brings after it a communion *in* CHRIST. These Stony-ground hearers never had root, and, as such, could not do otherwise than wither away. To the same purport is what is said concerning *the seed sown among thorns*. It is not supposed that the characters here alluded to, are the openly prophane, and such as are inattentive to divine things, but rather such as make much profession. They have received conviction in the head, of the importance of salvation, but from never having felt it in their heart, and no saving grace having passed upon them, this world's riches are preferred to the riches of eternity, and their hearts, like ground over-run with thorns, and wholly unfruitful. By the *good ground*, into which the seed is cast, is meant an heart renewed, and made good by sovereign grace, for every man's heart by nature is evil. And the different product from hence, is also wholly from the same grace, and not man's improvement. But it is blessed for the soul of that man, whose increase is but of the lowest kind, that all is of the same *quality*, though not of the same *quantity.* The drop of dew on the blade of grass, is as truly water as the ocean. And an union with CHRIST, makes the blessed, the humblest soul, as much as the highest. For it is all *of* JESUS, and *from* JESUS, and *to* JESUS, all the glory.

24 ¶ Another parable put he forth unto them, saying, The kingdom of heaven is likened unto a man which sowed good seed in his field:

25 But while men slept, his enemy came and sowed tares among the wheat, and went his way.

26 But when the blade was sprung up, and brought forth fruit, then appeared the tares also.

27 So the servants of the householder came and said unto him, Sir, didst not thou sow good seed in thy field? from whence then hath it tares?

28 He said unto them, An enemy hath done this. The servants said unto him, Wilt thou then that we go and gather them up?

29 But he said, Nay; lest while ye gather up the tares, ye root up also the wheat with them.

30 Let both grow together until the harvest: and in the time of harvest I will say to the reapers, Gather ye together first the tares, and bind them in bundles to burn them: but gather the wheat into my barn.

The LORD himself hath explained very fully, and very blessedly, this parable in the 36th, and five following verses, which supersedes the necessity of any observations from me. I therefore only detain the Reader to remark, that in this parable, the LORD comes closer home than in the former. In that parable, the world at large was spoken of as receiving the seed of the gospel, and the reception of it hath been shewn, by the greater part receiving it in the way-side, on stony ground, and amidst thorns. But in this parable of the Tares springing up among the Wheat, is meant the *professing* Church of CHRIST, where the children of the wicked One are mingling with the children of the kingdom. Here, therefore, they spring up together, and grow together: but from the first moment, however undiscerned by the eyes of men, as perfectly known to GOD from everlasting, as when ripened into their full state. The tares can no more become good seed, than good seed can become tares. They are from a different stamina, a totally different race. So JESUS explained it to his disciples, and, blessed be GOD, so the LORD's children find. And though they are *to grow together until the harvest,* and the Church of GOD, while on earth, will never be free from tares, yet *the* LORD *knoweth them that are his,* and by the sweet soul-refreshing dews of his Spirit, and the healing of the Sun of Righteousness upon their hearts, often the LORD giveth his people to know *whose they are, and to whom they belong.* Oh! the unspeakable mercy of being of the seed of CHRIST, and heirs of the kingdom. Reader! I beseech you to turn to those scriptures. Isaiah xliv. 3, 4, 5. Isaiah lix. 21. Gal. iii. 16—29.

31 Another parable put he forth unto them, saying, The kingdom of heaven is like to a grain of mustard seed, which a man took, and sowed in his field:

32 Which indeed is the least of all seeds: but when it is grown, it is the greatest among herbs, and becometh a tree, so that the birds of the air come and lodge in the branches thereof.

Different from all the Commentators I have seen, I cannot but think, that neither the great men of the earth, neither kings nor princes, are at all alluded to in this similitude; as if the Gospel, from small beginnings, attracted the notice of such men. But the simple beauty of this parable is, according to my view, that as a little leaven leaveneth the whole lump, so the grace of GOD, when put by the HOLY GHOST into the heart of a sinner, small and unnoticed as it is, produceth such vast things, that angels look with wonder and astonishment at the change which is wrought. Luke xv. 7.

33 Another parable spake he unto them; The kingdom of heaven is like unto leaven, which a woman took, and hid in three measures of meal, till the whole was leavened.

This parable, like the former, is meant to shew what wonderful works are wrought, when the grace of GOD, like leaven, sanctifieth the whole nature.

34 ¶ All these things spake Jesus unto the multitude in parables; and without a parable spake he not unto them:

35 That it might be fulfilled which was spoken by the prophet, saying, I will open my mouth in parables; I will utter things which have been kept secret from the foundation of the world.

I should apprehend, that what is here said, is figuratively said, with an eye to the vast difference in divine teaching, from the mere hearing the word of GOD. Every thing is a parable, even in the word of GOD, until the LORD is the teacher. Ezek. xx. 49.

36 Then Jesus sent the multitude away, and went into the house; and his disciples came unto him, saying, Declare unto us the parable of the tares of the field.

37 He answered and said unto them, He that soweth the good seed is the Son of man;

38 The field is the world; the good seed are the children of the kingdom; but the tares are the children of the wicked *one*.

39 The enemy that sowed them is the devil; the harvest is the end of the world; and the reapers are the angels.

40 As therefore the tares are gathered and burned in the fire; so shall it be in the end of this world,

41 The Son of man shall send forth his angels, and they shall gather out of his kingdom all things that offend, and them which do iniquity;

42 And shall cast them into a furnace of fire: there shall be wailing and gnashing of teeth.

43 Then shall the righteous shine forth as the sun in the kingdom of their Father. Who hath ears to hear, let him hear.

Our LORD's explanation of the parable of the Tares, is so plain and simple, that it can need nothing further by way of illustration, I only pray the LORD to give both Writer and Reader such a sense of it, that it may be found we have *the hearing ear*, and *the seeing eye*, to know these things which are freely given to us of GOD.

44 Again, the kingdom of heaven is like unto treasure hid in a field; the which when a man hath found, he hideth, and for joy thereof goeth and selleth all that he hath, and buyeth that field.

45 Again, the kingdom of heaven is like unto a merchant-man, seeking goodly pearls:

46 Who, when he had found one pearl of great price, went and sold all that he had, and bought it.

47 Again, the kingdom of heaven is like unto a net, that was cast into the sea, and gathered of every kind:

48 Which, when it was full, they drew to shore, and sat down, and gathered the good into vessels, but cast the bad away.

49 So shall it be at the end of the world: the angels shall come forth, and sever the wicked from among the just,

50 And shall cast them into the furnace of fire: there shall be wailing and gnashing of teeth.

The treasure may most probably be CHRIST, hid, in the field of the Scripture, from the wise and prudent, but revealed unto babes. The merchant-man seeking goodly pearls, may perhaps be designed to set forth the LORD JESUS CHRIST, who is seeking and must gather the goodly pearls, even his redeemed, which are the jewels of his mediatorial crown. Or if the merchant be designed to represent the spiritual merchant seeking CHRIST, as the pearl of great price, then it will shew, that the finding, and possessing him, includes all treasure; and gladly will a child of GOD then turn his back upon all the objects which might otherwise be desirable, in this waste and howling wilderness.

51 Jesus saith unto them, Have ye understood all these things? They say unto him, Yea, Lord.

52 Then said he unto them, Therefore every scribe *which is* instructed unto the kingdom of heaven is like unto a man *that is* an householder, which bringeth forth out of his treasure *things* new and old.

What a beautiful representation is here made of the SON of GOD! He calls his servants scribes, and points out how needful it must be, that those who were well instructed themselves, should be forward to instruct others.

53 And it came to pass, *that* when Jesus had finished these parables, he departed thence.

54 And when he was come into his own country, he taught them in their synagogue, insomuch that they were astonished, and said, Whence hath this *man* this wisdom, and *these* mighty works?

55 Is not this the carpenter's son? is not his mother called Mary? and his brethren, James, and Joses, and Simon, and Judas?

56 And his sisters, are they not all with us? Whence then hath this *man* all these things?

57 And they were offended in him. But Jesus said unto them, A prophet is not without honour, save in his own country, and in his own house.

58 And he did not many mighty works there because of their unbelief.

Reader! even now the offence of the cross is not ceased! And, the LORD be praised, it never shall. Oh! what a blessedness is it, that amidst all the unworthiness that is in us, there is none in CHRIST. LORD! grant that I may never be offended, but in the midst of the present perverse and crooked generation, be *strong in the* LORD, *and in the power of his might.*

REFLECTIONS.

READER! let you and I pause over this sweet Chapter, and mark the condescending love of JESUS, in thus adopting his discourse, under the imagery of parables, surely it serves to teach us the tenderness of his heart towards his redeemed, as if to come down to the humblest capacities of his people; and that none might err in the apprehension, he varies his subject by illustrating under various similitudes the important truths relating to his kingdom. But that all might be impressed of the everlasting line of distinction between his children, and the children of the wicked One, under whatever figure, or parable, he states the subject, JESUS never loseth sight of this. The good *seed,* or the *leaven,* the *treasure* hid in the field, or the *good* gathered into vessels, all are made to represent the very reverse of the *way-side* hearers, the *stony ground,* the *thorns,* and the *tares,* which uniformly set forth the state of the reprobate and the seed of the devil. In every part of this blessed Chapter, the LORD JESUS hath drawn, as with a sun-beam, the striking difference, and shewn that characters, springing from such different stocks, never can coalesce; so that the good seed may become tares, or the tares good seed. LORD JESUS! give thy people grace to discover, that amidst all their complaints of unprofitableness, and the like, still thy redeemed are thine, and the LORD will own them. Oh! for grace, to have all our fruit in JESUS, and the end everlasting life.

CHAP. XIV.

CONTENTS.

This Chapter opens with an account of Herod's having murdered John the Baptist. In the after part we have the relation of some of the miracles of CHRIST.

AT that time Herod the tetrarch heard of the fame of Jesus,

2 And said unto his servants, This is John the

Baptist; he is risen from the dead; and therefore mighty works do shew forth themselves in him.

3 For Herod had laid hold on John, and bound him, and put *him* in prison for Herodias' sake, his brother Philip's wife.

4 For John said unto him, It is not lawful for thee to have her.

5 And when he would have put him to death, he feared the multitude, because they counted him as a prophet.

6 But when Herod's birth-day was kept, the daughter of Herodias danced before them, and pleased Herod.

7 Whereupon he promised with an oath to give her whatsoever she would ask.

8 And she, being before instructed of her mother, said, Give me here John Baptist's head in a charger.

9 And the king was sorry: nevertheless for the oath's sake, and them which sat with him at meat, he commanded *it* to be given *her*.

10 And he sent, and beheaded John in the prison.

11 And his head was brought in a charger, and given to the damsel: and she brought *it* to her mother.

12 And his disciples came, and took up the body, and buried it, and went and told Jesus.

What a vast variety of solemn thoughts arise from this short, but affecting narrative of the death of John the Baptist. The cruelty of the actors, the implacable hatred of the human mind, towards this poor Prophet, the savage feelings of Herod's guests, and, above all, the LORD's providence in the appointment! what endless meditations arise from these, and the like subjects, suggested by the event. Oh! what a proof the whole brings of that solemn scripture : *The righteous shall rejoice when he seeth the vengeance, he shall wash his feet in the blood of the wicked. So that a man shall say, verily, there is a reward for the righteous, verily, he is a* GOD *that judgeth the earth.* Psalm lviii. 10, 11. Reader! pause over the subject. Who that would desire truly to know to what a state the human nature is reduced by the fall of man, must learn it, under divine teaching, from such savage instances as are here exhibited. What one man is capable of doing, all are; and, but for restraining grace, if temptations arose to prompt to like acts, would do. The seeds of every sin are in every heart, the same by the fall. Reader! do you believe this? Yes! if GOD the HOLY GHOST hath convinced you of sin. And until this is feelingly known in the heart, never will the infinitely precious redemption by the LORD JESUS CHRIST be understood or valued. Oh! how precious to them that believe is JESUS! 1 Pet. ii. 7. Hence a child of GOD reads this account of Herod, therefrom to abhor himself, and to love JESUS! 1 Cor. iv. 7.

13 When Jesus heard *of it*, he departed thence by ship into a desert place apart: and when the people had heard *thereof*, they followed him on foot out of the cities.

14 And Jesus went forth, and saw a great multitude, and was moved with compassion toward them, and he healed their sick.

15 And when it was evening, his disciples came to him, saying, This is a desert place, and the time is now past; send the multitude away, that they may go into the villages, and buy themselves victuals.

16 But Jesus said unto them, They need not depart; give ye to them to eat.

17 And they say unto him, We have here but five loaves, and two fishes.

18 He said, Bring them hither to me.

19 And he commanded the multitude to sit down on the grass, and took the five loaves, and the two fishes, and looking up to heaven, he blessed, and brake, and gave the loaves to *his* disciples, and the disciples to the multitude.

20 And they did all eat, and were filled: and they took up of the fragments that remained twelve baskets full.

21 And they that had eaten were about five thousand men, beside women and children.

I pray the Reader after he hath duly pondered the many blessed instructions contained in this miracle, to attend to one feature in our LORD's character, which can never be too often regarded, nor too affectionately valued; I mean the movement of CHRIST's heart upon this occasion, which is here sweetly noticed and testified, in the immediate act of healing the sick among the multitude. It ought to be our chief delight to notice, in every act of JESUS where it is more immediately recommended to our view, those actions of our LORD where his human feelings are brought forward to our observation. What can be so truly blessed as to mark the tendencies of CHRIST's love to his people, in that very nature of ours which he hath taken into union with the GODHEAD, and in which, and through which, the mercies of his divine nature flow to us in a way and manner which are peculiarly his own; that is to say, the mercies and compassion of the GOD-Man CHRIST JESUS! Oh! what an endless subject of joy ariseth to the mind of the redeemed, when properly considered from this one point of view! The mercies and compassions of my GOD and SAVIOR, are the mercies and compassions of GOD, for *He is One with the* FATHER *over all,* GOD *blessed for ever. Amen.* But they are no less the mercies and compassions of the Man CHRIST JESUS, for, *verily, He took not on him the nature of Angels, but he took on him the seed of Abraham,* and on purpose that *he might be a merciful and faithful High Priest in things pertaining to* GOD, *to make reconciliation for the sins of the people.* So that by this blessed compound of the two natures, his GODHEAD gives him an infinite fulness to supply all mercy towards his redeemed, and his Manhood gives him a fellow feeling, that those mercies come to us through an human channel, and in, and by both, they are the sweet, precious, and most affectionate compassions of the GOD-Man CHRIST JESUS, who is *the Head over all things to the Church, which is his body, the fulness of him which filleth all in all.* And, Reader! without amplifying, in this place, the subject, think what will be the communications of glory, if such be now the communications of grace, when *we shall see him as he is, and we shall know even as we are known!*

22 ¶ And straightway Jesus constrained his disciples to get into a ship, and to go before him unto the other side, while he sent the multitudes away.

23 And when he had sent the multitudes away, he went up into a mountain apart to pray: and when the evening was come, he was there alone.

Those retirings of the LORD are sweet incidents in his life, and they are held forth to the Church in strong endearments of character. But who shall undertake to describe them? Who shall take upon them to say, what passed in those hallowed seasons between CHRIST in his Mediator-character and the FATHER? We read of the transfiguration, Matt. xvii. 1—9. We read also of his agony in the garden, Luke xxii, 41—45. But here we pause. Every circumstance in the life of JESUS is, and must be, pregnant with somewhat great, but our part is in silence, and holy awe, to exercise our contemplation!

24 But the ship was now in the midst of the sea, tossed with waves: for the wind was contrary.

25 And in the fourth watch of the night Jesus went unto them, walking on the sea.

26 And when the disciples saw him walking on the sea, they were troubled, saying, It is a spirit; and they cried out for fear.

27 But straightway Jesus spake unto them, saying, Be of good cheer; it is I; be not afraid.

28 And Peter answered him and said, Lord, if it be thou, bid me come unto thee on the water.

29 And he said, Come. And when Peter was come down out of the ship, he walked on the water, to go to Jesus.

30 But when he saw the wind boisterous, he was afraid; and beginning to sink, he cried, saying, Lord, save me.

31 And immediately Jesus stretched forth *his* hand, and caught him, and said unto him, O thou of little faith, wherefore didst thou doubt?

32 And when they were come into the ship, the wind ceased.

33 Then they that were in the ship came, and worshipped him, saying, Of a truth thou art the Son of God.

Many very blessed instructions arise out of this short memorial of CHRIST's grace to his disciples, which we ought, through the LORD's teaching, to gather. The ship tossed with the waves, and the winds contrary, represents the case of the Church of JESUS at large, and the instance of believers in particular. It is such the LORD comforts in that sweet scripture: *Oh! thou afflicted, tossed with tempest, and not comforted—In righteousness shalt thou be established; thou shalt be far from oppression; for thou shalt not fear: and from terror; for it shall not come near thee.* Isaiah liv. 11, &c. And how often, amidst such frights as situations like the tossing of waves induce, is JESUS very near, as He was to his disciples, and we not conscious of it. *Hagar*, in the wilderness, could, and did say; *Thou* LORD *seeth me.* Gen. xvi. 13. But you and I too often forget the certain truth. I pray the Reader to remark in the case of *Peter's* faith, how *strong* that faith may be, and indeed is, when at the command of the Almighty Giver of it, the LORD calls it forth; but how *slender*, when the Lord suspends his powerful arm in the support of it. But do not, Reader, overlook the gentle words of JESUS, even in reproof. *Oh thou of little faith!* (said Jesus) *wherefore didst thou doubt?* The LORD did not say, Oh thou of *no* faith: for faith he had, through JESUS giving it to him; but his exercise of it was *little.* And let the Reader not fail to remark, the sequel of the whole : *When they were come into the ship, the wind ceased.* Yes! so is it always when JESUS makes himself known unto his people. *Fear not, I am with thee. Be not dismayed, I am thy* GOD. Look at that precious scripture. Isaiah xliii. 1, 2. I entreat the Reader, not to overlook the conviction wrought on the minds of the mariners of the GODHEAD of CHRIST by this event. They worshipped JESUS, and confessed who he was. The Reader will recollect also, how frequently this conviction was wrought on the multitude which followed CHRIST; and yet how shortly after the sense of it wore off. Luke iv. 22—29. Matt. xxi. 9. Mark xv. 13, 14.

34 And when they were gone over, they came into the land of Gennesaret.

35 And when the men of that place had knowledge of him, they sent out into all that country round about, and brought unto him all that were diseased :

36 And besought him that they might only touch the hem of his garment: and as many as touched were made perfectly whole.

How delightful is it to behold JESUS, in those interesting moments, when fulfilling the Prophet's prediction of him. It was one mark of his divine character, to heal all manner of sickness, and all manner of disease among the people. And here we behold the corresponding testimony. Isaiah xxxv. 4, 5, 6. Luke iv. 17, 18. But what I beg the Reader more particularly to observe, in this account of CHRIST, is, how fully it manifested his character as the GOD-man Messiah. Think, Reader, I beseech you, what an endearing representation this is of JESUS, that by his living so many years in this world as we do, and combating with the same exercises as we combat with; how blessedly suited he was, *having borne our sins, and carried our sorrows,* to sooth the sorrows in others, which he bore himself. Oh! how suited also now in glory, to recollect in his own trials what he felt, and to feel for others. The Apostle makes this the very basis of all comfort. *For in that he himself hath suffered being tempted: he knoweth how to succour them that are tempted.* Heb. ii. 18.

REFLECTIONS.

READER! let us gather a short lesson from the history of John the Baptist. To look at John, when falling a sacrifice at the instigation of a worthless woman, and to overlook the LORD in the appointment, is to consider second causes, and not the first; and very sure will it be, that we shall then make wrong conclusions. Here is a faithful servant of the LORD, borne down by oppression; and here is an incestuous woman triumphing in the godly man's death. But what follows? Aye, there's the grand concern. *Say ye to the righteous, it shall be well with him. Woe to the wicked, it shall be ill with him.*

Oh, for grace, to eye the LORD's sovereignty in all: for this alone will give energy to the lively actings of faith, and keep the soul in peace.

But let me turn from the servant to contemplate the Master! Oh, for grace to eye CHRIST, in the several blessed views here given of him; in feeding and supporting his people, and healing all their diseases. Precious LORD JESUS! do thou manifest thyself to my poor soul under that endearing character, as, JEHOVAH ROPHE, the LORD that healeth the people. And oh! for grace and faith in lively exercises upon his person, blood, and righteousness; that while JESUS is coming forth to bless, my soul through the HOLY GHOST, may be going forth to meet him; and like the people in this Chapter, may my faith be so strong in the LORD, that I may be convinced even the hem of CHRIST's garment, touched by faith, will make me perfectly whole. Amen.

CHAP. XV.

CONTENTS.

In this Chapter we have CHRIST's discourses with the scribes. The woman of Canaan, seeking to JESUS for her daughter: and the LORD feeding the multitude in the wilderness.

THEN came to Jesus scribes and Pharisees, which were of Jerusalem, saying,

2 Why do thy disciples transgress the tradition of the elders? for they wash not their hands when they eat bread.

3 But he answered and said unto them, Why do ye also trangress the commandment of God by your tradition?

4 For God commanded, saying, Honour thy father and mother: and, He that curseth father or mother, let him die the death.

5 But ye say, Whosoever shall say to *his* father or *his* mother, *It is* a gift, by whatsoever thou mightest be profited by me;

6 And honour not his father or his mother, *he shall be free.* Thus have ye made the commandment of God of none effect by your tradition.

7 *Ye* hypocrites, well did Esaias prophesy of you, saying,

8 This people draweth nigh unto me with their mouth, and honoureth me with their lips; but their heart is far from me.

9 But in vain they do worship me, teaching *for* doctrines the commandments of men.

It is worthy observation, how much men in all ages are disposed to rest in forms and customs, rather than know the power of godliness. Any thing, every thing shall be attempted or set up, if the LORD will relax in his demands. But what a precious thought is it to the believer in CHRIST, that neither washen nor unwashen hands, are any thing: but *faith which worketh by love.* One verse of scripture throws to the ground every thing of will worship. *The blood of* JESUS CHRIST *cleanseth from all sin.* So runs the glorious charter. And such in correspondence is the dependance of the faithful.

10 And he called the multitude, and said unto them, Hear, and understand:

11 Not that which goeth into the mouth defileth a man; but that which cometh out of the mouth, this defileth a man.

12 Then came his disciples, and said unto him, Knowest thou that the Pharisees were offended, after they heard this saying?

13 But he answered and said, Every plant, which my heavenly Father hath not planted, shall be rooted up.

14 Let them alone: they be blind leaders of the blind. And if the blind lead the blind, both shall fall into the ditch.

15 Then answered Peter and said unto him, Declare unto us this parable.

16 And Jesus said, Are ye also yet without understanding?

17 Do not ye yet understand, that whatsoever entereth in at the mouth goeth into the belly, and is cast out into the draught?

18 But those things which proceed out of the mouth come forth from the heart; and they defile the man.

19 For out of the heart proceed evil thoughts, murders, adulteries, fornications, thefts, false witness, blasphemies:

20 These are *the things* which defile a man: but to eat with unwashen hands defileth not a man.

I pass over the whole of this passage as being in itself too plain to need a Comment. But I beg to call the Reader's attention to that one verse in the middle of it. *Every plant* (saith JESUS), *which my heavenly Father hath not planted shall be rooted up.* Than which nothing can more decidedly shew, the everlasting and unchanging love of JESUS to his people. Planted by sovereign grace, made one in CHRIST, and receiving the distinguishing tokens of his love: it is impossible they who are thus planted by the LORD, can fall. But on the other hand every *one* which is not of this stock, is sure to fall. Oh! the blessedness of distinguishing grace. LORD! sweetly give grace to the improvement of thy people, that we may know where we are, and to whom we belong. And avert from thy redeemed, false teachers and false guides: that we may not be in danger of being led by the blind, and both fall into condemnation.

21 ¶ Then Jesus went thence, and departed into the coasts of Tyre and Sidon.

22 And, behold, a woman of Canaan came out of the same coasts, and cried unto him, saying, Have mercy on me, O Lord, *thou* son of David; my daughter is grievously vexed with a devil.

We here enter upon that beautiful history, of the woman of *Canaan*, whose faith is so highly commended by CHRIST. Every particular in it is interesting. The Evangelist saith, that she was a woman of *Canaan*; consequently a Gentile. *Mark* adds in his account of it, Mark vii. 26, that she was a *Syrophœnician;* that is, she belonged to that part of *Phœnicia* which bordered on *Syria.* She came from those coasts to seek after CHRIST. But who taught her of JESUS? And how came she to know that CHRIST was the SON of David? Surely none but GOD himself could be her teacher, or give her such faith as to follow JESUS. I pray the Reader, before he goes further, to turn to two scriptures in proof. Isaiah liv. 13, and John vi. 37—40. And when the Reader hath duly pondered these precious truths, let him behold JESUS directing his steps towards *Tyre* and *Sidon* to meet this woman, before that she was coming out of those coasts to meet CHRIST. Yes! for so the charter of grace runs: *It shall come to pass that before they call I will answer; and while they are yet speaking I will hear.* Isaiah lxv. 24. So sure, so very sure is that scripture: *If we love him, it is because he first loved us.* 1 John iv. 19.

But what was it that prompted this poor woman to come to CHRIST? *Her daughter was grievously vexed with a devil.* And who but JESUS could help her? The SON of GOD was manifested *that he might destroy the works of the devil.* 1 John iii. 8. How blessed is it to have such a deliverer to fly to, under distresses. If every mother, every father, whose children are under evil possessions, had the same knowledge of JESUS, and faith in JESUS, as this poor woman had: how would they hasten to his mercy-seat to spread their sorrows before him and seek his favor. I pray the Reader to notice how comprehensive her petition; and the ground upon which she asked for mercy. *Have mercy on me,* O LORD! CHRIST himself is mercy: the first born in the

womb of mercy. And the ground on which she hoped it was, that
JESUS is the *Son of David,* meaning, GOD in human nature. GOD
and man in one person; *Emmanuel* GOD with us. Let not the Reader
overlook this. Here is a poor woman, a Gentile, pleading for mercy,
with CHRIST, because he is CHRIST; while thousands who saw JESUS
daily, knew nothing of him! Whence could this be? Surely from
the LORD himself. So that we gather two grand truths from the case
of this woman, illustrated as it is, by her history; namely that GOD
and none other could have taught her of JESUS. And, secondly, that
that teaching infallibly led her to seek to CHRIST, as the CHRIST of
GOD. John vi. 45, 46.

23 But he answered her not a word. And his
disciples came and besought him, saying, Send her
away; for she crieth after us.

24 But he answered and said, I am not sent but
unto the lost sheep of the house of Israel.

But JESUS *answered her not a word.* What a discouragement was
here. Is this the LORD JESUS, who commanded every poor, weary,
and heavy laden sinner, to come to him, assuring them, that *they
should find rest unto their souls.* And doth JESUS remain silent, and
seemingly inattentive to the earnest cries of this poor creature?
Oh! ye that know the history of this woman, and behold that the end
of the LORD is very pitiful and gracious, learn from hence how to form
conclusions, when at any time, there is a silence at the heavenly
throne. JESUS both hears, and sees, and knows all your sorrows: yea,
himself it is, that measures out your portion of exercise; and is all
the while infinitely more disposed, to administer the needed comfort,
than you are to ask it. But he waits to be gracious: that is, waits the
properest time, which is the best time to answer his purpose, and your
real happiness. JESUS, therefore, for the present answers the poor
woman not a word. And this gives occasion to the disciples to interest themselves in her behalf. *Send her away: she crieth after us.*
They knew not what was in the LORD's intention. Ministers of
CHRIST, do well to bear the persons, and the wants of the LORD's
people in their prayers before the throne; and like their Master, in
his High Priestly office, go in before the mercy-seat, as JESUS doth,
with their names upon their breast and in their hearts. But here
they rest. They can go no further.

I am not sent, saith JESUS, *but to the lost sheep of the house of Israel.*
Commentators generally agree, that CHRIST, as the minister of the
Circumcision, meant to say by this, that his commission was only to
Israel. And on confirmation when he sent his disciples out to preach,
he commanded them *not to go in the way of the Gentiles.* Matt. x. 5,
6. But I am free to confess, that notwithstanding all this, I do not
conceive that the LORD JESUS could mean that his commission was
limited to the Jewish nation. *He came to seek, and save that which
was lost.* And what was lost, but his spouse, his Church, to whom
he betrothed himself, before all worlds? And was not the Gentile
Church, as much as the Jewish, included? Read those scriptures,
Isaiah xlix. 1—6. Song vi. 9. John x. 15, 16. Gal. iii. 28, 29.

The LORD's answer to the disciples, was therefore meant, for the further exercise of her faith.

25 Then came she and worshipped him, saying, Lord, help me.

26 But he answered and said, It is not meet to take the children's bread, and to cast *it* to dogs.

27 And she said, Truth, Lord: yet the dogs eat of the crumbs which fall from their master's table.

The poor woman, a true daughter of Abraham, *who against hope believed in hope,* still held out, under all discouragements; and therefore now ventures nearer to JESUS. She *worshipped him* in testimony of her belief in his GODHEAD; and the cry of the soul goes forth in the most vehement earnestness, saying, LORD *help me!* Oh! for grace on trying seasons, to be more clamorous, when discouragements abound; and to rest on JESUS, when every promise leading to JESUS seems shut up. *Though he slay me* (said one of old) *yet will I trust in him.* Job xiii. 15.

Still the exercise of her faith is not finished. JESUS now speaks for the first time to her; but it must have seemed what the LORD said as very cutting to the heart. *It is not meet to take the children's bread and cast it to dogs.* Think, Reader! how she felt, to hear those words drop from the lips of CHRIST. JESUS knew her, loved her, and from the first moment she cried to him; had all along determined to do for her, even more than she had asked; yet still, that faith the LORD had given her shall be tried. She is to stand forth, an everlasting monument in the Church of GOD, for her illustrious faith; and therefore let faith have her perfect work and lack nothing. And oh! what but grace could have enabled her to hold on and hold out; or have taught her to make that sweet reply to JESUS: *Truth, Lord! yet the dogs eat of the crumbs which fall from their master's table!*

28 Then Jesus answered and said unto her, O woman, great *is* thy faith: be it unto thee, even as thou wilt. And her daughter was made whole from that very hour.

Here finisheth the wonderful subject, in the LORD's manifested grace, and her soul's joy. *O woman, great is thy faith; be it unto thee even as thou wilt.* As if JESUS threw the reins of government into her hand, saying, as by the Prophet, *Concerning my sons, and concerning the work of my hands command ye me.* Isaiah xlv. 11. And was there ever a more finished instance of grace and mercy, not only in following up this daughter of *Abraham's* petition; but planting such faith in her heart, as might sustain so long, and painful a trial. Reader! I pray you, dismiss it not, until you have gathered some, at least of the many blessed instructions it contains, for your own private encouragement, under the lesser exercises of your faith.

And, *First.* Behold the sovereignty of Almighty grace, in this chosen vessel of GOD; and taken from the coasts of *Tyre* and *Sidon.*

How evident is it, that JESUS hath a Church, to be gathered from all nations. They shall come *from the east, and from the west, and from the north, and from the south.* And the certainty of their coming is in the covenant. *Thy people shall be willing in the day of thy power.* Psm. cx. 3.

Secondly. Mark the grace of the LORD, in disposing the way for this poor Gentile to come to CHRIST. By inducing afflictions of body, and giving grace in the soul, she is brought to JESUS. Oh! how often the LORD thus mercifully deals with his people.

Thirdly. Learn from the LORD's dealings with her, how to form proper judgment of his dealings with all his people. Though from the first, more disposed to grant than she to ask; yet to enhance the blessing, and to improve her faith, the mercy is suspended for a space. So JESUS doth by all. And sweet it is, when by waiting upon the LORD, we renew our spiritual strength.

Fourthly. Behold what humbleness of soul grace accomplisheth in the heart. Truth, LORD, said this poor member of CHRIST's mystical body, I am unworthy of children's fare. Reader! depend upon it, in proportion to our views of CHRIST's glory, such will be our views of our own unworthiness. It is CHRIST alone that shall be exalted. And now this poor Canaanite is sitting down with Abraham, Isaac, and Jacob, in the kingdom of our GOD, and of his CHRIST!

29 And Jesus departed from thence, and came nigh unto the sea of Galilee; and went up into a mountain and sat down there.

30 And great multitudes came unto him, having with them *those that were* lame, blind, dumb, maimed, and many others, and cast them down at Jesus' feet; and he healed them:

31 Insomuch that the multitude wondered, when they saw the dumb to speak, the maimed to be whole, the lame to walk, and the blind to see: and they glorified the God of Israel.

32 ¶ Then Jesus called his disciples *unto him,* and said, I have compassion on the multitude, because they continue with me now three days, and have nothing to eat: and I will not send them away fasting, lest they faint in the way.

33 And his disciples say unto him, Whence should we have so much bread in the wilderness as to fill so great a multitude?

34 And Jesus saith unto them, How many loaves have ye? And they said, Seven, and a few little fishes.

35 And he commanded the multitude to sit down on the ground.

36 And he took the seven loaves and the fishes, and gave thanks, and brake *them*, and gave to his disciples, and the disciples to the multitude.

37 And they did all eat, and were filled: and they took up of the broken *meat* that was left seven baskets full.

38 And they that did eat were four thousand men, beside women and children.

39 And he sent away the multitude, and took ship, and came into the coasts of Magdala.

We have here renewed instances of JESUS's grace, both to the souls and bodies of men. He manifested his power and GODHEAD, and proved his being the Messiah in fulfilling what had been prophesied of him. Isaiah xxxv. 5, 6. Isaiah lxi. 1, &c. But it would swell this work of the "Poor Man's Commentary" much beyond the limits proposed, to notice every miracle of the LORD JESUS, with observations, in a way of improvement. Of the LORD it must be truly said, as said the Psalmist ages before, who contemplated his coming; *his greatness is unsearchable.* Psm. cxlv. 3.

REFLECTIONS.

WHO can read in the opening of this Chapter, the pitiful substitution of outward acts of religion for the defect of inward purity, but with painful mortification, when we consider in such proofs to what a sad state of ruin, our whole nature is reduced by the fall? Alas! what are these Scribes and Pharisees, but representatives of all men in the Adam-race, until a work of mercy in salvation hath passed upon the soul? Do we not all draw nigh to GOD with our mouth, and honor him with our lips, while our hearts are far from him; until GOD the HOLY GHOST, hath revealed CHRIST to us, in his person, offices, and character, and *we are brought nigh by the blood of his cross?*

What a beautiful relief, from such a universal corruption of nature is the subject this Chapter introduceth us to, of the woman of *Canaan.* Oh! ye parents of perverse children, and children under the dominion of Satan; oh! may ye learn for them, for yourselves, yea, for the whole Church of CHRIST, how to come to JESUS. Who shall say what mercies JESUS is continually manifesting of the same kind? And if we feel interested, as that we cannot but feel interested, for our own, and their everlasting welfare, that neither we nor our offspring should remain under the worst of all distresses, even soul-distresses in Satan's influence; oh! let us come out of all the coasts of the *Tyre* and *Sidon* of this world, and look unto JESUS: and beholding his mercy here, let us hope for mercy for all Israel: for with him is *plenteous redemption.*

JESUS! do thou have compassion, LORD, as thou hadst in the days of thy flesh, and beholding the multitudes in the wilderness, send us not empty away, but feed us with thyself; and command a blessing upon thy bounty: for thou LORD art the bread of life, of which *whosoever eateth shall live for ever!*

CHAP. XVI.

CONTENTS.

The sign of Jonas, the leaven of the Pharisees and Sadducees guarded against; Peter's profession of CHRIST, *and the* LORD *foretelling his death, are the several subjects of this Chapter.*

THE Pharisees also with the Sadducees came, and tempting desired him that he would shew them a sign from heaven.

2 He answered and said unto them, When it is evening, ye say, *It will be* fair weather: for the sky is red.

3 And in the morning, *It will be* foul weather to day: for the sky is red and lowering. O ye hypocrites, ye can discern the face of the sky; but can ye not *discern* the signs of the times?

4 A wicked and adulterous generation seeketh after a sign; and there shall no sign be given unto it, but the sign of the prophet Jonas. And he left them, and departed.

It is very awful to behold men in an unwakened, unregenerate state, professing, like those Pharisees, great concern for religion. In all ages there have been multitudes amusing themselves, and deceiving others, on this ground. Signs from heaven, false interpretation of the Prophets, and men untaught by GOD the HOLY GHOST, setting up a system of instruction for others. To all such the cross of CHRIST will be as offensive as to the Pharisees of old. But to all such there will be no sign given but like that of *Jonas,* to offend them still more, and to work no work of grace.

5 And when his disciples were come to the other side, they had forgotten to take bread.

6 Then Jesus said unto them, Take heed and beware of the leaven of the Pharisees and of the Sadducees.

7 And they reasoned among themselves, saying, *It is* because we have taken no bread.

8 *Which* when Jesus perceived, he said unto them, O ye of little faith, why reason ye among yourselves, because ye have brought no bread?

9 Do ye not yet understand, neither remember the five loaves of the five thousand, and how many baskets ye took up?

10 Neither the seven loaves of the four thousand, and how many baskets ye took up?

11 How is it that ye do not understand that I spake *it* not to you concerning bread, that ye should beware of the leaven of the Pharisees and of the Sadducees?

12 Then understood they how that he bade *them* not beware of the leaven of bread, but of the doctrine of the Pharisees and of the Sadducees.

The caution the LORD gave to his disciples then, of a leaven in their doctrine, 1 venture to believe, was generally intended as a caution to all his disciples, in every age of the church. And never was there a period where the caution was more needful than now. Oh! what a leaven mixes in the present hour with the pure doctrines of CHRIST, and even in churches calling themselves Christian? Freewill, self-righteousness, improvements of grace, and conditional salvation with some, and the denial of the HOLY SPIRIT's agency, with the work of regeneration, and the justifying righteousness of the LORD JESUS CHRIST with others, to say nothing of numberless other corruptions which have crept in among men, to the great injury of *the faith* once *delivered unto the saints,* these too plainly prove that the precept of CHRIST, to beware of the leaven of deception and error in doctrine, is highly seasonable in the present day of the Church.

13 ¶ When Jesus came into the coasts of Cesarea Philippi, he asked his disciples, saying, Whom do men say, that I, the Son of man am?

14 And they said, Some *say that thou art* John the Baptist; some Elias; and others Jeremias, or one of the prophets.

15 He saith unto them, But whom say ye that I am?

16 And Simon Peter answered and said, Thou art the Christ, the Son of the living God.

17 And Jesus answered and said unto him, Blessed art thou, Simon Bar-jona: for flesh and

blood hath not revealed *it* unto thee, but my Father which is in heaven.

18 And I say also unto thee, That thou art Peter, and upon this rock I will build my church; and the gates of hell shall not prevail against it.

19 And I will give unto thee the keys of the kingdom of heaven: and whatsoever thou shalt bind on earth shall be bound in heaven; and whatsoever thou shalt loose on earth shall be loosed in heaven.

20 Then charged he his disciples that they should tell no man that he was Jesus the Christ.

The question JESUS here put to his disciples, is that grand and momentous question which every one should ask his own heart, for in the proper apprehension of it consists everlasting life. John xvii. 2, 3. Some read the words thus. Whom do men say that I am? Do they call me the SON of Man? Do they indeed know me in my human nature, the seed of the woman promised? Reader! it is blessed, yea very blessed, so to know him. Heb. ii. 16, 17, 18. The various opinions concerning CHRIST at that time, may serve to shew that there always hath been, and always will be, as now, great variety of notions concerning CHRIST. But, Reader! there can be but one right judgment, and that must be formed from divine teaching. And hence, when Peter for himself and his few faithful companions, declared that JESUS was the CHRIST of GOD, the LORD made this remarkable answer; that *flesh and blood could not reveal the glorious truth; and none but the Father which is in heaven.* I beg the Reader to pause over this account of CHRIST for his own sake, and see whether his knowledge of CHRIST comes from the same Almighty teaching. If, my brother, like *Peter*, you know and believe that CHRIST is the Christ of GOD, most evident it is, from what JESUS hath here said, that you have never learnt it from flesh and blood, but GOD himself hath been your teacher, and, like *Peter*, you are blessed in that knowledge also. See those sweet Scriptures; Matt. xi. 27. John vi. 45, 46. Gal. i. 15, 16. Ephes. i. 17, 18. 1 Cor. xii, 3. Ephes. iii. 14, &c. What follows in the promise made to Peter, is not simply to *Peter* as *Peter*, but as representing the LORD's body, his Church. CHRIST himself is the rock JEHOVAH hath laid in Zion. So the Prophet was commissioned to tell the Church. Isaiah xxviii. 16. And so *Peter* himself, in reference to CHRIST, explained it. 1 Pet. ii. 6, 7, 8. Hence when JESUS said, *upon this rock will I build my Church,* he meant himself, on whom *Peter* and all true believers are alike built, and from their union with CHRIST, neither hell nor corruption shall be able to prevail. By the keys of the kingdom of heaven, given to *Peter*, I venture to believe (but I do not presume to decide) is meant the power and prevalency of prayer, whensoever JESUS, by his outpouring of his Spirit, gives a spirit of prayer. And certain it is, that when the LORD the HOLY GHOST gives a spirit of grace and supplication to a child of GOD, the prayer, indicted by the *Spirit,* is in conformity to the will of GOD, and exactly in unison with the intercession of CHRIST. Hence the binding, or loosing, both in earth and heaven, must be secured, because all the Persons of the GOD-HEAD are engaged in the agency. *Whatsoever ye ask in my name,* (said JESUS,) *believing, he will give it you.* John xvi. 23.

21 ¶ From that time forth began Jesus to shew unto his disciples how that he must go unto Jerusalem, and suffer many things of the elders and chief priests and scribes, and be killed, and be raised again the third day.

22 Then Peter took him, and began to rebuke him, saying, Be it far from thee, Lord: this shall not be unto thee.

23 But he turned, and said unto Peter, Get thee behind me, Satan: thou art an offence unto me: for thou savourest not the things that be of God, but those that be of men.

Observe with what tenderness the LORD JESUS begins to prepare the minds of his disciples for the great event coming. Oh! the love of JESUS! But observe the mistaken views of *Peter* upon the occasion. No doubt it was love in Peter to the person of his LORD, which could not bear the thought of his dear LORD's sufferings. But alas! *Peter* what would have become of CHRIST's Church, if JESUS had not died to redeem it? I have often paused over the passage. Think what CHRIST said to his dear servant; *get thee behind me Satan!* Is this *Peter,* who, but a little before, JESUS, the SON of GOD, declared to be blessed? Never did the LORD JESUS use such language, and that to a child of GOD, and one of his own redeemed ones. But, Reader! while you and I consider, as in the instance of *Peter,* how a soul may be made blessed in the abundance of revelations, yet what temptations the same may fall into, when the LORD remits but a moment his teachings: and while we learn this from the character of this Apostle, let us yet abundantly more look unto the LORD JESUS in this instance, and see how his zeal for his Father's glory, and an holy love to his body, the Church, made him long for the hour, when, by his sufferings and death, he should accomplish redemption for his people. Oh! thou precious LORD JESUS! with what earnestness didst thou enter on this baptism of sufferings, and how wast thou straitened until it was accomplished!

24 Then said Jesus unto his disciples, If any *man* will come after me, let him deny himself, and take up his cross, and follow me.

25 For whosoever will save his life shall lose it:

and whosoever will lose his life for my sake, shall find it.

26 For what is a man profited, if he shall gain the whole world, and lose his own soul? or what shall a man give in exchange for his soul?

How graciously the LORD took occasion, from the mistaken views of *Peter*, to warn and teach all his disciples to be on their guard against all such influence. All the disciples, as well as *Peter*, were tainted with the same misapprehensions. And, Reader! are we not all? But ease, in this life, is not attainable with following the cross of JESUS. And the profit of the whole world, with the loss of the soul, would leave a man poor indeed.

27 For the Son of man shall come in the glory of his Father with his angels; and then he shall reward every man according to his works.

28 Verily I say unto you, There be some standing here which shall not taste of death, till they see the Son of man coming in his kingdom.

These verses are blended as if expressive of the same truth. Every coming of CHRIST is glorious, both when he comes first to awaken a soul, and in all the after visits of his grace, until he finally comes to take his redeemed home to glory. And JESUS puts his name, the *Amen*, the *faithful witness*, to the truth of it, that some then present would not, like holy *Simeon*, see death until they had seen CHRIST's kingdom of grace, leading to a sure kingdom of glory. And this was fulfilled on the day of Pentecost, and is fulfilled in every instance of a redeemed soul, when awakened *from darkness to light, and from the power of sin and Satan to the living* GOD.

REFLECTIONS.

LORD, I pray thee! keep my soul from every leaven, which, mingled with the compleat justifying righteousness of my LORD JESUS CHRIST, would rob my GOD of his glory, and my soul of happiness. And doth my GOD and SAVIOR demand of my poor soul who JESUS is, amidst the varieties of creeds and professions of the present day? Oh! for the teaching of GOD the HOLY GHOST, the revelation of GOD my Father, and the blessed manifestation of the SON of GOD to my heart, that I may bear a fixed, unalterable, and decided testimony, before Angels and Men, that thou art the CHRIST of GOD, the LORD, my righteousness. Oh! yes! thou HOLY ONE of Israel! thou art indeed the CHRIST of God, the Word of GOD, the Lamb of GOD, the wisdom of GOD, and the power of GOD, for salvation to every one that believeth. And oh, my honoured LORD, as thou hast said, flesh and blood cannot reveal it, and none but GOD the Father can give a spirit of wisdom and revelation in the knowledge of CHRIST, hath the LORD given to me this spirit of wisdom and revelation in the knowledge of my LORD; then let me take to myself the blessedness of the discovery, and *rejoice in hope of the glory of* GOD. Oh! for grace to savour the things which are of GOD, and not those which are of men. Give me, blessed JESUS, grace to follow thy cross, and learn all the necessary exercises of self-denial, that being conformed to thy image here; *I may be satisfied when I awake up after thy likeness hereafter!*

CHAP. XVII.

CONTENTS.

We have here an account of CHRIST's *Transfiguration. A Lunatic is healed by* JESUS. *The* LORD *again foretels his approaching death. The Tribute Money.*

AND after six days Jesus taketh Peter, James, and John his brother, and bringeth them up into an high mountain apart.

2 And was transfigured before them: and his face did shine as the sun, and his raiment was white as the light.

Three of the Evangelists have recorded this wonderful scene of CHRIST's glory. Mark ix. 2. Luke ix. 28. And three of the Apostles were present at it. One of them, *Peter*, was commissioned by the HOLY GHOST to give a new record of it just before his own death, to intimate the vast impression it had made upon his mind. 2 Pet. i. 16, &c. It is worthy remark, that JESUS should single out *Peter, James,* and *John,* to be with him at this display of his glory, who were to be present with him at his humiliation in the garden. No doubt it is the truest preparation to the followers of the LORD JESUS, to know CHRIST in his power, who are to be brought under exercises concerning his humiliation. Luke xxii. 28, 29, 30. I do not presume to add a word to what the Evangelists have here said of this transfiguration, by way of explaining what even my conception cannot equally form an idea of. We know that *the Word was made flesh, and dwelt among us.* John i. 14. And we know also, that *in Him,* that is, CHRIST, *dwelleth all the fulness of the* GODHEAD bodily. Coloss. ii. 9. All that we can possibly frame to ourselves of this transfiguration therefore is, that the GODHEAD shone forth in the manhood in a more than ordinary manner. The SON of GOD was pleased to manifest himself in his double-nature glory more than in the usual appearances of CHRIST in the days of his flesh. It was a moment of peculiar manifestation of the glories of his person. It was the personal glory of the GOD-Man, as GOD-Man, and every child of GOD must find cause to bless the LORD for the mercy. If the Reader will turn to the following scriptures, he will, perhaps, be led to discover somewhat similar. Exod. xxiv. Exod. xxxiii. 20. Isaiah vi. Ezek. i. 26, &c. Dan. x. 5, 6.

3 And, behold, there appeared unto them Moses and Elias talking with him.

Moses and *Elias* were seen, and it should seem were known by the Apostles, though the former had been dead *fifteen hundred years,* and the latter near *nine hundred.* I think we may safely infer from hence, that the Church of CHRIST are well known to each other in the several members of CHRIST's mystical body, and they who sleep in JESUS, as well as those alive in JESUS, have communion with their glorious Head. Sweet consideration to the believer. 1 Thess. iv. 13, &c. Rom. xiv. 8.

4 Then answered Peter, and said unto Jesus, Lord, it is good for us to be here : if thou wilt, let us make here three tabernacles ; one for thee, and one for Moses, and one for Elias.

It appears by what both *Mark* and *Luke* have related of this wonderful scene, the Apostle was in such a state of rapture that he knew not what he said. No doubt his whole soul was absorbed in the contemplation, and, like *Paul* upon another occasion, perhaps, not unsimilar, knew not whether he was in the body or out of the body. 2 Cor. xii. 1—4. The proposal of making tabernacles upon earth for those inhabitants of heaven, plainly shews in what a state *Peter's* mind was. But *Peter* might well say, it was good to be present at such a scene. And yet who should have thought, that a man present at such a manifestation of CHRIST's glory, and one who had before received the testimony of being blessed in the revelation GOD the FATHER had made to him concerning the Person of CHRIST, (see chap. xvi. 15—19.) would ever afterwards have denied CHRIST. (Matt. xxvi. 69—75.) Oh! that such an example may be commissioned of our GOD, to teach both Writer and Reader of this *Poor Man's Commentary,* what *Peter* himself, in the after stages of life declared, that *they that are kept, are kept by the power of* GOD, *through faith unto salvation.* 1 Pet. i. 5. Depend upon it, the safety of CHRIST's whole Church is in CHRIST, and not in ourselves.

5 While he yet spake, behold, a bright cloud overshadowed them ; and behold a voice out of the cloud, which said, This is my beloved Son, in whom I am well pleased ; hear ye him.

This is a most blessed proclamation, and infinitely precious to the Church of CHRIST. JEHOVAH had before, at the baptism of JESUS, given testimony to CHRIST's person and character, and here again confirms it. I stay not to make any observations concerning the splendor and glory of the scene, but rather to consider the blessedness of the thing itself. JEHOVAH bears testimony to CHRIST as the beloved SON of GOD. *One with the* FATHER *over all,* GOD *blessed for ever. Amen.* And again, as the begotten SON of GOD, to the purposes of salvation, *the brightness of the* FATHER's *glory, and the express image of his person.* And his being well pleased with Him, and in Him, confirms JEHOVAH's favor to the Church in CHRIST, being well pleased with Him as the Head of his body, the Church, and the Church in Him. *In whom I am well pleased.* Not only *with* Him, but *in* Him, that is, his whole Church, *in* Him, being always considered as part of himself, *members of his body, of his flesh, and of his bones. The* LORD *is well pleased for his righteousness' sake, he will magnify the law, and make it honorable.* Isaiah xlii. 21. So that when commanded *to hear him,* the Church is to accept CHRIST, in all the fulness of his complete salvation, both in his person, office, character, and relations, and to be so completely pleased with Him, as the LORD OUR RIGHTEOUSNESS, as JEHOVAH is pleased with Him, the glorious surety, sponsor, and complete justifying righteousness of his whole body, the Church, *the fulness of Him which filleth all in all.* Reader! Are you well pleased with JESUS? It is an important question. The soul that is so, makes JESUS, what JEHOVAH hath made him, the whole of salvation. Accepts CHRIST as all, looks to CHRIST for all. Pleads CHRIST in all, as the sole means of salvation. Not as procuring favor to the acceptation of our prayers, and tears, and repentance, and faith, but as the very cause, the very righteousness, in which the whole Church, and every individual of the Church, is accepted, and appears in before GOD. He that expressed himself in those words of scripture, felt this to the full. May it be my soul's language also. *I will go in the strength of the* LORD GOD: *I will make mention of thy righteousness, even of thine only.* Psm. lxxi. 16. Reader! what saith your experience to this statement? Oh! for grace, and the sweet influence of GOD the HOLY GHOST, always upon my heart, that as often as I read those words of GOD the FATHER, or they are brought to my recollection, concerning his testimony to GOD the SON, saying, *this is my beloved* SON *in whom I am well pleased, hear ye him,* may my soul be enabled to say, *and this* is my beloved SAVIOR, in whom I pray to be found well pleased, in life, and death, in time, and to all eternity! Amen.

6 And when the disciples heard *it,* they fell on their face, and were sore afraid.

7 And Jesus came and touched them, and said, Arise, and be not afraid.

8 And when they had lifted up their eyes, they saw no man, save Jesus only.

It is not to be wondered at that the disciples should be thus affected. GOD is awful, even in mercies. See how Israel was struck with fear on *Mount Sinai.* Exod. xx. 18—21. But see, Reader, the tenderness of JESUS. *He came and touched them,* Precious Redeemer! how hast thou, by the assumption of our nature, opened a way of communicating mercies to us, and lessening our fears. And Reader! I pray you to remark, that the very first words JESUS spake to his disciples after GOD the FATHER had commanded them to hear him, was, *be not afraid.* And doth it not follow, from hence, that such is the love of GOD our FATHER to the Church, in CHRIST, and knowing that all love is in the heart of CHRIST towards his people, thus he commands concerning him. And GOD the SON, having taking our nature for the express purpose, manifests that his whole heart towards them is love. And GOD the HOLY GHOST, from his everlasting love also to CHRIST, and his Church in him, takes care to make the whole effectual, in *directing the heart of the redeemed into the love of* GOD, *and into the patient waiting for* JESUS CHRIST! Oh! for grace, under those blessed assurances, to possess such faith in JESUS, as may raise our souls above all fears, while conscious of an union with CHRIST, and acceptance in CHRIST. The sudden departure of *Moses* and *Elias* may serve to teach us, that none but JESUS can be our abiding comfort. Every thing here below is short and transitory. Oh! what a blessed thought it is. JESUS hath said, *Lo! I am with you always,* Matt. xxviii. 20.

9 And as they came down from the mountain, Jesus charged them, saying, Tell the vision to no man, until the Son of man be risen again from the dead.

10 And his disciples asked him, saying, Why then say the scribes that Elias must first come?

11 And Jesus answered and said unto them, Elias truly shall first come, and restore all things.

12 But I say unto you, That Elias is come already, and they knew him not, but have done unto him whatsoever they listed. Likewise shall also the Son of man suffer of them.

13 Then the disciples understood that he spake unto them of John the Baptist.

There is somewhat very blessed in this prohibition of JESUS, concerning making known the vision. It doth not appear that the other disciples were made acquainted with it. *Peter* insists upon it much, after the LORD's return to glory, but not before. And the reason seems evident. The LORD's purposes are for his Church. They shall have, in due season, evidences enough, but to others, there is nothing that will carry conviction. So the Prophet declared, and so the Scriptures all along have shewn. Isaiah vi. 9. Acts xxviii. 22, to the end. Nothing can be more plain and evident, from this explanation of CHRIST, that the prophecy of Malachi, chap. iv. 5. concerning the coming of *Elijah*, had been grossly perverted by the Scribes. *John* the *Baptist* was indeed foretold by the Prophet *Isaiah*, in strong features of character, chap. xl. 3. and *Malachi* had been commissioned by GOD the HOLY GHOST, to speak of John also; chap. iii. 1. but the prediction of *Elijah's* coming, gave no authority to this expectation of the Scribes and Pharisees. *John* the *Baptist* could not be *Elias*, though he might be said to come in the spirit and power, with which he appeared, being commissioned, in like manner, by GOD the HOLY GHOST.

14 ¶ And when they were come to the multitude, there came to him a *certain* man, kneeling down to him, and saying,

15 Lord have mercy on my son ; for he is lunatick, and sore vexed : for oft times he falleth into the fire, and oft into the water.

16 And I brought him to thy disciples, and they could not cure him.

17 Then Jesus answered and said, O faithless and perverse generation, how long shall I be with you ? how long shall I suffer you? bring him hither to me.

18 And Jesus rebuked the devil: and he departed out of him: and the child was cured from that very hour.

19 Then came the disciples to Jesus apart, and said, Why could not we cast him out?

20 And Jesus said unto them, Because of your unbelief: for verily I say unto you, If ye have faith as a grain of mustard seed, ye shall say unto this mountain, Remove hence to yonder place; and it shall remove; and nothing shall be impossible unto you.

21 Howbeit this kind goeth not out but by prayer and fasting.

We have this miracle more particularly related by *Mark*, chap. ix. 14, &c. to which, therefore, I refer, as well as for the observations offered upon it, which will there be more fully considered. In the mean time, I only beg to detain the Reader with a short remark on the slenderness of the disciples' faith, in their inability to accomplish the cure of this child. This Epilepsy, or falling sickness, of the child's body, it should seem, had afforded handle to the devil to exercise his cruel devices on the child's soul; and no doubt the permission, as it laid the foundation for the greater manifestation of Christ's glory, was graciously ordered. But the slenderness of the disciples' faith, was simply this it should seem, not in their faith in Christ, but their exertion of that faith in this act of working miracles, as they had been commissioned to do. The Lord Jesus, when he said, O faithless, and perverse generation, did not speak to his disciples, for though they were indeed men of little faith, yet certainly not faithless. It was the men of that generation whom Jesus called faithless and perverse, for in *Mark's* account of this miracle, it appears, that from the inability of the servants of CHRIST, to heal the child, they began to triumph as though the same defect was in the Master, therefore JESUS called that generation faithless and perverse, But the weakness of the disciples' faith, opens a subject of encouragement to the timid disciples of JESUS, in every age of the Church, which, under grace, we ought to make improvement from. Let it be remembered therefore, that with respect to our own personal salvation, the smallest portions of faith, as they are *from* CHRIST, do prove an union *with* CHRIST, as truly as the largest gifts the LORD may be pleased to bestow upon his members. The drop of water in the dew, is as truly water as all the rivers of the world. It is the same in nature and in *quality*, though not in *quantity*. The same may be said in respect to faith. And this ought to comfort and encourage a poor child of GOD under weak faith, whose cries for an increase of faith are great and continual. Luke xvii. 5. Moreover those portions of faith, which are of the operation of the Spirit of GOD, however small and inconsiderable, yet carry with them the true marks of a child of GOD. *Unto you* (saith Paul to the Church) *it is given in the behalf of* CHRIST, *not only to believe on him, but also to suffer for his sake.* Philip. i. 29. Faith is the gift of GOD. And wheresoever this grace is given, it proves the possessor of it to be a child of GOD. For when Paul preached among the Gentiles, we are told, that *as many as were ordained to eternal life believed.* Acts xiii. 48. And as to the act of being justified by faith, it is plain from the whole tenor of Scripture, that while it is blessed to have strong and lively acting of faith on the person, work, and righteousness of GOD our SAVIOR, yet the babe in CHRIST, as well as the strong man in the LORD, is as truly justified, because it is CHRIST which justifieth, and not the strength of our faith in CHRIST which contributes thereto. *By him,* (saith Paul) that is, by CHRIST, *all that believe,* whether slender faith or strong faith, *all that believe, are justified from all things.* Acts xiii. 39.

22 ¶ And while they abode in Galilee, Jesus said unto them, The Son of man shall be betrayed into the hands of men :

23 And they shall kill him, and the third day he shall be raised again. And they were exceeding sorry.

I cannot allow those verses to pass without calling upon the Reader to remark, with me, how much the LORD JESUS seemed to delight in the prospect of his great accomplishment of redemption. Every feature in his character marks this. In proof, see Matt. xvi. 22, 23. Luke ii. 48, 49. Luke xii. 50. John xii. 27, 28. John xiii. 27.

24 ¶ And when they were come to Capernaum, they that received tribute *money* came to Peter, and said, Doth not your master pay tribute?

25 He saith, Yes. And when he was come into the house, Jesus prevented him, saying, What

thinkest thou, Simon? of whom do the kings of
the earth take custom or tribute? of their own
children, or of strangers?

26 Peter saith unto him, Of strangers. Jesus
saith unto him, Then are the children free.

27 Notwithstanding, lest we should offend them,
go thou to the sea, and cast an hook, and take up
the fish that first cometh up; and when thou hast
opened his mouth, thou shalt find a piece of
money: that take, and give unto them for me and
thee.

It should seem, that this tribute money was not what the publicans
gathered for the Roman emperors, but for the temple service. The
Son of God had no right to pay it, strictly speaking, for He himself
was Lord of the temple. Mal. iii. 1. Heb. iii. 6. But, as the Head
and Husband of his people, becoming debtor thereby to the whole
law, it was justly due. See Gal. iv. 4. Luke ii. 22. Exod. xxx.
12—15. Matt. iv. 15. But what a beautiful occasion Jesus took
therefrom to manifest his power and Godhead by the fish with
money. And, Reader! if to supply this pressing occasion, Jesus
wrought a miracle *then*, will he be inattentive to any of the wants of
his people *now*? Oh! how blessedly doth every incident in the
life of Christ, minister instruction, grace, and comfort?

REFLECTIONS.

What a lovely chapter is this to read to us the interesting events
in the life of Christ, when God the Holy Ghost is here leading the
Church by the hand, to contemplate Christ in his glory, and Christ
in his humiliation. We follow him, by faith, to the Mount of Transfiguration, and we hear him informing his disciples, soon after, of his
sufferings which were shortly to follow at Jerusalem! Precious Lord
Jesus! cause both views to have their gracious influences upon the
hearts of thy redeemed! Oh! may it be my portion to follow thee
often, by faith, both to the Mount of *Tabor*, and to the Garden of
Gethsemane. Surely every meditation will tend, under the teaching
of God the Holy Ghost, to strengthen my soul in the belief of Jesus.
What, though the privileges of thy people now, are not like those
highly favoured disciples, to behold *Moses* and *Elias* ministering to
my Lord, yet in Jesus himself I have all. In the sweet communion
with the Master, I shall miss not the absence of all his servants.
Yea! I shall rejoice to be alone with Jesus, having to communicate
to my Lord, and to receive from him those precious soul-transac-
tions, in a joy with which no lookers-on can meddle. It is blessed,
yea very blessed, my honored Lord, to behold the inability of thy
disciples, that my God and Savior's power and grace may be more
fully known. And whatever fears, from the weakness of faith in my
poor heart, and nature's feelings by reason of the remains of indwel-

ling-sin, may arise on entering the cloud, yet will my soul receive an holy joy, unspeakable, and full of glory, when I hear my God and FATHER's gracious voice proclaiming the divine approbation; *this is my beloved Son, in whom I am well pleased, hear ye him.*

CHAP. XVIII.

CONTENTS.

The Lord Jesus *is here teaching his disciples humbleness. He speaks of his own, and his* Father's *good pleasure, for the salvation of every one of his little ones. The Chapter is closed in a parable.*

AT the same time came the disciples unto Jesus, saying, Who is the greatest in the kingdom of heaven?

2 And Jesus called a little child unto him, and set him in the midst of them,

3 And said, Verily I say unto you, Except ye be converted, and become as little children, ye shall not enter into the kingdom of heaven.

4 Whosoever therefore shall humble himself as this little child, the same is greatest in the kingdom of heaven.

5 And whoso shall receive one such little child in my name receiveth me.

6 But whoso shall offend one of these little ones which believe in me, it were better for him that a millstone were hanged about his neck, and *that* he were drowned in the depth of the sea.

It is more than probable, the disciples, looking forward to a temporal kingdom, of their Master, (for it is most certain at this time and long after, they thought of no other; see Acts i. 6.) had often been parcelling out for themselves, some of the highest departments in it. Mark ix. 33, 34. Hence the method our Lord took to correct their error, was as gentle and affectionate, as it was wise and conclusive. Among the old writers, it was conjectured that this little child, was *Ignatius.* But there is no warrant for the conclusion. This antient father hath indeed, in his Latin Epistle to the Church at *Smyrna,* said, that " he saw Christ in the flesh, after his resurrection:" but this doth by no means warrant the former account of his being the child, which the Lord set in the midst of his disciples. But it is very blessed, (and the Reader I hope will not lose sight of it,) on what the Lord places the truest qualification for an entrance into his kingdom; namely, the conversion of the heart to God. For this proves an union with Christ, in the regeneration of the soul by God the

HOLY GHOST: and to offend one of CHRIST's little ones so regenerated; by despising them as CHRIST's, and to make light of the SPIRIT's work in their heart, subjects the despiser to everlasting misery. John iii. 3. Gal. iv. 6. Matt. x. 40, 41, 42.

7 ¶ Woe unto the world, because of offences! for it must needs be that offences come; but woe to that man by whom the offence cometh!

8 Wherefore if thy hand or thy foot offend thee, cut them off, and cast *them* from thee: it is better for thee to enter into life halt or maimed, rather than having two hands or two feet to be cast into everlasting fire.

9 And if thine eye offend thee, pluck it out, and cast *it* from thee: it is better for thee to enter into life with one eye, rather than having two eyes to be cast into hell fire.

10 Take heed that ye despise not one of these little ones; for I say unto you, That in heaven their angels do always behold the face of my Father which is in heaven.

11 For the Son of man is come to save that which was lost.

12 How think ye? If a man have an hundred sheep, and one of them be gone astray, doth he not leave the ninety and nine, and goeth into the mountains, and seeketh that which is gone astray?

13 And if so be that he find it, verily I say unto you, he rejoiceth more of that *sheep*, than of the ninety and nine which went not astray.

14 Even so it is not the will of your Father which is in heaven, that one of these little ones should perish.

Every word here is so plain, as to need no comment; and so blessedly spoken by CHRIST himself, as would be injured by me. I only beg to observe, upon the whole, what a charming thought it ought to be, to the humblest and poorest of CHRIST's little ones, while upon earth, that those who minister to them, as their Angels, are always in the view of beholding the face of GOD in heaven. Heb. i. 14. And let the Reader further observe upon this sweet and precious passage, that so earnest is GOD our FATHER, for the present and everlasting welfare of CHRIST's redeemed ones, that none of them, no not the least of them shall perish! Oh!' the safety of the whole Church of JESUS! Isaiah xxvii. 2, 3. John x. 27, 30.

15 Moreover if thy brother thould trespass against thee, go and tell him his fault between thee and him alone: if he shall hear thee, thou hast gained thy brother.

16 But if he will not hear *thee, then* take with thee one or two more, that in the mouth of two or three witnesses every word may be established.

17 And if he shall neglect to hear them, tell *it* unto the church: but if he neglect to hear the church, let him be unto thee as an heathen man and a publican.

18 Verily I say unto you, Whatsoever ye shall bind on earth shall be bound in heaven: and whatsoever ye shall loose on earth shall be loosed in heaven.

19 Again I say unto you, That if two of you shǎll agree on earth as touching any thing that they shall ask, it shall be done for them of my Father which is in heaven.

I pray the Reader to remark, the affection JESUS insists upon, to subsist between *brethren.* And indeed as they are members of CHRIST's body; brethren of JESUS, and of each other; one spirit moves in all. 1 Cor. xii. throughout.

20 For where two or three are gathered together in my name, there am I in the midst of them.

To the little infirmities, which from the remains of indwelling corruption, may, and will, occasionally break out, how precious is the direction of JESUS. Oh! that it were more generally adopted in the Church of CHRIST! And what an unanswerable argument doth the LORD here leave upon record, for the constant meeting together of his whole body, both in private and public ordinances. Zech. ii. 5, 10, 11. Matt. xx. 28.

21 ¶ Then came Peter to him, and said, Lord how oft shall my brother sin against me, and I forgive him? till seven times?

22 Jesus saith unto him, I say not unto thee, Until seven times : but, Until seventy times seven.

23 Therefore is the kingdom of heaven likened unto a certain king, which would take account of his servants.

24 And when he had begun to reckon, one was brought unto him, which owed him ten thousand talents.

25 But forasmuch as he had not to pay, his lord commanded him to be sold, and his wife and children, and all that he had, and payment to be made.

26 The servant therefore fell down, and worshipped him, saying, Lord, have patience with me, and I will pay thee all.

27 Then the Lord of that servant was moved with compassion, and loosed him, and forgave him the debt.

28 But the same servant went out, and found one of his fellow-servants, which owed him an hundred pence : and he laid hands on him, and took *him* by the throat, saying, Pay me that thou owest.

29 And his fellow-servant fell down at his feet, and besought him, saying, Have patience with me, and I will pay thee all.

30 And he would not : but went and cast him into prison, till he should pay the debt.

31 So when his fellow-servants saw what was done, they were very sorry, and came and told unto their lord all that was done.

32 Then his lord, after that he had called him, said unto him, O thou wicked servant, I forgave thee all that debt, because thou desirest me :

33 Shouldest not thou also have had compassion on thy fellow-servant, even as I had pity on thee ?

34 And his lord was wroth, and delivered him

to the tormentors, till he should pay all that was
due unto him.

35 So likewise shall my heavenly Father do also
unto you, if ye from your hearts forgive not every
one his brother their trespasses.

It was blessed for the Church, that GOD the HOLY GHOST put it
into the mind of *Peter*, to ask this question, which gave rise to one of
the most beautiful Parables of our LORD; and which, no child of GOD
would have lost for a world. The parable itself, in its first plain and
obvious sense, represents the boundless mercy of the LORD, in can-
celling a most enormous debt, even *ten thousand talents;* which,
counted by our *English* coin, would amount to no less a sum than fifty-
four millions and upwards, of our money. A sum almost incredible!
But what sum can represent the greatness of our mercies! What
insolvency come up to the insolvency of sin! But I confess, I cannot explain in my view the parable of our LORD, in reference to
this spiritual sense of it, unless with certain limitations.

The kingdom of heaven is well known to mean the Church of
CHRIST in the present dispensation. The parable saith, that the
LORD of this kingdom, that is, CHRIST, would take account of his servants: that is, his people, his Church, his chosen. Not the whole
world. For though by creation the earth is the LORD's, and all that
is therein; yet here the LORD is speaking of his redeemed. The *one*
brought to him in debt is the representative of *all.* And his debt was
so great, that the everlasting slavery of himself, and all the race
to which he belonged, could never cancel the debt nor pay it. In
this state, the LORD forgives him. Now the debt forgiven could never
be recalled. His cruelty to his fellow-servant, horrible as it was,
could never unsay what his LORD had said. Neither is the pardon
of our sins suspended upon our pardon of others. But the sense of the
Parable seems to be this: How truly undeserving must be all those
who are made partakers of the rich, full, and free salvation of GOD,
who in the view of their ten thousand talents forgiven, are unkind and
unforgiving to their fellow creatures. And in this sense the tormentors, to whom the unforgiving servant was delivered, will be a
source of disquietude to his mind, as long as the conscious sense of
his ingratitude shall remain. But though this must be agreeably to
the whole tenor of Scripture, the general sense of the Parable; yet
we are not authorized to strain the sense of the Parable too far. The
general scope of our LORD's meaning by it, is evidently this; to shew,
that as we hope for mercy, we are supposed to shew mercy: and
the consciousness of sins pardoned in CHRIST should prompt us, and
will prompt the heart of grace to be merciful to every one who bears
the image of CHRIST, and to forgive from our heart, every one his
brother their trespasses.

REFLECTIONS.

How truly blessed is it to have our hearts brought under divine
teaching, and made like the simplicity of a weaned child. See my
soul in the instance of these disciples of JESUS, how much our minds

are wedded to the concerns of this world. Oh! for grace to be converted, and become as little children, that we may be truly great in the kingdom of heaven.

Blessed LORD JESUS! may I never lose sight of this promise that thy presence is eminently manifested in the assemblies of thy people: for sure I am, that all the beauty and glory; all the power and efficacy; all the success and blessing, which can be derived from ordinances, can only be derived, because JESUS hath assured his Church, that wherever two or three are gathered together in his name, there he is in the midst of them, and that to bless them.

Thanks to my dear LORD for this beautiful and instructive Parable. Yea, LORD! my debt was so great, in ten thousand talents as made me insolvent for ever. In vain were it for me to say, LORD have patience with me and I will pay thee all. Never to all eternity, could I have done it. Oh! then add a grace more to the merciful forgiveness of all; and incline my heart to be merciful, even as my father which is in heaven is merciful! Precious JESUS! help me to imitate thee in all things!

CHAP. XIX.

CONTENTS.

The LORD JESUS *is here prosecuting his ministry ; healing the sick ; conversing with the Pharisees; receiving little children; discoursing with his disciples.*

AND it came to pass, *that* when Jesus had finished these sayings, he departed from Galilee, and came into the coasts of Judea, beyond Jordan;

2 And great multitudes followed him; and he healed them there.

3 ¶ The Pharisees also came unto him, tempting him, and saying unto him, Is it lawful for a man to put away his wife for every cause?

4 And he answered and said unto them, Have ye not read, that he which made *them* at the beginning, made them male and female,

5 And said, For this cause shall a man leave father and mother, and shall cleave to his wife: and they twain shall be one flesh?

6 Wherefore they are no more twain, but one flesh. What therefore God hath joined together, let no man put asunder.

7 They say unto him, Why did Moses then command to give a writing of divorcement, and to put her away?

8 He saith unto them, Moses, because of the hardness of your hearts, suffered you to put away your wives: but from the beginning it was not so.

9 And I say unto you, Whosoever shall put away his wife, except *it be* for fornication, and shall marry another, committeth adultery: and whoso marrieth her which is put away doth commit adultery.

There can be no question, but that the married state from the beginning of the creation of the world, was intended as a beautiful representation of the mystical union beween CHRIST and his Church. Gen. ii. 18—21 to the end, explained by Ephes. v. 23 to the end. And all the after stages, in the departure of our nature by adultery, could not destroy the first, and legitimate connection. JESUS betrothed his Church to himself for ever. Hosea ii. 19, 20. And though *Moses* as the LORD JESUS said, for the hardness of the hearts of the *Israelites*, did permit a bill of divorcement, yet not so will JESUS. His language is: *though thou hast played the harlot with many lovers, yet return unto me saith the* LORD. Jer. iii. 1. Deut. xxiv. 1—4. Hence the Church recovered by sovereign grace, sings aloud, *I will return unto my first husband.* Hosea ii. 6, 7.

10 His disciples say unto him, If the case of the man be so with *his* wife, it is not good to marry.

11 But he said unto them, All *men* cannot receive this saying, save *they* to whom it is given.

12 For there are some eunuchs, which were so born from their mother's womb: and there are some eunuchs, which were made eunuchs of men: and there be eunuchs, which have made themselves eunuchs for the kingdom of heaven's sake. He that is able to receive *it*, let him receive it.

How little do these men form proper conceptions in what the kingdom of heaven in grace is made, who have fancied the qualifications for the enjoyment of it consists in things outward; instead of that regeneration of the heart, which the LORD himself describes, as the best and only qualification, by the blood and righteoussness of JESUS CHRIST. Men may *make* themselves what they may in nature, but it is the LORD who alone *makes a new heart* in grace. John iii. 3. Ezek. xxxvi. 24—32.

13 ¶ Then were there brought unto him little children, that he should put *his* hands on them, and pray : and the disciples rebuked them.

14 But Jesus said, Suffer little children, and forbid them not, to come unto me: for of such is the kingdom of heaven.

15 And he laid his hands on them, and departed thence.

Strange it is that any should forbid godly parents from presenting their little ones to JESUS, when we see how positive the command of GOD was to bring children to the LORD the eighth day from their birth. Gen. xvii. 9—14.—Was the LORD so tenacious under the old dispensation to have little ones brought to him: and is He regardless under the new?

16 ¶ And, behold, one came and said unto him, Good Master, what good thing shall I do, that I may have eternal life?

17 And he said unto him, Why callest thou me good? *there is* none good but one, *that is*, God; but if thou wilt enter into life, keep the commandments.

18 He saith unto him, Which? Jesus said, Thou shalt do no murder, Thou shalt not commit adultery, Thou shalt not steal, Thou shalt not bear false witness,

19 Honour thy father and *thy* mother, and, Thou shalt love thy neighbour as thyself.

20 The young man saith unto him, All these things have I kept from my youth up: what lack I yet?

21 Jesus said unto him, If thou wilt be perfect, go *and* sell that thou hast, and give to the poor, and thou shalt have treasure in heaven: and come *and* follow me.

22 But when the young man heard that saying, he went away sorrowful: for he had great possessions.

23 Then said Jesus unto his disciples, Verily I

say unto you, That a rich man shall hardly enter into the kingdom of heaven.

24 And again I say unto you, It is easier for a camel to go through the eye of a needle, than for a rich man to enter into the kingdom of God.

25 When his disciples heard *it*, they were exceedingly amazed, saying, Who then can be saved?

26 But Jesus beheld *them*, and said unto them, With men this is impossible; but with God all things are possible.

I beg the Reader particularly to notice our Lord's answer to the question of this man, in calling Christ *good*. *Why callest thou me good?* As if Jesus had said, Thou knowest that there is, there can be none good but *one*, that is God. Hast thou then from the miracles I have wrought, received conviction that I am (and which is indeed the case) God. This seems to have been the sense of our Lord's question. And then, as if to deal with him as God, Jesus sends him to discover his ruined state, in the conviction of his own heart, from the breach of the commandments; and enumerates a few, as a decision for all. And so wholly untaught of the Spirit was this youth, that he knew nothing of the plague of his own heart, and therefore with the confidence of a poor, dark, blind, and ignorant mind, he declared, that he had kept the whole of God's law; when it was notorious from scripture, that he had broken the whole. James ii. 10. The Lord therefore only touched him a little more closely concerning one point, and which served to detect him in all. Oh! what a deceitful heart, the human heart is, and how incapable of doing any one thing towards its own salvation? Jerem. xvii. 9, 10, Rev. iii. 17.

27 Then answered Peter and said unto him, Behold, we have forsaken all, and followed thee; what shall we have therefore?

28 And Jesus said unto them, Verily I say unto you, That ye which have followed me, in the regeneration, when the Son of man shall sit in the throne of his glory, ye also shall sit upon twelve thrones, judging the twelve tribes of Israel.

29 And every one that hath forsaken houses, or brethren, or sisters, or father, or mother, or wife, or children, or lands, for my name's sake, shall receive an hundred fold, and shall inherit everlasting life.

30 But many *that are* first shall be last; and the last *shall be* first.

Reader! do not fail to observe the blessedness of those who follow CHRIST, in the regeneration? But in doing this, yet more particularly note the cause. It is for JESUS's sake, and by the LORD JESUS's righteousness. All *for* him and all *by* him. And in this redemption, the last and least, in the view of others, are first and greatest in the esteem of CHRIST. So essential it is to know him, whom to know is life eternal. Precious LORD! how reverse to the custom and manners of the world, is thy kingdom!

REFLECTIONS.

OH! thou glorious and gracious bridegroom of thy Church! Everlasting praises to thy name, it is not lawful for JESUS to put away his wife, whatever the world may do, for every cause. The LORD GOD of Israel hath said, that *he hateth putting away.* And while JESUS himself hath said by his Apostle, *Husbands love your wives, and be not bitter against them;* will JESUS be bitter against his? What! though she hath, since from everlasting he betrothed himself to her, fallen away, and sunk into misery and sin; will not JESUS recover her from this state? Yea, will it not be to his glory so to do? Yes! thou dear LORD! it will be to thy greater glory to recover her, than though she had never fallen. And the whole inhabitants of heaven will praise thee, and love thee the more also when thou shalt bring her home, cleansed from all her sins, in thy blood, and shalt present her to thyself *a glorious Church, not having spot, or wrinkle, or any such thing; but shall be without blame before thee in love!*

Blessed Master I would humbly enquire of thee concerning eternal life, as this youth; but not what good thing that I must do to attain it. For alas! if the possession of heaven could be obtained with only a single act of goodness; never to all eternity should I find it. *When I would do good, evil is present with me.* Oh! then for grace to know thee, to love thee, to follow thee, as my only good; my hope, my righteousness, my portion for ever! Amen.

CHAP. XX.

CONTENTS.

This Chapter contains, the Parable of the Laborers in the Vineyard: JESUS's discourse with the mother of Zebedee's children: and the cure of two blind men.

FOR the kingdom of heaven is like unto a man *that* is an householder, which went out early in the morning to hire labourers into his vineyard.

2 And when he had agreed with the labourers for a penny a day, he sent them into his vineyard.

3 And he went out about the third hour, and saw others standing idle in the market place,

4 And said unto them; Go ye also into the vineyard, and whatsoever is right I will give you. And they went their way.

5 Again he went out about the sixth and ninth hour, and did likewise.

6 And about the eleventh hour he went out, and found others standing idle, and saith unto them, Why stand ye here all the day idle?

7 They say unto him, Because no man hath hired us. He saith unto them, Go ye also into the vineyard: and whatsoever is right, *that* shall ye receive.

8 So when even was come, the lord of the vineyard saith unto his steward, Call the labourers, and give them *their* hire, beginning from the last unto the first.

9 And when they came that *were hired* about the eleventh hour, they received every man a penny.

10 But when the first came, they supposed that they should have received more; and they likewise received every man a penny.

11 And when they had received *it,* they murmured against the good man of the house,

12 Saying, These last have wrought *but* one hour, and thou hast made them equal unto us, which have borne the burden and heat of the day.

13 But he answered one of them, and said, Friend, I do thee no wrong: didst not thou agree with me for a penny?

14 Take *that* thine *is,* and go thy way: I will give unto this last, even as unto thee.

15 Is it not lawful for me to do what I will with mine own? Is thine eye evil, because I am good?

The kingdom of heaven, means the kingdom of grace, leading to the kingdom of glory. The man represented under the character of householder is God. Ephes. iii. 16. The vineyard is the Church. Isaiah v. 1, &c. The different seasons of hours intimate the different ages of the world, as well as the different ages of life. And by the market place, is intended the word and ordinances of the Gospel.

Idle persons may be found under the word and ordinances, as well as the diligent, who use the means of grace profitably. The day of hire means the day of life. The evening the close of it: and the wages of a penny, means not the merit of man but the gift of God. *For the wages of sin is death:* but it is the *gift* of God which is eternal life; and this *through* Jesus Christ *our* Lord. Romans vi. 23.

The equality of wages, is a beautiful illustration of the free and sovereign grace of God; because, strictly and properly speaking, it is all free: no merit, no pretensions of merit, in one more than another, making the smallest claim to favor. The Vineyard, the Church, and the Laborers in the Church, all the gift of God the Father, the purchase of God the Son, and the whole cultivation from the work of God the Holy Ghost. And however different the measures of grace, and strength, and ability given; yet the whole is the Lord's not theirs; and every thing speaks aloud that the whole efficiency is of him. *Not by might, nor by power, but by my Spirit, said the* Lord *of hosts.* Zech. iv. 6.

Now what a beautiful similitude is here, of the kingdom of grace! Such is the Church of Jesus, as a vineyard gathered out of the world's wide wilderness; chosen (as scripture expresseth it) by God the Father; purchased by God the Son; and set apart in the regenerating and purifying grace of God the Holy Ghost. Reader! at what age are you standing? Hath the Lord called you at the early morning of life, the mid-day, the afternoon, or evening? Are you *in* the vineyard of the Lord of Hosts? or are you still idle in the market-place? Oh! the unspeakable blessedness of knowing, under divine teaching, that we are *saved and called with an holy calling, not according to our works, but according to his own purpose and grace given us in* Christ Jesus *before the world began.* 2 Tim. i. 9.

16 So the last shall be first, and the first last: for many be called, but few chosen.

See the Note on Matt. xxii. 14.

17 ¶ And Jesus going up to Jerusalem took the twelve disciples apart in the way, and said unto them,

18 Behold, we go up to Jerusalem; and the Son of man shall be betrayed unto the chief priests and unto the scribes, and they shall condemn him to death.

19 And shall deliver him to the Gentiles, to mock, and to scourge, and to crucify *him;* and the third day he shall rise again.

I pray the Reader not to overlook our Lord's delight in speaking of his approaching death. This is the third time the Lord reminds his disciples of it within a few Chapters. Chap. xvi. 21, and Chap. xvii. 22, 23. And again in this place. Every act of Jesus testified his promptness to the work, as though he longed for it. *Lo! I come* (said Jesus) *to do thy will, O God. I delight to do it: yea, thy law is in the midst of my bowels.* And when *Peter* out of love (though a mistaken love) for his master, wished it to be otherwise; Jesus rebuked him, yea, called him *Satan,* for what he said. Never did the meek and loving Savior ever drop such an expression before: so very intent was he on finishing the work his Father gave him to do, and so much displeased was he with any one who wished it to be otherwise. Precious Lord Jesus! was this thine ardent love to thy spouse the Church, as one longing to bring her out of the prison-house of sin and Satan, though all the cataracts of divine wrath for sin were broken up, to be poured on thy sacred head!

20 ¶ Then came to him the mother of Zebedee's children with her sons, worshipping *him,* and desiring a certain thing of him,

21 And he said unto her, What wilt thou? She saith unto him, Grant that these my two sons may sit, the one on thy right hand, and the other on the left, in thy kingdom.

It is probable that this mother of *Zebedee's* children was *Salome.* Matt. xxvii. 46. Mark xv. 40. Both the mother and sons had no views at this time of any kingdom but a kingdom of this world. It is remarkable that the poor woman asked nothing for herself, but for her sons. Oh! how the feelings of nature exceed those of grace! How much more anxious parents are, to see their children rise to the enjoyment of the things of this world, than they are to see them made wise unto salvation for those to come.

22 But Jesus answered and said, Ye know not what ye ask. Are ye able to drink of the cup that I shall drink of, and to be baptised with the baptism that I am baptized with? They say unto him, We are able.

23 And he saith unto them, Ye shall drink indeed of my cup, and be baptized with the baptism that I am baptised with: but to sit on my right hand, and on my left, is not mine to give, but *it shall be given to them* for whom it is prepared of my Father.

What a tender answer of Christ! And true enough both *James* and *John* drank of the same cup though not to the dregs, as Jesus did in the after exercises of their life. *James* was the first of the Apostles who bore testimony to Christ, by his blood, Acts xii. 2. And *John* tells the Church in his banishment, of his sufferings for the testimony of Jesus. Rev. i. 9. I beg the Reader not to overlook our

LORD's expressions, concerning the sitting at his right hand in glory. *It is not mine to give but for whom it is prepared of my Father.* For I beg the Reader to notice, that the words put in between those words of CHRIST, *it shall be given to them,* are not in the original, neither ought they to have been introduced in the translation. And the doctrine without them is the pure doctrine of the Gospel. It is not mine to give but to those whom the Father hath given to me, in an everlasting covenant which cannot be broken. But *all whom the Father hath given me shall come to me, and him that cometh to me I will in no wise cast out.* And elsewhere JESUS expresseth the same blessed truth : for speaking to his Father he saith : *As thou hast given him power over all flesh : that he should give eternal life to as many as thou hast given him.* John vi. 37. John xvii. 2.

And what a glorious consideration is it that such a provision is made for the LORD's redeemed ones in the eternal purpose, council, and will of JEHOVAH : Father, Son, and Holy Ghost : nothing disposing to the gift of such unequalled mercy but the divine favour : and neither depending upon the merit of man, nor any of the after arrangements of life. Oh! the glories of grace! *Thanks be unto* GOD *for his unspeakable gift!*

24 And when the ten heard *it,* they were moved with indignation against the two brethren.

25 But Jesus called them *unto* him, and said, Ye know that the princes of the Gentiles exercise dominion over them, and they that are great exercise authority upon them.

26 But it shall not be so among you ; but whosoever will be great among you, let him be your minister ;

27 And whosoever will be chief among you, let him be your servant :

28 Even as the son of man came not to be ministered unto, but to minister, and to give his life a ransom for many.

In the conduct of the disciples towards *James* and *John,* we behold a renewed instance of the effects of our fallen nature. No man hath ever calculated, or can indeed calculate, the vast injury sustained by Satan's seduction of our first parents, and the whole race of human nature in them. Oh! how doth the thought of it tend to heighten the immense mercies in the recovery of the Church by CHRIST. Reader! see in the disciples of JESUS, the proof of a body of sin and death, though the soul be renewed by grace. They were men of like passions with ourselves. How many heart achs would it have saved me in days past, had I learnt of JESUS the humbling lesson he here taught them, in what the growth of grace consists: namely, in being more and more lowly in heart, from a conviction of unwor-

thiness, and more and more to see my need of JESUS. Precious example in this minister of salvation; who came *not to be ministered unto,*
but though LORD of all, became servant of all, and *who gave his life
a ransom for many.* John xiii. 14. Philip. ii. 7. 1 Timothy ii. 6.

29 ¶ And as they departed from Jericho, a great
multitude followed him.

30 And, behold, two blind men sitting by the
way side, when they heard that Jesus passed by,
cried out, saying, Have mercy on us, O Lord,
thou Son of David.

31 And the multitude rebuked them, because
they should hold their peace: but they cried the
more, saying, Have mercy on us, O Lord, *thou*
Son of David.

32 And Jesus stood still, and called them, and
said, What will ye that I should do unto you?

33 They say unto him, Lord, that our eyes
may be opened.

34 So Jesus had compassion *on them,* and touched their eyes: and immediately their eyes received
sight, and they followed him.

There is no doubt, but that the miracle JESUS wrought on those
men is the same which *Mark* takes notice of Chap. x. 46, and *Luke*
Chap. xviii. 35: although both those Evangelists mention but of *one* blind
man, while here *Matthew* speaks of *two.* But there is no contradiction
in the history. It is the fact of the miracle itself, each writer had in
view, and not the very circumstances of each. Many very precious
instructions arise out of it, which I pray GOD the HOLY GHOST to
bring home to the heart of his people. The grace of JESUS in the act;
the proof he thereby gave of his Messiahship. Isaiah xxxv. 5. The
place where it was wrought, near *Jericho,* the cursed city. Joshua
vi. 26. 1 Kings xvi. 34. JESUS bestows blessings; himself becoming
a curse for his people, that they might be made the righteousness of
GOD in him. 2 Cor. v. 21. The sovereign act of JESUS, in the freeness and fulness of his mercy, as a testimony of his GODHEAD; for on
the supposition of an eyeless socket, it is not simply giving sight to the
blind but a new creation. And who but GOD himself can do this?
The conduct of those blind, also hold forth many sweet instructions.
They were in the highway begging. It is good to be found in the
highway of ordinances, where JESUS passeth by. The cry of those
men under a sense of their misery, and JESUS's power, afford great
lessons to teach men how to pray, and not to faint. But who taught
them that JESUS was the Son of David; that is the Messiah which
should come? Who indeed, but he to whom they came could lead
them to himself? Observe also, how earnest, how clamorous they

were; and how they held on, spite of the unkind multitude who rebuked them. Oh! how earnest ought we to be, when we ask JESUS for the light of the soul. And if men revile, or would stifle our cries, may the LORD give us grace to be the more importunate; *have mercy on us, O LORD, thou Son of David!* And do thou blessed Master and LORD, give the grace to thy children, both to be sensible of our spiritual blindness; and to be as earnest in the cry of the soul for deliverance from it: and may that grace of thine in our hearts be more powerful to lead to thee, than all the world, or sin, or unbelief, to keep from thee. But may all thy redeemed, though blinded by sin, be so taught by grace, that they may besiege thy throne night and day, until the LORD hath heard and answered prayer; and then follow thee in the regeneration, *beholding with open face, as in a glass, the glory of the* LORD, *and be changed into the same image, from glory to glory, even as by the spirit of the* LORD. 2 Cor. iii. 18.

REFLECTIONS.

WHO can read in this Chapter, the striking Parable of the householder hiring laborers into his Vineyard, and not feel conviction at the free, sovereign, purposing, appointing, carrying on, and completing grace of GOD ? Is not the Vineyard of the LORD of hosts, his Church: and every plant in it of the LORD's right hand planting ? What! if JESUS sends his under servants his ministers to labor in his service; or calls his people to sit down under his shadow, do either lessen the right and property of the Almighty owner ? Is not the whole his, by gift, by purchase, by right, by conquest, and by power ? And is it not separated by redeeming grace from the world's wide wilderness, and fenced in with love ? Ye ministers of my GOD ! esteem it the highest honor, to labor within the sacred inclosure, and be more anxious to win souls than to win kingdoms. Ye children of the LORD ! whether in the early, mid-day, or later calls of his grace; bless GOD for the distinguishing mercy. Soon will the evening of life come; and the LORD of the Vineyard will call ye home, from his courts below to his heaven above.

Precious LORD JESUS ! I behold thee by the eye of faith in thine ascent to Jerusalem ! Yes ! truly there thou wast delivered for our offences and raised again for our justification ! Grant me dearest LORD to be more anxious to be brought under the continual baptisms of thy spirit, than to arrive at the highest temporal honors. A door-keeper in thy house, far exceeds the golden tents of the ungodly.

In the review of my LORD's mercy to those poor blind men, and the grace imparted to them to be so earnest with JESUS for bodily sight; teach me, thou gracious giver of eyes to the blind, to imitate their cries for spiritual apprehension of my LORD's person, work, and righteousness. Oh! for grace to see the king in his beauty, and to have my soul so awakened to desires after CHRIST, that I may follow my GOD and SAVIOR by faith here, till in open vision I *shall see him as he is, and dwell with him for ever!*

CHAP. XXI.

CONTENTS.

The LORD JESUS *is here described as riding into Jerusalem. He casteth the buyers and sellers out of the temple. We have also the account of the withered Fig-tree, and the parable of the husbandman.*

AND when they drew nigh unto Jerusalem, and were come to Bethphage, unto the mount of Olives, then sent Jesus two disciples,

2 Saying unto them, Go into the village over against you, and straightway ye shall find an ass tied, and a colt with her : loose *them*, and bring *them* unto me.

3 And if any *man* say ought unto you, ye shall say, The Lord hath need of them ; and straightway he will send them.

4 All this was done, that it might be fulfilled which was spoken by the prophet, saying,

5 Tell ye the daughter of Zion, Behold, thy king cometh unto thee, meek, and sitting upon an ass, and a colt the foal of an ass.

It is worthy remark, that the four Evangelists all notice this triumphal entrance of CHRIST into Jerusalem, five days before his death, as if to testify the prophecy concerning it. Isaiah lxii. 11. Zech. ix. 9. And it is worthy of still further remark, that none but CHRIST ever made such a public entry, and therefore the conclusion is undeniable. Behold! how distinguished from every other king, is Zion's king. No trumpets, no gorgeous apparel, no courtly attendants, but as the LORD himself was meek and lowly, every accommodation corresponded to the humble appearance! Such was, and is, JESUS !

6 And the disciples went, and did as Jesus commanded them.

7 And brought the ass, and the colt, and put on them their clothes, and they set *him* thereon.

8 And a very great multitude spread their garments in the way ; others cut down branches from the trees, and strawed *them* in the way.

9 And the multitudes that went before, and that followed, cried, saying, Hosanna to the son of

David: Blessed *is* he that cometh in the name of the Lord; Hosanna in the Highest.

But what was wanted in outward pomp, was amply made up in inward joy. And what, but the over-ruling power of GOD the SPIRIT, could have stirred up such a multitude to shout their Hosannas! Think how JESUS was welcomed to their hearts! See the Poor Man's Concordance, under the word *Hosanna*.

10 And when he was come into Jerusalem, all the city was moved, saying, Who is this?

11 And the multitude said, This is Jesus the prophet of Nazareth of Galilee.

What an astonishing effect was wrought on the city at this approach of JESUS, Though the LORD had been so long going in and out among them, yet so astonished were they at this entrance of our GOD and SAVIOR, that all men marvelled. Reader! have you never seen (I have) somewhat of the same kind in the present day, among the carnal and Christless, musing in their hearts when at any time hearing of JESUS! See a striking instance, John vii. 40 to the end. I pray the Reader to remark, with me, the unconscious evidence the multitude gave to the real person of CHRIST, the only true Nazarite of GOD. If my Reader hath near him my little penny publication of the "Poor Man's Concordance," I would beg him to turn to the article *Nazarene*, for an explanation of the important name of CHRIST, as the only true Nazarite. He will discover that the name is of an infinitely higher import than perhaps he at first might suppose.

12 ¶ And Jesus went into the temple of God, and cast out all them that sold and bought in the temple, and overthrew the tables of the money changers, and the seats of them that sold doves,

13 And said unto them, It is written, My house shall be called the house of prayer; but ye have made it a den of thieves.

14 And the blind and the lame came to him in the temple; and he healed them.

I pray the Reader to pause over this account of his adorable LORD. According to my view of things, perhaps there is not, among the miracles of CHRIST, hardly an higher proof of his GODHEAD. I wish the Reader to notice it as it deserves. To behold JESUS in the humble dress of a poor Jew, whipping the drove of cattle, with all the buyers and sellers, out of the temple, and overthrowing before him the counters of money, and the seats of the dove-sellers, and with such an holy countenance of zeal as none dared to oppose; surely it carried with it an invincible proof of his mighty power and authority! And I beg the Reader, upon this, and many similar occasions which have occurred, to observe how plainly he mingled with his human appearance, tokens of his divine. The blind and the lame coming to him for healing, afforded an additional testimony to his divine person and character.

15 And when the chief priests and scribes saw the wonderful things that he did, and the children crying in the temple, and saying, Hosanna to the son of David; they were sore displeased,

16 And said unto him, Hearest thou what these say? And Jesus saith unto them, Yea; have ye never read, Out of the mouths of babes and sucklings thou hast perfected praise?

What a blessed account is here, of the minds of those children being over-ruled by the divine power, thus to bear testimony to the person of Jesus. For to what other source can it be ascribed? It is probable that many of the parents of those children were among the money-changers, and the buyers and sellers, profaning the temple. And whence should those children have learnt of Christ's person and character as the Son of David? How have they been taught to sing Hosannah? Reader! do not fail to observe how the Lord accomplisheth his prophecies, by means the most unlooked for, and unexpected. *David,* by the spirit of prophecy, a thousand years before, had described this very event, that *by the mouths of babes and sucklings, the* Lord *would call forth praise.* And here we see it fulfilled. Psalm viii. 2.

17 And he left them, and went out of the city into Bethany; and he lodged there.

18 Now in the morning as he returned into the city, he hungered.

19 And when he saw a fig tree in the way, he came to it, and found nothing thereon, but leaves only, and said unto it, Let no fruit grow on thee henceforward for ever. And presently the fig tree withered away.

20 And when the disciples saw *it,* they marvelled, saying, How soon is the fig-tree withered away!

21 Jesus answered and said unto them, Verily I say unto you, If ye have faith, and doubt not, ye shall not only do this *which is done* to the fig-tree, but also if ye shall say unto this mountain,

Be thou removed, and be thou cast into the sea; it shall be done.

22 And all things, whatsoever ye shall ask in prayer, believing, ye shall receive.

Our LORD's departure into *Bethany* to lodge for the night, and his return in the morning, gave occasion for the display of another miracle, respecting the barren fig-tree. No doubt the design was to preach by it to the people. The leaves of a mere profession, without fruit in, and from CHRIST, will stand in no stead in the day of enquiry. Nothing short of an union with CHRIST's person, can bring up after it communion and interest in what belongs to CHRIST.

23 ¶ And when he was come into the temple, the chief priests and the elders of the people came unto him as he was teaching, and said, By what authority doest thou these things? and who gave thee this authority?

24 And Jesus answered and said unto them, I also will ask you one thing, which if ye tell me, I in likewise will tell you by what authority I do these things.

25 The baptism of John, whence was it? From heaven, or of men? And they reasoned with themselves, saying, If we shall say, From heaven; he will say unto us, Why did ye not then believe him?

26 But if we shall say, Of men; we fear the people; for all hold John as a prophet.

27 And they answered Jesus, and said, We cannot tell. And he said unto them, Neither tell I you by what authority I do these things.

28 But what think ye? A *certain* man had two sons; and he came to the first, and said, Son, go work to-day in my vineyard.

29 He answered and said, I will not: but afterward he repented, and went.

30 And he came to the second, and said likewise. And he answered and said, I *go*, sir: and went not.

31 Whether of them twain did the will of *his*

father? They say unto him, The first, Jesus saith unto them, Verily I say unto you, That the publicans and the harlots go into the kingdom of God before you.

32 For John came unto you in the way of righteousness and ye believed him not: but the publicans and the harlots believed him: and ye, when ye had seen *it*, repented not afterward, that ye might believe him.

33 Hear another parable: There was a certain householder, which planted a vineyard, and hedged it round about, and digged a winepress in it, and built a tower, and let it out to husbandmen, and went into a far country:

34 And when the time of the fruit drew near, he sent his servants to the husbandmen, that they might receive the fruits of it.

35 And the husbandmen took his servants, and beat one, and killed another, and stoned another.

36 Again, he sent other servants more than the first: and they did unto them likewise.

37 But last of all he sent unto them his son, saying, They will reverence my son.

38 But when the husbandmen saw the son, they said among themselves, This is the heir; come, let us kill him, and let us seize on his inheritance.

39 And they caught him, and cast *him* out of the vineyard, and slew *him*.

40 When the lord therefore of the vineyard cometh, what will he do unto those husbandmen?

41 They say unto him, He will miserably destroy those wicked men, and will let out *his* vineyard unto other husbandmen which shall render him the fruits in their seasons.

42 Jesus saith unto them, Did ye never read in the scriptures, The stone which the builders rejected, the same is become the head of the corner:

this is the Lord's doing, and it is marvellous in our eyes?

43 Therefore say I unto you, The kingdom of God shall be taken from you, and given to a nation, bringing forth the fruits thereof.

44 And whosoever shall fall on this stone shall be broken: but on whomsoever it shall fall, it will grind him to powder.

45 And when the chief priests and Pharisees had heard his parables, they perceived that he spake of them.

46 But when they sought to lay hands on him, they feared the multitude, because they took him for a prophet.

The whole of our Lord's discourse and reasoning is so plain, and self-evident, that I do not conceive it can be, in the smallest measure, necessary to enlarge upon it. I only detain the Reader, therefore, to remark upon the whole of what is here contained, that from our Lord's giving the preference to publicans and harlots, to that of self-righteous Scribes and Pharisees, we may safely conclude that nothing was more offensive to the Lord of life and glory, than a frame of mind which, of all others, is more immediately levelled against the leading doctrines of his gospel. Oh! for grace to be always aware of *the leaven* of the Scribes and Pharisees, which the Son of God himself declares *to be hypocrisy.* Luke xii. 1.

REFLECTIONS.

Pause, my soul, over this view of thy Redeemer! Did the Prophet, ages before Christ was born, call upon Zion to rejoice greatly, and Jerusalem to shout aloud, because her king was coming to her, meek and lowly, and having salvation; and did the Son of God, in his character as King of Zion, actually make his entry in the very manner the Prophet described; and did all those effects follow in confirmation of the glorious truth? And wilt not thou, my soul, join the heavenly Hosannas, and sing aloud, *blessed is He that cometh in the name of the* Lord, *Hosanna in the highest!*

And is it one and the same person who is here described as hungry, and needing the common sustenance to support nature, yea looking to a fig-tree to supply a pressing occasion? Oh! precious Jesus! how sweetly accommodating is thy lovely example, to the wants and exercises of thy people? Yes! thou dear Lord, it did indeed *behove thee to be made like unto thy brethren, that thou mightest be a merciful and faithful High Priest in things pertaining to* God. And having suffered being tempted, thou knowest how *to succour them that are tempted.*

Lord! give thy people grace to see, that while unawakened,

unregenerate sinners, like those husbandmen in the parable, though living in thy Church, and outwardly feasting upon the good things of thy vineyard, have no inward joy or communion with the Lord of his vineyard, there are those redeemed of the Lord whose right it is in Christ, and who will finally be brought home to the joy of their Lord ; while those miserable men will ultimately be destroyed, and have their portion with hypocrites in outer darkness, *where there will be weeping and gnashing of teeth.*

CHAP. XXII.

CONTENTS.

We have, in this Chapter, the Parable of the Marriage-feast, and Christ's discourses with the Scribes and Pharisees.

AND Jesus answered and spake unto them again by parables, and said,

2 The kingdom of heaven is like unto a certain king, which made a marriage for his son.

3 And sent forth his servants to call them that were bidden to the wedding : and they would not come.

4 Again he sent forth other servants, saying, Tell them which are bidden, Behold, I have prepared my dinner: my oxen, and *my* fatlings are killed, and all things are ready, come unto the marriage.

5 But they made light of *it*, and went their ways, one to his farm, another to his merchandise:

6 And the remnant took his servants, and entreated *them* spitefully, and slew *them.*

7 But when the king heard *thereof*, he was wroth : and he sent forth his armies, and destroyed those murderers, and burned up their city.

8 Then saith he to his servants, The wedding is ready, but they which were bidden were not worthy.

9 Go ye therefore into the highways, and as many as ye shall find, bid to the marriage.

10 So those servants went out into the highways, and gathered together all as many as they found, both bad and good : and the wedding was furnished with guests.

We shall enter, through the teaching of God the Holy Ghost, into the beautiful design of our Lord, in this parable, if we take with us, all the way we go through it, the leading features the Son of God hath drawn. The kingdom of heaven is uniformly meant to describe the kingdom of grace, in the present gospel state of the Church. The certain king, here spoken of, is God our Father. And the marriage is that union the Son of God hath been mercifully pleased, at the call of God his Father, to make with our nature, and with each Person in that nature, whom God the Father hath given to him, whose redemption Christ hath purchased, and God the Holy Ghost hath regenerated, for the purpose of grace here, and glory hereafter.

This marriage took place, in the plan and counsel of Jehovah, before all worlds. The Church was then presented by the Father, and fore-viewed by the Son, and sanctified in the will and design of God the Holy Ghost, when Christ betrothed her to himself for ever. And although, in the ordination of the divine will, this Church of Jesus was to be involved in the Adam-fall of our nature, in common with the whole race of men, yet the original connection could not be dissolved by this spiritual adultery, but rather afforded occasion for the Son of God to get more glory and honour by her recovery, in the wonderful means he accomplished in time, by the salvation he wrought for this purpose.

The Church, therefore, departing from her glorious husband, and having lost the image of God by sin, and having mingled with the heathen, and learned their works, this parable represents the King as sending forth his servants to bring his Church home to her lawful Lord and Husband again, notwithstanding all her baseness and unworthiness of departure.

The invitation to this purpose is represented under the image and similitude of a great dinner, in which a plentiful table is spread, the richest food is provided, servants are in waiting, and all with one voice say, *all things are ready, come to the marriage!* It were needless to observe, that the several parts of the parable, in the servants being again and again sent, and the contempt shewn by some, and the cruelty by others ; are meant to set forth the various ages of the Church, in which Patriarchs, Prophets, and Apostles, have ministered to this one end, and the events which have followed. These things are so plain, that every one who is acquainted with the Bible, cannot but know them. All that seems necessary for the least additional information on this subject, is to observe, that the final issue of the Lord's design, can neither be frustrated, nor unaccomplished. The Lord Jehovah, in his threefold character of persons, Father, Son, and Holy Ghost, hath made, for this, an effectual security. The Church is One with Christ, her Head and Husband, from all eternity. Hence every individual which constitutes a part in that mystical body, notwithstanding the after act in the Adam-nature, and Adam-fall, is secured from a pre-union with the Lord, her Husband, from everlasting ruin. Hence their effectual call and conversion is engaged for in covenant settlements. A secret union subsisted between Christ and his members from all eternity. And this brings up after it an open espousal of every one of them at the season of their conversion. *Thy people shall be willing in the day of thy power.* And hence they are carried safely on through all the periods of time, and will be brought home to a more public display of the divine love, at *the marriage supper of the Lamb in heaven.* Rev. xix. 9.

11 ¶ And when the king came in to see the guests, he saw there a man which had not on a wedding garment:

12 And he saith unto him, Friend, how camest thou in hither, not having a wedding garment? And he was speechless.

13 Then said the king to the servants, Bind him hand and foot, and take him away, and cast *him* into outer darkness; there shall be weeping and gnashing of teeth.

This man without a wedding garment, is the representative of all, be they many, or few, who are found, in the day of enquiry, without the garment of CHRIST's righteousness. The parable doth not say that he was without a garment, for no doubt he was cloathed, as many are, in a righteousness of his own. But his crime was, that it was not a *wedding* garment. A garment of his LORD's. A proof of his marriage, his union, and oneness with JESUS. This ought to be particularly attended to, and clearly understood. How often is it heard in the mouth of the untaught by GOD the HOLY GHOST, that this wedding garment is good works, an holy life, and charity, and the like. Alas! if our acceptance at CHRIST's table upon earth, or at his marriage supper in heaven, rested upon what some are so fond of talking of, but not a single son or daughter of Adam's fallen race ever knew; I mean good works and an holy life, no guests would be found for either. Neither doth this wedding garment consist in the adorning of a renewed soul by the graces of the HOLY SPIRIT, such as faith, repentance, or any, or all, of the sweet effects of the LORD's work in the soul. These are all blessed and essential things in the life of grace, and every child of GOD, called by grace, will he blessed in the enjoyment of them, but they are not CHRIST. These are the *effects*, not the *cause*; the *fruits* of regeneration, but not the *root* of salvation. The wedding garment, therefore, is none of these. And though it is blessed, yea very blessed, when grace is in lively exercise, to behold how true believers in CHRIST, from an union with CHRIST, act faith *upon* him, and live *to* him, and his praise; *adorning the doctrine of* GOD *our* SAVIOR *in all things*: yet these form no part in the wedding garment, which is wholly *of* CHRIST, wrought out *by* CHRIST, and is put on the believer *by* CHRIST. Every act of theirs is polluted, and must be cleansed in the blood of CHRIST, as well as their persons; for without this cleansing, neither the one, nor the other, can find acceptance before GOD. Reader! I pray you to seek for the teaching of GOD the HOLY GHOST, to have a clear apprehension of these things. And both in ordinances now, as well as the appearing before GOD hereafter, see to it, that you have this wedding garment, the want of which made this man speechless, and the possession of which, proves the betrothing of every child of GOD, by

which the whole body of CHRIST's church is made ready and prepared
by Him, as a bride adorned for her husband. Rev. xxi. 2. See
Ephes. v. 23 to the end.

14 For many are called, but few *are* chosen.

This close of the parable is the same with which JESUS closed
the one of the Laborers in the Vineyard, and is very striking and
solemn, but very obvious and plain upon the pure principles of the
gospel. *Calling*, by the outward sound of the word, and the being
chosen by the eternal purpose of sovereign grace, are very distinct
things. In preaching the Gospel, to a mixed multitude of hearers,
every one within the sound hears the gracious invitation which the
LORD gives to his Church; and, in one sense, it may be said the call
to the duties of life goes forth to the whole world, and is a command
from GOD, as a Sovereign, to hear and obey. But this *outward* call,
differs widely from the *inward* work, wrought by the HOLY GHOST
in the hearts of the redeemed, and which comes *not in word only,
but in power*. *Paul*, the Apostle, beautifully describes the difference; when speaking to the Church, he saith, *We are bound to give
thanks alway to* GOD, *for you brethren beloved of the* LORD, *because*
GOD *hath, from the beginning, chosen you to salvation through sanctification of the Spirit and belief of the truth, where unto he called you, by
our gospel, to the obtaining of the glory of our* LORD JESUS CHRIST.
Provision is made for this effectual calling of the LORD's people in
time, 2 Thess. ii. 13, 14. from their being chosen, in CHRIST, before
the foundation of the world. Ephes. i. 3, 4. 2 Tim. i. 9. So that the
whole process of grace, from the first awakenings of the soul, until
grace is consummated in glory, while all these prove the everlasting
love of GOD to his redeemed, in CHRIST, they become no less the
fruit of that love, and are the sure earnest of eternal glory. Rom. viii.
29, 30.

15 ¶ Then went the Pharisees, and took counsel
how they might entangle him in *his* talk.

16 And they sent out unto him their disciples
with the Herodians, saying, Master, we know that
thou art true, and teachest the way of God in truth,
neither carest thou for any *man;* for thou regardest
not the person of men.

17 Tell us therefore, What thinkest thou? Is it
lawful to give tribute unto Cesar, or not?

18 But Jesus perceived their wickedness, and
said, Why tempt ye me, *ye* hypocrites?

19 Shew me the tribute money. And they
brought unto him a penny.

20 And he saith unto them, Whose *is* this image
and superscription?

21 They say unto him, Cesar's. Then saith he unto them, Render therefore unto Cesar the things which are Cesar's; and unto God the things that are God's.

22 When they had heard *these words,* they marvelled, and left him, and went their way.

A sweet instruction ariseth from hence to the children of GOD. If JESUS was thus beset, wonder not that his people should be. Oh! how earnest are the ungodly to wound the followers of the LORD! Reader! pray consult that sweet scripture. John xv. 18—21.

23 ¶ The same day came to him the Sadducees, which say that there is no resurrection, and asked him,

24 Saying, Master, Moses said, If a man die, having no children, his brother shall marry his wife, and raise up seed unto his brother.

25 Now there were with us seven brethren: and the first, when he had married a wife, deceased, and, having no issue, left his wife unto his brother:

26 Likewise the second also, and the third, unto the seventh.

27 And last of all the woman died also.

28 Therefore in the resurrection whose wife shall she be of the seven? for they all had her.

29 Jesus answered and said unto them, Ye do err, not knowing the scriptures, nor the power of God.

30 For in the resurrection they neither marry, nor are given in marriage, but are as the angels of God in heaven.

31 But as touching the resurrection of the dead, have ye not read that which was spoken unto you by God, saying,

32 I am the God of Abraham, and the God of Isaac, and the God of Jacob? God is not the God of the dead, but of the living.

33 And when the multitude heard *this,* they were astonished at his doctrine.

It is worth observing, how the malice of both Sadducees and Pharisees was over-ruled to the LORD's glory and the comfort of his people. For had not those men brought forward this question, the Church would not have had the explanation, which it now hath, of this precious doctrine in this place; neither should we, most probably, have had those discoveries the LORD JESUS hath here given concerning himself at the bush of Moses. But what a blessed confirmation our LORD's answer to those men in this place is, to all the other unanswerable testimonies on this great point of the resurrection. JESUS hath put it on its own basis, and, from the covenant relation between CHRIST and his people, most fully shewn that GOD, that is (GOD in CHRIST) is not the GOD of the dead, but of the living, for all live to him; their souls, among the spirits of just men, made perfect, and their bodies, from an union with CHRIST, resting in this covenant hope of being raised at the last day. *For if the spirit of him that raised up JESUS from the dead, dwell in you, he that raised up CHRIST from the dead, shall also quicken your mortal bodies by his Spirit that dwelleth in you.* Rom. viii. 11.

34 But when the Pharisees had heard that he had put the Sadducees to silence, they were gathered together.

35 Then one of them, *which was* a lawyer, asked *him a question*, tempting him, and saying,

36 Master, which is the great commandment in the law?

37 Jesus said unto him, thou shalt love the Lord thy God with all thy heart, and with all thy soul, and with all thy mind.

38 This is the first and great commandment.

39 And the second *is* like unto it, Thou shalt love thy neighbour as thyself.

40 On these two commandments hang all the law and the prophets.

41 While the Pharisees were gathered together, Jesus asked them,

42 Saying, What think ye of Christ? whose son is he? They say unto him, *The son* of David.

43 He saith unto them, How then doth David in spirit call him Lord, saying,

44 The LORD said unto my Lord, Sit thou on my right hand, till I make thine enemies thy footstool?

45 If David then call him Lord, how is he his son?

46 And no man was able to answer him a word, neither durst any *man* from that day forth ask him any more *questions*.

It is very blessed to discover, that let Jesus be attacked by Pharisees or Sadducees, every thing tends to the Lord's glory, the promotion of his people's happiness, and the confusion of his enemies. Our Lord's conference with the Pharisees is of this kind, and so plain as to need no comment. But I would rather take occasion, from the Lord's question to the Pharisees, to propose the same, both to myself and Reader. What think ye of Christ, is the grand question of the whole subject contained in the word of God. And I beg the Reader to observe, Jesus doth not say, what think ye of *me*, but what think ye of Christ; that is, as God's Christ, the anointed, the sent, the sealed of the Father. For unless we have proper apprehension, both of his person and offices, in his double nature, and in his commission, our views of him will not be suitably formed. So that in this one question is involved a thousand others. What think ye of Christ? What think ye of his person, of his offices, characters, relations? What think ye of the completeuess, fulness, suitableness, all-sufficiency of his salvation? What think ye of Christ as to his worth, preciousness, beauty, glory? What, as to his value, importance, his absolute necessity, and the living without knowing him, and the dying without enjoying him? Oh! for the proper apprehension of Jesus! Oh! for the absolute and certain union with him, and interest in him! The soul that hath so learned Christ, will best know how to enter into the full sense of our Lord's question; and will best appreciate the being found in him, so as to render all other knowledge of no value, but the knowledge of Christ, the power of God, and the wisdom of God, for salvation to every one that believeth.

REFLECTIONS.

Blessed Lord Jesus! Was there ever condescension like thine, to marry our nature? To pass by the nature of angels, and to take on thee the seed of Abraham! And didst thou, Lord, so fix thy love upon thy Church, that though thou knowest from the beginning that our whole nature would deal very treacherously, yet this did not prevent thy gracious design, but thou didst determine to pay our dreadful debt, to rescue us out of the hand of every enemy, to disannul our agreement with sin, and to call back thy spouse, the Church, who, as a treacherous wife, had departed from her first husband? Did Jesus indeed, in the prosecution of this great design, send forth his servants in all ages of the Church; Patriarchs, Prophets, and Apostles, to call home his own, and to bring all his redeemed to the marriage supper of the Lamb in heaven? Oh! peerless, unequalled love! Oh! matchless sovereign mercy! Lord Jesus! grant that when thou comest in at the last day to see thy guests at thy table, my poor soul may not be found like the man without a wedding garment, and from being Christless now, I should be speechless then. But oh! thou dear LORD! may my soul be found of thee in that all-decisive hour, so adorned in thy spotless righteousness, that both now, and then, my soul may sing the holy triumphs of the Church, and find the blessedness of it. *I will greatly rejoice in the* LORD: *my soul shall be joyful in my* GOD: *for he hath cloathed me with the garments of salvation, he hath covered me with the robe of righteousness, as a bridegroom decketh himself with ornaments, and as a bride adorneth herself with her jewels.*

Dearest LORD JESUS! while Pharisees, and Herodians, and Sadducees, all confederate against thee; Oh! do thou cause my poor soul to be attached to thee more and more. Give me to enter into a proper apprehension of all the mysteries of faith, and the doctrine of the resurrection; that, convinced of an interest in the covenant of redemption made with *Abraham,* and the heirs with him of the promise, I may make the study of CHRIST, and the knowledge of CHRIST, the great essentials of everlasting life? and esteem CHRIST, and him crucified, the *one thing needful,* beyond all the knowledge of the earth. Oh! the blessedness of this living to CHRIST, and rejoicing in CHRIST, and making him, what GOD hath made him, the Alpha and Omega, the beginning and the end of salvation; convinced that *there is no other name under heaven, given among men, whereby we must be saved.*

CHAP. XXIII.

CONTENTS.

In this Chapter the LORD JESUS *is engaged in exhorting his disciples, and the multitude, against the doctrine of the Scribes and Pharisees. The Chapter closeth with* CHRIST's *pathetic lamentation over Jerusalem, as a City given up to destruction.*

THEN spake Jesus to the multitude, and to his disciples,

2 Saying, The scribes and the Pharisees, sit in Moses' seat:

3 All, therefore, whatsoever they bid you observe, *that* observe and do; but do not ye after their works: for they say, and do not.

4 For they bind heavy burdens and grievous to be borne, and lay *them* on men's shoulders; but they *themselves* will not move them with one of their fingers.

5 But all their works they do for to be seen of men: they make broad their phylacteries, and enlarge the borders of their garments,

6 And love the uppermost rooms at feasts, and the chief seats in the synagogues.

7 And greetings in the markets, and to be called of men, Rabbi, Rabbi.

8 But be not ye called Rabbi: for one is your Master, *even* Christ; and all ye are brethren.

9 And call no *man* your father upon the earth: for one is your Father, which is in heaven.

10 Neither be ye called masters: for one is your Master, *even* Christ.

11 But he that is greatest among you shall be your servant.

12 And whosoever shall exhalt himself shall be abased; and he that shall humble himself shall be exalted.

This chapter, if there were no other in the whole book of God, to alarm the mind on the awful consequence of Pharisaical righteous-ness, is enough, in itself, to awaken the most serious apprehensions on that account. Jesus, who knew what was in man, and to whose divine knowledge every heart was open, beheld in those men such false sanctity, that no language appeared sufficiently strong, to mark his severe displeasure at their conduct. Every thing done by them was done, the Lord said, with a view to the approbation of men. And the strong images of whited sepulchres, blind guides, and the like, which the Lord represented them by, may serve to shew in what a light he considered them. In these first verses of the chapter, the Lord Jesus cautions his hearers against the imitation of their con-duct. In the following he pronounceth the most awful woes upon them.

13 But woe unto you, scribes and Pharisees, hypocrites! for ye shut up the kingdom of heaven against men : for ye neither go in *yourselves*, neither suffer ye them that are entering to go in.

14 Woe unto you, scribes and Pharisees, hypo-crites! for ye devour widows' houses, and for a pretence make long prayer : therefore ye shall re-ceive the greater damnation.

15 Woe unto you, scribes and Pharisees, hypo-crites! for ye compass sea and land to make one proselyte, and when he is made, ye make him two-fold more the child of hell than yourselves.

16 Woe unto you, *ye* blind guides, which say, Whosoever shall swear by the temple, it is nothing;

but whosoever shall swear by the gold of the temple, he is a debtor!

17 *Ye* fools and blind : for whether is greater, the gold, or the temple that sanctifieth the gold ?

18 And, Whosoever shall swear by the altar, it is nothing ; but whosoever sweareth by the gift that is upon it, he is guilty.

19 *Ye* fools and blind : for whether is greater, the gift, or the altar that sanctifieth the gift?

20 Whoso therefore shall swear by the altar, sweareth by it, and by all things thereon.

21 And whoso shall swear by the temple, sweareth by it, and by him that dwelleth therein.

22 And he that shall swear by heaven, sweareth by the throne of God, and by him that sitteth thereon.

23 Woe unto you, scribes and Pharisees, hypocrites! for ye pay tithe of mint and anise and cummin, and have omitted the weightier *matters* of the law, judgment, mercy, and faith : these ought ye to have done, and not to leave the other undone.

24 *Ye* blind guides, which strain at a gnat, and swallow a camel.

25 Woe unto you, scribes and Pharisees, hypocrites! for ye make clean the outside of the cup and of the platter, but within they are full of extortion and excess.

26 *Thou* blind Pharisee, cleanse first that *which is* within the cup and platter, that the outside of them may be clean also.

27 Woe unto you, scribes and Pharisees, hypocrites! for ye are like unto whited sepulchres, which indeed appear beautiful outward, but are within full of dead *men's* bones, and of all uncleanness.

28 Even so ye also outwardly appear righteous unto men, but within ye are full of hypocrisy and iniquity.

29 Woe unto you, scribes and Pharisees, hypocrites, because ye build the tombs of the prophets,
and garnish the sepulchres of the righteous,

30 And say, If we had been in the days of our
fathers, we would not have been partakers with
them in the blood of the prophets.

31 Wherefore be ye witnesses unto yourselves,
that ye are the children of them which killed the
prophets.

32 Fill ye up then the measure of your fathers.

33 *Ye* serpents, *ye* generation of vipers, how can
ye escape the damnation of hell?

Here are no less than *eight* solemn woes denounced upon the very
men who trusted in themselves that they were righteous, and despised
others. And what made the woes more terrible, they were pronounced
by One that was meekness itself. And what is, if possible, yet more
awful, the same Almighty Judge, who cannot err, in the close of this
solemn denunciation, calls them by the several names which mark
their character, and explains the whole: *Ye serpents, ye generation of
vipers, how can ye escape the damnation of hell?* That is, ye cannot
escape it. The phrase is a stronger way of expressing a thing, by
way of question, than if in so many words the thing was said. We
have a similar method of speech by the Apostle. *How shall we escape,
if we neglect so great salvation.* Heb. ii. 3. That is, we cannot escape.
See also Mark viii. 36.

I very earnestly beg the Reader's close attention to the subject
contained in this chapter, concerning the Pharisees of our LORD's
day, and our LORD's decision of their character. I pray GOD the
HOLY GHOST to be the guide and teacher, both of him that writes,
and him that reads, that we may have a clear apprehension, on a
doctrine so truly important. It is one of the plainest doctrines in the
Bible, that the seed of the woman and the seed of the serpent, are in
their nature so directly opposed to each other, that there can be no
possibility of junction. Each is defineable by their very nature, and
must remain so, to all eternity. Now then, by serpents and a generation of vipers, the brood of the old serpent the devil is marked. And
hence from the beginning, the LORD GOD declared the everlasting
hatred this serpentine race should bear to the family of CHRIST. *I
will put enmity between thee and the woman : and between thy seed and
her seed.* Gen. iii. 15. Hence therefore, when the LORD JESUS saith :
*Ye serpents, ye generation of vipers ; how can ye escape the damna-
tion of hell?* The answer ariseth out of the question ; serpents and
vipers must be together : and it is fit they should. They cannot be
apart. And for the self-same reason that where CHRIST is there must
his members be ; so the old serpent, and all the hatch of his incubation
can never be separated from each other. See Matt. xii. 34. Rev. xii. 9.
John viii. 44.

I beg to detain the Reader one moment longer, on this momentous but solemn subject. Our LORD hath considered it so very important in itself, that he hath consumed the greater part of a long chapter upon it. And therefore it may well claim a little more of our serious consideration.

The Pharisees of our LORD's days, were so *generally*, yea, I might almost say so *universally* considered under this character, that we do not find one of them savingly converted to the LORD; *Nicodemus* only excepted. *Paul* the Apostle, was also a Pharisee, as he tells us himself, and drank into the spirit of self-righteousness as deep as most men. But then it should be remembered, that he was not in the days of our LORD's ministry. And by his conversion (as well as Nicodemus) he was proved not to be of that family, whom our LORD declared to be *a generation of vipers.* But it opens a solemn subject of consideration, that among all the Pharisees we read of, of that day; we read of none called by sovereign grace, saving that ruler of the Jews *Nicodemus.* John iii. 1, &c. John vii. 50. John xix. 39.

And wherefore this exclusion, but from the cause assigned? How should it be otherwise with those who in the Adam-fall received the serpent's seed, and for whom no provision was made for recovery in the seed of the woman, not having the union seed in CHRIST. (See Isaiah xliv. 3. Isaiah liii. 10. Isaiah lix. 21. Psm. xxii. 30, 31.) How should it be otherwise? Whereas the seed of CHRIST, though involved by *nature* in the Adam-transgression with the whole race; yet being one with CHRIST in *grace,* had security for their preservation from the everlasting ruin of the fall by virtue thereof: for *the root being holy, so also must be the branches.* For that portion of human nature united. to the GODHEAD, contained in it, the seed of holiness to all his children. Hence the promise runs to this amount in the charter of grace. *To Abraham and his seed were the promises made. He saith not, and to seeds as of many, but as of one; and to thy seed, which is CHRIST.* Gal. iii. 16. And hence also the seed of CHRIST are secured in all the covenant promises. And as it is said of *Levi,* on whom the promise was equally entailed with Abraham, that *he was in the loins of his father Abraham, when Melchisedec met him, and blessed him:* so was the whole Church in CHRIST, before the fall took place, in the Adam-generation: whereby every individual of the Church was preserved in CHRIST JESUS, and in time called. Jude 1.

One word more, and I will relieve the Reader's attention. How did this generation of vipers manifest their serpentine hatred to CHRIST, and bring upon themselves those awful denunciations? Not for their immoralities, for they prided themselves in being highly moral. Not for their neglect of their public or private worship. For they did both. Neither were they chargeable, as far as outward actions went, with the common vices of drunkenness, adultery, and the like. What was it then, which brought down upon them the LORD's severest judgments? Certainly, nothing more or less, than by this Pharisaical righteousness, teaching the people to slight the person and work of JESUS, as what were unnecessary for acceptance with GOD. They compassed sea and land the LORD told them, to make one proselyte, and when this was done, they made him two-fold more the child of hell, than themselves. That is, they labored to undermine the necessity of salvation by CHRIST, in setting up, and teaching others to do the same, a righteousness of their own: and thus by denying the fall of man, and the necessity of a recovery by grace, they set up the kingdom of Satan, and like children of hell, fought against the kingdom of grace.

Reader! pause over the awful subject! If such be the views which arise out of Pharisaical righteousness; we can no longer wonder at any of our LORD's expressions in this Chapter. And under the conviction, that nothing can be more in opposition to the very first principles of the Gospel; nothing more fatal to the humblings of grace; nothing which equally tends to make the cross of CHRIST of little worth, and the righteousness of CHRIST of no effect; I would say for myself, and every one, whose present and everlasting welfare I feel concerned,—From all self-righteousness, spiritual pride, hardness of heart, and contempt of thy word and commandments, Good LORD! deliver us!

34 ¶ Wherefore, behold, I send unto you prophets, and wise men, and scribes : and *some* of them ye shall kill and crucify ; and *some* of them shall ye scourge in your synagogues, and persecute *them* from city to city ;

35 That upon you may come all the righteous blood shed upon the earth, from the blood of righteous Abel unto the blood of Zacharias son of Barachias, whom ye slew between the temple and the altar.

36 Verily I say unto you, All these things shall come upon this generation.

These verses very properly follow here, in confirmation of the former. For as *Cain* the first murderer, began to shew this bitterness of spirit against *Abel;* so every persecution and blood shed, the cause of CHRIST had suffered, from his days to the end of the holy war, will be required of the serpent generation. Hence John expressly saith, in so many words, the reason wherefore *Cain* killed his brother *Abel,* was, because he belonged to that serpent family. *Not as Cain,* (saith he) *who was of* that wicked one, *and slew his brother.* 1 John iii. 12. To the same purport JESUS said, to some which were in his days: *Ye are of* your FATHER the DEVIL, *and the lusts of your Father ye will do. He was a murderer from the beginning.* John viii. 44.

37 O Jerusalem, Jerusalem, *thou* that killest the prophets, and stonest them which are sent unto thee, how often would I have gathered thy children together, even as a hen gathereth her chickens under *her* wings, and ye would not !

38 Behold, your house is left unto you desolate.

39 For I say unto you, Ye shall not see me henceforth, till ye shall say, Blessed *is* he that cometh in the name of the Lord.

Having much exceeded the limits to be observed in a work of this kind, in this Chapter, I reserve the comment on those verses to Luke xiii. 34. where we meet with the same pathetic lamentation of CHRIST.

REFLECTIONS.

PAUSE Reader! pause my soul, over the contents of this Chapter. Surely nothing can be more solemn, nothing more affecting. Behold the SON of GOD, who came to seek and save that which was lost; pronouncing sure and certain destruction upon a class of men, who in every age have stood up with pretensions for greater holiness than others, and like one of them in the Parable, all of them more or less ready to exclaim : GOD! *I thank thee that I am not as other men are!* Hear the LORD calling them serpents; a generation of vipers, which cannot escape the damnation of hell. And what were they considered in their department among men? How were they distinguished *then?* How are they known *now?*

The LORD calls them Pharisees. Men unhumbled in their minds. Who never felt the plague of their own heart. Uncircumcised in heart and ears. They never tasted the wormwood and the gall of a fallen state. They never were pricked to the heart under the deep conviction of a fallen state. And not feeling the want of CHRIST; they utterly despised him.

LORD JESUS! keep my soul humble at the foot of thy cross. Every day, and all the day, may I learn the infinitely precious consolations of salvation as alone in thee, and more and more from a deep sense of the want of thee, be led to see and enjoy my compleat interest in thee. And oh for grace like Paul, to count *all things but loss, for the excellency of the knowledge of* CHRIST JESUS *my* LORD : and to count *all things but dung, that I may win* CHRIST *and be found in him, not having mine own righteousness, which is of the law, but that which is through the faith of* CHRIST; *the righteousness which is of* GOD *by faith.* Oh! the blessedness that CHRIST is made of GOD to all his redeemed; *wisdom, righteousness, sanctification, and redemption, that he that glorieth may glory in the* LORD!

CHAP. XXIV.

CONTENTS.

We have in this Chapter the LORD JESUS *instructing his disciples, and in particular he foretells the destruction of the temple : and with it is blended the promise of his future coming.*

AND Jesus went out, and departed from the temple: and his disciples came to *him* for to shew him the buildings of the temple.

2 And Jesus said unto them, See ye not all these things? verily I say unto you, There shall not be left here one stone upon another, that shall not be thrown down,

It is worthy our observation, that this was the last visit JESUS made to the temple. So that when he left it, it was to return no more. And when JESUS left it, the glory was departed from it. The Prophet *Haggai* was commissioned by the LORD, to tell the people, that *the glory of this latter house should be greater than the former.* And it was made so in the presence of JESUS when he entered it, in substance of our flesh. Haggai ii. 9. But when the LORD of his temple departed, then what JESUS said in the close of the foregoing Chapter, was fulfilled: *your house is left unto you desolate.* Matt xxiii. 38. What a precious thought to all his redeemed; JESUS never leaves them! Heb. xiii. 5. Matt. xxviii. 20. This prediction of JESUS, we are told, was literally fulfilled when *Titus* sacked Jerusalem. For though the stones of the temple, were some of them of an enormous size, yet so it was, not one of them but what was broken or thrown down. The prophet Micah, had said, *Zion should be ploughed as a field.* Micah iii. 12. And here was the accomplishment. Reader! what an awful thing is it, even considered only in a temporal point of view, and as it respects nations to slight JEHOVAH's CHRIST? And how awful, in the day in which we live is it, to consider what a CHRIST despising generation is the present.

3 And as he sat upon the mount of Olives, the disciples came unto him privately, saying, Tell us, when shall these things be? and what *shall be* the sign of thy coming, and of the end of the world?

4 And Jesus answered and said unto them, Take heed that no man deceive you.

5 For many shall come in my name, saying, I am Christ; and shall deceive many.

6 And ye shall hear of wars and rumours of wars: see that ye be not troubled: for all *these things* must come to pass, but the end is not yet.

7 For nation shall rise against nation, and kingdom against kingdom: and there shall be famines, and pestilences, and earthquakes, in divers places.

8 All these *are* the beginning of sorrows.

9 Then shall they deliver you up to be afflicted, and shall kill you: and ye shall be hated of all nations for my name's sake.

10 And then shall many be offended, and shall betray one another, and shall hate one another.

11 And many false prophets shall rise, and shall deceive many.

12 And because iniquity shall abound, the love of many shall wax cold.

13 But he that shall endure unto the end, the same shall be saved.

14 And this gospel of the kingdom shall be preached in all the world for a witness unto all nations ; and then shall the end come.

While we consider the great events here spoken of, as having a peculiar and special reference, to the then age, and to the end of the Jewish state as a nation, we may, without violence, consider our LORD's words, as having a further respect to the events of his gospel, which followed. False Christs and false prophets, are signs always to be noticed in the Church history. Wars, and rumours of wars, are all ministering to CHRIST's kingdom. Every period in the Church to the present hour, hath been marked with these things. They are exercises to the faithful, and truly profitable, under the Spirit's teaching, to establish the heart in grace. Moreover, the expressions of *enduring to the end and being saved*, meant nothing more than a *temporal* deliverance; and when *the Gospel had been preached in all nations, the end then being come:* meant not the end of the world, but that when the disciples were gone forth after the day of Pentecost; this was the last sign of CHRIST's prophecy, concerning the overthrow of Jerusalem, and so the end of the Jewish state was come.

15 When ye therefore shall see the abomination of desolation, spoken of by Daniel the prophet, stand in the holy place, (whoso readeth, let him understand:)

16 Then let them which be in Judea, flee into the mountains:

17 Let him which is on the house-top not come down to take any thing out of his house:

18 Neither let him which is in the field return back to take his clothes.

19 And woe unto them that are with child, and to them that give suck in those days!

20 But pray ye that your flight be not in the winter, neither on the sabbath-day:

21 For then shall be great tribulation, such as

was not since the beginning of the world to this
time, no, nor ever shall be.

22 And except those days should be shortened,
there should no flesh be saved: but for the elect's
sake those days shall be shortened.

I cannot think with some, that the Prophet *Daniel* referred to some
image set up in the temple, by way of profaning it. For we read in
the history of those awful times, when Jerusalem was destroyed by
the Romans, that on the soldiers entering the temple and finding
no image there, as they had been accustomed to in their idolatrous
services, they ridiculed the Jewish religion, saying, that they worshipped the clouds. I rather am inclined to interpret the passage in
Daniel, which is called, *the overspreading of abominations, he shall
make it desolate*, Dan. ix. 27; as having respect to the Roman armies.
But be this as it may, the LORD JESUS pointed to this as the immediate
forerunner of the impending ruin. The verses which follow, are descriptive of great misery. But in the midst of this awful view, I beg
the Reader not to overlook that sweet verse of mercy to the elect.
Except *those days*, said JESUS, *be shortened*; (that is, the sweeping
destruction going forth at that visitation) *there should no flesh be saved:
but for the elect's sake*, said the Redeemer, *those days shall be shortened.*
Reader! do not overlook the mercy; and much less overlook the
LORD of the mercy. If the days had been lengthened out, as the
savage *Romans* wished, until the whole seed of Israel had been cut
off: from whence could there have been a race preserved for the pro-
pagating the seed of CHRIST, out of which the elect after the flesh
were to come? Here as in that beautiful similitude of the cluster in
which the new wine is found. Isaiah lxv. 8. Was one looking on,
which said: *destroy it not; for a blessing is in it. So, saith the
LORD, will, I do for my servant's sake, that I may not destroy them
all.* Reader! who shall say, from that hour to the present, and so on
to the end of time, how frequent and how numerous, the instances,
where mercy is shewn to the graceless, for the elect's sake, which in
the Adam race of nature, are to come forth from their loins. How
many among the unregenerate live on, and are preserved; because
CHRIST's seed after the flesh are appointed in their day and generation? Did the world but know this; or could the world but be made
sensible of the blessings they derive from CHRIST's seed; would they
persecute them as they now do, and like Pharaoh to Israel, often
make their lives grievous by reason of their bondage. Exod. ii. 23.
Oh! ye ungodly, ye careless, and christless people of this land!
What would ye do were the LORD to call home his own, and house
them all at once, from your persecutions? Surely you may truly
say with the Prophet: *Except the LORD of HOSTS had left unto us
a very small remnant, we should have been as Sodom, and we should
have been like unto Gomorrah!* Isaiah i. 9.

23 Then if any man shall say unto you, Lo,
here *is* Christ, or there; believe *it* not.

24 For there shall arise false Christs, and false

prophets, and shall shew great signs and wonders; insomuch that, if *it were* possible, they shall deceive the very elect.

I detain the Reader again, at this blessed statement of the LORD JESUS, concerning the safety of the elect. No signs nor wonders shall deceive *them*, our GOD saith; that is, shall deceive them to their injury, so as to hurt them really so in the present life, (see Romans viii. 28.) much less for the life to come, by any falling away. They may, and they will be frequently made the dupes of artifice, and the laughing stock of the world, and the drunkards' song. But this is no injury. And as they were chosen in CHRIST without respect to any thing of merit in themselves, before the world began; so are they secured in CHRIST to grace and glory. But let them remember, and remember it with all thankfulness, that all their safety here, and happiness hereafter, is not the result of their faith in CHRIST; but the sole purpose of their being elected in CHRIST. And the very reason wherefore they are kept in safety is, because they are chosen in CHRIST: so that their faith, and love, and joy in the LORD, are the *effects* of their election, and not the *cause*. Oh! the preciousness of this truth, and the security of GOD's people! Read that sweet scripture, Isaiah liv. 14 to the end.

25 Behold, I have told you before.

26 Wherefore if they shall say unto you, Behold he is in the desert; go not forth; behold, *he is* in the secret chambers; believe *it* not.

27 For as the lightning cometh out of the east, and shineth even unto the west; so shall also the coming of the Son of man be.

28 For wheresoever the carcase is, there will the eagles be gathered together.

I pause at this verse, respecting the carcase, and the gathering together of the eagles, to correct any error which might arise, as if it implied, that where CHRIST and his Gospel are, believers will flock. No doubt to CHRIST the gathering of the people shall be. But the term carcase, would but ill suit with the person and glory of CHRIST. I rather conceive that by carcase, is meant the slaughtered state of the Jews; and that the Roman soldiers, whose ensign was that of an eagle, would be assembled to their destruction.

29 ¶ Immediately after the tribulation of those days shall the sun be darkened, and the moon shall not give her light, and the stars shall fall from heaven, and the powers of the heaven shall be shaken:

30 And then shall appear the sign of the Son of

man in heaven : and then shall all the tribes of the earth mourn, and they shall see the Son of man coming in the clouds of heaven with power and great glory.

31 And he shall send his angels with a great sound of a trumpet, and they shall gather together his elect from the four winds, from one end of heaven to the other.

32 Now learn a parable of the fig tree : When his branch is yet tender, and putteth forth leaves, ye know that summer *is* nigh :

33 So likewise ye, when he shall see all these things, know that it is near, *even* at the doors.

34 Verily I say unto you, This generation shall not pass, till all these things be fulfilled.

35 Heaven and earth shall pass away, but my words shall not pass away.

The darkening of the sun and moon, and falling of the stars, are certainly meant in a figurative way; and were intended to imply, that on the dispersion of the Jews, those awful events should follow which the Prophet foretold, when *the* LORD *would cause the sun to go down at noon.* See the whole prophecy, Amos viii. 3 to the end. Neither when the LORD speaks of the SON of Man coming to judgment, could be meant, that *immediately* after the destruction of Jerusalem, would be the day of final judgment; but rather the judgment on the Jews, for rejecting the LORD of life and glory, and the sending of his Angels with the great sound of a trumpet, and gathering his elect, implies, his ministers going forth to preach the Gospel, which with the effect, is spoken of both by the Prophet and the Apostle. Isaiah xxvii. 13. Rev. xiv. 6. And the limitation of those events, to the then generation, in which CHRIST predicted them, is a plain proof to what they referred. For it was not full forty years after, when Jerusalem was destroyed; so that consequently many lived to see the accomplishment.

36 But of that day and hour knoweth no *man,* no, not the angels of heaven, but my Father only.

I desire to look at this verse singly, from the abuses made of it by the enemies to the GODHEAD of CHRIST. Had the Sceptic limited the sense of it, as it is evidently intended, to *the day of Jerusalem's destruction,* and not referred it to what it never was intended to have regard, to *the second* coming of CHRIST; he would have seen that the GOD-HEAD of CHRIST was neither honored nor dishonored in the business. As the GOD-Man CHRIST JESUS, all judgment is committed to CHRIST, on purpose that *all men should honor the* SON *even as they honor the*

FATHER. And he who alone is to be the judge of quick and dead, must know both the time and all the process connected with it. But on the occasion of Jerusalem's visitation, to which this verse refers, though CHRIST had so fully foretold the whole events which should take place, he doth not say the *year* was not known, for he himself had declared that that generation should not pass away till all were fulfilled; but our LORD's expressions are of that *day* and *hour*. And all consciousness of time was lost when the calamities took place on that devoted city.

37 But as the days of Noe *were,* so shall also the coming of the Son of man be.

38 For as in the days that were before the flood they were eating and drinking, marrying and giving in marriage, until the day that Noe entered into the ark,

39 And knew not until the flood came, and took them all away; so shall also the coming of the Son of man be.

40 Then shall two be in the field; the one shall be taken, and the other left.

41 Two women *shall* be grinding at the mill; the one shall be taken, and the other left.

42 Watch therefore, for ye know not what hour your Lord doth come.

43 But know this, that if the good man of the house had known in what watch the thief would come, he would have watched, and would not have suffered his house to be broken up.

44 Therefore be ye also ready : for in such an hour as ye think not the Son of man cometh.

45 Who then is a faithful and wise servant, whom his lord hath made ruler over his houshold, to give them meat in due season?

46 Blessed *is* that servant, whom his lord when he cometh shall find so doing.

47 Verily I say unto you, That he shall make him ruler over all his goods.

48 But and if that evil servant shall say in his heart, My lord delayeth his coming;

49 And shall begin to smite *his* fellow-servants, and to eat and drink with the drunken;

50 The lord of that servant shall come in a day when he looketh not for *him*, and in an hour that he is not aware of,

51 And shall cut him asunder, and appoint *him* his portion with the hypocrites, there shall be weeping and gnashing of teeth.

All that is here contained, though full of the highest instruction, yet, being so very plain and evident, will not require any comment more than its own beautiful order and simplicity. The readiness and watchfulness our Lord commanded in the prospect of the impending judgments he foretold, may by the same unanswerable reasoning be applied to the Lord's second coming to judgment, and to every man's departure out of life. For what, in fact, is the day of judgment to the whole world, but the day of death to every individual. Hence the only readiness is, being one with Christ, in an union with his person, regenerated by his spirit, washed in his blood, clothed in his righteousness, and habitually ready in the lively exercise of faith and hope, for the expectation of his coming; that when his Lord shall call, at midnight, or cock-crowing, or in the morning, he may arise at the joyful call, and mount up and meet the Lord in the air, and so for ever be with the Lord. Oh! the blessedness of that servant, *whom his* Lord *when he cometh shall find so doing!*

REFLECTIONS.

Blessed Lord Jesus! be thou everlastingly loved and adored, in that thou camest forth from the bosom of the Father, to make known the sacred purposes of his holy will and which were all purposed in Christ Jesus before the world began. And blessed be thy name for that love and grace in thine heart, in having taught thy people their safety amidst all the judgments going on in the world; and amidst all the deceptions of devils and men lying in wait to deceive. Yes! yes! thou dearest Lord, in this blessed Chapter we learn, that it is impossible so to deceive thine elect, or that any real injury can follow. Oh! Lord! give thy people grace to trace their mercies to the fountain head; and to know that their safety as well as their happiness, ariseth from their being chosen in thee, and not from any thing in themselves. And my soul, in a day like the present, let no reports of false christs, or false prophets at all move thee. Jesus will keep; Jesus will preserve; Jesus will secure his own. And the day is hastening, when *he will come to be glorified in his saints, and to be admired in all them that believe.* In that all-decisive hour, Lord grant that I may be found in thee, waiting thy approach, and *not be ashamed before thee at thy coming!* Amen.

CHAP. XXV.

CONTENTS.

In this Chapter we have the Parable of the Ten Virgins, and of the Talents; together with an account of the proceedings of the last day.

THEN shall the kingdom of heaven be likened unto ten virgins, which took their lamps, and went forth to meet the bridegroom.

2 And five of them were wise, and five *were* foolish.

3 They that *were* foolish took their lamps, and took no oil with them:

4 But the wise took oil in their vessels with their lamps.

5 While the bridegroom tarried, they all slumbered and slept.

6 And at midnight there was a cry made, Behold, the bridegroom cometh; go ye out to meet him.

7 Then all those virgins arose, and trimmed their lamps.

8 And the foolish said unto the wise, Give us of your oil; for our lamps are gone out.

9 But the wise answered, saying, *Not so;* lest there be not enough for us and you: but go ye rather to them that sell, and buy for yourselves.

10 And while they went to buy, the bridegroom came; and they that were ready went in with him to the marriage; and the door was shut.

11 Afterward came also the other virgins, saying, Lord, Lord, open to us.

12 But he answered and said, Verily I say unto you, I know you not.

13 Watch therefore, for you know neither the day nor the hour wherein the Son of man cometh.

By the kingdom of heaven, is not meant heaven itself, for there are no foolish virgins there, such as this Parable describes; but it is by way of comparison, to which the kingdom of grace in this life is said to resemble. The LORD describes *ten* virgins; *five* of whom were

Z 2

wise and *five* foolish. Not that the number *ten* hath any particular allusion; neither because they are divided into equal parts is it meant to say, that the number of the happy and of the miserable will be equal. But that the Parable our LORD hath judged proper to set forth under these images, may be the better understood. By the wise, are meant the wise unto salvation. And by the foolish those among the unawakened, careless, and christless professors, who are so foolish as to seek the gain of the world, rather than their own souls.

Now those virgins are alike described as going forth to meet the bridegroom. CHRIST is the bridegroom of his spouse the Church. By their going forth with their lamps, means going forth under a profession of CHRIST's religion. They that were foolish, took their lamps, that is, they had a mere profession, but no oil with them; they had none of the unction of GOD the HOLY GHOST upon them; were ignorant of their own lost estate before GOD, and though professing CHRIST, knew nothing of his saving power in their hearts. Whereas the wise, having been made wise unto salvation, had learnt their need of CHRIST, and were earnest to seek him.

While the bridegroom tarried, that is, while waiting in ordinances they all slumbered and slept. The Church describes herself in this frame; *I sleep, but my heart waketh.* Song v. 2. The slumbering of the LORD's people is not the sleep of death, but a deadness, of which GOD's people find but too much cause to complain. But the foolish virgins were never awakened, from being *dead in trespasses and sins.* The consequence of CHRIST's coming, must be supposed, as the Parable goes on to describe, as different as their different states unavoidably could not but produce. The *foolish* virgins, destitute of all vital godliness, unawakened, unregenerated, unacquainted with the plague of their own heart, and ignorant of the person, work, and glory of CHRIST; in all his saving offices, characters, and relations; and having nothing but a lamp of profession, were found in utter darkness, at the LORD's approach. While on the contrary, the wise virgins being furnished with the oil of grace, under the teaching of GOD the HOLY GHOST, and brought into an union with CHRIST, and communion in all that belonged to CHRIST, in regenerating, converting, justifying, and sanctifying mercy; thus prepared by the LORD, for the knowledge and enjoyment of the LORD; arise with holy joy, at the bridegroom's coming, and *enter with him into the marriage and the door is shut.*

The cry of the foolish virgins for admission, represents the state of all those who have no part nor lot in the matter. The LORD hath elsewhere described them, as well as in this parable, as those he knows not, that is, he knows them not, in any way of union or communion with him. And therefore he closeth the Parable with a recommendation to his redeemed, to be always on the watch-tower, unconscious at what day or hour, the LORD will come to take his redeemed home, that they may be found distinguished from those foolish virgins, void of all vital godliness.

14 ¶ For *the kingdom of heaven is* as a man travelling into a far country, *who* called his own servants, and delivered unto them his goods.

15 And unto one he gave five talents, to another two, and to another one ; to every man according to his several ability; and straightway took his journey.

16 Then he that had received the five talents went and traded with the same, and made *them* other five talents.

17 And likewise he that *had received* two, he also gained other two.

18 But he that had received one went, and digged in the earth, and hid his lord's money.

19 After a long time the lord of those servants cometh, and reckoneth with them.

20 And so he that had received five talents came and brought other five talents, saying, Lord, thou deliveredest unto me five talents: behold, I have gained beside them five talents more.

21 His lord said unto him, Well done, *thou* good and faithful servant; thou hast been faithful over a few things, I will make thee ruler over many things: enter thou into the joy of thy lord.

22 He also that had received two talents came and said, Lord, thou deliveredst unto me two talents: behold, I have gained two other talents beside them.

23 His lord said unto him, Well done, good and faithful servant; thou hast been faithful over a few things, I will make thee ruler over many things : enter thou into the joy of thy lord.

24 Then he which had received the one talent came and said, Lord, I knew thee that thou art an hard man, reaping where thou hast not sown, and gathering where thou hast not strawed :

25 And I was afraid, and went and hid thy talent in the earth: lo, *there* thou hast *that is* thine.

26 His lord answered and said unto him, *Thou* wicked and slothful servant, thou knewest that I

reap where I sowed not, and gather where I have not strawed:

27 Thou oughtest therefore to have put my money to the exchangers, and *then* at my coming I should have received mine own with usury.

28 Take therefore the talent from him, and give *it* unto him which hath ten talents.

29 For unto every one that hath shall be given, and he shall have abundance: but from him that hath not shall be taken away even that which he hath.

30 And cast ye the unprofitable servant into outer darkness: there shall be weeping and gnashing of teeth.

The LORD illustrates the same doctrine, as before, under another beautiful parable of a bountiful LORD, which is JESUS himself, committing different talents to his servants, and in the close, taking account of their improvement, or misimprovement, of the things committed to their charge. Two servants, to whom great charges were entrusted, are represented as making good use of their time and talents, and in the end receiving the approbation of their LORD. One, and to whom less was committed, is shewn to have proved unprofitable, and is condemned to utter darkness; and the talent entrusted to this man is said to be taken from him, and given to the servant which had most improved in his LORD's stewardship.

The obvious sense of this, as well as the former parable, renders all observations upon them unnecessary. I would only, therefore, beg it may be properly understood, that the rewards given to the faithful servant, must not be considered in a light contrary to the whole tenor of the gospel, as if any man merited divine favour. We must not strain the sense to this extent. *When we have done all, we are still unprofitable servants.* The grace of GOD cannot be made debtor to the services of man. The LORD is not moved to bestow his blessings on account of any supposed good in his creatures, neither is he restrained by our ill. *The gifts and callings of* GOD *are without repentance.* But the whole is with an eye to CHRIST. The talents here spoken of, given to the two former servants, were evidently the *gifts of grace,* and consequently the LORD's, and no merit in the receivers. Both the original stock and increase were the LORD's. LORD! (saith the Prophet,) *thou hast wrought all our works in us.* Isaiah xxvi. 12. But the One Talent the unprofitable servant received, could be only the *gift of nature,* for grace is that *good part* which cannot be taken away; whereas every thing in nature may, and at death must, and will. And the taking this talent from the slothful and unworthy, and giving it to the diligent, means to say, that the souls of the redeemed, who, through grace, abound in *spiritual* things, shall also, if needful, be blessed in the sanctified use of *temporal* things. *All are yours,* (saith the Apostle,) *whether the world, or life, or death, or things present, or things to come; all are yours, and ye are* CHRIST's, *and* CHRIST *is* GOD's. 1 Cor. iii. 22, 23, 24.

31 When the Son of man shall come in his glory, and all the holy angels with him, then shall he sit upon the throne of his glory:

32 And before him shall be gathered all nations: and he shall separate them one from another, as a shepherd divideth *his* sheep from the goats:

33 And he shall set the sheep on his right hand, but the goats on the left.

34 Then shall the King say unto them on his right hand, Come, ye blessed of my Father, inherit the kingdom prepared for you from the foundation of the world:

35 For I was an hungred, and ye gave me meat; I was thirsty, and ye gave me drink: I was a stranger, and ye took me in:

36 Naked, and ye clothed me: I was sick, and ye visited me: I was in prison, and ye came unto me.

37 Then shall the righteous answer him, saying, Lord, when saw we thee an hungred and fed *thee?* or thirsty, gave *thee* drink?

38 When saw we thee a stranger, and took *thee* in? or naked, and clothed *thee?*

39 Or when saw we thee sick, or in prison, and came unto thee?

40 And the King shall answer and say unto them, Verily I say unto you, Inasmuch as ye have done *it* unto one of the least of these my brethren, ye have done *it* unto me.

41 Then shall he say unto them on the left hand, Depart from me, ye cursed, into everlasting fire, prepared for the devil and his angels.

42 For I was an hungred, and ye gave me no meat: I was thirsty, and ye gave me no drink.

43 I was a stranger, and ye took me not in:

naked, and ye clothed me not: sick, and in prison, and ye visited me not.

44 Then shall they also answer him, saying,
Lord, when saw we thee an hungred, or athirst,
or a stranger, or naked, or sick, or in prison, and
did not minister unto thee?

45 Then shall he answer them, saying, Verily
I say unto you, Inasmuch as ye did *it* not to one
of the least of these, ye did *it* not to me.

46 And these shall go away into everlasting punishment: but the righteous into life eternal.

Here we enter on that part of our LORD's sublime discourse, on the
events of the last day, and in which the SON of GOD hath been pleased
to deliver himself on the momentous subject without a parable. And
most magnificent and solemn is the description. And when to this
be added the consideration, that every son and daughter of Adam
must be present, to receive the things done in the body, whether
good or bad, the subject becomes infinitely interesting indeed. There
can need no comment however. Every verse is plain. Every thing
described impossible to be misunderstood. And when GOD the HOLY
GHOST accompanieth the reading, or the hearing of it, with his grace,
it cannot fail of its impression in the heart.

I would only beg to observe upon it, that what is here represented
concerning the proceedings of the last day, refer chiefly, if not altogether, to the Church of the LORD JESUS, and not to the world at
large. All nations, indeed, are to be gathered before CHRIST, but then
what is described relates to the Church of CHRIST, as a Church professing CHRIST under the double character of the sheep and goats;
that is, the elect of GOD, and the non-elect. So that what JESUS
saith to each, is wholly spoken under these different views of character. And in confirmation of this grand and momentous truth, it
should be observed, that the sheep on the King's right hand, are
called upon, as the blessed of the FATHER, to come and inherit the
kingdom *prepared for them from the foundation of the world.* And
although, in infinite condescension and mercy, the King goes on to
speak of the exercise of those graces he had given them, in acts of
mercy shewn by them to his poor people, which are his representatives; yet these things were all subsequent to what was determined upon *before the foundation of the world.* A kingdom prepared from all eternity; and the persons for whom it was prepared,
being known and appointed, their possession of it could not depend
upon any of their after-actions in time. This would have been to
have put the *effect* for the *cause,* and to invert the very order of things
in the divine counsel. It is, indeed, very blessed to see, that the
LORD, who is himself the sole cause, appointed also the effect.
But plainly, the whole is the result of free sovereign grace, and not an
atom of merit in man, contributing, in the least degree, to the accomplishment.

Reader! pause over the subject, and ponder well the blessed contents! For what can be so truly blessed, as the contemplation of the provision the LORD made for his people, not only before they were born, but before the foundations of the earth were laid. I know that some dear children of GOD, yea, perhaps I might have said, by far the greater part of his children, on whom a work of grace is wrought, are looking more to the effect wrought *in* them, than the Almighty work wrought *for* them. But this should not be the case. Time will come, yea many a time circumstances do come, when redeemed souls lose sight of what is called their evidences; and where is their comfort then? Whereas, if we were always looking to the LORD JESUS, and JEHOVAH's covenant promises in him, and considered the security of this kingdom, which cannot be moved, and which hath been prepared for the Church and every member of CHRIST's body, from the foundation of the world; these are the LORD's evidences, in which we should find an everlasting source for joy. For so the promise runs. *Thou wilt keep him in perfect peace,* (or as the margin of the Bible very properly renders it, *peace, peace;* that is, peace for ever, peace upon peace, uninterrupted, and without end,) *whose mind is stayed on thee, because he trusteth in thee.* Isaiah xxvi. 3. LORD! I would say for myself, and every regenerated child of GOD! grant to us such blessed stayings upon thee, and arising wholly of what thou hast done, as the *sole cause;* and not in any thing which thy grace enables thy redeemed to perform, for all these can be but *the effect.* Oh! the unspeakable felicity of a kingdom not founded in time, but in eternity: not the result of man's merit, but GOD's gift; not depending upon creature attainments, but Creator faithfulness; and founded in the everlasting love of GOD the FATHER, the infinite merits, bloodshedings, and righteousness, of the LORD JESUS CHRIST, and the Almighty grace and efficient ministry of GOD the HOLY GHOST. And oh! how sweet are the words of the LORD JESUS, both here and elsewhere, while expressing the rich mercies thus prepared for his redeemed, before the foundation of the world, when he saith: *Fear not little flock, for it is your heavenly Father's good pleasure to give you the kingdom.* Luke xii. 32.

I hope the Reader will not be liable to any mistake, from the statement I have ventured to give, in pointing out the *cause* from the *effect.* Neither will he, I trust, be led to conceive, that I place no stress upon the *effects* of vital godliness, because I place so much upon the grand *cause* of all. This would be to pervert what I have intended. The LORD JESUS himself, is pleased to notice in his people the smallest exercise of those graces he hath given them; and he tells us, that he regards the cup of cold water, when we have nothing warmer to give, if given in the name of a disciple. Well therefore may we regard them also. And as CHRIST *personal* is no more upon earth to be ministered unto, as he was in the days of his flesh, Luke viii. 3. it is blessed when we feel a love to JESUS, to minister to any of his poor people, who are members of his *mystical* body. But still I must contend for the LORD's glory, as the sole cause of all. The foundation of a kingdom, and prepared from everlasting, is wholly in himself: and both the persons for whom this kingdom is prepared, and the graces wrought in them, as testimonies to the same, all ori-

ginate from the electing, redeeming, regenerating grace of GOD, in
CHRIST JESUS.

I detain the Reader a moment longer to remark, that from the
answer, and given with such seeming astonishment by the redeemed,
(called righteous, in the LORD's righteousness,) to the gracious words
of the king: LORD *when saw we thee an hungred and fed thee, &c.* it
appears that they had no consciousness of the oneness between CHRIST
and his people, in a manner equal to what it really is. And perhaps
no man alive, is, or can be able to conceive the intimate nearness between them. If we were, every child of GOD, would be more alive
than he is, even upon motives of selfishness to minister to one another.
One of the fathers of the Church *(Cyprian)* used to say, that this passage had never been understood; and the redeemed are all of them
represented as saying as much, when thus expressing their astonishment!

I do not think it necessary to enlarge, on the awful part of the representation given in this Chapter, of the condemnation of the unregenerate. That the sentence uttered by the king, *depart ye cursed;* is
spoken to such as were nominal Christians, is I think, too evident to be
doubted, in that JESUS saith, *I was an hungered and ye gave me no
meat:* which plainly proves that they dwelt among the LORD's people,
but had neither faith nor love for him, nor compassion for his members as such. In short the characters are contrasted. The righteous,
were righteous in CHRIST's righteousness; and through grace had been
savingly called, regenerated, justified, and sanctified; and had been
deeply humbled under a sense of their own utterly lost estate, and
had sought salvation only in CHRIST. The goats on the left hand, had
neither felt a sense of sin, nor a desire of salvation; they are supposed to have heard of CHRIST, but valued him not; priding themselves
in their own good works, or hoping that these would recommend them
to JESUS, and what was wanting, if there were any deficiency, he
might make up. So that their unhumbled hearts had never known any
thing of their own corruption; their acts of charity, if any, had never
been given with an eye to CHRIST: they had lived and died, as they
were born, and knew not the LORD. It is of such CHRIST speaks,
when he saith, *and these shall go away into everlasting punishment;
but the righteous into life eternal.*

REFLECTIONS.

LET both Writer and Reader, ponder well the weighty contents of
this Chapter, before they close the book, looking up to the great Author of his holy word, to commission it to their hearts, and to make it
a savour of life unto life, that the name of JESUS, may be *as ointment poureth forth!*

And oh! for grace, to be as the wise virgins, not going forth with
the lamp of a mere profession; which from not being fed, nor kept
alive by the LORD, cannot but go out in the midnight-hour. Neither
may my soul be as the unprofitable servant, whose end could be no
other but to be cast into outer darkness, *where there is weeping and
gnashing of teeth!* Oh! precious LORD JESUS! what a relief is it to
my soul that when thou shalt come in thy glory, and all thy holy
angels with thee, thy redeemed shall be set on thy right hand; and

their introduction into everlasting happiness, will then be proclaimed before a congregated world, to be the result of thy grace, not their merit. Yes! thou glorious Head of thy Church and people, it will be then seen that thou art the sole *cause* of all their salvation and joy, their everlasting portion and happiness, in time and to all eternity. LORD! grant in my heart all the blessed *effects* of thy love, that I may love thee and thy members, as streams from the fountain of thy love, and manifest whose I am and whom I serve, in the gospel of GOD's dear SON: and seeing that all thy redeemed have received *a kingdom which cannot be moved, we may have grace whereby we may serve* GOD *acceptably, with reverence and godly fear!*

C H A P. XXVI.

CONTENTS. ˙

We here enter upon the concluding scenes of CHRIST's *life. The Rulers conspire against* JESUS. *He celebrates his Passover. Judas betrayeth him; Peter denieth him; and all the disciples forsake him and flee.*

AND it came to pass, when Jesus had finished all these sayings, he said unto his disciples,

2 Ye know that after two days is *the feast of* the passover, and the Son of man is betrayed to be crucified.

I beg the Reader to attend very minutely, to the circumstances with which *Matthew*, the first Evangelist, in point of order, introduceth the subject of our LORD's sufferings. He saith, *When* JESUS *had finished all these sayings.* Perhaps he alluded to the finishing of his office in teaching. For as CHRIST in his character of Mediator, had *three* offices, prophet, priest, and king, he was uniformly carrying on one or other of these all the way through, during the whole of his ministry. He had therefore finished his teachings, as the *Prophet* of his people; and now he is about to enter more fully on his *Priestly* office, where he would be both the altar, sacrifice, and sacrificer. And when this was also finished, he would in a more open manner, than he had hitherto done, display his *Kingly* power in his ascension to glory, where the exercise of his sovereignty was to be shewn forth, in ruling his Church, until he had accomplished the destruction of his enemies, and brought home his redeemed to everlasting happiness.

As the interesting subject in the concluding scenes of our LORD's life, form so momentous a part in CHRIST's history, and as it is most essential to every child of GOD, to have the clearest apprehension of it, I hope I may be indulged in this " Poor Man's Commentary," to dwell upon each particular, with that attention it deserves; looking up to GOD the HOLY GHOST, to be the teacher both of Writer and Reader. And yet at the same time, that I may not swell the pages beyond their proper limits, I shall adopt a method, which I hope will answer this purpose very fully. I mean, that as the *four* Evangelists have re-

corded those solemn transactions, which took place, at the death of
CHRIST, it will not be necessary to repeat my observations in the same
way and manner upon every one; but connect the whole as one
history; and so divide the subject, that what I omit in my comment
on one part, may be introduced into the other. This will prevent
tediousness to the Reader, and yet allow of enlargement upon the whole,
so as under the LORD's blessing, to make the subject compleat.

I beg the Reader to observe, how CHRIST opens the subject himself,
and immediately directs the minds of his disciples to it, in calling
their attention to the Jewish Passover. This was the first public service in the appointment of the LORD, when the Church was first formed, in the memorable night of the people being delivered from Egyptian bondage. See Exod. xii. throughout. Now as GOD the HOLY
GHOST himself, by his servant Paul, explained this service in express
terms of application to the LORD JESUS, when the Apostle said CHRIST
our Passover is sacrified for us, therefore let us keep the feast. 1 Cor.
v. 7, 8. We cannot hesitate a moment in concluding that the first
institution of this service in the old Church, together with every sacrifice which followed under the law, had no other object in view than to
hold forth CHRIST. To him, every one of them pointed. In him, the
whole was compleated. He, and he alone, became the sum and substance of all; and all, as the HOLY GHOST, by the same Apostle
elsewhere saith in his writings, *were a shadow of things to come, but
the body is of* CHRIST. Coloss. ii. 17. Heb. x. 1.

When the Reader therefore hath diligently read over the interesting account given by all the Evangelists concerning the Passover, and
compared it with what is said concerning it at the first institution; I
would beg his closest attention to the whole subject, in the great
points of doctrine connected with it, and which will minister under
the LORD's teaching, to the proper apprehension of those grand features of character, in the person of the LORD JESUS CHRIST. See Mark
xiv. 1. Luke xxii. 1, &c. John xiii. 1. Compared with Exod. xii.
throughout.

And here the first and most prominent feature of character in the
LORD JESUS as our Passover, must be to consider him as our great
head, and representative of his Church and people. CHRIST, becoming our Passover, and dying for his redeemed in *time*, pre-sup-
poses an engagement for this purpose in eternity. And hence we find,
he is called *the lamb slain from the foundation of the world.* Rev.
xiii. 8. And to this amount the scriptures speak, when continually
and in every part, informing the Church of the everlasting covenant
made between the persons of the GODHEAD, before all worlds. By virtue of which, CHRIST, at the call of GOD the FATHER, as covenanted
for in the great purposes of redemption, stood up the glorious head,
representative, and high-priest of his people; taking their names and
their nature; undertaking for them to fulfill all righteousness, and
offering his soul an offering for sin. On the part of JEHOVAH, it was
agreed, that the whole persons of the GODHEAD would carry CHRIST,
in his human nature, through the wonderful undertaking; and when
accomplished, the glorious deliverer should see his seed with all the
blessed effects of his salvation, and have a Church to serve him,
where his praise should be sung, and his name adored, as long as the
sun and moon should endure, from one generation to another. And,

finally, bring home his chosen, to everlasting glory; when sin, Satan, death, and hell, should be brought under his feet. I stay not to quote at large the whole body of scripture, which, with one full voice come forth to confirm the great truth. I rather refer the Reader to look over those portions in his Bible for himself, which I have here referred to, and when he hath done, I will request him to follow me through those interesting records of our LORD's concluding scenes of his ministry and life, whose beauties will therefrom, I am persuaded, appear in their more plain and striking colors. Isaiah xlii. 1—8. Prov. viii. 22—31. Isaiah xlix. 1—9. Psm. xl. 1—7. compared with Heb. x. 1—22. John x. 18. On the part of JEHOVAH's covenant, see Psm. lxxxix. 2, 3, 4, 19—37. Isaiah xi. 1—9. John 3—34 to the end. Psm. cx. Isaiah liii. 10. Philip. ii. 6—12. Heb. xii. 2, &c. Rev. vii. 9 to the end.

3 Then assembled together the chief priests, and the scribes, and the elders of the people, unto the palace of the high priest, who was called Caiaphas,

4 And consulted that they might take Jesus by subtilty, and kill *him.*

5 But they said, Not on the feast *day,* lest there be an uproar among the people.

From what hath been observed before, in the introduction of this subject, in holding forth CHRIST, as the representative of his Church and people, we shall now enter upon it with a clearer apprehension, in beholding the chief priests here forming their council for killing JESUS. And although they had no consciousness, what instruments they were in the LORD's hand, for the accomplishing the sacred purposes of his will; yet they were (as *Peter* told some of them, after his soul was enlightened by the coming of the HOLY GHOST, on the day of Pentecost,) by wicked hands, doing all that they did, *by the determinate counsel and foreknowledge of* GOD. Acts ii. 23. See also to this purport, Acts iv. 27, 28. Acts xiii. 27, 28.

Reader! it is very blessed to behold CHRIST thus representing his redeemed as their head and husband; and the Chief Priests and Scribes, thus becoming GOD's instruments, for the purpose of bringing CHRIST into the very situation, where our sins must have brought us, but for his interposition. His being made both *sin* and a *curse* for us, became the only possible means, whereby we might be redeemed from both for ever. We shall have the clearest views of these grand points, as we prosecute the subject, if so be, the LORD the HOLY GHOST be our teacher! Matchless instructor! vouchsafe this blessing!

6 Now when Jesus was in Bethany, in the house of Simon the leper,

7 There came unto him a woman having an alabaster box of very precious ointment, and poured it on his head, as he sat *at meat.*

8 But when his disciples saw *it*, they had indignation, saying, To what purpose *is* this waste?

9 For this ointment might have been sold for
much, and given to the poor.

10 When Jesus understood *it*, he said unto them,
Why trouble ye the woman? for she hath wrought
a good work upon me.

11 For ye have the poor always with you; but
me ye have not always.

12 For in that she hath poured this ointment
on my body, she did *it* for my burial.

13 Verily I say unto you, Wheresoever this
gospel shall be preached in the whole world, *there*
shall also this, that this woman hath done, be told
for a memorial of her.

Some have thought, that this woman, is the same that is spoken of
in Luke vii. 37. And others have thought, that it was *Mary*, the sister
of *Lazarus*. John xii. 3. But I am too intent at present, to make any
enquiry here, who it was: it is the person of JESUS, who alone demands
our attention, while following him in those solemn moments. Reader!
mark what your Redeemer saith; the pouring this ointment on his
body, was in token of his *burial*. Yes! it was to this death of JESUS,
every thing referred. The moment the SON of GOD became incarnate,
and openly came forward as the Head and Surety of his Church, the
curse pronounced on man's fall, seized on him as the Sponsor.

Reader! I hope you have not forgotten the awful contents of it.
The *ground* was first *cursed* for man's sake. The nature of man was
doomed to sorrow and labor, in consequence thereof. *In sorrow shalt
thou eat of it all the days of thy life.* And death, was to close the
scene. *Dust thou art, and unto dust shalt thou return.* Gen. iii. 17,
18, 19. Hence therefore, the whole of this awful sentence attached
itself to CHRIST, when he freely offered himself the redeemer of his
Church and people. And what I beg the Reader particularly to
notice, and indeed, to us so highly concerned in the blessedness of
redemption by CHRIST, becomes more important than any other view
of the subject, is, that the curse in all its aggravated circumstances
lighting upon CHRIST, was wholly, in that he stood forth at the call of
his FATHER, as our surety. The SON of GOD taking our nature, would
not have subjected him to this curse, had he not volunteered to be
our surety. Great indeed was the grace, in the SON of GOD to become man. But this might have been done, and the same infinitely
glorious person he would have been, as he now is, had he never undertaken our redemption. But when he stood up at the call of GOD
our surety, *he* became responsible, while *we* who were the principals
in the debt were made free; CHRIST our surety took the whole upon
himself, and the LORD laid on him *the iniquity of us all.* Isaiah liii. 6.

14 ¶ Then one of the twelve, called Judas Iscariot, went unto the chief priests,

15 And said *unto them,* What will ye give me,
and I will deliver him unto you? And they
covenanted with him for thirty pieces of silver.

16 And from that time he sought opportunity
to betray him.

17 ¶ Now the first *day* of the *feast* of unleavened
bread the disciples came to Jesus, saying unto him,
Where wilt thou that we prepare for thee to eat
the passover?

18 And he said, Go into the city to such a man,
and say unto him, The Master saith, My time is
at hand; I will keep the passover at thy house
with my disciples.

19 And the disciples did as Jesus had appointed
them ; and they made ready the passover.

20 Now when the even was come, he sat down
with the twelve.

21 And as they did eat, he said, Verily I say
unto you, that one of you shall betray me.

22 And they were exceeding sorrowful, and
began every one of them to say unto him, Lord,
is it I ?

23 And he answered and said, He that dippeth
his hand with me in the dish, the same shall betray me.

24 The Son of man goeth, as it is written of him :
but woe unto that man by whom the Son of man
is betrayed ! it had been good for that man if he
had not been born.

25 Then Judas, which betrayed him, answered
and said, Master, is it I ? He said unto him, Thou
hast said.

26 And as they were eating, Jesus took bread,
and blessed it, and brake *it,* and gave *it* to the
disciples, and said, Take, eat ; this is my body.

27 And he took the cup, and gave thanks, and gave *it* to them, saying, Drink ye all of it;

28 For this is my blood of the new testament, which is shed for many for the remission of sins.

29 But I say unto you, I will not drink henceforth of this fruit of the vine, until that day when I drink it new with you in my Father's kingdom.

30 And when they had sung an hymn, they went out into the mount of Olives.

I reserve the view which this scripture opens of the traitor *Judas*, to the account given of it by *John*, where it is somewhat more enlarged upon. See John xiii. 18.

31 Then saith Jesus unto them, All ye shall be offended because of me this night : for it is written I will smite the shepherd, and the sheep of the flock shall be scattered abroad.

32 But after I am risen again, I will go before you into Galilee.

33 Peter answered and said unto him, Though all *men* shall be offended because of thee, *yet* will I never be offended.

34 Jesus said unto him, Verily I say unto thee, That this night, before the cock crow, thou shalt deny me thrice.

35 Peter said unto him, Though I should die with thee, yet will I not deny thee. Likewise also said all the disciples.

We shall very easily conceive, how likely it was, for the whole body of disciples to be offended, or as the original word is, *scandalized*, at the humiliation of Cʜʀɪsᴛ, if we all along keep in remembrance, that notwithstanding all the miracles Cʜʀɪsᴛ had wrought, and the discourses he had delivered to them; not one of them before the descent of the Hoʟʏ Gʜosᴛ, had any apprehension of any kingdom of Jᴇsᴜs, but an earthly kingdom. Even after he arose from the dead, they still harped upon the subject, Loʀᴅ ! *wilt thou at this time restore the kingdom of Israel?* meaning the overthrowing the Roman power, under whom Israel was then in tribute. Acts i. 6. And though every one of them (for Judas was now gone) as well as *Peter*, felt a confidence of attachment to Cʜʀɪsᴛ; yet certain it is, that when Cʜʀɪsᴛ was apprehended as he was soon after this by the Roman soldiers, all would have readily denied him, as *Peter* did, had the temptation been the same; neither but from CHRIST's intercession for them could they have stood in faith, for for the moment they all forsook him and fled.

36 ¶ Then cometh Jesus with them unto a place called Gethsemane, and saith unto the disciples, Sit ye here, while I go and pray yonder.

37 And he took with him Peter and the two sons of Zebedee, and began to be sorrowful and very heavy.

38 Then saith he unto them, My soul is exceeding sorrowful, even unto death: tarry ye here, and watch with me.

39 And he went a little farther, and fell on his face, and prayed, saying, O my Father, if it be possible, let this cup pass from me: nevertheless not as I will, but as thou *wilt*.

40 And he cometh unto the disciples, and findeth them asleep, and saith unto Peter, What, could ye not watch with me one hour?

41 Watch and pray, that ye enter not into temptation: the spirit indeed *is* willing, but the flesh *is* weak.

42 He went away again the second time, and prayed, saying, O my Father, if this cup may not pass away from me, except I drink it, thy will be done.

43 And he came and found them asleep again: for their eyes were heavy.

44 And he left them, and went away again, and prayed the third time, saying the same words.

45 Then cometh he to his disciples, and saith unto them, Sleep on now, and take *your* rest: behold, the hour is at hand, and the Son of man is betrayed into the hands of sinners.

46 Rise, let us be going: behold, he is at hand that doth betray me.

We have here CHRIST's entrance upon his sufferings, in the garden *Gethsemane*. The whole life of JESUS had been a life of sorrow, for of him, and him only, by way of emphasis, can it be said, that he was *a man of sorrows and acquainted with grief*. But here he is entering

more especially upon the great work of sorrow, for which he became
the surety of his people. And here it is therefore, that we need most
eminently the teaching of GOD the HOLY GHOST. I am aware how
very little a way our discoveries carry us, when following the steps
of JESUS by faith, into the garden of *Gethsemane*. If *Peter, James,*
and *John,* whom CHRIST took with him there, fell under such a
drowsiness as is described, how shall we hope to watch the footsteps
of JESUS to any great discoveries of such an awful scene? Nevertheless, looking up for the teachings and leadings of the HOLY GHOST, I
would beg the Reader to accompany me, in following by faith, the
LORD JESUS to *Gethsemane's* garden, in this dark and gloomy hour;
and may the LORD be our teacher in beholding the glory of CHRIST,
even in the depth of his soul travail, when he drank the cup of
trembling to the dregs, that we might drink the cup of salvation and
call upon the name of the LORD.

· And here Reader, carrying on the same important idea with us
all along, that in all CHRIST did, and all he suffered, he acted as the
surety and representative of his people, let us first consider the suitableness of the place.

It was a garden, in which JESUS entered, to commence the first onset
of suffering, when about to accomplish salvation by the sacrifice of
himself. And it should be remembered, that it was in a garden where
the devil first triumphed over our nature in the fall of man. Here
therefore, CHRIST enters for our recovery. There was indeed this
difference in the two places. Before the fall, this garden was an
earthly Paradise. But now, it is the gloomy *Gethsemane,* close to
the foul brook *Cedron,* into which all the filth of the sacrifices poured
their contents. It was the very place adjoining to that memorable spot
which good king Josiah polluted, by burning the vessels here, which·
had been used in idolatrous worship. 2 Kings xxiii. 4, 5, 6. The Jews
called it the valley of the children of *Hinnom* or *Topheth,* which was the
only word they had for hell, after the Babylonish captivity. *Scheol*
had been heretofore used for *hell.* Job xi. 8. This was the awful
spot where CHRIST in our nature entered when he went over the brook
Cedron. Now as Satan had conquered the first Adam in the garden,
and in him, made captive the whole race, and consequently in it the
whole Church; CHRIST shall there also, as his Church's representative,
begin to give the first deadly blow to sin and Satan. And although
from hence *he shall be taken* (as the Prophet said) *from prison and
from judgment; be cut off out of the land of the living, and for the
transgression of his people be stricken;* yet here shall the first overthrow to the kingdom of Satan be accomplished, and the victory of
CHRIST, in a wonderful way be displayed. Isaiah liii. 8,

As we prosecute this awful business, every step we take seems to
be more solemn and striking. The Evangelists who have described
the state of JESUS, have each of them used different words, by way
of expressing the feelings of JESUS. As if neither could find any language which fully came up to what those feelings really were. *Matthew* saith, that the LORD expressed himself as being *in soul exceeding
sorrowful, even unto death. Mark's* words are, that JESUS *began to
be sore amazed, and to be very heavy.* Mark xiv. 33. And it must be
allowed by those who are at all acquainted with the original scriptures,
the words in *Mark,* which our translators have rendered, *sore amazed,*

imply such an affright to the mind as when we say it makes the very hair stand on an end, and induceth a trembling and horror of the whole frame. *Luke,* still varying from both, but yet, if possible, in stronger terms than either, represents CHRIST in an *agony* or *combat;* though there was none near him until an Angel was sent from heaven to strengthen him. The sweat which forced itself through the pores of his sacred body, was as it were, *great drops of blood falling down to the ground.* Luke xxii. 43, 44. And this was at a time, when in the night, and in the open air, and when we are told that the servants of the High Priest in common-hall, had found it so piercingly cold, as had compelled them to make *a fire to warm themselves.* John xviii. 18. Pause Reader! Before we go further, let us humbly look up and enquire into the cause! Here is no account of any pains of body the Redeemer had yet entered upon! The horrors of crucifixion though in view, were not felt. Here was no person near CHRIST. JESUS was surrounded by no man. For though he had taken with him into the garden, *Peter* and the two sons of *Zebedee;* and though he had entreated them to watch with him, and pray that they might not enter into temptation; yet they were not near him! for we are told, that *they were withdrawn from him about a stone's cast.* Who withdrew them? What were they withdrawn for? Is it not plain, as JESUS said, that *this was the enemy's hour and power of darkness?* See Luke xxii. 41—45—53. and the Commentary upon the passage.

And what was the cause for which this Lamb of GOD was thus exercised? He who was *holy, harmless, undefiled, separate from sinners, and made higher than the heavens!* Heb. vii. 26. What can more decidedly confirm the scriptures of truth, than that as his Church's surety and representative, he *who knew no sin was made sin for us, that we might be made the righteousness of* GOD *in him.* 2 Cor. v. 21. *He* (as the Apostle saith) *hath redeemed us from the curse of the law, being made a curse for us.* Gal iii. 13. Here was the cause. It pleased JEHOVAH *to put him to grief.* The FATHER's hand was in the work. And hence the holy sufferer expressed himself in such strong words. *Save me, O* GOD! *for the waters are come in unto my soul. I sink in deep mire where there is no standing. I am come into deep waters, where the floods overflow me, &c.* Psm. lxix. 1, 2, 3. See also Psm. xxii. throughout. Psm. xxxviii. throughout.

Oh! ye my poor fellow sinners who never yet felt sin; behold the exceeding sinfulness in the soul travail of CHRIST JESUS! *Behold! (*he saith) *is it nothing to you, all ye that pass by: behold and see if there be any sorrow like unto my sorrow, wherewith the* LORD *hath afflicted me in the day of his fierce anger.* Lament. i. 12. LORD! let the contemplation fire my soul with love! They say, if in common life we bring the murderer of a dead man before the body, wonderful effects will follow; yea, that blood will flow afresh from the murdered, as if the unconscious body had sight of the murderer. Whether it be so or not; oh! for grace, dear JESUS, as my sins have induced thine agony and death, to delight to come before thee. And oh! let thy fresh flowing blood cleanse me, and cause my heart to bleed afresh, in the conciousness that by sin I have crucified my LORD!

47 ¶ And while he yet spake, lo, Judas, one of the twelve, came, and with him a great multitude

with swords and staves, from the chief priests and elders of the people.

48 Now he that betrayed him gave them a sign, saying, Whomsoever I shall kiss, that same is he: hold him fast.

49 And forthwith he came to Jesus, and said, Hail, Master; and kissed him.

50 And Jesus said unto him, Friend, wherefore art thou come? Then came they, and laid hands on Jesus, and took him.

51 And, behold, one of them which were with Jesus stretched out *his* hand, and drew his sword, and struck a servant of the high priest's, and smote off his ear.

52 Then said Jesus unto him, Put up again thy sword into his place: for all they that take the sword shall perish with the sword.

53 Thinkest thou that I cannot now pray to my Father, and he shall presently give me more than twelve legions of angels?

54 But how then shall the scriptures be fulfilled, that thus it must be?

55 In that same hour said Jesus to the multitudes, Are ye come out as against a thief with swords and staves for to take me? I sat daily with you teaching in the temple, and ye laid no hold on me.

56 But all this was done, that the scriptures of the prophets might be fulfilled. Then all the disciples forsook him, and fled.

We now arrive to that part in this momentous transaction, as is connected with the voluntary surrender of JESUS. The great feature in redemption, to give efficacy and merit to it, is the freeness of CHRIST in the work. On this JESUS had particularly dwelt, when he said: *Therefore doth my FATHER love me, because I lay down my life that I might take it again. No man taketh it from me. I have power to lay it down, and I have power to take it again. This commandment have I received of my FATHER.* John x. 17, 18. But I postpone the observations on this grand feature of CHRIST, to the review of the subject, in the Gospel of John. See John xviii. 4. for there we meet with it more strikingly.

57 And they that had laid hold on Jesus led *him* away to Caiaphas the high priest, where the scribes and the elders were assembled.

Every verse in the concluding scene of CHRIST's life is momentous. But the limits of this " Poor Man's Commentary," will not admit of our enlarging on the subject, as might be wished. Nevertheless, the apprehension of CHRIST, and the leading him away, are too important as points, in the wonderful subject, to be hastily passed by. He, who at a word of his mouth, smote to the ground the band of armed men which came to take him, (John xviii. 6.) cannot be supposed to have been bound and led away, but for the answering some important purpose. It may well merit therefore our attention.

In entering into a proper apprehension of this subject, always preserving in view and never losing sight of the voluntary sufferings of JESUS; let us first attend to what is said of CHRIST, under the spirit of prophecy. JESUS complains, of *the bulls of Basan compassing him around; and the dogs and assembly of wicked men inclosing him;* by which we plainly understand, that JESUS, as the *hind of the morning* was to be hunted, until he was *brought into the dust of death.* Psalm xxii. title of the Psalm, and 12—15 verses. Now the *binding* of CHRIST, was a part of the service of the sacrifice. Isaac his type was bound and put upon the altar. Gen. xxii. 9. And hence, all the sacrifices under the Jewish law were *bound* at the horns of the altar. Psm. cxviii. 27. But these things were all figurative of the. sins and iniquities of his people *binding* CHRIST. For as chains and fetters tye down the body : so sin and iniquity bend down the soul. Here CHRIST cries out, *Innumerable evils have compassed me about; mine iniquities have taken hold of me, so that I am not able to look up : they are more than the hairs of my head ; my heart hath failed me.* Psm. xl. 12. These are very precious views of CHRIST, when *restoring that he took not away.* Psm. lxix. 4. So that the *binding* of CHRIST, became a necessary part to set forth the *binding* of all the sins of his people on CHRIST, when JEHOVAH laid on him *the iniquity of us all.* And it is a very very precious thought, to the soul of every truly regenerated believer, that all the sins of his redeemed, without the omission of a single infirmity or sin; in thought, or word, or deed, were *laid upon* CHRIST, as the sacrifice was used to be *bound* on the altar. Hence, the High Priest, under the Jewish dispensation, was commanded to be thus particular, on the great day of atonement. *And Aaron shall lay both his hands upon the head of the live goat, and confess over him all the iniquities of the children of Israel, and all their transgression* in all their sins, putting them upon the head of the goat : *and shall send him away by the hand of a fit man* (a man of opportunity, as the margin hath it, and as CHRIST was) *into the wilderness,* as CHRIST was led away when bound. Levit. xvi. 21.

Reader ! do not overlook this grand feature in the person, office, and character of CHRIST. When CHRIST was bound and led away, he then fulfilled all that this type and shadow represented of him ; and the whole, and not a single sin, either of omission or commission, belonging to his redeemed was left out.

58 But Peter followed him afar off unto the high priest's palace, and went in, and sat with the servants to see the end.

59 Now the chief priests, and elders, and all the council, sought false witness against Jesus, to put him to death;

60 But found none: yea, though many false witnesses came, *yet* found they none. At the last came two false witnesses,

61 And said, This *fellow* said, I am able to destroy the temple of God, and to build it in three days.

62 And the high priest arose, and said unto him, Answerest thou nothing? what *is it which* these witness against thee?

63 But Jesus held his peace, and the high priest answered and said unto him, I adjure thee by the living God that thou tell us whether thou be the Christ, the Son of God.

64 Jesus saith unto him, Thou hast said: nevertheless, I say unto you, Hereafter shall ye see the Son of man sitting on the right hand of power, and coming in the clouds of heaven.

65 Then the high priest rent his clothes, saying, He hath spoken blasphemy: what further need have we of witnesses? behold, now, Ye have heard his blasphemy.

66 What think ye? They answered and said, He is guilty of death.

67 Then did they spit in his face, and buffeted him; and others smote *him* with the palms of their hands,

68 Saying, Prophesy unto us, thou Christ, Who is he that smote thee?

The HOLY GHOST, as if to stamp an everlasting reproach upon *Caiaphas*, hath pointed him out as awfully engaged in the office of High Priest, the year of CHRIST's crucifixion. JESUS was led away to *Annas*, then to *Caiaphas*. And *Caiaphas* was he that gave counsel to the Jews, that it was expedient that *one man should die for the people.* John xviii. 14. Right or wrong, this wretch determined the death of CHRIST. And the renting his cloaths in a seemingly holy indignation, was only covering over the malignity of his heart, by the horror he wished to express of blasphemy. But let not the Reader overlook the prophecies of this great transaction. Now was that scripture fulfilled, which JESUS spake by the spirit of prophecy, a thousand years before. *The assembly of the wicked have inclosed me.* Psm. xxii. 16. The LORD CHRIST answering to the adjuration of the High Priest is most blessed, and especially under the character of the SON of man!

69 Now Peter sat without in the palace; and a damsel came unto him, saying, Thou also wast with Jesus of Galilee.

70 But he denied before *them* all, saying, I know not what thou sayest.

71 And when he was gone out into the porch, another *maid* saw him, and said unto them that were there, This *fellow* was also with Jesus of Nazareth.

72 And again he denied with an oath, I do not know the man.

73 And after a while came unto *him* they that stood by, and said to Peter, Surely thou also art *one* of them; for thy speech bewrayeth thee.

74 Then began he to curse and to swear, *saying,* I know not the man, and immediately the cock crew.

75 And Peter remembered the word of Jesus, which said unto him, Before the cock crow, thou shalt deny me thrice. And he went out and wept bitterly.

Luke, hath related the denial of *Peter* in yet some more remarkable circumstances than either of the other Evangelists. I therefore shall postpone the interesting consideration of *Peter's* fall, and his recovery by grace, until we come to Luke's Gospel. See Luke xxii. 54, &c.

REFLECTIONS.

READER! in looking back upon the many wonderful events related in this Chapter, let us admire as well we may, the boundless love of the LORD JESUS, in the tender institution of his holy supper. For as the type and shadow of the Jewish Passover, was now for ever to cease, when He the true Christian Passover to which that service ministered, was sacrificed for us; it was an act of the highest love and mercy, in our dear Redeemer, to set up this precious ordinance in his Church, as a standing memorial of his death, until his coming again. And surely JESUS hath endeared it and recommended it by every affecting circumstance, when we consider the *time* when he instituted it; the *manner* in which he observed it himself, and commanded its *perpetual* observance by his people: with all the blessed effects he hath promised in it, from his gracious presence, in those holy seasons of communion: and the sure mercies, which shall accompany the faithful use of it. Oh! for grace, frequently thus to *set forth the* LORD'S *death till he come!*

And oh! thou dearest Redeemer! grant both the Writer and Reader the blessed unction of thine HOLY SPIRIT, as often as we follow thy steps by faith, to the garden of Gethsemane. Here may we oft resort in spirit, as JESUS in the days of his flesh oft resorted with his disciples.

And LORD grant, that we enter into thy retirings, and by watchfulness and prayer, go over in review again and again, the soul-agonies and soul-travails of JESUS: taking interest in all that we behold, of his sorrows for us and our salvation. Oh! for grace thus to read and thus to meditate on the person, work, offices, characters, and relations of the LORD JESUS CHRIST! To behold him, and to know him, who was made *sin for us who knew no sin; that we might be made the righteousness of* GOD *in him.*

CHAP. XXVII.

CONTENTS.

The Chapter opens with the relation of hurrying away the LORD JESUS *to Pilate; from thence to Herod.* CHRIST *is examined; Barabbas, a robber and murderer, is preferred before him. He is led away to be crucified. The awful signs attending his death. He is laid in the Sepulchre.*

WHEN the morning was come, all the chief priests and elders of the people took counsel against Jesus to put him to death:

2 And when they had bound him, they led *him* away, and delivered him to Pontius Pilate the governor.

It should seem pretty evident, that so intent were the Chief Priests and Elders, headed by *Annas* and *Caiaphas*, to destroy CHRIST, that they sat up all night in council: for *Luke* saith, *that as soon as it was day*, they were again assembled for this purpose. Luke xxii. 66. I interrupt the history for a moment, to remind the Reader, what a sweet observation the LORD JESUS made upon this eagerness of his enemies to kill him, when in answer to what Pilate said of his authority: *speakest thou not to me, said the poor proud worm, knowest thou not that I have power to crucify thee, and have power to release thee ?* JESUS *answered: thou couldst have no power at all against me, except it were given thee from above.* John xix. 10, 11. Oh! how truly blessed is it always to keep in view JEHOVAH's hand, and ordi- nation in the wonders of redemption! Blessedly also to this purport, is the word of the LORD's servants after attending to those of the Master. For in that prayer offered up by the whole college of Apostles, soon after the day of Pentecost, and which was answered by the LORD, *in the place being shaken where they were assembled;* we find those words, in making application of the second Psalm : *Why did the heathen rage, and the people imagine vain things ? The kings of the earth stood up, and the rulers were gathered against the* LORD *and against his* CHRIST. *For of a truth against thy holy child* JESUS *both Herod, and Pontius Pilate, with the Gentiles, and the people of Israel, were gathered together.* But then it is added; *For to do whatsoever thy hand, and thy counsel determined before to be done.* Acts iv. 25—28.

3 ¶ Then Judas, which had betrayed him, when he saw that he was condemned, repented himself, and brought again the thirty pieces of silver to the chief priests and elders,

4 Saying, I have sinned, in that I have betrayed the innocent blood. And they said, What *is that* to us? see thou *to that.*

5 And he cast down the pieces of silver in the temple, and departed, and went and hanged him- self.

6 And the chief priests took the silver pieces, and said, It is not lawful for to put them into the treasury, because it is the price of blood.

7 And they took counsel, and bought with them the potter's field, to bury strangers in.

8 Wherefore that field was called, The field of blood, unto this day.

9 Then was fulfilled that which was spoken by Jeremy the prophet, saying, And they took the thirty pieces of silver, the price of him that was valued, whom they of the children of Israel did value;

10 And gave them for the potter's field, as the Lord appointed me.

The awful termination of the life of the traitor, is very properly in- troduced here, as if to shew, that before the dreadful deed which was to follow his perfidy, in the death of his Master, had taken place; his own death, and that of the most horrible kind, in self-murder, at which, universally considered, nature, uninfluenced by the devil, must always shrink, should be accomplished. And as if abhorred, both of GOD and man; when having hanged himself, his very body shall have another mark of infamy, and his bowels shall gush out. Acts i. 18. I refer the Reader to the " Poor Man's Concordance," respecting the field bought with the traitor's money. See *Aceldama.* And the *repenting himself*, as it was very properly named, is proper to notice, for there was no act of GOD's grace in it but simply an horror of soul, in the consciousness of the dreadful deed he had committed; an agony of mind, which from the fearful expectation of misery for ever, compelled him to leap at once into hell, unable to bear the stings of a conscience worse than hell itself? The mistake as some have supposed, in applying to the Prophet *Jeremiah* what was delivered by *Zechariah* concerning the thirty pieces of silver, is easily rectified, by only supposing, what is most likely to have been the case, that *Zechariah's* prophecy on this subject, was gathered from some sermon of *Jeremiah;* or that, as hath been said, the four last Chapters of *Zechariah* had been written before *Jeremiah.* But in either case it doth not lessen the authority of the words themselves, or make the least alteration in their importance.

11 And Jesus stood before the governor: and the governor asked him, saying, Art thou the King of the Jews? And Jesus said unto him, Thou sayest.

12 And when he was accused of the chief priests and elders, he answered nothing.

13 Then said Pilate unto him, Hearest thou not how many things they witness against thee?

14 And he answered him to never a word; insomuch that the governor marvelled greatly.

15 Now at *that* feast the governor was wont to release unto the people a prisoner whom they would.

16 And they had then a notable prisoner, called Barabbas.

17 Therefore when they were gathered together, Pilate said unto them, Whom will ye that I release unto you? Barabbas, or Jesus which is called Christ?

18 For he knew that for envy they had delivered him.

19 When he was set down on the judgment seat, his wife sent unto him, saying, Have thou nothing to do with that just man : for I have suffered many things this day in a dream because of him.

20 But the chief priests and elders persuaded the multitude that they should ask Barabbas, and destroy Jesus.

21 The governor answered and said unto them, Whether of the twain will ye that I release unto you ? They said Barabbas.

22 Pilate saith unto them, What shall I do then with Jesus which is called Christ ? *They* all say unto him, Let him be crucified.

23 And the governor said, Why, what evil hath he done ? but they cried out the more, saying, Let him be crucified.

24 When Pilate saw that he could prevail nothing, but *that* rather a tumult was made, he took water, and washed *his* hands before the multitude, saying, I am innocent of the blood of this just person : see ye *to it.*

25 Then answered all the people, and said, His blood *be* on us, and on our children.

26 Then released he Barabbas unto them, and when he had scourged Jesus, he delivered *him* to be crucified.

We here enter upon the wonderful scene of CHRIST's trial. And here stands the LORD of life and glory, the judge both of quick and dead, before the unjust judge Pilate, *to witness a good confession.* 1 Timothy vi. 13. Every incident is of the highest moment to be regarded, and may the LORD, the HOLY GHOST, open to both Writer and Reader, the marvellous things which the Evangelist hath here recorded.

The court before which JESUS had stood the night before, was, or should have been, the *Sanhedrim,* that is, Seventy Elders of Israel; men in whom the spirit of GOD was, for so was the original appointment of this court. See Numb. xi. 16, 17. But in the time when JESUS stood before it, it appears that this court, was composed of Scribes and Pharisees, whom our LORD (who knew the heart of men) declared to be hypocrites. At the head of this council now presided as High Priest, *Caiaphas*. A man who had so little of the fear of GOD before his eyes, that in order to curry favor with the *Romans*, to whom *Judæa* was at this time under tribute, he very freely gave counsel, that it was expedient that one man should die for the people : lest the *Romans* should come and take away both the place and nation. So that this time-serving man, made no scruple to say, that the life of any individual was of no consequence, if by the sacrifice, the peace of the Romans could be obtained ! And though we perfectly well know, that it was GOD the HOLY GHOST prompted this High Priest, as High Priest, to utter these words in a way of prophecy, and in a very different sense from what the unfeeling speaker meant (and a most blessed prophecy it became, for the joy and comfort of the Church in all ages) ; yet they serve to shew at once the awfulness of his character. See John xi. 47—53. compared with Gen. xlix. 10.

But the power of the *Sanhedrim* was now, and for a considerable time before had been, abridged, *(Josephus*, the Jewish historian, saith, that *Herod* in the beginning of his reign had taken it away,) they were obliged to have recourse to the judgment seat of *Pilate*, for sentence of death upon the LORD JESUS; for as they told *Pilate*, *it was not lawful for them to put any man to death*. John xviii. 31. *Pilate's* conscience, as we perceive in the account here given by the Evangelist, was dreadfully alarmed, at this business. His wife also sent to tell him of her alarms. *Luke* in his relation of this history saith, that, in order to get rid of it, he sent CHRIST to *Herod*. Luke xxiii. 6, 7. And when the LORD was brought back to him again, *Pilate* tried and tampered with the Chief Priests and Elders all he could, to gain their favor, and yet be spared from the murder of CHRIST. And when nothing would do, but he must consent to the deed; with all the marks of horror, unable to conceal what passed within, he took water to wash his hands, as if to shew that he bore no part in the cruel transaction: and in the very moment he passed sentence of death on JESUS, proclaimed his innocence. Was there ever an instance in history of such conduct ?

It is time, however, to leave the unjust judge, and the awful *Sanhedrim* to themselves. Our meditation should be wholly directed to the LORD, in those solemn seasons here recorded. For in the history of JESUS, in every minute transaction of his life and death, for the salvation of his people, there is enough to employ our thoughts until we behold him coming in the clouds to judgment. Rev. i. 7. But there is one thought which ariseth out of what is here said by the people, and which is so intimately connected with the view of JESUS, that I would beg the Reader's patience, while I detain him for offering it. When Pilate said, *I am innocent of the blood of this just person, see ye to it : Then answered all the people and said : His blood be upon us and on our children.* They said it, no doubt, in a way of defiance : but like the speech of *Caiaphas*, which the LORD over-ruled to a very different purpose; did not the LORD, here also, answer it in mercy ? Are we not told that after the descent of the HOLY GHOST, on the day of *Pentecost*, when *Peter* charged the men of *Israel* with having by wicked hands, crucified and slain him, whom GOD had made both LORD and CHRIST; they were pricked in the heart, and said unto *Peter* and unto the rest of the Apostles : *men and brethren what shall we do ?* And do we not read, that a saving work of grace immediately passed upon some of them. And was not then the blood of CHRIST, though in a very different sense from what they meant, truly upon them? Yea, was not the very first prayer of JESUS on the cross to this purpose, when he said, *Father! forgive them, for they know not what they do?* And thus between the intercession of CHRIST, and the gifts of GOD the HOLY GHOST, there is a beautiful and gracious correspondence. Reader! do not overlook these things. Even the Jerusalem sinners, who embrued their hands in the blood of CHRIST are made partakers in the blessedness of salvation in his blood. What a thought to encourage every poor conscious sinner. See those scriptures: John vi. 37—64. Acts ii. 22 to the end.

But while we look at the bright side of this cloud, it is proper to meditate a moment on the reverse. Is not the Jewish nation even at this hour, as a nation reeking under the awful imprecation: *His blood be on us and on our children?* LORD I would say! Look upon thine antient people the Jews, and in mercy hasten that long promised day, when *the Deliverer shall arise out of Zion to turn away ungodliness from Jacob.* Romans xi. 26.

We ought not to overlook the patience and silence of JESUS, under the various provocations shewn to his sacred person, during the process of this part of the trial we have read. In the after circumstances of the LORD's sufferings, to which these were but the prelude, much shall we have to observe on this account, but for the present, it should not be passed by unnoticed, how the Lamb of GOD stood surrounded by those wolves of the night, waiting to suck his blood; and yet stood silent and answered nothing. It was predicted of him, that *he was oppressed and he was afflicted; yet he opened not his mouth: he was brought as a lamb to the slaughter, and as a sheep before her shearers is dumb, so he opened not his mouth.* And what a correspondence between the prediction and the event? Isaiah liii. 7.

But let us prosecute the solemn account. The cloud becomes more and more gloomy. When *Pilate* had scourged JESUS, he delivered him to be crucified.

27 Then the soldiers of the governor took Jesus into the common hall, and gathered unto him the whole band *of soldiers.*

28 And they stripped him, and put on him a scarlet robe.

29 And when they had platted a crown of thorns, they put *it* upon his head, and a reed in his right hand: and they bowed the knee before him, and mocked him, saying, Hail, king of the Jews!

30 And they spit upon him, and took the reed, and smote him on the head.

31 ¶ And after that they had mocked him, they took the robe off from him, and put his own raiment on him, and led him away to crucify *him.*

The indignities and cruelties shewn the person of our LORD, as the prelude to his crucifixion, formed no small part in the portion of sorrow; and we are too much interested in the whole, to pass the smallest circumstance by. For besides attending to those things in the bodily and soul anguish of the LORD JESUS; our own personal interest in them demands our attention.

Pilate, before he delivered the sacred person of JESUS to the Roman soldiers, scourged JESUS himself, or caused him to be scourged. And after this, as John relates, the soldiers scourged him, as was the custom of the *Romans*. John xix. 3. But after this scourging, they stripped him of his raiment, and put on him a scarlet robe; thus adding mockery to pain. And had the crown they put upon his head, been merely designed for laughter, they would not have chosen thorns, which, when driven into his flesh, must have occasioned exquisite suffering. Their spitting on him was intended to manifest the highest indignation and contempt. Among the Jews it was the greatest indignity imaginable. If a father spit in his daughter's face, so filthy was she considered thereby, that like the leper, the law enjoined the being shut out of the camp seven days. Numb. xii. 14.

Reader! let us for a moment pause over this awful scene, and behold the expediency and needs be of the whole. The Prophet had said, that it is *with his stripes we are healed.* Isaiah liii. 5. And hence JESUS must be scourged. The LORD himself had said by the spirit of prophecy, that he *gave his back to the smiters, and his cheeks to them that plucked off the hair:* and that *he hid not his face from shame and spitting.* Isaiah l. 6. And here we behold the accomplishment most compleatly. I pray the Reader to attend to what the LORD JESUS said by the spirit of prophecy concerning those things, and mark the sorrow of his soul. Psm. xxii. and lxix.

32 And as they came out, they found a man of Cyrene, Simon by name: him they compelled to bear his cross.

33 And when they were come unto a place called Golgotha, that is to say, A place of a skull,

34 They gave him vinegar to drink mingled with gall: and when he had tasted *thereof*, he would not drink.

35 And they crucified him, and parted his garments, casting lots: that it might be fulfilled which was spoken by the prophet, They parted my garments among them, and upon my vesture did they cast lots.

36 And sitting down they watched him there;

37 And set up over his head his accusation written, THIS IS JESUS THE KING OF THE JEWS.

38 Then were there two thieves crucified with him, one on the right hand, and another on the left.

39 And they that passed by reviled him, wagging their heads.

40 And saying, Thou that destroyest the temple, and buildest *it* in three days, save thyself. If thou be the Son of God, come down from the cross.

41 Likewise also the chief priests mocking *him,* with the scribes and elders, said,

42 He saved others ; himself he cannot save. If he be the King of Israel, let him now come down from the cross, and we will believe him.

43 He trusted in God; let him deliver him now, if he will have him : for he said, I am the Son of God.

44 The thieves also, which were crucified with him, cast the same in his teeth.

45 Now from the sixth hour there was darkness over all the land unto the ninth hour.

46 And about the ninth hour Jesus cried with a loud voice, saying, Eli, Eli, lama sabachthani? that is to say, My God, my God, why hast thou forsaken me ?

47 Some of them that stood there, when they heard *that,* said, This *man* calleth for Elias.

48 And straightway one of them ran, and took a spunge, and filled *it* with vinegar, and put *it* on a reed, and gave him to drink.

49 The rest said, Let be, let us see whether Elias will come to save him.

Let us follow JESUS to the cross; and as JESUS *suffered without the gate, that he might sanctify the people with his own blood ; let us go forth therefore unto him without the camp, bearing his reproach.* Heb. xiii. 12, 13. The first circumstance which strikes us in the hurrying away the LORD of Life and Glory to his execution, is the taking hold of a man of *Cyrene,* which they found in the way, whom they compelled to bear his cross. *John* saith, that JESUS bearing his cross went forth. John xix. 17. And *Matthew, Mark,* and *Luke,* observe, that this man of Cyrene, *Simon* by name, they compelled to bear it.

And both accounts no doubt are correct. For Jesus fainting beneath the cross, as probably he might, could go no further: and therefore this stranger is compelled to the office. There was no mercy intended to Jesus by this act; for had he died before they arrived at Calvary, as through suffering they feared he might, their triumph in his crucifixion would have been lost.

The views of the cross, in every direction and in every way, are too many to compress within a little compass: and as all the Evangelists call us to take our stand at the foot of the cross, and there *behold the Lamb of God taking away the sin of the world;* we shall, again and again, find occasion to meditate upon the endless subject. I shall for the present, therefore, request the Reader to take into his observation some of the first and most obvious sights which present themselves to our mediation of Christ crucified, which, while to the Jews it is *a stumbling block, and to the Gentiles foolishness; it is to them which are called both Jews and Greeks,* Christ *the power of* God, *and the wisdom of* God. 1 Cor. i. 23, 24.

And, *First:* it is very plain that the death of the cross was a *shameful* death. The malefactors were naked, who suffered this death. None but slaves could suffer it. No *Roman* was allowed by the laws to fall under it, be his crime what it might. Hence *Paul* speaking of it saith, *He humbled himself, and became obedient unto death, even the death of the cross.* Philip. ii. 8. But as Adam had made himself naked by sin, so Christ, in removing the curse, condescends to this shame, and *to do away sin by the sacrifice of himself.* Heb. ix. 26.

Secondly. The place where this was done, at *Golgotha,* a place of the unburied sculls of criminals. As if to intimate the very remains of those who died, or rather were put to death, in a spot of such infamy, their carcases might be exposed as dung upon the earth, abhorred both of God and men. Hence the Prophet speaking of one cursed of God, said concerning him, that they should not *lament for him, saying, Ah! Lord: or ah! his glory: but he should be buried with the burial of an ass, drawn and cast forth beyond the gates of Jerusalem.* Jerem. xxii. 18, 19. When Jesus therefore came to redeem from the curse of the law, being made a curse for us; he put himself in every situation into which our nature must everlastingly have fallen, but for his interposition : and as the law declared every one cursed which hanged on a tree, Jesus will take that curse to redeem his people from it. But as the prophecies concerning Christ declared by a strange and seeming contradiction, that though he was *cut off out of the land of the living* as a malefactor, and for *the transgression of the people should be stricken;* yet at the same time he should make *his grave with the wicked, and with the rich in his death:* the Lord over-ruled those wonderful contrarieties, that though Christ was crucified at *Golgotha,* he should be buried in a *garden,* yea, and in a new sepulchre, wherein *never man had lain.* See Gal. iii. 13. Isaiah liii. 8, 9. Luke xxiii. 50—53. See *Golgotha,* Poor Man's Concordance.

Thirdly. The infamy attending the crucifixion of Christ was increased, in that he was crucified between two thieves; yea, he himself, put in the middle of them, as if the most worthless of the three: thus fulfilling the prophecy of *being numbered with the transgressors.* Isaiah liii. 12. All that took place in the great events of Christ's death, was to fulfil the types and prophecies of him; and therefore this among the many, became most important to be attended to; and yet, but for the LORD's watching over it, nothing seemed more unlikely to have been accomplished.

Fourthly. The death of the cross was of all deaths the most painful. It was slow and lingering, violent and universally excruciating to the whole body. In the method used, the victim was placed upon the cross while on the ground, and the hands and feet stretched out as far as they might be made to extend, and nailed through the nervous parts to the timber. Then the cross with the wretched victim fastened to it, was raised up in an erect posture, and fixed into a hole prepared for the foot of it in the earth, which of consequence by the sudden jirk given to it could not fail to occasion the most dreadful pains. In this posture the unhappy sufferer remained suspended, the arms keeping up the whole weight of the body, until relieved by death. Sometimes, as in the case of the two thieves crucified with CHRIST, whether to aggravate their sufferings, or to put them the sooner out of misery, the soldiers brake their bones with blows. But the earlier death of JESUS prevented this last act of the *Roman* soldiers, we are told; for *they brake not his legs: but one of them with a spear pierced his side, and forthwith came there out blood and water.* Hereby leading to a double prophecy: *a bone of him shall not be broken.* And again another scripture saith: *they shall look on him whom they pierced.* Exod. xii. 46. Zech. xii. 10. John xix. 33—37.

And here let us pause over the solemn subject; and again look up by faith, and *behold the Lamb of* GOD *which taketh away the sin of the world!* Methinks we may, as we look up and behold that wonderous sight, contemplate JESUS as thus with arms extended, inviting his redeemed to come to him, as his arms are stretched forth to embrace them. And while his arms are thus open to receive, his feet are waiting for their coming. And with his head reclining, he looks down with his eyes of love, as welcoming their approach. And Reader! what a thought is it for every true believer in CHRIST to cherish, and never to lose sight of: JESUS in all this, hung on the cross not as a private person, but as the public head of his body the Church. For as certain as that you and I, were both in the loins of Adam, when he transgressed in the garden, and were alike implicated in his guilt and punishment; so equally are all the seed of CHRIST crucified with CHRIST, and interested in his salvation. For so the charter both of justice and of grace runs: *In the* LORD *shall all the seed of Israel be justified and shall glory.* Isaiah xlv. 25. For the further contemplation of the many wonderful events connected with the subject of CHRIST crucified, I refer the Reader to the other Evangelists. Mark xv. Luke xxiii. John xix.

50 Jesus, when he had cried again with a loud voice, yielded up the ghost.

51 And, behold, the veil of the temple was rent in twain from the top to the bottom; and the earth did quake, and the rocks rent;

52 And the graves were opened; and many bodies of the saints which slept arose,

53 And came out of the graves after his resurrection, and went into the holy city, and appeared unto many.

54 Now when the centurion, and they that were with him, watching Jesus, saw the earthquake, and those things that were done, they feared greatly, saying, Truly this was the son of God.

55 And many women were there beholding afar off, which followed Jesus from Galilee, ministering unto him :

There is somewhat very striking in this loud voice of Jesus. Not like one exhausted ; not as one dispirited ; but as a conqueror in the field of battle, retreating with his spoils. Jesus cried aloud, that all on earth, and all in heaven, and all in hell, might hear. *It is finished.* What is finished ? Redemption-work is finished. And from that moment the empire of sin, death, hell, and the grave, were vanquished. The most glorious views of that life and immortality, which Christ first brought to light by his gospel, were seen from the hill of Calvary, brighter than *Moses* saw on the heights of *Pisgah*, of the promised land. And that song was sung in heaven, which the beloved Apostle heard in vision : *thou wast slain, and hast redeemed us to* God *by thy blood.* Rev. v. 9.

The prodigies which attended this hour were all as if Christ had said, Ye are my witnesses. Significantly was the vail of the temple rent in twain, from the top to the bottom ; for the Lord Jesus had now opened a new and living way to the heaven of heavens, by his blood. Heb. ix. 6—12. Heb. x. 19—25. The earthquake and the rending of the rocks, were celebrations also of the glorious event. And the yawning of graves, and the coming forth from their tombs, the bodies of the saints, were no less memorable : what wonders were included in the redemption, by the death of Christ ! Neither was the conviction of the *Centurion* less splendid. Compelled by what he saw and felt, he acknowledged the Godhead of Christ. And compelled shall be the confession of all who deny that glorious truth now, in the day of grace, when the tremendous earthquakes and cataracts shall force the same from their pale and convulsed lips, in the great day of wrath.

56 Among which was Mary Magdalene, and Mary the mother of James and Joses, and the mother of Zebedee's children.

57 When the even was come, there came a rich man of Arimathea, named Joseph, who also himself was Jesus's disciple :

58 He went to Pilate, and begged the body of Jesus. Then Pilate commanded the body to be delivered.

59 And when Joseph had taken the body, he wrapped it in a clean linen cloth.

60 And laid it in his own new tomb, which he had hewn out in the rock: and he rolled a great stone to the door of the sepulchre, and departed.

61 And there was Mary Magdalene, and the other Mary, sitting over against the sepulchre.

The conduct and intention of those godly women; and of Joseph of Arimathea, the honorable counsellor, in embalming the body of CHRIST, will be noticed when we come to this part of the history, as related by the other Evangelists. See Mark xv. 43.

62 Now the next day, that followed the day of the preparation, the chief priests and Pharisees came together unto Pilate,

63 Saying, Sir, we remember that that deceiver said, while he was yet alive, After three days I will rise again.

64 Command therefore that the sepulchre be made sure until the third day, lest his diciples come by night, and steal him away, and say unto the people, He is risen from the dead: so the last error shall be worse than the first.

65 Pilate said unto them, Ye have a watch, go your way, make *it* as sure as ye can.

66 So they went, and made the sepulchre sure, sealing the stone, and setting a watch.

As *Matthew* is the only Evangelist, which hath noticed this conversation which took place between Pilate and the Chief Priests and Pharisees; it will be proper to propose the observations which l beg to offer upon it here. And I venture to persuade myself, that if the several circumstances, connected with the relation, are duly attended to, this plan proposed by the confederacy, of securing the body of CHRIST, tended to confirm the very truth, they meant to bring into question; and is in itself, if there were no other, a most decided testimony, in proof to the reality of the resurrection of JESUS.

For, *first:* by their application to Pilate for a watch, to guard the body of CHRIST, they prove that JESUS was truly dead, and laid in this new sepulchre. This is of no small consequence, in aid to all the other evidences we have of CHRIST's death and burial. And, *secondly;* they no less prove, by what passed, as related in the following Chapter, that the body of JESUS did not remain in the sepulchre, notwithstanding a guard of soldiers were purposely placed there to secure it. See Matt. xxviii. 11, 12, 13, 14. Here is a precious testimony, and from the mouth of CHRIST's enemies also, in confirmation of the resurrection which followed. And with respect to the story of the disciples taking away the body, it is in itself too childish and ridiculous to deserve even the relation of it. That a few poor timid disciples, who during their LORD's trial, and before any danger to themselves had even appeared, had all forsook JESUS and fled, should project such a scheme, as to come by surprize on a guard of *Roman* soldiers, who were placed at the sepulchre for no purpose but to watch the body of JESUS; and whose military discipline was the strictest in the world; and should actually take away the body, is one of the most extravagant suppositions, which ever entered the human mind. And to heighten the representation still more, it is added, that this was done while the soldiers were asleep. Soldiers and centinels asleep! And so it seems, that the evidence these soldiers gave of this transaction, of what had happened, was while they were asleep. A new way of giving testimony! Moreover, it is time to enquire, what possible motive these poor fishermen of Galilee could have to take away a dead body? Nothing can be more plain and evident than that the disciples of JESUS, at the time this transaction of CHRIST's death took place, knew not any more than their enemies, what the resurrection from the dead should mean. They had no other notions of CHRIST, notwithstanding all that JESUS had said to them, than that of a temporal prince; and when by his death, the hopes they had conceived of this kingdom were over, they would in a few days have returned to their former occupation again. In fact they did so. Besides, where could they have put the body? Was it stolen, and yet intended to be concealed? And if so what could be then accomplished by it? And can it be supposed for a moment, that when the soldiers all of them awaked from their sleep and found the body gone, and taken away by disciples; would the *Roman* soldiers, aided by the whole Jewish *Sanhedrim*, have suffered this handful of poor fishermen of *Galilee* to have remained a single hour, without giving up their plunder, and bringing them to immediate punishment.

I have not dwelt so circumstantially on this subject from any apprehension of its necessity, for my Reader's confirmation of *the faith once delivered to the saints;* but for the preciousness of any thing, and every thing connected with the resurrection of JESUS. Oh! the blessedness of knowing, and from divine teaching too; the certainty of that glorious truth, CHRIST *is risen from the dead.* And oh! when the conviction of that glorious truth is secured in the soul, by a testimony founded in the faithfulness of JEHOVAH; then in CHRIST's resurrection, the sure resurrection of his redeemed is included. *Blessed and holy is he that hath part in the first resurrection: on such the second death hath no power.* Rev. xx. 6.

REFLECTIONS.

READER! if there be an interesting moment in the life of JESUS while upon earth, to call forth the tenderest sympathy of his redeemed, in one instance more than another, surely it is here. Who indeed can, dry eyed, or without a weeping heart, follow the Redeemer from the hall of Pilate, to the Mount of Calvary, and behold the Lamb of GOD in those unequalled hours of suffering, offering his soul an offering for sin? Yea, who that from being enabled by the teaching of GOD the HOLY GHOST, to enter into the suitable apprehension of the mysterious subject, and stands convinced, that all which JESUS suffered, was the sinner's due, and must have been his sufferings to all eternity but for JESUS's interposition, can, unmoved, behold such scenes of sorrow? Reader! let you and I behold the Lamb of GOD, in this light! Let us listen to the declaration of JEHOVAH on this point, and while we look up at the cross of CHRIST, behold what but for his sufferings must have been our own; and then we shall rightly prize the voice of GOD, when he saith, speaking of CHRIST; *He was cut off out of the land of the living; for the transgression of my people was he stricken!*

Under these impressions, let us behold the LORD JESUS, the sinner's surety, 'taken from prison and from judgment. I see him bearing my sins, and my curse due to them; and hurried away to execution. An armed band seizing upon him; he is bound hand and foot as the sacrifice to the altar. The Scribes and Pharisees, like the bulls of *Bashan*, beset him around. He is made naked to his shame, publickly scourged, and his body torn with thorns, until the blood streamed in every direction. While the shouts of the unfeeling rabble, and the blows of the cruel soldiers, worry the Lamb of GOD to death. His cries on the cross loudly manifest what were the feelings of his soul; and above all, the frowns of Heaven when he hung upon the accursed tree, made the cup of trembling bitter indeed. Who that hears the words of JESUS, can enter into their full extent of sorrow. *Reproach hath broken my heart: I am full of heaviness. I looked for some to take pity, but there was none: and for comforters, but I found none!*

And must all this have been my case, had not JESUS been my surety? Yes! all, and every portion of it, and that for ever. For if the holy, and harmless, and undefiled Lamb of GOD, was made both sin and a curse for his people; certainly but for his taking both upon him, the sinner of every description must have borne the whole for himself. And when at death, the unregenerated sinner had received the awful sentence and is hurried away to punishment, that curse will light upon him, and remain upon him undone away to all eternity. Oh! the unspeakable felicity of being found in CHRIST, and having him as our surety, both now, in this day of grace, and thereafter in the day of judgment. Reader! may the LORD give us the faith of thus looking to the cross of CHRIST, and there behold JESUS as our surety! *Surely shall one say, in the* LORD *have I righteousness and strength: even to him shall men come, and all that are incensed against him shall be ashamed.*

CHAP. XXVIII.

CONTENTS.

In this close of the Gospel according to Matthew, we have the wonderful Relation of CHRIST's *Resurrection. The* LORD's *several Appearances to the Women and his Disciples:* CHRIST's *Commission to his Disciples, to preach his Gospel and baptize.*

IN the end of the sabbath, as it began to dawn toward the first *day* of the week, came Mary Magdalene, and the other Mary, to see the sepulchre.

2 And behold, there was a great earthquake: for the angel of the LORD descended from heaven, and came and rolled back the stone from the door, and sat upon it.

3 His countenance was like lightning, and his raiment white as snow:

4 And for fear of him the keepers did shake, and became as dead *men*.

5 And the angel answered and said unto the women, Fear not ye: for I know that ye seek Jesus, which was crucified.

6 He is not here: for he is risen, as he said. Come, see the place where the Lord lay.

7 And go quickly, and tell his disciples that he is risen from the dead; and behold, he goeth before you into Galilee: there shall ye see him, lo, I have told you.

8 And they departed quickly from the sepulchre with fear and great joy; and did run to bring his disciples word.

It is truly blessed to see, how every thing tended in proof to bring forward to the Church the evidences of our LORD's resurrection. The Prophets with one voice had predicted the event, which, until then, had never been heard of: and now the Evangelists come forward to attest the wonderful accomplishment. *Isaiah* had spoken of it. Isaiah xxvi. 19. *Ezekiel* had delivered by command a vision of it. Ezek. xxxvii. And *Jonah*, the LORD himself declared to be a type of it. Matt. xii. 38—40. And behold how minute the circumstances are to the confirmation of it. The morning was ushered in with the most portentous signs of it. While the godly women came at the dawn of day to visit the sepulchre, with the intention, as was the then custom, to embalm the body of our LORD: behold there was a great earthquake. An Angel from heaven came and rolled away the great stone from the door of the sepulchre. Reader! it must be the work of GOD, not simply to roll away, but to take out the stony heart from sinners, and to give an heart of flesh. And this GOD hath promised, and GOD doth perform, in the whole of his redeemed family. Ezek. xxxvi. 26. Let us pause over this account. Behold as an Angel from above came down to celebrate the triumph of the LORD JESUS, in our nature

over death and the grave; so the dead from beneath came up to
hail the glorious event, and both met together! Oh! the triumphs
of the resurrection! No wonder the Roman soldiers became as dead
men. And no wonder the lovers of JESUS should rejoice who came
to seek CHRIST. Reader! do not fail to observe, how very different
the same things operate upon different minds. While the graceless
tremble, the gracious will rejoice.

9 ¶ And as they went to tell his disciples, behold, Jesus met them, saying, All hail, and they
came, and held him by the feet, and worshipped
him.

10 Then said Jesus unto them, Be not afraid:
go, tell my brethren, that they go into Galilee,
and there shall they see me.

Oh! what a joyful meeting was here. And is it not so frequently
in life? Doth not JESUS meet and bless his people, even when at times
he is least expected? Oh! did I but always keep in remembrance
how near JESUS is, and looking on; what blessed enjoyments I should
have which are now overlooked and forgotten, by my poor forgetful
heart.

I must not omit calling the Reader's attention, to that gracious trait
of character in our LORD, when sending the women to his disciples
that they might inform them of the great event; he calls them *brethren.* One of the sacred Writers saith, that JESUS is not *ashamed to
call them brethren.* Heb. ii. 11. And what endears it more particularly at this time was, that now he was about to enter into his glory.
So that, if a child of GOD, any poor afflicted one of the LORD's family
was tempted by the enemy, or by the corruptions and unbelief of
his own heart, to question whether any change towards his people here
below, had taken place in the heart of JESUS, after he arose from the
dead; this silenceth at once every fear. For the very first message
he sent to his disciples after his resurrection was, *Go, tell my brethren.* And, to manifest the nearness and dearness of affection, into
which JESUS had brought his whole Church, both to himself and
Father, he said to Mary; *Go to my brethren, and say unto them, I
ascend unto my Father and your father; and to my* GOD *and your*
GOD. John xx. 17. Oh! what a lovely view of our all-lovely and
all-loving JESUS!

11 Now when they were going, behold, some
of the watch came into the city, and shewed unto
the chief priests all the things that were done.

12 And when they were assembled with the
elders, and had taken counsel, they gave large
money unto the soldiers,

13 Saying, Say ye, His disciples came by night,
and stole him *away* while we slept.

14 And if this come to the governor's ears, we will persuade him, and secure you.

15 So they took the money, and did as they were taught; and this saying is commonly reported among the Jews until this day.

I refer the Reader to what was observed in the preceding Chapter, on the subject of those verses. See 62 to the end.

16 ¶ Then the eleven disciples went away into Galilee, into a mountain where Jesus had appointed them.

17 And when they saw him, they worshipped him : but some doubted.

The only circumstance here of note to be attended to is, what is said that *some doubted.* What some? We read of no more but the *eleven* disciples being present, and how many can be supposed to be included in the phrase of *some* doubting? And what is to be understood by the *doubting* of any? Not surely that CHRIST was risen from the dead. For this interview at the mountain JESUS had appointed them, must have been some days after the day of our LORD's resurrection: during which time they had all seen CHRIST and all had had testimonies upon testimonies of the certainty of it. The unbelief of *Thomas* had been removed before this, and which was eight days, or rather the eighth day, from the day of CHRIST's resurrection. John xx. 26. The *doubting* here spoken of, therefore can mean no more, than that notwithstanding this meeting in *Galilee* was by the LORD's own appointment, (see Mark xiv. 28. and Mark xvi. 7.) and the whole *eleven* had seen CHRIST before (John xx. 26.); yet, now again, some of them for the moment doubted the reality of what they saw, overcome with holy joy and surprize, and supposing, as upon the former occasion, that *they had seen a spirit when they cried out for fear,* Luke xxiv. 37. This must be the meaning of the phrase. They beheld the LORD JESUS with the rest; and they had before received ample proof of his resurrection from the dead; but when JESUS appeared and the greater part immediately worshipped him with divine adoration, some were so struck with consternation as to appear like men in a state of suspense.

18 And Jesus came, and spake unto them, saying, All power is given unto me in heaven and in earth.

19 ¶ Go ye therefore and teach all nations, baptizing them, in the name of the Father, and of the Son, and of the Holy Ghost;

20 Teaching them to observe all things, whatsoever I have commanded you, and lo, I am

with you alway *even* unto the end of the world. Amen.

How truly gracious were the actions and words of JESUS, both to the strong and weak in faith, to confirm the one, and to remove all fears from the other! *All power is given unto me in heaven and in earth.* All power, as the supreme, universal, and eternal monarch of heaven and of earth. And this JESUS, as the SON of GOD, from his own essential nature and GODHEAD, possessed in common with the FATHER and HOLY GHOST from all eternity. But the power JESUS speaks of in this place, as *given unto him*, is as Mediator, GOD-Man, the Head of his body the Church: that *he should give*, as he elsewhere said, *eternal life to as many as were given him.* John xvii. 2.

And hence he now issues his commission as the glorious Head of his body the Church, and bids them go forth to teach and baptize. And, as if to impress his whole Church, with the glorious truth that salvation is the joint gift, and flowing from the joint love and mercy, of the three Almighty persons in the GODHEAD, which are one; JESUS enjoins the baptism of his people in their joint name, and as dedicated to their joint service, love, adoration, and praise. *And lo!* saith JESUS, as finally closing his commission with an assurance of his unceasing and everlasting presence; *lo! I am with you alway even unto the end of the world.* Which is not meant to say that the LORD's presence was to be with the disciples of JESUS merely to the end of their ministry, or their successors in his service; but for ever in the eternal world; here in grace and hereafter in glory. His perpetual presence securing their persons, defending their cause, rendering the whole of their labors effectual here upon earth, in bringing home his Church and people, and accomplishing the whole purposes of his salvation, in all the individual instances of it, for whom the whole was ordained in the ancient settlements of eternity, and bringing them all safe home to the everlasting abodes of glory.

And by way of seal to the truth, one of the names of CHRIST is added, Amen. *All the promises in him are yea, and in him Amen. He is the Amen: the faithful and true witness.* And this is the security. *That he who blesseth himself in the earth, shall bless himself in the Amen; the* GOD *of truth, and he that sweareth in the earth shall swear by the Amen, the* GOD *of truth.* See 2 Corinth. i. 20. Rev. iii. 14. Isaiah lxv. 16. See Poor Man's Concordance, *Amen.* •

Reader! the LORD give to you and to me grace, to mark CHRIST's name on this precious Gospel. And may the LORD himself write his Amen on our hearts. Isaiah li. 6. Rev. iii. 12, 13.

REFLECTIONS.

OH! for grace to receive and believe the record GOD hath given of his dear SON. Surely, the LORD hath furnished for his people, every evidence that GOD can give or man receive, to the truth of the resurrection of JESUS. By signs in heaven from above; and wonders in the earth beneath, was my LORD's triumph over death, hell, and the grave manifested. Every witness calls upon me, like the Angels to the women at the sepulchre; *Come! see the place where the* LORD *lay.* Yes! I would answer. My soul desires to take the wing of faith, and light down at the memorable sepulchre, and see the sacred spot! Yes! I would flee there, but not stay there, but hasten to look upwards after a risen and ascended SAVIOR! Yea! I would seek grace to pursue my researches after JESUS, until I beheld him in that bosom of JEHOVAH, where he hath lain from all eternity!

And now my honored LORD! my soul would lay low at thy footstool, and hail thee LORD of heaven and earth! Glorious, gracious, Almighty Head of thy Church and People! It is for thee to send forth thy servants, to call *thy sons from far and thy daughters from the ends of the earth!* Thy kingdom of grace shall be established until thou hast brought home all thy ransomed to thy kingdom of glory. Not one shall be left behind: but shall be brought under the baptisms of thy SPIRIT to the joint praise and honor of the holy Three in One, FATHER, SON, and HOLY GHOST. LORD! hasten thy gracious purposes; and confirm the sacred promises of thy will.

Farewel *Matthew,* faithful recorder of my LORD's history! Thanks to GOD the HOLY GHOST, for thy services in his Church in those written memorials of the conception, incarnation, birth, baptism, fastings, temptations, ministry, miracles, parables, prophecies, agonies, conflicts, sufferings, death, resurrection, and return to glory, of our LORD JESUS CHRIST! Blessed be my GOD and SAVIOR, in calling thee from the receipt of custom to be an Evangelist! Oh! may the ministry of thy word be made blessed to my soul, and to the souls of thousands. And then as thou broughtest home the LORD JESUS to thine house, and then madest him a feast with publicans and sinners; so ere long JESUS will take thee and me, and all his redeemed home, to *the marriage supper of the Lamb in heaven;* and feast our ravished souls, with the enjoyment of himself; and in him and through him, the whole persons of the GODHEAD in one unceasing banquet of holy joy for evermore. Amen and Amen.

THE GOSPEL ACCORDING TO

ST. MARK.

GENERAL OBSERVATIONS ON THE GOSPEL ACCORDING TO ST. MARK.

WE would enter upon this blessed Gospel, written by *Mark,* as we did that of *Matthew,* both, evidently, having been indicated by the Spirit of the living GOD, and with the same earnest waitings upon GOD the HOLY GHOST, to make it blessed, both to the Writer and to the Reader of this *Poor Man's Commentary.* And when we call to mind what are the blessed contents of it, every feeling of the soul

is called forth, in beholding the interesting records of the
LORD of life and glory. Oh! who can go over the wonderful
relation unmoved, which sets before us the life, ministry,
miracles, discourses, sufferings, death, resurrection, and ascension of the LORD JESUS CHRIST! Oh! LORD the Spirit,
be mercifully pleased to write the blessed contents in my
heart!

　Concerning *Mark*, the penman of this Gospel, we have
but little account. It is probable that he was one of the
seventy disciples, but it is not certain. He is spoken of by
Paul and *Peter.* And some have thought that *Peter* was engaged with *Mark* in forming the work. But one thing is certain; the HOLY GHOST gave the record. And it will be our
mercy, if the same Almighty LORD makes it a sweet savor to
our souls, that the name of JESUS may be *as ointment poured
forth!*

CHAPTER I.

CONTENTS.

The Evangelist enters upon his records of the LORD JESUS *with an
account of* John *the Baptist. To this follow the Baptism of* CHRIST,
*his temptation, preaching, the call of his Apostles; and the performing
miracles.*

THE beginning of the gospel of Jesus Christ,
　　the Son of God;

　2 As it is written in the prophets, Behold, I
send my messenger before thy face, which shall
prepare thy way before thee.

　3 The voice of one crying in the wilderness,
Prepare ye the way of the Lord, make his paths
straight.

　4 John did baptize in the wilderness, and preach
the baptism of repentance for the remission of
sins.

　5 And there went out unto him all the land of
Judea, and they of Jerusalem, and were all baptized of him in the river of Jordan, confessing
their sins.

　6 And John was clothed with camel's hair,
and with a girdle of skin about his loins; and he
did eat locusts and wild honey;

7 And preached, saying, There cometh one mightier than I after me, the latchet of whose shoes I am not worthy to stoop down and unloose.

8 I indeed have baptized you with water: but he shall baptize you with the Holy Ghost.

9 ¶ And it came to pass in those days, that Jesus came from Nazareth of Galilee, and was baptized of John in Jordan.

10 And straightway coming up out of the water, he saw the heavens opened, and the Spirit like a dove descending upon him:

11 And there came a voice from heaven, *saying*, Thou art my beloved Son, in whom I am well pleased.

It is remarkable, that in the opening of the Gospel according to *Mark*, he passeth over the wonderful event of CHRIST's miraculous incarnation and birth. Probably the HOLY GHOST so appointed, as *Matthew* and *Luke* had been so circumstantial in the relation of the mystery of GOD *manifest in the flesh*. But the Reader will do well to turn to those scriptures, and connect them with what the Evangelist hath here related. Matt. i. ii. chapters. Luke i. and ii. John i. throughout. 1 Tim. iii. 16. When the Reader hath accomplished this service, I would refer him to the 3d chapter of *Matthew's* Gospel, with the observations of the *Poor Man's Commentary* upon it, in relation to what is here said of *John the Baptist*. And also, in what follows in that chapter, in reference to the baptism of the LORD JESUS CHRIST; both subjects being there so largely dwelt upon as to render any enlargement here unnecessary. But I beg to detain the reader one moment longer, just to observe, that both in the beginning of the Gospel of JESUS CHRIST's, and the preaching of the *Baptist* as the forerunner of the LORD JESUS, the great and leading point of all John's ministry, in holding forth JESUS, was to shew the necessity of CHRIST's baptism of his redeemed with the HOLY GHOST. Reader! do not forget, that this vast and momentous principle in the gospel of salvation, as it concerns every individual heir of CHRIST's kingdom, is, after all, the great and distinguishing feature in the child of GOD. Paul put the question to the Church at *Ephesus;* and let you and I put it closely to our own consciences in the sight of GOD: *have you received the* HOLY GHOST *since ye believed?* Acts xix. 1—6 Oh! for the precious testimony of that *spirit of judgment, and spirit of burning*, whereby every truly regenerated believer is savingly witnessed to, in his own heart and conscience, that he is *born of* GOD! Isaiah iv. 2, 3, 4. Rom. viii. 14, 15, 16. Gal. iv. 6. John i. 12.

12 ¶ And immediately the spirit driveth him into the wilderness.

13 And he was there in the wilderness forty days, tempted of Satan; and was with the wild beasts; and the angels ministered unto him.

I refer the Reader to the observations made on CHRIST's temptations in Matt. iv. 3—11. And in addition to what is there offered, I would just beg to say, that very sweet are the consolations every child of GOD may draw, and indeed ought to draw, from those exercises of JESUS, when, at any time, brought under peculiar trials of his own. If the SON of GOD, when dwelling upon earth in substance of our flesh, was with the wild beasts, as well as tempted forty days of Satan, surely none of the members of his mystical body can wonder at their habitation and their exercises. And what can console a member of CHRIST's mystical body, under the sharpest conflicts, equal to the assurance, that JESUS, in our flesh, was all this, and more; purposely that he might be the better suited to administer relief to all the trials of his people. And while as GOD, his divine nature enabled him both to know and provide a largeness equal to all that might be needed for their relief, as man, his human nature gave him a fellow-feeling, that the mercies he imparted should be so loving and similar as one man is to another. The HOLY GHOST hath said as much, and infinitely more, when by his servant we are told; *for in that he himself hath suffered being tempted, he is able to succour them that are tempted.* Heb. ii. 18.

14 ¶ Now after that John was put in prison, Jesus came into Galilee, preaching the gospel of the kingdom of God.

15 And saying, The time is fulfilled, and the kingdom of God is at hand: repent ye, and believe the gospel.

16 ¶ Now as he walked by the sea of Galilee, he saw Simon and Andrew his brother, casting a net into the sea: for they were fishers.

17 And Jesus said unto them, Come ye after me, and I will make you to become fishers of men.

18 And straightway they forsook their nets, and followed him.

19 And when he had gone a little further thence, he saw James the *son* of Zebedee, and John his brother, who also were in the ship mending their nets.

20 And straightway he called them: and they

left their father Zebedee in the ship with the hired
servants, and went after him.

21 And they went into Capernaum; and straightway on the sabbath-day he entered into the synagogue, and taught.

22 And they were astonished at his doctrine, for
he taught them as one that had authority, and not
as the scribes.

These verses are almost the same as was noticed, Matt. iv. 17—22.
It appears from both accounts, that the Lord Jesus entered upon his
preaching with only those four Apostles at the first; and there should
seem to have been some interval between their call and the others.
But what a surprising call must it have been to those men; how unlooked for; and yet how powerful: instantly to leave all their earthly
concerns and connections to follow Jesus. Reader! it is still the
same in every instance where the claims of nature would thwart the
calls of grace. Painful to flesh and blood, as numberless circumstances are sometimes found, the plucking out an eye, or cutting off
an arm, are needful to be done if they stand in the way of Christ,
See that scripture, Luke xiv. 26, 27.

23 And there was in their synagogue a man
with an unclean spirit; and he cried out,

24 Saying, Let *us* alone; what have we to do
with thee, thou Jesus of Nazareth? art thou come
to destroy us? I know thee who thou art, the
Holy One of God.

25 And Jesus rebuked him, saying, Hold thy
peace, and come out of him.

26 And when the unclean spirit had torn
him, and cried with a loud voice, he came out of
him.

27 And they were all amazed, insomuch that
they questioned among themselves, saying, What
thing is this? what new doctrine is this? for with
authority commandeth he even the unclean spirits,
and they do obey him.

28 And immediately his fame spread abroad
throughout all the region round about Galilee.

We have here the first miracle Christ manifested in the relation of
*Mark's Gospel. The Son of God was manifested that he might destroy
the works of the devil.* And here he begins to overthrow both his

person and empire. This poor man, we are told, had an *unclean spirit*. Every man, by the fall, is under the dominion of sin and Satan. The children of GOD, as well as the whole race of men in the Adam-nature, in which they are born, are equally vassals and subjects to Satan. *For of whom a man is overcome, of the same is he brought into bondage.* 2 Pet. ii. 19. Hence therefore, we have all by nature an unclean spirit. Oh! for grace to be made sensible of this! Titus iii. 3—7. The next thing we meet with in this poor man's history is, that he was in the synagogue on the sabbath-day. Reader do not fail to remark, that notwithstanding this dreadful malady, he attended the worship of GOD. It is blessed to be found waiting at ordinances, whatever state the mind is in. Who would have thought, when he went into the synagogue under such a state of captivity to Satan, that he should come out so blessedly delivered by the Almighty power of GOD. Had he not been there, humanly speaking, he would have lost this opportunity of being healed. How sweet was that scripture fulfilled in this instance. Isaiah xlix. 24—28. The loud cry from the evil spirit, which had, at that time, the mastery over him, is worthy our closest observation in confirmation of the GODHEAD of CHRIST. Reader! do not fail to remark this! While thousands, who saw JESUS daily going about the streets of Jerusalem, knew not who he was, devils were compelled to give their unwilling testimony to his person and authority, and publickly to own him as the HOLY ONE of GOD! Oh! what will modern infidels to the GODHEAD of CHRIST have to say in the great day of his power; when devils themselves confessed their knowledge of him, even in the day of his flesh! Reader! remark with me also, the great awfulness of the blinded state of man by reason of sin, that even devils are not blinded, as sinners in nature are, to the knowledge of CHRIST. But let every child of GOD who reads my *Poor Man's Commentary*, and whose eyes the LORD hath opened, take sweet comfort in this; that while devils, in *head* knowledge, exceed in nature those whom, by their temptations, they have made blind at the fall, they never can receive in *heart*-influence what poor sinners recovered by sovereign grace, attain unto, both in an apprehension of, and interest in, the person, work, and glory of the LORD JESUS CHRIST. When the Reader hath duly pondered over these precious views of the case before us, I would request him to attend to another circumstance presented to us in it, namely, the acknowledgement the evil spirit made of CHRIST's power, and the dreadful alarm expressed in the apprehension that JESUS was come (as was indeed the case) to their destruction. Let every child of GOD here learn, what frights and fears devils are in, even in the midst of their cruel tyranny over our poor nature, which Satan, the Old Serpent, ruined at the Fall. Behold! in this instance, how, at the very approach of JESUS, they tremble. Oh! what confidence ought every child of GOD to feel in the consciousness of an interest in CHRIST. *No weapon formed against them can prosper. No temptation can take them,* but under it *the* LORD *will make a way for them to escape. And the* GOD *of peace* is engaged *to bruise Satan under their feet shortly.* See Isaiah liv. 17. 1 Cor. x. 13. Rom. xvi. 20. The victory of CHRIST in dispossessing the evil spirit, the recovery of the poor man, the astonishment of the whole congregation, and the rumour of such a miracle

circulating through the neighbourhood, these would furnish large subjects for our meditation. But I must study shortness, and therefore
refer the Reader to similar records of our LORD, where the improvements may be found to the same amount. See Mark v. And I
particularly request the Reader, if he hath the little penny number
by him of my *Poor Man's Concordance,* under the article *Nazarene,*
to consult it in this place.

29 And forthwith when they were come out of
the synagogue, they entered into the house of
Simon and Andrew, with James and John.

30 But Simon's wife's mother lay sick of a fever;
and anon they tell him of her.

31 And he came and took her by the hand, and
lifted her up; and immediately the fever left her,
and she ministered unto them.

32 And at even, when the sun did set, they
brought unto him all that were diseased, and them
that were possessed with devils.

33 And all the city was gathered together at the
door.

34 And he healed many that were sick of divers
diseases, and cast out many devils; and suffered
not the devils to speak, because they knew him.

35 And in the morning, rising up a great while
before day, he went out, and departed into a solitary place, and there prayed.

36 And Simon, and they that were with him,
followed after him.

37 And when they had found him, they said
unto him, All *men* seek for thee.

38 And he said unto them, Let us go into the
next towns, that I may preach there also; for
therefore came I forth.

39 And he preached in their synagogues throughout all Galilee, and cast out devils.

I refer the Reader for a comment on this passage, to what was
said on the same, Matt. viii. 14, &c.

40 And there came a leper to him, beseeching
him, and kneeling down to him, and saying unto
him, If thou wilt, thou canst make me clean.

41 And Jesus, moved with compassion, put forth *his* hand, and touched him, and saith unto him, I will: be thou clean.

42 And as soon as he had spoken, immediately the leprosy departed from him, and he was cleansed.

43 And he straightly charged him, and forthwith sent him away;

44 And saith unto him, See thou say nothing to any man; but go thy way, shew thyself to the priest, and offer for thy cleansing those things which Moses commanded, for a testimony unto them.

45 But he went out, and began to publish *it* much, and to blaze abroad the matter, insomuch that Jesus could no more openly enter into the city, but was without in desert places: and they came to him from every quarter.

The case of this leper is so fully considered, Matt. viii. 1—4. that it were unnecessary, in this place, to add any thing upon the subject.

REFLECTIONS.

READER! let us, while opening this precious record of the beginning of the Gospel of JESUS CHRIST, the SON of GOD, look up for grace from the Spirit of GOD, that the outward ministry of the word may be accompanied with inward instructions in our souls, *to make us wise unto salvation through the faith that is in* CHRIST JESUS. May the HOLY Three, which bear record in heaven, grant to us such sweet testimonies in our hearts and consciences of *the truth as it is in* JESUS, that we may enjoy that life eternal, to know the LORD JEHOVAH, FATHER, SON, and SPIRIT, to be *the only true* GOD *and* JESUS CHRIST *whom he hath sent.* Precious beginning of the Gospel, I would say; beginning, as it did, before all worlds, when *hid in* GOD, *who created all things by* JESUS CHRIST, and now made *manifest by the preaching of the everlasting gospel, to the intent that now, unto the principalities and powers in heavenly places, might be known by the Church the manifold wisdom of* GOD!

Here LORD I behold thy herald, the *Baptist*, preparing thy way before thee! Come, LORD, and bring my soul under the baptism of thy HOLY SPIRIT. Prepare me, by His enlightnings, to stand against the temptations of the devil. Oh! for the distinguishing calls of my LORD, as to his disciples. LORD! dispossess every unclean affection from my heart; and do thou reign there, and rule there, the

LORD of life and glory ! So will my soul, by thy grace, be made clean, though, in myself, polluted as the leper; and JESUS will be my LORD and my GOD, and my portion for ever!

CHAP. II.

CONTENTS.

The HOLY GHOST *is pleased to record, in this Chapter, the cure which the* LORD JESUS *wrought on the Man sick of the Palsy ;* CHRIST'S *call of* Matthew ; *his sitting at meat with Publicans ; and his divine Discourses at the Table. The Chapter closeth with an account of his passing through the Corn-field on the Sabbath-day.*

A ND again he entered into Capernaum after *some* days; and it was noised that he was in the house.

It is very blessed to behold the earnestness of the people in following JESUS. *Luke* saith, *they pressed upon him to hear the word of* GOD. Luke v. 1. Reader! are we as earnest to follow JESUS? Are the public offices, and the gates of great men crowded with persons, and shall not you and I delight to be found waiting at the pardon office of JESUS?

2 And straightway many were gathered together, insomuch that there was no room to receive *them*, no not so much as about the door: and he preached the word unto them.

3 And they come unto him, bringing one sick of the palsy, which was borne of four.

4 And when they could not come nigh unto him for the press, they uncovered the roof where he was: and when they had broken *it* up, they let down the bed wherein the sick of the palsy lay.

5 When Jesus saw their faith, he said unto the sick of the palsy, Son, thy sins be forgiven thee.

6 But there were certain of the scribes sitting there, and reasoning in their hearts.

7 Why doth this *man* thus speak blasphemies? who can forgive sins but God only?

8 And immediately when Jesus perceived in his spirit that they so reasoned within themselves, he said unto them, Why reason ye these things in your hearts?

9 Whether is it easier to say to the sick of the palsy, *Thy* sins be forgiven thee: or to say, Arise, and take up thy bed, and walk?

10 But that ye may know that the Son of man hath power on earth to forgive sins, (he saith to the sick of the palsy,)

11 I say unto thee, Arise, and take up thy bed, and go thy way into thine house.

12 And immediately he arose, took up the bed, and went forth before them all; insomuch that they were all amazed, and glorified God, saying, We never saw it on this fashion.

I stay not to remark, what might otherwise be very profitably attended to in the several circumstances of this man's case, the disease of his body; but I have so much to say in relation to the state of his soul, and the souls of GOD's people, who are all so highly concerned in what is here said, that I fear I shall trespass, and exceed the limits I ought to observe, before that I have said all I wish to say on a subject so abundantly interesting. But otherwise, here would be ample opportunity to enlarge upon such a subject, as a misery of nature, in the painful crippled state of a poor Paralytic, and the mercy of JESUS in healing him. But it is the palsy of the soul, which this of the body became a lively emblem of, that demands our special notice; and may the LORD render our contemplation of it profitable to our hearts. Think, Reader! what a crippled, benumbed, and helpless state our whole nature is reduced to by the fall! And behold, as in the instance of this man, he had no power of himself to come to CHRIST; so neither have we. See, in proof, John vi. 44. But what a beautiful lesson is read to us in the friends of this poor creature, in the earnest-ness with which they brought him to CHRIST. No throng, no ob-structions, will they allow to stop them. Even the house-top shall be opened, but CHRIST shall have him brought before him. Oh! that the LORD's people, who know, in their own cases, the blessedness of JESUS's grace, would feel somewhat of the same earnestness for the salvation of others. Methinks I would bring to ordinances, and also in private approaches, to the mercy seat, the whole of my carnal, graceless relations; and do as they did by this man, lay them down before the presence of JESUS. More than this I am not able to do; but thus far I am encouraged to do. And that compassionate LORD, who hath healed my crippled soul, can cure theirs.

And I pray the Reader to observe, how infinitely JESUS's love out-run their desires of favour. They brought the poor man to be healed only in his *body*, whereas JESUS extended his mercy also to the cure of the *soul*. And do not overlook the gracious manner in which the lord of mercy did it. *Son* (said JESUS) *thy sins are forgiven thee.* Did not JESUS mean, by the tender appellation, that he was, indeed, one of those children which the FATHER gave him in the everlasting covenant? One of those concerning whom Jesus hath already said, he will, at the last day, when presenting his Church to himself and Father, say; *behold I and the children whom thou hast given me.* Isaiah viii. 18. Heb. ii. 13. Reader! do not forget, in this view to remark, that a Son of Jesus may be, and frequently will be, deeply afflicted in body, while blessed in soul. Sickness, and the thousand other ailments of life, are not tokens of being *out* of the covenant, but rather of being *in* it. *Whom the* Lord *loveth,* it is said, *he chasteneth, and scourgeth every Son whom he receiveth.* Heb. xii. 6—8. And what I particularly beg the Reader to remark is, the unconsciousness of this relationship, in the poor man, until Jesus told him of it. So that though one of Christ's own, a son by adoption, and given to Christ, in an everlasting covenant, yet he himself knew it not, but was crippled with disease, and borne down with affliction. Let the sons and daughters of the Lord God Almighty, who, by regeneration, know themselves to be such, by adoption and grace, think of this, as they review this man's history. *If ye endure affliction,* saith the Holy Ghost, God *dealeth with you as with Sons.* The reasoning of the Scribes and Pharisees, though resulting from malice to Christ, was founded in what is right, concerning the thing itself. None but God can forgive sins. But here Jesus manifested that he was truly God, as well as man, by exercising this divine prerogative. And in confirmation that he was God who possessed this sovereign power, he instantly wrought a miracle, in nature, to cure the body, as he had wrought a miracle of grace in pardoning the soul. Look at this, ye people of God, and rejoice. Your Jesus is God; *One with the* Father *over all,* God *blessed for ever,* Amen. Look at this, ye that deny the Godhead of my Lord, and be ashamed. Oh! that the Lord may carry conviction to the unbeliever, in such a striking testimony of Christ's eternal power and Godhead, and cause the knee of the heart to bend before Jesus, crying out with the Prophet. *Who is a* God *like unto thee, that pardoneth iniquity, transgression, and sin!* Micah vii. 18. For other observations on this miracle, See Matt. ix. 2—8.

13 And he went forth again by the sea side; and all the multitude resorted unto him, and he taught them.

14 ¶ And as he passed by, he saw Levi the *son* of Alpheus sitting at the receipt of custom, and said unto him, Follow me. And he arose and followed him.

15 And it came to pass, that, as Jesus sat at meat in his house, many publicans and sinners sat also together with Jesus and his disciples: for there were many, and they followed him.

16 And when the scribes and Pharisees saw him eat with publicans and sinners, they said unto his

disciples, How is it that he eateth and drinketh
with publicans and sinners?

17 When Jesus heard *it*, he saith unto them,
They that are whole have no need of the physician, but they that are sick : I came not to call the
righteous, but sinners to repentance.

We had the relation of the call of *Levi*, or *Matthew*, in the preceding Gospel, See Matt. ix. 9. to which I refer for the observations
also.   I only again beg the Reader to remark, the wonderful properties of distinguishing grace.   Say what men will concerning it,
the truth itself stands where it always did, and always will.   *For,*
saith the HOLY GHOST, by his servant Paul, in the case of *Jacob* and
*Esau, the children being not yet born, and neither having done any
good or evil, that the purpose of GOD, according to election, might
stand; not of works, but of him that calleth, it was said, the elder
shall serve the younger; as it is written, Jacob have I loved, but
Esau have I hated.*   Rom. ix. 11—13.   Malachi i. 2, 3.   Hence
Matthew, Mary Magdalene, the *Thief* on the cross, and multitudes
have found CHRIST who sought him not ; while *Israel hath not obtained
that which he seeketh for.*   Rom. xi. 7.   What decided testimonies to
the doctrine of distinguishing grace ?

18 And the disciples of John and of the Pharisees used to fast : and they come and say unto
him, Why do the disciples of John and of the Pharisees fast, but thy disciples fast not?

19 And Jesus said unto them, Can the children
of the bridechamber fast, while the bridegroom is
with them ? as long as they have the bridegroom
with them, they cannot fast.

20 But the days will come, when the bridegroom shall be taken away from them, and then
shall they fast in those days.

21 No man also seweth a piece of new cloth on
an old garment : else the new piece that filled it up
taketh away from the old, and the rent is made
worse.

22 And no man putteth new wine into old
bottles : else the new wine doth burst the bottles,
and the wine is spilled, and the bottles will be
marred : but new wine must be put into new
bottles.

In addition to what was offered on this scripture, Matt. ix. 14, &c.
it may be further remarked, that in cases where the outward ministry
of the word is heard and received into the old unrenewed heart of
the Adam-nature, as the fermentation of new wine will burst the old
dried skins into which it is put, so men, unrenewed by the HOLY
GHOST, will burst with hatred, both against CHRIST and his people.
Perhaps no hatred is equal to that which the carnal mind fosters
against the people of GOD. And not simply the carnal, but the professor, in whose heart no saving work of grace hath been wrought.
It is painful to flesh and blood, sometimes, to meet the malice of the
ungodly and openly avowed profane. But the persecution of professors of godliness, in the Pharisees and Self-righteous, under the
cover of sanctity, comes with a deeper malignity. The LORD JESUS
himself noticeth this in *Judas.* Psalm lv. 12, &c.

23 ¶ And it came to pass, that he went through
the corn-fields on the sabbath-day; and his disciples began, as they went, to pluck the ears of
corn.

24 And the Pharisees said unto him, Behold,
why do they on the sabbath-day that which is not
lawful?

25 And he said unto them, Have ye never read
what David did, when he had need, and was an
hungred, he, and they that were with him?

26 How he went into the house of God, in the
days of Abiathar the high priest, and did eat the
shewbread, which is not lawful to eat but for the
priests, and gave also to them which were with
him?

27 And he said unto them, The sabbath was
made for man, and not man for the sabbath:

28 Therefore the Son of man is Lord also of
the sabbath.

There is somewhat uncommonly beautiful and interesting in this
view of JESUS and his disciples passing through the corn-fields; and
the discourse which arose out of it, from the disciples plucking the ears
of corn and eating them. The allusion which JESUS makes to the
hunger of *David* and his companions, in eating the shewbread, gives
a blessed spiritual application to the subject. On the LORD's day,
and every day, when hungry souls seek for CHRIST, the true shew-
bread, and the bread of life, where, but to the house of GOD, shall
they go for this spiritual sustenance? It is now indeed the most blessed
days of our High Priest, of which those of *Abiathar* were but a shadow. And the LORD JESUS hath made all his redeemed, both kings

and priests, to the Father. So that, when our spiritual *David*, and they that are with him, go into the house of GOD, the LORD sets a feast of fat things before them, in the enjoyment of his person, blood and righteousness, and saith, *Eat, O friends! drink, yea drink abundantly, Oh beloved!* Song v. 1. And I pray the Reader to observe, what our dear LORD saith in relation to the Sabbath, of which he himself is the LORD, that it was made for man. What man? Not only as a mere rest for the whole race of men, but for the LORD's people, as a sacramental ordinance of the LORD's *rest from the works of creation.* The rest is in CHRIST. Yea CHRIST himself *is the rest wherewith he causeth the weary to rest, and this is the refreshing.* Isaiah xxviii. 12. And hence the Psalmist saith, *return to thy rest* (thy Noah, thy Ark, the type of CHRIST). Psalm cxvi. 7. And hence the HOLY GHOST declares, *there is a rest* (JESUS himself) *which remaineth for the people of* GOD. Heb. iv. 9. So that the Sabbath was made for man, the renewed man, for the special persons of those interested in the LORD of the Sabbath, and to whom He is, peculiarly and personally, both the LORD of the Sabbath, and the Sabbath itself, in whom they rest, and who is their soul-refreshing. It is precious thus to eye CHRIST as the sum and substance of all; the ordinance, the shewbread, the Sabbath, and the LORD of it; in whose house, yea in himself, it is lawful, and lawful only to his priests to eat of Him, the bread of life, and live for ever. John vi. 48—58.

REFLECTIONS.

HAIL thou glorious LORD JESUS! Thou hast indeed, fully manifested thy power on earth to forgive sins; and as in this instance of the man with the palsy, thou hast healed the body, in confirmation of having saved the soul. Speak LORD but the word to my soul also, and sure I am of salvation. And oh! thou dear LORD, hast thou not taught, by thy freeness of thy call of *Levi,* that all thy calls on sinners, are the result of thy free sovereign grace, and not their deserts? Had *Levi* done any thing to merit thy favor? Yea, had he not done every thing to merit thy displeasure? And notwithstanding all his undeservings, was he called; and JESUS found of him, who sought him not? And is not JESUS as much now, in this day of his power, as then, in the days of his flesh, passing by, in ordinances, and in providences, and calling his redeemed from this world's custom, to follow him in the regeneration? And is it not JESUS who calls, and JESUS, who by his HOLY SPIRIT inclines, the hearts of them he calls to follow, and to take JESUS home, as this poor publican did, to their hearts and to their houses; and make JESUS a feast of his own bounties of the grace, JESUS gives them? Yea, is it not the wish and desire of every poor sinner, whom the LORD *makes willing in the day of his power,* to invite all poor sinners made sensible of sin, to come and sit down with JESUS and his disciples? What, though proud, unhumbled, self-righteous Pharisees, murmur at the grace of JESUS; let those who never felt the want of redemption, proudly reject it: but let every poor broken hearted sinner rejoice, in what the SON of GOD hath said: *I came not to call the righteous, but sinners to repentance.*

And let it please thee, my gracious GOD, to bless all thou receivest with thy favor, as thou didst *Levi.* Never, never, may any poor sinner fast, while Jesus is with them, and in his fulness they have enough for the supply of all their poverty. Never take a part of Jesu's-robe of righteousness, to mend their tattered rags, but receive a whole Christ as suited for a wholly ruined sinner; and be compleatly covered wth Christ's garment of salvation. Never receive the new wine of the Gospel, into the old skin of a withered nature: but may the Lord, who sitteth on the throne, making all things new, give the new heart, and the new nature together, and make all his redeemed new creatures in Christ Jesus! And be thou, dearest Lord, both the corn and the wine, and the oil, yea, the very sabbath of all thy people, till thou shalt bring them all home, to thyself, in glory!

CHAP. III.

CONTENTS.

We have here the case of the Man with the withered hand: the Call of the Apostles: the Scribe's Blasphemy: and the Lord Jesus *speaking of his relations.*

AND he entered again into the synagogue; and there was a man there which had a withered hand.

2 And they watched him whether he would heal him on the sabbath-day; that they might accuse him.

3 And he saith unto the man which had the withered hand, Stand forth.

4 And he saith unto them, Is it lawful to do good on the sabbath days, or to do evil? to save life, or to kill? but they held their peace.

5 And when he had looked round about on them with anger, being grieved for the hardness of their hearts, he saith unto the man, Stretch forth thine hand, and he stretched *it* out: and his hand was restored whole as the other.

6 And the Pharisees went forth, and straitway took counsel with the Herodians against him how they might destroy him.

In relation to the miracle here recorded, I refer the Reader for my observations upon it, to Matt. xii. 9, &c. When the Reader hath consulted what is there said, I beg his attention to behold the conduct of the Scribes and Pharisees upon the occasion. We are told, that *they watched* JESUS; not to adore him for his grace and mercy, but that *they might accuse him.* And as soon as the LORD had manifested his tender compassion to this poor man, they went forth, and *took counsel to kill him.* Now, Reader, do not overlook these things: for very awful as they are, they become precious testimonies to *the truth as it is in* JESUS. The LORD himself hath explained the cause. For while he saith, *My sheep hear my voice; and I know them and they follow me: and I give unto them eternal life.* John x. 27, 28. he saith to those that are not his sheep: *Why do ye not understand my speech? even because ye cannot hear my word. Ye are of your father the devil, and the lusts of your father ye will do.* John viii. 43—47.

No wonder JESUS *looked round about upon them with anger.* The seed of the woman, and the children of the wicked one, can never agree. And let it be remembered, that the destruction of the enemies of CHRIST, forms a part of CHRIST's mission as much as the salvation of his chosen. The hour of decision will come, when JESUS will *gather out of his kingdom all things that offend;* and while the redeemed shall *shine forth as the sun in the kingdom of their father,* the LORD will cast them that do iniquity into *the furnace of fire, where is wailing and gnashing of teeth.* Isaiah lxiii. 4. Matt. xiii. 36—43. Matt. xxv. 31 to the end.

7 But Jesus withdrew himself with his disciples to the sea: and a great multitude from Galilee followed him, and from Judea,

8 And from Jerusalem, and from Idumea, and *from* beyond Jordan: and they about Tyre and Sidon, a great multitude, when they had heard what great things he did, came unto him.

9 And he spake to his disciples, that a small ship should wait on him, because of the multitude, lest they should throng him.

10 For he had healed many; insomuch that they pressed upon him for to touch him, as many as had plagues.

11 And unclean spirits, when they saw him, fell down before him, and cried, saying, Thou art the Son of God.

12 And he straightly charged them that they should not make him known.

I pray the Reader to remark with me, of the LORD's over-ruling the mind, even of devils, to give their testimony, however unwillingly, to the GODHEAD of CHRIST. Let the Reader notice this, and observe their behavior upon the occasion, and the words they uttered. *When they saw him they fell down before him, and cried, saying, Thou art the* Son *of* God. Did ever devils acknowledge any authority less than God? Had they considered Christ (as many who affect to call themselves Christians do) as man only; would they have fallen down before him, and acknowledged him God? Reader do not forget this. Devils confess Christ to be God; while many, who would wish to be thought Christians, but can be so only in name, and because born in a Christian country, deny his Godhead, and are therefore more ignorant than devils. Oh! the blindness of the human mind! Reader! look to that blessed Scripture, and if so be, the Lord in mercy hath given you to know Christ, there read and discover the cause. Matt. xvi. 13—17. See also John xvii. 25, 26.

13 ¶ And he goeth up into a mountain, and calleth *unto him* whom he would: and they came unto him.

14 And he ordained twelve, that they should be with him, and that he might send them forth to preach,

15 And to have power to heal sicknesses, and to cast out devils:

16 And Simon he surnamed Peter;

17 And James the *son* of Zebedee, and John the brother of James; and he surnamed them Boanerges, which is, The sons of thunder:

18 And Andrew, and Philip, and Bartholomew, and Matthew, and Thomas, and James the *son* of Alpheus, and Thaddeus, and Simon the Canaanite.

19 And Judas Iscariot, which also betrayed him: and they went into an house.

See Matt. x. 1. See also *my Poor Man's Concordance*, on the subject of the *Apostles*.

20 And the multitude cometh together again, so that they could not so much as eat bread.

21 And when his friends heard *of it*, they went out to lay hold on him: for they said, He is beside himself.

Reader! what a lovely sight it must have been, to have beheld the crowded audiences of Jesus, when on earth. But you and I, may now throng his courts every day, and all the day. And very sure we shall be of welcome. Jesus will not look upon the humblest of his redeemed, with shyness. Sweetly the Psalmist sings of this: and so may you and I. See Psm. c. 4, 5.

22 And the scribes which came down from Jerusalem said, He hath Beelzebub, and by the prince of the devils casteth he out devils.

23 And he called them *unto him*, and said unto them in parables, How can Satan cast out Satan?

24 And if a kingdom be divided against itself, that kingdom cannot stand.

25 And if a house be divided against itself, that house cannot stand.

26 And if Satan rise up against himself, and be divided, he cannot stand, but hath an end.

27 No man can enter into a strong man's house, and spoil his goods, except he will first bind the strong man; and then he will spoil his house.

See Matt. xii. 24—30.

28 Verily I say unto you, All sins shall be forgiven unto the sons of men, and blasphemies wherewith soever they shall blaspheme:

29 But he that shall blaspheme against the Holy Ghost hath never forgiveness, but is in danger of eternal damnation:

30 Because they said, He hath an unclean spirit.

I beg the Reader's most earnest attention to this scripture. And I yet more earnestly beg that God the Holy Ghost, will be both his teacher and mine. Would you wish to know, in what the particular blasphemy against the Holy Ghost consisted? it should most evidently seem to have been in ascribing the merciful works of God the Spirit, to the agency of the devil. The Scribes and Pharisees, did not deny, but that Christ had cast out devils. And they could not but know, that no power but the power of God, could accomplish such acts. And yet, in the face of this very conviction, they blasphemously ascribed the gracious deeds, which so palpably proved the finger of God, to the agency of the devil. Here was blasphemy in the extreme. And what made it wholly unpardonable was this: that as a recovery from so malicious and obdurate a state, could never be accomplished but by the Holy Ghost's awakening true repentance in the soul; and there could be no hopes of such mercy; the sin continuing unlamented, must remain for ever unpardoned: and hence, eternal damnation could not but follow. The Lord pardon me if I err, but I humbly conceive that this is the sin of blasphemy, against the Holy Ghost, which is the Son of God, whose name is

Mercy, (Luke i. 72.) declared to be without forgiveness, both *in this world, and in the world to come.* Matt. xii. 32.

But as many a child of GOD, partly from the unbelief of his own heart, and partly from the temptations of Satan, hath been much distressed on this subject, lest he should have committed this unpardonable sin: and very many of the LORD's tried ones have I seen, sharply exercised on this account, during my poor feeble ministry; I hope the Reader will indulge me, if I enlarge somewhat more particularly on the subject. Perhaps the LORD may give me grace to write, and some poor buffeted soul to read, what I shall offer, and commission it to his or her comfort, and the LORD's glory.

I begin with observing, that I humbly conceive, this blasphemy against GOD the HOLY GHOST, which the men of this generation in the days of CHRIST's flesh committed, was peculiarly and personally chargeable on *them*. Not that I would be understood as supposing, or in the least intimating as if I supposed, that the sin itself, was so peculiar to that age only, as not capable of being committed in any other. Indeed, I rather think the contrary. When we meet with men in the present day, as well as hear of numbers in the intermediate time from CHRIST's days to ours, who from the same cause as those Scribes and Pharisees, in the presumptuous reasonings of their own hearts, have dared to contemn the most sacred truths of our holy faith; I cannot hesitate to conclude, that there is the same capability of committing this unpardonable sin *now*, as much as then. But while I say this, in order to guard against all unwarrantable misapprehensions on this point, I am inclined to think, that the sin itself, is peculiar, and that men of their complexion only, are liable to fall into it. And I beg to state the grounds, on which I have been led to form this conclusion.

The LORD JESUS, hath exempted no other species of blasphemy from forgiveness. He hath mercifully said, that *all manner of sins and blasphemies shall be forgiven unto men.* Yea, as if to denote, in yet more endearing characters, the love of his heart to his people, JESUS hath added, that *whosoever speaketh a word, against the* SON *of man it shall be forgiven him.* Not, that it is to be supposed, that the LORD intended thereby to intimate in the least, as if GOD the HOLY GHOST, was greater than GOD the SON: or that blasphemy against one person in the GODHEAD, was less sinful, than against the person of another. Not so. But to shew, that multitudes of sins, and blasphemies, against his person, had been, and should be, pardoned, while this one of blasphemy against the HOLY GHOST was for ever excluded from the possibility of pardon.

And the special nature of this blasphemy, which is declared to be unpardonable, will appear in yet more striking characters, if we consider, how every other hath been pardoned, and is uniformly represented, as pardonable through the whole word of GOD. Against the person of GOD the FATHER, in how many scriptures are his people said to have blasphemed his name, and yet mercy proclaimed to them. Ezek. xx. throughout, and Ezek. xxxvi. throughout. Against the person of GOD the SON, what blasphemies were uttered by numbers, who, like *Paul*, when in ignorance, were persecutors and blasphemers, and yet whose hearts were pricked at the day of Pentecost, and obtained mercy? And no less against the person, work, and glory, of GOD the HOLY GHOST; what proofs are there of multitudes, having long opposed, and resisted, the ministry of his holy word, and slighted the means of grace, and yet, have at length, been overcome by the LORD, in the day of his power? Hence it should seem, that the blasphemy against the HOLY GHOST, to which our LORD referred, and which he declared to be unpardonable, was a blasphemy, peculiar and personal: and had a special reference, to the Scribes, and Pharisees, with whom our LORD was conversing: and indeed the words imply as much: *Because they said, he hath an unclean spirit.*

And I cannot but venture to believe, that the thing itself, receives yet a further, and more decisive conclusion, to this point, when we consider the character of those, by whom this sin was committed. The LORD JESUS calls them, *a generation of vipers,* in the parallel passage, Matthew xii. 24—34, and intimates that it is impossible *for them being evil to speak good things.* And elsewhere, the LORD expresseth it more strongly: *ye are of your father the devil, and the lusts of your father ye will do. He was a murderer from the beginning, and abode not in the truth, because there is no truth in him. When he speaketh a lie, he speaketh of his own: for he is a liar and the father of it.* John viii. 44, 45. Now from hence, the conclusion is undeniable; that the generation and seed of the serpent, are in their very nature, not only liable to this sin, but *ordained to this condemnation.* Whereas *John* was commissioned by the HOLY GHOST to tell the Church; that *Whoever is born of* GOD *doth not commit sin* (unpardonable sin); *for his seed remaineth in him, and he cannot sin, because he is born of* GOD. *In this the children of* GOD *are manifest, and the children of the devil.* 1 John iii. 9, 10.

Now after all this statement, I cannot for my own part hesitate to conclude, that the unpardonable sin, in this peculiar species of blasphemy, here spoken of against the person and glory of GOD the HOLY GHOST, consists, in ascribing to the LORD JESUS, the being under the influence of an unclean spirit, when working miracles by the spirit of GOD. And though I do not presume to speak at all decidedly upon a point of such infinite importance, but would rather humbly ask, to be informed, than determine for others, yet I would venture to believe, that none of the children of GOD are permitttted to fall into it, but are kept from it *by the power of* GOD, *through faith, unto salvation.* And in proof of it, we find those fearful, timid souls, who tremble, lest, in the days of their unregeneracy, they should have fallen into it, are the most unlikely persons in the world to have committed it. Your fears more than half testify you have not. Those Scribes and Pharisees who had committed it, were hardened in the commission of it, and neither felt, nor regarded their sin and danger. Whereas your apprehensions flow from the humblings of grace, and manifest the truth of that scripture; *He keepeth the feet of his saints.* The LORD bless, as far as his truth is in it, what is here said, to every child of GOD.

31 ¶ There came then his brethren and his mother, and standing without sent unto him, calling him.

32 And the multitude sat about him, and they

said unto him, Behold, thy mother and thy brethren without seek for thee.

33 And he answered them, saying, Who is my mother, or my brethren?

34 And he looked round about on them which sat about him, and said, Behold my mother and my brethren!

35 For whosoever shall do the will of God, the same is my brother, and my sister, and mother.

For the Comment on this passage. See Matt. xii. 46, &c.

REFLECTIONS.

PRECIOUS LORD JESUS! do thou come by thy blessed Spirit into thy Church, and among thy people, now in the day of thy power, as thou didst in the days of thy flesh, into the synagogue; and there manifest, that thou art LORD of the Sabbath, by thine acts of grace and mercy, to the souls of thy redeemed. Many a withered hand and an unawakened heart, is there, of thy people for JESUS to heal. Oh! do thou speak, in the word, and by the word; and very sure will it be at thy bidding, the withered and the halt, yea the dead in trespasses and sins will come forth to life and health, and new creatures. And oh! blessed LORD! what read we here in this chapter? Do the very devils and unclean spirits proclaim thy power and GOD-HEAD? Oh then for grace, that all thy redeemed may know thee, from the least to the greatest. And do thou, dearest, and most compassionate LORD JESUS, give thy poor, fearful, and deeply exercised trembling ones, grace to see, that thou hast undertaken to keep them, from the unpardonable sin, in their union with thyself. Thy beloved Apostle hath said, under the authority of GOD the HOLY GHOST, that *whosoever is born of* GOD, *sinneth not, but he that is begotten of* GOD *keeepth himself and that wicked one toucheth him not.* Oh! let the sweet consolation of this, be made blessed to thy people; that while the malice of hell, is breaking out, in the minds of the children of darkness; all thy dear redeemed ones may know and rejoice, in the assurance, that they are *kept by the power of* GOD *through faith unto salvation.* Oh! the precious thought! CHRIST is not ashamed to call his people brethren. And as he condescends to own his poor relations in this life; so will he own them in the world to come. Never may my soul forget those sweet words of my LORD. *Whosoever* (saith JESUS) *shall do the will of* GOD, (and this is the will and work of GOD, *to believe on him whom he hath sent,) the same is my brother, and my sister, and mother.*

CHAP. IV.

CONTENTS.

We have in this Chapter, the Parable of the Sower; of the Seed in its secret growth: and JESUS, on the Lake in a Storm.

AND he began again to teach by the sea side: and there was gathered unto him a great multitude, so that he entered into a ship, and sat in the sea; and the whole multitude was by the sea on the land.

2 And he taught them many things by parables, and said unto them in his doctrine,

3 Hearken: Behold, there went out a sower to sow:

4 And it came to pass, as he sowed, some fell by the way side, and the fowls of the air came and devoured it up.

5 And some fell on stony ground, where it had not much earth; and immediately it sprang up, because it had no depth of earth:

6 But when the sun was up, it was scorched; and because it had no root, it withered away.

7 And some fell among thorns, and the thorns grew up, and choked it, and it yielded no fruit.

8 And other fell on good ground, and did yield fruit that sprang up and increased; and brought forth some thirty, and some sixty, and some an hundred.

9 And he said unto them, He that hath ears to hear, let him hear.

10 And when he was alone, they that were about him with the twelve asked of him the parable.

11 And he said unto them, Unto you it is given to know the mystery of the kingdom of God: but unto them that are without, all *these* things are done in parables:

12 That seeing they may see, and not perceive; and hearing they may hear, and not understand; lest at any time they should be converted, and *their* sins should be forgiven them.

13 And he said unto them, Know ye not this

parable? and how then will ye know all parables?

14 The sower soweth the word.

15 And these are they by the way side; where
the word is sown: but when they have heard,
Satan cometh immediately, and taketh away the
word that was sown in their hearts.

16 And these are they likewise which are sown
on stony ground; who, when they have heard the
word, immediately receive it with gladness;

17 And have no root in themselves, and so endure but for a time: afterward when affliction or
persecution ariseth for the word's sake, immediately
they are offended.

18 And these are they which are sown among
thorns; such as hear the word,

19 And the cares of this world, and the deceitfulness of riches, and the lust of other things entering in, choke the word, and it becometh unfruitful.

20 And these are they which are sown on good
ground: such as hear the word, and receive *it*, and
bring forth fruit, some thirty fold, some sixty, and
some an hundred.

I refer the Reader to the observations made on this Parable of
the Sower, and our LORD's own explanation of it. Matt. xiii. 3—23.
Every thing in it is so plain and obvious, as opened by CHRIST himself, as to supersede the necessity of remarks, by any Commentator.
The devil, who is the prince of the power of the air, is strongly
figured by the fowls devouring the seed sown; and the way-side and
stoney-ground hearers, so strikingly represent hearts of stone, unrenewed by grace, that the persecution such sustain, from the laughter
and ridicule of the carnal, may readily be supposed to render the
word of GOD unprofitable. None can bring forth good fruit but the
good ground made so by sovereign grace.

21 And he said unto them, Is a candle brought
to be put under a bushel, or under a bed? and
not to be set on a candlestick?

22 For there is nothing hid, which shall not be
manifested; neither was any thing kept secret, but
that it should come abroad.

23 If any man have ears to hear, let him hear.

24 And he saith unto them, Take heed what ye hear: with what measure ye mete, it shall be measured to you: and unto you that hear shall more be given.

25 For he that hath, to him shall be given: and he that hath not, from him shall be taken even that which he hath.

Our Lord, according to the Eastern method of instruction, dwelt much in figures and parables. We have a cluster of them here. The Gospel is as a light not to be hidden. Even among men the small taper of the night is never put under a covering. So the Lord will manifest his truths to his people. To them there is nothing hidden; neither is there any thing in the covenant of grace necessary for them to know, but what shall be made known to them. And, therefore, if any man hath his ears spiritually opened to hear, he shall hear. But to the unawakened, every thing must appear a Parable. And, saith our Lord, even to those whose ears are spiritually opened, still it is necessary to take heed what ye hear. No doubt, alluding to what the Lord elsewhere cautioned his people against, false Christ's, and false prophets, which should come so speciously, that, *if it were possible, they would deceive even the very elect.* See Matt. xxiv. 23—26.

I do not think with *some* Commentators, that these words, *with what measure ye mete it shall be measured to you,* refer to our dealings with men in our concerns with one another: for the Lord is speaking of our *hearing the word.* Neither do I think with *others,* that it hath reference to our dealings with God. As we deal with God, so say such, will God deal with us. In answer to which I say, the Lord forbid; for it would be our ruin indeed if so! But I humbly conceive, the words which follow explain the meaning; when it is said, *And unto you that hear shall more be given:* that is, if I apprehend right, in our dealings with ourselves; if the measure we mete with, according to the measure of the gift of Christ, of grace given to us, our spiritual understandings enable us to mete it in improvement; to you, that so hear, saith Jesus, more shall be given. *For to him that hath;* that is, that hath an awakened soul, by God the Holy Spirit to measure it, *more shall be given.* His vessel, opened and enlarged by grace, shall be filled. *But to him that hath not;* that is, where there hath been no work of God wrought upon the soul, *from him shall be taken away even that which he hath;* that is, of the outward ministry of the word. I do not presume to speak decidedly on the passage. I only humbly give the above as my view of it.

26 ¶ And he said, So is the kingdom of God, as if a man should cast seed into the ground:

27 And should sleep, and rise night and day, and the seed should spring and grow up, he knoweth not how.

28 For the earth bringeth forth fruit of herself; first the blade, then the ear, after that the full corn in the ear.

29 But when the fruit is brought forth, immediately he putteth in the sickle, because the harvest is come.

I consider this Parable, though short, yet as sweet, as either of our LORD's Parables in the illustration of his grace to his people. So is the kingdom of GOD, which is known by grace here, and glory hereafter, as if a man should cast seed into the ground; and sleep and rise, night and day, while the seed springeth and groweth he knoweth not how. We cannot err in considering this seed, as the incorruptible seed, which liveth and abideth for ever: and that it is so, is evident from its growth and quality. But the man who is said to cast seed into the ground, cannot mean our LORD JESUS CHRIST, for he neither slumbereth nor sleepeth; neither can it be ever said of him, that his seed springeth, and groweth he knoweth not how. Psm. cxxi. 4. Isaiah xxvii. 2, 3. His servants are said to minister to the Churches of the Spirit. Gal. iii. 5. And of them it may be truly said, the seed groweth they know not how. And although, all faithsul dispensers of the word, do watch over the spiritual plantation, and steep the word sown both in tears and prayers; yet, from their natural infirmity, they too often sleep, though not the sleep of spiritual death! The harvest however arrives not, to their consciousness, in the fields of their labors in numberless instances, until they themselves have fallen asleep in JESUS. Many a seed time, and many a day's labor, followed up with prayer, do faithful ministers of JESUS leave behind them, which are answered, when their poor bodies are mouldering in the grave.

And the latter part of the Parable, is not less beautiful than the former. *The earth bringeth forth fruit of herself;* that is, not the unrenewed heart of man, which the earth figuratively represents; but the renewed heart, now considered, as in the kingdom of grace, which this Parable is said to represent. It bringeth forth fruit void of the husbandman's care, who sleeps night and day, while the seed is growing he knoweth not how. A most precious and blessed proof of the SPIRIT's work in the heart; and that the whole is according to that sweet scripture: *Not by might, nor by power, but by my spirit, saith the* LORD. Zech. iv. 6. And the process of the whole proves the work wholly of the same. *First the blade, then the ear; after that the full corn in the ear.* As in nature, so in grace. The child, though perfect in all its parts, hath to grow from the *babe* to the *young man,* and at length to the *father in* GOD. And when grace is ripened for glory, like the fruit ripe for harvest, JESUS takes home his redeemed to him, to his harvest in heaven. Reader! do not overlook in the beauties of the Parable, the sweet enjoyment of a personal interest in it. The seed cast in the renewed heart, made so by grace, gives the sure earnest of the harvest. Though men sleep, and know not how the advance is made, JESUS both knows, gives the needed supply, and watches over the whole plantation. To you, to me, things may at times appear, as in a wintry dispensation. But to Jesus the progress is advancing. The promise is absolute from God the Father. *I will pour my spirit upon thy seed, and my blessing upon thine offspring.* Isaiah xliv. 3. Isaiah lix. 21. And a soul renewed in Christ, must be separated from Christ, before those promises can fail. Rom. viii. 39. Blessedly, therefore, the Apostle sings, to the full assurance of faith, when he saith, *Now he that hath wrought us for the selfsame thing is* God, *who hath also given unto us the earnest of the Spirit.* 2 Cor. v. 5.

30 ¶ And he said, Whereunto shall we liken the kingdom of God? or with what comparison shall we compare it?

31 *It is* like a grain of mustard seed, which, when it is sown in the earth, is less than all the seeds that be in the earth:

32 But when it is sown, it groweth up, and becometh greater than all herbs, and shooteth out great branches; so that the fowls of the air may lodge under the shadow of it.

33 And with many such parables spake he the word unto them, as they were able to hear *it*.

34 But without a parable spake he not unto them: and when they were alone, he expounded all things to his disciples.

These verses are so many different similitudes, to illustrate the progressive work of grace in the soul. A child of God is apt to make false conclusions, in forming his view of such scriptures, by what passeth in his own experience. He feels at times such a deadness to divine things, that he is at a loss to ascertain any growth in the divine life. But the truth is, the growth he is looking for, is to be found in the reverse of what he expects to find. He supposes to find *himself* more holy: whereas, the holiness, the Holy Ghost is ripening him in, is in Christ. He doth indeed make great progress, when, from making every day more discoveries of his own unholiness, he becomes more and more longing for the holiness in Jesus. When a sense of the remains of indwelling sin, makes him more out of love with himself, and more in love with Christ. This is indeed, from small beginnings, to arise to large attainments; because, as it begins in Christ, so it ends in Christ. And Christ is the tree of life, under whose branches, his people find both a banquet and a shadow. Song ii. 3, 4.

35 And the same day, when the even was come, he saith unto them, Let us pass over unto the other side.

36 And when they had sent away the multitude,

they took him, even as he was in the ship, and there were also with him other little ships.

37 And there arose a great storm of wind, and the waves beat into the ship, so that it was now full.

38 And he was in the hinder part of the ship, asleep on a pillow, and they awake him, and say unto him, Master, carest thou not that we perish?

39 And he arose, and rebuked the wind, and said unto the sea, Peace, be still; and the wind ceased, and there was a great calm.

40 And he said unto them, Why are ye so fearful? how is it that ye have no faith?

41 And they feared exceedingly, and said one to another, What manner of man is this, that even the wind and the sea obey him?

I refer to Matt. viii. 23—27. for observations on those verses.

REFLECTIONS.

READER! let you and I pass over numberless other considerations, which arise out of this Chapter, in order to attend to what is always, and ever must be, the first and last, and comprehensive object, and subject of every Chapter; the LORD JESUS CHRIST himself, and our salvation in him. He is both the Seed and Sower; that corn of pure wheat, cast into the ground of our hearts, which soil, when renewed by grace, brings forth, in all his redeemed, sure fruit; *some thirty fold, some sixty fold, some an hundred fold.* And he it is, to sow the pure seed in his Churches. And none sown by CHRIST can fall to the ground. What though his servants, and those who minister in the word and doctrine, too often find their labors in the way-side, and in thorny ground, and stony places, unproductive; yet, wheresoever JESUS sends his word, he saith himself, *it shall not return void, but it shall prosper in the heart to which he sends it.* To thee, then, LORD! let thy people look, both for direction, where to sow the seed, and from whom alone to expect a blessing. Sent and commissioned by thy sovereign power, *in due season, they shall reap if they faint not.*

Precious LORD JESUS! however to the unawakened and unregenerated all thy truths appear as parables, do thou speak thy sweet word to all thy redeemed, as they are able to bear it. And oh! do thou make it doubly sweet and blessed, when we are alone with thee, by expounding to us all things concerning thyself. And if we are called upon to enter upon the water, or pass through the fire with JESUS; oh! let the consciousness that JESUS is with us, hush all our fears, and make us more than conquerors, through thy grace helping us. LORD! do thou speak peace to our troubled souls, as thou didst to the troubled sea, by speaking pardon to our sins. Both winds and storms, and guilt and fear, must all be still at thy command

CHAP. V.

CONTENTS.

The LORD JESUS *healeth the Man possessed with a Legion: he cures the Woman with the Bloody Issue, and raiseth the Daughter of* Jairus.

AND they came over unto the other side of the sea, into the country of the Gadarenes.

2 And when he was come out of the ship, immediately there met him out of the tombs a man with an unclean spirit,

3 Who had *his* dwelling among the tombs: and no man could bind him, no, not with chains:

4 Because that he had been often bound with fetters and chains, and the chains had been plucked asunder by him, and the fetters broken in pieces: neither could any *man* tame him.

5 And always night and day he was in the mountains, and in the tombs, crying, and cutting himself with stones.

Notice hath been already taken of the country where this event took place. Matt. viii. 28. It will be unnecessary on that part to enlarge, but rather hasten to the consideration of the interesting case here recorded. Our LORD himself by the Evangelist, hath caused the several distressing circumstances of this poor *dæmoniac* to be related so particularly, as they refer to the sufferings of his *body*, that after mediating on the awful consequences of the fall, on that ground it will be profitable to attend to the more calamitous effects wrought by it on the *soul*. And here the description falls far short, of what it really is. Every man by nature, while in an unconverted state, is under the full sway and influence of an unclean spirit, as far as relates to himself. And was it not for restraining grace, of which the sinner is wholly unconscious, what tremendous evils, in ten thousand times ten thousand instances, would take place. We are by nature, and by the conquest Satan hath made over our nature, in bondage to sin with all its dreadful consequences. The flesh with its lusts, the world with its deceits, Satan with his devices, all govern with absolute sway. And add to these, we are justly exposed to the law of GOD, which we have all broken; the justice of GOD which every moment threatens punishment, the accusations of our own conscience, the fear of death, judgment, and eternity. This is the state and condition of every son and daughter of Adam, by the fall.

Moreover, as it is said of this poor creature, he had his dwelling among the tombs; no fetters could bind him, nor any man tame him; but he was always, night and day, in solitary places, crying, and cutting himself with stones; so is it with the unawakened, unregenerate sinner. Dead sinners, dead in trespasses and sins, dwell only with sinners, dead like themselves. The law of GOD loseth all its authority upon them. They acknowledge not its power; and as the law, however strong, cannot bind them, so neither can persuasions of men, or threats of GOD, have any influence upon them; but they are night and day, hastening on their own destruction, by a course of mad conduct, inevitably leading to it, except the grace of GOD interpose. Pause Reader! over the awful picture; and as you contemplate it, say, is it now your case; or was it once so? If you are now in grace, you will know that you was once unconscious of grace. And if you are not in grace, no doubt but that you are equally unconscious, of the bondage of sin and Satan, you are now in.

6 But when he saw Jesus afar off, he ran and worshipped him,

7 And cried with a loud voice, and said, What have I to do with thee, Jesus, *thou* Son of the most high God? I adjure thee by God, that thou torment me not.

8 For he said unto him, Come out of the man, *thou* unclean spirit.

Before we prosecute this poor creature's history, I must beg the Reader to stop, and remark with me, the sovereignty of CHRIST owned by the devils themselves. Reader! it is worthy your closest observation, in how many instances, during our LORD's ministry upon earth, this was done. Mark i. 23, 24. Luke iv. 41. Mark i. 34. One might have been led to hope, that such a testimony, evidently constrained as it was by Almighty power, would have stopped the presumptuous reasoning of those, who call themselves Christians, but by a strange misnomer; and yet own not the GODHEAD of our Almighty LORD. But the cause is explained. See Isaiah vi. 9, 10. And the awful consequence in another scripture, as blended with the sin. Acts xiii. 41.

But to return to the case of this man possessed with an evil spirit. As soon as he saw JESUS afar off, *he ran and worshipped him.* What was there in the appearance of the LORD JESUS, to have induced this effect? Our LORD, to every eye of common sense, appeared only as a poor Jew, consorting with the poorest of the people. And yet this man, whom no fetters could bind, nor reasoning tame, on the first sight of him, ran and worshipped him. And observe the loud cries, and earnest supplications of the devils, to be spared from torment, while as loudly confessing CHRIST's GODHEAD and oneness with the FATHER. Reader! behold from hence with what horror devils tremble at the person of CHRIST, while bowing before him! And Reader! do observe further, how will any and every poor sinner, who hath long been led captive by Satan at his will, when he first sees CHRIST, or hears of CHRIST, and taught who CHRIST is, by the HOLY GHOST, in spite of sin, and Satan, flee to JESUS, and seek deliverance by him, from all his sorrows?

I pray the Reader not to overlook what the devil said, *What have I to do with thee* JESUS! *thou* SON *of the most high* GOD? Devils wish not to have to do with *him*; but JESUS in our nature hath much to do with *them;* for his province it is to destroy them. Indeed, *the* SON *of* GOD *was manifested to destroy the works of the devil.* 1 John iii. 8. Well might they therefore dread his sovereign presence. But before this cry for forbearance, the word of the LORD had gone forth, for the destruction of Satan's empire over this poor man. JESUS had said, *Come out of the man, thou unclean spirit.* Reader! do not overlook the LORD's mercy, and the LORD's power. Oh! that every poor sinner, whom GOD the FATHER hath given to his SON, and whose redemption CHRIST hath purchased with his blood, may be led by GOD the HOLY GHOST, as this poor captive was, to flee to JESUS, sure as he is, of a spiritual deliverance.

9 And he asked him, What *is* thy name? and he answered, saying, My name *is* Legion: for we are many.

CHRIST's question could not have been for himself, but it seems to have been intended for the information of his disciples then with him, and for all his disciples to the end of time. The enemy we have to do with is truly a *legion;* multitudes of his soldiers in the lust of our flesh, and his dominion by them over the fallen nature he hath ruined, are at his command; which like a *Roman* legion, consisting as it did in the smallest computation of at least *six thousand,* are a formidable host for keeping in captivity that nature the devil first ruined. But, Reader! think herefrom, the greatness of his power, and the greatness of his mercy, which hath subdued all, and brought his people out. Oh! the grace and sovereignty in CHRIST JESUS!

10 And he besought him much that he would not send them away out of the country.

11 Now there was there nigh unto the mountains a great herd of swine feeding.

12 And all the devils besought him, saying, Send us into the swine, that we may enter into them.

13 And forthwith Jesus gave them leave. And the unclean spirits went out, and entered into the swine: and the herd ran violently down a steep place into the sea, (they were about two thousand,) and were choked in the sea.

14 And they that fed the swine fled, and told *it*

in the city, and in the country. And they went
out to see what it was that was done.

Much hath been said by infidels, on those verses, by way of cavil ;
but it hath only terminated to their own confusion and the LORD's
glory. Many very blessed truths are taught the Church by it, and
these if they were all, are sufficient to account for the LORD's permission of the devils entring into the herd of swine. As first what a
blessed evidence it afforded of CHRIST's GODHEAD. He who had power
to dispossess devils from one part of his creation, had power no less
to permit the possession of devils in another. Reader! think of this,
and turn to those scriptures. Jerem. v. 22. Luke xii. 4, 5. Moreover, hereby the LORD confirmed the holiness of his law. The swine
was unclean by the law; and by this permission, JESUS gave testimony to it. Levit. xi. 7. No method, according to our view of
things, could be more decisive to teach this, and enforce it also. And
as the Jews were very lax in their obedience to the law, in our LORD's
days, in the keeping those animals for others, if they partook not of
their flesh themselves; by this act of JESUS the law was strikingly
revived, to shew uncleanness ; and perhaps yet more with an eye to
himself, who came to fulfil the law, and do away the whole shadow
of it by the substance, in the sacrifice of himself.

In relation to the devils being permitted to possess the swine,
this was not to gratify them; but to answer CHRIST's purpose, Satan
obtained leave to tempt *Job*. But we know the sequel. The trial
ended to Job's joy, the LORD's glory, and Satan's confusion. See
Job i. 8—12. And who shall say, what blessed consequences followed, in the after circumstances of the Church, from this transaction,
both on Jew and Gentile, when CHRIST had finished redemption-work
and was returned to glory; and GOD the HOLY GHOST came down ?
Reader! let you and I, learn not to be wise above what is written,
but in all questionable cases; I mean, such as you and I cannot fully
explain, or such as sceptics make so; let us resolve all into that soul-
satisfying scripture, which forms at once both question and answer:
Shall not the judge of all the earth do right? Gen. xviii. 25.

15 And they come to Jesus, and see him that
was possessed with the devil, and had the legion,
sitting, and clothed, and in his right mind : and
they were afraid.

16 And they that saw *it* told them how it befel
to him that was possessed with the devil, and *also*
concerning the swine.

17 And they began to pray him to depart out
of their coasts.

I stay not so much to remark the terrible consternation, which this
demonstration of CHRIST's power must have induced on all beholders.
Such; but in an infinitely greater degree, will be the display of the
LORD's sovereignty, at the last day. But I would rather call the at-

tention of the Reader to the poor man, now no longer under *dæmoniac* influence, but sitting at the feet of JESUS, clothed, and in his right mind. A beautiful representation of all the redeemed of the LORD! For Reader! what is every truly converted child of GOD upon earth; yea, we may go further, and say what is every redeemed soul now in heaven, but once such as this man was, when under the dominion of sin and Satan? And now *washed, sanctified, justified, in the name of the* LORD JESUS, *and by the Spirit of our* GOD. 1 Cor. vi. 11. They of our brethen, now in heaven, gone before to glory: and they who are redeemed from among men still upon earth, in grace, are alike sitting at the feet of JESUS; clothed with the robe of his righteousness, and wearing the garment of his salvation. Oh! the unspeakable felicity of such a recovered state!

But let not the Reader overlook the awful conduct of the *Gadarenes;* in desiring JESUS to depart out of their coast. Is it possible, that any individual, when he saw the wonderful mercy shewn to this poor creature, could have wished the Great Author of such mercy to leave them? And yet *Matthew* in his relation of this miracle saith, that the *whole city* joined in the request, that JESUS would go out of their coasts. Matt. viii. 34. As long as this poor creature was under the possession of this evil spirit, he was a terror to the whole country. But yet it seems, they preferred the devil's raging among them, to that of the LORD JESUS manifesting his grace and mercy. But Reader! while you and I pity the poor deluded *Gadarenes,* let us look around among our own countrymen, and we shall discover equally distressing sights for pity. What daily manifestations are made of our fellow-creatures, living under the same awful influence, on whom the voice of JESUS's Gospel hath no controul? Multitudes like these *Gadarenes* do in effect, if not in words, say, to JESUS, *Depart from us: for we desire not the knowledge of thy ways!* Yea, Reader! to come a little nearer home. Have not you and I, in times past, said the same? Yea, is it not so now? Are we both sitting daily at the feet of JESUS, cloathed and in our right mind? Is it the language of your heart and mine, to JESUS? Do not LORD go away, neither suffer us to depart from thee, for *thou hast the words of eternal life!* These are solemn enquiries. Reader! do not dismiss them unanswered!

18 And when he was come into the ship, he that had been possessed with the devil prayed him that he might be with him.

19 Howbeit, Jesus suffered him not, but saith unto him, Go home to thy friends, and tell them how great things the Lord hath done for thee, and hath had compassion on thee.

20 And he departed, and began to publish in Decapolis how great things Jesus had done for him: and all *men* did marvel.

There is somewhat very affecting in this request of the poor man; and our LORD's refusal of his request merits our notice. What a wonderful change, grace had wrought upon him. He who but a few minutes before, was a terror to every body, is now so heavenly composed, that he desires never to leave JESUS. And is not this the case with every child of GOD, when savingly called *from darkness to light,* *and from the power of sin and Satan to the living* GOD? Surely, having once tasted that the LORD is gracious, we cannot but long to be *absent from the body, and present with the* LORD. But yet JESUS saith, this must not immediately be. Awakened sinners are to go home to their unawakened friends, and speak forth *the praises of him who hath called them out of darkness into his marvellous light.* They are to constitute a part of the LORD's Church upon earth, until the LORD's time shall come which he hath appointed to take them home to his Church above. JESUS must have a Church upon earth, as well as in heaven, as long as the earth remains. Neither can a redeemed soul live upon earth too long, while the LORD employs him to his glory and the Church's welfare. Reader! let this serve not merely to reconcile, but to make us happy in waiting *all the days of our appointed time, until our change come.* In the mean season, doing as JESUS commanded this poor man to do, if so be, like him, the LORD hath wrought a work of grace upon our hearts; tell our friends, yea tell all around, *what great things the* LORD *hath done for us, and hath had compassion on us.*

21 ¶ And when Jesus was passed over again by ship unto the other side, much people gathered unto him: and he was nigh unto the sea.

22 And, behold, there cometh one of the rulers of the synagogue, Jairus by name; and when he saw him, he fell at his feet,

23 And besought him greatly, saying, My little daughter lieth at the point of death: *I pray thee,* come and lay thy hands on her, that she may be healed; and she shall live.

24 And Jesus went with him; and much people followed him, and thronged him.

25 And a certain woman which had an issue of blood twelve years,

26 And had suffered many things of many physicians, and had spent all that she had, and was nothing bettered, but rather grew worse,

27 When she had heard of Jesus, came in the press behind, and touched his garment.

28 For she said, If I may touch but his clothes, I shall be whole.

29 And straightway the fountain of her blood was dried up; and she felt in *her* body that she was healed of that plague.

30 And Jesus immediately knowing in himself that virtue had gone out of him, turned him about in the press, and said, Who touched my clothes?

31 And his disciples said unto him, Thou seest the multitude thronging thee, and sayest thou, Who touched me?

32 And he looked round about to see her that had done this thing.

33 But the woman fearing and trembling, knowing what was done in her, came, and fell down before him, and told him all the truth.

34 And he said unto her, Daughter, thy faith hath made thee whole: go in peace, and be whole of thy plague.

35 While he yet spake, there came from the ruler of the synagogue's *house certain* which said, Thy daughter is dead: why troublest thou the Master any further?

36 As soon as Jesus heard the word that was spoken, he saith unto the ruler of the synagogue, Be not afraid, only believe.

37 And he suffered no man to follow him, save Peter, and James, and John the brother of James.

38 And he cometh to the house of the ruler of the synagogue, and seeth the tumult, and them that wept and wailed greatly.

39 And when he was come in, he saith unto them, Why make ye this ado, and weep? the damsel is not dead, but sleepeth.

40 And they laughed him to scorn: but when he had put them all out, he taketh the father and the mother of the damsel, and them that were with him, and entereth in where the damsel was lying.

41 And he took the damsel by the hand, and said unto her, Talitha cumi; which is, being interpreted, Damsel, I say unto thee, arise.

42 And straightway the damsel arose, and walked: for she was *of the age* of twelve years, and they were astonished with a great astonishment.

43 And he charged them straitly that no man should know it; and commanded that something should be given her to eat.

Both those interesting cases have been largely considered. Matt, ix. 18—26. to which I therefore refer. See also Luke viii. 41, &c.

REFLECTIONS.

OH! to what a desperate state is our whole nature reduced by the fall! Where Satan reigns, unrestrained by grace; see my soul, see in this man, (and while beholding look up and wonder at thy mercies) to what a length the human frame is capable of going in madness, while governed by devils! And what makes the subject yet more truly awful is, the consideration, that Satan's empire over our nature is a lawful empire: for as Scripture truly saith, *of whom a man is overcome of the same is he brought into bondage.*

But oh! the mercy of that promise : *Thus saith the* LORD : *ye have sold yourselves for nought, and ye shall be redeemed without money.* Hear, my soul, hear what is said. *Shall the prey be taken from the mighty; or the lawful captive delivered?* But *thus saith the* LORD : *even the captives of the mighty shall be taken away, and the prey of the terrible delivered : for I will contend with him that contendeth with thee, and I will save thy children.* And see, as in this instance, one of CHRIST's little ones though long held captive by Satan, yet gloriously delivered by the LORD JESUS CHRIST. And where is he now, who when recovered by grace on earth, sat at the feet of JESUS; but sitting with JESUS on his throne and kingdom of glory, in heaven? Oh! my soul, go tell all thy friends of this wonder-working SAVIOR!

Behold also the power, and sovereignty, of thy LORD, over unclean spirits, and unclean beasts. See what efficacy flows from JESUS, to the touch of faith in his divine person; yea, behold, how even the dead, JESUS raiseth. Never then call in question his power over all the uncleanness of thy nature, nor his grace to answer the desire of that faith, which he himself hath created. Thy deadness, and dying frames, JESUS can take away, and his command to arise must always be attended with power. He saith to thee, my soul, as to the ruler of the synagogue; be not afraid, only believe. LORD *I believe; help thou mine unbelief.*

CHAP. VI.

CONTENTS.

The LORD JESUS *is here spoken of with contempt by his country-men. He sends forth his Disciples. Herod hears of* CHRIST, *and is alarmed.* JESUS *feeds the Multitude. He is seen walking on the Sea. He heals the Sick.*

AND he went out from thence, and came into his own country; and his disciples follow him.

2 And when the sabbath-day was come, he began to teach in the synagogue: and many hearing *him* were astonished, saying, From whence hath this *man* these things? and what wisdom *is* this which is given unto him, that even such mighty works are wrought by his hands?

3 Is not this the carpenter, the son of Mary, the brother of James, and Joses, and of Judah, and Simon? and are not his sisters here with us? And they were offended at him.

4 But Jesus said unto them, A prophet is not without honour, but in his own country, and among his own kin, and in his own house.

5 And he could there do no mighty work, save that he laid his hands upon a few sick folk, and healed *them.*

6 And he marvelled because of their unbelief. And he went round about the villages, teaching.

I detain the Reader on those verses to remark, that what became in the view of the enemies of CHRIST matter of reproach, is, to the friends and followers of the Lamb, subject of heartfelt joy. *Is not this the carpenter,* say they? Yes! say I; and blessed be my LORD, for his grace and condescension, in being so. For I would have the Reader understand, that in CHRIST becoming a curse for his redeemed, it behoved him to undergo that curse in all its branches. The tenor of the curse pronounced at the fall, ran in those words: *In the sweat of thy face shalt thou eat bread;* meaning toil and labor. Had not JESUS therefore toiled and labored for his bread, this part of the curse would not have lighted upon him, neither could he then have been said to have borne it. But by laboring with his hands for his daily bread, he literally fulfilled that part of the curse. And though he might have fed himself as he fed others, by working a miracle; yet then could he not have come up, in this point, to the object intended. So far therefore is CHRIST's labor in the employment of a

carpenter, from lessening the authority of his mission, that without
it he would not have answered the character of our Redeemer, in redeeming us from *the curse of the law being made a curse for us.*
Gal. iii. 13.

Reader! hath it pleased the LORD in his providence, to place
you in a low estate. Look to him who when on earth had not where
to lay his head; and though the LORD, Creator and proprietor of all
things, lived and toiled, for his daily bread! See observations on
Luke ii. 51, 52.

7 ¶ And he called *unto him* the twelve, and began to send them forth by two and two: and gave
them power over unclean spirits;

8 And commanded them that they should take
nothing for *their* journey, save a staff only; no
scrip, no bread, no money in *their* purse:

9 But *be* shod with sandals; and not put on two
coats.

10 And he said unto them, In what place soever
ye enter into an house, there abide till ye depart
from that place.

11 And whosoever shall not receive you, nor
hear you, when ye depart thence, shake off the
dust under your feet for a testimony against them.
Verily I say unto you, It shall be more tolerable
for Sodom and Gomorrah in the day of judgement, than for that city.

12 And they went out, and preached that men
should repent.

13 And they cast out many devils, and anointed
with oil many that were sick, and healed *them.*

We have here the confirmation of what was before noticed on
Matt. x. 1, &c. the call and commission given to the Apostles. It
were well if all, who go forth in the Apostolic office, carried with
them such credentials of their authority.

14 And king Herod heard *of him;* (for his name
was spread abroad:) and he said, That John the
Baptist was risen from the dead, and therefore
mighty works do shew forth themselves in him.

15 Others said, That it is Elias, and others said,
That it is a prophet, or as one of the prophets.

16 But when Herod heard *thereof*, he said, It is John, whom I beheaded : he is risen from the dead.

17 For Herod himself had sent forth and laid hold upon John, and bound him in prison, for Herodias' sake, his brother Philip's wife : for he had married her.

18 For John had said unto Herod, It is not lawful for thee to have thy brother's wife.

19 Therefore Herodias had a quarrel against him, and would have killed him ; but she could not :

20 For Herod feared John, knowing that he was a just man, and an holy, and observed him ; and when he heard him, he did many things, and heard him gladly.

21 And when a convenient day was come, that Herod on his birth-day made a supper to his lords, high captains, and chief *estates* of Galilee ;

22 And when the daughter of the said Herodias came in, and danced, and pleased Herod, and them that sat with him, the king said unto the damsel, Ask of me whatsoever thou wilt, and I will give *it* thee.

23 And he sware unto her, Whatsoever thou shalt ask of me, I will give *it* thee, unto the half of my kingdom.

24 And she went forth and said unto her mother, What shall I ask ? and she said, The head of John the Baptist.

25 And she came in straightway with haste unto the king, and asked, saying, I will that thou give me by and by in a charger the head of John the Baptist.

26 And the king was exceeding sorry ; *yet* for his oath's sake, and for their sakes which sat with him, he would not reject her.

27 And immediately the king sent an execu-

tioner, and commanded his head to be brought.
And he went, and beheaded him in the prison,

28 And brought his head in a charger, and gave
it to the damsel: and the damsel gave it to her
mother.

29 And when his disciples heard *of it,* they
came and took up his corps, and laid it in a tomb.

In addition to what was remarked on the parallel passage, Matt. xiv.
1, &c. to which I refer the Reader, I would beg to observe, what
an awful view is here held forth to us, of the horrors of a guilty conscience. There was not the smallest resemblance between the LORD
JESUS CHRIST, and his servant and herald, *John* the Baptist. *John*
did no miracles : and the LORD JESUS was continually manifesting
his commission in this way. *John* came in a way of austerity and
fasting; but JESUS most endearing, and as the friend of publicans and
sinners; so that nothing could be more unlike each other. But *Herod*
was too much alarmed to mark the difference. This is *John,* said
he, whom I murdered. Reader! what must the everlasting horrors,
and self-reproaches of the miserable be, when in this life only their
consciences are so haunted before the time ?

30 ¶ And the apostles gathered themselves together unto Jesus, and told him all things, both
what they had done, and what they had taught.

31 And he said unto them, Come ye yourselves
apart into a desert place, and rest a while; for
there were many coming and going, and they had
no leisure so much as to eat.

32 And they departed into a desert place by
ship privately.

33 And the people saw them departing, and
many knew him, and ran afoot thither out of all
cities, and outwent them, and came together unto
him.

34 And Jesus, when he came out, saw much
people, and was moved with compassion toward
them, because they were as sheep not having a
shepherd: and he began to teach them many
things.

35 And when the day was now far spent, his
disciples came unto him, and said, This is a desert
place, and now the time *is* far passed :

36 Send them away, that they may go into the country round about, and into the villages, and buy themselves bread : for they have nothing to eat.

37 He answered and said unto them, Give ye them to eat, and they say unto him, Shall we go and buy two hundred pennyworth of bread, and give them to eat?

38 He saith unto them, How many loaves have ye? go and see. And when they knew, they say, Five, and two fishes.

39 And he commanded them to make all sit down by companies upon the green grass.

40 And they sat down in ranks by hundreds, and by fifties.

41 And when he had taken the five loaves, and the two fishes, he looked up to heaven, and blessed, and brake the loaves, and gave *them* to his disciples to set before them; and the two fishes divided he among them all.

42 And they did all eat, and were filled.

43 And they took up twelve baskets full of the fragments, and of the fishes:

44 And they that did eat of the loaves were about five thousand men.

45 ¶ And straightway he constrained his disciples to get into the ship, and to go to the other side before unto Bethsaida, while he sent away the people.

46 And when he had sent them away, he departed into a mountain to pray.

I shall only hint at one or two improvements, as they arise from this passage before us, having already noticed some of the principal things which are found in our LORD's miracle of feeding the multitude in the wilderness, in the similar relation of it. Matt. xiv. 1, &c. And first, it will be profitable to observe, what is said here of the Apostles, whom JESUS had sent forth to preach, returning with an account of their ministry : not by way of informing CHRIST what he already knew, but by way of praising him for the success of their labors. So should all ministers of JESUS. And what can be more engaging than the view of a faithful laborer in the Gospel, who hath gone forth in the LORD's strength in the day, returning to the LORD's praise in the night, and laying both himself and labors before the LORD for a blessing?

And let not the Reader overlook, as another interesting improvement, which ariseth from what is here said of CHRIST, compassion in beholding the fainting multitude. There is somewhat particularly striking in the manner in which it is related; JESUS was *moved with compassion toward them.* Reader! I know not what your feelings are, but I must confess that I receive a more than ordinary pleasure in such views of JESUS, as represent him *touched with our feelings;* for they certainly mean the feelings of JESUS in our nature, joined with the GODHEAD. Paul calls it *the bowels* of JESUS CHRIST. Phil. i. 8. Mercies and Compassions; not only GOD-mercies, but mercies in such a way, as are the mercies of the man also; and without the SON of GOD, having taken human nature into union with the GODHEAD, as GOD alone, he could not have felt. Reader! think what a view doth this apprehension of JESUS, in his two-fold nature, open to our everlasting joy, in a thousand instances which arise?

If I venture to hint at a *third* improvement from this passage, (many more might, but for swelling the pages,) it shall be only to observe, that if from a few loaves and fishes the LORD CHRIST made such a supply for so great a multitude, and left such an overplus, think, what infinite resources are with our GOD, for every occasion, to both the spiritual, and temporal necessities of his chosen? Very blessed is the Apostle's conclusion on this point, when he saith; *But my* GOD *shall supply all your need, according to his riches in glory by* CHRIST JESUS. Philip. iv. 19. See Matt. xiv. 22, 23.

47 And when even was come, the ship was in the midst of the sea, and he alone on the land.

48 And he saw them toiling in rowing; for the wind was contrary unto them: and about the fourth watch of the night he cometh unto them, walking upon the sea, and would have passed by them.

49 But when they saw him walking upon the sea, they supposed it had been a spirit, and cried out:

50 For they all saw him, and were troubled. And immediately he talked with them, and saith unto them, Be of good cheer: it is I; be not afraid.

51 And he went up unto them into the ship; and the wind ceased: and they were sore amazed in themselves beyond measure, and wondered.

52 For they considered not *the miracle* of the loaves : for their heart was hardened.

In addition to what was observed on this display of CHRIST's power, on the parallel passage, Matt. xiv. 24, &c. I would just beg to remark, what unceasing demonstrations the LORD gave of his GODHEAD. It should seem to have been done with a view to put to the blush the Infidel of after ages, as well as to comfort, and give confidence to his poor and humble believing Ones. Did the LORD JESUS make this provision for the present day of infidelity ? (I only ask the question.) As the LORD could not but know *the perilous times which in the last days should come,* when men, calling themselves Christians, would nevertheless *deny the* LORD *which bought them, and bring upon themselves swift destruction ;* did He mercifully furnish such testimonies of his GODHEAD, in the days of his flesh, as might afford peculiar strength to the faith of his people in the day of his power ? Indeed, indeed, I cannot but think there was much of CHRIST's intention, in the numberless proofs we so continually meet with, in those records of our LORD. And, I am the more inclined to this judgment, because we are told, that the disciples then, when at the time JESUS displayed such wonderful acts, were *sore amazed, and wondered ;* their *heart,* as it is said, being *hardened :* that is, I apprehend, they did not, for surely they could not for a moment doubt CHRIST's GODHEAD ; but they stood amazed, like men overwhelmed with what they saw and heard ; not knowing, as when in the Mount of Transfiguration, what to say. See Matt. xvii. 1, &c. See also my note on Matt. xxviii. 17.

53 And when they had passed over they came into the land of Gennesaret, and drew to the shore.

54 And when they were come out of the ship, straightway they knew him.

55 And ran through that whole region round about, and began to carry about in beds those that were sick, where they heard he was.

56 And whithersoever he entered, into villages, or cities, or country, they laid the sick in the streets, and besought him that they might touch if it were but the border of his garment : and as many as touched him were made whole.

I would appeal to the common sense and history of all mankind, whether the imagination can furnish a portrait so beautiful, so affectionate, and interesting, as is here drawn of our LORD JESUS CHRIST. The Prophet, ages before had said, *behold, your* GOD *will come and save you ! Then the eyes of the blind shall be opened, and the ears of the deaf be unstopped. Then shall the lame man leap as an hart, and* the tongue of the dumb sing. Isaiah xxxv. 4, 5, 6. And here we behold GOD indeed in the person of his dear SON, surrounded by the sick and diseased of every description and character, while as many as touched him were made whole. Oh! for grace, to come to Him now by faith; for surely, none whom GOD the HOLY GHOST shall lead to JESUS, will the LORD send empty away.

REFLECTIONS.

OH! thou who was in the form of GOD, and with whom it was no robbery to be equal with GOD! give me to see the blessedness of thy humiliation, in condescending to labor for thy daily bread, in order to remove the whole curse of the fall, in becoming a curse for thy people. Do thou, dearest LORD, give grace to all thy poor and toilsome family, to learn the blessedness of being conformed to thy lovely image in all things. Let all thy sent servants learn by thy Apostles how to return to JESUS, and lay before him the account of their ministry. In the awful history of *Herod*, give all thy people grace, to know how to value a peace of mind in JESUS, which nothing of this world's greatness can procure. And while thy redeemed behold their GOD and SAVIOR, feeding the thousands to the full with a scanty provision, and healing all the diseased with a word speaking; oh! let neither poverty nor sickness induce a moment's fear in the heart of thy people. Precious LORD! do thou realize, day by day, thy gracious and refreshing presence to our wants. And oh! for grace to have such views of GOD's CHRIST, and GOD's chosen, as GOD the FATHER hath set him forth by, in the word of his grace; and then will all the blessed effects of salvation be enjoyed by his redeemed, in villages, and cities, and countries upon earth; as the redeemed now enjoy in the city of our GOD in heaven.

CHAP. VII.

CONTENTS.

The Pharisees assemble to contend with CHRIST. JESUS *reproves them. He heals a poor child, and cures one that was deaf and dumb.*

THEN came together unto him the Pharisees, and certain of the scribes, which came from Jerusalem.

2 And when they saw some of his disciples eat bread with defiled, that is to say, with unwashen, hands, they found fault.

3 For the Pharisees, and all the Jews, except they wash *their* hands oft, eat not, holding the tradition of the elders.

4 And *when they come* from the market, except

they wash, they eat not. And many other things there be, which they have received to hold, *as* the washing of cups, and pots, brazen vessels, and of tables.

5 Then the Pharisees and scribes asked him, Why walk not thy disciples according to the tradition of the elders, but eat bread with unwashen hands?

6 He answered and said unto them, Well hath Esaias prophesied of you hypocrites, as it is written, This people honoureth me with *their* lips, but their heart is far from me.

7 Howbeit in vain do they worship me, teaching *for* doctrines the commandments of men.

8 For laying aside the commandment of God, ye hold the tradition of men, *as* the washing of pots and cups: and many other such like things ye do.

9 And he said unto them, Full well ye reject the commandment of God, that ye may keep your own tradition.

10 For Moses said, Honour thy father and thy mother: and, Whoso curseth father or mother, let him die the death:

11 But ye say, If a man shall say to his father or mother, *It is* Corban, that is to say, a gift, by whatsoever thou mightest be profited by me; *he shall be free.*

12 And ye suffer him no more to do ought for his father or his mother;

13 Making the word of God of none effect through your tradition, which ye have delivered: and many such like things do ye.

It will be highly profitable to the Reader, to observe the awful character of those Scribes and Pharisees, and to attend to what the LORD hath said of them. In the midst of their hatred and malice to JESUS, who appears equal to them for professions of holiness? Washing of hands, and cups, and pots, were harmless things in themselves, if they had been led therefrom to see the necessity of washing the heart. But, in the midst of this outside godliness, JESUS, who knew their inside corruption, represents it as most awful. The LORD hath indeed traced it to its source, and shewn, that they were of that seed which could not but sin. John viii. 44. Matt. xxiii. 15. It would have been well for the peace, yet not for the exercise of the LORD's people, if the Pharisee and Scribe generation had ceased with them. But though the Church hath been disturbed in all ages with such, yet it is to the profit of the LORD's household. For when at any time the LORD JESUS, and his great salvation, are by this Pharisaical generation, slightly regarded, (as in the present day) it tends the more, under grace, to endear CHRIST to the heart.

14 ¶ And when he had called all the people *unto him,* he said unto them, Hearken unto me every one *of you,* and understand :

15 There is nothing from without a man that entering into him can defile him : but the things which come out of him, those are they that defile the man.

16 If any man have ears to hear, let him hear.

17 And when he was entered into the house from the people, his disciples asked him concerning the parable.

18 And he saith unto them, Are ye so without understanding also ? Do ye not perceive, that whatsoever thing from without entereth into the man, *it* cannot defile him ;

19 Because it entereth not into his heart, but into the belly, and goeth out into the draught, purging all meats ?

20 And he said, That which cometh out of the man, that defileth the man.

21 For from within, out of the heart of men, proceed evil thoughts, adulteries, fornications, murders,

22 Thefts, covetousness, wickedness, deceit, lasciviousness, an evil eye, blasphemy, pride, foolishness :

23 All these evil things come from within, and defile the man.

I admire this discourse of the LORD JESUS to the people. And I cannot but admire it the more, because from the distinguishing manner in which it is said *he called them*, and introduced what he said to them, in charging them to hear that there were many of them his people, in contradistinction to the Pharisees around. And I cannot from hence help requesting the Reader to remark with me, how uniformly this distinction hath been preserved in the Church of CHRIST, in reading or preaching the word, from that time to the present hour. When we see (as that we cannot but see) in every congregation, *some* receiving the word with holy joy of the HOLY GHOST, as *Paul* testified the Church of the *Thessalonians* did: whilst *others*, like those *Pharisees*, seeking only to find fault; what can be more decisive in testimony to the same. And though many, like those *Pharisees*, are, as far as outward appearances go, apparently decent and moral in their lives and conversation with men; and others, in the religion of nature, seem to act up to the principles of external godliness, as high as natural strength can reach; yea, some of them make a profession of the Gospel, and are ready to compliment CHRIST to make up their deficiency; yet, in all these there is not an atom of regenerating grace; it is the old tang of the old nature, neither are they any of them savingly acquainted with the person, work, grace, and glory, of the LORD JESUS CHRIST. If the Reader wishes to have a true scriptural account of the real saving work of GOD the HOLY GHOST upon the heart, I refer him to the picture drawn by inspiration in the first Chapter of Paul's first Epistle to the Thessalonians. In verse the 4th, the Apostle states the knowledge of election. In the 5th, he shews how it was proved and made known. In verse the 6th, he shews the sure effects of it in themselves. And in the four verses which follow, he shews the evidences which were proved thereby to others.

24 And from thence he arose, and went into the borders of Tyre and Sidon, and entered into an house, and would have no man know *it:* but he could not be hid.

25 For a *certain* woman, whose young daughter had an unclean spirit, heard of him, and came and fell at his feet:

26 The woman was a Greek, a Syrophenician by nation; and she besought him that he would cast forth the devil out of her daughter.

27 But Jesus said unto her, Let the children first be filled: for it is not meet to take the children's bread, and to cast *it* unto the dogs.

28 And she answered and said unto him, Yes, Lord: yet the dogs under the table eat of the children's crumbs.

29 And he said unto her, For this saying, go thy way; the devil is gone out of thy daughter.

30 And when she was come to her house, she found the devil gone out, and her daughter laid upon the bed.

This miracle is largely dwelt upon, Matt. xv. 21.

31 And again, departing from the coasts of Tyre and Sidon, he came unto the sea of Galilee, through the midst of the coasts of Decapolis.

32 And they bring unto him one that was deaf, and had an impediment in his speech; and they beseech him to put his hand upon him.

33 And he took him aside from the multitude, and put his fingers into his ears, and he spit, and touched his tongue;

34 And looking up to heaven, he sighed, and saith unto him, Ephphatha, that is, Be opened.

35 And straightway his ears were opened, and the string of his tongue was loosed, and he spake plain.

36 And he charged them that they should tell no man: but the more he charged them, so much the more a great deal they published it;

37 And were beyond measure astonished, saying, He hath done all things well: he maketh both the deaf to hear, and the dumb to speak.

Some copies read this passage, concerning our LORD's progress, that JESUS went through *Sidon;* but as *Sidon* was further off from *Galilee* than *Tyre*, it is more than probable JESUS went not through it. However, this deaf and dumb man which they brought to JESUS, was not of either place. The miracle the LORD manifested in healing him, excited great astonishment among the people; but the spiritual sense of it seems to have been wholly overlooked by them. Nothing becomes more striking, in proof of a spiritual deafness and dumbness, than a poor unawakened sinner. He is like *the deaf adder, which stoppeth her ears at the voice of the charmer; charm he never so wisely;* for all the melody of mercy in the Gospel of CHRIST, nor all the harsh sounds of condemnation in the law of God, can affect his mind. And as he hears of nothing, either to allure, or to alarm, so no cry for salvation ever passeth his lips. I pray the Reader to notice, however, the solicitude of his friends in bringing him to JESUS. Gracious souls, who know the LORD, do well to bring to JESUS those who know him not. He that hath unstopped your ears, and opened your lips, can do the same by others. And while we qualify our prayers for the most graceless, by our LORD's standard, we cannot err. *Neither*, said JESUS, (while acting as the Great High Priest in interceding for his Apostles,) *pray I for these alone, but for them also which shall believe on me through their word.* John xvii. 20. Precious prayer! including the thousands then unborn of the Redeemer's family. JESUS's followers have here a very plain direction how to qualify their prayers, when visiting a mercy seat for the unawakened.

I beg the Reader, not to overlook the circumstance, in the miracle, of the LORD's taking the poor man aside from the multitude. Yes! when JESUS works an act of sovereign grace upon his people, for the most part he calls them aside from the world, yea, from themselves, from what they were before; and manifests himself in secret, and gives them to eat of the *hidden manna.* Rev. ii. 17. Neither do I think the actions of our adorable LORD were without signification. JESUS may be said to put his fingers into the ears of his redeemed, when he opens them to hear *the joyful sound.* He truly toucheth our tongues with the spittle of his mouth, when he looseneth our lips to speak his praise. And his looking up to heaven, in confirmation of what he saith, *My Father worketh hitherto, and I work.* John v. 17. is à sweet testimony of the Oneness in the FATHER and the SON, in all the parts of his divine mission. The sigh of CHRIST, and the *Ephphatha* or *Ethphatha* he pronounced with it, are beautiful proofs of his GOD-Man, Person, and Character. His power to open, and his sigh in testimony of his fellow feeling, were here beautifully blended. Reader! do not overlook it! Oh! what everlasting effects of sovereign grace must follow, when JESUS visits the souls of his redeemed with his great salvation!

REFLECTIONS.

READER! let us pause over the awful view of the deceitfulness of the human heart, as read to us in those Scribes and Pharisees! While full of uncleanness, and all manner of hypocrisy, see how they prided themselves on outside appearances!

But while such striking facts may serve to teach us, as they ought to teach us, the deepest humility, let a sense of it lead us to all-precious JESUS! Oh! how ought the consciousness of it to endear CHRIST to the heart. Gracious, and compassionate Redeemer! dispossess every evil, every unclean affection, from our souls. LORD! to thee belongs the curing, both of the spiritually deaf, and dumb. Oh! do thou pronounce the soul-renewing word, *Ephphatha!* and every faculty will obey thee. Thy people now will be astonished at the riches of thy grace, as they of old were at thy power, Thou hast indeed done all things well in time, and to all eternity. My poor deaf and dumb soul thou hast made to hear and speak; yea, thou hast raised it to a new life, when dead in trespasses and sins!

CHAP. VIII.

CONTENTS.

CHRIST *is here described in feeding the people by a miracle. He giveth Sight to a blind man, and sweetly discourseth with his disciples.*

IN those days the multitude being very great, and having nothing to eat, Jesus called his disciples *unto him,* and saith unto them,

2 I have compassion on the multitude, because they have now been with me three days, and have nothing to eat :

3 And if I send them away fasting to their own houses, they will faint by the way : for divers of them came from far.

4 And his disciples answered him, From whence can a man satisfy these *men* with bread here in the wilderness ?

5 And he asked them, How many loaves have ye ? And they said, Seven.

6 And he commanded the people to sit down on the ground : and he took the seven loaves, and gave thanks, and brake, and gave to his disciples to set before *them;* and they did set *them* before the people.

7 And they had a few small fishes : and he blessed, and commanded to set them also before *them.*

8 So they did eat, and were filled : and they took up of the broken *meat* that was left seven baskets.

9 And they that had eaten were about four thousand : and he sent them away.

In addition to the observations made on those miracles of JESUS feeding the multitude, see Matt. xv. 32. Mark vi. 35. I would here only detain the Reader, to remark how unceasingly that compassion of JESUS is still exercised, now in the day of his power; in feeding his redeemed spiritually here, in grace, and above, in glory. Let the Reader turn to the beautiful and interesting account which is given of his Church in glory, where CHRIST leads them *to fountains of living water.* Rev. vii. 17. And when he hath beheld, by faith, the Church above, let him look to the Church below, and see no less how JESUS still feeds them with his grace. He is himself the *living bread,* and the *living water.* John vi. 51. John iv. 14. and as he promiseth so his redeemed find; all who are fed by him, feel such fulness, that they hunger no more, neither thirst any more, after the empty, unsatisfying things, of time and sense; but find CHRIST's *flesh to be meat indeed,* and *his blood to be drink indeed.* Reader! shall we not both say, LORD! *evermore give us this bread!* LORD! evermore *give us this water, that we thirst not, neither* go elsewhere *to draw.* John vi. 34. John iv. 15.

10 ¶ And straightway he entered into a ship with his disciples, and came into the parts of Dalmanutha.

Matthew calls this place *Magdala.* Matt. xv. 39. but it should seem that *Magdala* was the larger, of which *Dalmanutha* formed a less place, in the same coasts.

11 And the Pharisees came forth, and began to question with him, seeking of him a sign from heaven, tempting him.

12 And he sighed deeply in his spirit, and saith, Why doth this generation seek after a sign ? verily I say unto you, There shall no sign be given unto this generation.

The sighing of CHRIST, *deeply in spirit,* as it is said he did, is no doubt of great signification. I do not presume to explain. Yet I venture to differ from every Commentator on the passage, who speak of it, as if JESUS was grieved at the hardness of the Pharisees' hearts, in not believing on him. Surely this could never be the case. For as JESUS knew them, and spake openly of them as a generation of vipers, which *could not believe;* how could the LORD be supposed to sigh on this account? See Matt. xxiii. throughout. But though I do not presume to assign the cause of the LORD's sighing deeply in spirit, I would beg to call the Reader's attention to the act itself, as a sweet testimony of his human affections. Oh! how truly blessed is it to discover, that JESUS was, and is, *partaker of flesh and blood;* and that in all things *it behoved him to be made like unto his brethren.* Heb. ii. 14—17.

13 And he left them, and entering into the ship again, departed to the other side.

14 Now *the disciples* had forgotten to take bread, neither had they in the ship with them more than one loaf.

15 And he charged them, saying, Take heed, beware of the leaven of the Pharisees, and *of* the leaven of Herod.

16 And they reasoned among themselves, saying, *It is* because we have no bread.

17 And when Jesus knew *it,* he saith unto them,

Why reason ye, because ye have no bread? perceive ye not yet, neither understand? have ye your heart yet hardened?

18 Having eyes, see ye not? and having ears, hear ye not? and do ye not remember?

19 When I brake the five loaves among five thousand, how many baskets full of fragments took ye up? They say unto him, Twelve.

20 And when the seven among four thousand, how many baskets full of fragments took ye up? And they said, Seven.

21 And he said unto them, How is it that ye do not understand?

If the whole body of the Apostles were with CHRIST, the one loaf was a scanty allowance. But yet, He who had wrought so great a miracle but just before, could soon supply. The disciples then were much of the same complexion as now, soon forgetful, to overlook and forget CHRIST's power. But the precept of CHRIST, to be careful of the leaven, both of the *Pharisees*, and of *Herod*, is very striking and important. The *Pharisee*-leaven hath been a deadly weed in the Church of CHRIST; that is, I mean the real Church of CHRIST, which hath produced much obstruction and entanglement to the pure seed. What leanness of soul it hath produced, and is now producing, in numbers of the hearts of GOD's people, who shall calculate? The leaven of *Herod*, and of the *Sadducees*, one should conceive, was like our *Free-thinkers*, despising all revelation. LORD! I would say, preserve thy Church from every false leaven.

22 ¶ And he cometh to Bethsaida; and they bring a blind man unto him, and besought him to touch him.

23 And he took the blind man by the hand, and led him out of the town; and when he had spit on his eyes, and put his hands upon him, he asked him if he saw ought?

24 And he looked up, and said, I see men as trees, walking.

25 After that, he put *his* hands again upon his eyes, and made him look up: and he was restored, and saw every man clearly.

26 And he sent him away to his house, saying, Neither go into the town, nor tell *it* to any in the town.

This *Bethsaida* is the town concerning which the LORD pronounced woe. Matt. xi. 21. And yet from thence came *Peter* and *Andrew* and *Philip*. John i. 44. Reader! it is blessed to observe how the Church of CHRIST is gathered from various places. Even *Jericho* had a *Rahab*. Joshua ii. 1 Heb. xi. 31. And what is more wonderful, from *Rahab*, after the flesh, sprung CHRIST. Matt. i. 5. And in what numberless instances do we find the children of the kingdom spring after the flesh, out of the loins of the carnal, who are not heirs of the promise. And again, on the contrary, how frequently the children of the kingdom are the progenitors of the ungodly. All which proves that grace is not hereditary. Such are among the mysteries of GOD!

I only detain the Reader over this miracle of the blind, here recorded, to whom JESUS gave sight, to remark, how the LORD was pleased to work this miracle by a progressive cure. It is not said in what state of blindness he was; whether without eyes, or only the eyes he had were totally void of vision. But I beg the Reader, once for all, to observe, and it is, in my view, a very important observation, always to have in remembrance, as well in this instance as in all others, of JESUS giving sight to the blind, that in cases where the sockets of the blind were eyeless, the LORD JESUS, in every cure, must have *created eyes*, as well as given sight. And this, by the way, became, in every instance, a complete demonstration of his GODHEAD, and proved him to be the Creator. Let the faithful believer never lose sight of it. And let the infidel, who denies the GODHEAD of CHRIST, explain the possibility, upon any of his infidel principles, if he can, how JESUS could create eyes, and yet not be GOD. The LORD challengeth the blind to come forward as his witnesses that he is GOD. And indeed if creation be, as it unquestionably is, the proof of GODHEAD, nothing can be an higher proof. Isaiah xliii. 8, 9, 10. See John ix. throughout. In the progressive cure of this man, no doubt the LORD was pleased to shew how *the path of the just is as a shining light, which shineth more and more unto a perfect day*. But we must not, from hence, conclude, that our being in CHRIST is obtained in a progressive manner, though our enjoyment of that being is increased by an increasing knowledge. Not so. The opening, or the creating of this man's eyes, became the consequence of a being in CHRIST, but the being itself was from all eternity. I am speaking upon the presumption of a *spiritual* sight, as well as a *bodily*, being given to this man.

27 And Jesus went out, and his disciples, into the towns of Cesarea Philippi: and by the way he asked his disciples, saying unto them, Whom do men say that I am?

28 And they answered, John the Baptist: but some *say*, Elias; and others, One of the prophets.

29 And he saith unto them, But whom say ye that I am? and Peter answereth and saith unto him, Thou art the Christ.

30 And he charged them that they should tell no man of him.

We never can be sufficiently thankful to the LORD for putting this question to his disciples. Neither can we too highly prize that grace the LORD gave *Peter* in the answer. Oh! for the same divine teaching, whereby alone the knowledge he had is attainable. See Matt. xvi. 13, &c.

31 And he began to teach them, that the Son of man must suffer many things, and be rejected of the elders, and *of* the chief priests and scribes, and be killed, and after three days rise again.

32 And he spake that saying openly. And Peter took him, and began to rebuke him.

33 But when he had turned about, and looked on his disciples, he rebuked Peter, saying, Get thee behind me, Satan: for thou savourest not the things that be of God, but the things that be of men.

Although, on the similar passage recorded by *Matthew*, I have made similar observations, and to which I refer, Matt. xvi. 22, 23. yet, if it be only to repeat them, they cannot be too often brought before us. Behold, Reader! in the instance of *Peter*, what man is! Who could give a more blessed testimony than *Peter* had just given, concerning his GOD and SAVIOR. And from whom did he learn it, but from GOD the HOLY GHOST? But how plain it is, that when *Peter* took JESUS, and began to rebuke him here, he learnt not this from that Almighty Teacher! Reader! let you and I learn the vast importance of being always under his blessed teachings, who teacheth not as man teacheth. And let us learn, moreover, from the instance of this great Apostle, how evident it is, that the people of GOD may be blessed of the LORD the SPIRIT to make blessed confessions at times, and yet at others, have indistinct views of some sweet and precious things of GOD.

34 And when he had called the people *unto him,* with his disciples also, he said unto them, Whosoever will come after me, let him deny himself, and take up his cross, and follow me.

35 For whosoever will save his life shall lose it; but whosoever shall lose his life for my sake, and the gospel's, the same shall save it.

36 For what shall it profit a man if he shall gain the whole world, and lose his own soul?

37 Or what shall a man give in exchange for his soul?

38 Whosoever therefore shall be ashamed of me and of my words in this adulterous and sinful generation: of him also shall the Son of man be ashamed, when he cometh in the glory of his Father with the holy angels.

I cannot suffer this blessed discourse of the LORD JESUS to pass unnoticed, though in the parallel passage, Matt. xvi. 24 to the end, (which see,) I have already remarked upon it. But it were a pity to let a single word of JESUS drop to the ground. A single soul is of more value than the whole world ; and for this plain reason : The time is coming, when the whole world, and all that is in it will be destroyed ; but the soul of every individual must live, either in happiness or misery, for ever. Reader! pause over the subject, and calculate, if possible, the value of a single soul. The creation of it called forth the council of the whole persons of the GODHEAD. The redemption of it cost CHRIST his blood. The regeneration of it was the work of GOD the HOLY GHOST, The everlasting happiness of it engageth the services of angels, and of men continually. Angels rejoice in heaven in the recovery of every sinner. Hell rageth in the event of their salvation. The soul hath a capability of grace here, and glory for ever. And therefore what a loss, incalculably great, must it be, that a being of such qualities, and so formed, should be exposed to everlasting destruction. Reader! Who is there, think you, capable of being ashamed of JESUS, and his words? *Never man spake like him!* Never any among the sons of men to be compared to JESUS! Ashamed of him! All nature might blush at the very thought. But yet, in fact, every son and daughter of men take shame at JESUS and his Gospel, who do not seek salvation in his name and righteousness only ; and every one who wishes to add unto, or take from, the finished salvation of the LORD JESUS CHRIST. LORD JESUS! grant that heaven and earth may now be able to witness for me, and JESUS himself will be my witness then ; that in thee alone all my hopes, wishes, joys, expectations, are. And, like *Paul*, may I be able to say with the same assurance of faith ; GOD *forbid that I should glory, save in the cross of our* LORD JESUS CHRIST, *by whom the world is crucified unto me, and I unto the world.* Gal. vi. 14.

REFLECTIONS.

My soul! see to it, that the frequent notice, the Gospel takes of those *Scribes* and *Pharisees*, the sworn foes to CHRIST, that thou do not overlook the important lesson to be drawn, from what is said of them. They were zealous in their profession, of what they called godliness ; but it was a godliness only of nature, unawakened by grace. It consisted in outside appearance, honoring GOD with the lips, while their hearts were far from him. My soul! see to it, that an union with CHRIST forms the basis of all thy worship. It is *with the heart, man believeth unto righteousness; and with the mouth, confession is made unto salvation.*

Precious LORD JESUS! do thou keep me, by thine Almighty power, through faith unto salvation. Give me to see, that from an ever-lasting union with thee, in a covenant which cannot be broken; here lies the security of grace, to suit the wants and circumstances of all thy people. JESUS will say, *Ephphatha!* to the unopened eyes and ears of all his children, born in the Adam-nature of blindness, deafness, yea, *dead in trespasses and sins.* Thine LORD, is the work to accomplish, and thine all the glory. Cause me daily to see thy glory, to hear thy voice, and my whole heart and soul to speak thy praise!

C H A P.   IX.

CONTENTS.

We have here the glorious Scene of CHRIST's *Transfiguration. The* LORD *begins to prepare the minds of his Disciples for his Death. The miracle of the Child healed of a Dumb Spirit. Our* LORD's *Discourse with his Disciples.*

AND he said unto them, Verily I say unto you, That there be some of them that stand here which shall not taste of death till they have seen the kingdom of God come with power.

I do not presume to speak decidedly upon so grand a subject, as this verse contains; but I venture to believe, that when the LORD JESUS saith, as in this verse, that there were some then present, whose lives would not end, until they had seen the kingdom of GOD come (by which is meant a conviction of CHRIST's person and character); the LORD JESUS meant, that there were some who now stood before him, that would live until CHRIST had fulfilled the whole purposes of his mission, and had returned unto glory, and the HOLY GHOST had come down, to establish the kingdom of GOD in grace upon the earth. See Acts ii. 36, 37.

2 ¶ And after six days Jesus taketh *with him* Peter, and James, and John, and leadeth them up into an high mountain apart by themselves: and he was transfigured before them.

3 And his raiment became shining, exceeding white as snow; so as no fuller on earth can white them.

4 And there appeared unto them Elias with Moses: and they were talking with Jesus.

5 And Peter answered and said to Jesus, Master, it is good for us to be here: and let us make three

tabernacles; one for thee, and one for Moses, and one for Elias.

6 For he wist not what to say : for they were sore afraid.

7 And there was a cloud that overshadowed them : and a voice came out of the cloud, saying, This is my beloved Son: hear him.

8 And suddenly, when they had looked round about, they saw no man any more, save Jesus only with themselves.

9 And as they came down from the mountain, he charged them that they should tell no man what things they had seen, till the Son of man were risen from the dead.

10 And they kept that saying with themselves, questioning one with another what the rising from the dead should mean.

11 And they asked him, saying, Why say the scribes that Elias must first come?

12 And he answered and told them, Elias verily cometh first, and restoreth all things; and how it is written of the Son of man, that he must suffer many things, and be set at nought.

13 But I say unto you, That Elias is indeed come, and they have done unto him whatsoever they listed, as it is written of him.

There doth not seem to be any connection in what went before, with what is here said of this wonderful scene of CHRIST's Transfiguration, since there was an interval of *six days* from the one to the other. But, no doubt, the glory must have been abundantly overwhelming. I presume not to enter into a description of what is not describable. In addition to what hath been offered in Matt. xvii. 1, &c. I would only beg the Reader further to remark with me, how frequently the LORD was pleased, both before his open manifestation, in substance of our flesh, and after he had publicly tabernacled among his people in human form, to make some special revelation of himself. Who that reads the frequent visits the LORD made to his Old Testament saints, sometimes in an human appearance, and sometimes in that of an angel, can doubt it. And what were all these, but as so many evidences how much he longed for the time of his accomplishing redemption to arrive? And what is it now, when by the influences of his blessed

Spirit, he makes himself known to his people, as their Redeemer, Husband, and Surety; otherwise than he doth to the world? I beg the Reader not to overlook the special *personal* glory here manifested of CHRIST, as the GOD-Man Mediator. It was not the glory of the essential GODHEAD, which the SON of GOD possesseth in common with the FATHER and the HOLY GHOST; but it was the *personal* glory of the union of GOD-and-Man Mediator. And who shall describe this glory? No wonder the minds of the Apostles were overpowered, with the splendor of such a scene.

Though I cannot, because I dare not, attempt to enter far into the subject of CHRIST's Transfiguration, being above the present unripe faculties of the human mind to reach; yet I venture to suggest to the Reader, some few improving reflections, which arise out of the same.

And, *First:* I would have the Reader observe from it, the tenderness of JESUS in preparing the minds of his few faithful followers, for the humiliation which was shortly to follow. Yet but a little while, and he whom they saw encircled in glory, with a light, which dazzled their view, and overwhelmed their senses, would be nailed to a cross and die, like one forsaken of GOD and man. By this manifestation, the LORD prepared them for the wonderful change. Reader! do not fail to make your improvement of it also. Hath JESUS manifested himself to you otherwise than he doeth to the world; never lose sight of it. Blend the Transfiguration and the Cross; and behold CHRIST in both.

Secondly. Learn, like the Apostles, to make those special and glorious views of JESUS, the ground work of assurance, against these seasons which may be dark and discouraging. *Peter* never lost sight of this scene, to his dying day. 2 Pet. i. 16, 17, 18. And *John* makes his knowledge of JESUS, the argument of comforting the whole Church. 1 John i. 1, 2, 3.

Thirdly. Learn to consider this manifestation, of the glory of the GOD-Man in the Mount of Transfiguration, as a sample, of what shall be the glorified bodies of all the saints of GOD. If in JESUS dwelt all the fulness of the GODHEAD bodily, surely we may safely conclude, that our bodies, which are now the temple of the HOLY GHOST, shall become glorious in JESUS: for it is said, *that he will change our vile bodies, that they may be fashioned like unto his glorious body according to the mighty working whereby he is able to subdue all things unto himself.* Philip. iii. 20.

Lastly, and above all. Let us never forget the preciousness and blessedness, of the testimony, given by JEHOVAH, in this transaction to the person, offices, and character of the LORD JESUS CHRIST. Oh! what a confirmation is this, to all the great purposes of salvation, in the infinite dignity, worth, and excellency, of our LORD JESUS CHRIST. LORD grant that JEHOVAH's good pleasure, may be my good pleasure; GOD's chosen, my chosen; GOD's delight, my delight.

14 ¶ And when he came to *his* disciples, he saw a great multitude about them, and the scribes questioning with them.

15 And straightway all the people, when they

beheld him, were greatly amazed, and running
to *him* saluted him.

16 And he asked the scribes, What question ye
with them?

17 And one of the multitude answered and said,
Master, I have brought unto thee my son, which
hath a dumb spirit;

18 And wheresoever he taketh him, he teareth
him; and he foameth, and gnasheth with his teeth,
and pineth away: and I spake to thy disciples
that they should cast him out; and they could not.

19 He answereth him, and saith, O faithless
generation, how long shall I be with you? how
long shall I suffer you? bring him unto me.

20 And they brought him unto him: and when
he saw him, straightway the spirit tare him; and
he fell on the ground, and wallowed foaming.

21 And he asked his father, How long is it ago
since this came unto him? And he said, Of a
child.

22 And ofttimes it hath cast him into the fire,
and into the waters, to destroy him: but if thou
canst do any thing, have compassion on us, and
help us.

23 Jesus said unto him, If thou canst believe,
all things *are* possible to him that believeth.

24 And straitway the father of the child cried
out, and said with tears, Lord, I believe; help
thou mine unbelief.

25 When Jesus saw that the people came running together, he rebuked the foul spirit, saying
unto him, *Thou* dumb and deaf spirit, I charge
thee, come out of him, and enter no more into
him.

26 And *the spirit* cried, and rent him sore, and
came out of him, and he was as one dead; insomuch that many said, He is dead.

27 But Jesus took him by the hand, and lifted him up; and he arose.

I hardly know among the miracles of JESUS, any, which opens more sweet, and precious instruction, and which under divine teaching may be rendered more profitable to the Church of CHRIST than this; and I hope therefore that the Reader will indulge me in enlarging upon it. Here is a tender father, with very slender faith, brings his child to CHRIST, to obtain a cure for him, under the possession of an evil spirit. The disciples who had in other instances, through the name, and by the authority of their divine Master wrought similar cures, here failed. It pleased the LORD, for the greater glory of CHRIST, the humbling of the Apostles, and the trying the faith of the father of the child, in his providence, so to order it. The poor man came, under great doubts and fears it is evident, by his manner of expression, probably tempted to fear that as the servants had failed, so might the Master. If (said he) *thou canst do any thing, have compassion upon us and help us.* To which our LORD made this remarkable answer; *If thou canst believe all things are possible to him that believeth.* No doubt the LORD JESUS accompanied his words with power; for immediately the man convinced of his little faith, and full of distress on account of his child, *cried out, with tears,* LORD! *I believe; help thou mine unbelief.* The event was as might be expected, JESUS healed the son and comforted the father.

The subject is too interesting not to follow it up, with suited observations: therefore the Reader will allow me to remark, what a sweet instruction it holds forth to persons of weak faith, to exercise more confidence in the LORD JESUS CHRIST. It should be observed, that this man had faith, though it was small. Now the smallest faith is not of human creation, it must be of GOD. And as all faith comes from JESUS, who is the author and finisher of faith; there is more cause to bless GOD, for the smallest degree of faith, than for all the riches of the world. For it implies an union with CHRIST, and interest in CHRIST. *As many as were ordained to eternal life believed.* Acts xiii. 48. And another scripture saith, that *by him all that believe,* that is, be they many or few, be they strong or weak, yet, as it is by JESUS and his great salvation, and not from the merits of their faith, *all that believe, are justified from all things.* Acts x. 43. So that the weak believer or the strong, the babe in CHRIST, or the father in GOD, are all alike as to their justification; though the joy in believing will differ, according to the weakness or strength of faith, in the believer. Reader! I beseech you, to take occasion, from what is here said of this poor man's faith, to make it in some measure a standard, by which to ascertain your own. Weak as his faith was, it still led him to JESUS. Doth your faith in CHRIST do this? He had a consciousness of the weakness of it, and begged of JESUS to increase it: LORD! said he, *I believe, help thou mine unbelief.* Do you feel this? and can a throne of grace witness for you, that you go there frequently with such petitions? This poor man not only sought an increase of it, but he sought it with tears. *Straitway,* saith the Evangelist, *the father of the child cried out with tears,* LORD! *I believe; help thou mine unbelief.* It is a blessed sign, when the heart is softened under grace, and a sense of unworthiness and unbelief, leads the heart to GOD to seek relief in Jesus. Reader! I would ask for myself, and if the Lord so please, may he give you grace also so to ask for yourself, as the Apostles did: Lord! *increase our faith.* Luke xvii. 5. But while the faith of an Apostle or a Patriarch, be desirable, let us learn to bless the Lord for what he hath bestowed. For, from the smallest degree of faith, we prove our call of God; and that we have eternal life abiding in us, *by the spirit which he hath given us.* 1 John iii. 24.

28 And when he was come into the house, his disciples asked him privately, Why could not we cast him out?

29 And he said unto them, This kind can come forth by nothing, but by prayer and fasting.

I have separated those verses, from the preceding, though they form a part of the same history; not by way of explaining them, for I very freely confess, that I do not apprehend the full sense and meaning of them: but by way of calling the Reader's attention to them, one point I think is very evident from our Lord's words, that when the disciples questioned the cause of their inability, our Lord doth not say, this kind can come forth by nothing but by prayer and fasting: in allusion to the evil spirit, for in the parallel passage, Matt. xvii. 20. Jesus directly refers it to a want of faith. Fastings and prayers are creature exercises. Our Lord cannot be supposed to assign to such the power of miracles. And evidently in the parallel passage of *Matthew*, the Lord ascribes the power rather to faith. The subject is however attended with too much difficulty to determine. Though I am inclined to think that by prayer and fasting, Jesus refers to himself, in whom alone all righteousness is fulfilled.

30 ¶ And they departed thence, and passed through Galilee: and he would not that any man should know *it.*

31 For he taught his disciples, and said unto them, The Son of man is delivered into the hands of men, and they shall kill him: and after that he is killed, he shall rise the third day.

32 But they understood not that saying, and were afraid to ask him.

I shall detain the Reader no longer, in an observation on these verses, than just to request him to notice, how tenderly the Lord began to open to them the subject of his death. He had noticed it slightly, in the preceding Chapter, verse 31; and here again he keeps up the remembrance of it. And let not the Reader fail to remark, that in both places, the Lord is pleased to connect together with his death, the certainty of his resurrection.

33 And he came to Capernaum; and being in the house, he asked them, What was it that ye disputed among yourselves by the way?

34 But they held their peace : for by the way they had disputed among themselves who *should be* the greatest.

35 And he sat down and called the twelve, and saith unto them, If any man desire to be first, *the same* shall be last of all, and servant of all.

36 And he took a child, and set him in the midst of them : and when he had taken him in his arms, he said unto them,

37 Whosoever shall receive one of such children in my name, receiveth me : and whosoever shall receive me, receiveth not me, but him that sent me.

Do not overlook in this passage, the GODHEAD of CHRIST. He knew their hearts. And though he asked them of the cause of their dispute, yet this was not for his information, but for their reproof. And I pray the Reader to observe, the very engaging method the LORD adopted to cure his disciples of all that mistaken pride he discovered in them. What a beautiful emblem of CHRIST's kingdom is represented in the humbleness, and docility of a little child ! *David* speaks of the state of his soul, under the consciousness of his nothingness, and abstraction from the vanity and pride of life, *as a weaned child.* Psm. cxxxi. 2. To a child of GOD, who hath really, and truly known and tasted the preciousness of JESUS; the breasts of the mother would no longer afford sweet milk ; but the bitterness of wormwood and gall is put upon them.

38 And John answered him, saying, Master, we saw one casting out devils in thy name, and he followeth not us : and we forbad him, because he followeth not us.

39 But Jesus said, Forbid him not : for there is no man which shall do a miracle in my name that can lightly speak evil of me.

40 For he that is not against us is on our part.

41 For whosoever shall give you a cup of water to drink in my name, because ye belong to Christ, verily I say unto you, he shall not lose his reward.

42 And whosoever shall offend one of *these* little ones that believe in me, it is better for him that a millstone were hanged about his neck, and he were cast into the sea.

I cannot offer a better improvement, on this very interesting passage, according to my view of it, and if so be the LORD the HOLY GHOST is the teacher, both of him that writes and him that reads, than to observe, that here is drawn, and by the LORD himself, the line of distinction, between what the Prophet, ages before declared, *the righteous and the wicked; between him that serveth* GOD *and him that serveth him not.* Malachi iii. 18. Every circumstance in the word of GOD, tends to the confirmation, that the two grand distinctions in life, how diversified soever they may appear to our dim sighted view, are formed between the Church of CHRIST and the ungodly world, the seed of the woman, and the spirit which worketh in the children of disobedience. The language of CHRIST is decisive, *He that is not against us, is on our part.* And the LORD hath very largely set the same solemn truth forth in all his discourses. The good seed and the tares, the sheep and the goats, the wise virgins and the foolish. And as they are perfectly distinct in their origin, their nature, and connection, so are they in all their progress, condition, and termination. There is nothing that can be called neutral, or of a middle state. To one or the other of these different kingdom all belong, and so will remain to all eternity. Reader! it is blessed, when under the Spirit's teaching, we discover our union with CHRIST, and consequently our interest in CHRIST. Luke xii. 32.

43 And if thy hand offend thee, cut it off: it is better for thee to enter into life maimed, than having two hands to go into hell, into the fire that never shall be quenched:

44 Where their worm dieth not, and the fire is not quenched.

45 And if thy foot offend thee, cut it off: it is better for thee to enter halt into life, than having two feet to be cast into hell, into the fire that never shall be quenched:

46 Where their worm dieth not, and the fire is not quenched.

47 And if thine eye offend thee, pluck it out: it is better for thee to enter into the kingdom of God with one eye, than having two eyes to be cast into hell fire:

48 Where their worm dieth not, and the fire is not quenched.

So very important, are those solemn and awful words, that the LORD JESUS was pleased thrice to repeat them. It may well become us to make as solemn an enquiry into their meaning. Perhaps the Reader will recollect, that they are a quotation from the close of *Isaiah's* prophecy. JESUS thus confirms the words of his servant, by giving the authority of the Master. In that prophetical chapter, with which Isaiah ends his ministry, he describes the result of the whole. When the LORD hath brought home his kingdom, and the new heavens and the new earth are formed; and all his redeemed are made Priests to GOD and the FATHER, in order to effect their minds with suitable impressions of distinguishing grace, they shall from time to time go forth and look upon the misery of the wicked, *for their worm shall not die, neither shall their fire be quenched.* Isaiah lxvi. 21 to the end. Now whether this prophecy referred to the Gospel Church, when *Jerusalem* was destroyed, or whether to the more spiritual state, when, as in the present day, the Jews nationally considered are given up to an unbelieving mind: *eyes that they should not see, and ears that they should not hear.* Rom. xi. 8. Or whether it hath a reference to the awful judgments of the last day, or whether the whole be included, and it refers to all taken together; in either sense the doctrine is the same. As in the case of the Parable of the *rich man* and *Lazarus,* the misery of the *former* was encreased in beholding the blessedness of the *latter;* so the terrors of hell, will be aggravated from a view of the felicity of heaven; and the glories of distinguishing mercy will make the redeemed ten fold more illustrious when looking over the battlements of heaven, they view the horrors of unredeemed transgressors.

49 For every one shall be salted with fire, and every sacrifice shall be salted with salt.

50 Salt *is* good: but if the salt have lost his saltness, wherewith will ye season it? Have salt in yourselves, and have peace one with another.

Various have been the sense given to those verses, by different writers. I presume not to speak upon them decidedly. All I shall propose, I would propose by way of humble enquiry, looking to GOD the SPIRIT to guide me and instruct me through the whole passage; and if I err, to pardon my errors, and suffer them not to be the means of leading others into the same.

And first, I humbly conceive, that as our LORD all the way through this discourse, from the 43rd verse, is speaking of the misery of hell, and the blessedness of heaven; I apprehend that he is still preserving the view of both in what he saith here of the person and the sacrifice. The *one,* is said to be salted with fire, the *other* is distinguished from this in being salted with salt. The *former, salted with fire,* it should seem (for I humbly ask the question) hath reference to those whose everlasting misery is expressed under the similitude of *a worm that dieth not, and the fire not quenched.* *Salted with fire* will then imply, that as the common salt hath power to preserve flesh from corruption, so this fire shall be, to preserve in being those persons from being consumed. And while, as was before said, the worm of a guilty conscience shall grow upon them with inexpressible anguish, they shall never die; the fire which is not extinguishable shall be as salt to preserve, while it shall burn with divine wrath to punish, and never go out; but *the smoke of their torment ascendeth up for ever and ever* Rev. xiv. 11.

In relation to the *latter ;* every sacrifice shall be salted with salt : I humbly conceive, that these sweet words have reference to the redeemed in CHRIST. It is a truth too well known, and too firmly ascertained to be questioned, that the whole law was but *a shadow of good things to come; but the body is* CHRIST. Hence, therefore, strictly and properly speaking, there was no real sacrifice, but the one offering of the body of JESUS CHRIST, once for all : for by that *one offering he hath perfected for ever them that are sanctified.* Heb. x. 1—14. So that every offering under the law, was offered, with an eye to CHRIST : and HE was the one glorious substance of all. Laying this down as a foundation, which cannot be questioned, we can now enter into some apprehension at least of our LORD's gracious words, if (as I have ventured to suppose) they refer to the redeemed in CHRIST : *Every sacrifice shall be salted with salt.* CHRIST the sacrifice, shall be offered by faith, with *the salt of the Covenant.* For so the LORD enjoined the Church when setting forth the sacrifice of CHRIST in type and shadow. *Every oblation of thy meat offering shalt thou season with salt: neither shalt thou suffer the salt of the Covenant of thy* GOD *to be lacking from thy meat offering : with all thine offerings thou shalt offer salt.* Levit. ii. 13. So that while the *salted with fire* acts upon the persons of the unredeemed, as salt to flesh to preserve in being, and yet in unextinguishable torments, the *salt of the Covenant* with which the sacrifice is offered, preserves to everlasting happiness the souls and bodies of the LORD's people ; being saved and accepted in CHRIST. Oh! LORD JESUS! say to my soul, and in saying it, confirm thy word unto thy servant, wherein thou hast caused me to hope; *have salt in yourselves.* Let never the salt of the Covenant of my GOD be lacking, but may JESUS in all his person, offices, grace, and spiritual seasonings, be in all my poor offerings : then shall I be as the salt of the earth, preserved in thee, and by thee, not only from the corruption of the world around, but the corruptions within, and have peace with thee, and all thy people.

REFLECTIONS.

LORD JESUS ! While I read thy gracious promise, at the opening of this Chapter, to some of thy faithful ones ; who, according to what was then said, did not taste death till they had seen this kingdom come with power ; I bless thee that though not present at thy Transfiguration ; yet seeing thee by faith, and knowing thee as the LORD OUR RIGHTEOUSNESS, all thy redeemed of the present day can say as holy Simeon of old, *mine eyes have seen thy salvation !*

Beholding thy rich mercy to the Child of the Poor Man, who, though his faith was so slender, yet thy grace was so great ; help me LORD ; yea, help all thy redeemed ones, to join in the same prayer, and may we experience the same mercy: LORD, *I believe ! help thou mine unbelief.*

Oh! for a spirit of humility among thy Church and People, that each may esteem other better than themselves : yea, may we all be content to be nothing ; yea, less than nothing, that JESUS, our adorable JESUS, may be all in all !

In the awful view of the unregenerate, in their *worm that dieth not,* and the *fire that is not quenched;* oh! give thy people grace to mark, and rightly prize, their distinguishing mercies. LORD! *how is it that thou hast manifested thyself unto us and not unto the world.* Oh! for the salt of the Covenant of my GOD! Oh! f)r the unspeakable blessedness in the interest in CHRIST's sacrifice! Oh! for the grace of GOD the HOLY GHOST, salting with the salt of his regenerating, cleansing, illuminating, strengthening, and confirming influence, my soul unto the day of eternal redemption!

CHAP. X.

CONTENTS.

Our Lord is here discoursing on the subject of divorcement. Little Children are brought to CHRIST. The LORD again speaks of his approaching Sufferings. JESUS passeth through Jericho.

AND he arose from thence, and cometh into the coasts of Judea by the farther side of Jordan: and the people resort unto him again; and, as he was wont, he taught them again.

2 ¶ And the Pharisees came to him, and asked him, Is it lawful for a man to put away *his* wife? tempting him.

3 And he answered and said unto them, What did Moses command you?

4 And they said, Moses suffered to write a bill of divorcement, and to put *her* away.

5 And Jesus answered and said unto them, For the hardness of your heart he wrote you this precept.

6 But from the beginning of the creation, God made them male and female.

7 For this cause shall a man leave his father and mother, and cleave to his wife;

8 And they twain shall be one flesh; so then they are no more twain, but one flesh.

9 What therefore God hath joined together, let not man put asunder.

10 And in the house his disciples asked him again of the same *matter*.

11 And he saith unto them, Whosoever shall put away his wife, and marry another, committeth adultery against her.

12 And if a woman shall put away her husband, and be married to another, she committeth adultery.

Our LORD's circuit in his ministry would lead, in the contemplation of it, to a most profitable subject. Unwearied in all his services, with zeal to his Father's glory, and his people's happiness, the sun watched his path by day, and the stars witnessed to his communion by night. It was no small distance JESUS had advanced in a little space. In the 8th Chapter we find him on the borders of *Tyre* and *Sidon* westward, and now he is arrived eastward on the coasts of *Judæa* by *Jordan*. Precious LORD! what a lesson, and what an example, to thy ministers and people! John ix. 4.

We have the Pharisees, the sworn foes to CHRIST, in this paragraph at their own trade again; not to receive instruction, but to entangle JESUS in his talk. They brought forward for his decision, that popular question already decided in their mind, but wishing to entrap CHRIST: the subject concerning Divorces. But how unworthy soever their designs were, the Church of CHRIST find cause to bless GOD that the question was put to CHRIST, since it gave occasion for his very sweet and gracious answer; by which the doctrine respecting divorces is put upon its just and unalterable foundation. If the reader will once more read over this paragraph, from the 2d to the 12th verse inclusive, I will then request his attention to the subject, according to our LORD's own statement.

And *first:* Our LORD most decidedly proves, that even in the cases where *Moses* permitted a divorcement, he allowed it not, without compelling the husband to write the bill with his own hand, before he put her away. As if to shew, that it should not be the hasty impulse of the moment, but the solemn and serious result of proper deliberation; thereby allowing an harsh and angry husband the time to relent. And even here, it was to be done with such coolness, turning over all the consequences, that the husband by the same law, however afterwards he might repent, was not by any means allowed to take her again. See Deut. xxiv. 1—4. And the LORD JESUS added that this law, which seemed rather to wink at such conduct than justify it, would never have been given by *Moses* but for the hardness of their hearts. So decidedly against all divorces was the tender and compassionate JESUS.

But, *secondly:* The LORD JESUS doth not stop here. His decision against all divorces arose from an higher authority still; for saith JESUS, from the beginning of the creation, GOD made them male and female; and declared that when joined in marriage, they were no longer twain, but one flesh: that GOD himself joined them together; and man dared not put them asunder. Here is an uncommonly strong argument in this statement by CHRIST: not only because marriage was of divine institution, and the separating man and wife solemnly prohibited by their Maker; but because in the first instance of wedlock, which ever took place in the creation of GOD, there was no possibility of the man's putting away his wife and taking another; for no other woman existed. One man, and one woman, the LORD had made, and no more: and from those two, made one by marriage, the race was to follow. So that here in the first marriage of our first parents, the LORD's holy will and pleasure concerning marriage was fully given,

as a pattern to all their children. I think this is so unalterably strong
and conclusive, that no appeal can be made against it. The popular
wish, and too general conduct of the Jews, in putting away their
wives, received our Lord's decided condemnation.

But we must not stop here. Divorcement received another decided
reproof from the very design of marriage : which was altogether
with a mystical allusion to Christ, and his Church. We have an
authority which cannot be questioned, that the marriage of our first
parents, *Adam* and *Eve*, in the garden of *Eden*, was altogether a type,
or more properly speaking, the shadow and representation of Christ's
marriage with his Church. A *type*, it might be said, because it set
forth what would be accomplished when the fulness of time was
come, and God sent forth his Son, made of a Woman, in marrying
our nature. And yet a *shadow* also, because it became the shade of
a prior substance, when before all worlds the Son of God did as the
Prophet described him, betroth his Church to himself for ever, Hosea
ii. 18, 19. *It was not good* that the God-Man Christ Jesus *should
be alone;* no more than Adam, in the Adam nature, in which he
was created : for then how would Christ have been the Bridegroom
of his Church without a Bride ? Jehovah therefore said, *I will make
him an helpmate for him.* Hence therefore of the Church to Christ,
as well as of Eve to her husband ; it is said, *therefore shall a man leave
his father and his mother and shall cleave to his wife : and they shall
be one flesh,* Gen. ii. 18 to the end. See Ephes. v. 23 to the end.

If the reader be not tired with the length of these observations on
this passage, I would wish to detain him, one moment longer, on the
subject of divorcement. You have seen the Lord Jesus decidedly
giving his disapprobation to all divorcement. Perhaps it will be
asked, yea it should be asked, as the most interesting question of all
others : Did ever Jesus put away his wife ? To which I venture most
humbly to say ; I trow not. Let the reader look over the word of God
for himself, (and never never can he be engaged in a question of higher
consequence,) and I persuade myself he will conclude with me, that
no bill of divorcement was ever given by Jesus to his Church. He
who by his servant *Paul* hath said ; *husbands love your wives, and be
not bitter against them,* would not be himself bitter against his,
Coloss. iii. 19.   Nay, the Apostle elsewhere saith, when speaking of
men's loving their wives as their own bodies, and he that loveth his
wife loveth himself, makes this blessed addition, *No man ever yet
hated his own flesh, but nourisheth and cherisheth it, even as Christ
the Church.* Ephes. v. 28, 29. Here's a beautiful scripture in point.
As no man ever hated his own flesh ; even though covered with sores
and wounds, so Jesus loved his Church, though leprous and unclean :
Oh ! precious, precious Lord Jesus ! Surely it becometh thee in all
things to have the pre-eminence !

And now, if the Reader feels interested (as well he may ; Lord,
let it engage my unceasing attention !) to look into the word of God
in the enquiry ; whether Jesus ever put away his Wife ; let him diligently search the whole Bible. The most striking passages which
seem to lean this way, are Jerem. iii. 8. Isaiah l. 1. Hosea ii. 2.
But the smallest attention, and especially when connected with the
whole body of scripture on the subject, very plainly (according to
my view,) declare the contrary. Let the Reader take with the 8th

verse of *Jeremiah*, the 3d, the 1st and 14th verses of the same chapter. Let him attend also to the manner of expression in the 50th chapter of *Isaiah*, and 1st verse, and he will perhaps be inclined to think with me, that the Lord challengeth any one to show the bill of divorcement; knowing there was none. And as for the passage in *Hosea*, chapter ii. and 2d verse; the whole chapter and the following are most decided in proof, that Jesus never did, as the Apostle Paul speaks elsewhere, *cast away his people which he foreknew.* Rom. xi. 1, 2. Our Lord's manner of speaking on this subject; where is the bill of your mother's divorcement, and the like; is not unsimilar to what he used to his disciples on another occasion. *At that day ye shall ask in my name; and I say not unto you that I will pray for you.* John xvi. 26. Now one might be led to think, in the first view of these words, as if Jesus meant to decline praying for them; whereas it is evident Jesus meant thereby to say more fully that he would.

The Reader will I hope forgive the length to which I have extended the subject, from the importance of it; and I shall now leave him to his own conclusions, under the pleasing assurance, that the Almighty Spirit of truth will guide both Writer and Reader into all truth, on this most sweet and interesting subject. Indeed, indeed it is blessed to hear the Lord, the God of Israel, say that *he hateth putting away.* Malachi ii. 14, 15, 16. And oh! what blessedness will in the end appear, when after all the treacherous departures of Jesus's Church, in all her spiritual adulteries, Jesus must, he will, yea, he cannot rest until he hath brought her home to his Father's house, and *presented her to himself a glorious Church, not having spot or wrinkle or any such thing, but that she shall be holy and without blemish.* Ephes. v. 27. Rev. xix. 5—9.

13 ¶ And they brought young children to him, that he should touch them; and *his* disciples rebuked those that brought *them.*

14 But when Jesus saw *it,* he was much displeased, and said unto them, Suffer the little children to come unto me, and forbid them not; for of such is the kingdom of God.

15 Verily I say unto you, Whosoever shall not receive the kingdom of God as a little child, he shall not enter therein.

16 And he took them up in his arms, put *his* hands upon them, and blessed them.

The same observations will meet us here, as Matt. xviii. 1, &c. Luke xviii. 15.

17 And when he was gone forth into the way, there came one running, and kneeled to him, and

asked him, Good Master, what shall I do that I may inherit eternal life?

18 And Jesus said unto him, Why callest thou me good? *there is* none good but one, *that is,* God.

19 Thou knowest the commandments, Do not commit adultery, De not kill, Do not steal, Do not bear false witness, Defraud not, Honour thy father and mother.

20 And he answered and said unto him, Master, all these have I observed from my youth.

21 Then Jesus beholding him loved him, and and said unto him, One thing thou lackest: go thy way, sell whatsoever thou hast, and give to the poor, and thou shalt have treasure in heaven: and come, take up the cross, and follow me.

22 And he was sad at that saying, and went away grieved: for he had great possessions.

23 ¶ And Jesus looked round about, and saith unto his disciples, How hardly shall they that have riches enter into the kingdom of God!

24 And the disciples were astonished at his words. But Jesus answereth again, and saith unto them, Children, how hard is it for them that trust in riches to enter into the kingdom of God!

25 It is easier for a camel to go through the eye of a needle, than for a rich man to enter into the kingdom of God.

26 And they were astonished out of measure, saying among themselves, Who then can be saved?

27 And Jesus looking upon them saith, With men *it is* impossible, but not with God: for with God all things are possible.

28 ¶ Then Peter began to say unto him, Lo, we have left all, and have followed thee.

29 And Jesus answered and said, Verily I say

unto you, There is no man that hath left house, or brethren, or sisters, or father, or mother, or wife, or children, or land, for my sake, and the gospel's,

30 But he shall receive an hundred fold now in this time, houses, and brethren, and sisters, and mothers, and children, and lands, with persecutions; and in the world to come eternal life.

31 But many *that are* first shall be last; and the last first.

In addition to the observations offered on the parallel passage, Matt. xix. 16, &c. I would beg to remark on the expression of Jesus beholding this young man, and as it is said, *loved him*, the words have no one reference whatsoever to the love Jesus beareth towards his people. There are various degrees of affection perfectly well known, felt, and understood by mankind. Even in the natural affinity of life, our love to one another is regulated by the particular character of relationship in which we stand. The Lord Jesus might be said, when beholding this youth, in whom the corruptions induced by the fall, had not broken out, in the more violent instances of notorious profligacy, as in the great mass of men, to love what he saw amiable. But then, it should be carefully distinguished what this love meant, from the love Jesus beareth to his people. The sequel of this youth's history, in going away sorrowful from Christ, and never more coming to Christ, as far as we are informed, very decidedly prove that no work of grace ever passed upon his heart. The love here spoken of differs altogether from the special affection the Lord Jesus bears to the persons of his redeemed, which are the gift of his Father, the purchase of his blood, and the objects of the everlasting love of God the Holy Ghost, in whom he puts the influences of his sovereign power and grace to make them wise unto salvation, through the faith that is in Christ Jesus.

The concluding part of this passage is uncommonly beautiful and interesting. While Jesus, in strong figures represents the total impossibility of the mere efforts of nature, rising above nature; he sets forth the ease and blessedness with which his redeemed, through his grace, will attain his kingdom. An huge camel might as soon pass through the eye of a needle, as for a rich man, rich in his own fancied goodness, swollen and bloated with his own Pharisaical righteousness, but never regenerated by grace, to enter into the kingdom of God. While on the other hand, every one of Christ's regenerated family, *poor in spirit, rich in faith, and heirs of the kingdom,* and who give proofs of the triumphs of grace over nature, leaving all for Christ, will enter with a full tide of glory into Christ's kingdom; being saved, *not by works of righteousness which they have done, but according to rich,* free and sovereign *mercy,* by the *washing of regeneration and renewing of the* Holy Ghost, *shed upon them abundantly through* Jesus Christ *our* Lord. Titus iii. 5, 6.

32 ¶ And they were in the way going up to Jerusalem; and Jesus went before them: and they were amazed; and as they followed, they were afraid: and he took again the twelve, and began to tell them what things should happen unto him,

33 *Saying*, Behold, we go up to Jerusalem; and the Son of man shall be delivered unto the chief priests, and unto the scribes; and they shall condemn him to death, and shall deliver him to the Gentiles:

34 And they shall mock him, and shall scourge him, and shall spit upon him, and shall kill him: and the third day he shall rise again.

I beg the Reader not to overlook the affection of JESUS in thus gradually preparing the disciples for his death. See Chap. viii. 31, and Chap. ix. 31, &c. It is a blessed trait of character of JESUS in confirmation of the leading feature of his office work as Mediator, the voluntary nature of it, that he longed for the accomplishment of the whole in his death. Hence we find him, Luke xix. 28, going before ascending up to Jerusalem. *I have a baptism* (said JESUS) *to be baptized with; and how am I straitened until it be accomplished.* Luke xii. 50. So to Judas. *What thou doest, do quickly.* John xiii. 37. And when Judas and the band came to apprehend him: JESUS *went forth and said unto them, whom seek ye? I am he.* John xviii. 4, 5. Blessedly is it said of him, that *he was led as a lamb to the slaughter; so free, so willing.* Isaiah liii. 7.

35 And James and John, the sons of Zebedee, come unto him, saying, Master, we would that thou shouldest do for us whatsoever we shall desire.

36 And he said unto them, What would ye that I should do for you?

37 They said unto him, Grant unto us that we may sit one on thy right hand, and the other on thy left hand, in thy glory.

38 But Jesus said unto them, ye know not what ye ask; can ye drink of the cup that I drink of? and be baptized with the baptism that I am baptized with?

39 And they say unto him, We can, and Jesus said unto them, Ye shall indeed drink of the cup

that I drink of; and with the baptism that I am baptized withal shall ye be baptized:

40 But to sit on my right hand, and on my left hand, is not mine to give; but *it shall be given to them* for whom it is prepared.

In addition to the observations made on the relation of this conversation, between Christ and the Sons of Zebedee. Matt. xx. 20. (which see;) I would only add, that as the petition of *James* and *John* plainly prove, they had at that time no knowledge in what Christ's kingdom consisted; so it is equally plain that our Lord's answer had no reference in the least to his power, but to the confirmation of the antient settlements of eternity. In the council of peace before all worlds, Christ's kingdom in the persons of his redeemed were all known, and their names numbered in the book of life. And hence, with an eye to this, the Prophet declared, that they should all *again* pass under the hand of him that telleth them. Jerem. xxxiii. 13. I beg the Reader not to overlook in this passage, as it was in the parallel one of *Matthew:* the words are in Italic, verse 40, *it shall be given to them*; which implies that they are not in the original. And if the verse be read without them, the sense will be in exact correspondence with what Jesus saith. John xvii. 2, that *he should give eternal life to as many as the* Father *had given him.*

41 And when the ten heard *it*, they began to be much displeased with James and John;

42 But Jesus called them *to him*, and saith unto them, Ye know that they which are accounted to rule over the Gentiles exercise lordship over them; and their great ones exercise authority upon them.

43 But so shall it not be among you: but whosoever will be great among you shall be your minister:

44 And whosoever of you will be the chiefest shall be servant of all.

45 For even the Son of man came not to be ministered unto, but to minister, and to give his life a ransom for many.

What a very lovely and unanswerable argument the Lord makes use of in those verses, to beget humbleness of soul. Who that beholds the Son of God leaving the bosom of his Father, and coming voluntarily to give himself an offering and a sacrifice for sin, can in the view of such an instance, assume distinction and pride!

46 ¶ And they came to Jericho: and as he went out of Jericho with his disciples, and a great num-

ber of people, blind Bartimeus, the son of Timeus,
sat by the highway side begging.

47 And when he heard that it was Jesus of Nazareth, he began to cry out, and say, Jesus, *thou*
son of David, have mercy on me.

48 And many charged him that he should hold
his peace : but he cried the more a great deal,
Thou son of David, have mercy on me.

49 And Jesus stood still, and commanded him
to be called: and they call the blind man, saying
unto him, Be of good comfort, rise; he calleth
thee.

50 And he, casting away his garment, rose, and
came to Jesus.

51 And Jesus answered and said unto him, What
wilt thou that I should do unto thee? the blind
man said unto him, Lord, that I might receive
my sight.

52 And Jesus said unto him, Go thy way : thy
faith hath made thee whole : and immediately he
received his sight, and followed Jesus in the way.

The miracle here recorded being particularly interesting, and
somewhat more largely treated, than in either of the other Evangelists, (See Matt. xx. 29. Luke xviii. 35.) I would beg the reader's
indulgence to notice some of the more striking features of it.

Jericho was the cursed city. Joshua vii. 26. 1 Kings xvi. 34; but
here the LORD will raise trophies to his grace. *Rahab* shall be called
from *Jericho ;* and thus blind *Bartimeus* shall form from thence an
everlasting monument in the Church, to the Redeemer's glory.

The first thing to be observed after the name, is the state and situation of this poor man. It doth not say so, but it is more than
probable that he was born blind. Born blind indeed he was in soul,
for this is the case of our nature universally speaking : and the SON of
GOD came to *give light to them that sit in darkness and the shadow of
death.* Isaiah xxxv. 5. Isaiah xlii. 6, 7. Isaiah xlix. 9. Isaiah
lxi. 1, compared with Luke iv. 18. I beg the Reader to consult
what was offered, Chap. viii. 22—26, on the subject of CHRIST, forming
a creation; in all such instances of blindness as he cured when the
eye had never been formed in the socket, or if destroyed. And
Reader ! is not every instance of every blindness when restored to
sight, an emblem of the sinner, yea, every sinner; when brought
*from darkness to light, and from the power of sin and Satan to the
living* GOD !

The next thing to be noticed in the case of this poor man, is the situation in which he sat by the highway side begging. Begging alms for the body, unconscious of the wants of the soul. What can be more pitiable than when we thus see beggars in our streets, earnest and importunate for the bread which perisheth; but unconcerned for that which endureth to everlasting life. Such was this man's state. Such is every man's state, though he waiteth on the highway of ordinances till Jesus pass by; and the Spirit of Jesus put a cry in his heart for spiritual light and understanding.

The *third* incident in the history of *Bartimeus* was the hearing of Jesus passing by, and the immediate effect wrought in his heart, putting a cry there; Jesus! *thou Son of David, have mercy on me!* Who told him that Jesus after the flesh, was the Son of David? And when he heard this, who informed him that it was under this character his people were to look for his mercy? Who but God the Spirit could have told him this; or put such a cry in his heart, which nothing should stifle, until the requested mercy had been granted him? Who, but must see the work of grace, upon this man's soul?

The *fourth* particular worthy our regard in the case, is the conduct of the people who endeavoured to stop his cry. What a striking representation this is of what is every day going on in the world. No sooner is a child of God brought under serious concern for his everlasting welfare, but false friends to poor sinners, and true enemies to the rich Savior, aim to stifle all conviction, and crush the infant desire of salvation at once in the soul. Oh! what sharp exercises have some gracious souls gone through, in their first awakenings from their carnal relations and neighbours, before that Christ hath been formed in the heart the hope of glory!

The *fifth* thing observable in the history, is the conduct of the poor man, on the endeavours of those around him to silence his cry; his earnestness became but the more increased. True grace, the more it is exercised, the more it will manifest itself: neither will an effectual call from the Lord ever cease, before that the prayer awakened by it and offered to the Lord, be answered in mercy. *Whom he did predestinate, them he also called; and whom he called, them he also justified; and whom he justified, them he also glorified.* Rom. viii. 30.

The standing still of Jesus, and calling the poor man, which are the next points to be noticed in this transaction, are most blessedly interesting indeed. Was there not *a needs be*, for Christ standing still; and calling him, similar to *Zaccheus* and the woman of *Samaria?* See Luke xix. 5. John iv. 4. Is not Jesus constrained by his very mission, to seek and save the lost? John vi. 37. Oh! what a subject of holy joy, such views of Christ furnish?

Neither do I think the poor man's instant arising, hastening to Jesus, and casting away his garment, (for the whole was Christ's grace in the man's heart, and not nature's powers,) are less interesting as the sweet effects proceeding from such a cause! Reader! think how blessed it must be, when at any time a poor sinner is enabled by the same grace as calls him, to hasten to that call; and to cast away every thing of his own; all his own righteousness, or what some men call righteousness, and which the word of God calls *filthy rags,* and come to Jesus, just as he is, poor and blind, and wretched, and needy; and receive all *from* Christ, since all is *in* Christ of pardon and salvation?

And what a beautiful close, to a most blessed and beautiful miracle doth the account end with : the poor man received his sight and followed Jesus in the way ; followed him no doubt, in the regeneration ; and having found Jesus so blessed in grace, is now sitting down with him for ever in glory. Oh! the preciousness of salvation! Oh! the unspeakable preciousness of such an Almighty Savior!

REFLECTIONS.

Blessed Bridegroom of thy Church ! how sweetly hast thou answered all the cavils of the *Pharisees*, and silenced all the fears of thy people, in teaching thy Church in the opening of this Chapter, that Jesus hath not put away his wife, notwithstanding all her shameful departures. Oh! for grace to cry out with the spouse, *my beloved is mine, and I am his!*

Praises to the condescending grace of the Son of God, who receiveth now, as he received then, in the days of his flesh, little children. So Lord must it be indeed thy grace to receive me, for I am but a child in understanding, and therefore I pray thee, thou tender Lord, to give me grace to sit at thy feet, and hear the blessed words which proceed out of thy mouth ! And as thou hast taught me in the solemn example of this apparently promising youth, who for the love of this world's gain, could so readily give up Christ. Oh! for grace, to be kept from *the love of money, which is the root of all evil.* Bring my soul under the continual baptisms of the Holy Ghost ; and let my whole rejoicings be in the consciousness of an interest in that ransom, which my God and Savior hath given for many.

Oh! thou glorious covenant of thy people ! Thou hast indeed proved thyself to be Jehovah's Covenant in all thy words and works. Lord ! I beseech thee give me grace to follow thee as *Bartimeus* did ; let me cast away, and cast off every thing of mine; for all must be, as I am myself, unclean. Lord, be thou all my salvation and all my desire ; give me spiritual sight, and enable me to follow thee in the way.

CHAP. XI.

CONTENTS.

The Lord Jesus *entereth Jerusalem in triumph.   The barren Fig Tree. *Christ's *Conversation with the Chief Priests.*

AND when they came nigh to Jerusalem, unto Bethphage and Bethany, at the mount of Olives, he sendeth forth two of his disciples,

2 And saith unto them, Go your way into the village over against you ; and as soon as ye be entered into it, ye shall find a colt tied, whereon never man sat ; loose him, and bring *him.*

3 And if any man say unto you, Why do ye

this? say ye that the Lord hath need of him; and straightway he will send him hither.

4 And they went their way, and found the colt tied by the door without in a place where two ways met; and they loose him.

5 And certain of them that stood there said unto them, What do ye, loosing the colt?

6 And they said unto them even as Jesus had commanded: and they let them go.

7 And they brought the colt to Jesus, and cast their garments on him; and he sat upon him.

8 And many spread their garments in the way: and others cut down branches off the trees, and strawed *them* in the way.

9 And they that went before, and they that followed, cried, saying, Hosanna; Blessed *is* he that cometh in the name of the Lord:

10 Blessed be the kingdom of our father David, that cometh in the name of the Lord: Hosanna in the Highest.

11 And Jesus entered into Jerusalem, and into the temple; and when he had looked round about upon all things, and now the eventide was come, he went out unto Bethany with the twelve.

Bethphage and *Bethany*, seem to have been somewhat like suburbs to Jerusalem; two little straggling villages joining to the city, the one ending like streets where the other began. From hence, and through these, the LORD was pleased to make a public entry into Jerusalem. The Prophet *Zechariah* foretold this; and as no king but Zion's King ever made such an entry, there can be no question concerning the prophecy, and the accomplishment of it. Zech. ix. 9.

I venture to think, that the disciples never gave a more decided token of their faith; perhaps none equal to it, during our LORD's ministry, than in thus going without hesitation, to take the colt according to his bidding. For, as the act itself was taking what was not their own, one might have expected that the disciples would have said so, when JESUS commanded them. But the manner in which he gave the order: his foretelling where they should find the colt, and the answer they were to give to the owners; *the* LORD *hath need of him;* as if intimating the LORD and proprietor of all things. These circumstances over-ruled their minds to an instant obedience. And it is probable, I think, that as the disciples never gave over, even till

CHRIST's death, their expectation of a temporal Kingdom, they might have been inclined to hope, that the LORD was now about to assume the government.

It is well worthy the Reader's remark, that the LORD JESUS went not to the Court, but to the Temple, as if to shew, that his kingdom was not of this world. Sweet consideration to the heart of the believer! So the Prophet described him; and so the LORD JESUS fulfilled the prophecy. Malachi iii. 1, 2. Nothing can be more decided in confirmation of CHRIST's character, than the over-ruling the minds of those little children to proclaim him for the CHRIST! And what could be more in point, in thus fulfilling that memorable prophecy. Psm. viii. 2. Surely, never did the LORD more signally silence the malice of his enemies, than when out of the mouths of unconscious children the GODHEAD and CHRISTSHIP of the Redeemer was thus acknowledged! If my Poor Man's Commentary should happen to fall into the hands of children; yea, even *little* children, or should be read in their hearing, I would beg the little ones of CHRIST's fold to notice this account; and I would beg the elders present to notice it to them. JESUS took delight in their testimony *then*, and so JESUS doth *now*. What can be more lovely than to hear the glory of the LORD *out of the mouth of babes and sucklings.* Mark x. 13—16. 2 Tim. iii. 15.

12 ¶ And on the morrow, when they were come from Bethany, he was hungry:

13 And seeing a fig tree afar off, having leaves, he came, if haply he might find any thing thereon: and when he came to it, he found nothing but leaves: for the time of figs was not *yet*.

14 And Jesus answered and said unto it, No man eat fruit of thee hereafter for ever: and his disciples heard *it*.

15 And they come to Jerusalem: and Jesus went into the temple, and began to cast out them that sold and bought in the temple, and overthrew the tables of the money-changers, and the seats of them that sold doves:

16 And would not suffer that any man should carry *any* vessel through the temple.

17 And he taught, saying unto them, Is it not written, My house shall be called of all nations the house of prayer? but ye have made it a den of thieves.

18 And the scribes and chief priests heard *it*, and sought how they might destroy him; for they

feared him, because all the people were astonished at his doctrine.

19 And when even was come, he went out of the city.

20 And in the morning as they passed by, they saw the fig tree dried up from the roots.

21 And Peter calling to remembrance, saith unto him, Master, behold the fig tree which thou cursedst is withered away.

22 And Jesus answering saith unto them, Have faith in God.

23 For verily I say unto you, that whosoever shall say unto this mountain, Be thou removed, and be thou cast into the sea; and shall not doubt in his heart, but shall believe that those things which he saith shall come to pass; he shall have whatsoever he saith.

24 Therefore I say unto you, What things soever ye desire when ye pray, believe that ye receive *them*, and ye shall have *them*.

25 And when ye stand praying, forgive, if ye have ought against any : that your Father also which is in heaven may forgive you your trespasses.

26 But if ye do not forgive, neither will your Father which is in heaven forgive your trespasses.

Every incident in this passage is interesting, and I beg the Reader's attention to it. And first, we are told that our LORD was hungry. Reader! never forget it, for it is among the most precious points of our holy faith, that the SON of GOD when he took into union with himself, our nature, took the whole of that nature in all the sinless infirmities of our nature, and was truly and properly Man as well as GOD. For had he not been so, he would not have suited for the purposes of redemption. An angel's nature would not have done ; for how would he then have felt as man, and known as man, what his people know and feel? JESUS hungered, wept, groaned, bled, died. And hence in those very feelings, knows the feelings of his people, in all these, and every other case. See Heb. ii. throughout.

The next thing to be noticed in this sweet passage, is the barren fig tree, and the LORD's condemning it to everlasting barrenness. But from the first view of the subject, we may well suppose that somewhat more than a mere fig tree is meant by it. No doubt the Jewish nation is referred to, which like this fig tree, had great shew

of religion, as this tree had leaves; but not an atom of fruit; yea,
rationally considered, they rejected the LORD of life and glory. But
the similitude reacheth to every other mere professor of the Gospel;
in every age of the Church, void of the fruit of CHRIST's righteousness.
And all such, from an awful representation in the present day, deceiving by the appearance of large full leaves of a profession without
fruit; and in the end will be found dried up from the roots, with the
curse of a broken law falling everlastingly upon them, untaken away
by CHRIST. Our LORD's observations to his disciples upon the occasion, are most sweet and precious. Faith in GOD; that is, in the
rich mercies of GOD in CHRIST, and the faithfulness of JEHOVAH's covenant promises in him, will remove all sin, and all difficulties; as if
Mount *Olivet*, which stood far from the sea, was carried at once into
it. Indeed, what cannot faith, which is the gift of GOD in CHRIST,
accomplish! See Heb. xi. See Matt. xxi. 18, &c. For the observation of CHRIST's driving the buyers and sellers out of the temple,
see John ii. 14.

27 ¶ And they come again to Jerusalem: and
as he was walking in the temple, there come to
him the chief priests and the scribes and the
elders.

28 And say unto him, By what authority dost
thou these things? and who gave thee this authority to do these things?

29 And Jesus answered and said unto them, I
will also ask of you one question, and answer me,
and I will tell you by what authority I do these
things.

30 The baptism of John, was *it* from heaven,
or of men? answer me.

31 And they reasoned with themselves, saying,
If we shall say, From heaven; he will say, Why
then did ye not believe him?

32 But if we shall say, Of men; they feared
the people: for all *men* counted John that he was
a prophet indeed.

33 And they answered and said unto Jesus, We
cannot tell: and Jesus answering saith unto them,
Neither do I tell you by what authority I do these
things.

, I am inclined to think, that those sworn enemies to CHRIST, who
are said here to have come to JESUS in the temple, demanding his authority, came in a public body, by way of confronting him; and as

those who were sent by the *Sanhedrim* for that purpose, and determined to silence him, and put an end to his preaching. The LORD JESUS had turned out the buyers and sellers from the temple, and had healed the blind and lame which came to him for that purpose into the temple; and was now teaching the people while walking about the temple, as was the custom in those days among a set of philosophers, who walked with the pupils as they taught them. Let the Reader figure to himself the LORD JESUS thus attacked, and observe the wisdom of the LORD in his answer. By directing not only the minds of his enemies to the subject of John's ministry, but also those to whom he was preaching his Gospel, the LORD took the most effectual method to throw to the ground their opposition, and establish his mission. They dared not admit *John's* ministry to be of divine appointment; for in so doing they would have acknowledged CHRIST, for the whole of *John's* office pointed to CHRIST. And most probably the congregation to whom JESUS was then preaching, had been among John's disciples; so that to have denied John's mission, would have been dangerous. The wretched state to which they were reduced, therefore, in confessing their ignorance, serves to shew the awful delusion under which those men were. And Reader, when we recollect that this transaction took place only a few days before CHRIST's death, the matter becomes yet more awful concerning them; for though put to silence and unable to answer CHRIST, they departed from him only with more determined hatred to seek his immediate death. Reader! You and I shall have read this account to very little profit, if it doth not teach us to what a desperate state the heart of man is capable of being hardened; and at the same time the distinguishing mercy of GOD in every instance where grace is given to believe the record GOD hath given of his dear SON! 1 John v. 10, 11.

REFLECTIONS.

READER! I would call upon you, as I would call upon myself; and may GOD the HOLY GHOST mercifully call upon both, to behold the LORD JESUS, in the opening of this chapter, as manifesting his double nature in his one glorious person, the GOD-Man Mediator; both in his unequalled humility when entering Jerusalem, in *having salvation, and yet lowly and riding upon an ass, and upon a colt, the foal of an ass.* And who less than GOD, could have exercised the knowledge of Omniscience so as to direct his disciples where to find the colt; and the power of inclining the minds of those the disciples were to meet, to fulfil CHRIST's wishes in the loan of the colt? Who less than GOD could have taught the children in the temple of CHRIST's person and character? And what power less than divine, could have constrained those babes to shout *Hosannah* to the glory of JESUS; when the elders, and many of them very probably the parents of those little ones, were doing all their malice could contrive, to stop their hymns of praise?

Reader! behold the barren fig tree! Observe its fruitless verdure! Figure to yourself the state of a church, a people, a family; yea, an individual, thus! And calculate if you can the awful state of appearing flourishing to the eye of man, while under the blighting curse of God. Oh! the tremendous sentence, could it be heard, concerning the unauthorized, uncalled, unsent minister, or graceless people: *No man eat fruit of thee for ever!*

Lord Jesus! increase our faith! let mountains of sin and unbelief be removed through faith in thy person, blood, and righteousness! And oh! let the malice of thy foes, and the opposition made by men to thee and thy Gospel, endear both to our heart. And grant such rich supplies of grace in the knowledge of thy person and work, that our faith may never be founded in *the wisdom of man, but in the power of* God.

CHAP. XII.

CONTENTS.

The Lord *is here teaching in Parables. The Pharisees and Herodians try to catch* Jesus *in his words. The* Lord *blessedly discourseth on the Resurrection, and with a Scribe: he cautions against the Scribes. The Chapter closeth with the* Lord's *Commendation of the Widow's Offering to the Treasury.*

AND he began to speak unto them by parables. A *certain* man planted a vineyard, and set an hedge about *it*, and digged *a place for* the winefat, and built a tower, and let it out to husbandmen, and went into a far country.

2 And at the season he sent to the husbandmen a servant, that he might receive from the husbandmen of the fruit of the vineyard.

3 And they caught *him*, and beat him, and sent *him* away empty.

4 And again he sent unto them another servant; and at him they cast stones, and wounded *him* in the head, and sent *him* away shamefully handled.

5 And again he sent another; and him they killed, and many others; beating some, and killing some.

6 Having yet therefore one son, his well beloved, he sent him also last unto them, saying, They will reverence my son.

7 But those husbandmen said among themselves, This is the heir; come, let us kill him, and the inheritance shall be ours.

8 And they took him, and killed *him*, and cast *him* out of the vineyard.

9 What shall therefore the lord of the vineyard do? he will come and destroy the husbandmen, and will give the vineyard unto others.

10 And have ye not read this scripture; The stone which the builders rejected is become the head of the corner:

11 This was the Lord's doing, and it is marvellous in our eyes?

12 And they sought to lay hold on him, but feared the people: for they knew that he had spoken the parable against them: and they left him, and went their way.

We had this parable, Matt. xxi. 33, to which I refer. But in addition to what was there observed, it may not be improper briefly to remark, that in this, as well as some other parables of CHRIST, we are to keep in remembrance as we pass through the several parts of it, that as it is a parable, we are not to strain the expressions beyond the figure intended; nor do more in the application of the whole than as evidently the LORD intended it in a general way. That the chief scope of it is to shew the LORD's ill-treatment from the Jewish nation is certain; and the several characters represented in the parable as plainly mark it out. The certain man here spoken of is GOD the FATHER; the vineyard as is elsewhere described, is the house of *Israel*, and the men of *Judah* his pleasant plant. Isaiah v. 7. The servants at different times said to be sent, are the Prophets, and faithful messengers preparatory to the coming of CHRIST, and his SON the LORD JESUS CHRIST. But when it is said that this *certain man went into a far country*; that this certain man, put a *may be* upon the reception his SON might receive; it *may be, they will reverence my* SON. These are parabolical expressions, and not to be construed in their exact literal sense and meaning. The LORD is every where, and always present; and therefore can neither be said to withdraw, nor go forth. Neither could the LORD be supposed to say, that there was a probability CHRIST would be reverenced by the nation, the Jews, to whom he was sent: for provision was only made for those to reverence CHRIST, of whom he himself spake, and every other: JESUS himself assigned the cause, wherefore they would not accept him. See John vi. 37. John viii. 43. But the parable is intended to shew the nation the Jews, in their national character. And the event, in the destruction of the Jewish nation, exactly corresponded to the predictions CHRIST here delivered. The whole nation was overthrown, and the people which survived the destruction of Jerusalem, were scattered over the face of the earth.

13 ¶ And they send unto him certain of the Pharisees, and of the Herodians, to catch him in his words.

14 And when they were come, they say unto him, Master, we know that thou art true, and carest for no man : for thou regardest not the person of men : but teachest the way of God in truth : Is it lawful to give tribute to Cesar, or not ?

15 Shall we give, or shall we not give ? but he knowing their hypocrisy said unto them, Why tempt ye me ? bring me a penny, that I may see *it.*

16 And they brought *it;* and he saith unto them, Whose *is* this image and superscription ? and they said unto him, Cesar's.

17 And Jesus answering said unto them, Render to Cesar the things that are Cesar's, and to God the things that are God's. And they marvelled at him.

It was said of the LORD JESUS, under the spirit of prophecy, that *with the hypocritical mockers were those that gnashed upon him with their teeth.* Psm. xxxv. 16. And here we behold them in deep design. If to the question of the lawfulness to give tribute to *Cæsar,* JESUS had said, no ; the *Herodians* would have apprehended him as an enemy to government. And if the LORD had justified *Cæsar's* claim, the whole nation of the Jews would have been against him, as they were all longing for deliverance from the yoke, and the very gatherers of the taxes were called publicans, and classed only as sinners. I beg the Reader not only to remark how much wisdom JESUS displayed in avoiding the trap which they had laid for him, but how blessedly he took occasion to remind them of what they owed to GOD. Who can indeed render to the LORD his due ?

18 ¶ Then come unto him the Sadducees, which say there is no resurrection ; and they asked him, saying,

19 Master, Moses wrote unto us, If a man's brother die, and leave *his* wife *behind him,* and leave no children, that his brother should take his wife, and raise up seed unto his brother.

20 Now there were seven brethren : and the first took a wife, and dying left no seed.

21 And the second took her, and died, neither left he any seed : and the third likewise.

22 And the seven had her, and left no seed, last of all the woman died also.

23 In the resurrection therefore, when they shall rise, whose wife shall she be of them? for the seven had her to wife.

24 And Jesus answering said unto them, Do ye not therefore err because ye know not the scriptures, neither the power of God?

25 For when they shall rise from the dead, they neither marry, nor are given in marriage, but are as the angels which are in heaven.

26 And as touching the dead, that they rise; have ye not read in the book of Moses, how in the bush God spake unto him, saying, I *am* the God of Abraham, and the God of Isaac, and the God of Jacob?

27 He is not the God of the dead, but the God of the living. Ye therefore do greatly err.

I detain the Reader, at the entrance, upon this most beautiful discourse, of the LORD JESUS, to remark to him, how graciously the LORD made every occasion minister to his glory, and his people's welfare. Here were the captious *Sadducees*, the free-thinkers of our LORD's generation, who came to him for no purpose, but to entangle JESUS in his talk. And observe, what a very blessed opportunity the LORD made of it, to speak upon that interesting subject, concerning the resurrection. It becomes a confirmation of that precious scripture; *Surely, the wrath of man shall praise thee, the remainder of wrath shalt thou restrain.* The LORD will use just so much of man's wrath, as shall minister to the LORD's purpose, in the promotion of his glory; and all that is over and above, as the violent stream at a mill, shall be turned into another channel. Psm. lxxvi. 10.

The junction of those different sects of men, *Sadducees* with the *Herodians*, was simply with a view to gall CHRIST. Every one will join in the attempt to crush CHRIST; however like *Herod* and *Pontius Pilate*, in other matters, they are at enmity between themselves. Luke xxiii. 12. So was it then, so is it now, and so will it be, during the whole of the present world. It is blessed to know this, and blessed to prove it. The most violent enemies against CHRIST, while the LORD was on earth, were the self-righteous Pharisees; and the greatest opposers to his purest truths now, are the same characters.

The question put by those men, was founded in consummate ignorance; and as our LORD told them, because *they knew not the scriptures;* that is, they knew nothing of the scripture, but the mere letter; and had never felt *the power of* GOD in them, by the LORD's teaching. *Seven* brethren marrying one and the same woman, or had the case been *seventy times seven* if possible, it would have been the same thing; for all the connections of nature in this life, are wholly for the purposes of this life, and are dissolved at death.

Our LORD therefore in declaring the children of the resurrection to be as the angels, gave a full and decisive answer to this, and every other question of the like nature. But the occasion was too fair to suffer it to pass unnoticed, as the subject might be made to minister to his people's comfort; and therefore the LORD JESUS not only proceeded in it, by way of establishing the certainty of the doctrine itself, but of throwing some divine light upon it, which have proved ever since, and ever will, until the whole come to be realized in glory, of the most blessed, and unspeakable joy to his Church.

The LORD takes only a single circumstance from the Old Testament scripture, in confirmation of the soul refreshing doctrine, as in itself more than sufficient for this purpose ; namely the call of GOD to *Moses* at the bush. No doubt it was JESUS himself, who in his covenant relation as GOD-Man Mediator, before his more open revelation of himself in that character, which spake to *Moses* at the bush. So *Stephen* believed. Acts vii. 30. where he calls him *an angel* (or *Messenger*) *of the* LORD. And so in fact the LORD JESUS himself intimated, when in his conference with the Jews, he declared his existence to have been before Abraham, and called himself *I* AM. Compare John viii. 58, with Exod. iii. 14. But passing this by, for the present if we consider what the LORD JESUS here saith to the Sadducees, we shall discover that nothing can be more decisive in confirmation of the resurrection. The LORD quotes the expressions made use of by the LORD to *Moses* at the bush. *I am the* GOD *of Abraham and the* GOD *of Isaac and the* GOD *of Jacob.* Now at the time that these blessed truths were delivered, these Patriarchs had been long dead, and their bodies mouldered into dust. And yet, GOD declares himself as much their GOD as ever. The LORD doth not say *I was* their GOD, when living in their bodies; but *I am* so now. A thing in itself impossible, if *Abraham,* though dead in body, was not then living in spirit. Hence the LORD adds, GOD *is not the* GOD *of the dead, but the* GOD *of the living :* and as Luke hath the words in his Gospel, it is added, *for all live unto him.* Luke xx. 38. And *Paul,* under the authority of the HOLY GHOST, was directed to teach the Church that whether believers lived, or died, they were the LORD's. *For* (said he) *to this end,* CHRIST *both died, and rose and revived, that he might be* LORD *both of the dead and living.* Rom. xiv. 8, 9. I pray the Reader by the way, to join this blessed passage with the two just before referred to. John viii. 58. with Exod. iii. 14, in confirmation that it was our LORD CHRIST who spake to *Moses* at the bush; and may the LORD give him a right understanding in all things.

Now then from the whole of this most blessed, and highly interesting passage, I venture to believe the following conclusions are undeniable. *First,* that the Patriarchs, *Abraham, Isaac,* and *Jacob,* were in their spirits, living in a state of separate existence from their bodies, at the time the LORD spake to *Moses* from the bush, when he called himself their GOD. *Secondly,* that the LORD in this call to *Moses,* declaring himself as he did in his covenant relationship to those Patriarchs, most fully and plainly implied his engagements with the whole persons of each, both soul and body ; and therefore the LORD could not be supposed to be understood, as solemnly acknowledging this relationship, which was made at a time when both existed together, if one part of the being of those persons was annihilated, never more to exist. *Thirdly*, the very recognizing this glorious title of the Patriarch's GOD in covenant, at a time their ashes were in the dust, solemnly confirmed the assurance of their resurrection. And, *fourthly*, the fulfilment of GOD's covenant made with those Patriarchs, depended upon the soul and body of each being again united; since not only without it, the covenant promises of GOD could only be with one part of their persons; but also the happiness of each could only be in part, if the body for ever remained separate from the soul. Reader! ponder well these things: give thyself wholly to them. In JESUS, behold the resurrection and the life, And oh! for grace from GOD the HOLY GHOST, to have *part in the first resurrection;. on such the second death hath no power!* Rev. xx. 6. See Mark xvi. 9. 1 Cor. xv. 20.

28 And one of the scribes came, and having heard them reasoning together, and perceiving that he had answered them well, asked him, Which is the first commandment of all?

29 And Jesus answered him, The first of all the commandments *is*, Hear, O Israel; The Lord our God is one Lord:

30 And thou shalt love the Lord thy God with all thy heart, and with all thy soul, and with all thy mind, and with all thy strength. This *is* the first commandment.

31 And the second *is* like, *namely* this, Thou shalt love thy neighbour as thyself. There is none other commandment greater than these.

32 And the scribe said unto him, Well, Master, thou hast said the truth: for there is one God; and there is none other but he:

33 And to love him with all the heart, and with all the understanding, and with all the soul, and with all the strength, and to love *his* neighbour as himself, is more than all whole burnt offerings and sacrifices.

34 And when Jesus saw that he answered discreetly, he said unto him, Thou art not far from the kingdom of God, and no man after that durst ask him *any question.*

If we were not well acquainted with the general character of the Scribes, we might be led to hope, that this man's question was with a better design than the Sadducees. But there is nothing neutral in the holy war. JESUS himself hath decided; *he that is not with me is against me.* Matt. xii. 30. But whether a friend or foe, our LORD hath blessedly taught the divine unity existing in a threefold character of persons, and followed it up with all its blessed consequences. The precious passage from one of the books of *Moses*, which the LORD refers to in proof, is in itself more than half confirmation of the glorious truth of the whole Bible, that the LORD JEHOVAH, the one Eternal and true GOD exists in a threefold character of persons; for otherwise, wherefore is Israel called upon to hear that the LORD thy GOD (that is, GOD in covenant) is one LORD! It never could have entered the apprehension of the human mind untaught of GOD, or any thing beside. But when the LORD was pleased to reveal himself, as in a great variety of parts in scripture he hath done, in his persons and in the covenant engagements between the persons of the GODHEAD, it formed in the LORD's grace great mercy to his people, to remind them at the same time of the unity of the Divine Essence. Reader! the LORD grant that you and I may so hear, and so love each and every person of the GODHEAD, and know them in all their office-characters and relations, that it may become a proof of our true regeneration of heart; since by nature there is no love, but enmity in us towards the Almighty Author of our being, till GOD *who commandeth the light to shine out of darkness, hath shined in our hearts, to give us the light of the knowledge of the glory of* GOD, *in the face of* JESUS CHRIST. 2 Cor. iv. 6.

35 ¶ And Jesus answered and said, while he taught in the temple, How say the scribes that Christ is the son of David?

36 For David himself said by the Holy Ghost, The LORD said to my Lord, Sit thou on my right hand, till I make thine enemies thy footstool.

37 David therefore himself calleth him Lord; and whence is he *then* his son? And the common people heard him gladly.

38 And he said unto them in his doctrine, Beware of the scribes, which love to go in long clothing, and *love* salutations in the market-places,

39 And the chief seats in the synagogues, and the uppermost rooms at feasts:

40 Which devour widows' houses, and for a pretence make long prayers: these shall receive greater damnation.

These observations of the LORD JESUS, unasked, and, as it should seem unexpected, because he had put all his enemies to silence, so as to presume to ask him no more questions, come in very sweetly after the former. Having there established the glorious mystery of One Eternal and Divine JEHOVAH existing in a threefold character of persons; the LORD JESUS here goes on to preach the second wonderful mystery of GOD *manifest in the flesh*. And in the question concerning CHRIST, at once *David's* LORD and *David's* Son, he confirms the doctrine most completely. Luke i. 32. 1 Tim. iii. 16. John i. 14: Rev. xvi. 22 : *Matthew* hath more largely given the LORD's discourse upon this occasion, in his condemnation of the Scribes and Pharisees. I therefore refer to it. Matt. xxiii. throughout.

41 ¶ And Jesus sat over against the treasury, and beheld how the people cast money into the treasury: and many that were rich cast in much.

42 And there came a certain poor widow, and she threw in two mites, which make a farthing.

43 And he called *unto him* his disciples, and saith unto them, Verily I say unto you, That this poor widow hath cast more in, than all they which have cast into the treasury:

44 For all *they* did cast in of their abundance; but she of her want did cast in all that she had, *even* all her living.

It is likely that when the LORD had caused all his foes to quit the field, he sat down with his disciples near the treasury door. Those who have described the Temple, speak of several chests which were placed there to receive the voluntary offerings of the people. This poor widow attracted the special notice of JESUS, How little was she conscious whose eye was upon her! How little did she think that this private retired act would be published to the very end of time in the Church of CHRIST, and be had in everlasting remembrance. Reader! what have we to cast into the LORD's treasury? Indeed, and in truth, nothing but what we have first received. We have too mites; soul and body: and these are both the LORD's. Oh! for grace to give both these; and JESUS looking on; JESUS disposing to the act, and JESUS accepting all to his glory. 1 Cor. vi. 19, 20.

REFLECTIONS.

PAUSE my soul over the many precious contents in this blessed chapter! Both the Jewish nation, and the Jewish church, have been as the LORD's vineyard. Oh! the boundless grace of JEHOVAH in setting apart that people with whom he deposited his Ordinances; *whose are the fathers, and of whom as concerning the flesh* CHRIST *came, who is over all* GOD *blessed for ever, Amen.* But oh! the wonderful provocations of Israel, in slighting the LORD's servants rising early and speaking, but regarding them not; till at length they killed the LORD of life and glory! But, Reader! are we then by nature or by practice better than they? Oh! no, in no wise. The LORD hath concluded all under sin, that the righteousness of GOD, which is by faith of JESUS CHRIST, might be given to them that believe. *Oh!* *the depth of the riches, both of the wisdom and knowledge of* GOD !

My soul! behold thy LORD attacked in every way, 'by men calling him *Rabbi ;* and professing great regard to his person, for his teaching the way of GOD in truth; and by *Pharisee* and *Sadducee,* by *Herodians* and by *Scribes,* aiming to catch him in his words! Oh! thou divine and Almighty Teacher, cause thy blessed truths in this chapter to sink deep into my heart! LORD! be thou everlastingly blessed for thy gracious discoveries concerning the glorious truths of thy resurrection. LORD! be thou my resurrection, and my life! Give me to know Israel's GOD in covenant as one LORD! And oh! give me grace to love Him in his threefold character of Person, FATHER, SON, and HOLY GHOST, *with all my heart, with all my soul, with all my mind, and with all my strength.* And in the love of GOD may my affections find sweet directions, to the love of my neighbour. So will David's LORD be my LORD, and his CHRIST my CHRIST. And like the poor widow, the LORD's treasury will have my whole living ; since all I have, and all I am, are the LORD's, and of His own only do I give him.

CHAP. XIII.

CONTENTS.

The LORD *foretells the Destruction of the Temple ; and the sad Calamities of the Jews. His solemn Cautions to his Disciples in the Expectation of those woeful Events.*

AND as he went out of the temple, one of his disciples saith unto him, Master, see what manner of stones, and what buildings *are here!*

2 And Jesus answering said unto him, Seest thou these great buildings? there shall not be left one stone upon another that shall not be thrown down.

3 And as he sat upon the mount of Olives over against the temple, Peter and James and John and Andrew asked him privately.

4 Tell us, when shall these things be? and what *shall be* the sign when all these things shall be fulfilled?

When we read, as in this scripture, of JESUS departing from the temple, and connect with it that it was his farewell departure, for he never again entered it, what solemn thoughts it awakens? When the LORD departs, woe to that land, woe to that house or family, where the LORD's gracious presence is not. No sooner had *Lot* departed from *Sodom* than the next account is the destruction of it. Gen. xix.

22—24. And who shall say how much the Christless owe in being saved from instant ruin, both in nations, and cities, and families, from the seed of CHRIST living in the midst of them.

This *second* temple, though so vastly inferior to the glory of the *first*, or *Solomon's* temple, so called, that the antient men who had seen the former, wept at beholding this latter. Ezra iii. 12, 13. And see the LORD's promise in consequence thereof. Haggai ii. 1—9. and which was literally fulfilled when the SON of GOD in our nature entered it: this second temple was a wonderful building. It had been repaired by *Herod*; and *Josephus*, the Jewish historian, saith, that some of the stones were of a magnitude even to *forty-five cubits* long, *five* high, and *six* broad. JESUS declared that such should be the desolation of the place, when the LORD visited it for the rejection of CHRIST, that not one of these immense stones should be left upon another. And we are told in history, that when *Titus*, under whose army *Jerusalem* was sacked, heard of this prophecy of CHRIST, he endeavoured to counteract it; but such was the impetuosity of his army, that no orders could restrain them, and CHRIST's prediction was literally fulfilled.

5 And Jesus answering them began to say, Take heed lest any *man* deceive you:

6 For many shall come in my name, saying, I am *Christ*; and shall deceive many.

7 And when ye shall hear of wars and rumours of wars, be ye not troubled: for *such things* must needs be; but the end *shall* not *be* yet.

8 For nation shall rise against nation, and kingdom against kingdom: and there shall be earthquakes in divers places, and there shall be famines and troubles: these *are* the beginnings of sorrows.

9 ¶ But take heed to yourselves: for they shall deliver you up to councils; and in the synagogues ye shall be beaten: and ye shall be brought before rulers and kings for my sake, for a testimony against them.

10 And the gospel must first be published among all nations.

11 But when they shall lead *you*, and deliver you up, take no thought beforehand what ye shall speak, neither do ye premeditate: but whatsoever shall be given you in that hour, that speak ye: for it is not ye that speak, but the Holy Ghost.

12 Now the brother shall betray the brother to death, and the father the son : and children shall rise up against *their* parents, and shall cause them to be put to death.

13 And ye shall be hated of all *men* for my name's sake : but he that shall endure unto the end, the same shall be saved.

14 ¶ But when ye shall see the abomination of desolation, spoken of by Daniel the prophet, standing where it ought not, (let him that readeth understand,) then let them that be in Judea flee to the mountains :

15 And let him that is on the housetop not go down into the house, neither enter *therein*, to take any thing out of his house :

16 And let him that is in the field not turn back again for to take up his garment.

17 But woe to them that are with child, and to them that give suck in those days !

18 And pray ye that your flight be not in the winter.

19 For *in* those days shall be affliction, such as was not from the beginning of the creation which God created unto this time, neither shall be.

20 And except that the Lord had shortened those days, no flesh should be saved : but for the elect's sake, whom he hath chosen, he hath shortened the days.

21 And then if any man shall say to you, Lo, here *is* Christ; or lo, *he is* there; believe *him* not.

22 For false Christs and false prophets shall rise, and shall shew signs and wonders, to seduce, if *it were* possible, even the elect.

23 But take ye heed: behold, I have foretold you all things.

24 ¶ But in those days, after that tribulation, the sun shall be darkened, and the moon shall not give her light.

25 And the stars of heaven shall fall, and the powers that are in heaven shall be shaken.

26 And then shall they see the Son of man coming in the clouds with great power and glory.

27 And then shall he send his angels, and shall gather together his elect from the four winds, from the uttermost part of the earth, to the uttermost part of heaven.

We have had the relation of this judgment of GOD upon Jerusalem, as predicted by our LORD, read to us in Matt. xxiv. throughout the greater part of it, together with observations. It will be the less necessary in this place to enlarge.

In addition to what was there offered, (to which I refer,) let me only request the Reader to consider the importance of the subject itself, which is recorded by *Luke* also, in the same, or similar solemn circumstances. See Luke xxi. throughout; and mark therefrom the awful judgment of GOD upon *Jerusalem*, the beloved city, in the midst of the LORD's mercies. And I take occasion therefrom, to request the Reader to make the nice, but proper distinction, between *Jerusalem* as a nation, and *Jerusalem* as the city of the LORD's inheritance. The HOLY GHOST useth very different words by way of expression, to denote the striking difference between the nation of the Jews, as the people with whom the LORD deposited the *covenant, and the giving of the law, and the service of GOD and the promises*, and the children of promise in CHRIST. The nation of the Jews are called indeed CHRIST's own; because it was his own nation after the flesh, and his own by creation and right. Thus it is said, that *he came to his own, and his own received him not.* John i. 11; meaning, that when CHRIST came into the world in the open manifestation of his office character, he came unto his own nation the Jews, and his own nation, as a nation, received him not. But in another part of the same Gospel, when it is said, that JESUS having loved his own which were in the world, he loved them unto the end. John xiii. 1. Here the word rendered *own*, is a very different word from the former, as every one who can read the original cannot but know. In the first chapter, where CHRIST is said to come to his own, the word means no more than that they were his own as a nation, to which as a Jew he belonged; or as the Creator of them, his own *goods*, his *property*. But the other word in the 13th chapter, is a word of peculiar and special nearness and relationship, as a man's own children, his spouse, his brethren; yea, *members of his body, of his flesh, and of his bones.* Such distinct views will serve to guide the Reader through this chapter, in beholding the miseries of *Jerusalem* with a different eye from what otherwise might be done; and shew at the same time, how CHRIST's love to his people is never interrupted by all the adverse circumstances to the ungodly.

And while I am upon the subject, I crave the indulgence of the Reader a little longer. In this solemn prediction of CHRIST, the LORD speaks of the awful events which were then coming on, as giving occasion for *false Christs and false Prophets to arise, which would, if it*

were possible, deceive even the very elect. Now that the security of the
Lord's people was not in themselves, is evident from our Lord's
expression. And indeed, most blessed was it then, that it was not so;
and blessed is it in every age of the Church of Christ that it is not
so; for if it were, the enemy would make sad havock of the Lord's
people, mingled as they are with the ungodly. Sometimes the elect
springing forth from the loins of ungodly parents in the Adam-nature
of existence; and sometimes the elect themselves having ungodly
children in the natural generation from father to son. Oh! how would
those natural ties, (yea, how often do those natural ties) send forth
their mature influence to the great obstruction of grace. Perhaps
some Reader of my *Poor Man's Commentary*, in this place, if a partaker of the grace of God in Christ Jesus, will enter into my meaning, and find cause therefrom while feeling the truth of it, to lift an
eye and heart also, to *the* God *of all his mercy!* Psm. lix. 10.

I would beg to add one observation more, and it shall be short, on
those desolating dispensations which the Lord foretold to his disciples,
as then hastening upon Jerusalem; and which was not confined to
that period, but attacheth itself to the people of God, in all ages of
the Church; namely, that the true followers of the Lord Jesus should
be *hated of all men for his name's sake.* Reader! I beseech you
look to this, as among the truest badge of character. Who is the
greatest hater of the Lord's faithful ones now? Who hates with the
bitterest hatred the lover of Jesus, that ascribes the whole of salvation
where Jehovah hath ascribed it, to the Lord Jesus Christ; and
makes his blood and righteousness the sum and substance of all?
Who hates such lovers of Jesus most? Not the openly profane; not
the infidel of any description or character: but the Pharisee, the self-
righteous Pharisee; the same class as was the Lord's bitterest foes in
the days of Christ's flesh, and are now the bitterest enemies to his followers, in the day of Christ's power.

28 Now learn a parable of the fig tree: When
her branch is yet tender, and putteth forth leaves,
ye know that summer is near:

29 So ye in like manner, when ye shall see
these things come to pass, know that it is nigh,
even at the doors.

30 Verily I say unto you, That this generation
shall not pass till all these things be done.

31 Heaven and earth shall pass away: but my
words shall not pass away.

32 But of that day and *that* hour knoweth no
man, no not the angels which are in heaven, neither the Son, but the Father.

This passage hath been noticed before. Matt. xxiv. 36. to which
I therefore refer. I only detain the Reader to remark in addition to
what was there observed, that when the Lord Jesus in this verse speaks

of the ignorance of the day and hour of those visitations, the words have not the smallest connection, as some have supposed, with the day of future judgment: but is wholly in reference to this destruction of Jerusalem. And concerning this event, those who lived to see it, and were involved in it, and survived it, could form no exact calculation we are told, by their historian, when it began, and when it ended; the miseries were so great and incalculable!

33 Take ye heed, watch and pray: for ye know not when the time is.

34 *For the Son of man is* as a man taking a far journey, who left his house, and gave authority to his servants, and to every man his work, and commanded the porter to watch.

35 Watch ye therefore; for ye know not when the master of the house cometh, at even, or at midnight, or at the cock-crowing, or in the morning:

36 Lest coming suddenly he find you sleeping.

37 And what I say unto you, I say unto all, Watch.

The close of this chapter gives occasion to extend our LORD's direction of watchfulness, not only to his disciples of that generation, but to the Church of GOD in all ages. It is blessed, yea, very blessed, for a child of GOD to be always on the look out for the second coming of CHRIST; or what is to the same amount, the day of a man's death. For though to every redeemed soul, in whose heart the work of grace hath been wrought, and being savingly converted from darkness to light, and from the power of sin and Satan to the living GOD; that soul is always in an habitual state of preparation, and always ready at a moment's call, to go forth at the Master's call into the world of spirits; yet it is blessed to be in an actual state, waiting, looking, longing for, and hastening to, as the Apostle speaks, for the LORD's coming. Reader! think what a blessed privilege this is, and beg of the LORD JESUS to be so found at his coming. 2 Peter iii. 12.

REFLECTIONS.

How little was it apprehended, either by the disciples or the multitude, that when JESUS went out of the temple, as is here represented in the opening of this chapter; he went out to return to it no more! Reader! so ought you, and I, to esteem ordinances, and our attendance on the house of prayer, each time as though it were our last. How differently would they be valued even by those who valued them most, if this thought were always uppermost in our minds?

Reader! while perusing the many awful events foretold by our LORD, in this chapter; how precious the thought! CHRIST's people were

safe in the midst of danger. It is wonderful until explained by God
the HOLY GHOST, how the LORD's people in all ages live, and are
carried on, and carried through, a thousand perils which apparently
seem to threaten destruction to them as well as the ungodly ; and yet
Noah-like they live out the storm, secured in the Ark CHRIST JESUS.
How may every child of GOD, yea, how ought every child of GOD to
take to himself the comfort of the LORD's assurance ; *I know the
thoughts I think towards you; thoughts of peace and not of evil, to
give you an expected end.* Precious LORD JESUS ! *thou art my hiding
place, thou shalt preserve me from trouble ; thou shalt compass me about
with songs of deliverance!*

CHAP. XIV.

CONTENTS.

We enter here upon the History of CHRIST's *Passion. The Chief
Priests conspire against him. A woman anoints the* LORD. *Judas
selleth* CHRIST, *and betrayeth him.* Peter *denieth him.*

A FTER two days was *the feast of* the passover
and of unleavened bread: and the chief
priests and the scribes sought how they might take
him by craft, and put *him* to death.

2 But they said, Not on the feast *day*, lest there
be an uproar of the people.

In addition to the observations made on the subject of the Passover,
Matt. xxvi. 2—20, &c. to which I refer the Reader, I beg to remark that *Mark* takes notice also, of the feast of *unleavened bread.*
It may be not amiss to consider, that those feasts were always together; in fact they were one and the same. See Exod. xii. 8, &c.
The Passover was finished in the first evening's solemnity, but the feast
of unleavened bread continued seven days. But what an awful picture is here given of the Chief Priests and Scribes! That at a season so
holy and sanctified for celebrating that great mercy of GOD to the
Church, in delivering the people from Egyptian bondage; those men
should then, of all other seasons, contrive the death of JESUS. They
indeed postponed their intentions for the moment, in carrying them
into execution, not out of tenderness to JESUS, not lest their solemn
services should be interrupted, but from the great affection the common people had to the person of JESUS, lest the LORD should be
rescued from them. Reader! pause over this part of the subject, and
behold in those men, the awful depravity of the human heart ! True,
indeed, it was necessary that CHRIST our passover should be then
sacrificed ; and they literally did that, and no more in the crucifying the LORD of life and glory, which GOD had before determined to
be done. Acts iv. 27, 28. But though the LORD's ordination was in
all, yet the deed itself, and the malice of the deed, was all their own;
and the chapter in the opening of it, gives us an awful representation
of the heart of man.

3 ¶ And being in Bethany in the house of Simon the leper, as he sat at meat, there came a woman having an alabaster box of ointment of spikenard very precious; and she brake the box, and poured *it* on his head.

4 And there were some that had indignation within themselves, and said, Why was this waste of the ointment made?

5 For it might have been sold for more than three hundred pence, and have been given to the poor. And they murmured against her.

6 And Jesus said, Let her alone; why trouble ye her? she hath wrought a good work on me.

7 For ye have the poor with you always, and whensoever ye will ye may do them good : but me ye have not always.

8 She hath done what she could: she is come aforehand to anoint my body to the burying.

9 Verily I say unto you, Wheresoever this gospel shall be preached throughout the whole world, *this* also that she hath done shall be spoken of for a memorial of her.

There is somewhat uncommonly interesting in this transaction, and as our LORD himself declared, that it was significant of his burial, our chiefest improvement of it should be with an eye to JESUS. •

Spikenard was in itself, we are told by naturalists, a small shrub not lovely to the view, but very grateful to the smell, (see my Poor Man's Concordance, *Spikenard*,) but when it was prepared into an ointment, it was very costly. This poor woman is supposed, and perhaps rightly so, to have been either *Mary*, the sister of *Lazarus*, (for this transaction was at *Bethany*,) or *Mary Magdalene*. But the LORD saith the act was symbolical. And what could be more striking, in allusion to his person and sacrifice, than this act of affection, excited, and altogether accomplished by the work of grace in her heart. *Spikenard* was very expressive of the person, and offices of CHRIST. Lowly and humble in himself, there was no beauty to desire him, yet the sweet *savour of his name is as ointment poured forth.* Song i. 3—12. Precious LORD JESUS! though thy people of the present day have not the privilege which this woman had, to anoint thine head at thy table, yet while they sit before thee, and by faith behold thee, we would say with the Church, *cause my Spikenard to send forth the smell thereof.* Every thing in thee, and from thee, is more precious than the mountains of frankincense. Thy person, thy blood, thy righteousness, are all lovely and refreshing.

10 ¶ And Judas Iscariot, one of the twelve, went unto the chief priests, to betray him unto them.

11 And when they heard *it*, they were glad, and promised to give him money. And he sought how he might conveniently betray him.

> If we compare what is here said, with what is related, John xiii. 27, of the devil's entering into *Judas*, we shall discover somewhat of the deliberate act of this son of perdition. No doubt the woman's pouring the ointment on CHRIST's head, acted as an incentive upon the mind of *Judas*, as we know the grace the LORD gives his people, calls forth the greater malice of their enemies. Acts vii. 54. Judas must have gone away from *Bethany* into *Jerusalem*, immediately after this transaction of the ointment, for the Chief Priests were at this time in council, (see verse 1,) and the traitor now joined the party; though to cover his diabolical purpose, he soon after returned and joined the disciples, and sat with them at the supper. Reader! pause over the view! Oh! who shall calculate the enormity of sin! Oh! who shall calculate the preciousness of distinguishing grace! See John xiii. 18.

12 ¶ And the first day of unleavened bread, when they killed the passover, his disciples said unto him, Where wilt thou that we go and prepare that thou mayest eat the passover?

13 ¶ And he sendeth forth two of his disciples, and saith unto them, Go ye into the city, and there shall meet you a man bearing a pitcher of water: follow him.

14 And wheresoever he shall go in, say ye to the good man of the house, The Master saith, Where is the guest-chamber, where I shall eat the passover with my disciples?

15 And he will shew you a large upper room furnished *and* prepared: there make ready for us.

16 And his disciples went forth, and came into the city, and found as he had said unto them: and they made ready the passover.

> It should not be forgotten, that the LORD with his disciples were still at *Bethany*, two miles from Jerusalem, and as the time was now arrived for the Passover, it became necessary for the disciples to return into the city, to make provision for it. For, according to the law in Jerusalem, the feast must be, and the Paschal Lamb slain, be-

tween the two evenings, and eaten at night. Hence the question the disciples put to CHRIST, and the LORD's answer as related in those verses. The Reader, I hope, will not fail to take notice how the LORD JESUS here again manifested his divine nature in foretelling his disciples who they should meet, and how they should be received : JESUS over-ruling this man's mind to accommodate the LORD and his disciples. By the disciples' *making ready the Passover*, I should apprehend they bought a lamb, for such no doubt were sold upon this solemn festival at Jerusalem, both to the inhabitants, and to the Jews which came to Jerusalem, to celebrate this feast; and as the law enjoined, they must have carried it to the court of the temple for slaughter, and there burnt the fat upon the altar, sprinkling the blood upon it, before they brought it home to the house where it was to be eaten. And I should apprehend also, that the roasting it whole, and the bitter herbs, and bread and wine, were all included in what is said of the disciples' making ready before that JESUS came in the evening to sit down with the twelve. See Exod. xii. throughout. Deut. xvi. 1—8.

17 And in the evening he cometh with the twelve.

18 And as they sat and did eat, Jesus said, Verily I say unto you, One of you which eateth with me shall betray me.

19 And they began to be sorrowful, and to say unto him one by one, *Is* it I? and another *said*, *Is* it I?

20 And he answered, and said unto them, *It is* one of the twelve, that dippeth with me in the dish.

21 The Son of man indeed goeth, as it is written of him : but woe to that man by whom the Son of man is betrayed? good were it for that man if he had never been born.

22 And as they did eat, Jesus took bread, and blessed, and brake *it*, and gave to them, and said, Take, eat : this is my body.

23 And he took the cup, and when he had given thanks, he gave *it* to them; and they all drank of it.

24 And he said unto them, This is my blood of the new testament, which is shed for many.

25 Verily I say unto you, I will drink no more

of the fruit of the vine, until that day that I drink
it new in the kingdom of God.

26 And when they had sung an hymn, they went
out into the mount of Olives.

Some have thought that *Judas* did not partake of this Passover, but
to me, I confess, there doth not seem the shadow of a doubt but that he
did. This first verse is decidedly in confirmation. And *in the evening*
JESUS *cometh with the twelve;* consequently Judas included: *and as
they sat and did eat* JESUS *said,* &c. But having very largely
dwelt upon this subject, in my *Poor Man's Concordance,* under the
article *Judas,* I rather refer to what is there said, than enlarge upon
it here.

Though I shall reserve the more striking circumstances concerning the traitor *Judas,* for one collected point of view, in what is said
of him, John xiii. 18, &c. yet I cannot help remarking to the Reader
in this place, the hardened state of this man's mind, which could so
coolly and deliberately return and take his place among the disciples, as though equally loving of his LORD, when he had then entered into an engagement with the Chief Priests to betray him. And
when, one by one, the disciples put the question to what JESUS had
said, that one of them would betray him, though conscious of his infamy, he should dare to brave the question also, and say, is it I? Oh!
the obduracy which sin occasions! *Matthew,* in his relation of this
solemn scene hath observed, that while the other disciples every one
of them, in putting the question to JESUS, called him LORD; Judas
called him *Rabbi.* And certain it is, that in the original the words
are different: the one is LORD, and the other *Rabbi* or Master. See
Matt. xxvi. 22 and 25. And as *Rabbi* or *Master* implies a nearness
and affection which the more distant name of LORD doth not convey,
to what an unequalled degree of infamy was the traitor by this time
arrived?

I refer to Matt. xxvi. 26, &c. for observations there offered on the
interesting view of the LORD JESUS and his disciples at this last supper.
But in addition to those, I would just remark, that the institution of
the holy supper seems to have been immediately made, as soon as
the paschal feast was finished; as if to intimate the superseding of the
one, in the establishment of the other. And it should be particularly remembered, that in the LORD's appointment of this ordinance,
in the breaking of the bread, and administering of the wine, the LORD
most expressly designed to convey the spiritual signification that his
body being broken and his blood shed, the emblems shewed forth
the twofold blessings intended, of pardon, mercy, and peace, in and
through the offering of the body of JESUS CHRIST once for all; and
also all the blessings of the covenant set forth and sealed in his blood,
and hence called *the New Testament in his blood.*

There is somewhat truly interesting in the hymn the LORD and his
disciples sung at the table. JESUS knew what the events of that
night would be. He had in contemplation *Gethsemane,* and all his
sorrows. But these things stopped not the *Hallel* the Jews always used
at the Passover. Some have thought that this *Hallel* was the 114th
Psalm, which celebrates the night of the Passover, and the going

forth from Egypt. Reader! Ought not our celebration of the LORD's Supper, in the contemplation of the LORD's love, be always accompanied with our *Hallel;* our song of Moses and the LAMB?

27 And Jesus saith unto them, All ye shall be offended because of me this night: for it is written, I will smite the shepherd, and the sheep shall be scattered.

28 But after that I am risen, I will go before you into Galilee.

29 But Peter said unto him, Although all shall be offended, yet *will* not I.

30 And Jesus saith unto him, Verily I say unto thee, that this day, *even* in this night, before the cock crow twice, thou shalt deny me thrice.

31 But he spake the more vehemently, If I should die with thee, I will not deny thee in any wise: likewise also said they all.

32 And they came to a place which was named Gethsemane: and he saith to his disciples, Sit ye here, while I shall pray.

33 And he taketh with him Peter and James and John, and began to be sore amazed, and to be very heavy;

34 And saith unto them, My soul is exceeding sorrowful unto death: tarry ye here, and watch.

35 And he went forward a little, and fell on the ground, and prayed that, if it were possible, the hour might pass from him.

36 And he said, Abba, Father, all things *are* possible unto thee: take away this cup from me: nevertheless, not what I will, but what thou wilt.

37 And he cometh, and findeth them sleeping, and saith unto Peter, Simon, sleepest thou? couldest not thou watch one hour?

38 Watch ye and pray, lest ye enter into temptation, the spirit truly *is* ready, but the flesh *is* weak.

39 And again he went away, and prayed, and spake the same words.

40 And when he returned he found them asleep again; for their eyes were heavy: neither wist they what to answer him.

41 And he cometh the third time, and saith unto them, Sleep on now, and take *your* rest: it is enough, the hour is come: behold, the Son of man is betrayed into the hands of sinners.

42 Rise up, let us go: lo, he that betrayeth me is at hand.

We have in some measure noticed what is here related by *Mark*, in the parallel passage by *Matthew*. But the contemplation is indeed in itself endless. Never was there a subject of equal importance proposed to the mind of men, or angels, as is brought before the Church in those concluding scenes of the life and ministry of the LORD JESUS CHRIST. Who is competent to describe the wonderful and mysterious subject? What faculty, either of men or angels, equal to enter into the full apprehension of it? It should seem very evident that as soon as JESUS arose to go from the table towards the Mount of Olives, *Judas* withdrew to hasten the business of delivering CHRIST into the hands of the Chief Priests: for soon after our LORD's agony in the garden, we find the traitor coming with a band of men to seize JESUS. It is impossible to convey by any form of words, what were the feelings of the disciples on this memorable occasion. The LORD's forewarning them of their taking offence at him that night; quoting a passage well known to them from the Prophets; and making application of it to himself, and them; his taking *Peter*, *James*, and *John* with him, while leaving the other disciples at some little distance from him, his being withdrawn from them (as *Luke* describes it,) about a stone's cast, kneeling down and praying, and charging them repeatedly to do the same; the agony they beheld CHRIST in, with numberless other circumstances of his being *sore amazed, in exceeding sorrow even unto death*. The renewed soul in CHRIST, under the teaching of GOD the HOLY GHOST, may indeed contemplate in humble wonder and adoration, and the most profound silence, the awful subject; but eternity itself will not be too long to unfold all the sublime circumstances involved in it, and connected with it. I would refer the Reader to that part of this solemn scene which relates to the temptations of Satan, in Luke xxii. 40, &c. for in that scripture the subject is somewhat more largely dwelt upon.

43 ¶ And immediately, while he yet spake, cometh Judas, one of the twelve, and with him a great multitude with swords and staves, from the chief priests and the scribes and the elders,

44 And he that betrayed him had given them a token, saying, Whomsoever I shall kiss, that same is he; take him, and lead *him* away safely.

45 And as soon as he was come, he goeth straightway to him, and saith, Master, master; and kissed him.

46 And they laid their hands on him, and took him.

47 And one of them that stood by drew a sword, and smote a servant of the high priest, and cut off his ear.

48 And Jesus answered and said unto them, Are ye come out as against a thief, with swords and *with* staves to take me?

49 I was daily with you in the temple teaching, and ye took me not: but the scriptures must be fulfilled.

50 And they all forsook him and fled.

51 And there followed him a certain young man, having a linen cloth cast about *his* naked *body ;* and the young men laid hold on him:

52 And he left the linen cloth, and fled from them naked.

I beg the Reader to observe, and to observe with the awakened attention so infinitely an interesting subject merits, the order in which the Lord Jesus proceeded in this business. The agonies in the garden were finished, the temptations to be endured there from the powers of darkness gone through; and now the Lord Jesus as one hastening with holy zeal to the close of his sufferings, calls upon his disciples to arise, and go to meet the traitor and his party for the execution. Reader! do not overlook this! Remember it is one of the great features in the merits of Christ's death the freeness and voluntary offer of the Lord. See John x. 17. Psm. xl. 6, 7, 8. He had said before to Judas at the table, *that thou doest do quickly.* But *no man at the table knew for what intent Jesus said this unto him.* John xiii. 27, 28. But we may learn from it, that it shewed the promptness of Christ's heart to the work. And though he knew the sorrows which it must induce, yet, *for the joy that was set before him, he endured the cross, despised the shame.* Yea, Jesus called the time, the hour of his glory. And as soon as the traitor had left the company, Jesus declared that *he was now glorified.* See John xiii. 31, 32. Reader! do not overlook these precious traits of character in the person of thy Redeemer! I request you never to lose sight of those *two* grand points, in the sufferings and death of the LORD JESUS. The *one* is, the infinite dignity of his person, GOD and Man in one. The *other* is the free-will offering of the LORD. Behold him under these views coming forth from the garden to meet the traitor, and crying out, *Rise up! let us go! lo! he that betrayeth me is at hand.*

It is a matter worth attention also, to observe how the traitor came, with a band of armed men. To take whom? The meek and lowly JESUS, in whose mouth was found no guile, and who *when he was reviled, he reviled not again.* But we must not overlook in this the LORD's hand. Here was JEHOVAH's purpose in all this. The HOLY GHOST, by the Psalmist had prophesied, that both *the heathen should rage, and the kings of the earth with the rulers take counsel together against the* LORD, *and against his* CHRIST, *his anointed.* Psm. ii. 1, 2. And here it is : *Herod* and *Pontius Pilate,* with the *Roman soldiers,* all *Gentiles,* or as they are called, the *Heathen,* shall have their hand in the death of CHRIST, as well as the rulers of the Jews. And wherefore ? Surely, because CHRIST died, both for Jew and Gentile ; and therefore both shall be involved in the guilt, as CHRIST is JEHOVAH's salvation for both *to the ends of the earth.* Isaiah xlix. 6.

As the season of the Passover was nearly, if not at the time of the full moon, unless it was a cloudy night, it should seem that they could not have needed lantherns; but yet the Evangelist *John,* in his relation of this circumstance, of *Judas* and the band, saith, that they came *with lantherns and torches and weapons.* John xviii. 3. And it is further remarkable, that not only the Roman soldiers, but the party which came with them, should be so ignorant of CHRIST's person, that Judas should think it necessary to give them a token, by way of discovering the LORD JESUS. But I rather think, that the horrible state of the traitor's mind was such, that though he had sold himself to this most detestable deed, yet his sense of CHRIST's GOD-HEAD was such, that as he knew what JESUS had before wrought in moments of danger, so he might accomplish the same and escape out of their hands. I pray the Reader, in confirmation of this, to turn to Luke iv. 28—30. John viii. 59. John x. 39. In short, the man was desperate, and acted desperately. He went *before the band,* (Luke saith,) and he repeated *Rabbi twice,* when he kissed CHRIST, as if to imply, how much he loved him. But what a heart-cutting answer the LORD JESUS's must have been to him, had he not been wholly graceless : *Judas!* (calling him by his name, as if to shew him that he not only knew him, but knew his whole heart,) *betrayest thou the* SON *of Man with a kiss?* Reader! ponder over the awful subject! Surely the HOLY GHOST hath designed in the history of this man, to shew to what a depth of iniquity the mind of man is capable of falling, See John xiii. 18, &c.

The one of them that stood by, John saith, was *Peter.* John xviii. 10, which drew his sword and cut off the ear of *Malchus.* It was a zeal to their Master which prompted all the disciples to declare their resolution to die with CHRIST. And here was a proof of it in *Peter.* The deed gave occasion for a new miracle to be wrought by CHRIST, in healing the wound, and restoring the ear ; but no miracle could affect the heart of those which were given up to a reprobate mind. See that awful scripture. Jude iv.

If we gather into one point of view, all that the LORD JESUS said, after this action of Peter's, in cutting of the ear of *Malchus*, we shall find large room for improvement. According to *Matthew's* account of this scene, JESUS first addressed *Peter: Put up again thy sword into his place*, &c. See Matt. xxvi. 52, &c. JESUS next addressed the multitude, according to Luke, chap. xxii. 51 : *Suffer ye thus far ; and he touched his ear and healed him.* He then remonstrated with the Chief Priests, and Captains of the temple, and Elders, in that they were come out as against a thief, to take him, and then asserted his supreme power in common with his Father, for deliverance, had he pleased; but declared the absolute necessity of the measure, for the accomplishment of the scriptures. And which by the way, I beg the Reader not to overlook, in relation to those numerous scriptures, which so largely dwell upon it. Psm. xxii. 69. Isaiah liii. Zech. xiii. 7, &c.

Mark is the only Evangelist which relates the circumstance of this young man following CHRIST, and he doth not give us the least traces to form any opinion who he was. But all the historians of this awful scene agree in describing the desertion of the whole body of disciples. Did *Peter* flee ? did *John* and *James* ? those who were in the Mount with CHRIST? they who were just before in the garden with him ? Alas! what is man, even the highest of men, if grace be suspended but for a moment? And how was it, the band of armed men, who seized upon the person of JESUS, and laid hold of this young man who fled from them naked, suffered the Apostles to escape? Read what *John* hath recorded of the words of the LORD JESUS at this time, and learn the cause.

If therefore ye seek me, (said JESUS,) *let these go their way, that the saying might be fulfilled which he spake of them which thou gavest me, I have lost none.* John xviii. 7, 8, 9. I shall have occasion, when we come to this passage, in the Gospel according to *John*, to speak more largely upon it; but, in the mean time, I would have the Reader observe, that from the miracle JESUS then wrought, of causing those who came to apprehend him to fall backward to the ground, (which take it altogether, is perhaps as great a miracle as the LORD JESUS ever wrought upon earth,) and the authority with which he pronounced these words : *if therefore ye seek me, let these go their way.* From both these concurring causes, the LORD JESUS secured the flight of his disciples. A certain authority accompanied what JESUS said : let *these go their way* ; that is, they shall go their way, *touch not mine anointed, and do my Prophets no harm.* Psm. cv. 15. Reader ! think how safe, how eternally safe and secure the LORD's people are, when the LORD gives command concerning them. Isaiah xxvii. 2, 3.

53 And they led Jesus away to the high priest : and with him were assembled all the chief priests and the elders and the scribes.

54 And Peter followed him afar off, even into the palace of the high priest ; and he sat with the servants, and warmed himself at the fire.

55 And the chief priests and all the council

sought for witness against Jesus to put him to death; and found none.

56 For many bare false witness against him, but their witness agreed not together.

57 And there arose certain, and bare false witness against him, saying,

58 We heard him say, I will destroy this temple that is made with hands, and within three days I will build another made without hands.

59 But neither so did their witness agree together.

60 And the high priest stood up in the midst, and asked Jesus, saying, Answerest thou nothing? what *is it which* these witness against thee?

61 But he held his peace, and answered nothing. Again the high priest asked him, and said unto him, Art thou the Christ, the Son of the Blessed?

62 And Jesus said, I am: and ye shall see the Son of man sitting on the right hand of power, and coming in the clouds of heaven.

63 Then the high priest rent his clothes, and saith, What need we any further witnesses?

64 Ye have heard the blasphemy: what think ye? and they all condemned him to be guilty of death.

65 And some began to spit on him, and to cover his face, and to buffet him, and to say unto him, Prophesy. And the servants did strike him with the palms of their hands.

We now enter upon the more immediate scene of this solemn process leading to Christ's death. Every minute circumstance merits our closest regard. Perhaps there is not the smallest indignity offered to the person of the Lord Jesus, but had a mystical meaning. May God the Holy Ghost go before, accompany, and follow, both the Writer of this *Poor Man's Commentary,* and the Reader of it, with his Almighty teaching! Amen.

And first: *Mark* relates, that no sooner had the soldiers apprehended Jesus, than they led him away to the High Priest. Now here, if I mistake not, there was much signification intended by God the Holy Ghost. For this was according to the law; in which the sacrifice was first to be brought unto the Priest, before it was offered. Levit. xvii. 5.

The next point to be noticed according to Mark's relation, is, that at the High Priest's palace where JESUS was led, the whole *Sanhedrim* were then assembled. *John* indeed, in his account states, that the band which led JESUS away, took him to *Annas* first, and that they had previously bound him. See Mark xv. 1. But let us here attend to Mark's relation of those transactions. We shall be better prepared hereafter for making suitable observations also on the account by *John*. It must have been late, and after the celebration of the Passover, when the Sanhedrim was thus assembled, so desperately bent were they to CHRIST's death. And although after that holy solemnity of the Passover, the Jews were prohibited from going abroad for the night, yet to crucify JESUS, this breach may be in their view passed over.

The process of trial which followed, was done with a view to cover over their proceedings, as if done most justly and legally; and as it became necessary to obtain the Roman Governor's sanction to CHRIST's death, without which, the sentence could not be carried into execution, they proceeded in a regular order, and sought for witnesses to condemn CHRIST.

The destruction of the temple, the refusing to give tribute to *Cæsar,* and the supposed blasphemy against GOD; all these charges were brought forward, but no witnesses could be found to substantiate or prove. But when to the adjuration of the High Priest, the LORD JESUS gave testimony to the GODHEAD of his person, and to the authority of his office, the whole assembly present decided, that he was guilty of death! And the consequence as is here related of the utmost indignities and cruelties manifested to his divine person immediately followed! Some began to spit upon him, some to buffet and mock him, and some to smite him with the palms of their hands. I beg the Reader not to overlook the LORD JESUS giving testimony to his GODHEAD. It was for this supposed blasphemy he was sentenced to die. John x. 33. Reader! let us pause over the solemn view, and looking unto the LORD JESUS encompassed with dogs, as he is described by the Prophet, *as the Hind of the morning,* hunting for his blood; let us as another Prophet saith, figure to ourselves JESUS himself speaking and saying to us: *behold and see! if there be any sorrow like unto my sorrow, which is done unto me wherewith the* LORD *hath afflicted me in the day of his fierce anger!* Lament. i. 12. Psm. xxii. throughout, and title.

66 ¶ And as Peter was beneath in the palace, there cometh one of the maids of the high priest:

67 And when she saw Peter warming himself, she looked upon him, and said, And thou also wast with Jesus of Nazareth.

68 But he denied, saying, I know not, neither understand I what thou sayest. And he went out into the porch; and the cock crew.

69 And a maid saw him again, and began to say to them that stood by, This is *one* of them.

70 And he denied it again: and a little after, they that stood by said again to Peter, Surely thou art *one* of them: for thou art a Galilean, and thy speech agreeth *thereto*.

71 But he began to curse and to swear, *saying*, I know not this man of whom ye speak.

72 And the second time the cock crew. And Peter called to mind the word that Jesus said unto him, Before the cock crow twice, thou shalt deny me thrice. And when he thought thereon, he wept.

For the history and effect of Peter's denial, I refer to Luke xxii. 54, &c.

REFLECTIONS.

READER! let us look up for the teachings of GOD the HOLY GHOST, while in the perusal of this sacred chapter, that all the blessed contents of it may be engrafted in our hearts. Who can read of the Jewish Passover, and here contemplate CHRIST our Passover sacrificed for us, and not earnestly desire to keep the feast. LORD JESUS! give to all thy redeemed which attend thy table, a portion of the same grace as filled the heart of this woman. Oh! for the Spikenard of the HOLY SPIRIT, to anoint the feet of JESUS at his table!

Lord! let thy sweet teaching be upon us, while reading the denial of *Peter*, and the desertion of all the Apostles, still to mark the essential difference between backsliding, and the total want of grace, as in the instance of the traitor *Judas*. LORD! give us grace to praise the great Author of his discriminating mercy! Dearest JESUS! let *Gethsemane* be ever dear to the remembrance of thy people. Here in faith would the souls of thy redeemed delight to roam and meditate thy soul-agony and conflicts and temptations. And LORD! when we see thee, taken from thence, to prison and to judgment! oh! for grace to behold thee, *as wounded for our transgressions, and bruised for our iniquities; the chastisement of our peace as upon thee, and by thy stripes we are healed.* Oh! the wonders of redemption, that He *who knew no sin, should be made sin for us;* that we, who knew no righteousness, *should be made the righteousness of* GOD *in Him!*

CHAP. XV.

CONTENTS.

The LORD JESUS *is here led away to Pilate. He is Condemned, and delivered to be Crucified. His Death and Burial.*

A ND straightway in the morning the chief priests held a consultation with the elders and scribes and the whole council, and bound Jesus, and carried *him* away, and delivered *him* to Pilate.

I detain the Reader in the very opening of this chapter, to remark with what hot lust those enemies of CHRIST hastened to suck his blood. It must have been little short of midnight before their assembly broke up; if not, (as I confess I am inclined to think,) they sat up all night until the morning; for *Matthew* in his relation of their proceedings saith, that when *the morning was come,* they led him *away to Pilate.* Matt. xxvii. 1, 2.

The most profitable view of these solemn transactions will be, I apprehend, to contemplate the sufferings of CHRIST, with an eye to our personal interest in them, and, as I verily believe, there is hardly a single circumstance, but what hath a mystical meaning, I pray GOD the HOLY GHOST, in his glorifying the LORD JESUS, that he will be graciously pleased to unfold them to our hearts.

And here, in the first instance, as recorded in this chapter, we are told that they *bound* CHRIST *and led him away* to Pilate. The binding CHRIST, had certainly a very striking allusion to his Church, for whom CHRIST was bound and crucified. By sin we are all bound over to the just judgment of Almighty GOD. In the captivity of Satan we are also bound, until CHRIST makes us free; and without his deliverance, in becoming sin, and a curse for us, every son and daughter of Adam is like the unprofitable servant spoken of in the parable, concerning whom the LORD saith, *take him and bind him hand and foot, and cast him into outer darkness, there shall be weeping and gnashing of teeth.* Matt. xxii. 13.

Now then, if the LORD JESUS will deliver his people out of captivity, he shall in all points personate those whom he delivers. He shall exclaim as in their person, *innumerable evils have compassed me about; mine iniquities have taken hold of me.* Psm. xl. 12. He shall be bound as a malefactor; yea, crucified between two thieves, as if the greatest of the three, standing as the sinner's surety: and thus he shall be bound, and led as a sacrifice, as *Isaac* was bound, and laid upon the altar. Gen. xxii. 9, and as the sacrifices are supposed to have been bound under the law, so here in this point, as in every other, fulfilling all righteousness. See Levit. iv. 7. Psm. cxviii. 37. Isaiah xlix. 24, 25. Hosea xiii. 14.

2 And Pilate asked him, Art thou the king of the Jews? and he answering said unto him, Thou sayest *it.*

3 And the chief priests accused him of many things: but he answered nothing.

4 And Pilate asked him again, saying, Answerest thou nothing? behold, how many things they witness against thee.

5 But Jesus yet answered nothing; so that Pilate marvelled.

We have here the LORD of life and glory arraigned at *Pilate's* bar, and witnessing, as the HOLY GHOST testifieth, *a good confession.* 1 Tim. vi. 13. And in this instance, as in the former, we behold strong mystical representations, in what JESUS suffered, to the circumstances of his people. The *silence of* CHRIST, to the many accusations of the Chief Priests, is strikingly descriptive of the sinner's state of guilt, whom JESUS then represented as their surety. It was said of Him, ages before his incarnation, that *he should be led as a lamb to the slaughter; and as a sheep before her shearers is dumb, so he opened not his mouth.* Isaiah liii. 7. In this, CHRIST represented the sinner; silent and abashed, under the sense of sin. For though in himself *he knew no sin,* yet was *he made sin for us.* 2 Cor. v. 21.

Pause Reader, over this view of thy Redeemer! Here is that Great Prophet, which so many ages before had been promised, as coming into the world, whom the LORD said *they should hear; and that every one which would not hear that Prophet, should be destroyed from among the people*: here he now stands, silent and accused, as a delinquent and malefactor, before *Pontius Pilate* and the Elders! Mark well, the striking difference, and then ask, in what sense are we to behold him, but as the surety of his people? Deut. xviii. 15. Acts iii. 22, and Acts vii. 37.

6 Now at *that* feast he released unto them one prisoner, whomsoever they desired.

7 And there was one named Barabbas, *which lay* bound with them that had made insurrection with him, who had committed murder in the insurrection.

8 And the multitude crying aloud, began to desire *him to do* as he had ever done unto them.

9 But Pilate answered them, saying, Will ye that I release unto you the king of the Jews?

10 For he knew that the chief priests had delivered him for envy.

11 But the chief priests moved the people that he should rather release Barabbas unto them.

12 And Pilate answered, and said again unto them, What will ye then that I shall do *unto him* whom ye call the King of the Jews?

13 And they cried out again, Crucify him.

14 Then Pilate said unto them, Why what evil

hath he done? and they cried out the more exceedingly, Crucify him.

Here is a beautiful meaning also, in allusion to the great purposes of redemption. The lot was to fall on *Jonah*, an eminent type of CHRIST, and he the only Israelite at that time in the ship, from *Joppa.* Jonah i. 7. The lot for the *Scape Goat*, was also determined the same way. Levit. xvi. 8. And JESUS being delivered *by the determinate counsel and foreknowledge of* GOD, *shall* be the one, on whom the whole voice of the people shall decide. Rev. xiii. 8. What striking allusions of a mystical nature are there in all these things!

15 ¶ And *so* Pilate, willing to content the people, released Barabbas unto them, and delivered Jesus, when he had scourged *him*, to be crucified.

16 And the soldiers led him away into the hall, called Pretorium; and they call together the whole band.

17 And they clothed him with purple, and platted a crown of thorns, and put it about his *head*.

18 And began to salute him, Hail, King of the Jews!

19 And they smote him on the head with a reed, and did spit upon him, and bowing *their* knees worshipped him.

20 And when they had mocked him, they took off the purple from him, and put his own clothes on him, and led him out to crucify him.

Before we enter upon this part of the awful events, in the cruelties exercised upon CHRIST's person, I beg the Reader to turn to the 18th chapter of Luke, 31—34, and read our LORD's prediction concerning them; then mark, one by one, the woeful account. And I request the Reader, yet more particularly, to observe through the whole, that he acted as the surety of his people. There certainly was, as I before remarked, a mystical meaning in all. For it forms a grand feature of our holy faith, that for the joy which was set before CHRIST, *he endured the cross, despised the shame, before that he sat down on the right hand of the Majesty on high.* JEHOVAH, which lay on him the iniquities of his people, *turned his glory into shame,* Psm. iv. 21, that the sin of his redeemed might be made appear *exceeding sinful.* Let the Reader attend to the shame, and reproaches, and cruelties, poured upon CHRIST, with an eye to this; and the blessedness of the whole will then appear, in their true colours.

The first act of cruelty which *Mark* takes notice of, exercised upon the sacred person of the LORD JESUS CHRIST, after *Pilate* had passed sentence of death upon him, and given him up into the hands of the

Roman soldiers, is that of scourging. *John,* in his Gospel, relates
that *Pilate* scourged CHRIST, or caused him to be scourged, before
this; when he did it with a view to release him. And no doubt that
this first scourging by *Pilate,* had been with no small severity.
Among the *Jews,* there was no permission to give stripes in any case
of delinquency, to above *thirty and nine,* lest, saith the law, *thy brother should seem vile unto thee.* Deut. xxv. 3. 2 Cor. xi. 24. But
CHRIST, our Brother, must be made vile, as the surety of his people,
who had made themselves vile by reason of sin, and therefore the *Gentiles,* into whose hands he shall fall, shall lay on stripes, without
number, as far as their savage cruelty shall incline them. And thus
CHRIST, both at the first and second scourging, shall be made vile,
that *we might be made the righteousness of* GOD *in him.* 2 Cor. v. 21.
Oh! the preciousness in this mystical allusion, concerning Him, and
his unequalled sufferings, *by whose stripes we are healed!*

The next view we have in *Mark's* Gospel, of our LORD, after
Pilate had delivered him up into the hands of the soldiers, is the
calling together the whole band, to insult him, and then clothing
him with purple, crowning him with thorns, spitting upon him,
striking him on the head, bending the knee before him in mockery,
and then unkinging him and unclothing him of his sham royalty,
before they led him away to crucify him. In every one of these
acts, more or less, we may, under divine teaching, discover the
LORD's hand, directing to some interesting circumstances of a mystical
nature, in allusion to the persons of CHRIST's redeemed, for whom
he became surety, and for whom he suffered.

The clothing him in *purple* was wholly in derision; but then it
should be remembered, that to do this, they first stripped him
and made him naked; and indeed so was he crucified. And what
so shameful as being wholly naked. But this also was necessary,
and highly significant; for as our first parents had made themselves
naked to their shame, in taking away the curse, CHRIST must be put
in their very law-room and place so as to fulfil all righteousness.

The *thorny crown,* had mock royalty been only intended, would
have been as well played off for their sport, with a crown of reeds!
But it was not sport, but cruelty, added to mockery, they meant; and
therefore *thorns* were chosen to be struck into his sacred head. Sinners
are threatened with having *their heads* and their *hairy scalp wounded,*
as enemies to GOD. Psm. lxviii. 21, &c. The LORD JESUS shall
therefore, as the sinner's surety, suffer in their stead. And forasmuch
as the curse pronounced at the fall, declared, that *thorns and thistles
should the earth bring forth* to the man. Gen. iii. 18. Here also
JESUS shall be pre-eminent in suffering, as he is in all things; and
shall be crowned with thorns, that the *Head* may feel, what in his
members the *Feet* only of his redeemed go through, in a thorny wilderness.

Little did those *Gentiles* consider, how they were by their mockery,
fulfilling JEHOVAH's design, in the setting forth these things. Insult and cruelty they intended, yet the LORD was then in reality
setting *his king upon his holy hill in Zion, and declaring the decree.*
Psm. ii. 6, 7. They bowed the knee in derision; but in truth then
began in a more open display that declaration of GOD, that when He

who was in the form of GOD, *and with whom it was no robbery to be equal with* GOD, *humbled himself to the death of the Cross, every knee should bow before him, and every tongue confess that* JESUS CHRIST *is* LORD, *to the glory of* GOD *the* FATHER. Philip. ii. 8—11. The purple robe and the thorny crown, and the reed for a sceptre, were the *insignalia* of this mock royalty. But whatever they meant, the LORD's purposes were fully answered: for the SON of GOD was at that moment, *the brightness of his* FATHER's *glory, and the express image of his person, whose sceptre of righteousness was the sceptre of his kingdom;* and concerning whom when the LORD JEHOVAH *bringeth in the first begotten into the world, he saith, and let all the Angels of* GOD *worship him.* Heb. i. 3—9.

21 And they compel one Simon, a Cyrenian, who passed by, coming out of the country, the father of Alexander and Rufus, to bear his cross.

22 And they bring him unto the place Golgotha, which is, being interpreted, The place of a scull.

23 And they gave him to drink wine mingled with myrrh: but he received *it* not.

24 And when they had crucified him, they parted his garments, casting lots upon them what every man should take.

25 And it was the third hour, and they crucified him.

26 And the superscription of his accusation was written over, THE KING OF THE JEWS.

27 ¶ And with him they crucify two thieves, the one on his right hand, and the other on his left.

28 And the scripture was fulfilled, which saith, And he was numbered with the transgressors.

29 And they that passed by railed on him, wagging their heads, and saying, Ah, thou that destroyest the temple, and buildest *it* in three days,

30 Save thyself, and come down from the cross.

31 Likewise also the chief priests mocking, said among themselves with the scribes, He saved others; himself he cannot save.

32 Let Christ the King of Israel descend now from the cross, that we may see and believe.

And they that were crucified with him reviled him.

33 And when the sixth hour was come, there was darkness over the whole land until the ninth hour.

34 And at the ninth hour Jesus cried with a loud voice, saying, Eloi, Eloi, lama sabachthani? which is, being interpreted, My God, my God, why hast thou forsaken me?

35 And some of them that stood by, when they heard *it*, said, Behold, he calleth Elias.

36 And one ran, and filled a spunge full of vinegar, and put *it* on a reed, and gave him to drink, saying, Let alone; let us see whether Elias will come to take him down.

37 And Jesus cried with a loud voice, and gave up the ghost.

In the relation which *John* gives, of their leading away CHRIST to be crucified, he saith, that JESUS *bearing his cross, went forth into a place, called the place of a skull.* But the three other Evangelists tell us, that this *Simon* the Cyrenian, they compelled to this labour. And no doubt, the relation by the whole is correct. For JESUS first went forth with it, but when they found him sinking under the burden, and fearing had he really died with fainting and loss of blood, before they arrived at *Golgotha*, their inhumanity would have lost the greatest triumph over him; they compelled the *Cyrenian* to bear the cross for him.

I beg to detain the Reader at this place, just to observe to him, what otherwise perhaps may not so immediately strike him, in tracing the unequalled sorrows of CHRIST, that it is not to be wondered at that the LORD JESUS should have fainted under the cross. For when we consider what he had already undergone of pain and fatigue, and loss of blood, and agonies, the only astonishment is, that he had not sunk under the pressure before. They who have studied the map of Jerusalem and its vicinity, and have marked the ground over which the LORD JESUS was hurried up and down from one place to another, have shewn that CHRIST actually walked the day of his Crucifixion, and the night immediately before it, many a mile, perhaps not less than seven, without rest or intermission. And add to these, the LORD JESUS, six days before the Passover visited *Bethany*, and was closely engaged every portion of the time, from that period to his death. John xii. 1. And *Luke* saith, that he abode in the *Mount of Olives by night*, and in the morning *early* the people came to hear him in the temple. Luke xxi. 37, 38. And from the moment of his being apprehended to his death, after all these fatigues and sufferings, there was no interval allowed for sleep. Well might the Prophet say, we have caused him *to serve with our sins, and wearied him with our iniquities.* Isaiah xliii. 24. Oh! ye that are weary and heavy laden with sin! come to this wearied SAVIOR. He knows your feelings by his own!

In respect to the painful and ignominous death of the Cross, I refer to the observations made in the Commentary on Matt. xxvii. But in addition, I would just remark, that such were the cruelties exercised upon the occasion, that the malice of hell seems to have been at study, to make the whole the most aggravated and full of torture. Yet what I chiefly beg the Reader not to lose sight of, in beholding the Cross, is the wonderful coincidence of circumstances so over-ruled by the LORD, as that every thing done to CHRIST, or suffered by CHRIST, should have a mystical allusion, to the great design for which he offered his soul an offering for sin. Under this view of the subject, what but GOD's sovereignty could have brought about such an event, that in their despising the offices of CHRIST, I mean his *Priestly,* *Kingly,* and *Prophetical* offices, they should have used the very same words, in which CHRIST complained of those reproaches, a *thousand years* before those events were accomplished. *All they that see me* (said CHRIST by the spirit of prophecy,) *laugh me to scorn, they shoot out the lip, they shake the head, saying, he trusted on the* LORD *that he would deliver him; let him deliver him, seeing he delighted in him;* Psm. xxii. 7, 8. the Evangelists have recorded those very words, as among the taunts and reproaches of the multitude. The Reader will not fail, I hope to recollect, that the LORD of life and glory was then in very deed, saving his people from their sins by the gracious act of thus offering himself in sacrifice. And their testimony though very differently intended by them, was in fact overruled by the LORD to the same. *He saved others,* (said they) *himself he cannot save.*

Blessed Lamb of GOD! enable thy people to have these things always in remembrance; and never, oh! never may we fail to connect with the view, the intimate concern thy Church and people all have in the wonderful events of this day. But for this thy gracious interposition, thy Church in every individual of it, must have been bound hand and foot, as JESUS was for them, and hurried away to the Judge. Silent as JESUS was; must we all have stood at that tremendous bar. And after sentence had been passed, hell in an army, would have seized upon us, and driven we must have been from the presence of GOD, into regions of endless despair. Oh! the unspeakable mercy of GOD in JESUS CHRIST.

38 And the veil of the temple was rent in twain from the top to the bottom.

39 And when the centurion, which stood over against him, saw that he so cried out and gave up the ghost, he said, Truly this man was the Son of God.

40 There were also women looking on afar off, among whom was Mary Magdalene, and Mary

the mother of James the less, and of Joses, and
Salome :

41 (Who also, when he was in Galilee, followed
him, and ministered unto him;) and many other
women which came up with him unto Jerusalem.

Amidst the prodigies which distinguished the death of CHRIST, the
renting the vail of the temple was not the least. I am led to view
it indeed as of great moment; and as such, would request to call the
Reader's attention to it somewhat more particularly. The Reader
should be told that in the temple there was a vail of separation between
the holy and the most holy place. The HOLY GHOST, by his servant
the Apostle, hath thought proper to give the Church some account
of it. Heb. ix. 3—12. This vail then, by some invisible hand, was
rent in twain, from the top to the bottom, at the moment CHRIST cried
with a loud voice and gave up the ghost. And as this was at the 9th
hour, that is, three of the clock in the afternoon, which was the time
of the evening sacrifice, I pause, to remark how astonished the Priest,
who was at that very hour with the people present then in the outer
temple, must have been to have seen it, by which the inner temple
appeared at once open to his and their view!

This vail was not simply torn, or separated in part, but rent in twain,
and that from the top to the bottom. Yes! by the death of CHRIST,
the separation between GOD and his people was now for ever removed.
JESUS had then opened a new and living way by his blood. Before
this, the vail of separation kept back the people. It was impossible
to go in; yea, dangerous to LOOK in : and the High Priest himself,
could not enter without blood, and that only once in a year. Hence,
therefore, the SON of GOD having now accomplished redemption by
his blood, he hath himself entered as our forerunner, and opened a
new and living way for all his redeemed to follow; and the vail of
separation, both to Jew and Gentile can be found no more. Precious
LORD JESUS! I would say for myself, and all his redeemed; blessed
for ever be thy name; thou hast removed by thy death all vails which
stood in the way of our access to GOD. And thou wilt remove all
the remaining vails of darkness, sin, and corruption, which are in us.
The vail of death, and the covering cast over all faces, thou wilt
utterly do away, now *thou hast swallowed up death in victory, and the
rebuke of thy people thou hast taken away from off all the earth, for the
mouth of the* LORD *hath spoken it.* Isaiah xxv. 7, 8.

42 ¶ And now when the even was come, because it was the preparation, that is, the day
before the sabbath,

43 Joseph of Arimathea, an honourable counsellor, which also waited for the kingdom of God,
came, and went in boldly unto Pilate, and craved
the body of Jesus.

44 And Pilate marvelled if he were already

dead : and calling *unto him* the centurion, he asked him, whether he had been any while dead ?

45 And when he knew *it* of the centurion, he gave the body to Joseph.

46 And he bought fine linen, and took him down, and wrapped him in the linen, and laid him in a sepulchre which was hewn out of a rock, and rolled a stone unto the door of the sepulchre.

47 And Mary Magdalene, and Mary *the mother* of Joses, beheld where he was laid.

Excepting the enquiry which *Pilate* made of the Centurion by way of being assured of the certainty of Christ's death, we have the same account given by *Matthew* as is here related by *Mark*. I therefore refer to the observations which were then offered. But, if I detain the Reader a moment longer on those verses, it shall be only to invite him to contemplate the tomb of Jesus. Never did death before detain such a prisoner. But, Reader ! it is the joy of his redeemed that he then did. For it is *by death* Christ *hath destroyed him that had the power of death; that is, the Devil : and delivered them, who through fear of death, were all their life time subject to bondage.* Heb. ii. 14, 15. But what a funeral is here ! The sacred body begged, and then perfumed. A few following the procession, and but a few; and those by stealth as it were. But, Reader ! as the death of Christ was of the highest importance to the everlasting salvation of his Church, so his burial became essential both to prove that death, and to answer the prediction of prophecies concerning it. See Isaiah liii. 9. Psm. xxii. 15. Matt. xii. 40. Hosea xiii. 14. Jerem. xxxi. 26. Rev. i. 13—18. Psm. xxiii. 4. Reader ! let you and I frequently in solemn meditation visit the Sepulchre of Jesus ! Sacred garden of the most blessed thoughts ! From hence, the first distinct prospect was given of the upper and brighter world. Here Jesus the resurrection and life of his redeemed taught them to look up, and by faith enter upon the possession of those mansions which he is gone before to prepare for them, until he shall come again to receive them to himself, that where he is, there they may be also. Hail ! thou risen and exalted Savior ! In thy triumphs over death, hell, and the grave, we already can and do sing the Apostle's song : *Oh ! death where is thy sting ! O grave where is thy victory !*

REFLECTIONS.

Reader ! let us not hastily pass away from this most solemn and interesting chapter. It is profitable to follow the footsteps of the Lamb whithersoever he goeth. And while from the High Priest's palace, to the palace of Pilate, we attend the lowly Redeemer, marking his footsteps with his blood, oh ! for grace to ponder well the cause of all his sufferings. The Holy Ghost in one line of his blessed word, hath explained the whole. Christ hath once suffered for sins; the just for the unjust, that he might bring us to God.

Reader! do not overlook that every hand, both Jew and Gentile, were embrued in his blood; yea, above all, behold the hand of JEHO-VAH engaged in the vast design. Look at the cross, and hear the voice of the LORD, calling to the sword to awake. *Awake, O sword, against my shepherd, and against the man that is my fellow, saith the* LORD *of* HOSTS! *Smite the shepherd, and the sheep shall be scattered!*

Reader! let us both, as lovers of JESUS, attend the funeral. This is the office of near and dear friends. Remember, he is still the same, and the covenant in his blood cannot be dissolved by death. And in the contemplation of our own death, and our sure resurrection in JESUS, let us say with *Job, Oh! that thou wouldst hide me in the grave, that thou wouldst keep me secret until the wrath be past; that thou wouldst appoint me a set time, and remember me!*

CHAP. XVI.

CONTENTS.

CHRIST'S *Resurrection, and his Appearance to* Mary Magdalene *and to others. The* LORD *giveth his Commission to his Apostles; and returned unto Glory.*

A ND when the sabbath was past, Mary Mag-dalene, and Mary the *mother* of James, and Salome, had bought sweet spices, that they might come and anoint him.

Reader! let us pause at the very entrance on this precious chapter, with which the HOLY GHOST is pleased that *Mark* should finish his Gospel. Every word is big with events, in recording the wonderful history of our LORD's resurrection, and may well merit the closest attention of his people. The sabbath was past, we are told, and the LORD of the sabbath (Mark ii. 28.) had rested from his *own* works. Heb. iv. 10. and that blessed scripture but little understood, yet most highly significant, was now to be immediately accomplished. Jerem. xxxi. 26. Those godly women, still unconscious of the great things in which they themselves were so highly interested, had bought sweet spices, (and so had *Nicodemus,* John xix. 39.) with intention of em-balming the body of JESUS. Reader! behold how the LORD was pleased to keep those whom he loved in ignorance for a while, of a subject which when made known, filled their hearts *with a joy unspeakable and full of glory.* Let you and I, from hence learn to estimate our mercies, and desire with *Paul,* to know CHRIST, *and the power of his resurrection.* Philip. iii. 10, 11.

2 And very early in the morning, the first *day* of the week, they came unto the sepulchre at the rising of the sun,

3 And they said among themselves, Who shall roll us away the stone from the door of the se-pulchre?

4 And when they looked, they saw that the stone was rolled away ; for it was very great.

There is somewhat very striking in the short, but sweet account, of the rising of the sun. It became a beautiful representation of the rising of the sun in nature; to shadow forth Him, who is the sun of righteousness in grace. Well might the created sun arise to his glory, who was, and is, the Creator of all things. Mal. iv. 2. The difficulty those women apprehended, from the great stone at the door of the sepulchre, stopping their way, and the removal of it they knew not how, may suggest to us, how much better to his people the LORD is, than all their fears. But, Reader, though you and I follow those women to the tomb of JESUS by faith, yet we shall have no cordial belief in the resurrection of JESUS, until the LORD hath not only caused the stone to be rolled away from the door, but He himself hath taken it out of our heart. It can be nothing short of an Almighty work to do this. *The first day of the week* with every child of GOD in being brought acquainted with the resurrection of JESUS, is the first day of a new life and salvation together. Hence Paul's prayer for the Church, which I beg the Reader not to pass from those verses till he hath read. Ephes. i. 15, to the end.

5 And entering into the sepulchre, they saw a young man sitting on the right side, clothed in a long white garment; and they were affrighted.

6 And he saith unto them, Be not affrighted : Ye seek Jesus of Nazareth, which was crucified : he is risen ; he is not here : behold the place where they laid him.

7 But go your way, tell his disciples and Peter that he goeth before you into Galilee: there shall ye see him, as he said unto you.

8 And they went out quickly, and fled from the sepulchre; for they trembled and were amazed: neither said they any thing to any *man :* for they were afraid.

The Jewish Sepulchres were all made large, not only to admit many bodies being placed by the side of each other; but also for the entrance of the friends, who might indulge the pleasing melancholy of visiting them. I pass over several very interesting circumstances related here, to call the Reader's attention to the tenderness expressed to *Peter* among the other disciples, in calling him by name. The LORD JESUS well knew how exceedingly the consciousness of having denied CHRIST had operated upon the heart of the Apostle, and therefore he will have the message sent to *Peter* more particularly by name : *Go tell his disciples and Peter !* Oh ! what grace is in the heart of CHRIST. Had the message been sent to the disciples, only as

disciples, *Peter* might have been tempted to fear, that on account of
his shameful conduct, he was no longer a disciple, and as such, not
included in it.   But being particularly named, how very blessedly he must have felt this renewed attention in his LORD.   Reader!
do not dismiss the very gracious testimony, such a view of JESUS
brings with it, to the hearts of all the LORD's disciples.   We learn
most evidently from it, that the LORD's grace is not restrained by our
unworthiness; neither is it bestowed for our deservings.   CHRIST's
love, and not ours, is the only standard for CHRIST's mercy to his
people.   And I would beg to call the Reader's attention to another
most blessed instruction, this conduct of the LORD JESUS holds
forth, in the immediate regard he shewed to his disconsolate disciples.
The first thing the LORD JESUS had respect to, when he arose from
the dead, was to send his Angel to comfort his disciples with the
assurance of his love, while he informed them of his resurrection.
Go tell my disciples and Peter!   Disciples still, and brethren still, for
John's relation is to the same amount. John xx. 17.   So that his Almighty power, by which he arose from the dead, Rom. i. 4. and his
altered state made no alteration in his love.   He is still the same
JESUS, and the same brother as before.   Oh! for grace to have this
always in remembrance!

9 ¶ Now when *Jesus* was risen early the first
day of the week, he appeared first to Mary Magdalene, out of whom he had cast seven devils.

10 *And* she went and told them that had been
with him, as they mourned and wept.

11 And they, when they had heard that he was
alive, and had been seen of her, believed not.

I cannot help pausing over this view of CHRIST's grace to *Mary Magdalene,* that she should have the honor of beholding the LORD of life
and glory the first of all his redeemed, after he rose from the dead.
And as the Evangelist adds, *out of whom he had cast seven devils.*
Doth it not seem to intimate, in that GOD the HOLY GHOST hath
thought proper, to have this act of grace of JESUS mentioned at the
same time, as if the LORD would thereby encourage, and comfort
any, and every one, of his more than ordinarily distressed members,
to this conclusion, that where *sin aboundeth, grace shall much more
abound?*   All CHRIST's redeemed shall have the love-tokens of JESUS;
but the one which Satan most afflicts, CHRIST will more abundantly
comfort.

12 After that, he appeared in another form unto
two of them, as they walked, and went into the
country.

13 And they went and told *it* unto the residue:
neither believed they them.

14 Afterward he appeared unto the eleven as

they sat at meat, and upbraided them with their unbelief and hardness of heart, because they believed not them which had seen him after he was risen.

We never can sufficiently bless the LORD for his gracious condescension, in those repeated appearances he made to his disciples. But how astonishing is it to behold their great unbelief. No doubt for the greater confirmation of the faith the LORD had so appointed it; for it wholly removes the ridiculous charge of the Jews, that while the soldiers slept, the disciples should have taken away the body of CHRIST from the sepulchre; when we find that evidence upon evidence did not prove sufficient for a while to bring those poor timid disciples into the heart's conviction of our LORD's being risen from the dead. See Matt. xxviii.

15 ¶ And he said unto them, Go ye into all the world, and preach the gospel to every creature.

16 He that believeth and is baptized shall be saved; but he that believeth not shall be damned.

17 And these signs shall follow them that believe: In my name shall they cast out devils; they shall speak with new tongues;

18 They shall take up serpents; and if they drink any deadly thing, it shall not hurt them; they shall lay hands on the sick, and they shall recover.

It should seem, from the relation of this final commission the LORD gave to his disciples, that it was not all delivered at this morning and evening of the day of his resurrection, but in the different meetings which JESUS graciously made with them during the forty days he went in and out before them, to the day he returned to glory. And the commission itself of going into the whole of the then known world, and preaching the Gospel to every creature, carried with it the full glorious tidings of salvation in his blood, and righteousness both to Jew and Gentile. See Isaiah xlix. 1—6. And while the LORD thus taught them that the door of salvation was to be opened to the people of GOD, which were scattered abroad, the Gospel itself implied that CHRIST himself in his person, work, grace, blood-shedding, and righteousness, became JEHOVAH's one and only ordinance of salvation, to every one which believeth; to the Jew first, and also to the Gentile. CHRIST in himself is comprehensive of the whole Gospel. In *Matthew's* relation of this, it is added, they were to baptize the people, in the joint name of the FATHER, SON, and HOLY GHOST, intimating thereby, that to the joint love, and grace, and mercy, of the HOLY THREE in ONE, the whole blessings of redemption flow. See 1 Pet. i. 2, compared with Numbers vi. 22, to the end. 2 Cor. xiii. 14.

19 ¶ So then after the Lord had spoken unto them, he was received up into heaven, and sat on the right hand of God.

20 And they went forth, and preached every where, the Lord working with *them*, and confirming the word with signs following. Amen.

Mark sums up the glorious event of CHRIST's ascension, and the HOLY GHOST's descension, in a comprehensive manner indeed, in these two verses. But his testimony of those wonderful acts was all that the HOLY GHOST thought proper to make use of by his ministry. The events themselves are more largely followed up in the relation in the Acts of the Apostles, to which, therefore, I refer. For the present, it will be sufficient to observe, that *Mark's* testimony is confirmed by the LORD's testimony, in those gracious signs which followed. And the LORD JESUS's name, like the sign and seal of a charter, the AMEN, closeth *Mark's* Gospel, as the Verily, the faithful witness of Heaven. Rev. iii. 14. Isaiah lxv. 16.

REFLECTIONS.

READER! while you and I hasten, with the ardent love of those godly women, to the Sepulchre of JESUS, and hear with the ear of faith, as they heard in sense, the invitation of the Angel; *Come see the place where the* LORD *lay.* Oh! for the teaching of GOD the HOLY GHOST, to follow JESUS from the cross to the throne, and behold where the LORD lay from all eternity, in the bosom of the FATHER.

Send down, thou risen and exalted SAVIOR, all those precious gifts thou art returned on purpose to impart! And as in the case of *Mary Magdalene,* such grace was manifested; so in the instance of all thy redeemed ones, prove, thou dearest LORD, that thou art *exalted as a Prince and a* SAVIOR, *for to give repentance to Israel, and forgiveness of sins.* Oh! the blessedness of receiving the power of CHRIST's resurrection, in the heart and conscience, when the LORD works with his holy word, and *confirms that word with signs following.* May the souls of all the LORD's redeemed family, thus find the sweet testimonies to the truth of our LORD's resurrection; when *first* GOD *our* FATHER *having raised up his* SON JESUS, *hath sent him to bless us in turning away every one of us from our iniquities.*

And now FAREWELL *Mark!* thou faithful Evangelist; surely thou hast well done the work of one, and *made full proof of thy Ministry.* For the testimony of thy Gospel is in the hearts of thousands, *to the truth as it is in* JESUS, *through the power of the* HOLY GHOST. Precious is the *written* Word, when confirmed as an *engrafted* Word, by the SPIRIT's grace in the heart; and when that Almighty LORD, sets to his seal, in the heart, that GOD *is true.* All the faithful will thank thee, *Mark,* for thy labour of love, as they daily read the wonders recorded by thee of JESUS. And all will find cause, who are taught of GOD, to say as *Paul* did concerning thee, though not called to the service of the sanctuary, as he was; for *he is profitable to me in his ministry!*

Precious LORD JESUS! while we thank the servant, we bow down with unspeakable thanksgiving to the MASTER! Be thou everlastingly loved, and praised, and adored, in thy Person, Work, Offices, Characters, and Relations. *Men shall be blessed in thee, and all nations shall call thee blessed.* Praised be the FATHER, SON, and HOLY GHOST, for all Covenant love, in JESUS CHRIST! Amen.

THE GOSPEL ACCORDING TO

ST. LUKE.

GENERAL OBSERVATIONS ON THE GOSPEL ACCORDING TO ST. LUKE.

IN entering upon this blessed Book of GOD, which carries with it, through every Chapter and verse, proofs of divine inspiration, I would beg the Reader to look up with me to the Almighty LORD, which both directed and guided *Luke's* pen, for grace to attend to it, with that reverence and godly fear, as is suitable and becoming to such precious Memoirs of our LORD and SAVIOR JESUS CHRIST. Surely, Reader, the HOLY GHOST would not have raised up the several Evangelists to this sacred service, neither have added the Gospel of *Luke* to those of *Matthew*, and *Mark*, but for the most blessed purposes. Oh! that they may all be unitedly made *a sweet savor, to make manifest his knowledge to his people in every place.*

Some have thought that *Luke* was one of the seventy disciples. It is possible he might have been so. And others have supposed, that he is the same person whom *Paul* calls *the beloved Physician.* Col. iv. 10. But there is no certainty whether either be right; the whole is conjecture.

Neither is it determinable, with any greater assurance, at what time *Luke* wrote this Gospel. Some make it as early as within *fifteen* years after our LORD'S ascension: So *Beza* saith in his Manuscript Copy: while others date it as late as *twenty-seven*. *Eusebius*, in his Ecclesiastical History, relates, that the Apostle *John* read it when finished, and gave his sanction to it. But GOD's people have a yet higher authority of its truth, when the HOLY GHOST, in his divine teaching, gives to his regenerated children the testimony of its holy doctrines in their own hearts and consciences. I cannot upon this occasion help making an earnest request to my Reader, that he will make this the grand standard of decision, concerning the whole scriptures of God; namely, that when the Holy Ghost teacheth *in* them, and *by* them, this forms of itself the truest test of their divine authority. May the Lord the Spirit do this, by this precious portion of his Holy word, we are now entering upon, and render it in his Almighty Hand, the blessed instrument of good to his people. Amen.

CHAPTER I.

CONTENTS.

We have an Introduction by the Evangelist, in the opening of this Gospel. To which follows the Account of John the Baptist, as the Harbinger of Christ. An Angel appears to Zacharias, and to the Virgin Mary: the Hymn of Mary on the Occasion: the Birth of John the Baptist, and the Prophecy thereon of Zacharias.

FORASMUCH as many have taken in hand to set forth in order a declaration of those things which are most surely believed among us,

2 Even as they delivered them unto us, which from the beginning were eye witnesses and ministers of the word;

3 It seemed good to me also, having had perfect understanding of all things from the very first, to write unto thee in order, most excellent Theophilus,

4 That thou mightest know the certainty of those things wherein thou hast been instructed.

I do not think it necessary to detain the Reader with any long observation on this preface. The reasons *Luke* assigns for entering upon this solemn service, plainly shew that the hand of the Lord was upon him. The certainty of the truths he was about to deliver, arose, not only from being with others *eye witnesses* of them, but he, and they, are said to have been *ministers of the word;* thereby intimating that he considered himself called to it by the Lord; for he saith, that *it seemed good to him.* Who this *Theophilus* was, is not certain; but it should seem to have been One taught of God, by what is said of his instruction in the faith. And hence we learn, *for* whom the Gospel is designed, and *to* whom God the Holy Ghost sends it; similar to what *Paul* said in his preaching, *Men and Brethren, Children of the stock of Abraham, and whosoever among you feareth God, to You is the word of this salvation sent!* Acts xiii. 26. Gal. iii. 29. Reader! if God the Spirit so commissions His word of salvation to your heart and mine, this will be a blessed testimony to us both, not only of the truth of his holy scriptures, but also of our personal interest in them. And this will be what the same Apostle said to the Church of the *Thessalonians*, the highest proof of our election of GOD, when his Gospel comes unto us, *not in word only, but also in power, and in the* HOLY GHOST, *and in much assurance.* 1 Thess. i. 4, 5.

5 THERE was in the days of Herod, the king of Judea, a certain priest named Zacharias, of the course of Abia: and his wife *was* of the daughters of Aaron, and her name *was* Elisabeth.

6 And they were both righteous before God, walking in all the commandments and ordinances of the Lord blameless.

7 And they had no child, because that Elisabeth was barren, and they both were *now* well stricken in years.

8 And it came to pass, that while he executed the priest's office before God in the order of his course,

9 According to the custom of the priest's office, his lot was to burn incense when he went into the temple of the Lord.

10 And the whole multitude of the people were praying without, at the time of incense.

11 And there appeared unto him an angel of the Lord standing on the right side of the altar of incense.

12 And when Zacharias saw *him*, he was troubled, and fear fell upon him.

13 But the angel said unto him, Fear not, Zacharias: for thy prayer is heard; and thy wife Elisabeth shall bear thee a son, and thou shalt call his name John.

14 And thou shalt have joy and gladness, and many shall rejoice at his birth.

15 For he shall be great in the sight of the Lord, and shall drink neither wine nor strong drink; and he shall be filled with the Holy Ghost, even from his mother's womb.

16 And many of the children of Israel shall he turn to the Lord, their God.

17 And he shall go before him in the spirit and power of Elias, to turn the hearts of the fathers to the children, and the disobedient to the wisdom of the just; to make ready a people prepared for the Lord.

18 And Zacharias said unto the angel, Whereby shall I know this? for I am an old man, and my wife well stricken in years.

19 And the angel answering said unto him, I am Gabriel, that stand in the presence of God; and am sent to speak unto thee, and to shew thee these glad tidings.

20 And, behold, thou shalt be dumb, and not able to speak, until the day that these things shall be performed, because thou believest not my words, which shall be fulfilled in their season.

21 And the people waited for Zacharias, and marvelled that he tarried so long in the temple.

22 And when he came out, he could not speak unto them: and they perceived that he had seen a vision in the temple: for he beckoned unto them, and remained speechless.

23 And it came to pass, that as soon as the days of his ministration were accomplished, he departed to his own house.

24 And after those days his wife Elisabeth conceived, and hid herself five months, saying,

25 Thus hath the Lord dealt with me in the days wherein he looked on *me*, to take away my reproach among men.

Here *Luke* begins his relation of the wonderful events concerning the Person, Character, Offices, and Relations of the LORD JESUS CHRIST. And he begins the subject with the date of those transactions, which was in the days of One of the *Herods*. And it is worthy the Reader's remark, that as this *Herod*, who was at this time deputy King, under the Roman Emperor, the prophecy of Jacob when a dying was now to be fulfilled. He had said, that *the sceptre should not depart from Judah, nor a lawgiver from between his feet, until Shiloh come.* Gen. xlix. 10. And here we find the sceptre indeed departed, for *Herod*, a foreigner, was King. Deut. xvii. 15.

The birth of *John*, though singularly accomplished, differed widely from that of the LORD JESUS; for though wonderful, it was not miraculous. And the introduction in the opening of this Gospel, in the particulars of it, appears to have been on purpose to mark the striking dissimilarity. We shall have occasion in the course of this chapter to notice this. In the mean time, let us observe the method the LORD was pleased to adopt to bring *Zacharias* acquainted with it. He was, in the course of his ministry, attending the temple service, when an angel appeared to him. This is the first open vision which the HOLY GHOST had favored the Church with, from the close of the Old Testament prophecy by *Malachi*. *Zacharias*, astonished at the sight and message of the angel, is tempted to doubt, and is struck dumb for his unbelief. But what I particularly request the Reader to remark, in proof that the birth of *John* differs altogether from that of the LORD JESUS CHRIST, is, that though the wife of *Zacharias* was indeed now aged, and had been hitherto barren, yet the event of *John's* birth was altogether the result wholly of natural causes, and from natural means; and though *John* was a child of promise, as *Isaac* was, yet in his conception and birth there was nothing miraculous, or contrary to the ordinary course of nature more than his. Gen. xviii. 10 to 14. Gal. iv. 28.

When the Reader hath properly noted this, that no more honor be given to the servant than the LORD hath given him, the Reader may properly pause, and consider the greatness of the Man, and the greatness of the Office, in the which he was designed to minister. Like *Jeremiah*, ordained from the womb, he was filled with the HOLY GHOST, for the purpose of this office, in ministering to the LORD JESUS CHRIST. Jerem. i. 5. And when it is said, as that it is said, that *he should be great in the sight of the* LORD, plainly this means, that he was so in the sight of Him to whom he became a forerunner. And hence we find the LORD JESUS bearing testimony to his character, that he was not only a Prophet, and more than a Prophet, but that among them born of women, none had been greater than he. Matt. xi. 11. See John i. 23, &c.

I detain the Reader to make one observation more, in order to have suitable apprehensions of the vast difference between the servant, and Him that sent him. It is said here, concerning the office of *John*, that *he should go before the* LORD JESUS CHRIST, *in the power and spirit of Elias, to turn the hearts of the fathers to the children, and to make ready a people prepared for the* LORD. Reader! do not overlook, that all that is here said, is said only of *John's* ministry, as an instrument to this blessed work, and no further. *John* never did, nor could, convert or turn a single soul. This is Creator-work, and not creature. The LORD who made the heart, can only turn the heart. But *John*, by ministering in the LORD's name, became the LORD's instrument in the great work. And I beg the Reader to notice, and with the just attention it deserves, what is said of *John*, *in making ready a people prepared for the* LORD. Yes! *John's* ministry, like all other servants, could be blessed to no other than the LORD's people: they whom the FATHER gave to his dear SON, before the world was formed, and whom GOD the HOLY GHOST had engaged to make willing in the day of his power, were *prepared* for JESUS as his redeemed; and grace here, and glory hereafter, *prepared* for them *in* CHRIST, from everlasting. How blessedly all the great truths of God harmonize!

26 ¶ And in the sixth month the angel Gabriel was sent from God unto a city of Galilee named Nazareth,

27 To a virgin espoused to a man whose name was Joseph, of the house of David; and the virgin's name *was* Mary.

28 And the angel came in unto her, and said, Hail, *thou that art* highly favoured, the Lord *is* with thee : blessed *art* thou among women.

29 And when she saw *him,* she was troubled at his saying, and cast in her mind what manner of salutation this should be.

30 And the angel said unto her, Fear not Mary; for thou hast found favour with God.

31 And, behold, thou shalt conceive in thy womb, and bring forth a son, and shalt call his name JESUS.

32 He shall be great, and shall be called the Son of the Highest : and the Lord God shall give unto him the throne of his father David :

33 And he shall reign over the house of Jacob for ever ; and of his kingdom there shall be no end.

34 Then said Mary unto the angel, How shall this be, seeing I know not a man ?

35 And the angel answered and said unto her, The Holy Ghost shall come upon thee, and the power of the Highest shall overshadow thee : therefore also that holy thing which shall be born of thee shall be called the Son of God.

36 And, behold, thy cousin Elizabeth, she hath also conceived a son in her old age : and this is the sixth month with her who was called barren.

37 For with God nothing shall be impossible.

38 And Mary said, Behold the handmaid of the Lord; be it unto me according to thy word : and the angel departed from her.

As the miraculous conception forms so grand and momentous a doctrine of our most holy faith, in the firm assurance of which is involved every thing that is important in the Gospel; I persuade myself that I shall have the free indulgence of my Reader to enter upon it very fully, and on true spiritual grounds to look into the whole relation of it, while looking up to God the Holy Ghost to be the teacher both of myself and Reader, in examining the several interesting particulars contained in it. Could it be supposed but for a moment, that the human nature of Christ had been produced in the ordinary way of generation among men, though it were admitted at the same time, that the mission of Christ as far exceeded all other Prophets, as the heavens are higher than the earth; still this were nothing. For then, after all, the dignity of Christ's person would have been no greater than that of any other Prophet; and his communications from God would have been in no other way than theirs. The office indeed, might have been greater, and his communications from God greater, and his usefulness more extensive. But, as to nature and person, Christ would have been upon a level with all that went before. Whereas, between Christ and *Moses*, the greatest of all Prophets under the Old Testament; and Christ, and *John the Baptist*, declared to be the greatest of all born among women, under the New; the *former* is said to be but as a servant to Christ, the Son, in the house of God: and the *latter* declares himself not worthy to unloose the latchet of the shoes of Christ. See Heb. iii. 1—6. John i. 15—34. Reader, ponder over these things by the way. See Commentary on Matt. iii. 1—4.

I have, in my *Poor Man's Commentary*, on the first chapter of *Matthew*, ver. 18. stated, somewhat largely, my views, according to scripture testimony, on the miraculous conception. But, as the subject is infinitely important, and the Church of God cannot be too clearly, nor fully established, in the most perfect conviction of this fundamental truth of our most holy faith; I would very earnestly beg the Reader's indulgence, taking advantage, from the long contents concerning it, in this chapter, to consider it yet a little more particularly. And I am free to confess, that an anxiety, for the rising generation in this kingdom, on the momentous doctrines of the Gospel, prompt me the more earnestly to this service. Never, in my view, was there a day since the Reformation, when the only principles, which make *the glorious Gospel of the ever blessed* God truly blessed, were in equal danger to be frittered away, by the carelessness of some, and the artfulness of others, who affect to call themselves *rational* Christians. I humbly beg to bear my testimony to *the truth, as it is in* Jesus, to this fundamental article of the real Christian's creed, in the evidences of the miraculous conception. And when I have stated in order, the scriptural account of this momentous doctrine, I shall leave the whole to the Reader's own mind, that he may *compare spiritual things with spiritual :* and that, under the teaching of God the Holy Ghost, his faith may be found, not to rest *in the wisdom of man, but in the power of* God.

And first: I beg him to observe with me, that with the Promise, which came in with the Fall; it was said, *the seed of the Woman should bruise the Serpent's head.* And in conformity to this, when, in the after age of the Church, the Lord entered into covenant with *Abraham*; the tenor of this covenant was conveyed in terms agreeably to this promise; that *in his seed should all families of the earth be blessed.* Gen. xii. 3. *Now,* saith the Holy Ghost by Paul, when explaining both those Scriptures, and shewing their connection; *now to Abraham, and his seed were the promises made: he saith not, and to seeds, as of many, but as of One, and to thy seed which is* Christ. Gal. iii. 16. Words, as plain these, as language can furnish, in proof that the human nature, which the Son of God should take into union with him, thereby forming one Person, even Christ, should be *the seed of the woman.* *Peter,* in his sermon, on the day of *Pentecost,* quotes a passage from one of the prophetical Psalms of *David,* in confirmation. He first shews that *David* king of Israel could not possibly mean himself; and then saith, that *David* being a prophet, knew that God *had sworn with an oath to him, that of the fruit of his body according to the flesh, he would raise up* Christ *to sit upon his throne.* Acts ii. 30. compared with Psm. cxxxii. 11. and Luke i. 31, 32. And these scriptures most plainly shew, that Christ, after the flesh, should be of *the seed of the woman.*

The next point to be attended to, in forming suitable and becoming apprehensions of this great mystery, is, to examine into what the holy scriptures taught, concerning the Incarnation of the Son of God. And here we discover the Prophets, commissioned by the Holy Ghost, informing the Church, that the event should be altogether new, and mysterious; such as never had taken place in the annals of the world. One of them cried aloud to the Church, saying: that *the* Lord *himself would give them a sign.* *Behold,* (said he,) *a virgin shall conceive, and bear a Son, and shall call his name Immanuel.* *Which* (saith an Evangelist in after days, under the same authority) *being interpreted, is* God *with us.* Compare Isaiah vii. 14. with Matt. i. 23. Another Prophet, in allusion to the same blessed promise, declared, that *the* Lord *hath created a new thing in the earth; A woman shall compass a man.* Jerem. xxxi. 22. And the Lord Jesus himself by the spirit of prophecy, confirms them both, in what he had long before delivered to the Church; when in that precious Psalm, which principally means himself, he had said; *For thou hast possessed my reins: thou hast covered me in my mother's womb. I will praise thee; for I am fearfully and wonderfully made: marvellous are thy works, and that my soul knoweth right well. My substance was not hid from thee, when I was made in secret, and curiously wrought, in the lowest parts of the earth.* Psm. cxxxix. 13, 14, 15. Fearfully and wonderfully made indeed, when considered with an eye to Christ, by the sovereign agency of God, in the womb of the Virgin; here called, in prophetical language, *the lowest parts of the earth.* But the terms are by no means applicable to the universal generation of mankind. Great as the Lord's power is, in all his works of creation; yet the stated order of the Lord, in those acts of his appointment, do away the expressions of fear and wonder. Now, these scriptures taught the Church to expect the birth of Him, whom they refer to, as coming out of the ordinary course of nature; and in a way, such as the Incarnation of the Son of God, by the miraculous conception only, can explain.

From hence we go on to what the Evangelist hath recorded in this chapter. An angel is sent to the virgin *Mary*, to announce the wonderful event. His salutation implied somewhat of infinite moment. *Hail thou that art highly favored!* Highly favored indeed! And not simply, in the grace imparted to her, of GOD's everlasting love; personally considered in redeeming mercy, as distinguished in calling her, with an holy calling, from the Adam state of nature, in which she was born; for this blessing she had in common with all the children of GOD; but highly favored, in this singular instance of grace, which never could be enjoyed by any other; in being chosen, as the woman, whose seed should bruise the serpent's head.— Concerning the chastity of *Mary*, in respect to her virgin state, none but unblushing infidels could for a moment question. For unless it could be supposed, that GOD the HOLY GHOST, for more than seven hundred years before the event was to take place, should have caused such a prophecy to be made, as that of the conception of a virgin; and then, be regardless of the accomplishment: unless this could be supposed, which is impossible, we cannot but suppose, that the LORD watched over his own promise, and made all due arrangement, that it should come to pass.

Assuming this point also granted, and still prosecuting the mysterious subject, we next have to consider another branch, requiring explanation. The Virgin *Mary*, though in herself in perfect chastity, yet certainly derived from the Adam-nature, in which she was born, taints of the same corruption from that race of fallen man, of whom it is said, by the testimony of the HOLY GHOST himself, *there is none holy, no not one*. It therefore becomes necessary to enquire, how He, who was conceived in the Virgin's womb, by the miraculous power of GOD, was preserved free from that contagion; so as to be, as he is blessedly described, *holy, harmless, undefiled, separate from sinners, and made higher than the heavens?* Heb. vii. 26. This question becomes exceedingly momentous. And blessed be GOD we have, in scripture, the most satisfying answer to it.

The word of GOD teacheth, that all the persons of the GODHEAD were engaged in the formation of the human nature of CHRIST. Concerning GOD the FATHER, it was said by CHRIST, under the spirit of prophecy, ages before his incarnation : *A body hast thou prepared me.* Compare Psm. xl. 6. with Heb. x. 5. And that GOD the SON had a hand in it is evident, for the HOLY GHOST by *Paul* saith; that He *took* not on him the nature of angels, but the seed of *Abraham*. And again, He *took* of flesh and blood. Heb. ii. 14. 16. And in this Chapter we have the wonderful relation of the part which GOD the HOLY GHOST had in the work, in his *overshadowing power*.

When the Reader hath duly pondered these sublime considerations, I would beg of him to be very attentive to what the Evangelist hath recorded in this Chapter. The angel answered the modest enquiry of *Mary*, how the thing he spoke of should be; by saying, *The* HOLY GHOST *shall come upon thee : and the power of the Highest shall overshadow thee.* By which we plainly learn, that this overshadowing power became the sole act of generation. And this is in exact correspondence to what was said by the angel to *Joseph*. *For that* (said he) *which is conceived in her, is of the* HOLY GHOST. Matt. i. 20. Here then, the whole is explained. The act of conception from the HOLY GHOST must be holy; because it is solely *from*, and wrought *by*, the LORD himself, who is holy. Had there been the intervention of an human father, no doubt, that in this case, defilement must have followed; for it is by this corruption is derived in all generations, from father to son. But in this instance, GOD the HOLY GHOST is the agent; and therefore, as the angel said, that *holy thing* which shall be born of thee, shall be called the SON of GOD. This then was *the tabernacle which* GOD *pitched, and not man.* Heb. viii. 2. This *the stone cut out without hands:* that is, without human hands. Dan. ii. 45.

And I beg the Reader to observe with me, yet further, in confirmation of this most blessed, and wonderful truth; how the HOLY GHOST hath been pleased to word the mysterious subject. *A virgin shall conceive.* Yes! But not by man! She shall bring forth a son. Yes! But not by human begetting. The HOLY GHOST shall overshadow her. THEREFORE, (that is, his Almighty agency being the sole cause) THAT HOLY THING (not that holy person, for then there would have been two persons in one CHRIST; but that holy thing) *shall be called the* SON *of* GOD. Oh! how precious is this discovery! And further: When GOD sends forth his SON, he is said to be *made* of a woman; not *begotten*, but *made:* and which, though *made* of the substance of the *seed* of the woman; yet being made by the HOLY GHOST, cannot but be holy. So that as nothing is derived by generation, from the impurity of our nature, the sole agency being of GOD; that *holy thing* is in nature holy, and of consequence the SON of GOD.

Now Reader, pause over the wonderful subject! Put the whole together in one collected point of view. Behold, how very full and clear the several terms made use of, in representing this great truth, are; that the Church-might have all suitable, and becoming apprehensions (as far as our capacities at present are capable in apprehending) of so great a mystery. Call to mind the vast preparations made for this one purpose: the union of GOD and man in one person, through a long succession of generations, from the fall of man to the coming of CHRIST. Yea, before the earth was formed, or JEHOVAH, in his threefold character of person, went forth in acts of creation. Then CHRIST was set up, as the head of his body the Church, from everlasting. Prov. viii. 22, 23. And from the first promise in the Bible, concerning the seed of the woman, until we behold it fulfilled in the uncreated word being made flesh, and dwelling among us; we trace the whole scope of scripture, pointing and directing, like so many rays of light, converging to this one centre. Had the human nature of CHRIST been formed out of nothing, or from the dust of the earth, as *Adam* was; where would have been his relationship to his people? Or, had the human nature of CHRIST been taken from any part of man, as *Eve* was, from the rib of *Adam;* this would have been a relationship no doubt, but nothing more mysterious than the former instance. But, to form the Human Nature of CHRIST from the seed of the woman, by conception, without man, and wholly by the power of GOD; this was a sign indeed, from GOD: this was a new thing in the earth; and a mystery, surpassing all human foresight and contrivance. Well might the Apostle, in the contemplation, exclaim: *Great is the mystery of godliness:* GOD *was manifest in the flesh.* 1 Tim. iii. 16.

Largely as I have trespassed, I must not dismiss the vast subject before that I have first called the Reader to remark with me, and to remark it in terms suited to its infinite importance, the very blessed doctrine connected with it, of the *atonement*. For, the miraculous conception, once confirmed, brings up after it, the evident intention from it, of CHRIST's sacrifice. The SON of GOD becoming incarnate, implied the design, of *making his soul an offering for sin.* This one act preached more fully than ten thousand sacrifices on Jewish altars; that *without shedding of blood, there was no remission.* Surely, all the branches of revelation, concerning GOD, might have been accomplished, (as far as revelation was necessary,) without such an event as the miraculous conception. But if CHRIST, and CHRIST only, can do away sin, by the sacrifice of himself, a body must be given him. Psm. xl. 6—8. Blessedly doth GOD the HOLY GHOST bear testimony to this, by his servant the Apostle: *In all things* (said he) *it behoved him to be made like unto his brethren, that he might be a merciful, and faithful High Priest, in things pertaining to* GOD, *to make reconciliation, for the sins of the people.* Heb. ii. 17. See the Commentary there.

39 ¶ And Mary arose in those days, and went into the hill country with haste, into a city of Juda;

40 And entered into the house of Zacharias, and saluted Elisabeth.

41 And it came to pass, that, when Elisabeth heard the salutation of Mary, the babe leaped in her womb; and Elisabeth was filled with the Holy Ghost:

42 And she spake out with a loud voice, and said, Blessed *art* thou among women, and blessed *is* the fruit of thy womb.

43 And whence *is* this to me, that the mother of my Lord should come to me?

44 For, lo, as soon as the voice of thy salutation sounded in mine ears, the babe leaped in my womb for joy.

45 And blessed *is* she that believed: for there shall be a performance of those things which were told her from the Lord.

46 And Mary said, My soul doth magnify the Lord,

47 And my spirit hath rejoiced in God my Saviour.

48 For he hath regarded the low estate of his
handmaiden : for, behold, from henceforth all generations shall call me blessed.

49 For he that is mighty hath done to me great
things: and holy *is* his name.

50 And his mercy *is* on them that fear him,
from generation to generation.

51 He hath shewed strength with his arm ; he
hath scattered the proud in the imagination of
their hearts.

52 He hath put down the mighty from *their*
seats, and exalted them of low degree.

53 He hath filled the hungry with good things,
and the rich he hath sent empty away.

54 He hath holpen his servant Israel, in remembrance of *his* mercy;

55 As he spake to our fathers, to Abraham and
to his seed, for ever.

56 And Mary abode with her about three
months, and returned to her own house.

Many very beautiful, and highly interesting things, arise before
our view, in those scriptures; but I must study shortness. The babe
leaping in the womb of *Elizabeth*, was certainly more than the ordinary effects of natural causes. In the after circumstances of the Baptist's life, every thing testified to the sanctification of the man, as the
forerunner of his Lord. Hence therefore, as if moved by a divine
impulse, at the approach of Christ, though not manifested openly,
the babe leaped in the womb for joy. Let the Reader recollect, what
the angel said of *John*, Luke i. 15. And I cannot but request the
Reader to observe with me, that the salutation *Elizabeth* gave to *Mary*,
was in the same words as the angel saluted the Virgin with; *Blessed
art thou among women.* But the thing is explained, for we are told,
that *Elizabeth was filled with the* Holy Ghost. And let not the
Reader forget *Elizabeth's* testimony concerning Him, of whom she
spake, when she said, and *blessed be the fruit of thy womb!* neither
the source from whence she said it, being filled with the Holy Ghost.
So then, here is God the Holy Ghost, by the mouth of *Elizabeth*,
confirming the whole word of Scripture, to the testimony of the
Godhead, and Manhood of Christ; that He is the blessing of Jehovah, to the Church: *Men shall be blessed in him; and all nations
shall call him blessed.* Psm. lxxii. 17, 18, 19.

The song of *Mary* is full of the breathings of a soul under the influence of the Holy Ghost. How blessedly she speaks of God her
Savior; evidently shewing, that she had a perfect apprehension of

what the Prophets had taught, concerning the miraculous conception; and therefore knew, that the child then in her womb was, in one and the same moment, her Son and her Savior! And how blessedly she speaks of the low estate, both in the temporal poverty of her father's house, and the spiritual reduced estate, by reason of sin, to the whole race of *Adam*. And the personal dignity to which she, a poor, young, and humble Virgin, was exalted. *He that is mighty* (said she) *hath done to me great things*. Great indeed, and, until that period, never heard of before; and never to be again wrought in the earth. And how beautifully she ends her hymn of praise, in singing the sure deliverance of the Church, by this stupendous event. *He hath holpen* (said she) *his servant Israel:* meaning, He hath redeemed the Church of God, in the Israel of God, his chosen; thus confirming the Covenant made with Abraham, that *in his seed should all the families of the earth be blessed*. Gen. xii. 3. with Gal. iii. 16.

57 ¶ Now Elisabeth's full time came that she should be delivered; and she brought forth a son.

58 And her neighbours and her cousins heard how the Lord had shewed great mercy upon her; and they rejoiced with her.

59 And it came to pass, that on the eighth day they came to circumcise the child; and they called him Zacharias, after the name of his father.

60 And his mother answered and said, Not *so;* but he shall be called John.

61 And they said unto her, There is none of thy kindred that is called by this name.

62 And they made signs to his father, how he would have him called.

63 And he asked for a writing table, and wrote, saying, His name is John: and they marvelled all.

64 And his mouth was opened immediately, and his tongue *loosed*, and he spake, and praised God.

65 And fear came on all that dwelt round about them: and all these sayings were noised abroad, throughout all the hill country of Judea.

66 And all they that heard *them* laid *them* up in their hearts, saying, What manner of child shall this be! and the hand of the Lord was with him.

It was a custom among the Jews, though we do not find in the word of Gᴏᴅ a precept to this effect, to give the child a name at circumcision. And it was also customary, for the person, who performed the act of circumcision, to accompany it with a blessing. So that it could be no ordinary character that did it, and very generally it was the father. See Gen. xvii. 23. But the dumbness of *Zacharias,* it is most likely, prevented in the present instance, his performing the service. For the name which those present intended to give the child, seems to imply as much. And when they made signs to his father on the subject, it is said, that he asked for a writing table for this purpose; that is, he made signs to have a writing table, so to do; for the dumbness of *Zacharias* was still upon him, until the name of *John* was fully given, according to the angel's declaration. (See verse 13.) *Elizabeth's* determining this name for her son, might have been taught her from her husband, who probably, notwithstanding his loss of speech, might have had the ability of informing her by sign, somewhat of the vision he had received. But I confess, that I am rather inclined to think, that the chastisement for unbelief on *Zacharias,* deprived him of this ability; and that *Elizabeth,* being full of the Hᴏʟʏ Gʜᴏsᴛ, (see ver. 41.) derived her knowledge from an higher source. The immediate liberation given to *Zacharias's* tongue when the prediction of the angel was fulfilled, became an additional testimony to the whole of this wonderful affair. And we may well suppose, as is here recorded, the astonishment produced in the minds of all that heard it.

67 ¶ And his father Zacharias was filled with the Holy Ghost, and prophesied, saying,

68 Blessed *be* the Lord God of Israel: for he hath visited and redeemed his people,

69 And hath raised up an horn of salvation for us in the house of his servant David;

70 As he spake by the mouth of his holy prophets which have been since the world began;

71 That we should be saved from our enemies, and from the hand of all that hate us;

72 To perform the mercy *promised* to our fathers, and to remember his holy covenant;

73 The oath which he sware to our father Abraham,

74 That he would grant unto us that we, being delivered out of the hand of our enemies, might serve him without fear,

75 In holiness and righteousness before him, all the days of our life.

76 And thou, child, shalt be called the prophet of the Highest: for thou shalt go before the face of the Lord to prepare his ways;

77 To give knowledge of salvation unto his people, by the remission of their sins,

78 Through the tender mercy of our God; whereby the day-spring from on high hath visited us,

79 To give light to them that sit in darkness and *in* the shadow of death, to guide our feet into the way of peace.

Reader! before you enter upon your observations of *Zacharias's* prophecy, pause at the threshold, to notice the grace of the LORD towards him, in removing from him his affliction. Well was it for *Zacharias:* well is it for all the LORD's people, his grace waits not their deservings, but flows from his own free love. And you should observe also, that no sooner is his tongue untied from the consequence of his unbelief, but the LORD loosens both heart and tongue to speak the LORD's praise; and to proclaim the LORD's mercy. And how doth he praise the LORD? Do not fail to observe, it is as the GOD of Israel: Israel's GOD in covenant. All, and every part of redemption is, *to perform the mercy promised.* Yes! For the LORD's CHRIST is *the mercy promised:* the first born in the womb of mercy; the whole of mercy; yea, mercy itself in the full. For there is no mercy, but in CHRIST. Every thing which can be called mercy, must have CHRIST in it, or it is no mercy be it what it may. It must have its very nature from CHRIST; its sweetness from CHRIST, its value from CHRIST, and its everlasting continuance from CHRIST. And hence *Zacharias* harps upon this sweet string; that it was *to perform the mercy promised,* and to fulfil JEHOVAH's covenant and oath, in all the blessings of CHRIST, for evermore. And let not the Reader fail to observe, with what holy rapture the father *Zacharias* addresses his son, though an infant, under the divine influence of the same spirit of prophecy: and having spoken of the LORD, now speaks of His harbinger. And this, by the way, is no small testimony in what office and character the HOLY GHOST, by *Zacharias,* declared John's commission: (see Malachi iii. 1.) as a messenger going before the LORD, of His temple. Who, less than GOD, can have a temple? Who, but the SON of GOD in our nature, can be called *the* LORD of his temple? Oh! the preciousness of those unnumbered attestations, all over the word of GOD, to the GODHEAD of CHRIST, the truth as it is in JESUS!

80 And the child grew, and waxed strong in spirit, and was in the deserts till the day of his shewing unto Israel.

It is a blessed account of *John,* in the close of the chapter. He grew, and was in the deserts, until he entered upon his ministry. Untaught of men, unacquainted even with the person of his LORD, until taught of the HOLY GHOST, how to know him; but then giving the highest attestation to the greatness of CHRIST's character, while declaring the littleness of his own. See John i. 19—34.

REFLECTIONS.

READER! let you, and I, at the very portal of this precious Gospel, stand and pause, before we hastily enter into the perusal of its blessed contents, and look up, and praise the Almighty Author, of His holy word, for such a profusion of mercies, as are here made known unto us; while we entreat the same glorious LORD to be our teacher, into a right understanding of those mysteries of godliness, to make us *wise unto salvation, through faith which is in* CHRIST JESUS. Was it not enough to have given the Church the inspired records, concerning our LORD, in the precious relation by *Matthew* and *Mark*; but would our bountiful LORD add the Gospel, according to *Luke*, and *John* also? Oh then! do thou, blessed LORD the HOLY GHOST, accompany the whole with thy divine teaching, that we may know the things, which are so freely given us of GOD; *comparing spiritual things with spiritual.*

Behold, Reader, in this chapter, the unbelief of *Zacharias.* Behold the faith of *Mary* and *Elizabeth!* To what, or to whom, shall we ascribe these things, but to distinguishing grace? Oh! may it be our happiness, *to believe the record, which* GOD *hath given of his dear* SON. And while we have faith, to this testimony of GOD; may we never lose sight of what the HOLY GHOST hath taught by his servant, the Apostle; when he saith, *Unto you it is given to believe in his name.*

Reader! let us ponder over, again and again, the wonderous subject here recorded, of the miraculous conception. Let us view the distant prophecies, so many ages before, declaring the unheard of, unthought of, event: and then behold, as related in this Chapter, the accomplishment; until our souls are warmed with the contemplation, and we feel constrained to cry out with the Apostle, *Great is the mystery of godliness,* GOD *was manifest in our flesh!* And oh! for grace to join in those hymns, both of *Mary* and *Zacharias,* from a personal interest in the same subject. Surely our souls may well rejoice in GOD our SAVIOR, when *through the mercy of our* GOD *the day-spring from on high hath visited us.*

C H A P. II.

CONTENTS.

The birth of CHRIST. *His Circumcision.* Simeon's *Prophecy of* CHRIST, *and the declaration of* Anna *concerning him.* JESUS *teaching in the Temple, at the age of twelve years.*

AND it came to pass in those days, that there went out a decree from Cesar Augustus, that all the world should be taxed.

2 *(And* this taxing was first made when Cyrenius was governor of Syria.)

3 And all went to be taxed, every one into his own city.

4 And Joseph also went up from Galilee, out of the city of Nazareth, into Judea, unto the city of David, which is called Bethlehem; (because he was of the house and lineage of David :)

5 To be taxed with Mary his espoused wife, being great with child.

6 ¶ And so it was, that, while they were there, the days were accomplished that she should be delivered.

7 And she brought forth her first-born son, and wrapped him in swaddling clothes, and laid him in a manger; because there was no room for them in the inn.

The Evangelist hath thought proper to note the reign of *Cæsar Augustus,* and also to distinguish a striking circumstance of the very period when the taxing the persons, (not their property,) first began.: both which were important, to mark the æra of the birth of CHRIST. First, in confirmation of *Daniel's* prophecy, which declared, that in the days of the *fourth* great monarchy, *the* GOD *of heaven should set up a kingdom which should never be destroyed.* And, secondly, *Micah* declared the town of Bethlehem was the place where CHRIST should be born. See Dan. ii. 44, 45. Micah v. 2. Now the Roman kingdom, under which CHRIST after the flesh was born, was the *fourth* from the Babylonish captivity, that is the time of Daniel's prophecy. And but for the enrolling the names of the subjects of this empire, humanly speaking, nothing could have brought *Mary,* a poor young woman, betrothed to a poor carpenter, working for his daily bread, from *Galilee* to *Bethlehem,* for this purpose. So the LORD over-ruled these events; and so the Evangelist therefore hath recorded them. And as this taxing implied, the compleat government the Roman empire had obtained over *Judæa :* the dying *Jacob's* prophecy was now fulfilled, and CHRIST was come. Gen. xlix. 10. The poverty of CHRIST's birth, corresponded to the object of his becoming incarnate. Cast out into a stable, formed a striking testimony, in correspondence with all that followed, that as he put himself in the state and circumstances of his Church, which he came to redeem, it was proper he should represent us here also, as in all other points: for we, by reason of sin, were cast out, as the prophet described, in the day we were born, and left to perish, but for the LORD passing by, and bidding us live. Ezek. xvi. 4, 5, 6.

8 And there were in the same country shepherds abiding in the field, keeping watch over their flock by night.

9 And, lo, the angel of the Lord came upon them, and the glory of the Lord shone round about them; and they were sore afraid.

10 And the angel said unto them, Fear not: for, behold, I bring you good tidings of great joy, which shall be to all people.

11 For unto you is born this day, in the city of David, a Saviour, which is Christ the Lord.

12 And this *shall be* a sign unto you; Ye shall find the babe wrapped in swaddling clothes, lying in a manger.

13 And suddenly there was with the angel a multitude of the heavenly host praising God, and saying,

14 Glory to God in the highest, and on earth peace, good will toward men.

When we consider the humble appearance in which CHRIST was born, how blessed is it to see the glorious attestation, which was given at the same time, of the greatness of his person. Angels, (and it should seem a multitude, though one only came forward to the Jewish shepherds, to be the speaker,) came from heaven to proclaim the wonders of his birth, and the end of it in salvation. I beg the Reader to remark the burden of their message: *Glory to* GOD; *peace and good will to men.* Yes! the whole glory is GOD's; because it is all founded in GOD; carried on in GOD; compleated in GOD; and man is but the receiver of the mercies. Oh! that this was well understood by men! What an end would it put to all the pharisaical righteousness, and pride of men!

15 And it came to pass, as the angels were gone away from them into heaven, the shepherds said one to another, Let us now go even unto Bethlehem, and see this thing which is come to pass, which the Lord hath made known unto us.

16 And they came with haste, and found Mary and Joseph, and the babe lying in a manger.

17 And when they had seen *it,* they made known abroad the saying which was told them concerning this child.

18 And all they that heard *it*, wondered at those things which were told them by the shepherds.

19 But Mary kept all these things, and pondered *them* in her heart.

20 And the shepherds returned, glorifying and praising God for all the things that they had heard and seen, as it was told unto them.

It doth not appear that those shepherds, though struck with astonishment, both at the vision of angels and in their visit to *Bethlehem*, at what they had seen and heard, were savingly converted to the faith. They are said to have returned praising God, and spreading the report abroad. But we hear no more of them. *Mary* is said to have pondered these things in her heart. Sweet view of grace; which is silent and retired, waiting on the LORD!

21 ¶ And when eight days were accomplished for the circumcising of the child, his name was called JESUS, which was so named of the angel before he was conceived in the womb.

22 And when the days of her purification, according to the law of Moses, were accomplished, they brought him to Jerusalem, to present *him* to the Lord;

23 (As it is written in the law of the Lord, Every male that openeth the womb shall be called holy to the Lord;)

24 And to offer a sacrifice, according to that which is said in the law of the Lord, A pair of turtle doves, or two young pigeons.

It is blessed, yea, very blessed, to behold CHRIST being put into our law-room and place, thus entering upon his work in redeeming his people. As such, circumcision was the first rite in the Church, for admission into the covenant. See Gen. xvii. 10 to 14. CHRIST therefore, by virtue of this rite, became a debtor to the whole law to fulfil it. This proved him to be under the law, and a son of *Abraham*, according to the flesh. And his presentation in the temple, became a further testimony. And with CHRIST the rite ceased for ever. For as CHRIST, by virtue of it, became a debtor to the whole law, and fulfilled it in his own person, so he virtually freed his Church from the rite for ever. Hence the Apostle saith, *Behold I Paul, say unto you, that if ye be circumcised,* CHRIST *shall profit you nothing. For I testify again to every man that is circumcised, that he is a debtor to do the whole law.* Galat. v. 1 to 6. See Levit. xii. 3 to 6. Exod. xiii. 2. Numb. iii. 13,

25 And, behold, there was a man in Jerusalem whose name *was* Simeon; and the same man *was* just and devout, waiting for the consolation of Israel: and the Holy Ghost was upon him.

26 And it was revealed unto him by the Holy Ghost, that he should not see death before he had seen the Lord's Christ.

27 And he came by the spirit into the temple; and when the parents brought in the child Jesus, to do for him after the custom of the law,

28 Then took he him up in his arms, and blessed God, and said,

29 Lord, now lettest thou thy servant depart in peace, according to thy word:

30 For mine eyes have seen thy salvation,

31 Which thou hast prepared before the face of all people;

32 A light to lighten the Gentiles, and the glory of thy people Israel.

33 And Joseph and his mother marvelled at those things which were spoken of him.

34 And Simeon blessed them, and said unto Mary his mother, Behold, this *child* is set for the fall and rising again of many in Israel; and for a sign which shall be spoken against;

35 (Yea, a sword shall pierce through thy own soul also) that the thoughts of many hearts may be revealed.

Concerning this man, the HOLY GHOST hath given blessed testimony. And the revelation made to him, doth not seem to have been of an ordinary kind, as is the case with all that are regenerated and sanctified: but in a way of prophecy, so as to comfort therefrom others. And the LORD that gave him such strong assurances, that he should not die till he had seen CHRIST, must have led him to the temple at the very time CHRIST was there; and also taught him, that this was CHRIST. Reader! think how blessed it is to be taught of GOD. See that promise. Isaiah liv. 12. with John vi. 45. And what a beautiful hymn of praise and faith, and holy joy! How strong the faith of Old Testament saints. They had no fears of death, when once they had seen CHRIST. GOD's covenant love, and CHRIST's salvation, were the same to them, living or dying. The astonishment

excited in the minds of *Joseph* and *Mary*, was not, I apprehend, as if
what *Simeon* had said, was altogether unheard of or not considered by
them before; but rather, their wonder was continually kept up, in
the expectation of the marvellous things which was predicted to be
wrought by CHRIST.

36 And there was one Anna, a prophetess, the
daughter of Phanuel, of the tribe of Aser: she
was of a great age, and had lived with an husband
seven years from her virginity;

37 And she *was* a widow of about fourscore and
four years, which departed not from the temple,
but served *God* with fastings and prayers night
and day.

38 And she coming in that instant gave thanks
likewise unto the Lord, and spake of him to all
them that looked for redemption in Jerusalem.

This woman was very aged indeed, according to the general age
of people in those days. For supposing she had married as early as
fifteen, and seven years in marriage, and eighty-four years a widow,
she could not be less than one hundred and six years. And yet we
find her constant abode was in the temple, in deep humility of soul.
The HOLY GHOST's testimony by her of CHRIST, is worthy regard.

39 And when they had performed all things according to the law of the Lord, they returned into
Galilee, to their own city Nazareth.

40 And the child grew, and waxed strong in
spirit, filled with wisdom : and the grace of God
was upon him.

I detain the Reader at those verses, in order to call his attention
to what is said of CHRIST concerning his growth in nature, and
waxing strong in spirit. It forms a subject of interesting enquiry.
I pray the LORD the HOLY GHOST to guide the mind, both of Writer
and Reader, into a proper apprehension of the mysterious subject.

Now let it be first considered, that CHRIST in his human nature
was to stand in the precise state and place of that nature he came to
redeem. *It behoved him to be made like unto his brethren in all
things.* He came to redeem his people from the curse, *being made a
curse for them.* Hence he is said to have been made *in the likeness
of sinful flesh.* In the *likeness* of it only : not himself sinful, for *he
knew no sin*; but was *holy, harmless, undefiled, separate from sinners,
and made higher than the heavens.* Standing thus; though holy, in
our nature, and the representative of all his people, the moment he
entered our world, the consequences of the curse attached itself to
him, and seized upon him. Hence, he took all the sinless infirmi-

ties of our nature; was born a child; became subject to misery and sorrow; to labor and travail; and as *Adam's* doom for sin was pronounced upon him, and all his children, CHRIST in putting away sin by the sacrifice of himself, subjected himself to eat bread, in the sweat of his brow, until he was brought into the dust of *death.* Psm. xxii. 15. Hence, therefore, this explains at once, wherefore it became necessary for CHRIST to stand in the very state and place of the nature he came to redeem. It was as the representative and surety of his Church and People. The mere taking of our nature into union with the GODHEAD, without this, would not have answered the purpose. It would have been indeed a wonderful act of condescension in the SON of GOD so to have done: but then, had he came forth as the first earthly *Adam* came forth, in the perfection of his manhood at once, this would not have suited our case and circumstances; neither would it have answered for us in removing the curse. No! The SON of GOD, if he will be our surety, must put himself in our circumstances; must be born an infant; must gradually advance to manhood; must wax strong in spirit, and be filled with wisdom, and have the grace of GOD upon him. And these things blessedly prove to us, that it was a real and true body, the SON of GOD took into union with himself, in all points like ours, *yet without sin:* so that both in body and in soul he was manifested to be the same as we are.

From these premises let us go on further, and we shall discover, that agreeably to this assumption of our nature, for the purposes of redemption, JESUS became subject to all the sorrows of it, and to all the labors of it. His reputed father was a poor man, who worked for his daily bread. JESUS therefore did the same. Hence we hear him upbraided, *Is not this the Carpenter's Son? Is not this the Carpenter?* Matt. xiii. 55. Mark vi. 3. And so truly low in circumstances, that he could not, as the children of better condition among the Jews did, learn to read the Prophets, for the HOLY GHOST from the mouth of his enemies hath given us this testimony, that he never learnt from human teaching. *The Jews marvelled, saying, how knoweth this man letters having never learned?* John vii. 15. And no doubt, though it is not recorded in so many words, but from the earliest period of his life, as soon as ability enabled him to work for his bread, to the time he entered on his ministry at the age of thirty years, his lot was cast among that class of labor which belongs to the greatest part of mankind. Reader! so far is this from lessening the dignity of our LORD's character, that without it he would not have filled in the whole of the office of our great Mediator. The curse pronounced on the fall, comprized in it three grand points. *First,* a nature of frailty and infirmity. *Secondly,* a toilsome life, midst thorns and briers. And, *thirdly,* death. When the SON of GOD undertook to be his Church's surety, and to redeem his Church, he engaged for all these, and all these he fulfilled. Oh! how precious to my soul is the consideration. *He who knew no sin was made sin for me,* that I (who know no righteousness in myself,) *may be made the righteousness of GOD in him.* 2 Cor. v. 21.

41 Now his parents went to Jerusalem every year at the feast of the passover.

42 And when he was twelve years old, they went up to Jerusalem, after the custom of the feast.

43 And when they had fulfilled the days, as they returned, the child Jesus tarried behind in Jerusalem; and Joseph and his mother knew not *of it.*

44 But they, supposing him to have been in the company, went a day's journey, and they sought him among *their* kinsfolk and acquaintance.

45 And when they found him not, they turned back again to Jerusalem, seeking him.

46 And it came to pass, that after three days, they found him in the temple, sitting in the midst of the doctors, both hearing them, and asking them questions.

47 And all that heard him were astonished at his understanding and answers.

48 And when they saw him, they were amazed: and his mother said unto him, Son, why hast thou thus dealt with us? behold, thy father and I have sought thee sorrowing.

49 And he said unto them, How is it that ye sought me? wist ye not that I must be about my Father's business?

50 And they understood not the saying which he spake unto them.

As in the preceding verses we were introduced into an acquaintance with CHRIST's abased state, so here we are brought into a short, but blessed view of his exaltation and glory. The men of Israel were obliged to go up three times in a year before the LORD at Jerusalem, at the great feasts; but the women were not enjoined to this service. Deut. xvi. 16. However, we find *Mary*, on this occasion, accompanying her husband at the Passover. *Nazareth* was distant from *Jerusalem* about three days journey. It is refreshing to behold, how holy men of old delighted in attending the feasts at Jerusalem. And as they were figurative of Gospel mercies, especially the *Passover*, there can be no doubt but that the HOLY GHOST accompanied those services with a sweet savor of CHRIST. And the LORD JESUS, at twelve years of age, accompanying his mother and *Joseph*, becomes a blessed recommendation to the children of believing parents to have an early relish for divine things. Neither doth the conduct of *Joseph* and *Mary*, seeking for JESUS among their kinsfolk and acquaintance, bring with it a subject of less profitable instruction. Where should we seek JESUS, but among his people? Song i. 7, 8.

But the most interesting part in what is here said, is the engagement in which *Joseph* and *Mary* found JESUS, after a three days' search in the midst of the doctors, and the answer the LORD made to *Mary's* question. *How is it that ye sought me? Wist ye not that I must be about my* FATHER'S *business?* And though they understood not the saying, yet, Reader! You and I, under divine teaching, may. What business could the LORD JESUS then be upon, but the very business which brought him first from heaven, in the redemption of his Church and People? Here then was the opening of it. Here a breaking forth for the moment appeared of that *zeal which for his* FATHER'S *house had eaten him up.* Psm. lxix. 9. and which afterwards appeared in full glory. John ii. 12. to the end. A more decided proof could never be desired, in testimony of CHRIST'S mission, than in such an instance. JESUS gently reproved both his mother and *Joseph* by his answer, in that, after all that had been told them, and especially his mother, they should not instantly have concluded where he was, and how engaged. *Wist ye not that I must be about my* FATHER'S *business?* As if JESUS had said, in the temple, my FATHER'S house, I enter upon that business for which I became incarnate; to fulfil the whole law; to satisfy divine justice; to bring in an everlasting righteousness; and by conquering sin, Satan, death, hell, and the grave; to save my people from their sins!

51 And he went down with them, and came to Nazareth, and was subject unto them: but his mother kept all these sayings in her heart.

52 And Jesus increased in wisdom and stature, and in favour with God and man.

The Reader will have all suitable apprehensions of what is contained in these verses, if he keeps in view the recollection of the GODHEAD, and of the Manhood of CHRIST. In his human nature he was, as hath been before observed in this Chapter, a true and proper man, *in all points as we are, yet without sin.* And had he not been so, he could not have been a true and proper surety. In this nature therefore, he was subject to Mary and Joseph, in all subordination. And in this nature, he increased in wisdom and stature, and in age also, (as it is rendered in the margin of our Bibles,) and in favor with GOD and man. For as the holiness and purity of his life became daily greater in accession, so of consequence it increased in favor both in the eye of GOD and man, as tending more and more to perfection. But in his divine nature there could be no increase, being in the essential properties of JEHOVAH, *one with the* FATHER *over all* GOD *blessed for ever. Amen.* If men of no grace would read their Bibles with candour only, (for with more than this, untaught of GOD, they never can,) and recollect, that *the faith once delivered to the saints,* contemplates the person of CHRIST in his two-fold nature of GOD and

Man united; they might from the same candour be led to suppose, that in all those passages, such as is contained in these two verses, it is the simple humanity of CHRIST only, which the HOLY GHOST is treating of. But what becomes a *stone of stumbling, and a rock of offence*, to Infidels of every description and character, is to the faithful among the sweetest and most precious testimonies of his suitability and fitness as the CHRIST of GOD. Yes! thou dearest LORD! thy humble birth, thy laborious life, in eating bread by the sweat of thy brow, in fulfilling all righteousness, and in thy ignominious death, even the death of the cross, mark thee as the very Lamb *slain from the foundation of the world!* Hail! thou LORD of all, while servant of all! To thee shall *every knee bow, and every tongue confess, that* JESUS CHRIST *is* LORD *to the glory of* GOD *the* FATHER. Amen.

REFLECTIONS.

READER! how little did the Roman Emperor *Augustus*, or his deputy *Cyrenius*, conceive, that the over-ruling power of GOD so arranged the taxation, that the chief object to which it should minister, should be to bring the Virgin *Mary* to *Bethlehem*, and mark the precise period of the birth of CHRIST! How unconscious were the Jewish shepherds, when keeping watch over their flocks by night, until the message from heaven informed them of the wonderful event of the arrival of the SAVIOR! And oh! the astonishing mystery, when GOD, who hath recorded from all eternity the names of his redeemed in the book of life, brings them acquainted with the unspeakable mercy, and manifests himself to them otherwise than he doeth to the world. Reader! can You and I mark down our personal knowledge of these things, so as with *Simeon* or *Anna* declare, our eyes have seen CHRIST's salvation; and speak of the LORD JESUS to all them *that look for redemption in Jerusalem?*

Precious LORD JESUS! when I behold thy obscure birth, thy low circumstances and mean accommodation, a manger only to receive thee in thine entrance into this our world, and no room for thee in the inn; oh, what a lively representation was there in this, of all the future circumstances of thy life. Truly didst thou say, and the truth holds equally good in all ages; *Blessed is he whosoever is not offended' in thee!* My soul! delight thou more and more in the sweet testimonies of thy LORD's humanity, while beholding him at the same time possessing all the proofs of GODHEAD. For by both only could JESUS be suited for thee as thy Surety, Husband, and SAVIOR. Oh! the preciousness of that mystery, which without controversy is great, GOD *was manifest in the flesh.*

CHAP. III.

CONTENTS.

The Introduction of John the Baptist, *with the Time of his Entrance on his Ministry　His Testimony of* CHRIST. *Our* LORD's *Baptism and Genealogy.*

NOW in the fifteenth year of the reign of Tiberius Cesar, Pontius Pilate being governor of Judea, and Herod being tetrarch of Galilee, and his brother Philip tetrarch of Iturea, and of the region of Trachonitis, and Lysanias the tetrarch of Abilene,

2 Annas and Caiaphas being the high priests, the word of God came unto John the son of Zacharias in the wilderness.

The Evangelist having in the two preceding Chapters, faithfully recorded the wonderful events of CHRIST's incarnation and birth, now enters upon the wonderful history also of CHRIST's ministry, in order to prosecute it to the end. But in doing this he makes a long stride. The *fifteenth* year of the reign of *Tiberius Cæsar*, became nearly parallel to the *thirtieth* year of CHRIST, when the LORD JESUS entered on his ministry, (verse 23,) so that from the *twelfth* year, in which the last Chapter represents CHRIST, as found in the midst of the doctors, in his FATHER's business, to the period of his entrance on his public ministry, *Luke* passeth by in silence. Reader! think of this, and conceive, if it be possible, how the holy soul of the LORD must have been exercised, during the many years in the society of the ungodly, before the time arrived for making himself known to Israel. If *Lot* was vexed, as it is said he was, *with the filthy conversation of the wicked*, 2 Peter ii. 7, 8. what must CHRIST have experienced? Pause over the contemplation. For my own part, I cannot but conclude, that here, in this part of the Redeemer's life, in the private circumstances of it, as well as when coming forward to his public ministry, he was fulfilling all righteousness, and acting in all departments, and in all offices, for his people. For consider, CHRIST being the very same in nature as we are, *(yet without sin,)* in being exercised with the same feelings as ours, his holy soul must have felt, (only in a ten thousand times higher degree,) what we feel, when once our souls are renewed by grace, at what we behold, and hear, and see, in the sins of others. And as the LORD JESUS came to bear the sins of all his people, how must he have felt at what he saw and heard of his redeemed in their infirmities and sins? And is it not in this sense, as well as in every other, he is said *to have took our infirmities, and bore our sicknesses?* Matt. viii. 17. For let it be remembered, that as his holy nature was not liable to be affected with any disease in himself, personally considered, by sickness, as well as by sin, his knowledge of both must have been one and the same. And the scripture account is, that he was made in the *likeness* of sinful flesh. Romans viii. 3. and was made sin when he knew no sin, 2 Cor. v. 21. Such views of CHRIST are exceedingly precious! And I cannot but hope that the Reader will have his mind suitably exercised, in contemplating the LORD JESUS under characters so truly endearing, whenever he is led to reflect on the long interval from the birth of CHRIST, to the more open display of his Person, Work, and Labors, at his entrance on his public ministry!

I only detain the Reader one moment longer at these verses, just to remark, that the characters here spoken of, I mean of *Cæsar*, *Pontius Pilate, Herod, Philip, Lysanias, Annas,* and *Caiaphas,* would never have found place for record in the word of God, but for the more perfectly ascertaining the period of John's ministry, and the appearance of Christ. This *Tiberius Cæsar* was the third of the *Cæsars* which were Emperors of *Rome.* Christ was born under the reign of the *second* of the name, *Augustus Cæsar:* and the Reader may at once conclude how contemptible the whole were in the view of the Church, since nothing more is said of either, than just by way of recording the period in their reign, which opened in the ministry of John the Baptist to the advent of Christ. And the grand point, as it related to the Gospel of Christ, and which the mention of their names was designed to prove, was, that now *Judæa* was brought into subjection to the *Roman* power, the prediction of the dying Patriarch *Jacob* was fulfilled; *the sceptre was departed from Judah, and the lawgiver from between his feet,* and consequently *the Shiloh was come!* Gen. xlix. 10.

3 And he came into all the country about Jordan, preaching the baptism of repentance for the remission of sins;

4 As it is written in the book of the words of Esaias the prophet, saying, The voice of one crying in the wilderness, Prepare ye the way of the Lord, make his paths straight.

5 Every valley shall be filled, and every mountain and hill shall be brought low: and the crooked shall be made straight, and the rough ways *shall be* made smooth:

6 And all flesh shall see the salvation of God.

7 Then said he to the multitude that came forth to be baptized of him, O generation of vipers, who hath warned you to flee from the wrath to come?

8 Bring forth therefore fruits worthy of repentance, and begin not to say within yourselves, We have Abraham to *our* father: for I say unto you, that God is able of these stones to raise up children unto Abraham.

9 And now also the ax is laid unto the root of the trees: every tree therefore which bringeth not forth good fruit is hewn down, and cast into the fire.

10 And the people asked him, saying, What shall we do then?

11 He answereth and saith unto them, He that hath two coats, let him impart to him that hath none; and he that hath meat, let him do likewise.

12 Then came also publicans to be baptized, and said unto him, Master, what shall we do?

13 And he said unto them, Exact no more than that which is appointed you.

14 And the soldiers likewise demanded of him, saying, And what shall we do? and he said unto them, Do violence to no man, neither accuse *any* falsely; and be content with your wages.

15 ¶ And as the people were in expectation, and all men mused in their hearts of John, whether he were the Christ, or not;

16 John answered, saying unto *them* all, I indeed baptize you with water: but one mightier than I cometh, the latchet of whose shoes I am not worthy to unloose: he shall baptise you with the Holy Ghost and with fire:

17 Whose fan *is* in his hand, and he will thoroughly purge his floor, and will gather the wheat into his garner; but the chaff he will burn with fire unquenchable.

18 And many other things in his exhortation preached he unto the people.

19 ¶ But Herod the tetrarch, being reproved by him for Herodias his brother Philip's wife, and for all the evils which Herod had done,

20 Added yet this above all, that he shut up John in prison.

21 ¶ Now when all the people were baptized, it came to pass, that Jesus also being baptised, and praying, the heaven was opened,

22 And the Holy Ghost descended in a bodily shape like a dove upon him, and a voice came

from heaven, which said, Thou art my beloved
Son ; in thee I am well pleased.

Having very largely dwelt upon the most prominent features of the
person and office of John the Baptist, on the parallel account given
of him in *Matthew's* statement, Chap. iii. 1 to the end; I think it
unnecessary to enlarge on the subject here, but rather refer the
Reader *to my Poor Man's Commentary*, in that place. In addition
to what was there offered, I would only beg further to observe, on what
is here said of the consternation into which *John's* ministry threw
his auditory, whether he was the CHRIST, or not; certain it was, that
a general expectation had been raised about this very time, by all
orders of the people, for the coming of the *Messiah*. The prophecies
concerning CHRIST, *when* he should appear, according to *Daniel's*
seventy weeks, was now arrived : Dan. ix. 24. *where* he should be
born, according to *Micah*, had been fulfilled in CHRIST's instance.
Micah v. 2. Matt. ii. 4, 5, 6. John vii. 42. And his forerunner,
which *Malachi* described, now arrested their attention. Malachi iii. 1.
So that it is not to be wondered at, that the multitude of the people
which read their prophets, pondered over *John's* preaching. See
John i. 19 to 34. I beg the Reader's particular attention to what was
offered on the subject of CHRIST's baptism, and the testimony of the
three heavenly witnesses on that occasion, as stated Matt. iii. 16, 17.

23 ¶ And Jesus himself began to be about thirty
years of age, being, as was supposed, the son of
Joseph, which was *the son* of Heli,

24 Which was *the son* of Matthat, which was
the son of Levi, which was *the son* of Melchi, which
was *the son* of Janna, which was *the son* of Joseph,

25 Which was *the son* of Mattathias, which was
the son of Amos, which was *the son* of Naum,
which was *the son* of Esli, which was *the son* of
Nagge,

26 Which was *the son* of Maath, which was *the
son* of Mattathias, which was *the son* of Semei,
which was *the son* of Joseph, which was *the son* of
Juda,

27 Which was *the son* of Joanna, which was
the son of Rhesa, which was *the son* of Zorobabel,
which was *the son* of Salathiel, which was *the son*
of Neri,

28 Which was *the son* of Melchi, which was
the son of Addi, which was *the son* of Cosam,

which was *the son* of Elmodam, which was *the son* of Er,

29 Which was *the son* of Jose, which was *the son* of Eliezer, which was *the son* of Jorim, which was *the son* of Matthat, which was *the son* of Levi,

30 Which was *the son* of Simeon, which was *the son* of Juda, which was *the son* of Joseph, which was *the son* of Jonan, which was *the son* of Eliakim,

31 Which was *the son* of Melea, which was *the son* of Menan, which was *the son* of Mattatha, which was *the son* of Nathan, which was *the son* of David,

32 Which was *the son* of Jesse, which was *the son* of Obed, which was *the son* of Booz, which was *the son* of Salmon, which was *the son* of Naasson,

33 Which was *the son* of Aminadab, which was *the son* of Aram, which was *the son* of Esrom, which was *the son* of Pharez, which was *the son* of Juda,

34 Which was *the son* of Jacob, which was *the son* of Isaac, which was *the son* of Abraham, which was *the son* of Thara, which was *the son* of Nachor,

35 Which was *the son* of Saruch, which was *the son* of Ragau, which was *the son* of Phalec, which was *the son* of Heber, which was *the son* of Sala,

36 Which was *the son* of Cainan, which was *the son* of Arphaxad, which was *the son* of Sem, which was *the son* of Noe, which was *the son* of Lamech,

37 Which was *the son* of Mathusala, which was *the son* of Enoch, which was *the son* of Jared, which was *the son* of Maleleel, which was *the son* of Cainan,

38 Which was *the son* of Enos, which was *the son* of Seth, which was *the son* of Adam, which was *the son* of God.

I detain the Reader, at the very entrance on this genealogy concerning CHRIST, to call his particular attention to the manner in which *Luke* introduceth *Joseph*, as the *supposed* father of CHRIST. Than which form of words, nothing can be stronger in proof, that it was a mere supposition only, and not in reality. And the insertion in Luke's Gospel of the direct descent of CHRIST after the flesh, in a regular order from *Adam* to *Joseph*, as *Matthew* had before done from *Abraham* to *Mary*, was evidently intended for no other purpose than as a testimony to the great point, that CHRIST was the seed of the Woman. With Joseph, CHRIST had no connection. But it was a common mode of expression with the Jews, to call the man *father* which brought up a child. Hence *Joseph* became the *supposed* father. And if the Reader will compare Matt. i. 16. with what is said here, verse 23, he will discover somewhat of this very custom. In Matthew, *Joseph* is said to have been begotten of Jacob, so that *Jacob* was his real father. But according to Luke, *Heli* was his father, and so he was, that is his *reputed* father, by virtue of *Joseph* being betrothed to *Mary* his daughter. So that these things explain the several expressions, according to Jewish customs.

In respect to the life of CHRIST, at his entrance upon his ministry, being then about *thirty years of age;* I have already, in the former part of this chapter, offered a short observation upon it. In addition, I would only just remark, that the precise period, for CHRIST being made manifest unto Israel, had been so strikingly marked from the beginning, that to this point several weighty circumstances evidently had reference. The law enjoined, that from thirty years, and upward, until fifty years, the sons of *Levi* should enter into the host. Numb. iv. 2, 3. JESUS, though not of *Levi*, but of *Judah*, yet being Him, in whom the Priesthood centered, and was completed, shall therefore so enter. And although his ministry extended but to the half week of *Daniel's* prophecy, that is, just three years and a half; yet so much worn was He, by hard service, cruel treatment, and hard fare, that the Jews supposed him to have been fifty. Dan. ix. 27. John viii. 57. And in type also, Joseph is said, when prefiguring CHRIST, to have gone at that age in before Pharaoh. Gen. xli. 46. Some have gone further in discovering, or in supposing they have discovered, many shadows in scripture, of this substance of CHRIST's ministry, in relation to the period of three years and a half. See Dan. xii. 7. with Rev. xii. 14. James v. 17. with Luke iv. 25. But I presume not to decide upon the subject.

In respect to this genealogy, I do not think it necessary to enlarge. The correctness of it is unquestionable; and the intention of it is plain. It is essential, yea most essential to the Church's peace and welfare, to be well informed, and as the Apostle saith, to remember also that JESUS CHRIST *is of the seed of David*. 2 Timothy ii. 8. So that in going over this, it is not, as may be said of many, *giving heed to fables, and endless genealogies which minister questions, rather than godly edifying:* but here is a subject, which leads to the fountain head of mercy, in tracing Him, *who is made not after the law of a carnal commandment, but after the power of an endless life.*

REFLECTIONS.

READER! where are all those proud monarchs, in the *Cæsars,* and *Pilates,* and *Herods,* of the day; whose looks frowned men for the moment into fear; and whose words, and actions, made men tremble throughout the earth? The flood of time hath gone over them, and they are no more! But He, who as a *little stone cut out without hands,* hath broken them all in pieces, and, as foretold, is become a mountain, and hath filled and is filling the earth. Behold the humbleness and austerity of his herald the Baptist. Then see the low estate of the SON of GOD. And in the midst of all that debasement, poverty, and meekness of character, hear the voice from heaven attesting to the glories of his person, while the HOLY GHOST bore testimony to the same; *Thou art my beloved Son! In thee I am well pleased.* Oh! for grace to be well pleased also with his person, work, offices, character, and relations! Precious LORD JESUS! truly thou art the seed of the woman; and in thee *shall all the seed of Israel be justified, and shall glory!*

CHAP. IV.

CONTENTS.

CHRIST'S *Temptations. His Preaching in the Synagogue. He casteth out a Devil, and cureth many that were sick.*

AND Jesus, being full of the Holy Ghost, returned from Jordan, and was led by the Spirit into the wilderness,

2 Being forty days tempted of the devil. And in those days he did eat nothing: and when they were ended, he afterward hungered.

3 And the devil said unto him, If thou be the Son of God, command this stone that it be made bread.

4 And Jesus answered him, saying, It is written, That man shall not live by bread alone, but by every word of God.

5 And the devil taking him up into an high mountain, shewed unto him all the kingdoms of the world in a moment of time.

6 And the devil said unto him, All this power

will I give thee, and the glory of them: for that is delivered unto me: and to whomsoever I will I give it.

7 If thou therefore wilt worship me, all shall be thine.

8 And Jesus answered and said unto him, Get thee behind me, Satan: for it is written, Thou shalt worship the Lord thy God, and him only shalt thou serve.

9 And he brought him to Jerusalem, and set him on a pinnacle of the temple, and said unto him, If thou be the Son of God, cast thyself down from hence:

10 For it is written, He shall give his angels charge over thee to keep thee:

11 And in *their* hands they shall bear thee up, lest at any time thou dash thy foot against a stone.

12 And Jesus answering said unto him, It is said, Thou shalt not tempt the Lord thy God.

13 And when the devil had ended all the temptation, he departed from him for a season.

It was one part of the covenant of redemption, that the human nature of CHRIST should be anointed to the arduous work, which the SON of GOD, when taking into union with himself that holy portion of our nature, for this vast purpose, engaged to do. Hence those scriptures: Isaiah xi. 1, 2. Psm. lxxxix. 19—24. Heb. i. 8, 9. with Psm. xlv. 6, 7. And what makes this subject most blessed is, that the spirit of JEHOVAH not only rested *upon* CHRIST, but was *in* CHRIST. Holy men of old, and the Prophets of GOD, spake as they were moved by the HOLY GHOST. The influence given to them was limited at certain times, and greater or less as occasion required; but GOD gave not *the spirit by measure unto* CHRIST. He always spake the words of GOD. So that in every other person, the HOLY GHOST was as in a vessel, but in CHRIST as a fountain. In JESUS, full, overflowing. *To every one of us,* saith the Apostle, *is given grace, according to the measure of the gift of* CHRIST. 2 Pet. i. 21. John iii. 34. Ephes. iv. 7.

We shall do well, in our entrance upon the subject of CHRIST's temptations to observe, how immediately after his baptism, temptations began. And we shall do well also to observe, how every thing tended to heighten those temptations with the LORD JESUS, in long and severe fasting; and in a wilderness uninhabited but with wild beasts. Reader! it is one of the most endeared views of JESUS, which the HOLY GHOST hath given us, when we behold him going through the same exercises, and being assaulted with the same fiery trials his people are made acquainted with; inasmuch as these things carry with them a palpable evidence, that he knoweth all our feelings by his own. All the angels of light cannot give us that assistance, neither can they enter into our feelings, because their nature is not human. But JESUS's affections are like our own, only infinitely heightened, both from the greatness and holiness of his nature, and his own personal experience in his humanity. It was a precious love-token of our LORD, and, if I do not greatly mistake, intended to act in this way, when after his resurrection, in appearing to them, he saw and felt for their fright, and comforted their minds into this assurance, from fellow-feeling. *A spirit hath not flesh and bones as ye see me have.* Luke xxiv. 39. It will be well both for the Writer and Reader in all their temptations, while reading those of the LORD JESUS CHRIST, to keep this thought in view.

The limits I must observe in a work of this kind, will not allow me to lead the Reader through all the several particulars which might otherwise be noticed in our LORD's temptations. It will be sufficient to observe, that under three great branches are included all sorts of sin, to which the devil tempted CHRIST in our nature, and which *John* calls *the lust of the flesh, and the lust of the eye, and the pride of life.* 1 John ii. 16. If the Reader will examine the several different artifices of *Satan,* here used by the accursed enemy to seduce CHRIST, he will find that all may be classed under one or other of these. But I am more concerned that both myself and Reader may have suitable apprehensions of the *cause* of those temptations of the LORD JESUS, when acting as our surety and representative, than to attempt exploring what human intellect, in the present unripe state of things, can never arrive at, and in a subject so deep and mysterious as the temptations of JESUS.

And we shall at once get into very precious and blessed discoveries of this most interesting subject, such as the temptations of CHRIST are, when, under the HOLY GHOST's teaching, we behold CHRIST as sustaining those attacks from *Satan* on our account. By the fall of man, our whole nature was become the lawful captive of the devil. See Isa. xlix. 24, 25, 26. Here then JESUS enters the field in our behalf, and goes into the very territories of *Satan,* to rescue our nature from his dominion. And when the devil had discharged the whole of his artillery, he departed for a season. We find his renewed attacks in the garden of *Gethsemane,* the particulars of which are related to us, Luke xxii. to which I refer the Reader. But in this part of his temptations in the wilderness, we behold him giving out, and CHRIST victorious.

Let not the Reader however, even for the present, dismiss the subject, before that he hath first, under the HOLY GHOST's teaching, taken with him one or two improvements arising from the same, which may the LORD make profitable.

And *first,* let it be remembered, it is said of CHRIST, *that though He were a Son, yet learned he obedience by the things which he suffered.* Heb. v. 8. From hence we may safely conclude, that it was in our nature CHRIST sustained the attacks of Satan; and therefore his per-

sonal knowledge and fellow-feeling of our nature, give his redeemed
an interest in that knowledge and fellow-feeling, upon every occasion of trial. *For in that he himself hath suffered, being tempted,
he knoweth how to succour them that are tempted.* Heb. ii. 18.

Secondly. To this should be added, that though JESUS is now in
glory, yet is He the same JESUS still. It is not his nature that is
changed, but his state. And He is now in glory, as the head of his
body the Church, and consequently as an head, he knows and feels
what every one of his members feel. Every attack of *Satan,* on the
humblest of his people, JESUS is perfectly acquainted with. And if
JESUS, in the days of his flesh, *offered up strong crying and tears,
and was heard in that he feared,* how sure, how very sure is it, that
he will hear and answer all the cries of his redeemed!

And *thirdly,* to add no more, and what according to my view of
things, becomes as sweet a thought as any, all that mercy, help,
compassion, and the like, which JESUS will impart to the tempted
state of his members below, will be his JESU-love, that is, his GOD-
man love, made everlastingly secure and full, to all the unnumbered
wants of his whole tried family upon earth, by virtue of his GODHEAD;
but at the same time no less most graciously suited, to be communicable to them by virtue of his manhood, in flowing in one and the same
nature from his heart to theirs, in an endless succession of love and
kindness.

14 ¶ And Jesus returned in the power of the
Spirit into Galilee: and there went out a fame of
him through all the region round about.

15 And he taught in their synagogues, being
glorified of all.

16 ¶ And he came to Nazareth, where he had
been brought up: and, as his custom was, he went
into the synagogue on the sabbath day, and stood
up for to read.

17 And there was delivered unto him the book
of the prophet Esaias. And when he had opened
the book, he found the place where it was written,

18 ¶ The Spirit of the Lord *is* upon me, because
he hath anointed me to preach the gospel to the
poor; he hath sent me to heal the broken-hearted,
to preach deliverance to the captives, and recovering of sight to the blind, to set at liberty them
that are bruised,

19 To preach the acceptable year of the Lord.

20 And he closed the book, and he gave *it*
again to the minister, and sat down. And the

eyes of all them that were in the synagogue were fastened on him.

21 And he began to say unto them, This day is this scripture fulfilled in your ears.

22 And all bare him witness, and wondered at the gracious words which proceeded out of his mouth. And they said, Is not this Joseph's son?

We shall enter into *some* of the very blessed things contained in this scripture, (but ah! how small a part,) if we do as we are commanded, while waiting on the HOLY-GHOST's teaching, *compare spiritual things with spiritual.* 1 Cor. ii. 13. By turning to the writings of the Prophet *Isaiah*, chap. lxi. 1, &c. we are taught to expect CHRIST as there represented. And here we behold CHRIST exactly answering to the description. JESUS reads the passage, confirms thereby the character of Him that was to come into the world; and then appeals to their own senses for the application to himself.

It were to do little short of going over the life of CHRIST, to follow JESUS in all the parts of this most precious Sermon. Indeed it may be considered but as an abridgement of his whole Gospel. Sweet as it would be, and the most interesting discourse capable of being offered, yet that pleasure I must suppress, while remembering the limits suited to a *Poor Man's Commentary.* But though constrained to pass over all observations on CHRIST's Sermon, yet I do very earnestly beg the Reader not to overlook the decided testimony the people gave, in consequence thereof, to the truth of his divine character. For it is said, that *all* bare him witness. There seemed to be for the moment, one general common consent, that He was the CHRIST. I beg the Reader not to lose sight of this; and the more so, from what follows in a few verses after.

23 And he said unto them, Ye will surely say unto me this proverb, Physician, heal thyself: whatsoever we have heard done in Capernaum, do also here in thy country.

24 And he said, Verily I say unto you, No prophet is accepted in his own country.

25 But I tell you of a truth, Many widows were in Israel in the days of Elias, when the heaven was shut up three years and six months, when great famine was throughout all the land;

26 But unto none of them was Elias sent, save unto Sarepta *a city* of Sidon, unto a woman *that was* a widow.

27 And many lepers were in Israel in the time of Eliseus the prophet; and none of them was cleansed saving Naaman the Syrian.

28 And all they in the synagogue, when they heard these things, were filled with wrath,

29 And rose up, and thrust him out of the city, and led him unto the brow of the hill whereon their city was built, that they might cast him down headlong.

30 But he, passing through the midst of them, went his way,

31 And came down to Capernaum, a city of Galilee, and taught them on the sabbath days.

32 And they were astonished at his doctrine: for his word was with power.

And here we find how the tone of their sentiments is changed. *All they in the synagogue were now filled with wrath,* and endeavoured to push him on to the brow of the hill of their city, in order to destroy him. Reader! when you have duly pondered the subject, and marked the great change, I beseech you to pause, and if it be possible, find out the cause. It was at one and the same meeting this vast alteration of conduct in the people took place. There could have been no one circumstance of a change in CHRIST, either in his person or behaviour. And what was it, think you, filled the minds of this people with wrath, which before had borne witness at *the gracious words which proceeded out of his mouth?* Are you able to discover the cause? surely nothing can be plainer. The simple reason was, in the *former,* JESUS preached his Gospel in the *general* features of it. In the latter, JESUS preached the same Gospel in the *special* and *particular* application of it. In the *one,* he held forth the glories of his person, in his offices, character, and relations. In the *latter,* the personal interest his people alone have in it. In a word, CHRIST preached in the close of what he had before delivered, that doctrine, which ever hath, and ever must, and ever will give disgust to all carnal men; and which, though CHRIST himself be the preacher, (as we here see fully proved,) will never cease to be odious; even the doctrine of GOD's sovereignty, in opposition to the pride of the free will of man; and hence CHRIST shall experience what all his servants, in all ages of the Church have experienced, the most bitter resentment instantly arising against it. But, Reader! while making due observation on those striking passages, in explaining the cause of that change of behaviour towards the LORD JESUS CHRIST, do not fail at the same time to mark down in suitable characters, what a blessed testimony the SON of GOD hath here given, in proof of that fundamental, glorious, and incontrovertible doctrine of GOD. See Matt. xi. 25, 26. John xvii. 2, 3, 9. Rom. ix. 6. to the end.

33 ¶ And in the synagogue there was a man which had a spirit of an unclean devil; and cried out with a loud voice,

34 Saying, Let *us* alone; what have we to do with thee, *thou* Jesus of Nazareth? art thou come to destroy us? I know thee who thou art; the Holy One of God.

35 And Jesus rebuked him, saying, Hold thy peace, and come out of him. And when the devil had thrown him in the midst, he came out of him, and hurt him not.

36 And they were all amazed, and spake among themselves, saying, What a word is this! for with authority and power he commandeth the unclean spirits, and they come out.

37 And the fame of him went out into every place of the country round about.

We have the relation of this miracle, in very nearly the same words, Mark i. 23, &c. I refer therefore to the observations on it there offered.

38 And he arose out of the synagogue, and entered into Simon's house, and Simon's wife's mother was taken with a great fever; and they besought him for her.

39 And he stood over her, and rebuked the fever; and it left her: and immediately she arose and ministered unto them.

40 Now when the sun was setting, all they that had any sick with divers diseases brought them unto him; and he laid his hands on every one of them, and healed them.

41 And devils also came out of many, crying out, and saying, Thou art Christ the Son of God. And he rebuking *them,* suffered them not to speak: for they knew that he was Christ.

42 And when it was day, he departed and went into a desert place: and the people sought him,

and came unto him, and stayed him, that he should not depart from them.

43 And he said unto them, I must preach the kingdom of God to other cities also: for therefore am I sent.

44 And he preached in the synagogues of Galilee.

We have the record of these things, Matt. viii. 14. &c. I refer the Reader thither.

REFLECTIONS.

READER! let it be our wisdom, in all our meditations on the sufferings and exercises of CHRIST, to connect with them the cause. *He was wounded for our transgressions: he was bruised for our iniquities: the chastisement of our peace was upon him; and by his stripes we are healed!* And while we think of those things, let us in all our lesser exercises bless GOD, when at any time called to the fellowship in suffering of his SON JESUS CHRIST. *My brethren* (saith James) *count it all joy, when ye fall into divers temptations.* And, no doubt, when the strength of CHRIST is made perfect in our weakness, there is great cause of joy, to glory even in our infirmities, when the power of CHRIST doth rest upon us.

Reader! think what a sermon CHRIST's first sermon was, as recorded here, which he preached after his ordination by the unction of the HOLY GHOST, in the Jewish synagogue? Oh! that all preachers of the word of GOD were to follow CHRIST's example, and thereby prove that the spirit of the LORD, according to the measure of the gift of CHRIST, was upon them. Might we not hope, that from the same blessed cause, as by the master, so by his servants, gracious effects would follow; and the LORD's cause would be glorified in the earth. But let all such not fail to do as CHRIST did. However offensive to carnal reason, and to the free will of men, let the sovereignty of GOD be proclaimed. Many widows, and many *lepers* there may be in Israel now, as of old; but until GOD sends his word, there will be no commission to heal. Oh! do thou, blessed JESUS, who in the days of thy flesh didst heal all the diseases of thy people, now in the day of thy power manifest the sovereignty of thy grace and salvation, and preach by thy blessed spirit, as then in the synagogues of Galilee. Amen.

CHAP. V.

CONTENTS.

We have in this Chapter the LORD JESUS *teaching the People: the miraculous Draught of Fishes; the Leper cleansed; a Man with a Palsy healed; and the Call of* Matthew.

A ND it came to pass, that, as the people pressed
upon him to hear the word of God, he stood
by the lake of Gennesaret,

2 And saw two ships standing by the lake: but
the fishermen were gone out of them, and were
washing *their* nets.

3 And he entered into one of the ships, which
was Simon's, and prayed him that he would thrust
out a little from the land. And he sat down, and
taught the people out of the ship.

I pray the Reader to pause over this interesting account of the
LORD's preaching, and the eagerness of the people to hear Him, *who
spake as never man spake.* Let the Reader figure to himself the
thronging multitude, pressing upon him, and hanging upon his very
lips, to catch the gracious words which proceeded out of his mouth.
Doth it not remind the Reader of what is said of CHRIST, Psm. xlv.
2. *Grace is poured into thy lips!* And of what the Church, in her
rapturous view of JESUS, hath said; *Let him kiss me with the kisses of
his mouth.* Song i. 2. So precious, so very precious are all the words
and manifestations of JESUS, that the Church could hang upon CHRIST's
lips for ever.

4 ¶ Now when he had left speaking, he said
unto Simon, Launch out into the deep, and let
down your nets for a draught.

5 And Simon answering said unto him, Master,
we have toiled all the night, and have taken nothing, nevertheless at thy word I will let down the
net.

6 And when they had this done, they inclosed
a great multitude of fishes; and their net brake.

7 And they beckoned unto *their* partners which
were in the other ship, that they should come and
help them. And they came, and filled both the
ships, so that they began to sink.

8 When Simon Peter saw *it,* he fell down at
Jesus' knees, saying, Depart from me; for I am a
sinful man, O Lord.

9 For he was astonished, and all that were with
him, at the draught of the fishes which they had
taken:

10 And so *was* also James, and John, the sons of Zebedee, which were partners with Simon. And Jesus said unto Simon, Fear not; from henceforth thou shalt catch men.

11 And when they had brought their ships to land, they forsook all, and followed him.

Very many blessed things are contained in this short history of the miraculous draught of fishes. I might call upon the Reader to remark with me, what kindness to the poor fishermen, who had toiled all night and caught nothing, in thus immediately providing for them and their households. I might observe also, what a beautiful application was hereby made of the LORD's sermon. These, and other remarks, might be gathered from it of an instructive nature. But I pass by all these, in order to call the attention of the Reader to a point, yet vastly more momentous; namely, the testimony which this miracle of the LORD JESUS carried with it to the mind of *Peter* of the GODHEAD of CHRIST. For the Apostle's falling down at the feet of JESUS and crying out, *Depart from me, for I am a sinful man, O Lord,* was altogether expressive what his views of JESUS at that time were. *Peter,* it should seem, at the moment recollected what the LORD had said to *Moses* in the Mount. *Thou canst not see my face, for there shall no man see me and live.* Exod. xxxiii. 20. And under these impressions, holy men concluded, that the sight of GOD must produce instant death. Hence *Manoah,* in after ages, when the angel of the LORD appeared to him and his wife, and did wonderously, expected death : *We shall surely die,* (said he,) *because we have seen GOD.* Judges xiii. 22. *Peter* felt all this, and under a conscious sense of sin, desired the LORD to depart from him. The Apostle was convinced, that nothing short of an Almighty power could have produced such a miracle,as was then shewn, and therefrom drew his conclusion of the GODHEAD of CHRIST. I hope the Reader will as readily, and from the same power as taught *Peter,* be led to the same conclusion, and then the passage will appear in all its beauty. See Matt. xvi. 13—17.

12 ¶ And it came to pass, when he was in a certain city, behold, a man full of leprosy ; who seeing Jesus, fell on *his* face, and besought him, saying, Lord, if thou wilt, thou canst make me clean.

13 And he put forth *his* hand, and touched him, saying, I will; Be thou clean; and immediately the leprosy departed from him.

14 And he charged him to tell no man : but go, and shew thyself to the priest, and offer for thy

cleansing according as Moses commanded, for a testimony unto them.

15 But so much the more went there a fame abroad of him: and great multitudes came together to hear: and to be healed by him of their infirmities.

16 And he withdrew himself into the wilderness, and prayed.

For observations on the history of the leper, See Matt. viii. 2, &c.

17 ¶ And it came to pass on a certain day, as he was teaching, that there were Pharisees and doctors of the law sitting by, which were come out of every town of Galilee, and Judea, and Jerusalem: and the power of the Lord was *present* to heal them.

18 And, behold, men brought in a bed a man which was taken with a palsy: and they sought *means* to bring him in, and to lay *him* before him.

19 And when they could not find by what *way* they might bring him in because of the multitude, they went upon the housetop, and let him down through the tiling with *his* couch into the midst before Jesus.

20 And when he saw their faith, he said unto him, Man, thy sins are forgiven thee.

21 And the scribes and the Pharisees began to reason, saying, Who is this which speaketh blasphemies? Who can forgive sins, but God alone?

22 But when Jesus perceived their thoughts, he answering said unto them, What reason ye in your hearts?

23 Whether is easier to say, Thy sins be forgiven thee; or to say, Rise up and walk?

24 But that ye may know that the Son of man hath power upon earth to forgive sins, (he said unto the sick of the palsy,) I say unto thee, Arise, and take up thy couch, and go unto thine house,

25 And immediately he rose up before them, and took up that whereon he lay, and departed to his own house, glorifying God.

26 And they were all amazed, and they glorified God, and were filled with fear, saying, We have seen strange things to day.

I cannot suppose that the cure of the man with the palsy was at the same time as those doctors were present; for *Mark*, in his relation of this miracle, doth not notice their presence; and moreover it is said, in the close of the wonderful act, the lookers on were all amazed, and they glorified GOD. A circumstance never ascribed to those men, who only came to entrap CHRIST, and to accuse him. Concerning this miracle of the paralytic, I have very largely dwelt upon it, Mark ii. 2 to 12, to which therefore I refer.

27 ¶ And after these things he went forth, and saw a publican, named Levi, sitting at the receipt of custom: and he said unto him, Follow me.

28 And he left all, rose up, and followed him.

29 And Levi made him a great feast in his own house: and there was a great company of publicans and of others that sat down with them.

30 But their scribes and Pharisees murmured against his disciples, saying, Why do ye eat and drink with publicans and sinners?

31 And Jesus answering, said unto them, They that are whole need not a physician; but they that are sick.

32 I came not to call the righteous, but sinners to repentance.

33 And they said unto him, Why do the disciples of John fast often, and make prayers, and likewise *the disciples* of the Pharisees; but thine eat and drink?

34 And he said unto them, Can ye make the children of the bridechamber fast, while the bridegroom is with them?

35 But the days will come, when the bridegroom shall be taken away from them, and then shall they fast in those days.

36 And he spake also a parable unto them ; No man putteth a piece of a new garment upon án old; if otherwise, then both the new maketh a rent, and the piece that was *taken* out of the new agreeth not with the old.

37 And no man putteth new wine into old bottles ; else the new wine will burst the bottles, and be spilled, and the bottles shall perish.

38 But new wine must be put into new bottles ; and both are preserved.

39 No man also having drunk old *wine* straightway desireth new : for he saith, The old is better.

We have this passage almost literally, Matt. ix. 9, &c. I refer therefore to the observations which were then offered. The last verse indeed is an addition to the subject, and only made by *Luke;* but the sense and doctrine is the same. It should seem to have been a proverbial expression, and well understood in a wine country like that of *Judæa.* But the spiritual sense of it, in application to our Lord's discourse, appears to have been thus : No man having drunk into the spirit of the faith of the old disciples, the Patriarchs, and Prophets, concerning Christ, will desire to taste of any other. That which was from the beginning, and in which the fathers among the faithful all lived and died, is the old wine of God's covenant love. And he which hath drank into this will drink of no other. Christ's *love is better than wine!* Song i. 2.

REFLECTIONS.

Reader! think what privileges the men of that generation possessed, which had Christ himself for their preacher! He, who was himself the whole of the covenant, to be the messenger, and administrator of it also! Well might the people press upon him to hear the word of God! And, Reader! see how immediately after the sermon was finished, he kindly rewarded the attendance of his disciples with the supply of fishes. What a testimony at the same time of his being Lord and proprietor, both of earth and sea. Lord! let such a display of thy sovereignty have the same effect on my heart, as on that of *Peter;* not to say Lord! depart from me, but to impress my mind as his was, that I may say, *Thou art my* Lord *and my* God!

Oh! for grace, when I read of this *leper,* and hear of the mercy shewn to the *paralytic,* to have faith in my God! Yes! blessed Jesus, all power is thine to cleanse both the leprosy of soul and body ; and to remove the crippled state of all thy redeemed, until *the lame man shall leap as an hart, and the tongue of the dumb sing.* Like *Levi,* Lord! I would take thee home to my house, to my heart, and invite other poor sinners to the banquet of my God. No Pharisaical fastings would I set up, by way of recommending myself to the LORD; but rejoice in this, CHRIST came not to call the self-righteous, but sinners to repentance. No patched up garments, no new wine of the Gospel to receive in the old skin of nature; but pray that He who sits upon the throne, making all things new, while He himself remains eternally and unchangeably the same, would make my heart new, and renew a right spirit within me. LORD JESUS! do thou all this, and more; and cause thou me to drink of the old wine of thine everlasting love, *which goeth down sweetly, causing the lips of those that are asleep to speak!*

CHAP. VI.

CONTENTS.

JESUS *passing through the Corn Fields on the Sabbath, and his Disciples eating the Ears of Corn, called forth the Anger of the Pharisees.* JESUS's *Answer. He healeth the withered Hand: calleth the Disciples: performeth Miracles, and preacheth.*

AND it came to pass on the second sabbath after the first, that he went through the corn fields; and his disciples plucked the ears of corn, and did eat, rubbing *them* in *their* hands.

2 And certain of the Pharisees said unto them, Why do ye that which is not lawful to do on the sabbath-days?

3 And Jesus answering them said, Have ye not read so much as this, what David did, when himself was an hungred, and they which were with him;

4 How he went into the house of God, and did take and eat the shewbread, and gave also to them that were with him; which it is not lawful to eat but for the priests alone?

5 And he said unto them, That the Son of man is Lord also of the sabbath.

In the two former Evangelists, *Matthew* and *Mark*, we have the circumstance here mentioned by *Luke* also related. See Matt. xii. 1. Mark ii. 23. It is always profitable to attend to what the LORD JESUS hath said, on every occasion of discourse. These *Pharisees*, however undesignedly, have been very useful in calling forth the LORD's observations in answer to their cavils.

6 ¶ And it came to pass also on another sabbath, that he entered into the synagogue and

taught: and there was a man whose right hand was withered.

7 And the scribes and Pharisees watched him, whether he would heal on the sabbath day; that they might find an accusation against him,

8 But he knew their thoughts, and said to the man which had the withered hand, Rise up, and stand forth in the midst. And he arose and stood forth.

9 Then said Jesus unto them, I will ask you one thing; Is it lawful on the sabbath days to do good, or to do evil? to save life, or to destroy *it?*

10 And looking round about upon them all, he said unto the man, Stretch forth thy hand. And he did so; and his hand was restored whole as the other.

11 And they were filled with madness; and communed one with another what they might do to Jesus.

This miracle is recorded by both the preceding Evangelists; and observations were offered on both, to which I now refer. See Matt. xii. 9. and Mark iii. 1.

12 ¶ And it came to pass in those days, that he went out into a mountain to pray, and continued all night in prayer to God.

I would beg to notice this verse by itself. There is somewhat very striking in those scriptures which relate to our Lord's retiring for the purpose of prayer. The sample he hath caused to be left upon record, John xvii. throughout, may in some measure lead our minds into an apprehension of our Lord's employment, upon those solemn occasions. The Evangelist in this place gives two striking features of it. He was alone. And he was all night in communion. Oh! for grace to be like him. And may he give his people *songs in the night!*

13 And when it was day, he called *unto him* his disciples: and of them he chose twelve, whom also he named apostles;

14 Simon, (whom he also named Peter,) and Andrew his brother, James and John, Philip and Bartholomew,

15 Matthew and Thomas; James the *son* of Alpheus, and Simon called Zelotes;

16 And Judas *the brother* of James, and Judas Iscariot, which also was the traitor.

CHRIST's call of his Apostles we have noticed, Matt. x. 1. and again Mark iii. 14. See Matt. x. 1, &c. and my *Poor Man's Concordance,* on the subject.

17 ¶ And he came down with them, and stood in the plain, and the company of his disciples, and a great multitude of people out of all Judea and Jerusalem, and from the sea coast of Tyre and Sidon, which came to hear him, and to be healed of their diseases;

18 And they that were vexed with unclean spirits: and they were healed.

19 And the whole multitude sought to touch him: for there went virtue out of him, and healed *them* all.

Here is a beautiful view of JESUS, and his College of Apostles, coming down from the mount where He had ordained them. Can we suppose the ordination service to have been less solemn than that of the Prophet *Jeremiah?* see chap. i. throughout. True, *Judas* was among them; but this became no bar to the LORD's special sanctification of the rest; while JESUS well knew, when he called the traitor, that he was a devil, and consequently unsanctified. John vi. 70, 71. Solemn consideration!

20 ¶ And he lifted up his eyes on his disciples, and said, Blessed *be ye* poor; for your's is the kingdom of God.

21 Blessed *are ye* that hunger now: for ye shall be filled. Blessed *are ye* that weep now: for ye shall laugh.

22 Blessed are ye, when men shall hate you, and when they shall separate you *from their company,* and shall reproach *you,* and cast out your name as evil, for the Son of man's sake.

23 Rejoice ye in that day, and leap for joy: for, behold, your reward *is* great in heaven: for

in the like manner did their fathers unto the prophets.

24 But woe unto you that are rich? for ye have received your consolation.

25 Woe unto you that are full! for ye shall hunger. Woe unto you that laugh now! for ye shall mourn and weep.

26 Woe unto you when all men shall speak well of you! for so did their fathers to the false prophets.

27 But I say unto you which hear, Love your enemies, do good to them which hate you,

28 Bless them that curse you, and pray for them which despitefully use you.

29 And unto him that smiteth thee on the *one* cheek, offer also the other; and him that taketh away thy cloke forbid not *to take thy* coat also.

30 Give to every man that asketh of thee; and of him that taketh away thy goods ask *them* not again.

31 And as ye would that men should do to you, do ye also to them likewise.

32 For if ye love them which love you, what thank have ye: for sinners also love those that love them.

33 And if ye do good to them which do good to you, what thank have ye? for sinners also do even the same.

34 And if ye lend *to them* of whom ye hope to receive, what thank have ye? for sinners also lend to sinners, to receive as much again.

35 But love ye your enemies, and do good, and lend, hoping for nothing again; and your reward shall be great, and ye shall be the children of the Highest: for he is kind unto the unthankful and *to the* evil.

36 Be ye therefore merciful, as your Father also is merciful.

37 Judge not, and ye shall not be judged: condemn not, and ye shall not be condemned; forgive, and ye shall be forgiven;

38 Give, and it shall be given unto you; good measure, pressed down, and shaken together, and running over, shall men give into your bosom: for with the same measure that ye mete withal, it shall be measured to you again.

39 And he spake a parable unto them, Can the blind lead the blind? shall they not both fall into the ditch?

40 The disciple is not above his master: but every one that is perfect shall be as his master.

41 And why beholdest thou the mote that is in thy brother's eye, but perceivest not the beam that is in thine own eye?

42 Either how canst thou say to thy brother, Brother, let me pull out the mote that is in thine eye, when thou thyself beholdest not the beam that is in thine own eye? Thou hypocrite, cast out first the beam out of thine own eye, and then shalt thou see clearly to pull out the mote that is in thy brother's eye.

43 For a good tree bringeth not forth corrupt fruit; neither doth a corrupt tree bring forth good fruit.

44 For every tree is known by his own fruit: for of thorns men do not gather figs, nor of a bramble bush gather they grapes.

45 A good man, out of the good treasure of his heart, bringeth forth that which is good; and an evil man, out of the evil treasure of his heart, bringeth forth that which is evil: for of the abundance of the heart his mouth speaketh.

46 And why call ye me Lord, Lord, and do not the things which I say?

47 Whosoever cometh to me, and heareth my sayings, and doeth them, I will shew you to whom he is like:

48 He is like a man which built an house, and digged deep, and laid the foundation on a rock: and when the flood arose, the stream beat vehemently upon that house, and could not shake it: for it was founded upon a rock.

49 But he that heareth, and doeth not, is like a man that without a foundation built an house upon the earth, against which the stream did beat vehemently, and immediately it fell, and the ruin of that house was great.

This is the same sermon as CHRIST preached, and which is recorded in *Matthew's* Gospel, chap. v. vi. vii. And having very largely dwelt upon the principal parts of it in that place, I do not think it necessary to enlarge upon it here. I would beg the Reader just to remark, how CHRIST in this sermon specially and peculiarly addressed his disciples, when he pronounced those blessings with which he opened his discourse.

Perhaps in the 39th verse, here are certain proverbial expressions of CHRIST, which, as they were not in the sermon recorded by *Matthew*, were not spoken by our LORD at that time, but at another occasion, but introduced in this place by *Luke*. See Matt. xv. 14. But our LORD's discourse in this Chapter, being in itself very plain, and for the most part having been explained in the Commentary on Matt. v. I think it needless to enlarge.

REFLECTIONS.

BLESSED LORD! as oft as I pass through the corn fields, whether on the Sabbath day or any other, may the recollection of thine unequalled tenderness and condescension, in those seasons here represented, lead me to the contemplation of thy grace and love to thy disciples. And while I behold thy followers rubbing the ears of corn and eating them, I would call to mind how JESUS was broken and bruised for our sins, and his body given as the bread of life for all his redeemed. Oh! for grace to feed on thee by faith, until I come to see thee as thou art, and dwell with thee for ever! And do thou, LORD, to all my withered and dying circumstances, do by me as this poor man in the synagogue; let JESUS speak but the word, and sure I am of being healed. And let thine effectual calling on my poor heart, cause me to follow thee, as did thy faithful disciples: surely, LORD, if virtue went out of thee, when upon earth, and healed them all, the efficacy is not lessened in the day of thy power! Oh! for that distinguishing grace which JESUS pronounceth to be blessed, which though found by them that are poor in themselves, and among the hungry and the mourners, are found rich in faith before GOD, and heirs of the kingdom. Standing firm on the rock CHRIST JESUS, they shall ride out every storm, and find CHRIST a sure sanctuary in the day of wrath.

CHAP. VII.

CONTENTS.

We have here the Cure of the Centurion's Servant: the raising of the Widow's Son; CHRIST's Answer to the Messengers of John the Baptist; and Mary anointing CHRIST's Feet.

NOW when he had ended all his sayings in the audience of the people, he entered into Capernaum.

2 And a certain centurion's servant, who was dear unto him, was sick, and ready to die.

3 And when he heard of Jesus, he sent unto him the elders of the Jews, beseeching him that he would come and heal his servant.

4 And when they came to Jesus, they besought him instantly, saying, That he was worthy for whom he should do this:

5 For he loveth our nation, and he hath built us a synagogue.

6 Then Jesus went with them; and when he was now not far from the house, the centurion sent friends to him, saying unto him, Lord, trouble not thyself: for I am not worthy that thou shouldest enter under my roof;

7 Wherefore neither thought I myself worthy to come unto thee: but say in a word, and my servant shall be healed.

8 For I also am a man set under authority, having under me soldiers, and I say unto one, Go, and he goeth; and to another, Come, and he cometh; and to my servant, Do this, and he doeth *it*.

9 When Jesus heard these things, he marvelled at him, and turned him about, and said unto the people that followed him, I say unto you, I have not found so great faith, no, not in Israel.

10 And they that were sent, returning to the house, found the servant · whole that had been sick.

Capernaum was much frequented by CHRIST, indeed it is called his own city. Hence the condemnation, Matt. xi. 23. The account here given of this centurion, differs in some points from the relation given by *Matthew:* but both are correct. *Matthew* doth not notice the elders of the Jews first coming to CHRIST in his behalf: but it should seem that the *centurion* sent them first, and then hearing that JESUS was coming to him, he hastened towards CHRIST, as is here described, to testify his unworthiness of the LORD's condescension. I have somewhat largely made observations on this gracious act of CHRIST, in Matt. viii. 5, &c. to which I refer.

11 ¶ And it came to pass the day after, that he went into a city called Nain : and many of his disciples went with him, and much people.

12 Now when he came nigh to the gate of the city, Behold, there was a dead man carried out, the only son of his mother, and she was a widow ; and much people of the city was with her.

13 And when the Lord saw her, he had compassion on her, and said unto her, Weep not.

14 And he came and touched the bier; and they that bare *him* stood still : and he said, Young man, I say unto thee, Arise.

15 And he that was dead sat up, and began to speak : and he delivered him to his mother.

16 And there came a fear on all : and they glorified God, saying, That a great prophet is risen up among us; and, That God hath visited his people.

17 And this rumour of him went forth throughout all Judea, and throughout all the region round about.

This city of *Nain* lay near Mount *Tabor*, and not very remote from *Capernaum*. The case of this poor widow, and her dead son,

is not noticed by either of the Evangelists, except Luke, and therefore it may be proper to attend to it somewhat more particularly. The
history is but short, yet it is wound up to the most finished description of sorrow. This youth was not an infant, whose endearments
had not therefore been long, so as by time to work deeper holdfast
in the affections; but one arrived to manhood, in the flower of his age,
and capable of recompensing a mother's care. And what made the
loss more bitter, he was her *only* son; so that in his death she had
been stripped of all. And, as if all this was not enough to weigh her
down with overmuch sorrow, she was a widow; so that she had no
husband to bear a part with her in the affliction, and to drink a portion of the sorrowful cup. Yea, an husband *dead*, and child too, so
that she was desolate.

The scriptures have noticed the distress of such bereaving providences, as among the heavy calamities of life. Jer. vi. 26. Zech.
xii. 10. And we find this case attracted the attention of the Son
of God. *When the* Lord *saw her, he had compassion on her.* Reader!
what a sweet thought it is to relieve the sorrows of the Lord's people,
that the eye of Jesus is always upon them. And his knowledge of
their distresses is not only as God, but his feeling for them is as man.
Blessedly is it said of him, *in that he hath suffered being tempted,*
he is able to succour them that are tempted. Heb. ii. 18.

The miracle he wrought in raising this young man from the dead,
became the fullest and most decided evidence of his own sovereign
power and Godhead. For although there are on record in scripture, several instances of the Lord's servants, for the confirmation
of the faith, working such miracles, yet not one without first praying
to the Lord to justify them as his servants, in the accomplishment
of such deeds. But in the instance before us, here is the immediate
act of Jesus, saying, *Young man, I say unto thee, arise!* I beg the
Reader to notice this, with that due attention so decided a testimony
gives to the Godhead of Christ. John x. 37, 38. The improvements
to be drawn from this miracle of Jesus, are very many; but it would
swell our little work into too great a bulk to notice all. Yet, I cannot
allow myself and Reader to leave it altogether, without first observing, what a most lovely view it affords of the tenderness and compassion of Christ. Truly was it said of him by the Prophet, *He*
hath borne our griefs, and carried our sorrows. And I would request
the Reader, while beholding this affection of character to his people
while on earth, to remember that He is the same Jesus now in heaven.
And the most blessed part of the subject is, that He not only knows
what the exercises of his redeemed are, as God; but He knows also,
and feels for them as man. That union of God and man in One Person, gives him both the power to know all, and the fellow-feeling
to administer the suited relief to all; and in such a way, as without
this union of the two natures, could not have answered our wants,
and his glory, as Mediator. Oh! the preciousness of such views
of Christ!

Reader! allow me to add one thought more on this glorious miracle
of our God and Savior. Think what a testimony it carries with it
concerning Him, and his Almightiness of character, as the resurrection and the life. Surely, He who raised the widow's son, can and will
raise the members of his own mystical body, at the last day. They

shall arise by virtue of their union with Him. All that are in their graves shall hear his voice, and come forth. But the dead in CHRIST shall rise first. For thus the charter of grace runs. *He shall quicken your mortal bodies by his spirit that dwelleth in you.* Read in confirmation those precious scriptures : Isaiah xxvi. 19. John v. 28, 29. 1 Thess iv. 16. Romans viii. 11.

18 ¶ And the disciples of John shewed him of all these things.

19 And John calling *unto him* two of his disciples, sent *them* to Jesus, saying, Art thou he that should come? or look we for another?

20 When the men were come unto him, they said, John Baptist hath sent us unto thee, saying, Art thou he that should come? or look we for another?

21 And in the same hour he cured many of *their* infirmities and plagues, and of evil spirits; and unto many *that were* blind he gave sight.

22 Then Jesus answering said unto them, Go your way, and tell John what things ye have seen and heard; how that the blind see, the lame walk, the lepers are cleansed, the deaf hear, the dead are raised, to the poor the gospel is preached.

23 And blessed is *he,* whosoever shall not be offended in me.

24 And when the messengers of John were departed, he began to speak unto the people concerning John, What went ye out into the wilderness for to see? A reed shaken with the wind?

25 But what went ye out for to see? A man clothed in soft raiment? Behold, they which are gorgeously apparelled, and live delicately, are in kings' courts.

26 But what went ye out for to see? A prophet? Yea, I say unto you, and much more than a prophet.

27 This is *he,* of whom it is written, Behold, I send my messenger before thy face, which shall prepare thy way before thee.

28 For I say unto you, Among those that are born of women, there is not a greater prophet than John the Baptist: but he that is least in the kingdom of God is greater than he.

29 And all the people that heard *him*, and the publicans, justified God, being baptized with the baptism of John.

30 But the Pharisees and lawyers rejected the counsel of God against themselves, being not baptised of him.

31 And the Lord said, Whereunto then shall I liken the men of this generation! and to what are they like?

32 They are like unto children sitting in the market-place, and calling one to another, and saying, We have piped unto you, and ye have not danced; we have mourned to you, and ye have not wept.

33 For John the Baptist came neither eating bread, nor drinking wine: and ye say, He hath a devil.

34 The Son of man is come eating and drinking; and ye say, Behold, a gluttonous man and a wine bibber, a friend of publicans and sinners!

35 But wisdom is justified of all her children.

We have already noticed this message of John to the Lord Jesus, together with Christ's answer; and his testimony concerning John. Matt. xi. 1, &c. I refer the Reader therefore to the observations there offered.

36 ¶ And one of the Pharisees desired him that he would eat with him: and he went into the Pharisee's house, and sat down to meat.

37 And, behold, a woman in the city which was a sinner, when she knew that *Jesus* sat at meat in the Pharisee's house, brought an alabaster box of ointment.

38 And stood at his feet behind *him*, weeping, and began to wash his feet with tears, and did

wipe *them* with the hairs of her head, and kissed his feet, and anointed *them* with the ointment.

39 Now when the Pharisee which had bidden him saw *it*, he spake within himself, saying, This man, if he were a prophet, would have known who and what manner of woman *this is* that touched him: for she is a sinner.

40 And Jesus answering, said unto him, Simon, I have somewhat to say unto thee; and he saith, Master, say on.

41 There was a certain creditor which had two debtors: the one owed five hundred pence, and the other fifty.

42 And when they had nothing to pay, he frankly forgave them both. Tell me therefore, which of them will love him most?

43 Simon answered and said, I suppose that *he* to whom he forgave most: and he said unto him, Thou hast rightly judged.

44 And he turned to the woman, and said unto Simon, Seest thou this woman? I entered into thine house, thou gavest me no water for my feet: but she hath washed my feet with tears, and wiped *them* with the hairs of her head.

45 Thou gavest me no kiss: but this woman, since the time I came in, hath not ceased to kiss my feet.

46 My head with oil thou didst not anoint: but this woman hath anointed my feet with ointment.

47 Wherefore I say unto thee, Her sins which are many, are forgiven; for she loved much: but to whom little is forgiven, *the same* loveth little.

48 And he said unto her, Thy sins are forgiven.

49 And they that sat at meat with him began to say within themselves, Who is this that forgiveth sins also?

50 And he said to the woman, Thy faith hath saved thee, go in peace.

The interesting account which *Luke* hath recorded, concerning our LORD's dining with a *Pharisee*, and which gave rise to the very beautiful history of this pardoned sinner, merits our particular attention, and the more so, as this is the only Evangelist who hath preserved the relation of it to the Church. I beg the Reader's indulgence upon the subject.

And first, whatever motive this *Pharisee* had, of inviting CHRIST to eat with him, is not so material to regard, as it is to remark the gracious condescension of JESUS, in accepting so readily the invitation. Reader! do not fail to notice it down for constant use, in the memorandums of your heart, that if JESUS so promptly went at the first invitation to eat with a *Pharisee*, will he not, think you, readily come at the repeated requests of his people?

Turn to those sweet scriptures in confirmation, and then may you and I give that condescending LORD the frequent invitation to come and dwell with us, and make his abode with us. Isaiah lxv. 24. Rev. iii. 20, 21. Isa. lviii. 9.

Secondly, Let us look at this poor woman. The Evangelist makes the Reader feel much interested in her history, from the manner in which he hath introduced the subject: *And, behold! a woman in the city which was a sinner!* Surely every conscious sinner, at the first hearing of such an one visiting CHRIST, cannot but feel anxious to know what reception she met with, and how she succeeded. So that at once, you and I, knowing that we are sinners, take part in all that concerned her in her approaching JESUS, and anxiously wait the event.

I pause however to observe, that according to my views of this woman's history, I do not think, as some have done, that this woman was *Mary Magdalene;* for their circumstances do not correspond. *Mary Magdalene* no doubt was, like this woman, a sinner, for the LORD is said to have cast out of her *seven devils.* Mark xvi. 9. but there is not a word of the kind said here, neither should it seem, according to the account before us, that this woman had ever had any interview before with JESUS. Moreover, the very name *Mary Magdalene* implies, that she was of *Magdala,* or if by *Magdalene* it be supposed was meant a loose woman, still this might be on account of the place, because *Magdala* was proverbial for women of no chastity. Whereas this transaction was in *Galilee.* Neither do I conceive, that this woman is the same with the sister of *Lazarus,* mentioned John xii. 3. for here this poor sinner lay at CHRIST's *feet,* and washed them with her tears; but there, the *Mary John* speaks of, poured the ointment on CHRIST's *head.* And the *former* is said to have been done in the house of this *Pharisee;* whereas the *latter* was in the house of *Lazarus* and his sisters. So that the history is not one and the same. Neither is this instance the same with that mentioned Matt. xxvi. 6, 7. for the event concerning this poor sinner in the *Pharisee's* house, must have taken place a considerable time before CHRIST's farewell supper; but that recorded by *Matthew,* and *Mark* xiv. 3. was only the evening before CHRIST's apprehension. I venture therefore to believe, though I do not presume to speak decidedly upon the subject, that this poor sinner was a different person from either of the *Maries,* noticed by the other Evangelists, and that she had never before had any interview with JESUS.

Let us now attend to what is related of her behaviour in her approaches to JESUS. Every circumstance which is said concerning her by the Evangelist, is expressive in proof of a real work of grace wrought upon her heart. And who shall say whether, as in the instance of *Zaccheus*, and that of the woman of *Samaria*, CHRIST's eating with the *Pharisee* was not wholly intended on her account, and for the instruction of the Church, in all the future generations of it, by her history. See Luke xix. 1—10. John iv. 4—42. I beg the Reader particularly to notice, amidst the several features of a true sorrow of soul for sin, in this woman's behaviour; the self-loathing and abhorrence of her own filthiness, and the ardent love which her kisses expressed to the person of the SON of GOD! Reader! in all the marks of genuine repentance, depend upon it, these are the strongest. It is not our tears, nor our prayers, nor our attempted reform; no, nor our faith, considered as any act of our's, which can bring any glory to GOD, or peace to ourselves. A broken and a contrite heart becomes a blessed *effect* from GOD's grace there planted. But it is GOD's grace and CHRIST's blood which are the *cause;* and the change wrought by that grace and blood is the *effect.* Every thing is beautiful in order. Faith and repentance are precious *fruits* of the HOLY SPIRIT. But CHRIST, and CHRIST alone, becomes the *cause* of salvation.

Our next view of this beautiful memoir, is to look at *Simon the Pharisee.* Though he invited CHRIST to his house, yet it is evident, from his suspicions of CHRIST's character, that he had no high opinion of him in his heart. The gracious allowance of JESUS to this poor sinner wounded his pride. Had she touched the Pharisee's garment, he would have thought himself defiled. But JESUS the SON of GOD was pleased with the act. Reader! think of this. JESUS is glorified when his people are sanctified in him. His holiness suits their uncleanness. His riches their poverty.

But it is high time to look to JESUS, and observe his grace and mercy on this occasion. And first, I beg the Reader to take notice how plainly our dear LORD's conduct towards the *Pharisee,* proved the GODHEAD of his person. The Pharisee had made it up in his mind, that if JESUS were a Prophet, he would have known who, and what manner of woman this was, for she was a sinner. Not that this knowledge belonged to the ordinary Prophets; but to JESUS, as the LORD GOD of the Prophets, it did belong, and his omniscience marked his character. Rev. xxii. 6. Hence therefore JESUS, by telling *Simon* what was in his heart, manifested his eternal power and GODHEAD. Reader! mark this first down in thine heart, or rather beg of GOD the HOLY GHOST to do it for thee. John xvi. 13, 14. 1 Cor. xii. 3.

Next observe the very wise and gracious manner which the LORD JESUS adopted in manifesting himself as GOD, in pardoning iniquity, transgression, and sin, and to make the wounded soul of this poor sinner to rejoice. Under the similitude of a beautiful figure, which the *Pharisee* might not immediately see through, the LORD JESUS taught, that the debtor of five hundred pence, or the debtor of fifty, when both unable to pay, were equally insolvent before GOD, the Almighty creditor; and that it must be an act of free grace to pardon either. Here *Simon,* with all his fancied righteousness, confessing, as he could not but do, that he had many infirmities, in the midst of all; and this poor sinner, with her conscious compleat unworthiness, stood upon a level; and therefore if the LORD forgave both, both were debtors to his free bounty. And then when JESUS had extorted this confession from the proud self-righteous *Pharisee*, he proceeded to apply. And the Evangelist hath most beautifully set this forth, in terms so plain and evident, as can need no explanation.

One thing more I would beg the Reader particularly to notice, namely, the grace CHRIST manifested, and the authority he exercised in forgiving her sins. And this the LORD twice said, that there might be no possible mistake in a point of so much consequence. Oh! how truly blessed is the view! I beg the Reader to look to a similar passage on this ground, Mark ii. 3—12. Let the Reader observe how the LORD expresses himself to the woman, *thy faith hath saved thee.* And to the Pharisee concerning her. *For she loved much.* In both which expressions we are not to suppose JESUS meant, that either her faith, or her love, both which were the LORD's gifts, could be her merit, or the cause of her pardon. These were from the workings of grace in her heart, so that the LORD's love and mercy were the *cause,* and the workings in her heart the *effect.* And as her pardon was great, because her sins were great, her love and thankfulness were the more. Such are among the many precious things this lovely history furnisheth, to the praise of the LORD's grace, the joy of poor sinners, and the casting down the pride of all Pharisees. And, Reader! think where that precious soul of her's is now, amidst the spirits of just men made perfect, surrounding his throne in glory, who once lay at his feet when upon earth in tears. Blessedly *Paul* speaks to this subject, concerning those recovered by grace among the redeemed, from among men upon earth, when he saith, *And such were some of you! but ye are washed, but ye are sanctified, but ye are justified in the name of the* LORD JESUS, *and by the* SPIRIT *of our* GOD. 1 Cor. vi. 11.

REFLECTIONS.

MY soul! behold thy LORD, in the many sweet views of Him presented in this chapter. See him in his mercy, hastening to the relief of the centurion's servant. Behold him manifesting what the HOLY GHOST had marked of his character, when exercising his sovereign authority as GOD, blended with the tenderness of his manhood, at the gate of the city *Nain.* Oh! who that beheld my GOD and SAVIOR, in that moment of turning the widow's tears into joy, and raising her son from the dead, but would have cried out with the Prophet, and echoed to his blessed words, *behold! your* GOD *is come to save you!* And who that beheld the poor penitent in the house of the proud Pharisee, and the gracious mercy and condescension of JESUS to her sorrows, but would have hailed the happy hour of GOD's faithful promise confirmed; *I even I am he that blotteth out thy transgressions, and will not remember thy sins.*

And is it not the same in the present hour? Is the LORD's arm shortened that he cannot save? Is his ear grown heavy, that he cannot hear? Precious, precious LORD JESUS! how sweet to my soul the assurance, that as thy person, so thy purpose admits of no change. JESUS CHRIST! the same yesterday and to day, and for ever.

C H A P. VIII.

AND it came to pass afterward, that he went
throughout every city and village, preaching
and shewing the glad tidings of the kingdom of
God : and the twelve *were* with him,

2 And certain women which had been healed of
evil spirits and infirmities, Mary called Magdalene, out of whom went seven devils,

3 And Joanna, the wife of Chuza, Herod's
steward, and Susanna, and many others which
ministered unto him of their substance.

It must have been very blessed to have followed the Lord Jesus
in this circuit of his preaching. Our Great High Priest and Bishop
going through his diocese, attended by the twelve, proclaiming the
glad tidings of the kingdom. Reader! do not forget, however, that
spiritually, the same is daily doing now. Matt. xxviii. 19, 20. Concerning those women, it will be proper to observe, that having received from the Lord Jesus spiritual mercies to their souls, as well as
temporal mercies to their bodies, they gladly ministered to Jesus of
their time and substance. It is remarkable, that none of the Evangelists have recorded this great miracle shewn to *Mary Magdalene,*
they only speak of the thing itself being done ; but have not mentioned, as in other cases, the time. That this *Mary Magdalene* was not
the woman noticed in the preceding chapter, hath been shewn
there. And to which it may be added here, in confirmation of the
same, that she is said to have gone about with Christ in this circuit of
preaching : whereas Jesus dismissed the woman in *Simon's* house,
when he said, Go in peace. *Joanna* and *Susanna,* no doubt, were
persons of some property ; and it is blessed to behold, such as the
Lord hath dealt bountifully by, in temporals, as well as spirituals,
ministering to the necessities of Christ and his family. The Corpus
Christi, that is, the body of Christ, in his mystical members, is
in every place ; and Jesus takes every act done to them, in his name,
as done to himself. See, in proof, Matt. xxv. 40. Mark ix. 41, 42.

4 ¶ And when much people were gathered together, and were come to him out of every city,
he spake by a parable :

5 A sower went out to sow his seed : and as he

sowed, some fell by the way side; and it was
trodden down, and the fowls of the air devoured
it.

6 And some fell upon a rock; and as soon as it
was sprung up it withered away, because it lacked
moisture.

7 And some fell among thorns; and the thorns
sprang up with it, and choked it;

8 And other fell on good ground, and sprang
up, and bare fruit an hundred fold. And when he
had said these things, he cried, He that hath ears
to hear, let him hear.

9 And his disciples asked him, saying, What
might this parable be?

10 And he said, Unto you it is given to know
the mysteries of the kingdom of God: but to
others in parables; that seeing they might not
see, and hearing they might not understand.

11 Now the parable is this: The seed is the
word of God.

12 Those by the way side are they that hear:
then cometh the devil, and taketh away the word
out of their hearts, lest they should believe, and
be saved:

13 They on the rock *are they* which, when they
hear, receive the word with joy; and these have
no root, which for a while believe, and in time of
temptation fall away.

14 And that which fell among thorns are they
which, when they have heard, go forth, and are
choked with cares and riches and pleasures of *this*
life, and bring no fruit to perfection.

15 But that on the good ground are they which,
in an honest and good heart, having heard the
word, keep *it*, and bring forth fruit with patience.

16 ¶ No man, when he hath lighted a candle,
covereth it with a vessel, or putteth *it* under a bed;

but setteth *it* on a candlestick, that they which enter in may see the light.

17 For nothing is secret that shall not be made manifest: neither *any thing* hid that shall not be known and come abroad.

18 Take heed therefore how ye hear: for whosoever hath, to him shall be given; and whosoever hath not, from him shall be taken even that which he seemeth to have.

19 Then came to him *his* mother and his brethren, and could not come at him for the press.

20 And it was told him *by certain* which said, Thy mother and thy brethren stand without desiring to see thee.

21 And he answered and said unto them, My mother and my brethren are these which hear the word of God, and do it.

The parable of the sower is so fully explained by our LORD himself, that it can need no farther comment. For the observations made on the whole discourse of CHRIST, in those verses, I refer the Reader to the parallel passages, Matt. iii. 13, &c. Mark iv. 1, &c. Matt. v. 15. Matt. xii. 46.

22 Now it came to pass on a certain day, that he went into a ship with his disciples: and he said unto them, Let us go over unto the other side of the lake. And they launched forth.

23 But as they sailed he fell asleep: and there came down a storm of wind on the lake; and they were filled *with water*, and were in jeopardy.

24 And they came to him, and awoke him, saying, Master, master, we perish. Then he arose, and rebuked the wind, and the raging of the water: and they ceased, and there was a calm.

25 And he said unto them, Where is your faith? and they, being afraid, wondered, saying one to another, What manner of man is this! for he commandeth even the winds and water, and they obey him.

In addition to the observations made on this situation of CHRIST and his disciples on the lake, Matt. viii. 23 to 27, I would only just remark, that exercises, like these, for trial, are among the most precious tokens of divine love. It is blessed to be brought into difficulties, where those difficulties afford a better opportunity for the larger display of divine strength, made perfect in human weakness. When nature is unable to help, grace becomes more sweet and valuable. And, however it may be a paradox to the world, yet it is not so with the people of GOD; they know the blessedness of the apostle's state, and can fully ascribe to his sentiments, when he saith, *Most gladly will I glory in my infirmities, that the power of* CHRIST *may rest upon me; for when I am weak, then am I strong.* 2 Cor. xii. 9, 10.

26 ¶ And they arrived at the country of the Gadarenes, which is over against Galilee.

27 And when he went forth to land, there met him out of the city a certain man, which had devils long time, and ware no clothes, neither abode in *any* house, but in the tombs:

28 When he saw Jesus, he cried out, and fell down before him, and with a loud voice said, What have I to do with thee, Jesus, *thou* Son of God most high? I beseech thee torment me not.

29 (For he had commanded the unclean spirit to come out of the man. For oftentimes it had caught him: and he was kept bound with chains and in fetters; and he brake the bands, and was driven of the devil into the wilderness.)

30 And Jesus asked him, saying, What is thy name? and he said, Legion: because many devils were entered into him.

31 And they besought him, that he would not command them to go out into the deep.

32 And there was there an herd of many swine feeding on the mountain: and they besought him that he would suffer them to enter into them: and he suffered them.

33 Then went the devils out of the man, and entered into the swine: and the herd ran violently down a steep place into the lake, and were choked.

34 When they that fed *them* saw what was

done, they fled, and went and told *it* in the city,
and in the country.

35 Then they went out to see what was done ;
and came to Jesus, and found the man out of
whom the devils were departed, sitting at the feet
of Jesus, clothed, and in his right mind: and they
were afraid.

36 They also which saw *it,* told them by what
means he that was possessed of the devils was
healed.

37 Then the whole multitude of the country of
the Gadarenes round about, besought him to depart from them: for they were taken with great
fear.   And he went up into the ship, and returned
back again.

38 Now the man out of whom the devils were
departed, besought him that he might be with
him: but Jesus sent him away, saying,

39 Return to thine own house, and shew how
great things God hath done unto thee.   And he
went his way, and published throughout the whole
city, how great things Jesus had done unto him.

I have so largely dwelt upon the circumstances of this history, in
the parallel account given of it by *Mark,* that I think it needless to
enlarge upon the subject in this place.   I beg to refer the Reader to
Mark v. 1 to 20.

40 And it came to pass, that, when Jesus was
returned, the people *gladly* received him; for they
were all waiting for him.

41 And, behold, there came a man named
Jairus, and he was a ruler of the synagogue; and
he fell down at Jesus' feet, and besought him that
he would come into his house :

42 For he had one only daughter, about twelve
years of age, and she lay a dying.   But as he
went the people thronged him.

43 And a woman having an issue of blood

twelve years, which had spent all her living upon physicians, neither could be healed of any,

44 Came behind *him*, and touched the border of his garment; and immediately her issue of blood stanched.

45 And Jesus said, Who touched me? When all denied, Peter, and they that were with him, said, Master, the multitude throng thee, and press *thee*, and sayest thou, Who touched me?

46 And Jesus said, Somebody hath touched me: for I perceive that virtue is gone out of me.

47 And when the woman saw that she was not hid, she came trembling, and, falling down before him, she declared unto him, before all the people, for what cause she had touched him, and how she was healed immediately.

48 And he said unto her, Daughter, be of good comfort: thy faith hath made thee whole: go in peace.

49 While he yet spake, there cometh one from the ruler of the synagogue's *house*, saying to him, Thy daughter is dead: trouble not the Master.

50 But when Jesus heard *it*, he answered him, saying, Fear not: believe only, and she shall be made whole.

51 And when he came into the house, he suffered no man to go in, save Peter, and James, and John, and the father and the mother of the maiden.

52 And all wept, and bewailed her, but he said, Weep not: she is not dead, but sleepeth.

53 And they laughed him to scorn, knowing that she was dead.

54 And he put them all out, and took her by the hand, and called, saying, Maid, arise;

55 And her spirit came again, and she arose

straightway: and he commanded to give her meat.

56 And her parents were astonished, but he charged them that they should tell no man what was done.

Both these cases here recorded, are incorporated one in the other; and so they are in the same history of each, given by *Matthew* and *Mark.* I have largely insisted upon the interesting particulars, Matt. ix. 18 to 26, to which I refer. If the Reader will allow me to make a short observation, in addition to what was there offered, it would be to say, that in the case of the woman touching CHRIST's garment, with such lively actings of faith, we may remark upon it, that such will ever be the result of that true faith, which is the operation of the Spirit of GOD. Those who attend ordinances, who express delight in them, and seemingly love to hear of JESUS: but in whose heart no saving change from nature hath taken place; may *press* upon CHRIST, as the throng here did: but the personal knowledge of CHRIST, and faith in CHRIST, is like this woman truly *touching* him.

The miracle of CHRIST, in raising the ruler's child, not only became a decided testimony of his eternal power and GODHEAD, but it served to teach all his redeemed family, that amidst all their dead and dying circumstances, that power secures for them the resurrection of grace here, and glory hereafter.

REFLECTIONS.

BEHOLD! ye poor and afflicted of the LORD's tried ones, how JESUS, the SON of GOD, when he humbled himself to be made man, condescended to have his wants supplied by the bounty of his people. Oh! how hath he dignified the path of honest poverty by his bright example! Never, then, forget what *Paul* was commanded to tell the church: *Ye know,* said he, *the grace of our* LORD JESUS CHRIST; *that though he was rich, yet for your sakes he became poor, that ye, through his poverty, might be made rich.* Blessed LORD! while I read thy sweet parable of the sower, oh for grace to discover that the pure seed of thy Gospel is sown in my heart, by thy sovereign power: and, from the fallow ground of my poor heart being turned up, and planted with thy grace, the fruit of thy righteousness may, in thee, and through thee, be brought forth an hundred fold. Enable me to embark with thee, thou dearest LORD, in the roughest sea, never being alarmed as long as GOD-incarnate is with me in the storm; who guides the helm of all my affairs, and will rebuke both wind and tide. And blessed be my GOD, my SAVIOUR, my HOLY ONE! JESUS, the SON of GOD, hath dispossessed the enemy from my heart; and now let me, as this poor *Gadarene,* sit at the feet of JESUS, cloathed in my LORD's robe of righteousness, and in my right mind. Yea, LORD, if, like the poor woman, deeply and long diseased, or even as the ruler's daughter, dead, JESUS can and will recover. He saith himself, *I am the resurrection and the life. He that liveth and believeth in me, shall never die. Amen.*

CHAP. IX.

CONTENTS.

The Lord Jesus *is here sending forth his Apostles. An Account of Herod.* Jesus *feedeth the Multitude in the Wilderness.* Peter's *blessed Confession of* Christ. *The Transfiguration. The Lunatic healed.* Jesus *going through* Samaria.

THEN he called his twelve disciples together, and gave them power and authority over all devils, and to cure diseases.

2 And he sent them to preach the kingdom of God, and to heal the sick.

3 And he said unto them, Take nothing for *your* journey, neither staves, nor scrip, neither bread, neither money, neither have two coats apiece.

4 And whatsoever house ye enter into, there abide, and thence depart.

5 And whosoever will not receive you, when ye go out of that city, shake off the very dust from your feet for a testimony against them.

6 And they departed, and went through the towns, preaching the gospel, and healing every where.

The two former Evangelists have given us an account of our Lord's ordination of his apostles; Matt. x. 1, &c. Mark, iii. 14, vi. 7; and there is somewhat truly interesting in the relation of it. But certainly the commission, at this time, must have been very limited. For the apostles themselves, had but imperfect notions of their Lord's kingdom of grace, leading to his kingdom of glory. So strongly were their minds rivetted in the Jewish nation of a temporal kingdom, that not even the death of Christ had power to do away the impression. See, in proof, Acts i. 6, 8.

7 ¶ Now Herod the tetrarch heard of all that was done by him : and he was perplexed, because that it was said of some, that John was risen from the dead;

8 And of some, that Elias had appeared : and of others, that one of the old prophets was risen again.

9 And Herod said, John have I beheaded : but who is this of whom I hear such things? and he desired to see him.

We have noticed this man before, Matt. xiv. 1, and Mark vi. 14. Were it not for his connection with scripture history, how little would his name have been known in the present hour: but how little to be regarded now, but for the instruction his awful character holds forth? Oh how plain is it that purple and fine linen, and faring sumptuously every day, have nothing to do to make up happiness! A guilty conscience, and the fear of death, are enough to throw down all the props of such outside splendor.

10 And the apostles, when they were returned, told him all that they had done. And he took them, and went aside privately into a desert place belonging to the city called Bethsaida.

11 And the people, when they knew *it*, followed him: and he received them, and spake unto them of the kingdom of God, and healed them that had need of healing.

12 And when the day began to wear away, then came the twelve, and said unto him, Send the multitude away, that they may go into the towns and country round about, and lodge, and get victuals: for we are here in a desert place.

13 But he said unto them, Give ye them to eat. And they said, We have no more but five loaves and two fishes; except we should go and buy meat for all this people.

14 For they were about five thousand men. And he said to his disciples, Make them sit down by fifties in a company.

15 And they did so, and made them all sit down.

16 Then he took the five loaves, and the two fishes, and looking up to heaven, he blessed them, and brake, and gave to the disciples to set before the multitude.

17 And they did eat, and were all filled; and there was taken up of fragments that remained to them twelve baskets.

For shortness sake, I would refer the Reader to what hath been already offered, by way of improvement, on this miracle of CHRIST, Matt. xiv. 14, &c. and Mark vi. 30 to 46.

18 ¶ And it came to pass, as he was alone praying, his disciples were with him: and he asked them, saying, Whom say the people that I am?

19 They answering, said, John the Baptist; but some *say*, Elias; and others *say*, that one of the old prophets is risen again.

20 He said unto them, But whom say ye that I am? Peter answering, said, The Christ of God.

21 And he straitly charged them, and commanded *them* to tell no man that thing;

22 Saying, The Son of man must suffer many things, and be rejected of the elders, and chief priests, and scribes, and be slain, and be raised the third day.

23 And he said to them all, If any *man* will come after me, let him deny himself, and take up his cross daily, and follow me.

24 For whosoever will save his life shall lose it: but whosoever will lose his life for my sake, the same shall save it.

25 For what is a man advantaged, if he gain the whole world, and lose himself, or be cast away?

26 For whosoever shall be ashamed of me, and of my words, of him shall the Son of man be ashamed, when he shall come in his own glory, and *in his* Father's, and of the holy angels.

27 But I tell you of a truth, there be some standing here, which shall not taste of death, till they see the kingdom of God.

We have the whole of what *Luke* relates in those verses, Matt. xvi. 13, &c. and Mark viii. 27. I refer the Reader to both.

28 ¶ And it came to pass about an eight days after these sayings, he took Peter, and John, and James, and went up into a mountain to pray.

29 ¶ And as he prayed, the fashion of his

countenance was altered, and his raiment *was* white *and* glistering.

30 And, behold, there talked with him two men, which were Moses and Elias;

31 Who appeared in glory, and spake of his decease, which he should accomplish at Jerusalem.

32 But Peter, and they that were with him, were heavy with sleep: and when they were awake, they saw his glory, and the two men that stood with him.

33 And it came to pass, as they departed from him, Peter said unto Jesus, Master, it is good for us to be here: and let us make three tabernacles, one for thee, and one for Moses, and one for Elias: not knowing what he said.

34 While he thus spake, there came a cloud, and overshadowed them: and they feared as they entered into the cloud.

35 And there came a voice out of the cloud, saying, This is my beloved Son: hear him.

36 And when the voice was past, Jesus was found alone. And they kept *it* close, and told no man in those days any of those things which they had seen.

Having largely considered the subject of these verses, Matt. xvii. 1, and Mark ix. 1 to 13, I do not wish to trespass farther by enlarging upon it.

37 ¶ And it came to pass, that on the next day, when they were come down from the hill, much people met him:

38 And, behold, a man of the company cried out, saying, Master, I beseech thee look upon my son: for he is mine only child.

39 And, lo, a spirit taketh him, and he suddenly crieth out: and he teareth him, that he foameth again, and bruising him, hardly departeth from him.

40 And I besought thy disciples to cast him out; and they could not.

41 And Jesus answering, said, O faithless and perverse generation, how long shall I be with you, and suffer you? Bring thy son hither.

42 And as he was yet a coming, the devil threw him down, and tare *him*. And Jesus rebuked the unclean spirit, and healed the child, and delivered him again to his father.

43 And they were all amazed at the mighty power of God; but while they wondered every one at all things which Jesus did, he said unto his disciples,

44 Let these sayings sink down into your ears: for the Son of man shall be delivered into the hands of men.

45 But they understood not this saying, and it was hid from them, that they perceived it not: and they feared to ask him of that saying.

46 ¶ Then there arose a reasoning among them, which of them should be greatest.

47 And Jesus, perceiving the thought of their heart, took a child, and set him by him,

48 And said unto them, Whosoever shall receive this child in my name, receiveth me: and whosoever shall receive me, receiveth him that sent me: for he that is least among you all, the same shall be great.

The Reader will meet my humble observations on these verses in the similiar ones, Mark ix. 14, &c.

49 And John answered and said, Master, we saw one casting out devils in thy name; and we forbad him, because he followeth not with us.

50 And Jesus said unto him, Forbid *him* not; for he that is not against us is for us.

There is somewhat very singular in what is here said. Who this man was is not at all noticed, or even hinted at, by any of the Evangelists. *Mark* takes notice of him indeed; but leaves us wholly in the dark concerning him. See Mark ix. 38. Some have supposed that he was one of *John's* disciples; and, therefore, in the expectation of Christ, from a lively apprehension of Christ's mission, went about preaching in his name, although he had not as yet come to Christ. But be this as it may, I beg the Reader not to overlook the Lord's gracious answer to *John.* Oh! who shall say how many there are of Christ's little ones hid away and unknown by the world, but yet well known and well regarded by Jesus Christ!

51 ¶ And it came to pass, when the time was come that he should be received up, he stedfastly set his face to go to Jerusalem,

52 And sent messengers before his face: and they went, and entered into a village of the Samaritans, to make ready for him.

53 And they did not receive him, because his face was as though he would go to Jerusalem.

54 And when his disciples, James and John, saw *this,* they said, Lord, wilt thou that we command fire to come down from heaven, and consume them, even as Elias did?

55 But he turned, and rebuked them, and said, Ye know not what manner of spirit ye are of.

56 For the Son of man is not come to destroy men's lives, but to save *them.* And they went to another village.

I apprehend, by the time being come that Jesus should be received up, is not meant that his public ministry in preaching was now nearly over; for, according to all calculation, the crucifixion of Christ was, at least, six months after. But, probably, it means, that it was now arrived when he should ascend from *Galilee* to *Jerusalem;* for after this, we do not find our Lord again in *Galilee.* The indisposition in the *Samaritans* to receive Jesus, it is possible, might arise from their discovering our Lord's wishes to go up to *Jerusalem.* And this they construed into a partiality for the temple, at the holy city, in preference to the mountain of *Samaria,* for worship. Reader! observe, I do not decide upon it: I only offer my conjecture. See John iv. 9 to 29. But whether I am correct or not in this view of the subject, one point I beg the Reader not to overlook, the striking contrast of our Lord's mind to that of the apostles' *James* and *John.* They were for calling fire from Heaven to resent the insult offered to Jesus. But Jesus himself manifested nothing but meekness and love. Oh! how blessed, how very blessed is it to behold Jesus pre-eminent in mercy, as he is pre-eminent in greatness!

57 And it came to pass, that, as they went in the way, a certain *man* said unto him, Lord, I will follow thee whithersoever thou goest.

58 And Jesus said unto him, Foxes have holes, and birds of the air *have* nests; but the Son of man hath not where to lay *his* head.

59 And he said unto another, Follow me, but he said, Lord, suffer me first to go and bury my father.

60 Jesus said unto him, Let the dead bury their dead: but go thou and preach the kingdom of God.

61 And another also said, Lord, I will follow thee; but let me first go bid them farewell which are at home at my house.

62 And Jesus said unto him, No man having put his hand to the plough, and looking back, is fit for the kingdom of God.

We have similar observations in Matt. viii. 19, &c, But there we read CHRIST was in *Capernaum;* and here he is on his way to *Jerusalem.* Moreover that conversation which JESUS had, as *Matthew* relates it, was with a scribe soon after his descent from the mountain: but here our LORD had taken his farewell of *Galilee,* no more to return thither. However, the words are the same, and the observations arising from them the same.

REFLECTIONS.

THINK, my soul, of the vast honour, the high privilege, the distinguished dignity of the apostles of thy GOD and SAVIOR! Sent forth, as his ambassadors, to call his redeemed Israel to the blessings of reconciliation and peace! Oh! ye servants of the LORD, what an honour was your's to cast out devils, to heal the sick, and preach the Gospel! But what an awful contrast in the character of *Herod!* And yet who that had seen the poverty of the poor fishermen of *Galilee,* and beheld the purpled luxuries of the *Tetrarch,* but would have connected every thing blessed with the latter, and misery with the former? See, Reader, how JESUS instantly supplied a wilderness with food: and think, then, how soon the wilderness frames of his people he can make to blossom as the rose! Oh! my soul, what a view was that which the disciples *Peter, John,* and *James,* had of JESUS in the Mount of Transfiguration! But what was this, in point of glory, to that which all the church of GOD will see, and thou among the number, when he shall come in the mount Zion, *to be glorified in his saints, and to be admired in all them that believe ?* Behold CHRIST's power in healing the lunatic. Behold how JESUS predicted his sufferings when he should be crucified in weakness. Oh! for grace, that all the precious sayings of JESUS may sink down into my ears! And grant, dearest LORD, that while Samaritans refuse to receive thee; and the dead, in trespasses and sins, are too busily employed in burying their dead, to find time or inclination to follow thee, I may be found with having put my hand to the gospel plough; and never to look back, but follow my LORD in the regeneration, and enter with him into his kingdom.

CHAP. X.

CONTENTS.

The LORD *appoints other Seventy also to go before him.* CHRIST *pronounceth a woe upon* Chorazin *and* Bethsaida. JESUS *in sweet Communion with his* FATHER. *The Parable of the Samaritan.* Martha *reproved.*

AFTER these things, the Lord appointed other seventy also, and sent them two and two before his face into every city and place whither he himself would come.

2 Therefore said he unto them, The harvest truly *is* great, but the labourers *are* few: pray ye therefore the Lord of the harvest, that he would send forth labourers into his harvest.

3 Go your ways: behold, I send you forth as lambs among wolves.

4 ¶ Carry neither purse, nor scrip, nor shoes: and salute no man by the way.

5 And into whatsoever house ye enter, first say, Peace *be* to this house.

6 And if the Son of peace be there, your peace shall rest upon it: if not, it shall turn to you again.

7 And in the same house remain, eating and drinking such things as they give: for the labourer is worthy of his hire, go not from house to house.

8 And into whatsoever city ye enter, and they receive you, eat such things as are set before you:

9 And heal the sick, that are therein, and say unto them, The kingdom of God is come nigh unto you.

10 But into whatsoever city ye enter, and they receive you not, go your ways out into the streets of the same, and say,

11 Even the very dust of your city, which cleaveth on us, we do wipe off against you : notwithstanding, be ye sure of this, that the kingdom of God is come nigh unto you.

12 But I say unto you, That it shall be more tolerable in that day for Sodom than for that city.

I do not presume to say as much, but it doth seem not improbable that these seventy disciples were, in conformity to what is said, Numb. xi. 16, 24, 25, or, perhaps more properly speaking, those of the Old Testament were figurative of the New. See Exod. xxiv. 1—9. And the twelve tribes of Israel were descriptive of the twelve apostles, Rev. xxi. 10 to 21. But I beg the Reader not to overlook what is said of these men being sent into every city and place, whither CHRIST *himself would come.* Yes, without his presence, and his power, all their labours were nothing, John xv. 5. We have much of the same expressions in *Matthew,* to which I refer, Matt. x. 5 to 15.

13 Woe unto thee, Chorazin! woe unto thee, Bethsaida! for if the mighty works had been done in Tyre and Sidon, which have been done in you, they had a great while ago repented, sitting in sackcloth and ashes.

14 But it shall be more tolerable for Tyre and Sidon at the judgement than for you.

15 And thou, Capernaum, which art exalted to heaven, shall be thrust down to hell.

16 He that heareth you, heareth me: and he that despiseth you, despiseth me : and he that despiseth me, despiseth him that sent me.

There is somewhat very awful in these verses : to think that the preaching of JESUS himself should have no effect ! And, Reader, it may well be supposed, that the heaviest judgments will light on those whose advantages have been greatest, but have rejected them : and, in this sense, we may be tremblingly alive for our British *Chorazin* and *Bethsaida.* The grace of GOD, it may be truly said, hath, in the outward ministry of the word, appeared unto all men; but, alas! *who hath believed the report, or to whom is the arm of the* LORD *re-*

vealed? Ordinances and means of grace do exalt our nation, as *Capernaum* was exalted to heaven; but will not the neglect and abuse of them sink down to hell?

17 ¶ And the seventy returned again with joy, saying, Lord, even the devils are subject unto us through thy name.

18 And he said unto them, I beheld Satan as lightning fall from heaven.

19 Behold, I give unto you power to tread on serpents and scorpions, and over all the power of the enemy : and nothing shall by any means hurt you.

20 Notwithstanding, in this rejoice not, that the spirits are subject unto you : but rather rejoice because your names are written in heaven.

I beg the Reader to pause over these verses; not so much to observe the joy of the seventy at the success of their ministry, as to behold the Lord Jesus in this almightiness of character. We are not made acquainted when it was that Jesus beheld the fall of Satan. Whether before the foundation of the world, when Satan was cast out of heaven, see Jude 6. Rev. xii. 7 to 12. or whether in the overthrow of his kingdom and influence, by Christ, and his Gospel in covenant promises, Psm. lxxxix. 19 to 23. And the power Jesus communicated to his disciples, opens to the view a very blessed contemplation. For is it not so to all his redeemed? Mark xvi. 18. Acts xxviii. 5. 1 Cor. x. 13. Rom. xvi. 20. But when the Reader hath paid all due attention to these scriptures, I would beg to call his notice yet more earnestly to what the Lord told his disciples, as opening to a much greater cause of joy, than even the devils being made subject to us through his name : namely, that the names of Christ's redeemed are written in heaven. Here, Reader, is a subject of holy joy indeed ; and which secures all the blessedness of the life that now is, and of that which is to come, see Rev. xiii. 8. Nothing can more decidedly prove that the choice of God to eternal life, is special, personal, and particular. Names written, implies persons known, and everlastingly secured. So that the Father's gift, the Son's purchase, and the Holy Ghost's work of grace, are the result of everlasting love; and render the event of salvation and happiness as a thing not liable to any doubt or uncertainty. See those scriptures, Jerem. xxxiii. 13. John vi. 37 to 40. Philip. iv. 3. Rev. xx. 12 to 15.

21 ¶ In that hour Jesus rejoiced in spirit, and said, I thank thee, O Father, Lord of heaven and earth, that thou hast hid these things from the wise and prudent, and hast revealed them unto

babes: even so, Father; for so it seemed good in thy sight.

I desire to refer the Reader for my observations on this verse to Matt. xi. 25, 26.

22 All things are delivered to me of my Father: and no man knoweth who the Son is, but the Father; and who the Father is, but the Son; and *he* to whom the Son will reveal *him*.

The subject contained in this verse, short as it is, is so infinitely great and sublime, that though I could not dare to pass by it altogether unnoticed, yet I know not how to presume the offering my faint and imperfect observations upon it. I shall, indeed, but barely touch on the deep things contained in it; and no farther than may, under the LORD's teaching, lead the Reader's mind, with my own, to the consideration of the very sweet and precious instructions which arise out of it.

The *all things* delivered to CHRIST, of his FATHER, is a comprehensive expression, to denote the office and authority of CHRIST, as mediator. This part I do not allude to in respect to the depth of mystery contained in this verse; for though such is the infinite fullness of CHRIST, that neither men nor angels can have capacities competent to conceive, yet this is not the most wonderful doctrine which this verse calls the church to contemplate. *No man knoweth who the* SON *is but the* FATHER: and, in like manner, *who the* FATHER *is but the* SON. Here are depths indeed of mystery. We are told by the Evangelist *John*, that *no man hath seen* GOD *at any time*, but that *the only begotten* SON, *which is in the bosom of the* FATHER, *he hath declared him*, John i. 18. So that nothing can be more plain, than that it became impossible for the creation of GOD to know any thing of JEHOVAH, in his three-fold character of persons, but by the immediate act of the SON, begotten into his mediatorial character, GOD-Man in one person, thereby to reveal him. By this voluntary act of the SON of GOD, and by this humbling himself, in order to make this revelation through the medium of the manhood, he hath done that, which, without this union of nature, never could have been done. And by this act, he hath brought in a new glory to the GODHEAD, in that his creatures have now a knowledge of the FATHER, SON, and SPIRIT; and which opens to the felicity of GOD's intelligent creation to all eternity. Our LORD's expression is striking: *No man knoweth who the* SON *is but the* FATHER: that is, as SON of GOD. It is GOD only, that can know GOD. For though the persons in the GODHEAD are revealed, sufficiently plain in proof, as articles of faith, yet none knoweth how the SON is SON but the FATHER. It is the FATHER only who knoweth the SON, as a person of equal dignity and glory with himself. And so, in like manner, *No man knoweth who the* FATHER *is save the* SON. The personal apprehension of each is to each, FATHER, SON, and SPIRIT, can be known only as such in their essential nature and GODHEAD, by each other. And when JESUS adds, and *he to whom the* SON *will reveal him*: that is, in making such a revelation of him, as he came purposely to make, and the enlightened soul, by grace, is capable of receiving.

Reader! ponder over the wonderful mystery; and, while looking into the vast depth, rather feel astonishment at the condescending grace of the LORD, in that we are enabled to apprehend so much, instead of marvelling that we know no more. It is very blessed that the SON of GOD hath come to make known such stupendous things, which, without his having taken upon him our nature, and in that nature made such gracious revelations of the mystery of GOD, and of the FATHER, and of CHRIST, never could have been discovered to all eternity. *Thanks be unto* GOD *for his unspeakable gift!*

Though I passed by the consideration of the *all things*, delivered by the FATHER to CHRIST, at the opening of this verse, in order to attend the more particularly to the momentous doctrine contained in the latter part of it, yet let not the Reader overlook either the sweetness or the fullness of the blessed expression. JESUS, in his Mediator-character, here considers himself as the Great and Almighty Trustee of heaven; and that he is thus full in himself, and by the FATHER's appointment, in order to give out, in all the departments of nature, providence, grace, and glory, to the supply of all. And CHRIST's invitation is founded upon his ability, see Matt. xi. 27 to 30. So that as all the promises, all grace, all the blessings of the covenant, all government; in short, the whole, and every part of supply for all things, can only be found in CHRIST; there can be no possibility of obtaining any thing either for time or eternity, but in him. And what tends to endear this state of things still more, is, that as all things are delivered from the FATHER to the SON, in seeking all things from CHRIST, we honour the FATHER by seeking for the SON. For as the FATHER puts honour upon CHRIST, in thus constituting him universal and everlasting LORD, so every poor needy creature, who looks by faith to CHRIST for his supply, puts honour upon him also. Reader! think of this in all approaches to CHRIST: and depend upon it, that whenever your poor heart is made joyful in CHRIST, and enriched by supplies from him, CHRIST is glorified in you, in giving out of his fullness, and gets praise from the riches of his grace in making all his people happy in him. *Thanks be unto* GOD, *who always causeth us to triumph in* CHRIST! 2 Cor. ii. 14.

23 ¶ And he turned him unto his disciples, and said privately, Blessed *are* the eyes which see the things that ye see:

24 For I tell you, That many prophets and kings have desired to see those things which ye see, and have not seen *them;* and to hear those things which ye hear, and have not heard *them.*

I beg the Reader to notice the grace of JESUS. With what tenderness and affection the LORD JESUS marks his own! It was the longing of the Old Testament saints to see CHRIST's day. *Moses* was both prophet and king in *Jesurun:* and how he earnestly desired even but to see the hallowed spot, where he knew, by faith, CHRIST; his *dweller in the bush,* should one day come, and accomplish salvation. Deut. iii. 23 to 27. And as *Peter* told the Jews in his sermon, *All the prophets, from* Samuel, *and those that followed ;* with *David,* and the good Kings of Israel, who foretold of Christ, desired to see his day: and, like *Abraham,* in the prospect *rejoiceth, and was glad.* Acts iii. 24. John viii. 56. Hebrew xi. 13. Reader! hath Jesus ever said the same privately to you, as he did here to his disciples?

25 ¶ And, behold, a certain lawyer stood up, and tempted him, saying, Master, what shall I do to inherit eternal life?

26 He said unto him, What is written in the law? how readest thou?

27 And he answering, said, Thou shalt love the Lord thy God with all thy heart, and with all thy soul, and with all thy strength, and with all thy mind; and thy neighbour as thyself.

28 And he said unto him, Thou hast answered right: this do, and thou shalt live.

29 But he, willing to justify himself, said unto Jesus, And who is my neighbour?

30 And Jesus answering, said, A certain *man* went down from Jerusalem to Jericho, and fell among thieves, which stripped him of his raiment, and wounded *him,* and departed, leaving *him* half dead.

31 And by chance there came down a certain priest that way; and when he saw him, he passed by on the other side.

32 And likewise a Levite, when he was at the place, came and looked *on him,* and passed by on the other side.

33 But a certain Samaritan, as he journeyed, came where he was; and when he saw him, he had compassion *on him.*

34 And went to *him,* and bound up his wounds, pouring in oil and wine, and set him on his own beast, and brought him to an inn, and took care of him.

35 And on the morrow, when he departed, he took out two pence, and gave *them* to the host, and said unto him, Take care of him : and whatsoever thou spendest more, when I come again, I will repay thee.

36 Which now of these three, thinkest thou, was neighbour unto him that fell among the thieves?

37 And he said, He that shewed mercy on him. Then said Jesus unto him, Go, and do thou likewise.

There can be no doubt but that this lawyer's question was not with a view to learn from CHRIST, but to confound CHRIST; for it is said that *he tempted him*. And what a body of such critics have the servants of JESUS been tempted with ever since! How admirably our LORD sends the man to the law for conviction! When the law is used as CHRIST here useth it, the HOLY GHOST makes it a schoolmaster to CHRIST. *By the law is the knowledge of sin,* Rom. iii. 20 ; so that JESUS sent this lawyer to the law for self-condemnation. But how the man aimed to evade the force of it! He saith nothing about the love of GOD, but questions about his neighbour. The method the LORD took with this lawyer is both beautiful and striking: and though we have no authority to conclude the discourse ended in any saving work upon his heart, yet it could not but silence him with confusion. But, leaving the lawyer, it will be more for our purpose to observe some of the many precious things contained in this most interesting account of the wounded traveller and the kind *Samaritan*. Reader! we shall do no violence to the subject before us, if we behold, in this certain man going down from *Jerusalem* to *Jericho,* our own nature in every individual instance of it, leaving the holy city, which *Jerusalem* represents, and going down to the cursed city, *Jericho,* so declared in the Scriptures of GOD, Nehem. xi. 1. Joshua vi. 26. 1 Kings xvi. 34. As then this man, leaving the holy city, fell among thieves, which stripped him, wounded him, and left him half dead, so our nature, by the fall, is robbed by Satan, stripped of original righteousness, is made a whole mass of disease with the wounds of sin, and left more than half dead by the great enemy of souls. In soul—that is, *spiritual* death, truly *dead in trespasses and sins.* Ephes. ii. 1. And in body, exposed to *natural* death, certain and sure : and unless relieved, as this poor man was, during the present life, as certain of *eternal* death, both of body and soul for ever. Such is the awful state of every man by nature.

Our LORD describes the passing by of a *Priest* and a *Levite,* beholding the wounded traveller. The former immediately went on, seemingly regardless of his misery. The *latter* went and looked on him, but passed by on the other side. Probably, by these different characters, both equally unfriendly, might be meant, in allusion to our fallen helpless nature, the inability of either law or sacrifices, under the law, to heal the wounds of sin. But a certain Samaritan, JESUS describes as doing all the needful offices, nor departing from the wretched creature until he had brought him to an inn of safety. All commentaries, without hesitation, have considered this *Samaritan* as representing the LORD JESUS CHRIST. And there can be no doubt but that he, and he only, proved the divine Samaritan to our ruined nature. Yet, in the first view of the subject, CHRIST, in his human nature, was not a *Samaritan*, but a *Jew*. And moreover, if we trace the subject higher, and look at the SON of GOD, when first assuming our nature, he was indeed no Samaritan, that is, not a stranger, but from being the head, and husband of his Church, when he stood up as such, at the call of GOD, before all worlds, he, and he alone, was the nearest of all relations from all eternity. And his *journeying*, as is here represented, might be supposed to mean his coming down from the *Jerusalem* above, which is the mother of us all, to the *Jericho* of this world, brought under the curse by reason of the fall. But be this as it may, he proved the *Samaritan* to our nature. It is said that he saw him. Yes! JESUS beheld his Church from all eternity. CHRIST saw the Church when presented to him by his FATHER, before all worlds, in her native glory, in excellency in him. She was, from all eternity, a king's daughter, all glorious within, being GOD the FATHER's gift to his dear SON. JESUS saw her, loved her, delighted in her, for so the Scriptures speak : see Psm. xlv. 13, 14. Psm. xxi. 1, 2. Prov. viii. 22, 30, 31. But the seeing our nature in the deplorable state of a robbed and wounded man here described, is in allusion to our *Adam*-nature, and time-state of sin and ruin, into which, by *Satan*, we are involved. And here comes in all those precious blessed offices the history represents, which so exactly corresponds to the mercies of CHRIST. If the *Samaritan* went to the wounded man, and poured in oil and wine, and bound up his mangled body, set him on his own beast, and brought him to an inn, and took care of him, JESUS still more. The SON of GOD, in our nature, hath remembered us in our lowest estate, *for his mercy endureth for ever.* He hath indeed not barely poured in the oil and wine, to heal the wounds of sin, but the precious balsam of his own blood. He hath set us not on his own beast, but borne us in his arms, and carried us in his bosom. He hath brought us to his Church, to the richest inn of plentiful provisions, in means of free and sovereign grace and ordinances of gospel worship; and having washed our wounds in the fountain he hath opened for sin and for uncleanness, he hath took care of us with all this care. And now, though as on the morrow of departure he is returned to glory, he hath commanded all his servants, who minister in his name, to be attentive to our wants, assuring them and us, that at his return, which he will assuredly make good his promise in coming, he will make ample amends to recompence all done for us during his stay. The *two-pence* spoken of, is in allusion to a *Roman* coin, about fifteen-pence in value, to our *English* money. Some have considered this two-pence as in allusion to the two Testaments; and some to the two ordinances of Baptism and the LORD's Supper. But perhaps this may be fanciful. Yet though it were not necessary, nor perhaps proper, to strain the history to every minute point, it may be well to gather from the whole, under divine teaching, what the Lord Jesus evidently intended from such a striking illustration of our ruin, and his mercy over us ; so that every poor sinner, made sensible by grace of his lost estate by nature, and his wounded, ruined condition by *Satan*, may cry out, when contemplating Christ in the display of such mercy as is here set forth, and say, Lord Jesus! thou divine Samaritan, pass by and behold me, in my desperate circumstances, like this poor traveller. Pour in the precious balsam of thy blood, take me to thy Church, and heal me! The confession of the lawyer could be no other than what the Lord extorted from him. But it is not said that any other effect was wrought by it upon his mind.

38 ¶ Now it came to pass, as they went, that he entered into a certain village : and a certain woman, named Martha, received him into her house.

39 And she had a sister called Mary, which also sat at Jesus' feet, and heard his word.

40 But Martha was cumbered about much serving, and came to him, and said, Lord, dost thou not care that my sister hath left me to serve alone? bid her therefore that she help me.

41 And Jesus answered, and said unto her, Martha, Martha, thou art careful and troubled about many things :

42 But one thing is needful : and Mary hath chosen that good part, which shall not be taken away from her.

It should seem, that after this conversation with the lawyer, our Lord and his disciples moved onward in their walk. According to the account given by *John*, Jesus and his disciples were returning from *Jerusalem*, at this time after the feast of tabernacles: and they were now entering *Bethany*, the town of *Lazarus* and his sisters. See John vii. 10. The conversation here recited is but short, but it is very striking. The contrast between these sisters, in their different pursuits, is finely set forth by the Lord himself. Oh! what a folly is the diligence of even the most inoffensive employments, bounded by the prospects of this life, when compared to *the desire of the one thing needful.* The Reader will not fail to remark, that Christ himself is that good part alluded to, which never can be lost. All else may : all else will. God, our Father, hath given the Church nothing to have, and hold for ever, but his dear Son. And this first, and best, and comprehensive gift, which includes every other, is given never to be recalled. *Mary's* choice of this is not to be supposed as if resulting from her own natural affection. *If we love him,* it is because *he first loved us.* Nature untaught, uninfluenced by the grace of

GOD, would never make choice of CHRIST to all eternity. But when the LORD's choice of his redeemed, which is always accompanied with the grace of the LORD in the heart, directs the soul to JESUS; then, like *Mary*, our choice flowing from the LORD's choice, and our love issuing as a stream from the fountain of his love, we are made everlastingly secure in the grace of GOD in CHRIST; and CHRIST, with his fulness, becomes a portion to live upon in time, and to all eternity, and which can never be taken away.

REFLECTIONS.

READER! in pondering the several weighty and important things contained in this chapter, let us both look again and again to the Almighty Author of his holy word, to accompany our reading of it with his gracious teaching. JESUS, when he sent forth the seventy disciples here spoken of, to the work to which he called them, sent them forth only to the city, or place, whither he himself would come. And without the LORD's presence with us, what can we hope to enjoy of the LORD's grace and blessing? We see in *Chorazin* and *Bethsaida* the awful event of Gospel Ordinances, unaccompanied with the divine favor. LORD! in mercy grant the doom of *Capernaum* may never fall on our *British* Israel!

Amidst this awful view, help me, thou dear LORD JESUS, help every truly regenerated Reader to rejoice in what thou hast said of *Satan's* fall, as lightning from Heaven. Oh! for a heart renewed by grace to sing that song which *John* once heard in vision : *Now is come salvation and strength, and the kingdom of our GOD, and the power of his CHRIST; for the accuser of our brethren is cast down, which accused them before our GOD day and night.* And oh! the greater joy still, than that of treading on serpents and scorpions, to know our names are written in Heaven. Secured by this in GOD the FATHER's everlasting love, we are One with CHRIST, and CHRIST with us; and sealed by GOD the HOLY GHOST, unto the day of eternal redemption. Oh! HOLY FATHER! taught by thy dear SON, let every renewed soul praise thee, that though these things be hidden, from men who are worldly wise, and prudent in their own eyes, yet hast thou revealed them unto babes. All which we humbly and thankfully refer unto thine own sovereign will and pleasure. *Even so, FATHER, for so it seemed good in thy sight!*

Precious LORD JESUS! give us grace to hail thee, thou great Samaritan! Surely it is thou, and thou alone, which fully answereth to the character, thou thyself hast drawn, when from heaven thou camest down to this our world, to seek and save that which was lost. LORD! thou wilt bring thy whole redeemed home, though wounded by Satan, and dead in trespasses and sins! And oh! for grace, that until that hour comes for thy return, thy people may not be found like *Martha* cumbered with the many things of this unsatisfying, dying, sinful state; but through thy grace giving the power, like *Mary*, we may chuse that good part which *cannot be taken away.*

C H A P. XI.

CONTENTS.

We have in this Chapter our LORD *teaching his Disciples to pray.*
He works a Miracle in casting out a Devil. He preacheth to the
People; and pronounceth a Woe upon the Scribes and Pharisees.

AND it came to pass, that, as he was praying
in a certain place, when he ceased, one of
his disciples said unto him, Lord, teach us to pray,
as John also taught his disciples.

2 And he said unto them, When ye pray, say,
Our Father, which art in heaven, hallowed be
thy name. Thy kingdom come. Thy will be
done, as in heaven, so in earth.

3 Give us, day by day, our daily bread.

4 And forgive us our sins; for we also forgive
every one that is indebted to us. And lead us not
into temptation; but deliver us from evil.

5 And he said unto them, Which of you shall
have a friend, and shall go unto him at midnight,
and say unto him, Friend, lend me three loaves;

6 For a friend of mine in his journey is come
unto me, and I have nothing to set before him?

7 And he from within shall answer and say,
Trouble me not: the door is now shut, and my
children are with me in bed; I cannot rise and
give thee.

8 I say unto you, Though he will not rise and
give him, because he is his friend, yet because of
his importunity he will rise and give him as many
as he needeth.

9 And I say unto you, Ask, and it shall be
given you; seek, and ye shall find; knock, and
it shall be opened unto you.

10 For every one that asketh receiveth; and he
that seeketh findeth: and to him that knocketh it
shall be opened.

11 If a son shall ask bread of any of you that

is a father, will he give him a stone? or if *he ask*
a fish, will he for a fish give him a serpent?

12 Or if he shall ask an egg, will he offer him
a scorpion?

13 If ye then, being evil, know how to give
good gifts unto your children : how much more
shall *your* heavenly Father give the Holy Spirit to
them that ask him?

It should be observed in this place, that though the form of
prayer here delivered by *Luke*, differs not in any thing material from
that recorded by *Matthew*, chap. vi. 9. yet JESUS was now in *Judea*;
whereas, then he was in *Galilee*. And moreover, the prayer was then,
according to *Matthew*, delivered in the midst of CHRIST's *preaching*.
Here we are told, he himself was *praying*. I need not tell the
Reader (indeed the limits and designs of this Poor Man's Commentary
would not permit me,) how much hath been said for and against the
use of this prayer by the LORD's people. Doubtless it is a very
blessed, a very comprehensive prayer, and every petition in it truly
spiritual ; and contains, more or less, every thing of what the prayer
of the faithful ought to be. And, according to what *Luke* hath here
said, it should seem to decide the point. He doth not use the same
expression as *Matthew* did, when recording the words of CHRIST :
After this manner, therefore, pray ye ; but he positively saith, *When*
ye pray, say, Our FATHER, &c.

Our LORD beautifully illustrates the holy importunity of prayer,
under the figure of a friend arising at midnight ; and at length prevailing over all the arguments brought against him by his unwearied
earnestness, which will take no refusal. The LORD loves a fervency
in spirit. Scripture hath furnished several striking instances of its
effect and success. Gen. xxxii. 9 to 12, and 24 to 29. Luke xviii.
1 to 8.

14 ¶ And he was casting out a devil, and it
was dumb. And it came to pass, when the devil
was gone out, the dumb spake ; and the people
wondered.

15 But some of them said, He casteth out
devils through Beelzebub, the chief of the devils.

16 And others, tempting *him*, sought of him a
sign from heaven.

17 But he, knowing their thoughts, said unto
them, Every kingdom divided against itself is
brought to desolation ; and a house *divided* against
a house falleth.

18 If Satan also be divided against himself, how shall his kingdom stand? because ye say that I cast out devils through Beelzebub.

19 And if I by Beelzebub cast out devils, by whom do your sons cast *them* out? therefore shall they be your judges.

20 But if I with the finger of God cast out devils, no doubt the kingdom of God is come upon you.

21 When a strong man armed keepeth his palace, his goods are in peace:

22 But when a stronger than he shall come upon him, and overcome him, he taketh from him all his armour wherein he trusted, and divideth his spoils.

23 He that is not with me is against me: and he that gathereth not with me scattereth.

24 When the unclean spirit is gone out of a man, he walketh through dry places, seeking rest; and finding none, he saith, I will return unto my house whence I came out.

25 And when he cometh, he findeth *it* swept and garnished.

26 Then goeth he, and taketh *to him* seven other spirits more wicked than himself; and they enter in, and dwell there: and the last state of that man is worse than the first.

I have very largely dwelt on this subject in the parallel passage, Matt. 24 to 30. I therefore refer the Reader to it.

27 And it came to pass, as he spake these things, a certain woman of the company lifted up her voice, and said unto him, Blessed *is* the womb that bare thee, and the paps which thou hast sucked.

28 But he said, Yea, rather, blessed *are* they that hear the word of God, and keep it.

There is somewhat very singular in this relation. *A certain woman of the company.* What company? Not of the company of them who charged CHRIST with casting out devils through *Beelzebub*. Probably of the people that, it is said, wondered at JESUS's miracle, which he had, just before this discourse, wrought, (ver. 14). This woman, it should seem, was so struck with the miracle, and the discourse which followed, that she could not contain expressing her astonishment in the words here recorded. But from our LORD's answer, it doth not appear as if JESUS regarded her as one of his people. Natural feelings will sometimes ascend great heights: but nature is not grace. Numbers heard JESUS, and wondered at the gracious things which proceeded out of his mouth: but here the whole ended. Oh! Reader! how sure is it that the saving effectual call of every sinner is of GOD!

29 ¶ And when the people were gathered thick together, he began to say, This is an evil generation: they seek a sign; and there shall no sign be given it, but the sign of Jonas the prophet.

30 For as Jonas was a sign unto the Ninevites, so shall also the Son of man be to this generation.

31 The queen of the south shall rise up in the judgement with the men of this generation, and condemn them: for she came from the utmost parts of the earth to hear the wisdom of Solomon: and, behold, a greater than Solomon *is* here.

32 The men of Nineve shall rise up in the judgement with this generation, and shall condemn it: for they repented at the preaching of of Jonas: and, behold, a greater than Jonas *is* here.

33 No man, when he hath lighted a candle, putteth *it* in a secret place, neither under a bushel, but on a candlestick, that they which come in may see the light.

34 The light of the body is the eye; therefore when thine eye is single, thy whole body also is full of light; but when *thine eye* is evil, thy body also *is* full of darkness,

35 Take heed therefore, that the light which is in thee be not darkness.

36 If thy whole body therefore *be* full of light, having no part dark, the whole shall be full of

light, as when the bright shining of a candle doth
give thee light.

Our LORD's discourse in this place, illustrated as it is by those beautiful histories of *the Queen of the South,* and *the Men of Nineveh,* deserves our awakened attention. JESUS plainly shows that his Gospel,
in his own open and free preaching of it, became a candle placed
most conveniently for giving light, and not obscurely hid. But such
was the prejudice of darkened nature, that the very light arising out
of it, like the vicious humours of the body, only tended to render it
indistinct. Both the *Queen of the South,* and the Men of *Nineveh,*
must alike arise to condemn the generation before whom CHRIST
preached. For the former came from a vast distance to hear the mere
wisdom of a man; but they passed by in their own streets with contempt, and staid not to hear the wisdom of the SON of GOD. And the
latter fell down in sorrow and sackcloth, at the preaching of *Jonas,*
from a single sermon; whereas, the repeated discourses of JESUS
were utterly disregarded by them, and despised.

37 ¶ And as he spake, a certain Pharisee besought him to dine with him. And he went in,
and sat down to meat.

38 And when the Pharisee saw *it,* he marvelled
that he had not first washed before dinner.

39 And the Lord said unto him, Now do ye
Pharisees make clean the outside of the cup and
the platter; but your inward part is full of ravening and wickedness.

40 *Ye* fools, did not he that made that which is
without, make that which is within also?

41 But rather give alms of such things as ye
have; and, behold, all things are clean unto
you.

We had an account of JESUS eating with a *Pharisee,* chap. vii. 36,
which see. And here is the relation of another. Our LORD took all
occasions to manifest the object for which he came on earth. And
certainly we have abundant reason to bless our gracious LORD for this
condescension; for this dinner party, as well as the former visit to the
Pharisee's house, afford some very sweet and profitable instructions.
Our LORD's shewing in what real uncleanness consists, is a rich sermon
taught us at this *Pharisee's* table.

42 But, woe unto you, Pharisees! for ye tithe
mint and rue, and all manner of herbs, and pass
over judgement, and the love of God: these
ought ye to have done, and not to leave the other
undone.

43 Woe unto you, Pharisees! for ye love the uppermost seats in the synagogues, and greetings in the markets.

44 Woe unto you, scribes and Pharisees, hypocrites! for ye are as graves which appear not, and the men that walk over *them* are not aware *of them.*

45 Then answered one of the lawyers, and said unto him, Master, thus saying, thou reproachest us also.

46 And he said, Woe unto you also, *ye* lawyers! for ye lade men with burdens grievous to be borne, and ye yourselves touch not the burdens with one of your fingers.

47 Woe unto you! for ye build the sepulchres of the prophets, and your fathers killed them.

48 Truly ye bear witness, that ye allow the deeds of your fathers; for they indeed killed them, and ye build their sepulchres.

49 Therefore also said the wisdom of God, I will send them prophets and apostles, and *some* of them they shall slay and persecute:

50 That the blood of all the prophets which was shed from the foundation of the world, may be required of this generation;

51 From the blood of Abel, unto the blood of Zacharias, which perished between the altar and the temple: verily I say unto you, It shall be required of this generation.

52 Woe unto you, lawyers! for ye have taken away the key of knowledge: ye enter not in yourselves. And them that were entering in ye hindered.

I am inclined to think that though *Luke* hath recorded in this place those words of CHRIST, yet they were not spoken in the house of the *Pharisee.* For we do not read, that when this *Pharisee* desired JESUS to dine with him, that there were any others invited. And if not, how should such a company as it should seem of the *Scribes* and *Pharisees* have been so gathered, as for the LORD to preach to.

Moreover, *Matthew* hath related this discourse nearly in the same words as if delivered in the temple ; so that unless our Lord preached it twice, once in the temple, and now again in the house of the Pharisee, it should rather seem, that *Luke* hath only recorded it in this place after the Pharisee's dinner, and not as in the *Pharisee's* house. But I pray the Reader to observe, that here, as upon all other doubtful occasions, I never speak decidedly. Let the sermon have been preached whereever it might have been, it is a solemn one indeed ; and, coming from him who searcheth the heart, and trieth the reins, the contents of it are enough to make the ears of them that hear it to tingle with alarm at the awful state of such awful characters ! See Matt. xxiii. 13 to the end.

53 And, as he said these things unto them, the scribes and the Pharisees began to urge *him* vehemently, and to provoke him to speak of many things;

54 Laying wait for him, and seeking to catch something out of his mouth, that they might accuse him.

I beg the Reader to attend to the expressions in these verses. We read that those sworn foes of Christ began to urge him and to provoke him ; but we do not read that Jesus felt hurt. What the Lord said, no doubt, was, as the former part of his discourse, full of denunciations against those whited sepulchres, as he called them : but *no guile was found in his mouth.* Precious Lord Jesus ! give thy people grace to consider thine unequalled meekness, in *enduring such contradiction of sinners against thyself that we may never be weary nor faint in our minds.* Heb. xii. 3.

REFLECTIONS.

Dearest Lord Jesus ! I would say for myself, and all thy redeemed family, teach us to pray, and with what words to come before the Lord, in all our soul exercises, and wants, and conflicts, and trials. Do thou, dear Lord ! by the sweet influences of thine Holy Spirit, both spread thy fulness, cause us to feel our need, excite a spiritual appetite, and open a constant source of communion, *that, from thy fullness, we may all receive and grace for grace !* And oh ! for a fervor in prayer, awakened by the Holy Ghost ! that, like the friend at midnight, and *Jacob* at *Bethel,* never may we go to the mercy-seat, and come away empty; but, like the great father of the praying seed, in the same spirit of faith to tell our God, *I will not let thee go, except thou bless me.* And, oh Lord ! grant that neither the *Queen of the South,* nor *the Ninevites,* may bring reproach upon thy people ! No Solomon like our Solomon—no preaching of *Jonah* like the preaching of our Lord Jesus Christ ! Precious Master ! let neither the awful state of *Pharisee* blindness, nor the wretched delusion of *Jewish* ignorance, be in the lot of thy redeemed, in all generations of thy Church. Oh! for grace to sit at thy feet, to hear thy word! that through the blessed illumination of GOD the HOLY GHOST, *our whole body,* as thou hast said, *being full of light, and having no part dark, the whole may be full of light!* JESUS, the sun of righteousness, shining *as when the bright shining of a candle doth give the people light.*

CHAP. XII,

CONTENTS.

JESUS *is here preaching to the People. A Man from the throng complains to him of his Brother. The* LORD *takes occasion therefrom to reprove Covetousness, and discourseth on several Subjects.*

IN the mean time, when there were gathered together an innumerable multitude of people, insomuch that they trode one upon another, he began to say unto his disciples first of all, Beware ye of the leaven of the Pharisees, which is hypocrisy:

2 For there is nothing covered, that shall not be revealed; neither hid, that shall not be known.

3 Therefore whatsoever ye have spoken in darkness, shall be heard in the light; and that which ye have spoken in the ear in closets, shall be proclaimed upon the housetops.

4 And I say unto you my friends, Be not afraid of them that kill the body, and after that have no more that they can do.

5 But I will forewarn you whom ye shall fear: Fear him, which after he hath killed, hath power to cast into hell; yea, I say unto you, Fear him.

6 Are not five sparrows sold for two farthings, and not one of them is forgotten before God?

7 But even the very hairs of your head are all numbered: fear not therefore: ye are of more value than many sparrows.

8 Also I say unto you, Whosoever shall confess me before men, him shall the Son of man also confess before the angels of God:

9 But he that denieth me before men, shall be denied before the angels of God.

10 And whosoever shall speak a word against the Son of man, it shall be forgiven him: but unto him that blasphemeth against the Holy Ghost, it shall not be forgiven.

11 And when they bring you unto the synagogues, and *unto* magistrates, and powers, take ye no thought how or what thing ye shall answer, or what ye shall say,

12 For the Holy Ghost shall teach you, in the same hour, what ye ought to say.

I cannot help remarking, upon the several discourses of JESUS, how very much his doctrine is directed against the Pharisees. Let any man gather, from the Gospels, the whole discourses of JESUS, and observe how large a part is spent in condemning that class of persons: and the reason is plain. No set of men whatever, no, not even the openly-profane, are as sworn foes to the full and finished salvation of JESUS as the Pharisees. For by setting up a righteousness of their own, or, what results from the same source, the unhumbled pride of human nature, in part they do, by so much lessen the vast importance of CHRIST and his redemption. Either the whole mass of men are dead in trespasses and sins, or they are not. If they are not, what need have they of a Savior? If they are, what an impudent attempt is it in the Pharisee, of any generation, to set himself up as a part-Savior! Pharisees, in the days of our LORD, were his most deadly foes; and Pharisees, in modern times, are the most deadly foes to his people. Our LORD's discourse, in those verses, very plain and simple as it is, seems to have been founded on the prospect he saw in his Church, what opposition his chosen ones would meet with, all the way through, from that class of people. *Beware ye of the leaven of the Pharisees, which is hypocricy.*

13 ¶ And one of the company said unto him, Master, speak to my brother, that he divide the inheritance with me.

14 And he said unto him, Man, who made me a judge, or a divider, over you?

15 And he said unto them, Take heed, and beware of covetousness; for a man's life consisteth not in the abundance of the things which he possesseth.

16 And he spake a parable unto them, saying,

The ground of a certain rich man brought forth plentifully:

17 And he thought within himself, saying, What shall I do, because I have no room where to bestow my fruits?

18 And he said, This will I do: I will pull down my barns, and build greater; and there will 1 bestow all my fruits and my goods.

19 And I will say to my soul, Soul, thou hast much goods laid up for many years; take thine ease, eat, drink, *and* be merry.

20 But God said unto him, *Thou* fool, this night thy soul shall be required of thee: then whose shall those things be, which thou hast provided?

21 So *is* he that layeth up treasure for himself, and is not rich toward God.

How little this man from the crowd knew of JESUS, or of his business in this world! Sweetly doth the example of JESUS here teach, and ministers especially, to be disentangled from the concerns of the world, and to sit aloof from them as much as possible. It is blessed, however, to observe, how the LORD, took occasion from the request made to him, to raise a very interesting and blessed discourse. This rich fool, in CHRIST's parable, is but too often realized, and found to be a true character in the world. I have often thought what a most consummate fool this man must have been to speak thus to his soul. Why, the soul can neither eat nor drink. All the stores in barns, laid up by the worldling, cannot profit the soul. And what a selfish wretch, to talk of laying up, instead of saying, I will make new barns in the hungry bodies of the poor around me: I will make them my store-houses and my barns! But oh! thou dearest LORD JESUS! is not every man thus by nature, until taught by thy HOLY SPIRIT, of the true treasure which thou causest thy people to inherit in making rich towards GOD? Reader! think, if it be possible, how many die as this rich fool died; who, in the midst of their childish pursuits, are suddenly called away to their awful account! Surely it will be one among the wonders of eternity, the mistaken calculations of such men. And will it not tend to aggravate their misery in eternity in having then a full view of the awful delusion under which they lived and died? in passing by, while upon earth, the cries of common nature, and foolishly hoarding what never gave them real happiness here, but treasured up wrath against the day of wrath hereafter? Compare those Scriptures, Prov. viii. 18 to 21. Job xxi. 7 to 12.

22 ¶ And he said unto his disciples, Therefore I say unto you, Take no thought for your life,

what ye shall eat; neither for the body, what ye shall put on.

23 The life is more than meat, and the body *is more* than raiment.

24 Consider the ravens: for they neither sow nor reap; which neither have storehouse nor barn; and God feedeth them: how much more are ye better than the fowls?

25 And which of you, with taking thought, can add to his stature one cubit?

26 If ye then be not able to do that thing which is least, why take ye thought for the rest?

27 Consider the lilies how they grow: they toil not, they spin not; and yet I say unto you, that Solomon in all his glory was not arrayed like one of these.

28 If then God so clothe the grass, which is to-day in the field, and to-morrow is cast into the oven; how much more *will he clothe* you, O ye of little faith?

29 And seek not ye what ye shall eat, or what ye shall drink, neither be ye of doubtful mind.

30 For all these things do the nations of the world seek after: and your Father knoweth that ye have need of these things.

31 But rather seek ye the kingdom of God; and all these things shall be added unto you.

Every word in this lovely discourse of JESUS is truly blessed. The images and figures are divinely chosen to represent the interesting subject the LORD had in view. The flower of the field is more strikingly expressive of dependence on the LORD's providence, in allusion to his exposed ones, than that of the garden would have been. For the *latter* is fenced in and watched over, but the *former* is open to the foot of every traveller, and may be bitten off by any beast in his forage. So, in like manner, the fowls of the air differ widely from those of the barn. They have no caterer, no store-house, no shelter; and the bush they roost on one night, may be taken away before the next. Sweetly, by these images, JESUS teaches his apparently unprovided for family, that not one of them is forgotten before GOD. Reader! pray turn to that most blessed Scripture, Isaiah xxvii. 2, 3; and beg of GOD the HOLY GHOST to write it down for you, for common use, in the hourly memorandums of your heart. *In that day, sing ye unto her* (the Church). *A vineyard of red wine : I, the* LORD, *do keep it. I will water it every moment, lest any hurt it : I will keep it night and day.*

32 Fear not little flock; for it is your Father's good pleasure to give you the kingdom.

33 Sell that ye have, and give alms: provide yourselves bags which wax not old, a treasure in the heavens that faileth not, where no thief approacheth, neither moth corrupteth.

34 For where your treasure is, there will your heart be also.

35 Let your loins be girded about, and *your* lights burning;

36 And ye yourselves like unto men that wait for their lord, when he will return from the wedding; that, when he cometh and knocketh, they may open unto him immediately.

37 Blessed *are* those servants whom the lord when he cometh, shall find watching: verily, I say unto you, That he shall gird himself, and make them to sit down to meat, and will come forth and serve them.

38 And if he shall come in the second watch, or come in the third watch, and find *them* so, blessed are those servants.

39 And this know, that if the good man of the house had known what hour the thief would come, he would have watched, and not have suffered his house to be broken through.

40 Be ye therefore ready also: for the Son of man cometh at an hour when ye think not.

41 ¶ Then Peter said unto him, Lord, speakest thou this parable unto us, or even to all?

42 And the Lord said, Who then is that faithful and wise steward, whom *his* lord shall make ruler over his household, to give *them their* portion of meat in due season?

43 Blessed *is* that servant whom his lord when he cometh shall find so doing.

44 Of a truth I say unto you, That he will make him ruler over all that he hath.

45 But, and if that servant say in his heart, My lord delayeth his coming; and shall begin to beat the men servants and maidens, and to eat and drink, and to be drunken;

46 The lord of that servant will come in a day when he looketh not for *him*, and at an hour when he is not aware, and will cut him in sunder, and will appoint him his portion with the unbelievers.

47 And that servant, which knew his lord's will, and prepared not *himself*, neither did according to his will, shall be beaten with many *stripes*.

48 But he that knew not, and did commit things worthy of stripes, shall be beaten with few *stripes;* for unto whomsoever much is given, of him shall be much required; and to whom men have committed much, of him they will ask the more.

I shall have no occasion to offer much comment on this very blessed discourse of Jesus. His language is so plain as to need none. I shall only here and there call the Reader's attention to some of the more striking expressions the Lord is pleased to use. There is somewhat very interesting in Jesus calling his Church a *little* flock. Little, in comparison of the world's wide wilderness; but when all brought home by electing, redeeming, and effectual calling in grace, here in the present life, and to glory above, the Church is said to be a *multitude which no man could number*, Rev. vii. 9. The Lord hath been pleased to dignify his Church with several very striking names; but all highly descriptive. A *beautiful* flock, Jerem. xiii. 20. A flock of *slaughter*, Zech. xi. 4 to 7. An *holy* flock, Ezek. xxxvi. 38. And by his same servant, most blessedly doth he call it, *My flock*, Ezek. xxxiv. 17. All which prove the special and peculiar character of the Lord's people, 1 Pet. ii. 9. And it is equally worthy the Reader's attention what Jesus saith in relation to *the kingdom*. It is said to be *given*. *Fear not, little flock, it is your heavenly Father's good pleasure to give you the kingdom*. So that it is not man's purchase by merit, but God's gift by grace. And it is not only a gift, but a free gift, and wholly the result of God's good pleasure, Isaiah xliii. 21, Matt. xi. 26. Jesus's direction to his disciples, to wean themselves from earth and earthly connections, is very striking. And the figure of a man with his loins girded, and his light burning, is a beautiful allusion to servants of the east; whose long vestures were always tucked up, and fastened to their girdles, when in waiting, that they might be able to run with speed, when their master's services required it. And this explains to us what the Prophet saith of the ministers of the Gospel, whose feet are uncovered when they run on the mountains, Isaiah lxii. 7. But the most lovely of all the similitudes in this discourse of JESUS, is that in which he describes himself as *girding himself, and coming forth to serve his faithful servants, whom he will make to sit down to meat.* It is indeed impossible to form equal apprehensions of the grace and humility of the LORD JESUS. He who washed his disciples' feet, when in the moment he knew himself to be LORD of all, and all things were given into his sovereign hand, who shall calculate the wonderful extent of such grace? But without straining the expressions to the utmost limits, in beholding JESUS serving *them,* whose very happiness must be made up of serving *him,* it may serve to shew, in some measure, the overflowing love of his heart, which is wholly theirs; and every act of it directed for their happiness here, and to all eternity, Song ii. 14.

49 I am come to send fire on the earth, and what will I, if it be already kindled?

50 But I have a baptism to be baptized with, and how am I straitened till it be accomplished?

51 Suppose ye that I am come to give peace on earth? I tell you, Nay; but rather division:

52 For from henceforth there shall be five in one house divided, three against two, and two against three.

53 The father shall be divided against the son, and the son against the father, the mother against the daughter, and the daughter against the mother; the mother-in-law against her daughter-in-law, and the daughter-in-law against her mother-in-law.

Various have been the judgment of the godly concerning those expressions of our LORD, in the opening of this paragraph. What fire the LORD JESUS alluded to, doth not seem decidedly plain, so as to determine whose judgment is correct amidst the various opinions which have been formed, in relation to it. Some have conceived that it had respect to the work of GOD the HOLY GHOST, Isaiah iv. 4. Malachi iii. 2. And others refer it to the consequent persecution which followed CHRIST's preaching: and they conclude that the words of JESUS so explain it. And in relation to the baptism JESUS speaks of, equal difficulty, in point of determination, hath arisen. It could not mean the baptism of water, for this CHRIST had gone through. Neither of the HOLY GHOST, for JESUS was full of the HOLY GHOST, Luke iv. 1. The general tide of commentators runs in the supposition that he re-

ferred to our LORD's sufferings. But I confess it doth not strike me
in that point of view; for what was the whole life of JESUS upon
earth any more than a baptism? if so, from sorrows and exercises.
But I leave the decision of it with the LORD, only begging to observe,
that if JESUS was so straitened for the accomplishment of this baptism, whatever it might be, how ought the LORD's people to be on the
continual look out, and humble waitings, for the baptisms of GOD the
HOLY GHOST?

54 And he said also to the people, When ye
see a cloud rise out of the west, straightway ye
say, There cometh a shower: and so it is.

55 And when *ye see* the south wind blow, ye say,
There will be heat; and it cometh to pass.

56 *Ye* hypocrites, ye can discern the face of the
sky, and of the earth; but how is it that ye do
not discern this time?

57 Yea, and why, even of yourselves, judge
ye not what is right?

58 When thou goest with thine adversary to the
magistrate, *as thou art* in the way, give diligence
that thou mayest be delivered from him; lest he
hale thee to the judge, and the judge deliver thee
to the officer, and the officer cast thee into prison.

59 I tell thee, Thou shalt not depart thence till
thou hast paid the very last mite.

We have those Scriptures already noticed, Matt. xvi. 2, and Matt.
v. 25, to which I refer.

REFLECTIONS.

READER! the HOLY GHOST is blessedly teaching the Church, in
this chapter, sweet lessons of grace and of providence. In the view
of the multitude pressing upon JESUS to hear the word of GOD, we
are taught how precious ordinances are, where the LORD is present
to bless them. And in the discourse of JESUS on the LORD's care
over the birds of the air, and his glory displayed in the lilies of the
field, we learn how everlastingly secure and provided for must be
his redeemed ones. And in the contemplation of the foolish worldling, how strikingly doth JESUS shew the little value of riches, unsanctified by the blessing of the LORD. And should these reflections
meet the eye of one of the LORD's timid fold, oh! for GOD the
SPIRIT, to make that sweet Scripture blessed. *Fear not, little flock,
it is your* FATHER's *good pleasure to give you the kingdom.* Hail!
thou blessed Master of thine household, which promiseth such rich
rewards to thy waiting servants! But wilt thou indeed condescend

to such acts of humbleness as to gird thyself, and serve them?.
Was it ever heard of in the annals of mankind that ever a Lord did
so? *Solomon* was struck with astonishment, that he, whom the
heaven of heavens could not contain, should visit the house he had
built with his presence. But what would this eastern prince have
said, had he beheld JESUS the SON of GOD washing the feet of poor
fishermen? Oh! for grace *to know that love of* CHRIST, *which
passeth knowledge, that we may be filled with all the fullness of* GOD!

CHAP. XIII.

CONTENTS.

The LORD *is here discoursing to the People. He speaks of the
Galileans, and of the Barren Fig-Tree. He cureth a Woman of
her Infirmity. Makes a circuit through the Villages; and laments over
Jerusalem.*

THERE were present at that season, some that
told him of the Galileans, whose blood Pilate
had mingled with their sacrifices.

2 And Jesus answering, said unto them, Suppose ye that these Galileans were sinners above all
the Galileans, because they suffered such things?

3 I tell you, Nay; but, except ye repent, ye
shall all likewise perish.

4 Or those eighteen, upon whom the tower in
Siloam fell, and slew them, think ye that they
were sinners above all men that dwelt in Jerusalem?

5 I tell you, Nay; but, except ye repent, ye
shall all likewise perish.

We have no account of this discourse of JESUS by any other of
the Evangelists. It will be proper, therefore, to notice it in this place.
And it is remarkable also, that no historian hath noticed this act of
Pilate. It differs from one related by the writer of the Jewish
history, concerning *Pilate's* slaughter of certain Samaritans; so that
it cannot be the same. The contempt *Pilate* manifested to their sacrifices, serves to shew the awfulness of his character. This pool of
Siloam hath been supposed to have been the same with the waters
of *Shiloah*, Isaiah viii. 6; and others make it the same as the pool of
Bethesda, John v. 2. But these are but conjectures. I rather would
call the attention of the Reader to what may be considered as im-
provable from the whole passage. The repentance JESUS speaks of,
I humbly conceive not to be intended as if it was an act of their
mind, and in their own power; for this would be contrary to the
whole tenor of the Gospel. It is the act of sovereign grace to work

this in the sinner's mind. And all the persons' of the GODHEAD are engaged in the gracious work of creating it in the mind of the people. GOD the FATHER pledgeth himself to give it, Ezek. xxxvi. 24 to 27. CHRIST is said to be *exalted as a Prince and a Savior for to give repentance to Israel, and forgiveness of sins,* Acts v. 31. And no less GOD the HOLY GHOST is said to be *a spirit of grace and supplication,* that they on whom it is poured, may *look unto him whom they have pierced, and mourn,* Zech. xii. 10. Hence, as this is GOD's work, and not man's, and repentance is but an *effect* of this work, and not the *cause,* it never was meant, neither could it be expected, as a means of bringing sinners into a salvable state, but rather an evidence of their being brought. So that when the LORD saith, *Except ye repent, ye shall all likewise perish;* this included *Jerusalem* sinners, as well as the sinners of *Galilee;* yea, all mankind in whom no saving change was wrought. For according to the unalterable language of CHRIST, without the new birth, and which (as a *great* principle includes the *less,*) comprizeth *repentance also towards* GOD, *and faith in the* LORD JESUS CHRIST, there could be no salvation. John iii. 3. Acts xx. 21. Reader! do not fail to mark in this discourse of the LORD JESUS, with which this Chapter opens, how sweetly CHRIST is preached, even where at the first view, we might least have expected him.

6 ¶ He spake also this parable: A certain *man* had a fig-tree planted in his vineyard; and he came and sought fruit thereon, and found none.

7 Then said he unto the dresser of his vineyard, Behold, these three years I come seeking fruit on this fig-tree, and find none; cut it down; why cumbereth it the ground?

8 And he answering, said unto him, Lord, let it alone this year also, till I shall dig about it, and dung *it.*

9 And if it bear fruit, *well;* and if not, *then* after that thou shalt cut it down.

They who read this parable of the LORD JESUS, through the medium of the *free-will* mind, (which every man by nature is strongly tinctured with,) will consider that this representation of the barren fig-tree, is intended to set forth the free will and ability of the human heart to accomplish his own salvation; while they who going upon the scriptural bottom of *free grace,* admit not for a moment the possibility of GOD's grace depending upon man's will, and therefore refer the whole into the sovereignty of GOD.

In the view of opinions so diametrically opposite, in order for the discovery with whom the truth is, (for both cannot be right,) and for the better apprehension of our LORD's design, it may be proper to consider upon what occasion JESUS spake this parable, and to whom it was addressed.

Now we find, that the LORD had been discoursing on the general apostacy of human nature, and had declared, that all men, without a saving change by grace wrought upon their hearts, would perish. And, in the further illustration of this doctrine, JESUS added this parable. A barren fig-tree is represented as in the vineyard, that is, the Church of GOD, (See Isaiah v. 1—7.) which under the highest cultivation, even of our LORD's own personal ministry, for *three years*, (the time which at the delivery of this parable, JESUS had laboured in his word and doctrine,) had produced nothing. The sentence by the owner of the vineyard is then given; *Cut it down, why cumbereth it the ground.* The dresser of the vineyard is represented as interceding for another year; and then consenting to the destruction of it, if still remaining fruitless.

If the Jewish nation be considered as this barren fig-tree, every thing in the parable bears a just resemblance to the several features of it. The children of Israel as a nation and people, had all along Church privileges. *To them,* (saith Paul,) *according to the flesh, pertained the covenant, and the giving of the law, &c.* But *they,* (saith he,) *are not all Israel, which are of Israel.* Rom. ix. 3—6. Outward privileges are perfectly distinct things from inward grace. *Capernaum* was exalted to heaven in advantages of this kind; but her end the LORD said, should be to be brought down to hell. Matt. xi. 20—24. In like manner this barren fig-tree was doomed for destruction; and as CHRIST predicted, the event actually took place, when the Jewish nation, as a nation, was soon after overthrown by the *Roman* army, verse 35. And to this agrees the whole purport of the Bible. When GOD created our nature, it was, as the LORD himself saith, *a noble vine, and wholly a right seed.* But, when in the Adam-nature of the fall, *it was turned into a degenerate plant of a strange vine,* of consequence nothing but *blossoms as the dust,* and *grapes of gall,* could it bring forth. See Jerem. ii. 21. Isaiah v. 24. Deut. xxxii. 32. Intercessions for the sparing such corrupt stock, form no part in the covenant of grace. JESUS himself saith, *Every plant which my heavenly FATHER hath not planted shall be rooted up.* Matt. xv. 13.

But, who then is this dresser of the vineyard? Not the LORD JESUS CHRIST, I venture to believe. For we do not find among all the offices of the LORD JESUS, enumerated in scripture, such an one as a vine-dresser mentioned. But we read indeed, in allusion to Gospel days, that the LORD would appoint *the sons of the alien to be the Church's plowmen and vine-dressers,* as so many degrading employments, whilst all the LORD's people should be named *the priests of the* LORD, *and men should call them the ministers of our* GOD. Isaiah lxi. 5, 6. Rev. i. 6. But, not to dwell upon these things, it cannot for a moment be supposed, that, on the presumption this barren fig-tree represented the Jewish nation, CHRIST is here set forth by himself as the dresser. For in that case, his all-prevailing office of Intercessor must have failed; the nation soon after (and as he himself predicted,) being cut down. A doctrine which the most violent *free-will* men will hardly venture to think possible.

The question again recurs, if the LORD JESUS himself be not meant by him, in the character of this dresser, whom doth the LORD mean? I venture to say in answer, though not to decide, may it not be all such as in the warmth of their natural feelings, overstep the modesty

of grace, and intercede, without being taught so to do by the LORD.
Such was *Abraham,* when he interceded for *Sodom;* and led away by
nature, he asked for *Ishmael* before he knew *Isaac.* Gen. xvii. 18.
Gen. xviii. 23, &c. Such was *Moses,* in the case of *Israel.* Exod.
xxxii. 31, 32. And *Paul* felt somewhat of the same nature. Rom.
ix. 3. All this is nature, not grace. And in the highest characters
such remains of nature are found. But none of those things belong
to Him, or are found in his offices, whose decision is, *All that the*
FATHER *giveth me shall come to me, and him that cometh to me I will
in no wise cast out.* John vi. 37. The glorious advocacy of JESUS, is
in exact conformity to covenant settlements. It is liable to no perad-
ventures, no questions, no doubts. And how solemn soever the doctrine of this parable is, yet far better is it that GOD's sovereignty
should be seen in it, than that man's pride should be gratified, in
rendering that questionable which JEHOVAH's word and oath hath made
certain; and leaving the intercession of the LORD JESUS at an hazard,
whether GOD's free grace, or man's free will, shall finally triumph!

10 ¶ And he was teaching in one of the synagogues on the sabbath.

11 And, behold, there was a woman which had
a spirit of infirmity eighteen years, and was bowed
together, and could in no wise lift up *herself.*

12 And when Jesus saw her, he called *her to
him,* and said unto her, Woman, thou art loosed
from thine infirmity.

13 And he laid *his* hands on her: and immediately she was made straight, and glorified God.

14 And the ruler of the synagogue answered
with indignation, because that Jesus had healed on
the sabbath day, and said unto the people, There
are six days in which men ought to work: in them
therefore come and be healed, and not on the
sabbath day.

15 The Lord then answered him, and said, *Thou*
hypocrite, doth not each one of you on the sabbath loose his ox or *his* ass from the stall, and lead
him away to watering?

16 And ought not this woman, being a daughter
of Abraham, whom Satan hath bound, lo, these
eighteen years, be loosed from this bond on the
sabbath day?

17 And when he had said these things, all his adversaries were ashamed : and all the people rejoiced for all the glorious things that were done by him.

How lovely is it to see JESUS so mercifully engaged on his own day! Oh! what a lesson, beyond a thousand precepts, to his servants who minister in his word and ordinances, to be active on those holy occasions in holding forth their divine Master.

There are numberless beauties in this miracle of our LORD, not one of which ought to be overlooked, but under the HOLY GHOST's teaching brought home to our hearts. And, first; let such as are too easily prevailed upon to stay from ordinances for trifling sicknesses, and frivolous excuses, behold this poor woman, whom eighteen years' infirmity, and when bowed together, unable to lift up herself, could not keep back from the synagogue. Oh! who shall calculate the mass of sin on this one account only, in this CHRIST-despising day of our sinful country! Let any of CHRIST's little ones, of long infirmity, look at this woman and take comfort. She was a daughter of *Abraham*, no doubt spiritually so, and yet how long and deeply exercised! Let them consider this. Next look to JESUS. He called her before she called on him! Yes! it is sweet to trace the openings of grace. There is no warmth, no love in the sinner's heart, till JESUS puts it there. Observe the instant power of JESUS. Oh! how soon, thou dear LORD, canst thou make thy people whole! And, observe the blessed effects in the poor woman's heart. She glorified GOD. This will always be the sure consequence of grace. When the LORD leads us to see our mercies, the same grace leads us to acknowledge them.

But, Reader! mark the contrast, in the ruler of the Synagogue. Was there ever such barefaced impudence, and hypocrisy! To pretend to a reverence for the Sabbath; and yet manifest such bitterness against the LORD of the Sabbath. But how blessed the answer of JESUS! And how blessedly the matter turned to the disgrace of the ruler, and to the triumph and glory of CHRIST. I cannot pass away from the view of this man, and those adversaries of JESUS that were present, without begging the Reader to remark with me, how much the LORD's preaching was directed against this class of people. His threatenings are all against Scribes and Pharisees, hypocrites. Publicans and harlots the LORD encouraged to come to him; but those Pillars of the temple as they considered themselves, the LORD pronounced upon the whole of them the most awful woe. Matt. xxiii. 13, to the end.

But the most beautiful part in the miracle remains to be noticed. This poor woman was a daughter of *Abraham*; but yet Satan had bound her! Yes! she, and every son and daughter of *Abraham*, though they belong to CHRIST, in the union-grace of the Church, being chosen in CHRIST, before the world began; yet are they all involved in the *Adam*-fall of nature, until CHRIST claims his own, and brings them out. Reader! what saith your apprehension of the truth of GOD to this statement? Certainly you cannot but know the bondage of sin and Satan, whether eighteen years, or as many more or less, if one like the SON of Man hath made you free. Bowed together you once was, and unable to lift up yourself, if so be JESUS's power and sovereignty in grace you have felt, I pray you to read that sweet Psalm cxlii. and see the case described; and then let your heart answer to yourself, what you know of it, by soul experience.

18 Then said he, Unto what is the kingdom of God like? and whereunto shall I resemble it?

19 It is like a grain of mustard seed, which a man took and cast into his garden: and it grew, and waxed a great tree; and the fowls of the air lodged in the branches of it.

20 And again he said, Whereunto shall I liken the kingdom of God?

21 It is like leaven, which a woman took and hid in three measures of meal, till the whole was leavened.

Our LORD's figures and similitudes are most beautiful and striking. The *grain of mustard seed,* and the *leaven,* are both to the same purport, to show how the small, and, to human observation, the unperceived entrance of grace into the heart, induceth such wonderful effects! Blessed JESUS! be thou the sweet leaven of my soul; for sure I am the blessed influences of thy Spirit will leaven the whole of my nature!

22 And he went through the cities and villages, teaching, and journeying toward Jerusalem.

23 ¶ Then said one unto him, Lord, are there few that be saved? and he said unto them,

24 Strive to enter in at the strait gate: for many, I say unto you, will seek to enter in, and shall not be able.

25 When once the master of the house is risen up, and hath shut to the door, and ye begin to stand without, and to knock at the door, saying, Lord, Lord, open unto us; and he shall answer and say unto you, I know ye not whence ye are:

26 Then shall ye begin to say, We have eaten and drunk in thy presence, and thou hast taught in our streets.

27 But he shall say, I tell you, I know you not

whence ye are; depart from me all *ye* workers of iniquity.

28 There shall be weeping and gnashing of teeth, when ye shall see Abraham, and Isaac, and Jacob, and all the prophets in the kingdom of God, and you *yourselves* thrust out.

29 And they shall come from the east, and *from* the west, and from the north, and *from* the south, and shall sit down in the kingdom of God.

30 And, behold, there are last which shall be first, and there are first which shall be last.

The whole of this passage will be at once abundantly clear, if we consider the very different characters which the LORD JESUS describes under those striking particulars; and whom he had in view. JESUS is here drawing that line of everlasting discrimination, between those who have indeed all the advantages of Gospel privileges, but who never felt their power; and the true seed of *Abraham, Isaac,* and *Jacob,* who are in the Covenant of Redemption. If the Reader will only attend to the features the LORD hath marked, he will at once discern them. They strive to enter in; but it is in their own strength. They plead the privileges they have had of ordinances; they have eaten and drunk in CHRIST's presence; yea, many had heard CHRIST preaching; and yet there is not one atom of grace in all this. These are all *outward* things, and may be very punctually attended, and yet never bring the heart to GOD. Gentiles who never heard of CHRIST may be brought into a saving acquaintance with CHRIST; while those Jews, who professed their apprehension of JEHOVAH, from being favored with the principles of revelation even in the midst of the blaze of the Gospel, should be so wholly unconscious of its power. So that the *Gentiles,* which were last and afar off, become first; while the Jews, who were first in Gospel privileges, were last, in rejecting the counsel of GOD, against their own souls,

31 The same day, there came certain of the Pharisees, saying unto him, Get thee out, and depart hence; for Herod will kill thee.

32 And he said unto them, Go ye, and tell that fox, Behold, I cast out devils, and I do cures to-day and to-morrow, and the third *day* I shall be perfected.

33 Nevertheless, I must walk to-day, and to-morrow, and the *day* following: for it cannot be that a prophet perish out of Jerusalem.

34 O Jerusalem, Jerusalem, which killest the
prophets, and stonest them that are sent unto thee;
how often would I have gathered thy children together, as a hen *doth gather* her brood under *her*
wings, and ye would not!

35 Behold, your house is left unto you desolate;
and verily I say unto you, Ye shall not see me
until *the time* come when ye shall say, Blessed *is*
he that cometh in the name of the Lord.

I pass over every thing in this passage, as being of a plain and
self-evident nature, to attend to what our LORD hath said, concerning
Jerusalem, the beloved city. JESUS here expressly refers to some
period, antecedent to his tabernacling openly in *Jerusalem*. And I
beg the Reader not to overlook it, neither hastily pass it by. But
when was it that JESUS would have done those frequent acts of mercy
to his beloved *Jerusalem* before the period of his coming openly in our
flesh? Though we cannot follow the question in all its bearings, yet
we must conclude that those frequent manifestations of JEHOVAH in
the Old Testament which we read of, must have been in the Person
of CHRIST. And let the Reader observe further, what love must
there have been in the heart of CHRIST, thus to have watched over
his Church, by the secret workings of his holy Spirit, through so long
a period before his coming. And when the Reader hath duly pondered these things, let him think what the LORD JESUS is carrying on
now, over his people, in the ten thousand times ten thousand instances of his affection, which he sheweth to them, *otherwise than he
doth to the world?* Every ordinance of JESUS, is with this express
view, in order to lead his redeemed into an apprehension of his love
for them, and his grace to them, as evidences of his good will. Are
not all these similar tokens to those of JESUS over *Jerusalem*, when
with the tenderness of an hen over her little brood, she spreads
her wings to shelter them from all danger?

But while we behold the beauty of the Scripture, thus explained
with an eye to JESUS, in his watchful care over his Church, as his
Church and people, let the Reader no less notice how CHRIST is here
describing the ruin of *Jerusalem*, as a *nation* and *people* unconnected
with his Church (except in outward privileges), and to whom were
never extended the real union of interest with the Church in CHRIST
her LORD. *How often* (saith JESUS) *would I have gathered thy children together, and ye would not.* Not gathered them in grace, for the
Pharisees to whom JESUS was then speaking, and concerning whom he
was then speaking, were never children of grace, and consequently
never to be gathered. Neither is JESUS speaking of gathering *to*
CHRIST; but gathering *together*, nationally considered. Had they,
as a nation and people, received CHRIST, instead of crucifying *the*
LORD *of life and glory*, they would have been saved as a *nation*, and
the Romans not have taken away (as they afterwards did) both the
nation and *people*. How totally ignorant must those men be, who

construe our LORD's expressions here concerning *Jerusalem*, into a sense with which it hath no connection; and, instead of considering it as our LORD's lamentation over the *temporal* ruin which was coming upon his countrymen, as a nation, which he foresaw and foretold, take a latitude from it, as if a man might outstay the time of grace, and lose, contrary to GOD's design, his own eternal salvation. It is a *national*, not an *individual* ruin, CHRIST referred to. It is a *temporal*, not an *eternal* business, the LORD is speaking of. It is the *house* that is left to them desolate, not the *soul*. Here is not a word of grace in all this, in reference to a man's making his peace with GOD; but so acting by an *outward* profession as to secure the peace of the *nation*. And when that desolation came upon Jerusalem, then was the LORD's words fulfilled, *When the sinners in Zion were afraid;* and they were constrained to cry out, *Blessed is he that cometh in the name of the* LORD! Isaiah xxxiii. 14.

REFLECTIONS.

READER! let us both, as we contemplate the LORD's visitations on those *Galileans* and men of *Siloam*, gather improvement from what JESUS hath said, and solemnly remember, that without faith and repentance, which are both the gifts of GOD, and arising from the LORD's regenerating the heart, we shall all likewise perish. And, Reader! in the barren fig-tree, growing without fruit within the pale of GOD's vineyard, the Church, let us behold the awful state of all those who have a name to live, but yet are virtually dead before GOD. Oh! the blessedness of being found trees of the LORD's planting, made fat and fruitful by his blessing!

Precious LORD JESUS! do thou graciously come into our synagogues, thy Churches, on thine own day, and every day in thine ordinances! Oh! how many of thine, like this daughter of *Abraham*, are bound in the *Adam*-nature of sin by *Satan*! And wilt thou not, dear LORD! call them all to thee? lay thine Almighty hand upon them, and make them whole? All thy redeemed will glorify thee for all the gracious manifestations of thy love. And do thou, dearest LORD! give thy people to see thy unremitting watchfulness and care over them. All the tenderness and solicitude of the hen cannot describe the boundless love of JESUS, in gathering his little ones to him, and covering them with his wings, while thy faithfulness and truth become their shield and buckler. And oh! thou gracious GOD of our salvation, cause us to note down, in the strongest characters, thy distinguishing grace! While nations and individuals, like *Jerusalem* of old, become Gospel despisers, and perish, and refuse to have thee to reign over them, do thou, LORD! strongly impress the wonderous truth upon the hearts of all thy redeemed, that it is all of grace wherein they differ, and that to thy grace they may cheerfully ascribe all the glory.

CHAP. XIV.

CONTENTS.

The LORD JESUS *dineth with a Pharisee. He healeth a Man of the Dropsy. He puts forth a Parable. Describes his Gospel under the Similitude of a great Supper; and adds a blessed Discourse.*

AND it came to pass, as he went into the house of one of the chief Pharisees to eat bread on the sabbath-day, that they watched him.

2 And, behold, there was a certain man before him which had the dropsy.

3 And Jesus answering, spake unto the lawyers and Pharisees, saying, Is it lawful to heal on the sabbath-day?

4 And they held their peace. And he took *him*, and healed him, and let him go;

5 And answered them, saying, Which of you shall have an ass or an ox fallen into a pit, and will not straightway pull him out on the sabbath-day?

6 And they could not answer him again to these things.

Our LORD, we find, frequently visiting the Pharisees, though from the complexion of that sect, none of them had the least regard to his person or doctrine. Here we find, in the midst of this seeming kindness to JESUS, they watched him; that is, they waited to reproach him. It is not said how this man with the dropsy came to the house of the Pharisee; but it afforded a blessed occasion for the display of the LORD's grace and power, and their resentment. That the cure JESUS wrought made them angry, is evident, from the LORD's answer. We find a similar instance in the preceding chapter, Luke xiii. 15. See also Matt. xii. 9—14.

7 ¶ And he put forth a parable to those which were bidden, when he marked how they chose out the chief rooms; saying unto them,

8 When thou art bidden of any *man* to a wedding, sit not down in the highest room, lest a more honourable man than thou be bidden of him;

9 And he that bade thee and him come and say unto thee, Give this man place; and thou begin with shame to take the lowest room.

10 But when thou art bidden, go and sit down in the lowest room; that when he that bade thee cometh, he may say unto thee, Friend, go up higher: then shalt thou have worship in the presence of them that sit at meat with thee.

11 For whosoever exalteth himself shall be abased; and he that humbleth himself shall be exalted.

Reader! what a lovely quality is grace, which truly makes men great, in making them humble; and induceth the very reverse of nature, which, by the fall, hath made all mankind proud, when, by reason of sin, it ought to have made all humble. In the unequal pattern of the LORD JESUS, we are made to see what true humbleness is. He who was LORD of all, became servant to all; and in the same hour, when he knew that the FATHER had given all things into his hands, actually stooped down, and did wash the feet of poor fishermen. See John xiii. 3 to 5. Reader! do not, if possible, ever lose sight of this. Was there ever an instance of the kind known among the great ones of the earth? And let me ask, was there ever an instance of real greatness like this, of unequalled humility? Did ever the SON of GOD in our nature look more lovely, more blessed, and call forth the affections of his people in a more awakened manner than upon this occasion? Oh! for grace to copy what none can ever equal! Precious JESUS! let me never forget this scene, but gladly take the lowest room in recollection of thee! And, Reader! let such a precept, backed by such an example, have its due weight with both our hearts: and let us be comforted with this assurance, JESUS, who thus stooped *then*, will be gracious *now*. LORD! the lower thou wilt come down to our wants, the higher thou wilt be exalted to our love and praise. See Philip. ii. 5—11.

12 ¶ Then said he also to him that bade him, When thou makest a dinner or a supper, call not thy friends, nor thy brethren, neither thy kinsmen, nor *thy* rich neighbours: lest they also bid thee again, and a recompence be made thee.

13 But when thou makest a feast, call the poor, the maimed, the lame, the blind:

14 And thou shalt be blessed; for they cannot recompense thee; for thou shalt be recompensed at the resurrection of the just.

15 And when one of them that sat at meat with him heard these things, he said unto him, Blessed *is* he that shall eat bread in the kingdom of God.

Our Lord's directions are here specially given to his people. It is true, Jesus addressed the man at whose house he then was; but as the Lord speaks of the resurrection of the just, the justified soul in Christ must be meant by the expression; and therefore it was such the Lord had in view. And with respect to the recompense spoken of, it will be indeed an ample recompense in that great day of God to be noticed by Christ, in having so loved his members, when upon earth, as his members. Who shall calculate the joy? Our Lord hath more particularly explained it, Matt. xxv. 34—40. All other recompense, and which the self-righteous are seeking after, will be an awful retribution. 1 Cor. iv. 7.

16 ¶ Then said he unto him, A certain man made a great supper, and bade many;

17 And sent his servant at supper time to say to them that were bidden, Come; for all things are now ready.

18 And they all with one *consent* began to make excuse. The first said unto him, I have bought a piece of ground, and I must needs go and see it: I pray thee have me excused.

19 And another said, I have bought five yoke of oxen, and I go to prove them: I pray thee have me excused.

20 And another said, I have married a wife, and therefore I cannot come.

21 So that servant came and shewed his lord these things. Then the master of the house, being angry, said to his servant, Go out quickly into the streets and lanes of the city, and bring in hither the poor and the maimed, and the halt, and the blind.

22 And the servant said, Lord, it is done, as thou hast commanded, and yet there is room.

23 And the lord said unto the servant, Go out into the highways and hedges, and compel *them* to come in, that my house may be filled.

24 For I say unto you, That none of those men which were bidden shall taste of my supper.

Our Lord took occasion, from the observation of one that sat at the Pharisee's table with him, to deliver this precious discourse. It is much to the same purport as that sermon delivered, Matt. xxii. 2, &c.

The prophet Isaiah was taught by the HOLY GHOST to represent the Gospel under the figure of a royal feast, Isaiah xxv. 6. The only difference in the representation is, that in one place it is called a *dinner*, and here the LORD calls it a *supper*. Perhaps, the *former* was in allusion to the early manifestations of grace; and the *latter* to intimate the final revelations in the person of CHRIST himself. Heb. i. 1, and ix. 26.

By the certain man, no doubt the LORD JESUS meant GOD the FATHER; for CHRIST is GOD's salvation to the ends of the earth, Isaiah xlix. 6. And by the servant sent to call them that were bidden, must mean CHRIST; for so GOD speaks of him, Isaiah xlii. 1, &c. And in the great work of redemption, for the recovery of his Church from the ruin into which, by her Adam-nature, she was fallen, CHRIST came as JEHOVAH's servant, Philip. ii. 6, 7. This being *bidden* can mean nothing more than the *outward* ministry of GOD's word to the Jewish nation. With them were committed *the covenants, and the giving of the law, and the service of* GOD, *and the promises*. But *all are not Israel which are of Israel*, Rom. ix. 4, 6. For when CHRIST *came to his own;* that is, his own nation, *his own received him not*. John i. 11. So that the special distinguishing grace, which distinguished the people, differed widely from this outward call; that being accompanied with an *inward* work upon the heart, inclining them to come. Psm. cx.

The different excuses form a most apt representation of the several causes, which prevent, according to the view of natural causes, all the unawakened and unregenerated world from coming to CHRIST. The piece of ground, and the yoke of oxen, and the married state, are strikingly expressive of the three great causes John describes: namely, *the lust of the flesh, the lust of the eyes, and the pride of life*. 1 John ii. 16. Under one or other of these all of the unrenewed of mankind may be found. And what an awful state the whole is!

The dismission of the servant to the highways, and lanes, and streets of the city, to call in the poor, and the maimed, and the halt, and the blind, is, in the language of the Gospel, to shew that GOD hath given *the heathen to* CHRIST *for an inheritance, and the uttermost part of the earth for his possession*, Psm. ii. 8. And the characters here described are to be considered *spiritually*. It is the poor in spirit, it is the maimed by sin, it is the halt in the faculties of soul, and the blind, who by nature are strangers to CHRIST, and all whose minds, by the gracious call of GOD, are brought into a sense of their lost and utterly helpless state in themselves, which are here set forth. And what a beautiful view doth the representation afford of the infinite fullness of GOD's provision, that when multitudes are brought, and are feasted with grace and salvation, the LORD sends again to use an holy violence, and to compel every poor, needy, self-condemned, and sensible sinner to come, that CHRIST's house may be filled.

Reader! pause over this delightful view! Behold and observe what the language of grace saith, *Yet there is room*. Yes, there is room as there was *then*, so *now*, in the fullness of covenant settlements formed among the whole persons of the GODHEAD before the world was made. The thousands that were then unborn when JESUS spake this parable, and which have since been born in nature, and new born in grace, have found the blessed truth to their soul's everlasting joy: and still room for the thousands yet to be born until the consummation of all things, equally interested in the covenant of promise. Room in the everlasting love of all the persons in the GODHEAD, chosen by GOD the FATHER, preserved in JESUS CHRIST, and called by the gracious and regenerating mercy of GOD the HOLY GHOST. And as there hath always been, and is, and always will be, room for all whom the FATHER hath given to the SON, both Jew and Gentile, for all the purposes of manifesting grace here; so is there, and everlastingly must be, room in the upper and brighter world of glory hereafter, for all the blessings prepared for the Church of GOD, in that eternal kingdom of GOD and the LAMB.   John xiv. 2, 3.

There is no difficulty of apprehension, concerning those who were first bidden to the feast, but by their contempt of it for ever rejected, if we keep in view that the chief scope from the parable, is to shew the difference of *outward* means to *inward* grace.   The Gospel hath been, and from the very necessity of the case must be, openly published and proclaimed, like the public bell, which causeth to assemble, in the hearing of all.   But herein is the wisdom and equity of GOD manifested.   The enemies of GOD and his CHRIST reject the counsel of GOD against their own souls.   CHRIST is the one ordinance of heaven, and the only one for the recovery of our *Adam*-nature from the ruins of the fall.   If this be slighted and despised, there is no other, Acts iv. 12.   The Scribes and Pharisees fell under this condemnation; and those Scriptures in them were fulfilled.   *Many are called, but few chosen.   Go to this people, and say, Hear ye indeed, but understand not: and see ye indeed, but perceive not.*   Isaiah vi. 9. Matt. xiii. 14, &c.   And thus the sovereignty of JEHOVAH is manifested, and their rejection of his appointed means becomes an everlasting testimony to his justice.

25 ¶ And there went great multitudes with him: and he turned, and said unto them,

26 If any *man* come to me, and hate not his father and mother, and wife, and children, and brethren, and sisters, yea, and his own life also, he cannot be my disciple.

As my view of this Scripture, in those two verses, differs altogether from every Commentator which I have read upon it, I beg the Reader's indulgence to be somewhat more particular in his attention to my remarks.   I shall very freely state the sense which I have of the passage; and if I err, I pray the LORD to forgive the unintentional error, and guard the Reader from adopting it.

It is plain, from the occasion in which JESUS delivered himself on this subject of hatred to our nearest relations, in the bonds of nature, that he meant to inculcate the higher claims of grace; and, as great multitudes were then following him, the LORD gave them to understand, that the life of a real disciple of his, was attended with greater sacrifices than they at first might suppose.   But few have considered the term of *hatred* to mean any thing more, than, in a comparative way, and similar to that passage in *Matthew*, not to love any person or thing *more* than Christ, or *equal* with Christ. Matt. x. 37. But *first* I would observe, that the word in the original, which in our Testament is translated *hate*, will admit of no softer expression. It is one of the plainest words in the Greek language, as every one conversant with the original cannot but allow. And *secondly*, it should be further observed, that the doctrine is not the language of the New Testament only, but of the Old. *Israel* was enjoined to have no pity upon the friend, which was as a man's own soul, if that friend enticed him to leave the Lord: *Thine hand* (saith the law) *shall be first upon him, to put him to death, and then the hand of all the people.* See Deut. i. 13, throughout. And the hatred which the Lord Jesus is here speaking of, is wholly commanded upon this principle: namely, that any of those tender affinities of *nature* rise up to the injury of the more important claims of *grace*. And they must be indeed really and truly objects of hatred to the soul, if they have a tendency, or make use of their influence to thwart the soul in pursuits of the divine life.

And what, in my view, tends most clearly to prove this, and to throw a light upon the whole doctrine, is the concluding sentence in the passage, in which Jesus, having declared the necessity of hating the nearest ties in nature, if opposing the pursuits of grace, hath added, *Yea, and his own life also.* Here the point, according to my apprehension, is at once shown. For if a man is to hate his own life, namely, his corrupt, unregenerate, unrenewed part, because he feels daily an opposition in this body of sin and death, to the holy desires of the renewed soul, nothing can be more plain than that Jesus meant exactly what the words express: and in following Christ in the regeneration, there will be daily cause of hatred arising in the soul, to the remains of indwelling and corrupt affections, which oppose the soul, and too often bring the soul into leanness, and distress, and sorrow.

And I would ask every real believer, every truly regenerated soul of the Lord's people, whether, on this very account, he doth not groan daily, being burthened? Let him determine the question with his own conscience! let him study the subject, as it relates to holy men of old gone before. What were the woes of *Isaiah*, the self-reproaches of *Job*, of *David*, of *Paul*, but on this account? See Isaiah vi. 5. Job xlii. 6. Psm. li. 2, 3. Romans vii. 23, 24. Men who have taken up, with a flimsy view of godliness, and not learnt, from divine teaching, the plague of their own heart, may, in the pride of their heart, be content with a Pharisaical righteousness, and *talk* of what they never truly *enjoyed* in themselves, a progressive holiness; but he who is learning in the school of God the Holy Ghost, to be more and more in love with Jesus, will learn from the same lesson, practically, to be more and more out of love with himself, and while he hates the world, and sin, and Satan, he will hate his own life also from the same cause; namely, the opposition he meets with from that quarter; and as *Job* expresses it, will *abhor himself, and repent in dust and ashes.*

And, Reader! suffer me to add, (however largely I have already trespassed,) is it not this self-hatred, by reason of a body of sin and death, which makes, in part, a cause for the true believer to be reconciled to the prospect of death? Yea, doth not Jesus sweetly and graciously over-rule even this malady of nature to the higher prospects of grace, and cause his faithful ones to feel as *Paul* did, and rejoice in the hope as he rejoiced, in the desire to *depart, and to be with* Christ, *which is far better?* Philip. i. 23. But I proceed no further. I am free to confess that the language of our Lord, in this memorable passage, strikes me in the sense in which I have represented it. Here, therefore, I leave it with the Lord, and to the Reader's reflection, under the divine teaching.

27 And whosoever doth not bear his cross, and come after me, cannot be my disciple.

28 For which of you, intending to build a tower, sitteth not down first, and counteth the cost, whether he have *sufficient* to finish *it?*

29 Lest haply, after he hath laid the foundation, and is not able to finish *it*, all that behold *it* begin to mock him,

30 Saying, This man began to build, and was not able to finish.

31 Or what king, going to make war against another king, sitteth not down first, and consulteth whether he be able with ten thousand to meet him that cometh against him with twenty thousand?

32 Or else, while the other is yet a great way off, he sendeth an ambassage, and desireth conditions of peace.

33 So likewise, whosoever he be of you that forsaketh not all that he hath, he cannot be my disciple.

34 Salt *is* good : but if the salt have lost his savour, wherewith shall it be seasoned?

35 It is neither fit for the land, nor yet for the dunghill ; *but* men cast it out. He that hath ears to hear, let him hear.

All these are so many beautiful illustrations of one and the same thing ; namely, of the wisdom and safety of counting the cost, in every undertaking, before we enter upon any. The builder and the warrior are strong figures to explain : and what builder, like the Christian, who is building for eternity? What warrior like him that contends for everlasting life? And unless the LORD JESUS CHRIST be the Founder of the one, and the General of the other, what success can follow? And in application to what went before, they both are beautiful. See on ver. 34. Mark ix. 49, 50.

REFLECTIONS.

READER! let us not turn away too hastily from this beautiful chapter, and those soul-teaching, and soul-refreshing discourses of CHRIST. While the *Pharisees* watched JESUS, to find somewhat offensive, as according to their corrupt hearts they would have made it, let you and I listen to his heavenly doctrine, and behold, with delight and joy, his mercies to the body in healing the man with the dropsy, while mingling sweet words for consolation to the soul. and oh! for grace in contemplating CHRIST thus discoursing at the *Pharisee's* table! to be earnest to discourse of JESUS at our own! What can be more suited, more grateful, more blessed than, while partaking of the LORD's bounties, to speak of the LORD's love? and while sitting with our family at *our* supper, to mingle with our food gracious conversation of the LORD's?

Reader! do not overlook the very wonderful condescension of JESUS in the various methods the LORD was pleased to adopt in setting forth the plentiful provisions of his Gospel. What a feast indeed of fat things it is! What bowels of mercy and grace in the Great Provider! And what company are the guests invited? such as the great ones of the earth would not look at, much less consort with. Oh! how utterly lost, how utterly inexcusable must those be who refuse such great salvation! Hasten, my soul! hasten, Reader! for it is the poor and the maimed, the most sensibly wretched and miserable, that are most welcome.

And doth my LORD say that his followers must be self-haters, must bear a cross, must hate all which would stop the way? Oh! for grace to be of that happy number! LORD! help me to pluck out an eye, cut off an arm, leave all for JESUS and his great salvation, so that I may be found the true disciple of the LORD! Amen.

CHAP. XV.

CONTENTS.

The LORD is here teaching by Parables. Here are three contained in this Chapter; namely, the Lost Sheep, the Lost Piece of Money, and the Prodigal Son.

THEN drew near unto him all the publicans and sinners for to hear him.

2 And the Pharisees and scribes murmured, saying, This man receiveth sinners, and eateth with them.

The imagination can hardly form to itself a more striking portrait than what those verses represent. Figure to yourself, Reader, a company of poor, despised outcasts of society, in a body, of publicans and sinners, drawing nigh, with looks of hope and desire to CHRIST, as if to say, Can there be mercy for us? And on the other side of the representation, look at the proud, disdainful, self-righteous Pharisees and Scribes withdrawing from the LORD, with countenances of the most sovereign contempt, as if JESUS and his company should pollute their holiness. *This man* (say they) *receiveth sinners, and eateth with them.* Precious JESUS! Well is it for me that thou dost; for what must have become of me had this not been the case? How truly lovely doth the SON of GOD appear by such marvellous condescension! And what can more endear CHRIST to his people?

3 And he spake this parable unto them, saying,

4 What man of you, having an hundred sheep, if he lose one of them, doth not leave the ninety and nine in the wilderness, and go after that which is lost, until he find it?

5 And when he hath found *it,* he layeth *it* on his shoulders rejoicing.

6 And when he cometh home, he calleth together *his* friends and neighbours, saying unto them, Rejoice with me: for I have found my sheep which was lost.

7 I say unto you, That likewise joy shall be in heaven over one sinner that repenteth, more than over ninety and nine just persons which need no repentance.

The grace of heaven, in the reception of sinners, is proclaimed in every part of the Bible. Here it is eminently illustrated by our LORD himself, under the similitude of the most beautiful parables. I would not, methinks, strain Scripture into the most distant idea of any thing fanciful; neither suppose what was never intended; but I cannot help observing, that, according to my views, the LORD JESUS intended, by the *three* striking parables in this chapter, more immediately to set forth and represent the office work and character of each glorious person of the GODHEAD, as they have manifested their love, and grace, and mercy, to our fallen nature. It is a well-known and fully-allowed truth, in the doctrine of the pure *faith, once delivered to the saints,* that our salvation is the joint work, resulting from the joint love and mercy of the whole persons of the GODHEAD; each glorious person concurring, co-operating in the work. It is a blessed subject to trace the subject in all: and here, if I mistake not, the LORD JESUS, by a beautiful parable, sets it forth.

The first parable in the chapter is contained in the verses just read, in which Christ himself is represented in his well-known character and office-work of a *shepherd*. The Lord represents his Church as one sheep of an hundred : and the Church, in point of bulk, compared to the whole creation of God, is but as one world to many. Hence called a *little* flock, Luke xii. 32. Sometimes called a *beautiful* flock, Jerem. xiii. 20. The flock of *slaughter,* Zech. xi. 4—7. Jesus himself calls it *one* flock, and of which there is but *one* shepherd, John x. 16. Song vi. 9. And the Lord Jesus hath a variety of names, all descriptive of him, as the Shepherd of his people. Jehovah's Shepherd, Zech. xiii. 7. *One* Shepherd, Ezek. xxxiv. 23. The *good* Shepherd, John x. 11. The *great* Shepherd, Heb. xiii. 20. The *chief* Shepherd, 1 Pet. v. 4. And as in this chapter, so in others, and particularly in the writings of *Ezekiel*, a whole chapter is made use of in describing the Lord seeking out his sheep, and bringing them home from wandering, when scattered upon the mountains, and upon the face of the earth, Ezek. xxxiv.

The joy of the shepherd, when taking home his lost sheep, affords a most delightful representation of Jesus, in manifesting that his happiness is blended with that of his redeemed ; and that he cannot enlarge his grace and mercy to any of his wanderers in bringing them home, without glorifying himself in their salvation. And the joy of his neighbours and friends, probably meaning angels and the inhabitants of heaven, is also a beautiful testimony how much the whole pure creation of God take part in the Redeemer's triumphs. And as it is said, that at creation, *the morning stars sung together, and all the sons of* God *shouted for joy :* so at redemption, the multitude before the throne are represented as *singing their hallelujahs to* God *and the Lamb.* Job. xxxviii. 7. Rev. vii. 9, 10, &c.

8 ¶ Either what woman, having ten pieces of silver, if she lose one piece, doth not light a candle, and sweep the house, and seek diligently till she find *it ?*

9 And when she hath found *it*, she calleth *her* friends and *her* neighbours together, saying, Rejoice with me: for I have found the piece which I had lost.

10 Likewise I say unto you, There is joy in the presence of the angels of God over one sinner that repenteth.

Here, if I do not err, is represented, under the similitude of a lost piece of money, our lost estate by nature. And, without torturing the figure, may be not unaptly supposed, by the lighting of a candle, and sweeping the house until it be found, is represented the blessed office of God the Holy Ghost, in enlightening, regenerating, and renewing grace. Our whole nature, when first formed in the image of God, had the pure impression. But in the Adam-apostacy, like a lost piece of money, the image was marred. It is the work of God

the SPIRIT to restore : and this is effectually done, when, by illuminating grace, *he commandeth the light to shine in the heart to give
the light of the knowledge of the glory of* GOD *in the face of* JESUS
CHRIST. 2 Cor. iv. 6. And the same blessed effects are said to follow
upon this occasion of recovery, as in the former. Holy joy breaks
forth afresh in the streets of the new Jerusalem, with more rapture,
on every instance of a sinner raised from the *Adam*-fall to the image of
GOD in CHRIST, than over the unchanging state of the elect angels, who
never fell, and therefore needed no repentance.

11 And he said, A certain man had two sons :

12 And the younger of them said to *his* father,
Father, give me the portion of goods that falleth
to me. And he divided unto them *his* living.

13 And not many days after, the younger son
gathered all together, and took his journey into a
far country, and there wasted his substance with
riotous living.

14 And when he had spent all, there arose a
mighty famine in that land : and he began to be
in want.

15 And he went and joined himself to a citizen
of that country ; and he sent him into his fields to
feed swine.

16 And he would fain have filled his belly with
the husks that the swine did eat : and no man gave
unto him.

17 And when he came to himself, he said, How
many hired servants of my father's have bread
enough and to spare, and I perish with hunger!

18 I will arise and go to my father, and will
say unto him, Father, I have sinned against
heaven, and before thee,

19 And am no more worthy to be called thy
son: make me as one of thy hired servants.

20 And he arose and came to his father. But
when he was yet a great way off, his father saw
him, and had compassion, and ran, and fell on his
neck, and kissed him.

21 And the son said unto him, Father, I have

sinned against heaven, and in thy sight, and am no more worthy to be called thy son.

22 But the father said to his servants, Bring forth the best robe, and put *it* on him; and put a ring on his hand, and shoes on *his* feet;

23 And bring hither the fatted calf, and kill *it;* and let us eat and be merry:

24 For this my son was dead, and is alive again; he was lost, and his found. And they began to be merry.

25 Now his elder son was in the field: and as he came and drew nigh to the house, he heard musick and dancing.

26 And he called one of the servants, and asked what these things meant?

27 And he said unto him, Thy brother is come: and thy father hath killed the fatted calf, because he hath received him safe and sound.

28 And he was angry, and would not go in: therefore came his father out and intreated him.

29 And he answering said to *his* father, Lo, these many years do I serve thee, neither transgressed I at any time thy commandment; and yet thou never gavest me a kid that I might make merry with my friends:

30 But as soon as this thy son was come, which hath devoured thy living with harlots, thou hast killed for him the fatted calf.

31 And he said unto him, Son, thou art ever with me, and all that I have is thine.

32 It was meet that we should make merry and be glad: for this thy brother was dead, and is alive again; and was lost, and is found.

In this parable we have the same blessed doctrine read to us, by way of magnifying the riches of grace, as in the two former. And if those before may be supposed, without violence to the subject, to represent the office character of CHRIST and the HOLY GHOST, we may, with equal safety, conjecture that here is particularly represented the clemency and grace of GOD the FATHER, who is the FATHER of mercies, and the GOD of all comfort.

The certain man here spoken of, can mean no other than GOD the FATHER; for although, properly speaking, it was neither the person of the FATHER, nor the person of the HOLY GHOST, which took the nature of manhood, yet it should be considered, that this is but a parable, and therefore, to answer the purposes of the similitude intended from it, the LORD JESUS so represents GOD the FATHER.

The two sons are very generally supposed to be meant, by CHRIST, as the two branches of the Church, the elder as the *Jew,* and the younger as the *Gentile.* I cannot conceive that this was our LORD's design; indeed it is not correct. The Jew is not elder, for, strictly and properly speaking, both Jew and Gentile form but one Church; and this Church was given to CHRIST, and the Church chosen in CHRIST before the foundation of the world. See Psm. ii. Ephes. i. 4. Prov. viii. 22 to the end. Isa. xlix. 6. Ephes. iii. 5 to 11. I rather think, that by the two sons, one always living in the house, and the other departing, are meant the elder living in the constant use of ordinances, without any saving effect; and the younger living without ordinances, and *without hope, and without* GOD *in the world,* till brought home, and made nigh, *by the blood of* CHRIST. Ephes. ii. 12, 13.

I must not allow myself to swell the pages of my *Poor Man's Commentary* with enlarging, by many observations, on this most beautiful and highly-finished parable; but otherwise, here is enough to call up the most awakened feelings of the mind. Indeed, they are already called up, as the several parts of the parable arise to our view in our LORD's own precious words. I shall only beg to point out what our LORD might be supposed to mean in some of the terms and characters made use of, by way of illustrating the LORD's great design. The younger son, in the ruined state of our *Adam-* nature, when brought to penury, and joining himself to a citizen of that country, is finely described. Ruined sinners, unawakened by grace, will join themselves to any thing and every thing, rather than return to GOD. There never was, there never can be, in any son or daughter of *Adam,* the least disposition to seek GOD, before that GOD first seeks us. The wandering strayed sheep will wander and stray for ever, if not brought home. So true is the Apostle's words: *If we love him, it is because he first loved us.*

By this citizen, I understand a man of this world; *not a citizen of the saints and of the household of* GOD. Ephes. ii. 19. The text saith, a citizen of *that country;* that is, this country, this world, a man of the world, under whatever character he be considered; whether a professor, a minister, of the *letter,* and not of the *spirit.* A poor miserable sinner, like this prodigal, when all his substance is spent, and he finds himself in want, will join himself to any person or congregation, with a view to ease his misery; for in this unawakened state he yet knows not the LORD. And as this citizen sent him into the field to feed the swine, and he would fain have filled his belly with the husks, which the swine did eat, and no man gave to him, so the sinner is sent by such into the field of his labors to feed as swine feed on husks, that is, the shell and carcase of religion, outside things, an attempted reform of life and manners, which never did nor never can bring real comfort to the soul. And though the poor wretch would fain have satisfied himself with these things, yet he could not. And no man gave them to him. No services, no ministry of this kind, can satisfy a soul whom the LORD, by sharp soul afflictions, is preparing for himself. Reader! I beseech you pause a moment over this view of the subject. Whether I have or have not fully explained it, yet depend upon it, this part of the parable is not the least beautiful and striking, if considered in this light. And who shall calculate the number of precious souls, that from day to day continue under their bondage frames, while joining themselves to such citizens of this country, and who can send them no where for soul satifaction but into the fields of their ignorance, that they may feed with the swine on the mere husks of Pharisaical righteousness?

And when he came to himself; that is, when grace first entered his soul; for all before this, he had been but in the phrenzy of a ruined state, and unconscious both of his cause of misery and the means of cure. Like *Ephraim,* grey hairs were upon him, but he knew it not. The spots of death were covering him, and he ignorant of any disease.

I detain the Reader at this part of the parable just to remark, that the first awakening of a sinner, like this prodigal, *dead in trespasses and sins,* is, as far as it concerns the personal mercy vouchsafed the sinner, to his own apprehension, one of the greatest, if not the very greatest act ever to be shewn a child of GOD to all eternity. For all the after-stages of grace is but a progressive going on, from grace to glory, and in heaven itself, from one degree of glory to another. But until this quickening of the soul by GOD the HOLY GHOST is done, there is no real spiritual life formed in the soul. And notwithstanding that soul is given of GOD the FATHER to the SON, before all worlds, and GOD the SON hath betrothed the person of this gift of the FATHER to himself, from everlasting, yet until GOD the SPIRIT hath graciously wrought his sovereign work also, and brought forth the soul into actual life of union with CHRIST, there is no possibility of any one act of spiritual life, or of spiritual enjoyment in the soul. So that this great, this vast, this momentous work of regeneration, is, to the personal joy of the poor sinner, the greatest work ever to be received in time or to all eternity. For it is lifting the sinner over the gulph, which, without passing, would separate for ever. It is passing from death to life; from nothing to every thing; from the service and kingdom of Satan to the glorious liberty of the sons of GOD. Reader! what saith your personal experience to these things? Hath such an act of sovereign grace passed upon you? Are you born again?

I must not enlarge on the several features of the parable in what remains to be noticed. Our LORD's own words need no explanation. The son's return, the father's reception of him, the joy of his house and family upon the occasion, are all very blessedly shewn. And the clothing him with the robe of salvation, putting on the ring of marriage, and the feet shod with the preparation of the Gospel of peace; all these, in illusion to the mercies of redemption, are too plain to need enlargement. See another beautiful representation of the same grace and mercy, Jeremiah xxxi. 18, &c. But if I may trespass one moment longer, it shall be to observe, what, perhaps, at first view, may not be so immediately plain to every Reader; I mean concerning the unjust and unreasonable anger of the elder brother. And this view of the character, according to our LORD's description of him if there were no other, would form a sufficient discovery to know who CHRIST meant. For surely one should think none but the devil himself could envy the mercy and grace shewn to a poor sinner. And yet we find the *Scribes* and *Pharisees* were indignant beyond measure at our LORD's favourable reception of poor sinners. *This man* (said they) *receiveth sinners, and eateth with them.* And who is it now that takes most offence at the free and full preaching of the Gospel ? Not the world at large; for the pleasurable part of the world, the busy part of the world, the high in rank of the world, all these are, for the most part, like *Gallio, they care not for such things.* But it is the self-righteous *Pharisee,* like the elder brother in the parable, who wishes to be no further obliged to CHRIST than according to his view is barely necessary. This is the character which takes most offence at the preaching of a free and full Gospel ; and, like the brother whom the LORD JESUS describes, takes the confidence to say, *Lo, these many years do I serve thee, neither at any time transgressed I thy command.* Of all the awful deceptions of the human mind, this, perhaps, is the greatest ; and it is worthy the most serious consideration, that against such CHRIST expresseth himself most angry. Matt. xxiii. throughout.

I must detain the Reader yet further to explain my view of the father's answer to the elder son, when he said to him, *Son ! thou art ever with me, and all that I have is thine.* What can be supposed is meant by this ? I apprehend, nothing more than the portion of worldly goods which came to him by lot, as it is said before, that when the younger son went away, he divided unto them his living. Hence, all that he had of this world's portion, like another *Esau,* was his, the fatness of the earth, and his dwelling therein ; for these things he chiefly desired. Gen. xxvii. 39. Here is not a word said of spiritual things, no gracious manifestations, no awakenings from sin, and conversions of the heart to GOD, through the Spirit; but simple outward privileges and sensual gratifications. The father calls him son. Yes; so he was in *nature,* but not by *adoption* and *grace.* See Luke xvi. 25. Oh! the felicity of one like the younger brother, brought home by a saving conversion of the heart to GOD. In all such cases, it is indeed very might, right, and our bounden duty, that the whole redeemed creation of GOD should make merry and be glad, when thus a brother, *who was dead, is alive again, who was lost, and is found.*

REFLECTIONS.

READER ! let us not hastily pass away from the review of this most blessed chapter, but ponder over again and again the sweet and gracious contents. And as from divine teaching in the Scriptures of eternal truth, we discover that the whole three persons in the GOD-HEAD have mercifully concurred in the salvation of the Church, let us delight upon any and every occasion, to behold an illustration of their joint grace and favor, whenever the word sets forth their office-work, as manifested to the souls of the LORD's people.

Precious LORD JESUS! do we not behold thee in that lovely and endearing representation thou hast here drawn of the tender and affectionate shepherd? Surely the fold, the Church, is thine, both by the FATHER's gift, thine own purchase, and the conquest of thine HOLY SPIRIT. And when one of thy little ones wander from thee, wilt thou not seek it on the mountains, until thou shalt find it? and when thou hast found it, wilt thou not bring it home, as here described, on thy shoulders, rejoicing? Is it not JESUS's joy, as well as the happiness of his redeemed, when this is done? Blessed be my LORD, my Shepherd, who, when in the *Adam*-nature of my fallen state, I had wandered on the dark mountains, JESUS sought me out, and found me; and hath not only brought me home, but now watches over me for good, and feeds me, and sustains me, and causeth me to lie down in green pastures.

And no less, thou HOLY and eternal SPIRIT, GOD the HOLY GHOST, do I pray for grace from thee, to look up to thee, and bless thy Almighty Name, that when, like a piece of lost money, I was fallen in the nature of sin, thou didst, by thy sweeping judgments and enlightening grace, find me, and restore me to the image of GOD in CHRIST. *Spirit of Truth! do thou lead me into all truth!*

And oh! thou FATHER *of mercies, and* GOD *of all comfort!* receive me, LORD, as the father in the parable did his returning prodigal. *I have gone astray like a sheep that is lost.* But thou, in thy rich mercy, hast received me; and by thy grace in me, caused me to return. Thy bowels of love yearned over me in my lost estate, *for thy mercy endureth for ever.* And now, LORD! through thy grace, I shall go out no more. Thou hast killed for me indeed the fatted calf, and clothed me with the robe of CHRIST's righteousness. Oh! for grace to live to thy glory, daily crying out with the Apostle, *Now thanks be unto* GOD *for his unspeakable gift!*

CHAP. XVI.

CONTENTS.

We have in this Chapter our LORD's *account of an unjust Steward; and* CHRIST's *Observation upon the History. The Relation, also, of the Rich Man and* Lazarus.

AND he said also unto his disciples, There was a certain rich man which had a steward; and the same was accused unto him, that he had wasted his goods.

2 And he called him, and said unto him, How is it that I hear this of thee? give an account of thy stewardship: for thou mayest be no longer steward.

3 Then the steward said within himself, What

shall I do? for my lord taketh away from me the stewardship: I cannot dig, to beg I am ashamed.

4 I am· resolved what to do, that, when I am put out of the stewardship, they may receive me into their houses.

5 So he called every one of his lord's debtors *unto him,* and said unto the first, How much owest thou unto my lord?

6 And he said, An hundred measures of oil. And he said unto him, Take thy bill, and sit down quickly, and write fifty.

7 Then said he to another, And how much owest thou? and he said, An hundred measures of wheat. And he said unto him, Take thy bill, and write fourscore.

8 And the lord commended the unjust steward, because he had done wisely: for the children of this world are in their generation wiser than the children of light.

9 And I say unto you, Make to yourselves friends of the mammon of unrighteousness; that, when ye fail, they may receive you into everlasting habitations.

10 He that is faithful in that which *is* least, is faithful also in much: and he that is unjust in the least, is unjust also in much.

11 If therefore ye have not been faithful in the unrighteous mammon, who will commit to your trust the true *riches?*

12 And if ye have not been faithful in that which is another man's, who shall give you that which is your own?

13 No servant can serve two masters: for either he will hate the one, and love the other; or else he will hold to the one, and despise the other; ye cannot serve God and mammon.

I differ from all writers who class this account here given, of an unjust steward, among the *parables* of Christ. To me, I confess, it

differs altogether from the plan and design of all our LORD's parables, and cannot, I think, be explained upon any principles whatever in relation to GOD, as the certain rich man here spoken of, or
any of the LORD's stewards. I am led to conclude, that it is a real
history, which JESUS knew, and from which the LORD took occasion
to raise instructions of profit to his people.

The certain rich man, cannot mean GOD, for though he, and he
only is rich; and all mankind are, in a certain sense his stewards;
yet his servants, who are the stewards of the mysteries, are anointed
with the HOLY GHOST, and as such, are faithful. 1 Cor. iv. 1, 2. And
although it may be said that *Judas* is an exception, yet none of the
characters given in the history of this unjust steward, answer to him.
But it is highly probable, that both the rich man and this unjust
steward, were men of this world; for the *servant*, acting with the
worldly policy he did, and the *master* commending that policy, very
strongly prove that they were both under the sole influence of
worldly motives; but CHRIST's stewards are not of this world. John
xvii. 16.

The mistake in supposing that GOD is the rich man intended to
be set forth, perhaps arose from the general scope of our LORD's parables
on this ground; and also from supposing, that when JESUS said the
Lord commended the unjust steward, he meant GOD the FATHER, or
himself the LORD JESUS CHRIST. But not to observe how impossible
this could be, from causes too plain to insist upon, if the Reader will
read the whole attentively, he will find that it is the steward's Lord
which commended him for his worldly wisdom, in providing an home
to go to, when he was turned out of his, and not the LORD JESUS.
What shall I do? (said the steward,) for *my Lord* taketh away from
me the stewardship. It is the same Lord which is said to commend
him, and that for his policy.

And that this is the case, is still farther evident from our LORD's
words which follow, where JESUS speaks to his disciples by way of
making improvement from this history. He speaks in the *first* person when speaking of himself; but when speaking of the Lord of this
steward, he speaks of him in the *third* person. I say unto you (saith
CHRIST) make to yourself friends of the mammon of unrighteousness, &c. Whereas, when JESUS summed up the close of this man's
history, he said of him: And the Lord (that is the Lord of this unworthy servant) commended the unjust steward because he had done
wisely. And here ends the relation of the history; for the next
words are CHRIST's first observation upon it: *For the children of this
world are, in their generation, wiser than the children of light.* A
strong, but melancholy truth: and the children of light, to their
sorrow, but too fully know it; for while men of the world are up
and alive to every worldly artifice and contrivance, like this unjust
steward, the children of GOD are cold, and lifeless, and barren in
their grand concerns. And the reason is plain. Instead of walking
by faith, we are too much engaged by sight. We are more flesh
than spirit; have more of nature than grace. LORD, *increase our
faith!*

But the most difficult part of this subject remains yet to be considered; for when our LORD adds, *And I say unto you, make to yourselves friends of the mammon of unrighteousness, that when ye fail they*

may receive you into everlasting habitations. Certainly it requires
much wisdom from the Lord, and much attention to Christ's expressions, to have a clear apprehension of his meaning. Some have
supposed our Lord recommends, that by being generous to the poor,
in the wise use of riches, which is the *mammon* of this world, that
we should make to ourselves friends from those acts of mercy. But
this would be like the Pharisees indeed, to seek God's favor by good
deeds, and to bolster up the mind with pride, instead of lowering the
soul in humility. Christ never preached a doctrine of this kind,
but the reverse. Neither are the friends which Jesus exhorts his
disciples to make, the poor whom they relieved by their bounty;
for their good wishes go but a little way towards the soul's salvation;
and they have no habitations, much less *everlasting* habitations, to
receive their benefactors into, when they need them. I am free to
confess, that no small difficulty lies in our way to enter into the full
sense of our Lord's meaning; while I venture to believe, that the
friends the Lord Jesus recommends his disciples to make, in order
that they may be received, when they themselves fail, into everlasting habitations, cannot possibly mean that their wise use of riches
will procure them. But amidst all the difficulty in explaining this
passage, I conceive some light may be thrown upon it, from considering the drift of our Lord in the whole discourse.

It should be considered, that our Lord had been shewing how an
unjust man, by worldly policy, contrived to get some men like himself to take him into their houses, when his Lord turned him out of
his. Now (saith Jesus) as this man made himself friends of a worldly
nature, do you seek to make to yourselves friends in grace. And as
none but God can provide you with a perfect security of this kind,
seek the Lord's friendship, detached *from* (for so the word may be
rendered), that is, while you are in the midst of *the mammon of unrighteousness;* and from the body of sin and death you carry about
with you, and from the remains of indwelling sin which is in you,
and in all the world around you, that when ye fail, as that all things
out of Christ must shortly fail, they may receive you; that is, God,
in covenant in Christ, may receive you into everlasting habitations. If this sense be admitted, the doctrine is agreeable to the whole
tenor of the Gospel. And then, from the same kind of reasoning,
the proverbial expressions which follow in the succeeding verses,
may be explained on the same principles.

14 ¶ And the Pharisees also, who were co-
vetous, heard all these things, and they derided
him.

15 And he said unto them, Ye are they which
justify yourselves before men; but God knoweth
your hearts; for that which is highly esteemed
among men, is abomination in the sight of God.

It was very natural to expect the hatred of the Pharisees would
be called forth from our Lord's discourse. Pulling down to the ground
the haughty pretensions of such men to divine favor, could not but

excite their bitterest displeasure. And, Reader! what is it now? Let a real child of God venture to call in question the apparent zeal of the present day, and whisper only his doubts in the same words as JESUS hath here used: that what is *highly esteemed among men, is abomination in the sight of* God, and it will be well if he escapes as JESUS then did, with the derision only and scorn of the self-righteous *Pharisee.*

16 The law and the prophets *were* until John: since that time the kingdom of God is preached, and every man presseth into it.

17 And it is easier for heaven and earth to pass away, than one tittle of the law to fail.

18 Whosoever putteth away his wife, and marrieth another, committeth adultery: and whosoever marrieth her that is put away from *her* husband, committeth adultery.

The last of those verses hath been very fully considered in the subject, Mark x. 1, &c. And the first of them in the doctrine, hath been also somewhat noticed, Matt. xi. 12. But on this subject I would take occasion in this place to add, that the pressing into the kingdom of God could never be meant by our LORD as intimating an *holy pressure.* That multitudes flocked to hear *John* preach, and so they did to hear CHRIST, is true; but this, for the most part, was mere curiosity, and, as JESUS told them, for *the loaves and fishes.* John vi. 26. The kingdom of heaven *suffering violence,* means more, a persecution from the world than from the haste which mere sermon followers run to hear them, or from the earnest petitions of truly-awakened souls, who seek acceptance in CHRIST. And our LORD evidently in this place, as well as in the parallel one of *Matthew,* meant to say, that while his sheep knew his voice, and followed him, and he gave to them eternal life, the great mass of the CHRIST-despising age he was going in and out among, only pressed upon him to hear, but not to regard. See Matt. xi. 16—26, and note.

19 ¶ There was a certain rich man, which was clothed in purple and fine linen, and fared sumptuously every day:

20 And there was a certain beggar, named Lazarus, which was laid at his gate full of sores,

21 And desiring to be fed with the crumbs which fell from the rich man's table; moreover the dogs came and licked his sores.

22 And it came to pass, that the beggar died, and was carried by the angels into Abraham's

bosom. The rich man also died, and was buried:

23 And in hell he lifted up his eyes, being in torments, and seeth Abraham afar off, and Lazarus in his bosom:

24 And he cried, and said, Father Abraham, have mercy on me, and send Lazarus that he may dip the tip of his finger in water, and cool my tongue: for I am tormented in this flame.

25 But Abraham said, Son, remember that thou in thy life-time, receivedst thy good things; and likewise Lazarus evil things: but now he is comforted, and thou art tormented.

26 And beside all this, between us and you there is a great gulf fixed; so that they which would pass from hence to you, cannot: neither can they pass to us that *would come* from thence.

27 Then he said, I pray thee therefore, father, that thou wouldest send him to my father's house:

28 For I have five brethren: that he may testify unto them, lest they also come into this place of torment.

29 Abraham saith unto him, They have Moses and the prophets; let them hear them.

30 And he said, Nay, father Abraham: but if one went unto them from the dead, they will repent.

31 And he said unto him, If they hear not Moses and the prophets, neither will they be persuaded though one arose from the dead.

We have here a most interesting relation, given by our LORD under the similitude of a parable, in a wonderful contrast between a rich man clothed in *Tyrian* purple, and a poor man as miserably wretched in respect to this world's good, as the possibility of the human state could admit. Yet, notwithstanding these outward circumstances, the poor man is shewn to have been a child of GOD, and an heir of the kingdom, while the rich man was found to have been a child of the devil, and an heir of hell. The circumstances of both are drawn by CHRIST in the most striking and finished manner; and the improvements the LORD intended from the representation to the Church, are too plain to need a comment.

Every thing in the picture of the poor man but one feature corresponds to CHRIST himself; and were it not for that one striking particularity, we might be led to conclude that the LORD JESUS is the Lazarus of the parable. But that one wholly precludes such an application; for though the LORD JESUS was poor indeed, yet not a beggar: for had he been so, be could not have answered the law; which suffered no beggar in Israel. But in every other sense, the humbled and debased state of CHRIST was in correspondence to Lazarus., *He was wounded for our transgressions, and bruised for our iniquities.* His death, his ascension to glory, and the rejection of his name and Messiahship, brought on the awful judgments which followed. But on these points we need not enlarge in this parable.

The awful close to the rich man's luxury, and the cries uttered by him in hell, are strongly marked. And the total impossibility of any recovery from thence, is not only read here, but through all the word of GOD. There can be no change without grace in the heart; and where there is no grace, there is no salvation. See an equally awful account, Psm. xlix. 6—14.

REFLECTIONS.

READER! in beholding the character of this unjust steward, let us learn to seek from GOD grace, that we may be found faithful. And let us, in putting the question to our own hearts, which he put to every one of his Lord's debtors, do the reverse of what he recommended, and instead of lessening our account, learn to discover that they far exceed our own views of them. Oh! thou blessed LORD! I owe thee more in nature, providence, and grace, than any calculation can number. So much so, O LORD! that I am insolvent for ever. But, LORD! let thy grace still exceed even my unworthiness. Oh! grant that I may be received into thine everlasting habitations!

Blessed JESUS! cause me to learn, in the history of this rich glutton, how short-lived all pamperings of the flesh are; and what an awful close terminates the career of all who live without GOD, and without CHRIST, in the world. And let me be content to be as *Lazarus,* poor, if need be, here below, if *rich in faith, and an heir of the kingdom.* Be thou, dear LORD! my portion, and then all is well. Every state sanctified in CHRIST is, and must be, blessed. LORD! grant that I may exercise an holy jealousy in all; and by making thee what GOD the FATHER hath made thee, both *Alpha* and *Omega;* my LORD may be the first in all my desires, and the close of all my joys; for then in life and death, both here and hereafter, JESUS will be my everlasting portion.

CHAP. XVII.

CONTENTS.

Some very blessed Discourses of CHRIST *are contained in this Chapter. The History of the Ten Lepers. Some of* CHRIST's *Prophecies.*

THEN said he unto the disciples, It is impossible but that offences will come: but woe *unto him* through whom they come!

2 It were better for him that a millstone were hanged about his neck, and he cast into the sea, than that he should offend one of these little ones.

It was exceedingly to be wished that the carnal and ungodly part of mankind were to consider this. If they did, would they dare to do as they now too often do, to smite the LORD's little ones? But whether they will regard this counsel or not, let no child of GOD forget how highly JESUS prizeth the humblest and poorest of his people. *Whoso toucheth you, toucheth the apple of his eye.* Zech. ii. 8.

3 ¶ Take heed to yourselves: If thy brother trespass against thee, rebuke him; and if he repent, forgive him.

4 And if he trespass against thee seven times in a day, and seven times in a day turn again to thee, saying, I repent; thou shalt forgive him.

5 And the apostles said unto the Lord, Increase our faith.

6 And the Lord said, If ye had faith as a grain of mustard seed, ye might say unto this sycamine tree, Be thou plucked up by the root, and be thou planted in the sea; and it should obey you.

There is somewhat very striking in this prayer of the Apostles, and the suddenness of it, and the occasion upon which they so expressed themselves, is also striking. It should seem that they were astonished at the infinite benignity the LORD JESUS had just expressed on the subject of forgiveness; and in the moment, as if longing to be always in the exercise of it, they begged for an increase of faith, by which alone they knew they might practise it. Reader! let us daily do the same; and ask our dear and compassionate JESUS for larger tokens of this precious faith. 2 Pet. i. 1; that on the view of the divine mercy of the LORD JESUS to our daily offences, we may find grace to exercise bowels of mercy to the infirmities of our brethren. Read that sweet Scripture by way of strengthening this lovely grace. Coloss. iii. 12, 13.

7 But which of you, having a servant plowing, or feeding cattle, will say unto him by and by, when he is come from the field, Go, and sit down to meat?

8 And will not rather say unto him, Make ready wherewith I may sup, and gird thyself, and serve me, till I have eaten and drunken; and afterward thou shalt eat and drink?

9 Doth he thank that servant because he did the things that were commanded him? I trow not.

10 So likewise ye, when ye shall have done all those things which are commanded you, say, We are unprofitable servants : we have done that which was our duty to do.

This is a beautiful illustration in the supposed case of a servant ploughing, or feeding cattle, (which were among the lowest offices with the Jews. Isaiah lxi. 5.) to shew how utterly unprofitable, as it relates to the LORD, are the best services of the best men. And as this was particularly spoken to the Apostles, it should seem that JESUS had an eye to the ministers of his word and ordinances. Oh! how low, how very low before GOD, must every man lay, both ministers and people, who, taught of GOD the HOLY GHOST, have learnt their own nothingness, unworthiness, and short coming. Reader! depend upon it, if the blood of the Lamb was not sprinkled upon our most holy things, our very prayers would come up unholy before the LORD. Read that solemn Scripture, Exod. xxviii. 38. and behold there how the Great High Priest, under the law, typified CHRIST, our Almighty High Priest, under the Gospel. Oh! the blessedness of being *accepted in the Beloved!* Eph. i. 6.

11 ¶ And it came to pass, as he went to Jerusalem, that he passed through the midst of Samaria and Galilee.

12 And as he entered into a certain village, there met him ten men that were lepers, which stood afar off:

13 And they lifted up *their* voices, and said, Jesus, Master, have mercy on us.

14 And when he saw *them*, he said unto them, Go, shew yourselves unto the priests. And it came to pass, that, as they went, they were cleansed.

15 And one of them, when he saw that he was healed, turned back, and with a loud voice glorified God,

16 And fell down on *his* face at his feet, giving him thanks. And he was a Samaritan.

17 And Jesus answering, said, Were there not ten cleansed? but where *are* the nine?

18 There are not found that returned to give glory to God, save this stranger.

19 And he said unto him, Arise, go thy way: thy faith hath made thee whole.

Our LORD was now, for the last time, going to Jerusalem, for the blessed purpose of finishing his redemption-work, by his sacrifice and death. It is very probable, that these ten men had heard of JESUS's mercy to poor lepers, and therefore, in a body, presented themselves all at once before him. But though coming to him as they did, like lepers conscious of their uncleanness, they stood afar off. See Matt. viii. 1, &c. Levit. xiii. 46. If my Reader hath the Poor Man's Concordance by him, I would refer him to consult it, under the word *Master*, for a full apprehension of that name as especially applicable to JESUS. I beg the Reader to observe the method the LORD JESUS was pleased to adopt in the healing of these men. JESUS said unto them, *Go, shew yourselves unto the priests.* Now this was GOD's command in the Old Testament dispensation, by way of the priests ascertaining the reality of the disease itself. See Levit. xiii. 2, 3. We may suppose, therefore, that in the case of these ten men, the thing had been already done; for they were shut out, in consequence of the disease, from civil and religious communion. When, therefore, the LORD JESUS commanded them to go and shew themselves to the priests, this was in conformity to the precept when the leprosy was healed. See Levit. xiv. 2, 3; and as a thing already done. What a beautiful view doth this give us of CHRIST's power and GODHEAD? No wonder, therefore, that when, by faith, they all, with one consent, departed to go to the priest, they were healed as they went. Reader! you and I may gather instruction here. It is blessed to be found in the way and in the use of means which the LORD hath appointed. But it is blessed also, as we go, to watch and discover the sovereign power and goodness of the LORD without means.

The striking character of the one, which instantly returned to JESUS on the discovery of his cure, opposed to the nine, which, if they went as JESUS had commanded them to the priests, returned not to thank their benefactor, is full of instruction. It is evident that this Samaritan had a lively sense who CHRIST was, by the display of this miracle. None but God could heal the leprosy. This, in his instance, CHRIST had done: and consequently in this view, CHRIST was GOD. And as such, with a loud voice that all around might hear, he glorified him. And now no longer unclean, he did not stand afar off, but fell down on his face at the feet of JESUS. But the most remarkable feature to be noticed in this miracle, as it related to this man, is that the LORD JESUS said unto him, his faith had made him whole. How is this? The whole ten were healed by CHRIST: and was there then any thing *special* in this man's case? I would not

be understood as speaking decidedly upon the subject; but I am
inclined to think that there was, and that those persons differed widely
in their characters, and in the mercy received. They were all healed
of the leprosy of the body; but this man only of both leprosy of
soul and body. And hence the different effects. When the *ten* felt
their cure, nine of them had all they desired, all they asked for. But
in this man, grace entered his soul, and healed a far deeper and more
dreadful leprosy there; and, therefore, led by that awakening grace
in the heart, he had for ever done with Jewish priests and legal
sacrifices, and fled to CHRIST the author and finisher of his salvation.
Reader! if my views be right, we see at once the effect of distinguishing grace. Nine lepers, or in nine thousand, if only healed in *body*,
will rise from beds of sickness as they lay down, never discerning the
hand of that LORD, whose name is JEHOVAH ROPHE: *I am the* LORD
that healeth thee. Exod. xv. 26. But the poor sinner, who feels and
knows the leprosy of the *soul*, no sooner finds that CHRIST hath made
him whole, but falls at his feet with a loud voice of thankfulness.
Oh! the mercy of mercies, JESUS CHRIST. He goes no more *to the
law of a carnal commandment, but to* JESUS, the High Priest, *made
after the power of an endless life.* Heb. vii. 16.

20 ¶ And when he was demanded of the Pharisees when the kingdom of God should come, he
answered them, and said, The kingdom of God
cometh not with observation :

21 Neither shall they say, Lo, here ; or lo,
there : for, behold, the kingdom of God is within
you.

Every enquiry of those Pharisees was with an evil design. But the
LORD hath taken occasion from them to raise instructions to his people.
Reader! while the men of that generation were looking for a temporal
kingdom, and carnal men like them of every generation, have no
higher object in view! Oh! that it may be our mercy to understand
our dear LORD's words. The kingdom of the LORD JESUS CHRIST is
set up in the hearts of his redeemed. It is from the gift of GOD the
FATHER, the finished salvation of the LORD JESUS CHRIST, and the
saving work of GOD the HOLY GHOST. Hence Paul speaks of it, Rom.
xiv. 17, 18.

22 And he said unto the disciples, The days
will come when ye shall desire to see one of
the days of the Son of man, and ye shall not
see *it*.

23 And they shall say to you, See here, or see
there: go not after *them*, nor follow *them*.

24 For as the lightning, that lighteneth out of
the one *part* under heaven, shineth unto the other

part under heaven; so shall also the Son of man be in his day.

25 But first must he suffer many things, and be rejected of this generation.

26 And as it was in the days of Noe, so shall it be also in the days of the Son of man.

27 They did eat, they drank, they married wives, they were given in marriage, until the day that Noe entered in the ark; and the flood came and destroyed them all.

28 Likewise also as it was in the days of Lot: they did eat, they drank, they bought, they sold, they planted, they builded;

29 But the same day that Lot went out of Sodom, it rained fire and brimstone from heaven, and destroyed *them* all:

30 Even thus shall it be in the day when the Son of man is revealed.

31 In that day, he which shall be upon the housetop, and his stuff in the house, let him not come down to take it away; and he that is in the field, let him likewise not return back.

32 Remember Lot's wife.

33 Whosoever shall seek to save his life shall lose it; and whosoever shall lose his life shall preserve it.

Our LORD took occasion, from this ill-designed question of the Pharisees, to instruct his people in respect to the day of visitation, partly, perhaps, with an eye to the destruction of *Jerusalem*, and partly in relation to the last day. All shall be sudden and unexpected as the days of the flood, or as the destruction of *Sodom* and *Gomorrah*. I cannot help noticing what JESUS saith respecting the destruction of the cities of the plain; that in the same day that Lot went out of *Sodom* it rained fire and brimstone from heaven, and destroyed them all. If the Reader will turn to the account of this awful event, as it is related by Moses, (Gen. xix. 24.) he will there observe, that it is said, that *the* LORD *rained from the* LORD *out of heaven*; a strong expression, as if JEHOVAH the FATHER answered what that glorious person (which seems to have been CHRIST himself,) who was present to this destruction as soon as *Lot* had entered *Zoar*, declared; and both concurred in the judgment. And let not the Reader overlook that such, JESUS saith, will be the final overthrow at the second coming of Christ. Beautifully the Lord refers to the awful consequence of an hankering after any thing when the judgments of God are abroad, as in the instance of the wife of *Lot.* It is blessed to sit loose and detached to any thing, and to every thing here below, that when the angel of death comes, we may be ready to fly with him to our *Zoar,* Christ Jesus!

34 I tell you, in that night there shall be two *men* in one bed; the one shall be taken, and the other shall be left.

35 Two *women* shall be grinding together; the one shall be taken, and the other left.

36 Two *men* shall be in the field; the one shall be taken, and the other left.

37 And they answered and said unto him, Where, Lord? and he said unto them, Wheresoever the body *is,* thither will the eagles be gathered together.

In these figures, the Lord very plainly and fully confirms his doctrine of distinguishing grace. And every thing in life as decidedly answers to our Lord's discourse. What a blessed account of it Jesus hath given! Matt. xi. 25, 26. And what a testimony the experience of God, in all ages, bears to it! 2 Timothy ii. 19. Reader! let not you or I put the unnecessary question, Where, Lord? For every where, and in all things, where the carcase of the ungodly is, destruction, like the eagle, will smell the scent afar off: and wheresoever Jesus is, thither will his people fly, *as doves to their windows.* Isaiah lx. 8.

REFLECTIONS.

Oh! thou blessed Lord Jesus! well is it said by thee, that offences will come. Yes! thou, dear Lord! art thyself, to every carnal, unawakened sinner, *a stone of stumbling, and rock of offence.* Thy humble birth, thy meek deportment, thy cross, thy despised followers, to those who looked for temporal prosperity, was indeed an offence that nothing but sovereign grace could overcome. Blessed be that distinguishing grace of my God bestowed upon my poor heart, that I am no longer offended in thee!

Oh! for grace to every sensible, awakened sinner, to come to Jesus under the leprosy of sin. Would to God, I would say, like the poor captive servant in *Syria,* that all such were with my Lord, the Lord God of the prophets, that is Lord over Israel, Jesus. He can heal all of their leprosy of sin. Blessed Jesus! make all thy people sensible of this, according to the covenant promise *in the day of thy power.*

My soul! seek not for Christ's kingdom, in the mere outward things of observation; but seek it in the power of grace within, in the Lord's empire in the heart. Seek it in the Father's testimony of his dear

Son; seek it in the complete, full, all-sufficient, and all-justifying righteousness, and blood shedding of the Lord Jesus Christ : and seek it in the precious, blessed, regenerating, and renewing grace of God the Holy Ghost. Here Jesus manifests his distinguishing love and mercy in the taking of one, and leaving the other; for while *many are called, few are chosen.*

CHAP. XVIII.

CONTENTS.

This Chapter contains the Relation of the Importunate Widow. The Parable of the Pharisee *and* Publican. *Children brought to* Christ. *Our* Lord's *Discourses; and the History of the Blind Man, near* Jericho.

A ND he spake a parable unto them *to this end,* that men ought always *to* pray, and not to faint ;

2 Saying, There was in a city a judge, which feared not God, neither regarded man :

3 And there was a widow in that city ; and she came unto him, saying, Avenge me of mine adversary.

The scope of this beautiful parable is not to insist upon the necessity of prayer; for the Lord's people are supposed to be a praying people. Psm. xxvii. 8. No sooner doth grace at regeneration enter the heart, than the new-born soul breathes in prayer. *Behold, he prayeth!* is the first account the Lord himself gives at the conversion of *Paul.* Acts ix. 11. But it is the perseverance in prayer, the holy vehemency and importunity of a soul in prayer, which, like *Jacob,* will not leave the mercy-seat without a blessing. Gen. xxxii. 26. This is the great point, which the Lord Jesus so graciously teaches his redeemed and exercised ones, by the design of this parable. He who best knows how matters go on at the court of heaven, here instructs all his people how to hold on, and hold out, upon earth, until the needed mercy is obtained. *In due time we shall reap if we faint not.* Gal. vi. 9. Reader! do not overlook this great design of the parable. Neither forget who it is that designed it. He who is the Almighty Advocate at the throne, in whose hands all petitions are lodged, and from whose prevalency in his priestly office, blood-shedding and righteousness, all success must be obtained. It is Jesus, all-precious Jesus, that thus recommends; and, in that recommendation, gives grace to perform. This God-man directs his people to carry all their sorrows, exercises, trials, temptations, fears, and unbelief to him, at his pardon-office, and there wait. And he gives an instance, by the similitude of a parable, how sure they are to succeed.

The Lord first gives the outlines of character in an unjust judge. The portrait Jesus draws of him, is but in two features; but the Lord

hath so strongly marked them, that they convey the whole countenance, both of head and heart. *He feared not* GOD, *neither regarded
man.* What an awful character in himself! and how unsuited for the
office of a magistrate! It is true indeed, that every man by nature,
and while remaining in a state of unregeneracy, hath not the fear of
GOD before his eyes; but here is a monster of iniquity that sets GOD
at defiance. Not content with living regardless of GOD, he prided
himself in the contempt of GOD. He was arrived at that consummate
degree of impudence as to boast of it; for he scrupled not to give his
own character, in openly declaring, that *he feared not* GOD, *nor regarded man.* To this infamous man a poor defenceless widow was compelled to bring her cause. What hope could there be that one who
made no conscience of his ways would listen to her petition? Can any
that have thrown off the fear of GOD be well disposed towards man?

The parable goes on : *And there was a widow in that city* (saith
JESUS), *and she came to him, saying, Avenge me of mine Adversary.*
Reader! do attend to the several features of character in which JESUS
hath drawn her picture; and if, with an eye to the Church, in the case
of every individual of CHRIST's mystical body, you consider the subject
(for very evidently it was in this light JESUS intended it), the matter
will become more striking. It is CHRIST's poor, despised, oppressed
followers, the LORD meant by this widow. Not indeed that, in the
strictest sense of the word, the Church is a widow, for CHRIST, her
husband, is not dead, for he ever liveth. But the Church is called
a widow. Lament. i. 1. And while CHRIST is absent from her, she
is considered as one in a widowed state. John xiv. 18. It is said that
JESUS will come and bring home his wife to the marriage-supper of
the Lamb. Rev. xix. 9. Hence, therefore, during the present day
of grace, the Church may be considered as in the city of an unjust
judge; and surrounded with many adversaries, both from within and
without; and continually longing to be delivered from their power.
It is the case of all the LORD's tried ones.

4 And he would not for a while: but afterward
he said within himself, Though I fear not God,
nor regard man :

5 Yet because this widow troubleth me, I will
avenge her, lest by her continual coming she
weary me.

It is on this point the LORD particularly lays the stress of the
whole parable. Here is an unjust judge, one who is regardless both
of GOD and man; fears not the one, nor loves the other; and yet, from
the unceasing importunity and clamorous demands of a poor woman,
determines in himself that he will do as she desired. From hence
the LORD JESUS draws his unanswerable conclusion of the efficacy
of prayer in the saints of GOD. It is as if the LORD JESUS had said,
See what perseverance will do. Here's an unjust, unfeeling, time-
serving wretch, at length over-ruled, overawed, snd actually compelled to do a violence to his own feelings. *I will* (saith he) *avenge
her :* not to save her, but to ease myself.

6 And the Lord said, Hear what the unjust judge saith.

7 And shall not God avenge his own elect, which cry day and night unto him, though he bear long with them?

8 I tell you, That he will avenge them speedily, nevertheless, when the Son of man cometh, shall he find faith on the earth?

Now our LORD most blessedly makes application of the parable. *Hear* (saith CHRIST), *hear what the unjust judge saith.* As if JESUS had said, Hear, my poor afflicted redeemed ones, what an unfeeling judge saith, when overcome by the ceaseless and unremitting importunity of a poor widow, and take comfort and encouragement in all your approaches to the throne. After such an instance as this, never never despond. *And shall not* GOD *avenge his own elect?* There is an uncommon beauty and strength in the expression, *His own elect.* Not simply an elect, but GOD's elect; not only a chosen seed, but GOD's chosen, and which GOD delights to call his own. Not simply a people set apart, and set apart *for* GOD, but set apart by GOD himself. His *own* elect. I cannot say enough in endeavouring to point out to the people of GOD the blessedness, and the peculiarity of the expression. *His own elect.* They are his. And they are his choice, his elect. And they are so *before* all others, and in preference to all others. And the FATHER gave them to his dear SON, not only before all others, and in preference to all others, but as a choice manifestation of his love. In short, his own elect. Reader! pause over the blessed thought, for it is a very blessed thought! and learn, that amidst all the cavils and disputes of infidels, that GOD hath an elect, and which are specially and personally his own. And learn, at the same time, that though they are GOD's elect, yet are they as this poor widow was, much oppressed by the adversary; yea, they have many adversaries: and do not forget also, that as they are GOD's own, GOD cannot but regard them.

And (saith Jesus) *shall not* GOD *avenge his own elect which cry day and night unto him, though he bear long with them?* Shall this timeserving wretch, this unjust judge, be at length overcome to do, what he delighted not to do; and shall not GOD do that, which is his glory and his pleasure to do? Shall this poor widow prevail with an unjust judge, and shall not the married wife of JESUS prevail with a just Father? Shall a cruel unfeeling man be at length overcome, and shall not a merciful tender GOD be gracious? Is it possible to suppose, that she, who had no one to speak for her, and no interest in the mind of this earthly judge to aid her petition, should yet at length by importunity succeed; and shall not the poor of JESUS's family be successful who have CHRIST to speak for them, and have in the very bosom of GOD our FATHER an advocate in his own everlasting love, which in CHRIST must ensure their acceptance? *Yea,* saith JESUS, (thus putting a blessed positive emphasis upon it,) *I tell you, he will avenge them speedily.* But, Reader! what a humbling thought is it at

the close of the parable in the LORD's question, when JESUS saith;
Nevertheless, when the SON *of Man cometh shall he find faith on the
earth?* It is a kind of question which carrieth with it its own answer,
as if he had said; No! he will not. For, notwithstanding all the
covenant faithfulness and promises of GOD in CHRIST JESUS, who is
there that lives up to the enjoyment of the whole by faith? Reader!
what a reproach is it to the truly regenerated soul, that JEHOVAH's
word and oath, with all CHRIST's precious salvation, should be so
little rested upon by faith?

9 ¶ And he spake this parable unto certain
which trusted in themselves, that they were righteous, and despised others:

10 Two men went up into the temple to pray :
the one a Pharisee, and the other a publican.

11 The Pharisee stood and prayed thus with
himself, God, I thank thee, that I am not as other
men *are,* extortioners, unjust, adulterers, or even
as this publican.

12 I fast twice in the week, I give tithes of all
that I possess.

13 And the publican standing afar off, would
not lift up so much as *his* eyes unto heaven, but
smote upon his breast, saying, God, be merciful
to me a sinner.

14 I tell you, This man went down to his house
justified *rather* than the other: for every one that
exalteth himself shall be abased: and he that humbleth himself shall be exalted.

Here is another beautiful parable of our LORD's, and the occasion
for which he spake it is declared. I do not think it necessary as in the
former, to enlarge upon the several features of it. Every circumstance
in both the characters CHRIST hath drawn, is descriptive of the different ground for which they stood for seeking acceptance with GOD.
And it should be observed, in order to give weight to the design of
our LORD's teaching, that the *Pharisee* and *Publican* are as much living
characters now, as then, in the days of our LORD. Every man is a
Pharisee that is seeking acceptance with GOD either whole or in part,
who prides himself upon his own good deeds, and prayers, and sa-
craments, and almsgiving; and hath recourse to CHRIST no further
according to his will than to make up (if there should be any) his
own deficiency. And every man may be called a *Publican,* in the
sense of this parable, who from the teaching of GOD the SPIRIT hath
been led to behold the *Adam*-nature in which he was born, and
the condemnation in which he is involved, both by original, and by

actual transgression; and led by the HOLY GHOST to GOD in CHRIST, acknowledgeth himself unmeriting forgiveness, while in sorrow and contrition he seeks it. Justification is of GOD in CHRIST. And therefore the self-condemned, and not the self-righteous, find justification before GOD.

15 And they brought unto him also infants, that he would touch them: but when *his* disciples saw *it,* they rebuked them.

16 But Jesus called them *unto him,* and said, Suffer little children to come unto me, and forbid them not: for of such is the kingdom of God.

17 Verily I say unto you, Whosoever shall not receive the kingdom of God as a little child, shall in no wise enter therein.

We have a parallel passage, Matt. xviii. 1, &c. to which I refer; and shall only in addition observe in this place, what an endearing and tender representation is given of our LORD JESUS CHRIST, in such a beautiful and interesting trait of character, in thus folding in his divine arms little children. What an encouragement for believing parents to bring their offspring often before him!

18 And a certain ruler asked him, saying, Good Master, what shall I do to inherit eternal life?

19 And Jesus said unto him, Why callest thou me good? none *is* good, save one, *that is* God.

20 Thou knowest the commandments, Do not commit adultery, Do not kill, Do not steal, Do not bear false witness, Honour thy father and thy mother.

21 And he said, All these have I kept from my youth up.

22 Now when Jesus heard these things, he said unto him, Yet lackest thou one thing; sell all that thou hast, and distribute unto the poor, and thou shalt have treasure in heaven; and come, follow me.

23 And when he heard this, he was very sorrowful: for he was very rich.

24 And when Jesus saw that he was very sorrowful: he said, How hardly shall they that have 'riches enter into the kingdom of God!

25 For it is easier for a camel to go through a needle's eye, than for a rich man to enter into the kingdom of God.

26 And they that heard *it*, said, Who then can be saved?

27 And he said, The things which are impossible with men are possible with God.

28 Then Peter said, Lo, we have left all, and followed thee.

29 And he said unto them, Verily I say unto you, There is no man that hath left house, or parents, or brethren, or wife, or children for the kingdom of God's sake,

30 Who shall not receive manifold more in this present time, and in the world to come life everlasting.

Both *Matthew* and *Mark* have recorded, and nearly in the same words, this interview which JESUS had with this ruler. Matt. xix. 16. Mark x. 17. I refer to the observations there offered upon it. Every incident in our LORD's ministry becomes interesting, but to notice the whole would lead into endless discourses. Truly it must be said, and without a figure concerning the person and work of the LORD JESUS, *there is no end of his greatness.*

31 ¶ Then he took *unto him* the twelve, and said unto them, Behold, we go up to Jerusalem, and all things that are written by the prophets concerning the Son of man shall be accomplished.

32 For he shall be delivered unto the Gentiles, and shall be mocked, and spitefully intreated, and spitted on:

33 And they shall scourge *him*, and put him to death; and the third day he shall rise again.

34 And they understood none of these things; and this saying was hid from them, neither knew they the things which were spoken.

I request the Reader to remark with me how graciously the LORD JESUS, by little and little, as they were able to bear it, prepared the minds of his disciples for the great events which were now coming on, and very shortly to be accomplished at *Jerusalem*. The Passover, which was now at hand, the LORD JESUS well knew would be his last.

And I beg the Reader to observe yet further, how sweetly Jesus directed their minds to the study of those scriptures which referred to him on the subject, that when the great events foretold should be accomplished, they might the better be enabled to compare the prediction with the event. And let me add, that the Reader will do well to be occupied in the same. For this purpose, let him consult those scriptures to which in the prophets we may suppose Christ here referred, Isaiah liii. Psms. ii. xxii. and lxix. Isaiah l. Dan. ix. 24, 25, 26. Zech. xi. 12, 13. These holy records will be truly blessed, when opened to us by God the Holy Ghost; if we take them with us in our hands, and feel their power in our hearts, when by and by we come on to that part of *Luke's* Gospel, where we follow the Lord Jesus Christ from the garden to the hall of Pilate, until we take our stand at the foot of the cross. Oh! the preciousness of entering into an heartfelt participation of those momentous truths, when with the eye of faith we behold the Lord Jesus as *Paul* describes him, *witnessing before Pontius Pilate a good confession.* 1 Tim. vi. 13.

35 And it came to pass, that, as he was come nigh unto Jericho, a certain blind man sat by the way side begging:

36 And hearing the multitude pass by, he asked what it meant?

37 And they told him, That Jesus of Nazareth passeth by.

38 And he cried, saying, Jesus, *thou* Son of David, have mercy on me.

39 And they which went before rebuked him, that he should hold his peace; but he cried so much the more, *Thou* Son of David, have mercy on me.

40 And Jesus stood and commanded him to be brought unto him. And when he was come near, he asked him,

41 Saying, What wilt thou that I shall do unto thee? and he said, Lord, that I may receive my sight.

42 And Jesus said unto him, Receive thy sight: thy faith hath saved thee.

43 And immediately he received his sight, and followed him, glorifying God. And all the people, when they saw *it,* gave praise unto God.

The history of this miracle hath been so largely dwelt upon, in the review taken of it in *Mark's* Gospel, x. 46. that I need only refer the Reader to it in that place.

REFLECTIONS.

READER! let us both beg of GOD the HOLY GHOST, for his sweet and gracious office it is, to lead to the mercy-seat, to endite our prayers when there, and to give us every thing suited to that sacred place; that He will of his rich mercy so help us in our infirmities, that we may be enabled to do as JESUS here commands, *always pray and not faint.* And oh! what unanswerable motives the LORD hath here furnished us with, in beholding a cruel, time-serving, unfeeling judge, at length prevailed upon to give way to a poor widow's unceasing importunity; when we call to mind that the LORD to whom we go in CHRIST, is our righteous, gracious, compassionate tender FATHER; and who himself hath expressly said: *It shall come to pass that before they call I will answer, and while they are yet speaking I will hear!* Oh! for faith, *to believe the record* GOD *hath given of his dear* SON!

LORD hide pride from our eyes, that no child of thine may be tinctured with pride, like this haughty blinded *Pharisee;* but give to all thy redeemed grace to be humbled like this poor *Publican,* that with self-contrition as his, we may each smite upon his breast as he did, saying, GOD *be merciful to me a sinner!*

And oh! for the continual teachings and leadings of the HOLY GHOST, that as babes desiring the sincere milk of the word, we may come to JESUS; and never be sorrowful, as the young man rich in this world was, when called upon to leave all for CHRIST. Do thou, blessed LORD! do by us as by the blind man near *Jericho,* put a cry on our heart, and the more the ungodly rebuke for following JESUS, the more may our souls cry aloud for him, until JESUS heareth and answereth prayer, opens all the blinded senses of our spiritual faculties, and gives us grace to follow him in the regeneration; that we may glorify the LORD upon earth, and praise him to all eternity in heaven.

CHAP. XIX.

CONTENTS.

Of Zaccheus *the Publican. The Parable of the Talents.* JESUS *entereth* Jerusalem, *and goeth immediately to the Temple.*

AND *Jesus* entered and passed through Jericho:

I pause over this verse, short as it is, to remark how much in point of doctrine is contained in it. JESUS entered into *Jericho,* and passed through it. We read of nothing done in it by the LORD in a way of grace. Were there none of the LORD's family here? Time was when a precious jewel of CHRIST's crown was found in it. But there is nothing said now! Is not this loudly preaching distinguishing grace? I beg the Reader to turn to those scriptures, Joshua ii. and vi. chapters. 1 Kings xvi. 34. Heb. xi. 31.

2 And, behold, *there was* a man named Zaccheus, which was the chief among the publicans, and he was rich.

3 And he sought to see Jesus, who he was; and could not for the press, because he was little of stature.

4 And he ran before, and climbed up into a sycamore tree, to see him: for he was to pass that *way*.

5 And when Jesus came to the place, he looked up, and saw him, and said unto him, Zaccheus, make haste, and come down: for to-day I must abide at thy house.

6 And he made haste, and came down, and received him joyfully.

7 And when they saw *it*, they all murmured, saying, That he was gone to be guest with a man that is a sinner.

8 And Zaccheus stood, and said unto the Lord, Behold, Lord, the half of my goods I give to the poor: and if I have taken any thing from any man by false accusation, I restore *him* fourfold.

9 And Jesus said unto him, This day is salvation come to this house, forasmuch · as he also is a son of Abraham.

10 For the Son of man is come to seek and to save that which was lost.

The key to open this gracious history is in the close of it. Salvation coming to the house of *Zaccheus* is explained, when the LORD saith, *Forasmuch as he also is the son of Abraham.* Gal. iii. 29. Numberless are the beauties in this short memoir of *Zaccheus.* But in a *Poor Man's Commentary,* I must all along study shortness. We are told that his name was *Zacchai;* but whether a Jew, or Gentile, is not said. It was a name well known among the Jews, and as such, he might have been by nature of the seed of *Abraham.* But whether this, or not, certain it is by the event of CHRIST's calling him to salvation, that he was according to grace *a child of promise.* Gal. iv. 28. But we are told that he was a publican, and chief of the order. And how odious this office of a tax-gatherer was, may easily be inferred from what our LORD himself said concerning such. For when JESUS had occasion to remark the character of a man more than ordinarily wicked, he said, *let him be unto thee as an heathen man, and a publican.* Matt. xviii. 17. Such was the man as is here represented, whom CHRIST distinguished among a great multitude, and called by sovereign grace *from darkness to light; and from the power of sin and Satan to the living* GOD!

I must not stay to go over every particular, in the relation of this wonderful display of grace. A few only of the more striking circumstances I would beg the Reader to attend to. *Zaccheus*, we are told, sought to see JESUS, who he was. And those who read the history slightly, may suppose that this was mere curiosity. Perhaps, indeed, *Zaccheus* himself thought no other. But *Zaccheus* was not first in the intention of this business. It was JESUS sought to see *Zaccheus*, before that Zaccheus thought of seeing him; yea, directed his steps through *Jericho*, purposely to meet *Zaccheus*. And, as this was the day appointed from all eternity for this interview between CHRIST and this man, all the steps leading to the accomplishment of it were marked, over-ruled, and made to minister to this one great end. Oh! the preciousness of preventing grace! What an huge volume may be read by an enlightened eye, in every man's life, when once the day-light of regeneration hath opened the spiritual sight, to see the instances exemplified in his own history. To behold, yea, and to trace them unfolded and explained by GOD the HOLY GHOST, when as *Jude* expresses it, we see ourselves *sanctified by* GOD *the* FATHER, *preserved in* JESUS CHRIST, *and called*, Jude 1. Reader! do you know any thing of these unspeakable mercies in your own history? Can you look back and see how *preserving* grace *in* JESUS CHRIST kept you until *called to* JESUS CHRIST; and all this from the *sanctification* of GOD the FATHER in his eternal purpose concerning you! Ephes. i. 4.

I beg the Reader to observe with me, some at least of the predisposing causes leading to this meeting of the SAVIOR with the sinner. The poor man is prompted to go to the place where JESUS was to pass. Little of stature, and a great throng around CHRIST, he is led to climb a tree, that he might have a full view of him. The SON of GOD comes there, beholds Zaccheus, who no doubt, though he went to see CHRIST, never once conceived that CHRIST would see him. The LORD calls to him, calls him by name, bids him come down, invites himself to his house, tells him that he must to-day abide with him; and *Zaccheus* finds his heart instantly disposed to come down from the tree, and to receive CHRIST joyfully.

Now, while the Reader makes every due observation on this wonderful transaction, as it relates personally to *Zaccheus*, I would have him, methinks, (and every poor sinner like him and myself,) consider also, what a blessed subject is folded up in it, for the spiritual improvement of all the LORD's family; and for whose comfort, encouragement, and instruction, we may fairly conclude GOD the HOLY GHOST caused it to be recorded.

When poor sinners, like this publican, feel a desire to see CHRIST, in his word, in his ordinances, and in the various means the LORD hath appointed, as JESUS passeth by, though such are unconscious that very often it is the LORD working upon their minds to awaken desire, and bring about an interview; yet how blessed is it in the after stages, from certain discoveries, which at the time did not strike the mind, to perceive, that it was the LORD's predisposing grace, which led to all. And though such are little in knowledge, little in the apprehension of their sins, and a want of CHRIST, as this man was little in stature; yet neither the pressure of the world, the pressure of time, or the pressure of a multitude, shall keep back from CHRIST, when the hour is come for bringing souls to the presence of CHRIST, however before unknown by them, or unregarded. It is truly blessed to be brought into acquaintance with those things, after we are brought into acquaintance with the LORD JESUS CHRIST.

But what I would yet more particularly entreat the Reader to regard, in this striking history of the conversion of the publican, is, the grace of JESUS manifested to him. Do not lose sight of this. JESUS, from everlasting, had his eye upon this man. The Church in every individual was chosen in CHRIST. Ephes. i. 4. Their names written in the Book of Life. Rev. xiii. 8. Luke x. 20. All CHRIST's sheep were given to him by the FATHER. John x. 27—29. And every one of them must again pass under the hand of him that telleth them. Jerem. xxxiii. 13. Now then the hour was come for the recovery of this poor Publican from the *Adam*-nature transgression in which he was born, and in which he was involved. And JESUS, who came upon earth to seek and save that which was lost, disposeth every plan leading to the accomplishment of his purpose, as might best minister to his own glory and *Zaccheus's* welfare. CHRIST prompts the heart of *Zaccheus*, perhaps he knew not why, (or if a sense of sin had been previously awakened by grace in his heart, this leads him) to an earnest desire of seeing JESUS. The poor man hastens to the place where JESUS was that day to pass. And the LORD that sent him there, goes there to meet him. But this transaction must not be private. Many shall know it, and behold the whole. The thing shall be recorded, that future generations of the Church may be told it, and rejoice in it also. *Zaccheus* therefore climbs a tree. Probably, he concluded that he should be not seen by any one. But this afforded the very means of making the whole more public. When JESUS arrived to the spot, he looked up, saw *Zaccheus*, knew him as his FATHER's gift, called him by name, told him to come down, and that hastily; invited himself to his house, from the necessity of the case, and inclined the heart of this publican sinner to an instant acceptance of his Almighty Guest, who came down and received him joyfully.

And, Reader! such is the case in every instance of CHRIST's redeemed! JESUS, from everlasting, hath arranged every step for the accomplishment of this great end, when the hour is come for calling home his own to the knowledge and enjoyment of his grace. The time *when*, the place *where*, the manner *how*, all these and every other are so ordered and disposed, that not one thing can fail. Oh! what a refreshing consideration it ought to be to the Church of GOD. During the whole days and years of their unregeneracy, the eye of JESUS is unceasingly watching over them. And when the love-calls of his HOLY SPIRIT go forth, like *Zaccheus*, if lifted up with Pharisaical pride, self-righteousness, ambition, worldly pursuits, and the numberless other obstructions, which before kept them from CHRIST; down they come, and lay low at JESUS's feet; and then take the SAVIOR home to their house, and to their heart, and receive him joyfully. Reader! are you personally acquainted with this soul-work? Do you know any thing of the love-calls of JESUS? It is impossible not to know them, if you have ever heard them. The soul that hears the voice of JESUS, though he never heard it before, will know it among ten thousand; yea, the sweet sound will never be forgotten by him. When JESUS first speaks to a sinner, which was before dead in trespasses and sins, it is a *loud* voice. John v. 25. a *powerful* voice, Psalm xxix. 3—11. a *still small* voice, 1 Kings xix. 9—14. a *sweet, loving, winning* voice, Song v. 2. and it is a *personal* voice, Prov. xxii. 19. It will be well for the Reader, if his heart find a correspondence to these scriptures.

The joyful reception *Zaccheus* gave to the SAVIOR; the murmurs of the Scribes and Pharisees; the open confession of the Publican, with his wish to make a fourfold restitution to any he had injured; and the declaration of JESUS in respect to the object for which he came into the world; these are all so many beautiful additions in the history, if the limits I must observe would allow me to enlarge. But I forbear. The LORD bless the whole by his grace, and cause the example shewn in *Zaccheus*, to have the suited effect upon all his people.

11 ¶ And as they heard these things, he added and spake a parable, because he was nigh to Jerusalem, and because they thought that the kingdom of God should immediately appear.

12 He said therefore, A certain nobleman went into a far country to receive for himself a kingdom, and to return.

13 And he called his ten servants, and delivered them ten pounds, and said unto them, Occupy, till I come.

14 But his citizens hated him, and sent a message after him, saying, We will not have this *man* to reign over us.

15 And it came to pass, that when he was returned, having received the kingdom, then he commanded these servants to be called unto him, to whom he had given the money, that he might know how much every man had gained by trading.

16 Then came the first, saying, Lord, thy pound hath gained ten pounds.

17 And he said unto them, Well, thou good servant: because thou hast been faithful in a very little, have thou authority over ten cities.

18 And the second came, saying, Lord, thy pound hath gained five pounds.

19 And he said likewise to him, Be thou also over five cities.

20 And another came, saying, Lord, behold, *here* is thy pound, which I have kept laid up in a napkin :

21 For I feared thee, because thou art an austere man: thou takest up that thou layest not down, and reapest that thou didst not sow.

22 And he saith unto him, Out of thine own mouth will I judge thee, *thou* wicked servant. Thou knewest that I was an austere man, taking up that I laid not down, and reaping that I did not sow:

23 Wherefore then gavest not thou my money into the bank, that at my coming I might have required mine own with usury?

24 And he said unto them that stood by, Take from him the pound, and give *it* to him that hath ten pounds.

25 (And they said unto him, Lord, he hath ten pounds.)

26 For I say unto you, That unto every one which hath shall be given; and from him that hath not, even that he hath shall be taken away from him.

27 But those mine enemies, which would not that I should reign over them, bring hither, and slay *them* before me.

In this parable we have an illustration in part of CHRIST's method of government in his kingdom. I take it for granted, that without a comment the Reader will immediately understand CHRIST himself is the nobleman here represented. Having finished redemption-work, he is returned to glory; and in the appointed season will come to judgment. Acts iii. 21. John v. 25—29. Acts x. 42.

But it is not so clear who is meant by the *Ten Servants*, which are here appointed to occupy till CHRIST shall come. Not the Apostles I should think; for they were *twelve* in number. And, even if it be supposed that *Judas* is the *one* who is represented as the slothful and unprofitable servant, in this case the remainder would be *eleven*, and not twelve. Neither do I conceive, as some have thought, that the servants here spoken of, mean the Ministers of the Word and Ordinances; for although, as in the instance of *Judas,* the call to the office doth not imply a call by grace; yet the occupying and improving the trust must carry with it the blessing of GOD qualifying; and the reward given, in the different degrees to the faithful servants, doth not bear correspondence to the scripture account of the last day. Neither doth it seem that by the *ten servants* is meant the world at large. For though, no doubt, the whole creation may be said in this sense to minister to the LORD's service; yet here appears to be some special and personal acts of servitude implied in their labors.

If I venture to give my views of our LORD's meaning, I pray that it may be considered I rather propose them by way of enquiry, than in a way of decision. But I am inclined to think, by the *ten servants* (in which I conclude our LORD hath only put a certain number for an indefinite,) are intended by the LORD JESUS to distinguish his redeemed from the *Adam*-nature out of which he hath brought them; and those of the *Adam*-nature who stand upon their own bottom. And I am inclined to this opinion, because though *ten* servants are mentioned, we hear only of *two* classes, though *three* persons are called when the LORD cometh to reckon with them. And those two classes plainly mean the different states of *nature* and *grace.*

To each servant was given a pound; by which is meant the equality of the outward ministry of the word. All brought under the sound of the Gospel may be said, in the language of the parable, to have the same charge, *Occupy till I come.* By the improvement, the different situations are marked between those, who through grace, from an union with CHRIST, increased their riches; and the man who void of grace, stood upon his own creature bottom, and consequently made no advance. The faithful servants represent those, who in the use of the blessed means afforded them, rejoice in the prospect of their LORD's coming, and, through grace, are found waiting in hope of eternal life by JESUS CHRIST our LORD. The unprofitable servant hath his pound no less, in hearing the Gospel of salvation; but is averse to the method of GOD's free grace in CHRIST, and rejects the counsel of GOD against his own soul. Both these characters differ from the world at large, in that they are called by the Gospel to occupation; and as such are brought into a state of service. The rejection of the *one,* becomes the cause of just condemnation; while the acceptation of the *other* tends to magnify the riches of free grace; and *both* illustrate the equity of the divine will. Had the posterity of *Adam* continued in the state of uncorrupt nature in which *Adam* was formed; a state of happiness suited to that state would have followed, as *Adam* before his fall enjoyed. But, when by that fall transgression entered into the world, it was a merciful dispensation to have the trust of that occupation, as the parable calls it, of the means of grace; and the rejection of it, which the man who kept the pound laid up in a napkin represents, justly induceth the whole condemnation which followeth. Reader! what a mercy is it to discover our grace-union with CHRIST, which brings up after it an interest and communion in all that belongs to CHRIST! The close of the parable in CHRIST's own words is full to this point. *To every one that hath,* that is, that hath union with CHRIST, shall be given. JESUS hath engaged for all his redeemed. Every thing which is in CHRIST, as the head of his body the Church, is for them. In Him all is secured. But the *seeming* possessor, he who hath all the advantages of the outward means of grace, and yet, from no union with CHRIST, hath in reality no grace; all those outward privileges will shortly cease and be taken away! And CHRIST's destruction of all such will follow.

I shall only detain the Reader with just remarking, that in the margin of our old Bibles, (and our *old* Bibles, like old gold, are precious things,) the word *pound* is said to be *twelve ounces and half*, which at five shillings an ounce of our money, would be *three pounds twelve shillings and six-pence.* I believe that this is tolerably correct. The word *Mina,* (or more properly MaNeH) being of that value. But if it was a gold coin, (and there is nothing said that it was not,) the pound in that case would be an hundred drachms, which was worth near *eighty pounds,* and in silver near *eight pounds.* But our dear LORD in worldly circumstances was poor, and in his days and his company, as one of them said, and all might have said the same, *silver and gold have I none,* Acts iii. 6. it is more than probable JESUS alluded to the common Maneh, which was neither gold nor silver, but ordinary coin, and as the margin of our Bible renders it, *three pounds twelve and six-pence !*

28 ¶ And when he had thus spoken, he went before, ascending up to Jerusalem.

29 And it came to pass, when he was come nigh to Bethphage, and Bethany, at the mount called *the mount* of Olives, he sent two of his disciples,

30 Saying, Go ye into the village over against *you :* in the which at your entering ye shall find a colt tied, whereon yet never man sat : loose him, and bring *him hither.*

31 And if any man ask you, Why do ye loose *him?* thus shall ye say unto him, Because the Lord hath need of him.

32 And they that were sent went their way, and found even as he had said unto them.

33 And as they were loosing the colt, the owners thereof said unto them, Why loose ye the colt?

34 And they said, The Lord hath need of him.

35 And they brought him to Jesus : and they cast their garments upon the colt, and they set Jesus thereon.

36 And as they went, they spread their clothes in the way.

37 And when he was come nigh, even now at

My grace is sufficient for
\ee: for My strength is
ade perfect in weakness.

2 Corinthians xii. 9.

Sᴛ. LUKE.   477

\.\.\. ᴜᴄꜱᴄᴇɴᴛ ᴏʀ the mount of Olives, the whole multitude of the disciples began to rejoice and praise God with a loud voice, for all the mighty works that they had seen;

38 Saying, Blessed *be* the King that cometh in the name of the Lord: Peace in heaven, and glory in the highest.

39 And some of the Pharisees from among the multitude said unto him, Master, rebuke thy disciples.

40 And he answered and said unto them, I tell you, that if these should hold their peace, the stones would immediately cry out.

The entrance of the Lᴏʀᴅ Jᴇꜱᴜꜱ into Jerusalem, is recorded by all the Evangelists, as if in confirmation of the prophecies. Isaiah lxii. 11. Zech. ix. 9. Some short observations were made on it in Matthew xxi. and Mark xi. but, from the importance of the thing itself, it will be proper in addition to what hath been there brought before the Reader, yet further to remark some of the more prominent features attending it. And, *first,* I do not think it unlikely that Gᴏᴅ the Hᴏʟʏ Gʜᴏꜱᴛ had an eye both to Cʜʀɪꜱᴛ's triumphs, and Cʜʀɪꜱᴛ's humiliations, at those memorable spots, *Bethphage,* and the Mount of *Olives;* when *David,* who was an illustrious type of the Lᴏʀᴅ Jᴇꜱᴜꜱ, went there bare-footed, 2 Sam. xv. 30. The humiliations of the Lᴏʀᴅ Jᴇꜱᴜꜱ were the highest of his glories. And I would in the *next* place, beg the Reader to remark with me, how the Lᴏʀᴅ Jᴇꜱᴜꜱ, in preparing for his triumphal entrance into the holy city, gave evidences of his divine nature, in telling the disciples where they should find the colt, and overruling the mind of the owners to lend the beast to Cʜʀɪꜱᴛ. And what I would yet more particularly desire the Reader to remark with me, are the circumstances which attended our Lᴏʀᴅ's entry into *Jerusalem.* What but Gᴏᴅ working upon the human mind, could in one and the same moment overrule so great a multitude, to make the air ring with their *Hosannas;* and literally to call Him what their scriptures of the Prophets had foretold of the *Messiah,* in the very hour the Scribes and Pharisees were ripening their schemes to destroy him? And, what but the same Almighty grace, acting to the same purpose, could have caused the mouths of unconscious children, in spite of their Jewish parents, to proclaim a truth their tender years could not understand. According to my view of this subject, yea, to every man's view of the subject, who will look at it as it really is, it forms one of the most palpable and decided testimonies, as far as outward evidence can go, to the glories of Cʜʀɪꜱᴛ's person; and is such, as our Lᴏʀᴅ himself most blessedly observed upon it, so full in point, as if resisted, became enough to make the stones exclaim.

41 ¶ And when he was come near, he beheld the city, and wept over it,

42 Saying, if thou hadst known, even thou, at least in this thy day, the things *which belong* unto thy peace! but now they are hid from thine eyes.

43 For the days shall come upon thee, that thine enemies shall cast a trench about thee, and compass thee round, and keep thee in on every side,

44 And shall lay thee even with the ground, and thy children within thee: and they shall not leave in thee one stone upon another: because thou knewest not the time of thy visitation.

This view of the Lord Jesus is most lovely and endearing. We behold him here touched with the feelings of our nature, dropping tears over the beloved city, in contemplating her approaching ruin. And to be sure nothing can endear Christ so tenderly to the heart, as when we behold him manifesting *the man of sorrows, and acquainted with grief.* It is blessed to know him, blessed to go to him, blessed to pour out our hearts before him, when the soul is taught by God the Holy Ghost, how much Jesus enters into the concerns of his people, and, from his fellow-feeling, makes their concerns his own. This is to know him as God, to know him as Man, and to draw nigh to him in the union of both.

But who should have thought that this very character of Jesus, of God, and Man, in one person, which renders him so dear to his faithful, could have prompted his enemies therefrom to call his God-head in question? Who would have believed it possible, had not matter of fact proved it, that the tears which Jesus shed over Jerusalem, when he contemplated her sure ruin as *a city*, should have been mis-construed, as though Christ lamented over any of *his people* there, as if they had outlived the day of grace, to whom in numberless instances, (as witness the Jerusalem sinners converted at the day of *Pentecost*,) the day of grace was not then arrived?

And yet such is the blindness and perversity of men, untaught of God the Holy Ghost, that by putting a wrong construction on the words and actions of Christ, they make that lamentation of Jesus over a beautiful and beloved city, given up to destruction, in a *temporal* way, as if Jesus wept over the people concerning a *spiritual* ruin; and render the words of Christ as if referring to the *everlasting* welfare of the people, which only could be meant to the *present* desolation of the city. *If thou hadst known*, (saith the Lord,) *even thou,* (the bloody city of Jerusalem, which hath been the slaughter-house of all the Prophets,) (see chapter xiii. 31, 32, 33. and also Matt. xxiii. 34 to the end,) *the things which belong to thy peace; but now they are hid from thine eyes. For the days shall come upon thee, that thine enemies shall cast a trench about thee, and compass thee round, and keep thee in on every side; and shall lay thee even with the ground, and thy children within thee; and they shall not leave in thee one stone upon another, because thou knewest not the time of thy visitation.*

Now, let any man read these words of the LORD JESUS, and say, whether these things do not wholly relate to *Jerusalem* as a city, as a nation given up to ruin. And wherefore? But because she knew not, *nationally* considered, the time of her visitation. The Prophets with one voice had foretold of CHRIST: CHRIST himself had come in conformity to the whole tenor of prophecy: the nation, nationally considered, had rejected the LORD of Life and Glory; killed the Prophets, and JESUS knew would shortly embrue their hands in his blood. The time of visitation as a city therefore is now over; the rulers as such are given up to an incurable blindness. Had the nation received CHRIST, as CHRIST, though only in an *outward* profession, for no more was, or could have been expected from them; then, as a nation, they would still have remained. JESUS saw this rejection, deplored the awful consequence, and wept over the city, in beholding the whole, in consequence thereof, as given up to destruction. This is the plain and evident meaning of the passage.

But what hath this to do with individuals, in relation to their *everlasting salvation?* Who would from hence draw a conclusion, that an individual of the persons given to CHRIST by the Father, may outlive the day of grace, and the things which might at one season have ministered to his peace, at another be for ever hid from his eyes? What hath the peace of a nation, as a nation, to do with the peace of GOD? Is it not notorious, that *five thousand* of those Jerusalem-sinners, who joined the rabble and the multitude of the people in crucifying CHRIST, were pricked to the heart on the day of Pentecost, were baptised and sanctified by the HOLY GHOST? And yet these were among the persons then in Jerusalem, when our LORD wept over it, and expressed himself in those memorable words. A positive proof that they were not meant in the general destruction. So very plain and palpable is the fact, that CHRIST's apostrophe referred wholly to the *city*, and not to the *people*. JESUS had many of His there, at the moment when he thus expressed himself; and who, though they were then insensible of the LORD, yet when the HOLY GHOST, according to CHRIST's most sure promise, at the day of Pentecost came upon them, were converted and saved.

Reader! I have been the more particular in my view of this passage, because it hath been, and still is, and will be, in the apprehension of unenlightened free-will men, a favorite portion to bring forward, in justification as they think, to shew that men may outlive the day of grace; but with which those blessed words of our LORD hath nothing to do. And it would be well with such men, whether preachers or hearers, to attend to what our LORD saith in another place on the same subject; and which, if rightly considered, would shew them that such a gracious blessed provision is made for all the LORD's redeemed ones, that the day of grace can never end with them, until grace hath brought them home, and is consummated in glory. *All that the FATHER giveth me shall come to me, and him that cometh to me I will in no wise cast out.* John vi. 37.

45 ¶ And he went into the temple, and began to cast out them that sold therein, and them that bought;

46 Saying unto them, It is written, My house is the house of prayer; but ye have made it a den of thieves.

47 And he taught daily in the temple, but the chief priests and the scribes, and the chief of the people sought to destroy him,

48 And could not find what they might do: for all the people were very attentive to hear him.

I refer the Reader for my observations on those verses to the similar passage, Matt. xxi. 12—14.

REFLECTIONS.

BLESSED LORD JESUS! do I behold thee, mine honored LORD, entering and passing through *Jericho*, the cursed city? Yes! I do. And is it, my soul, to be wondered at, when I know that that HOLY LORD, who knew no sin, was yet content to be made both sin and a curse, that his redeemed might be made the righteousness of GOD in Him? And was there a poor *Zaccheus* near *Jericho*, one of CHRIST's, a son of *Abraham*, that JESUS went purposely to seek? And will not JESUS still seek his own, wherever they are scattered, in the present cloudy and dark day? Oh! yes! JESUS will call them down from every lofty imagination, or raise them up from every fallen state; for *the* SON *of* Man *is come to seek and save that which was lost.*

Almighty King! thou art indeed a nobleman gone to receive to thyself a kingdom, and to return LORD! give me grace to occupy till thou shalt come. The truest occupation, my honored LORD, is to live on thee, and to be everlastingly receiving of thy fulness, and grace for grace. And when my LORD shall come, shall I not, as those babes of Israel, hail thee with Hosannas; yea, with shouts and acclamations of praise? *Blessed, for ever blessed be He that cometh in the name of the* LORD.

And, oh! thou tender compassionate LORD! May my soul often call to remembrance thy tears over Jerusalem. JESUS wept! Oh! the largeness of mercies in the heart of the GOD-Man CHRIST JESUS. What shall ever keep my soul from going to Him, who knoweth my frame by his own; and whose mercies are the mercies of both GOD and man in one. Oh! the privilege of a throne of grace! Oh! the blessedness of such an High Priest!

CHAP. XX.

CONTENTS.

The Chief Priests and the Scribes demand of CHRIST *his Authority for his Ministry. The* LORD *puts them to silence. He adds a Parable. In answer to a* Sadducee, JESUS *discourseth on the Resurrection.*

AND it came to pass, *that,* on one of those days, as he taught the people in the temple, and preached the gospel, the chief priests and the scribes came upon *him,* with the elders,

2 And spake unto him, saying, Tell us by what authority doest thou these things? or who is he that gave thee this authority?

As we are now drawing nigh the solemn scenes of CHRIST's sufferings and death, the Evangelist relates to the Church the increasing opposition made by the sworn foes to CHRIST, against his person and doctrine. This chapter opens with telling us, that now the chief priests and scribes, with the elders, came upon him, in a collected body, to attack him. Hitherto they had smothered their base designs under cover, as if they would question him for information; but now their plan for his destruction is nearly ripened, they throw off all courtesy, and imperatively demand his authority, both for his miracles and doctrines. Reader! do not overlook the folly as well as the wickedness of the question. Miracles spake for themselves. None but GOD could do the work which JESUS did. So *Nicodemus* wisely judged. John iii. 2. And every man of common sense must judge the same.

3 And he answered and said unto them, I will also ask you one thing; and answer me:

4 The baptism of John, was it from heaven, or of men?

5 And they reasoned with themselves, saying, If we shall say, From heaven; he will say, Why then believed ye him not?

6 But, and if we say, Of men: all the people will stone us; for they be persuaded that John was a prophet.

7 And they answered, That they could not tell whence *it was.*

8 And Jesus said unto them, Neither tell I you by what authority I do these things.

I should not detain the Reader over these verses, for they are too plain to need a comment, were it not that I wish to remark to him, how very suited the LORD's answer was to the menacing question of those designing men. How graciously the LORD teacheth his people by his lovely example, to avoid the captious conduct of the ungodly. Men of the same principles as those Scribes and their companions, are in every generation. And as they are all alike enemies to the pure truths of the Gospel, the faithful cannot be too earnest in seeking grace, to avoid all unnecessary conversation, which *minister questions rather than godly edifying.* 1 Tim. 1. 4.

9 ¶ Then began he to speak to the people this parable; a certain man planted a vineyard, and let it forth to husbandmen, and went into a far country for a long time.

10 And at the season, he sent a servant to the husbandmen, that they should give him of the fruit of the vineyard: but the husbandmen beat him, and sent *him* away empty.

11 And again he sent another servant: and they beat him also, and entreated *him* shamefully, and sent *him* away empty.

12 And again he sent a third: and they wounded him also, and cast *him* out.

13 Then said the lord of the vineyard, What shall I do? I will send my beloved son: it may be they will reverence *him* when they see him.

14 But when the husbandmen saw him, they reasoned among themselves, saying, This is the heir: come, let us kill him, that the inheritance may be our's.

15 So they cast him out of the vineyard, and killed *him*. What therefore shall the lord of the vineyard do unto them?

16 He shall come and destroy these husbandmen, and shall give the vineyard to others. And when they heard *it*, they said, God forbid.

17 And he beheld them, and said, What is this then that is written, The stone which the builders rejected, the same is become the head of the corner?

18 Whosoever shall fall upon that stone shall be broken; but on whomsoever it shall fall, it will grind him to powder.

19 ¶ And the chief priests, and the scribes, the same hour sought to lay hands on him; and they feared the people: for they perceived that he had spoken this parable against them.

This parable of the LORD JESUS, though addressed to the people, the Chief Priests and Scribes perfectly well understood was meant for them. They were the husbandmen our LORD had in view, among whom the Church of GOD, as a beautiful vineyard had been long planted, even from the days when the Church was brought out of Egypt; but in vain, from them as a nation had fruit been sought for. Reader! do not from hence, however, suppose that the real Church of the LORD was unproductive to GOD's glory, during all this period. For even in the worst of times, when the prophet *Elijah* thought himself alone, as the servant of the LORD; there were *seven thousand in Israel*, which grace had reserved from the general corruption. 1 Kings xix. 14—18. And in all ages as *Isaiah* remarked in his days, and *Paul* in his, *there is a remnant according to the election of grace.* Isaiah x. 22. Rom. xi. 5. But JESUS is here describing under the similitude of a Parable, the *professing Church* of Israel, nationally considered, of which those Priests and Scribes were the supposed Husbandmen, under GOD the rightful owner. And in this sense what a pointed parable it was! And how justly true, in the destruction of the many faithful servants of the LORD, which in the several ages had been sent to them. And though the great and concluding instance of the whole, in the killing the SON was not in the moment CHRIST was then speaking, actually accomplished; yet intentionally it was done, and that by some of the very persons, in whose hearing JESUS delivered the parable. CHRIST had the whole process in view, which he knew would soon be accomplished; and therefore prophetically describes the thing as really fulfilled. I beg the Reader to remark, what an effect for the moment, the relation had upon their guilty minds. For when JESUS said, the Lord of the vineyard will come and destroy those husbandmen, and give his vineyard to others; they cried out under the impression of indignation against themselves, GOD *forbid!* Yes! Reader, there are moments in the lives of the ungodly, in which conscience will do her office, and compel the sinner to give sentence against himself. And I beg the Reader yet further to remark, how very sweetly JESUS is described as beholding them, and calling their attention to a well known scripture in confirmation of what he had said. Psm. cxviii. 22. By which the LORD led them again to their studies, for their further conviction of the truth. Oh! what aggravated condemnation to men, that with the word of GOD in their hands, are enemies to GOD's CHRIST in their hearts! Our LORD's observation respecting himself as a stone, in men's falling upon it and being broken, or the stone falling upon them and grinding them to powder, is very striking. To fall upon CHRIST, is when

JESUS becomes *a stone of stumbling and a rock of offence*, 1 Pet. ii. 8. When the carnal heart takes offence at CHRIST and his salvation, in setting up their own righteousness in whole or in part, this is to fall on CHRIST, and not to build upon CHRIST. And very awful is the condition of both, in rejecting the LORD of Life and Glory. Precious LORD JESUS! I would say, be it my portion, that blessedness, thou hast pronounced to him, *who is not offended in thee!* Matt. xi. 6.

20 And they watched *him,* and sent forth spies, which should feign themselves just men, that they might take hold of his words, that so they might deliver him unto the power and authority of the governor.

21 And they asked him, saying, Master, we know that thou sayest, and teachest rightly, neither acceptest thou the person *of any,* but teachest the way of God truly:

22 Is it lawful for us to give tribute unto Cesar, or no?

23 But he perceived their craftiness, and said unto them, Why tempt ye me?

24 Shew me a penny, Whose image and superscription hath it? they answered and said, Cesar's.

25 And he said unto them, Render therefore unto Cesar the things which be Cesar's, and unto God the things which be God's.

26 And they could not take hold of his words before the people: and they marvelled at his answer, and held their peace.

I beg the Reader to observe the eagerness with which those awful characters followed up their pursuit, in hunting after the life of JESUS. The Evangelist saith, that it was *the same hour.* Like the malice of the men, which in after days sought to destroy *Paul,* who vowed neither *to eat or drink, till they had killed him.* Acts xxiii. 12. But let not the Reader overlook in every minute circumstance which attended the death of the LORD JESUS, the hand of JEHOVAH in all. This is a grand part in the whole transaction. Isaiah liii. 10. John xix. 10, 11. Acts ii. 23. iv. 27, 28. The attempt of those men in the instance here mentioned, was with a view to bring an accusation against him, to the Roman government. The nation of the Jews at that time, was under bondage to this power. And the whole body of the people were looking forward to the coming of the *Messiah,* to deliver them from it. Nothing therefore could exceed the art of those men. They therefore now send spies, which should address JESUS very courteously; *Rabbi!* (say they,) *we know that thou sayest and teachest rightly, neither acceptest thou the person of any, but teacheth the way of* GOD *in truth.* Thus in flattering words, they covered over their evil design. Either way, by CHRIST'S answer, they made sure to entangle him. For if he confessed the authority of the *Roman* government, they concluded he would lose his popularity among those who considered him as the *Messiah.* And if he denied the *Roman* power of tribute, they would have hurried him away to *Pontius Pilate* the governor. Precious JESUS! how truly wert thou all along manifested to be *the hind of the morning,* when, according to thine own language, *many bulls compassed thee, and strong bulls of Bashan beset thee round!* Psm. xxii. title, and 12th verse.

27 ¶ Then came to *him* certain of the Sadducees, which deny that there is any resurrection; and they asked him,

28 Saying, Master, Moses wrote unto us, If any man's brother die, having a wife, and he die without children, that his brother should take his wife, and raise up seed unto his brother.

29 There were therefore seven brethren, and the first took a wife, and died without children,

30 And the second took her to wife, and he died childless.

31 And the third took her; and in like manner the seven also: and they left no children, and died.

32 Last of all the woman died also.

33 Therefore in the resurrection whose wife of them is she? for seven had her to wife.

34 And Jesus answering, said unto them, The children of this world marry, and are given in marriage:

35 But they which shall be accounted worthy to obtain that world, and the resurrection from the dead, neither marry, nor are given in marriage:

36 Neither can they die any more: for they are equal unto the angels: and are the children of God, being the children of the resurrection.

37 Now that the dead are raised, even Moses shewed at the bush, when he calleth the Lord the

God of Abraham, and the God of Isaac, and the God of Jacob.

38 For he is not a God of the dead, but of the living : for all live unto him.

39 Then certain of the scribes answering, said, Master, thou hast well said.

40 And after that, they durst not ask him any *question at all.*

The error of the *Sadducees* being founded in the first principles of doctrine, that, with the termination of the present state, man falleth into his original nothing, could not but bring after it, like so many links in the chain, error in all the after consequences. Their views being wholly carnal, they considered that CHRIST would be greatly puzzled on the supposition of a resurrection; how a woman, which in this life had been the wife of seven men, could be disposed of in another. This childish notion, however, hath not been confined to the age of the Sadducees, for some calling themselves *Rational* Christians, have in their light philosophical moments ventured to call in question doctrines of an higher nature; respecting the resurrection of CHRIST from the dead, and his return to heaven the same identical body as he lived on earth. But what is there the human mind, untaught of GOD, is not capable of setting up in opposition to the revealed truths of the Gospel? But leaving men of such principles, as well as the *Sadducees* of old; I beg the Reader to observe with me, how sweetly the LORD JESUS took occasion from their ignorance, to raise a subject of the highest improvement to all his people. For what can be more blessed than CHRIST'S own declaration, that *the children of* GOD, namely, the redeemed in the covenant, are *the children of the resurrection.* For by virtue of their union with CHRIST, they are included in all that is communicable from CHRIST : He the head, and they the members, of his body. Hence their resurrection is not the simple effect of sovereign and Almighty power, for thus all the dead shall arise ; but the children of the resurrection being children of GOD in covenant, will arise from their oneness and union with CHRIST. To this purport speaks GOD the HOLY GHOST, by the Apostle. Rom. viii. 11. *If the spirit of him that raised up* JESUS *from the dead dwell in you, he that raised up* CHRIST *from the dead, shall also quicken your mortal bodies by his Spirit that dwelleth in you.* CHRIST is the efficient cause. His blessed Spirit secures the resurrection of their bodies. He saith himself by the spirit of prophecy, when the LORD is promising the Mediator this covenant blessing : *Thy dead men, saith* GOD, *shall live. Together* (saith He) *with my dead body shall they arise.* Isaiah xxvi. 19. So that it is from the union with the LORD, as the members with the head ; the resurrection of his people is effected. *Thy dew* (saith he) *is as the dew of herbs,* which after a winter-like death, gives a warmth like the dew of the morning, and *the earth will give up* CHRIST'S *dead* ones. And as it was the Spirit of CHRIST which first quickened the souls of his redeemed from the death of sin, so is it the same Spirit, from their union with him, which reanimates their bodies at the resurrection. Oh! the preciousness of a oneness with CHRIST! Reader! what a miserable hope is the doctrine of the *Sadducees,* and the philosophical creed of the *rational* christian, as he affects to call himself, compared to this!

41 And he said unto them, How say they that Christ is David's son?

42 And David himself saith in the book of Psalms, The LORD said unto my Lord, Sit thou on my right hand,

43 Till I make thine enemies thy footstool.

44 David therefore calleth him Lord, how is he then his son?

45 Then in the audience of all the people he said unto his disciples,

46 Beware of the scribes, which desire to walk in long robes, and love greetings in the markets, and the highest seats in the synagogues, and the chief rooms at feasts:

47 Which devour widows' houses, and for a shew make long prayers: the same shall receive greater damnation.

Our LORD, having now for ever driven from the field of disputation, the whole body of Scribes, Pharisees, and Sadducees, takes occasion to lead to a subject highly interesting, that he might not only instruct his Church in that great doctrine of his double nature, GOD and Man, in One Person; but at the same time, pass his farewell sentence of condemnation upon the Scribes of that day, and the Pharisees, and self-righteous of every day, in all future generations; JESUS therefore puts forth a question respecting the relationship between *David* king of Israel and the Messiah, which was foretold as *David's* SON after the flesh. He takes for granted, that none among them had any question, as to the coming of CHRIST; but he questions, if they knew in what sense it was that he was *David's* SON. They were struck dumb at the question; and from not being taught of GOD, were unable to answer it. But, Reader! how truly blessed is our privilege, when taught of GOD. You and I perfectly know, and are assured, from that infallible teacher, that CHRIST is both the *root* and the *offspring* of *David.* For as GOD, *One with the* FATHER *over all* GOD *blessed for ever;* he is, and must be GOD: David's *root,* and the *maker* of all things. And as man he is the *offspring,* which as a *branch,* was promised to grow out of his roots: Isaiah xi. 1. Precious JESUS! hadst thou not been *both,* what would have become of me? LORD I hail thee, as the LORD my righteousness! Reader! do not hastily turn away from the solemn sentence CHRIST pronounceth on the

Scribes of old. Awful as the case of all sinners must be, who live and die in their sins; yet of all the tremendous judgments pronounced on the Christless, you see, by Christ's own words, the greater damnation will be on those who from self-righteousness, lessen in their esteem the infinitely precious value of Christ's blood and salvation; as if the necessity of Christ's sufferings were not so highly needed to recommend them to God! Isaiah lxv. 5.

REFLECTIONS.

Reader! observe in the opening of this Chapter, with what determined hatred the Chief Priests, and Scribes, and Elders, came upon Christ! What had Jesus done? He had preached the Gospel to the poor; and had gone about, healing all manner of sickness and all manner of disease among the people. And was this the cause of all their hatred and malignity? Yes! truly; and cause enough, to Satan and his seed. Look into the world now. Is the offence of the cross ceased? Oh no! Let any of Christ's servants in the present hour preach the Gospel the master preached; and hold forth salvation alone in his name, throwing to the ground all goodness and righteousness of men, and declaring, that Christ's blood and merits are the sole cause of acceptance before God; and the same effects will follow. The whole body of modern Pharisees will rise up, and like the hornet's nest will buz about to sting if they can.

What an awful, but just parable, hath Jesus here delivered of the vineyard and the husbandmen. The very enemies of Christ were compelled to acknowledge the application of it. How truly awful it is, to behold a professing Church wholly destitute of godliness. Husbandmen like foxes of the desert, destroying, but not cultivating, the Lord's vineyard!

Reader! The Holy Ghost hath not recorded the events in this Chapter for nothing. Let you and I learn, both from *Pharisee*, and *Sadducee*, to discover the melancholy state of a mind unenlightened by grace; and if so be, the Lord is our teacher, to bless God that we are the children of the resurrection. Blessed Lord! do thou reveal thyself in a covenant way, as the God of *Abraham*, and the God of *Isaac*, and the God of *Jacob*, to my soul; and then shall I live unto thee, and live in thee, and derive all life from thee, for ever and ever.

CHAP. XXI.

CONTENTS.

The Lord Jesus *foretells the Destruction of the Temple. He answers the anxious Questions of his Disciples, in fortifying their Minds with suitable Advice for the approaching Trials.*

AND he looked up, and saw the rich men casting their gifts into the treasury.

2 And he saw also a certain poor widow casting in thither two mites.

3 And he said, Of a truth I say unto you, that this poor widow hath cast in more than they all.

4 For all these have of their abundance cast in unto the offerings of God: but she of her penury hath cast in all the living that she had.

By JESUS looking up is not meant to say that the treasury was on an elevated spot, for *Mark* tells us that *he sat over against it.* It was near to the temple, and placed there most probably for conveniency, that those who were going to or from the temple might bring their alms. Our LORD furnisheth a lovely example of a poor widow, in her rich and costly offering. How little is understood of the nature of true charity. A man may give thousands, and yet have no real charity towards GOD. And another may give but little, yea, nothing, and yet in the LORD's sight be very bountiful. And the reason is plain. Where the love of GOD in CHRIST is in the heart, this, like a fountain, will diffuse streams from the same source all around. But, where that first and pre-disposing cause of all that is good is wanting, the motive cannot be right, and therefore nothing of good can follow. Hence thousands may be bestowed, and no true charity accompanying. And a precious child of GOD, like *Peter,* may have nothing to give, and yet in GOD's sight be a most liberal soul. Acts iii. 6.

5 ¶ And as some spake of the temple, how it was adorned with goodly stones, and gifts, he said,

6 *As for* these things which ye behold, the days will come in the which there shall not be left one stone upon another, that shall not be thrown down.

7 And they asked him, saying, Master, but when shall these things be? and what sign *will there be* when these things shall come to pass?

This prophecy of the LORD JESUS, and the accomplishment of it, is most wonderful. The greatness of the building, and the huge stones of which it was composed rendered it the most improbable thing upon earth. And yet, from the Jews' own historian, we learn that it was literally fulfilled.

8 And he said, Take heed that ye be not deceived; for many shall come in my name, saying, I am *Christ;* and the time draweth near, go ye not therefore after them.

9 But when ye shall hear of wars and commotions, be not terrified: for these things must first come to pass; but the end *is* not by and by.

10 Then said he unto them, Nation shall rise against nation, and kingdom against kingdom:

11 And great earthquakes shall be in divers places, and famines, and pestilences; and fearful sights, and great signs shall there be from heaven.

12 But before all these they shall lay their hands on you, and persecute *you*, delivering *you* up to the synagogues, and into prisons, being brought before kings and rulers for my name's sake.

13 And it shall turn to you for a testimony.

14 Settle *it* therefore in your hearts, not to meditate before what ye shall answer:

15 For I will give you a mouth and wisdom, which all your adversaries shall not be able to gainsay nor resist.

16 And ye shall be betrayed both by parents, and brethren, and kinsfolks, and friends; and *some* of you shall they cause to be put to death.

17 And ye shall be hated of all *men* for my name's sake.

18 But there shall not an hair of your head perish.

19 In your patience possess ye your souls.

20 And when ye shall see Jerusalem compassed with armies, then know that the desolation thereof is nigh.

21 Then let them which are in Judea flee to the mountains; and let them which are in the midst of it depart out; and let not them that are in the countries enter thereinto.

22 For these be the days of vengeance, that all things which are written may be fulfilled.

23 But woe unto them that are with child, and to them that give suck in those days! for there shall be great distress in the land, and wrath upon this people.

24 And they shall fall by the edge of the

sword, and shall be led away captive into all nations; and Jerusalem shall be trodden down of the Gentiles, until the times of the Gentiles be fulfilled.

Both *Matthew* and *Mark* have related the same prophecy of CHRIST; and our LORD's predictions in both Evangelists were nearly the same. I refer therefore to them, to avoid the swelling our pages beyond the limits I must observe. See Matt. xxiv. throughout, and Mark xiii. in like manner.

25 ¶ And there shall be signs in the sun, and in the moon, and in the stars; and upon the earth distress of nations, with perplexity; the sea and the waves roaring;

26 Men's hearts failing them for fear, and for looking after those things which are coming on the earth: for the powers of heaven shall be shaken.

27 And then shall they see the Son of man coming in a cloud with power and great glory.

28 And when these things begin to come to pass, then look up, and lift up your heads, for your redemption draweth nigh.

29 And he spake to them a parable; Behold, the fig-tree, and all the trees:

30 When they now shoot forth, ye see and know of your ownselves that summer is now nigh at hand.

31 So likewise ye, when ye see these things come to pass, know ye that the kingdom of God is nigh at hand.

32 Verily I say unto you, This generation shall not pass away till all be fulfilled.

33 Heaven and earth shall pass away: but my words shall not pass away.

34 And take heed to yourselves lest at any time your hearts be overcharged with surfeiting and drunkenness, and cares of this life, and *so* that day come upon you unawares.

35 For as a snare shall it come on all them that dwell on the face of the whole earth.

36 Watch ye therefore, and pray always, that
ye may be accounted worthy to escape all these
things that shall come to pass, and to stand before
the Son of man.

I include the whole of those verses into one view, and in addition
to what hath been already observed upon the subject, in the former
Evangelists, I have only to guard the Reader against making unscrip-
tural and improper application, as if those things referred to the last
day of CHRIST's final coming to judgment. To correct this, the LORD
declared, that, the generation then present should not be all dead,
until the events he foretold were come to pass: Similar to our LORD's
expression, Matt. xvi. 28. And this was literally the case; for *John*,
the beloved Apostle, outlived it; and numbers besides there must have
been of those who were little children at the time our LORD so prophesied.

37 And in the day time he was teaching in the
temple; and at night he went out, and abode in
the mount that is called *the mount* of Olives.
38 And all the people came early in the morning to him in the temple for to hear him.

What a beautiful view, in a short compass, is here given of the
LORD JESUS CHRIST! Never fatigued, nor weary in his labor of love,
though in body sometimes, as we find, (John iv. 6.) obliged to sit to
rest himself. And, in the period we are now arrived at in his history,
JESUS knew what exercises, both of soul and body, were opening before him. Blessed LORD! the temple bare witness to thy fatigue by
day, and the Mount of Olives of thy exercises and communion by
night. Oh! how truly lovely and engaging thus to behold CHRIST,
while acting as the Surety and Representative of his people!

REFLECTIONS.

MY soul! in beholding this poor widow, whose charity of soul the
LORD himself hath recorded, and made her history memorable in his
Church for ever; learn how very costly and precious in thy JESUS's
sight, is the love of man, when flowing from the love of GOD. Oh!
who would not wish, among the children of the LORD, to give a cup of
cold water, when we have nothing warmer to offer, in the name of
a disciple, than to build alms-houses, and give thousands, without
an eye to CHRIST.

Blessed LORD! how truly awful was thy prediction concerning the
once beloved city; and how truly verified was the whole! Most
fully was GOD the FATHER's sentence accomplished on *Jerusalem*,
when he said, in relation to his dear SON, *For the nation and kingdom
that will not serve thee shall perish.* And, in the instance of Jerusalem!
how awfully fulfilled. LORD, grant that all thy redeemed ones, preserved by sanctifying grace, and gathered out of the city of destruc-

tion, may be enabled by thy renewing mercy and free salvation, to watch and pray; and be accounted worthy in the alone blood and righteousness of JESUS, to escape all these things, and *to stand before the Son of Man!*

CHAP. XXII.

CONTENTS.

An Account of the Passover. Judas engageth to betray CHRIST. *The* LORD's *Supper instituted.* CHRIST *apprehended, and led away to the High Priest's House.* Peter *denieth* CHRIST. *The* LORD JESUS *brought before the Council.*

NOW the feast of unleavened bread drew nigh, which is called the Passover.

2 And the chief priests and scribes sought how they might kill him: for they feared the people.

We are now entering upon the most sublime, the most solemn and interesting subject which the mind of a truly regenerated child of GOD can possibly contemplate. It is indeed endeared to every heart. I have been always led to consider the wonderful events recorded in this chapter as of the tenderest nature, since the LORD brought me in any measure acquainted with himself. And at every renewed opportunity of going over the sacred contents, I would look up for renewed teachings of GOD the HOLY GHOST, that I may discover somewhat increasingly precious to my view, in the person and offices of JESUS, that may render the subject increasingly interesting. LORD! I would say, shed those sweet influences in the present moment!

Of the *Passover* I have already had occasion to notice, Matt. xxvi. and shall again have somewhat further to offer as we enter upon it. But for the present I pass it by, in order to attend to what is related of *Judas* in the following verses.

3 ¶ Then entered Satan into Judas, surnamed Iscariot, being of the number of the twelve.

4 And he went his way, and communed with the chief priests and captains, how he might betray him unto them.

5 And they were glad, and covenanted to give him money.

6 And he promised, and sought opportunity to betray him unto them in the absence of the multitude.

I beg the Reader to be particular in remarking what is here said of the traitor, in relation to the *time*, in which *Satan* is said to have entered into him. If the Reader compares what is here said with the other Evangelists' account, he will discover that it was *two days* before the Passover. *Matthew* saith, that CHRIST was then in *Bethany*, in the house of *Simon* the *leper*. Matt. xxvi. 2—6. And *John* saith, that CHRIST and his disciples were at supper. John xiii 2. Now this Supper could not have been the LORD's *Supper*, for JESUS instituted the LORD's Supper in the room of the Jewish *Passover*: and this he did not do before that he had, according to his earnest desire, celebrated it once more with his disciples. Neither could this Supper have been the *Passover*, for it was two days after this, when the LORD sent *Peter* and *John* to *prepare for the Passover*. And, moreover, this Supper was at *Bethany*, two miles from *Jerusalem*. And the Passover could no where be observed but *in Jerusalem*. See Deut. xvi. 2, 5, 6, 16. So that all these circumstances are in full proof, that the Supper *John* speaks of was not the *Passover*, neither the Supper of the LORD.

Now *John* is express to declare, that it was at this Supper in *Bethany*, JESUS gave the sop to *Judas* Iscariot, after which Satan entered into him. And *Luke* in this place saith, that this was *before* the *Passover;* and *Matthew* dates the time; it was *two days before the Passover.* Matt. xxvi. 2, 6, 16, 17. If the Reader be careful to put all these things together, he cannot hesitate to conclude, that *Satan's* entrance into the traitor was *two days* before the *Passover.*

And this point being very fully ascertained and confirmed, we shall next as compleatly discover, notwithstanding weak and injudicious Christians would wish to have it otherwise, that *Judas*, after this, partook both in the *Passover* and the LORD's *Supper*. And here again I request the Reader's close attention, in order to have a clear apprehension of the fact.

When the disciples, which had been sent from *Bethany* to prepare the *Passover*, had made all things ready, we are told, that, in the evening, JESUS came with the twelve. Mark. xiv. 17. And both *Matthew* and *Luke* are express in saying, that, when the hour was come, he sat down, and the *twelve Apostles with him.* Verse 14. Matt. xxvi. 20. And the relation, as given by the Evangelists, *Matthew*, *Mark*, and *Luke*, of the services, both of the *Passover*, and the LORD's institution of his Supper, very fully prove the presence and participation of *Judas*, in common with the rest of the Apostles. The ordinance of the *Passover* is related in this chapter, from the 15th to the end of the 18th verse. Then commenceth the service of the LORD's Supper. At the close of which, and not before, JESUS declares that the hand of the traitor was then with him on the table. How long after *Judas* remained is not said; but this statement by those three Evangelists, most decidedly prove, that the traitor took his place at the table, perhaps the better to cover his design, and was a partaker in both ordinances.

And, indeed, I cannot discover the shadow of a reason, wherefore any of the LORD's faithful ones should take offence at it, or wish it otherwise. Nay, I humbly conceive, that the LORD JESUS had a special design in it, for his own glory, and his Church's happiness. I will explain myself—

It is certain, that when the LORD chose *Judas* to the office of an Apostle, he knew him to be a devil, for so the LORD said, *Have not*

I chosen you twelve? and one of you is a devil! He spake (said the Evangelist) *of Judas Iscariot, the Son of Simon, for he it was that should betray him, being one of the twelve.* John vi. 70, 71. If therefore the LORD chose him into the Apostleship, under such circumstances, shall it appear surprizing, that he admitted him to the Passover and Supper? Having granted the *greater*, can we wonder at the *less.*

Moreover, we find, that during the whole time of our LORD's ministry, *Judas* exercised the commission of an Apostle, in common with the rest. We read, (Luke ix. 1—6.) that the LORD sent out the *twelve* to cast out devils, heal the sick, and preach the kingdom of GOD; consequently *Judas* must have been included. Had this man been restrained from the exercise of the same power as the *eleven*, surely it mu·t have been perceived by the rest, and they would have known it. And yet we find, that *Judas*, though all the while, as our LORD termed him, a devil, had carried himself so deceitfully, (2 Cor. xi. 13, 14, 15.) that when at the table, and at the close of CHRIST's ministry, JESUS declared that one of the twelve would betray him, they were so unconscious of his real character, that they anxiously enquired which of them it should be?

Now then, if the LORD JESUS, (who, as John saith, *knew all men, and needed not that any should testify of man, for he knew what was in man.* John ii. 25.) was thus pleased, for wise and great purposes, though unknown to us, yet well known to him, to choose a devil to mix up with his Apostles, yea, for aught we know to the contrary, to exercise the same functions as they did; what greater causes could there be to keep him from ordinances than from the Apostleship? Did he not enjoy higher privileges as an Apostle, than in partaking of the Passover, or Supper of the LORD? And is it not highly probable that our adorable JESUS had some gracious design in the appointment, which, instead of militating to evil should be overruled to good. I humbly conceive this to be the case; and I beg the Reader's patience while I state my further views upon this part of the subject also.

And here, first, I would remark, that this traitor, this devil, as the LORD called him, though chosen to be a Minister, and an Apostle, was never called to be a partaker of grace, neither he himself ever regenerated by the HOLY GHOST. Let this be well considered. And, that the Church of GOD might not err in forming just views of his real character, GOD the HOLY GHOST, by the mouth of *Peter*, was pleased to shew to what the Apostleship of Judas extended. *He was numbered with us,* (said Peter,) *and had obtained* PART *of this ministry.* Acts i. 17. Part of this ministry! Yes! such a part, and such only, as a devil might obtain. And what is that? An *outside* part; the form of office; the mere exercise of the function. Nothing of grace. No one gift of the Spirit. Such as men, unordained by the HOLY GHOST, unregenerated in heart *may*, and the LORD only knows how often *do* exercise; but which have no tendency to their own sanctification. Such was Judas! A devil he was, and a devil he remained, notwithstanding his associating with the Apostles while on earth, until the measure of his iniquity was filled; and then, as we are told, he went *to his own place!* Acts i, 25. And, however awful the view to the Church of JESUS, yet, the Great Head of it hath prepared his redeemed to expect similar instances, and by our

LORD's manner of speaking, not a few beside that of *Judas*, which shall be unfolded at the last day. *Many* (saith JESUS) *will say to me in that day*, LORD! LORD! *have we not prophesied in thy name, and in thy name cast out devils, and in thy name done many wonderful works. And then will I profess unto them I never knew you; depart from me, ye that work iniquity.* Matt. vii. 22, 23.

But it were not doing justice to the subject to stop here. May we not also suppose, that the LORD JESUS had a further design of mercy to his Church and people in the appointment of a *Judas* among his Apostles? He well knew that his Church would never be free, while in a militant state, from false Apostles, and false Prophets. JESUS not only foretold his redeemed this, but prepared them how to form conclusions concerning them. Tares, he said, should grow together with the good seed, until the harvest. Goats should be found with the sheep. But, in the midst, the *precious and the vile* are still perfectly distinct; and never, no never can coalesce. Tares never can become good seed, neither can sheep become goats. The seed of the woman, and the seed of the serpent cannot join. Hence therefore, if JESUS, in that little handful of his people, the eleven Apostles, purposely chose a *Judas* to mingle, well may the Church be satisfied in the midst of the heathen, when they consider that the LORD *endured such a contradiction of sinners against himself, lest they should be weary, and faint in mind.*

Reader! learn from hence, that the Church of CHRIST is not polluted from the mingling of the ungodly in her sweetest and most sacred ordinances. The *Passover*, and the *Supper* of the LORD, lost no savor to the Apostles, from the presence of *Judas!* They had JESUS with them, and that was all they needed. And if you or I, in his house, or at his table, meet JESUS in the ordinance, our joys will suffer no lessening from any unhallowed objects around. If GOD the HOLY GHOST will lead my way *forth by the footsteps of the flock, where the Great Shepherd feeds his sheep;* Song i. 8. though *Judas* himself dared to be present, there my soul should be found. Job i. 6. And however I would seek out that ministry, and that people, where CHRIST alone is exalted, yet sure I am, however barren the means, yet led by the LORD, I shall go in and out, and find pasture. JESUS will prepare *a table before me in the presence of mine enemies, he will anoint my head with oil, and make my cup run over.* Psm. xxiii. 5.

7 ¶ Then came the day of unleavened bread, when the passover must be killed.

8 And he sent Peter and John, saying, Go, and prepare us the passover, that we may eat.

9 And they said unto him, Where wilt thou that we prepare?

10 And he said unto them, Behold, when ye are entered into the city, there shall a man meet you bearing a pitcher of water: follow him into the house where he entereth in,

11 And ye shall say unto the good man of the house, The Master saith unto thee, Where is the guest-chamber, where I shall eat the passover with my disciples?

12 And he shall shew you a large upper room furnished: there make ready.

13 And they went, and found as he had said unto them: and they made ready the passover.

14 And when the hour was come, he sat down, and the twelve apostles with him.

15 And he said unto them, With desire I have desired to eat this passover with you before I suffer:

16 For I say unto you, I will not any more eat thereof, until it be fulfilled in the kingdom of God.

17 And he took the cup, and gave thanks, and said, Take this, and divide it among yourselves:

18 For I say unto you, I will not drink of the fruit of the vine, until the kingdom of God shall come.

19 ¶ And he took bread, and gave thanks, and brake it, and gave unto them, saying, This is my body which is given for you: this do in remembrance of me.

20 Likewise also the cup after supper, saying, This cup is the new testament in my blood, which is shed for you.

21 But behold, the hand of him that betrayeth me is with me on the table.

22 And truly the Son of man goeth as it was determined: but woe unto that man by whom he is betrayed!

23 And they began to enquire among themselves, which of them it was that should do this thing.

24 And there was also a strife among them which of them should be accounted the greatest.

25 And he said unto them, The kings of the Gentiles exercise lordship over them; and they that exercise authority upon them are called bene-factors.

26 But ye *shall* not *be* so: but he that is greatest among you, let him be as the younger; and he that is chief, as he that doth serve.

27 For whether *is* greater, he that sitteth at meat, or he that serveth? *is* not he that sitteth at meat? but I am among you as he that serveth.

28 Ye are they which have continued with me in my temptations.

29 And I appoint unto you, a kingdom, as my Father hath appointed unto me;

30 That ye may eat and drink at my table in my kingdom, and sit on thrones judging the twelve tribes of Israel.

31 And the Lord said, Simon, Simon, behold, Satan hath desired *to have* you, that he may sift you as wheat:

32 But I have prayed for thee, that thy faith fail not: and when thou art converted, strengthen thy brethren.

33 And he said unto him, Lord, I am ready to go with thee both into prison, and to death.

34 And he said, I tell thee, Peter, the cock shall not crow this day before that thou shalt thrice deny that thou knowest me.

35 And he said unto them, When I sent you without purse, and scrip, and shoes, lacked ye any thing? and they said, Nothing.

36 Then said he unto them, But now, he that hath a purse, let him take *it,* and likewise *his* scrip: and he that hath no sword, let him sell his garment, and buy one.

37 For I say unto you, That this that is written must yet be accomplished in me. And he was

reckoned among the transgressors: for the things concerning me have an end.

38 And they said, Lord, behold, here *are* two swords. And he said unto them, It is enough.

39 And he came out and went, as he was wont, to the mount of Olives; and his disciples also followed him.

I have not interrupted the precious narrative, both of the cele-bration of the *Passover*, the institution of the LORD's *Supper*, and the Redeemer's divine discourse, both before, and with those services, and after. The account, as here given by *Luke*, carries on the subject to the moment when the LORD JESUS arose from the table, and went for the last time to the Mount of *Olives*. But, the Reader must be aware, that numberless incidents beside those which *Luke* hath here recorded, took place at this memorable season. Here it was, at this table, JESUS delivered in part that sweet discourse which *John* hath recorded in the xivth, xvth, and xvith chapters of his Gospel. Accord-ing to my apprehension of those solemn transactions, I conceive that JESUS, viewing the deep sorrow of heart expressed in the counte-nances of the eleven Apostles, after the traitor was gone out, begun that most blessed Sermon, as related by John, xivth chapter. *Let not your heart be troubled*, &c. And when the LORD had concluded that chapter, he arose, as *Luke* here describes, and went forth to-wards the Mount of *Olives*. And I am inclined to suppose, that, as JESUS was passing along, beholding the rich luxuriant vines which spread their branches on the ground, he continued his discourse, and took occasion to describe himself under this similitude with his people, and then begun at the words *John* hath recorded in the opening of the xvth Chapter, and thus prosecuting his blessed Sermon through the whole to the end of the xvith Chapter. And then offered up the prayer Chapter xvii. Whether this be rightly placed, according to order, I venture not to determine. But, certain it is, that somewhere about this time the LORD JESUS preached this farewell Sermon to his dear disciples; and as a dying Father, encircled by his family, the LORD thus took leave of them as a body together. I remember, in the writings of *Luther*, that highly honored servant of the LORD, concerning this loving Sermon of JESUS, he saith, " Never since the world began was there such a precious, costly, sweet, and heavenly banquet feast conversation and discourse, as this of JESUS' Supper with his disciples."

The Reader will observe, that I have not ventured to say more on the services of the *Passover*, and the Institution of the Supper, than barely to point out, according to *Luke's* account of it, at what verse the service of the *Passover* ended, and that of the Holy Supper began. But I leave him to his own meditations on both, under the hope that GOD the HOLY GHOST will unfold and explain to him the whole in order. CHRIST was here doing away for ever the *one*, and establishing the *other*. It was the *last* Passover ever to be observed in the Church of GOD; for CHRIST the true Passover was now come;

and the shadow of the ordinance wholly ceased. And it was the *first*
Supper in commemoration of CHRIST's death, and which was instituted
for a perpetual remembrance of the same, until time should be no
more.   Under the impressions of all these high ideas, and infinitely
more than our faculties are competent to conceive, the LORD JESUS
abolished the *one,* and established the *other;* and enjoined the sweet
service of the Supper in those endearing words, *This do in remem-*
brance of me !

In remembrance of thee ! O Lamb of God ! I would say in words
similar to the Church, as she spake of her beloved Jerusalem; *If I*
forget thee, let my right hand forget her cunning ! If I do not re-
member thee, let my tongue cleave to the roof of my mouth ; yea, if I
prefer not the meditation of JESUS *and Gethsemane above my chief*
joy ! Psalm cxxxvii. 5, 6.

For observations from verse 23, to verse 30, inclusive, see Matt. xix.
27 to the end.

On the subject of *Peter's* temptation, fall, and recovery, I purpose
to gather the whole into one view, in the latter part of this chapter,
where we have the circumstances more fully recorded ; and offer a few
observations.   But I would in this place just remark, what a most
interesting view is given the Church in this short but striking account of *Peter's* danger, and CHRIST's all-sufficiency.   Think how the
LORD's eye is everlastingly watching over his redeemed.   This was
an hour of deep sorrow ; but JESUS forgets his own sorrows, to attend
to the exercises of his tried ones.   *Satan* desired to have Peter, that he
might sift him as wheat. Yes ! that deadly foe desires to cast the whole
Apostles, yea, the whole Church of CHRIST into hell. Rev. ii. 10.
And observe *Peter's,* and the whole Church's safety, *I have prayed*
for thee ! Reader ! above all things keep this in everlasting view.   It
is not our prayers, our tears, our strivings, our strength !   The devil
laughs at the whole, for they are no more than a feather to the wind,
in the hour of temptation !   Precious LORD ! it is thy Advocacy, thy
Blood, thy Covenant righteousness, which becomes the security of
thy people !   And what a sweet thought to every child of GOD in a
trying hour ; there is more in JESUS, in point of deservings for his
redeemed, than there is of undeservings in all their persons.   JESUS
hath more to plead in himself and his merit for poor sinners, whom
the FATHER hath given to him, than all their unworthiness hath to say
against them !   Reader ! never lose sight of this !

40 And when he was at the place, he said unto
them, Pray, that ye enter not into temptation.

41 And he was withdrawn from them about a
stone's cast, and kneeled down, and prayed,

42 Saying, Father, if thou be willing, remove
this cup from me: nevertheless, not my will, but
thine, be done.

43 And there appeared an angel unto him from
heaven, strengthening him.

44 And being in an agony, he prayed more earnestly: and his sweat was at it were great drops of blood falling down to the ground.

45 And when he rose up from prayer, and was come to his disciples, he found them sleeping for sorrow;

46 And said unto them, Why sleep ye? rise and pray, lest ye enter into temptation.

I enter upon those verses with an holy awe and reverence! Who is competent to apprehend, much less to explain, the soul-agony of CHRIST, in this tremendous season. JESUS himself called it the hour of the enemy's triumph, and *the power of darkness.* His disciples were withdrawn from him; Satan desperately bent against him: and JESUS bearing the whole sins of his redeemed in his own person. And, as if that was not enough, the justice of GOD beholding him, as the sinner's Surety, voluntarily coming forward, the Representative and Head of his Church, to be made both a sin and a curse for his people, that they might be made the righteousness of GOD in him. These outlines of the subject, (for our present capacities are incapable of apprehending any thing more, than the merest outlines of a subject whose dimensions are infinite,) may, in some measure, serve to shew what an unequalled season of agony and soul-conflict this was to the Great Redeemer. We are told, that, on CHRIST's entrance upon his public ministry, after his baptism, when led up by the Spirit into the wilderness to be tempted of the devil, when the devil had ended those temptations, he departed from him *for a season.* Luke iv. 13. And now, at the close of his ministry, the devil came again with ten-fold fury.

But, had the temptations of hell been all which the LORD JESUS sustained in those tremendous hours, these might easily have been borne, compared to what the SON of GOD in our nature, and as the Surety of his Church and people, had to encounter. The dreadful part the LORD fell under, and which brought him to the ground in agonies and prayer, was, the frowns of Heaven; in the curse he bore, and the FATHER's judgment due to sin in consequence of it. The HOLY GHOST hath in one short verse described it, and none but GOD the HOLY GHOST could describe it: when under the Spirit of prophecy, JESUS said, *Thy rebuke hath broken my heart!* Psalm lxix. 20. It is impossible in our researches on this subject to go very far. We know that the curse pronounced on the fall was, *In the sweat of thy face shalt thou eat bread.* Gen. iii. 19. But, in sustaining this curse, who would have concluded, that a bloody sweat should follow? All men, more or less, taste of the fruit of *Adam's* sin, and not only the laboring part eat bread in the sweat of the brow; but the rich and the mighty, some way or other, know the bitterness of it. But while the earth brings forth thorns to all, JESUS only was *crowned* with them. While men sweat in sorrow, JESUS only sweats a bloody sweat. Precious LORD! in all things thou must have the pre-eminence! Coloss. i. 18.

I have, in the best manner I am able, noticed the different terms the Evangelists make use of concerning CHRIST's agony in the garden of *Gethsemane.* See Matt. xxvi. 38. He calls it the soul of CHRIST being *exceeding sorrowful even unto death. Mark* expresses it, being *sore amazed, and very heavy.* Mark xiv. 34. And *Luke* renders it *agony,* as one that was at strife, for such is the original. And yet CHRIST was alone. What strife then could this be? Nay, who shall answer the question. An angel appeared from heaven to strengthen him. An angel! Did He who was the image of the invisible GOD, and with whom it was no robbery to be equal with GOD, need aid from his creatures? So the word of truth states it; but who is competent to explain a fact so mysterious. Reader! ponder well the subject. *Angels desire to look into it.* 1 Peter i. 12. surely never, never was there a period in all the annals of mankind, since time began to be numbered, (the cross of CHRIST excepted, and this was but the close to it) of equal moment with this soul conflict of CHRIST in the garden of Gethsemane!

Reader! would you see sin in its true light! This is the mirror. The drowning of the whole world at the flood; the destruction of Sodom by fire; the ten thousand hospitals of mankind; yea, the whole earth considered as one great mass of misery; and even hell itself, with its everlasting burnings, all form no equal manifestations of the malignity of sin, compared to CHRIST bearing the curse and punishment of sin, when in the garden he bore agonies, and on the cross he died, *the just for the unjust, to bring his people to* GOD. And, therefore, let my soul, let your soul, yea, let every reflecting soul, think what ultimately must be the everlasting state and condition of every sinner who dies out of CHRIST, with his sins unpardoned, his soul uncleansed, his spirit unregenerated, and the whole weight and pressure of his iniquity bearing upon his own soul! If CHRIST was thus brought into such an agony, while bearing only the transgressions of others; what must be the terrors of those who bear their own? If, to use our LORD's own words, *such things were done in the green tree,* where there was nothing to give fuel to fire, *what shall be done in the dry?* where, like combustible matter, it wants but the spark to set the whole in a blaze, to burn for ever! Luke xxiii. 31.

I feel constrained to detain the Reader one moment longer over this most solemn passage, just to observe the state of the disciples at this awful crisis. When JESUS, in the midst of his agony, came to them who had been withdrawn from him by some supernatural power, it is said, that he found them *sleeping for sorrow!* And both *Matthew* and *Mark* have recorded, that, at this time this was repeatedly the case, at CHRIST's going from them, and returning to them again. Matt. xxvi. 40, 43, 45. Mark xiv. 37, 40, 41. Reader! observe the expression, *sleeping for sorrow!* We know full well, that sorrow, deep sorrow, will prevent sleep; but it must be unusual sorrow indeed to induce sleep. But it should seem very plain, that the Apostle's sleep was a sleep into which they were cast by the powers of hell. JESUS himself said, that this was the hour of the enemies' triumph, and the powers of darkness; and it seems more than probable, that *Satan* had drenched those few faithful servants of the LORD in a stupidity and heaviness to sleep on purpose, that all human comfort should be withdrawn at this awful time from CHRIST; and CHRIST left alone to combat in this unparalleled struggle!

47 And while he yet spake, behold, a multitude, and he that was called Judas, one of the twelve, went before them, and drew near unto Jesus, to kiss him.

48 But Jesus said unto him, Judas, betrayest thou the Son of man with a kiss?

49 When they which were about him saw what would follow, they said unto him, Lord, shall we smite with the sword?

50 And one of them smote the servant of the high priest, and cut off his right ear.

51 And Jesus answered and said, Suffer ye thus far. And he touched his ear, and healed him.

52 Then Jesus said unto the chief priests, and captains of the temple, and the elders, which were come to him, Be ye come out, as against a thief, with swords and staves?

53 When I was daily with you in the temple, ye stretched forth no hands against me: but this is your hour, and the power of darkness.

54 Then took they him, and led *him,* and brought him into the high priest's house. And Peter followed afar off.

We now are called upon to another view of the Redeemer. I beg the Reader's close attention. Every word is big with importance. And, *first,* Judas, with the band coming to apprehend CHRIST. But what a band of such armed men to lay hold of one poor unarmed man? Had they conceived that JESUS was nothing more than man, is it likely that they would have taken so great a body? And wherefore did *Judas* give such a signal for the apprehension of CHRIST? And *Matthew* adds to this account, that *Judas,* who made this the signal for the seizing of CHRIST, said to the soldiers, that when he had kissed CHRIST, they should *hold him fast.* Matt. xxvi. 48. Wherefore were all these precautions, but from a conviction, that CHRIST was more than man. Surely, in the very moment they seized the LORD of life and glory, the minds of the greater part of the party were struck with condemnation. *Judas* could not forget the miracles of CHRIST. He had known his Master escape from the hands of his enemies, when they sought to throw him over the hill of the city.

Luke iv. 29, 30, 31. Hence he charged them to bind him, and lead him away safely. Mark xiv. 44. Reader! pause here to remark, how the LORD was overruling their malice to his own glory. CHRIST was now accomplishing the whole predictions of the prophets. Though the voluntary offering of the LORD JESUS formed a most momentous part in the great efficacy of his sacrifice, yet the sacrifice, according to the law, must be bound. Psalm cxviii. 27. Hence *Isaac*, a type of CHRIST, was bound and laid upon the altar. So that to answer both purposes, CHRIST's willingness, and their holding him fast, we have JESUS' voluntary surrender of himself, and their binding him.

And, *secondly*, I beg the Reader not to overlook what is said of the whole band, both of Jews and Gentiles, as engaged in this apprehension of CHRIST. By the spirit of prophecy, ages before these events came to be fulfilled, it was said, that, *the kings of the earth, and the rulers, should take counsel together, against the* LORD, *and against his anointed.* Psalm ii. 1, 2, 3. Here we behold the accomplishment. And GOD the HOLY GHOST, by the mouth of *Peter*, sweetly explains the whole, and applies it. Acts iv. 19—28. Compare with Psalm xxii. the title of it, and the 12th and 16th verses explain each other.

And, *thirdly*, I pray the Reader to observe, that though all along, as the mock trial which follows proves, their intention was to deliver CHRIST over to the *Roman* power; yet to the High Priest he shall be first led. And wherefore? Aye! there's the point. They saw not the LORD's hand in all this; but the sacrifice of CHRIST must be bound, must be led away, as all sacrifices under the law were, to the High Priest, and both Jew and Gentile must be engaged in the great work. So that the hurrying the LORD JESUS, from the High Priest to the Governor, and from the hall of *Pilate*, to the Mount of *Calvary*, shall be in confirmation of that glorious scripture, *He is brought as a lamb to the slaughter, and as a sheep before her shearers is dumb, so he openeth not his mouth.* Isaiah liii. 7.

55 And when they had kindled a fire in the midst of the hall, and were set down together, Peter sat down among them.

56 But a certain maid beheld him as he sat by the fire, and earnestly looked upon him, and said, This man was also with him.

57 And he denied him, saying, Woman, I know him not.

58 And after a little while, another saw him, and said, Thou art also of them. And Peter said, Man, I am not.

59 And about the space of one hour after, another confidently affirmed, saying, Of a truth this *fellow* also was with him: for he is a Galilean.

60 And Peter said, Man, I know not what thou sayest. And immediately, while he yet spake, the cock crew.

61 And the Lord turned, and looked upon Peter. And Peter remembered the word of the Lord, how he had said unto him, Before the cock crow, thou shalt deny me thrice.

62 And Peter went out and wept bitterly.

The subject of *Peter's* fall, and recovery by grace, which the sacred historian hath so particularly noticed in those verses, both merit our most earnest attention. There can be no doubt, but that the HOLY GHOST meant it should be held forth to the Church, for the special improvement of the LORD's people in all ages; and it would be an unpardonable neglect under such an impression, if we were to pass it by.

The best service, I apprehend, which I can do the Reader, will be by a short commentary to mark under both parts in his fall, and in his recovery by sovereign grace, the striking features contained in the history; looking to the LORD the HOLY GHOST to make the review of it profitable to both Writer and Reader.

And here, in respect to the subject of *Peter's* fall, I would observe the greatness of that fall. Every thing tended to aggravate it. The person of *Peter*, so dear to JESUS; the time and place in which this foul denial was committed; the little provocations to it at the instance of a poor servant maid, and such like characters: add to these, the peculiar privileges *Peter* had enjoyed above all the other Apostles, excepting *James* and *John*. He had seen CHRIST's glory in the Mount. He had been an eye witness to his agonies in the garden. One or two miracles of a private nature, which JESUS wrought, he had been present at; and once, at the command of CHRIST, his faith had been so strong in the first warmth of his love, that he had attempted to walk to JESUS on the water. And yet, amidst all these distinguishing mercies, and forewarned as he was by CHRIST, he not only denied CHRIST, but persisted in the denial, though the first crow of the cock told him of his perfidy; yet on he went, and at length proceeded by oaths to such a desperate state of confirmation to the lie, as took off all pretence that it might have been the effect of surprize or inadvertency. Reader! behold in this instance what man is in his highest attainments! Surely, in the view of so great an Apostle, (for a great Apostle he was,) we cannot but learn, that the best of men are but men, and the greatest of men may fall. The corruptions of nature are the same in all. And the only difference between one man and another, is what grace makes, and not man's merit. LORD JESUS! impress this great truth on my heart, that I may have a full sense of that sweet scripture, and which *Peter*, in the after stages of life more fully learnt under the HOLY GHOST, they *that are kept, are kept by the power of* GOD *through faith unto salvation.* 1 Peter i. 5.

, Let us attend now, in a few words, to the improvements to be drawn from *Peter's* recovery. From whence we no less learn, that as the best of men cannot keep themselves from falling, so neither, when fallen, can they raise themselves, but their recovery is the sole effect of sovereign grace. In proof of this, in the instance of *Peter*, we are told, that he heard the *first* crowing of the cock without manifesting any emotion. But, when at the *second* crowing of the cock, *the* LORD *turned and looked upon Peter*, that look entered his soul. *He went out and wept bitterly*. That his repentance was true and sincere, all the after events in the Apostle's life proved. But these were the *effects*, and not the *cause*. One of the Fathers, (I think it was *Chrysostom*,) hath made a beautiful observation upon the blessings which accompanied the LORD's word with the LORD's power. For, as Peter heard the cock crow, and seemingly unconcerned, so sinners hear the word of GOD, and remain regardless. But when the LORD's grace enters the heart, as the eye of JESUS darted upon Peter, then all the blessed effects follow. Reader! do not overlook the gracious, tender, loving, (what shall I call it,) forgiving look of JESUS to *Peter*. Surrounded as CHRIST then was, with the hell-hounds waiting for his blood, still he forgot not poor *Peter!* Oh! the compassions of JESUS! LORD! manifest them to my soul!

63 And the men that held Jesus mocked him, and smote *him*.

64 And when they had blindfolded him, they struck him on the face, and asked him, saying, Prophesy, who is it that smote thee?

65 And many other things blasphemously spake they against him.

66 And as soon as it was day, the elders of the people, and the chief priests, and the scribes came together, and led him into their council, saying,

67 Art thou the Christ, tell us. And he said unto them, If I tell you, ye will not believe:

68 And if I also ask *you*, ye will not answer me, nor let *me* go.

69 Hereafter shall the Son of man sit on the right hand of the power of God.

70 Then said they all, Art thou then the Son of God? and he said unto them, Ye say that I am.

71 And they said, What need we any further witness? for we ourselves have heard of his own mouth.

I will only for the present in this place beg the Reader to notice the cruelties exercised on CHRIST's person, and the blasphemy they were guilty of to his divine offices. In their mockery, they insulted his *Kingly* office. In their blindfolding him, his *Priestly*: for there were to be no blemishes in those who ministered in holy things. And in demanding who smote him, they did despite to his *Prophetical*. But, amidst all these reproaches, we hear no murmur. Yea, no answer, until demanded whether he was the Son of God. And, oh! how blessed the good confession; *Ye say that : I am.* For so it should be stopped. Precious Lord! in what a blessed view is this testimony of the Lord in all the hearts of his redeemed!

REFLECTIONS.

Reader! let us ponder well the precious contents of this most precious Chapter. Behold! how Jesus delighted in his *last* Passover, and *first* Supper! *With desire* (said that dear Lord,) *I have desired to eat it with you before I suffer.* And doth he not still desire sweet communion with his people *now*, as he did *then ?* Doth not Jesus say the same concerning his Word, his Ordinances, his Table, his Supper? And doth not the Lord, from the first moment of beholding his Church, long for the season of the conversion of each, and the comfort of all, until the whole redeemed are brought home to glory? Oh! then how sweet to follow up the Lord's desires with our own; and while Jesus is coming forth to bless, You and I may, through his grace, be going forth to meet him.

Reader! pause over the awful character of *Judas!* Behold the different features of *Peter!* Contemplate from everlasting the cause in the sovereignty of grace, and if so be we can find in our own souls, tokens of rich, free, unmerited love, causing us to differ from the traitor, in being children of promise; oh! for grace to ascribe all the glory to Him, to whom alone all is due. Lord! how is it, we may well say, *that thou hast manifested thyself unto us, and not unto the world!*

Praised be thy dear name, in that Jesus the Son of God took upon him to answer for his people, by which the Holy One of Israel was reckoned among the transgressors. And shall not thy redeemed be accounted righteous in thee, before God ? My soul! all the ransomed in Zion are authorized to this conclusion. Bless thy God and Savior for this unspeakable mercy. It is Jehovah that hath so concluded, and therefore make it thy conclusion also; for so the charter of grace runs to the Church's joy. *For he hath made him to be sin for us, who knew no sin, that we might be made the righteousness of God in him.*

CHAP. XXIII.

CONTENTS.

The Lord Jesus is hurried away before Pilate, and accused. He sends Christ to Herod; where he is mocked, and sent back to Pilate. The unjust Governor condemns him to Death; and Christ is led away to Execution. The Lord's Death and Burial.

AND the whole multitude of them arose, and led him unto Pilate:

2 And they began to accuse him, saying, We found this *fellow* perverting the nation, and forbidding to give tribute to Cesar, saying, that he himself is Christ, a King.

3 And Pilate asked him, saying, Art thou the King of the Jews? and he answered him and said, Thou sayest *it*.

4 Then said Pilate to the chief priests, and *to* the people, I find no fault in this man.

5 And they were the more fierce, saying, He stirreth up the people, teaching throughout all Jewry, beginning from Galilee to this place.

6 When Pilate heard of Galilee, he asked whether the man were a Galilean?

7 And as soon as he knew that he belonged unto Herod's jurisdiction, he sent him to Herod, who himself also was at Jerusalem at that time.

8 And when Herod saw Jesus, he was exceeding glad: for he was desirous to see him of a long *season*, because he had heard many things of him: and he hoped to have seen some miracle done by him.

9 Then he questioned with him in many words; but he answered him nothing.

10 And the chief priests and scribes stood, and vehemently accused him.

11 And Herod, with his men of war, set him at nought, and mocked *him*, and arrayed him in a gorgeous robe, and sent him again to Pilate.

12 And the same day Pilate and Herod were made friends together, for before they were at enmity between themselves.

It forms a very interesting part, in my view of those solemn scenes, to observe how the Lamb of God is worried before his death, in those many wearisome journies he is compelled to make, in walking from one place to another to gratify the malice of his enemies. And I beg the Reader to observe with me, that, as in all those places CHRIST received the same contempt and mockery, at the house of the *High Priest,* and at the palaces of *Pilate* and *Herod,* whether the whole was not intended for the greater humiliation of the Son of God, because, in that humiliation, the vast merit of his redemption-work consisted. It was the Son of God, as God, vacating, or emptying himself of his own personal glory, as God-Man-Mediator, which constituted the infinite preciousness of his undertaking, as our Surety, and which gave such an infinite, and never to be fully recompensed value, both to his active and passive righteousness, both to his doing and dying. I would entreat the Reader, methinks, to pass over, in this sublime subject, every other consideration, to attend wholly to this one. The part which those wretched characters, *Pilate* and *Herod,* with the whole Jewish crew, wreaking their malice upon the person of Christ, is a matter of no moment to regard, compared to this one. This forms the blessedness of the whole subject. This renders the whole so inexpressibly great and glorious. For the more the child of God is enabled by the Holy Ghost to enter into a suitable apprehension of this distinguishing feature of character in our Lord, as Redeemer, the infinitely higher will the merit of his sacrifice rise in his esteem.

13 And Pilate, when he had called together the chief priests, and the rulers, and the people,

14 Said unto them, Ye have brought this man unto me, as one that perverteth the people: and, behold, I, having examined *him* before you, have found no fault in this man, touching those things whereof ye accuse him:

15 No, nor yet Herod: for I sent you to him; and, lo, nothing worthy of death is done unto him.

16 I will therefore chastise him, and release *him.*

17 (For of necessity he must release one unto them at the feast.)

18 And they cried out all at once, saying, Away with this *man,* and release unto us Barabbas:

19 (Who for a certain sedition made in the city, and for murder, was cast into prison.)

20 Pilate therefore, willing to release Jesus, spake again to them.

21 But they cried, saying, Crucify *him,* crucify him.

22 And he said unto them the third time, Why, what evil hath he done? I have found no cause of

death in him : I will therefore chastise him, and let *him* go.

23 And they were instant with loud voices, requiring that he might be crucified. And the voices of them, and of the chief priests, prevailed.

24 And Pilate gave sentence, that it should be as they required.

25 And he released unto them him that for sedition and murder was cast into prison, whom they had desired; but he delivered Jesus to their will.

If I pause over those verses, it shall be only to detain the Reader with remarking what an awful character this time-serving judge *Pilate* must have been. He declared JESUS guiltless, and yet proposed by way of a milder punishment, to scourge him. He pronounced sentence of death upon CHRIST in the same breath that he declared him innocent! With what horrors must the soul of *Pilate* behold JESUS at the last day, when his body shall arise at the voice of the archangel and the trump of GOD, to receive from the LORD his sentence of everlasting misery? Rev. i. 7.

26 And as they led him away, they laid hold upon one Simon, a Cyrenian, coming out of the country, and on him they laid the cross, that he might bear *it* after Jesus.

27 ¶ And there followed him a great company of people, and of women, which also bewailed and lamented him.

28 But Jesus turning unto them, said, Daughters of Jerusalem, weep not for me, but weep for yourselves, and for your children.

29 For, behold, the days are coming in the which they shall say, Blessed *are* the barren, and the wombs that never bare, and the paps which never gave suck.

30 Then shall they begin to say to the mountains, Fall on us; and to the hills, Cover us.

31 For if they do these things in a green tree, what shall be done in the dry?

I refer to the observations proposed in *Matthew* and *Mark's* Gospel, on the cruelties exercised on CHRIST's person, after sentence of death was passed upon him. See Matt. xxvii. 27. Mark xv. 16. Let the Reader in this place remark the tenderness of the LORD JESUS, in forgetting his own sorrows to regard the sorrows of his people. *Luke* is the only Evangelist which hath recorded this affectionate address of JESUS to the daughters of Jerusalem. Is it not (for I do not speak decidedly on the subject) as a prophecy of the LORD, in relation to the sorrows hastening upon *Zion's* sons in the approaching destruction of Jerusalem? Zech. xii. 10. But their weeping at the view of the LORD JESUS, was as might be expected. For who could dry-eyed behold the Lamb of GOD surrounded thus with hell-hounds, waiting to suck his blood? Nature alone, untaught of grace, hath some remains of feeling to shew that it is not totally void of humanity. It is said of *Austin*, that before his conversion, he delighted to hear *Ambrose* speak of the sufferings of CHRIST, and always wept at hearing the relation. But this may be, and yet not grace. *Ezekiel* had such hearers. Ezek. xxxiii. 32.

32 And there were also two other malefactors led with him to be put to death.

33 And when they were come to the place which is called Calvary, there they crucified him, and the malefactors; one on the right hand, and the other on the left.

In reading the former of those verses, I beg the Reader to observe, that a stop should be put after the word *other*: for then the sense of the passage will be clear. *And there were also two other:* (which were) *malefactors*. For the LORD JESUS himself was no malefactor. *He did no sin, neither was guile found in his mouth.* 1 Peter ii. 22. He stood forth indeed in the eye of the law, being the Surety of his people, and their Representative, as the greatest of all malefactors. Yea, JEHOVAH considered him as such. But, though laden with the sins of all his people, yet there was no shadow of sin in him. Sin was put *upon* him, not *in* him. The LORD *laid on him*, it is said, *the iniquity of us all*, that is, the Church. Isaiah liii. 6. Reader! do you discover the blessedness of the distinction? If so, think how compleat must be his sacrifice! For this purpose, GOD would have him loaded with all sin, and with all the possible shame of sin, as sin had made his Church marked to our shame, so CHRIST, the Surety, shall bear both. And hence the conclusion the HOLY GHOST makes from hence, for the everlasting joy of the Church, *He made him to be sin for us who knew no sin*, that *we might be made the righteousness of GOD in him.* 2 Cor. v. 21,

34 Then said Jesus, Father, forgive them: for they know not what they do. And they parted his raiment, and cast lots.

For the cries of JESUS on the cross, see the whole collected into one view. John xix. 30.

35 And the people stood beholding. And the rulers also with them derided *him*, saying, He saved others; let him save himself, if he be Christ, the chosen of God.

36 And the soldiers also mocked him, coming to him, and offering him vinegar,

37 And saying, If thou be the king of the Jews, save thyself.

I pray the Reader, again and again to mark the insults offered to the person of the Redeemer in his *offices*. As the Church by sin had put an affront on all the characters of her LORD, Jesus, in redeeming her, shall sustain in his own person those insults. Hence the rabble mocked at his office as the Great *Prophet* of his people, when they smote him, and said unto him, *prophecy, thou* CHRIST, *who is he that smote thee.* So again, in his *Priestly* office ; the derision of the rulers in all those instances of pardon, JESUS had shewn (Mark ii. 5—12.) was blasphemously used, when, as in the passage before us, they said, *He saved others, himself he cannot save.* Think, Reader! what an awful instance was here! And his *Kingly* office, the Roman soldiers insulted, when they said, as they offered CHRIST the predicted vinegar, (see Psalm lxix. 21.) *If thou be the king of the Jews, save thyself.* Reader! do not fail to behold the hand of JEHOVAH in these solemn transactions. Both *Jew* and *Gentile* shall bear part in those insults offered to CHRIST's person and offices. For the LORD JESUS was at that moment redeeming his whole Church, both *Jew* and *Gentile. The heathen was his for an inheritance,* now CHRIST was set as king on *his holy hill of Zion.* Psalm ii. throughout. Never did the glory of the LORD JESUS shine out more fully! Never did CHRIST more fully prove his suretyship-character as now, when his glorious offices were thus set at nought and despised.

38 And a superscription also was written over him in letters of Greek, and Latin, and Hebrew, THIS IS THE KING OF THE JEWS.

39 And one of the malefactors, which were hanged, railed on him, saying, If thou be Christ, save thyself and us.

40 But the other answering, rebuked him, saying, Dost not thou fear God, seeing thou art in the same condemnation?

41 And we indeed justly; for we receive the due reward of our deeds: but this man hath done nothing amiss.

42 And he said unto Jesus, Lord, remember me when thou comest into thy kingdom.

43 And Jesus said unto him, Verily I say unto thee, to-day shalt thou be with me in paradise.

Of the titles on the cross, I refer to John xix. 19. But, as *Luke* is the only Evangelist which hath recorded the abundant mercy shewn to the dying thief, I shall beg to make a short observation upon it here. *Matthew* and *Mark* are both express to shew, that those men which were crucified with JESUS, joined the rabble to insult CHRIST. And *Luke* saith, that one of them reproved his hardened companion; owned CHRIST for a Savior; found mercy from CHRIST; and received the assurance of being that day with him in Paradise. And, no doubt, the whole relation of the Evangelists is correct. *Both* thieves at the first, when nailed to the cross, joined the cry against our LORD; until *one* of them, struck by divine conviction, had his heart suddenly changed, and cried out for mercy. JESUS snatched him as from the very brink of hell, and as a trophy of his rich, free, and sovereign grace, took him with him to heaven. I beg the Reader not to pass away from the view of such wonderful love, until that he hath feasted his soul with the contemplation. Here was no merit, no pre-disposition, no service, no ordinance, no means, neither baptism nor the LORD's supper; but, on the contrary, every thing of demerit, a life of infamy, and within a short period all over, and dying under the hand of justice. And yet such an one the SON of GOD took with him at once to everlasting joy! What will any man call this? Was CHRIST, or was He not, in this instance, the whole of salvation? And is He not so in every other?

44 And it was about the sixth hour. And there was darkness over all the earth until the ninth hour.

45 And the sun was darkened, and the veil of the temple was rent in the midst.

46 And when Jesus had cried with a loud voice, he said, Father, into thy hands I commend my spirit. And having said thus, he gave up the ghost.

47 Now, when the centurion saw what was done, he glorified God, saying, Certainly this was a righteous man.

48 And all the people that came together to that sight, beholding the things which were done, smote their breasts, and returned.

49 And all his acquaintance, and the women that followed him from Galilee, stood afar off, beholding these things.

I have no power to conceive, and much less to describe, the awful prodigies which attended the cross of CHRIST. The cries of JESUS; the darkness which at mid-day covered the land; the rending of the vail of the temple in twain from the top to the bottom; the yawning of the graves; the dead bodies of saints which had mouldered to dust arising, going into the holy city, and appearing unto many; the *Centurion* himself compelled to acknowledge CHRIST for the SON of GOD; and the rabble which came to the sight of CHRIST crucified, smitten at what they saw and heard, returning under horrors; these are events soon recorded, but never to be fully contemplated. For my own part, I would pray for continual grace to take my stand by faith at the foot of the cross, and with the Evangelists in my hand, go over again and again the marvellous subject, according to the plain, simple, and unvarnished manner in which those holy and inspired men have related it. And I would above all contemplate Him, who by that death procured my life; until, like *Paul*, I found grace to say as *Paul* said, and to feel as *Paul* felt; *to know nothing among men save* JESUS CHRIST, *and him crucified;* and from the same heartfelt conviction as his, knowing it is *the power of* GOD, *and the wisdom of* GOD, *for salvation to every one that believeth.* 1 Cor. ii. 2. 1 Cor. i. 24.

But, Reader! with all these high objects before us, let us take one view more of the LORD JESUS on the cross, and look over the heads of men and devils to behold what is the highest and most momentous object to contemplate in the whole, I mean the hand of GOD the FATHER in this wonderful transaction. The Scriptures of GOD teach us, that *it pleased* JEHOVAH *to bruise him:* it was He that *put him to grief.* Isaiah liii. 10. Here then was the grand part which put a finishing wound to the soul agonies and bodily pains of CHRIST. It was the hand of GOD which pierced most deeply in the Redeemer's heart. This clenched the work. This drove the nail of bitterness home to the head. *The iron entered into his soul.* Psm. cv. 18.

Angels are incompetent to explain the mysterious subject; and surely it never can be the province of man. But, it appears from the whole tenor of revelation on *those deep things of* GOD, that the whole burden of sin, and the curse due to sin, meeting together, and with the whole wrath of JEHOVAH against sin, like a mighty cataract in the sluices of divine displeasure, were poured forth on the person of CHRIST. The darkness at mid-day intimated somewhat of it. For this darkness, which was altogether supernatural, could not be, as hath been said by some, as if to shew the FATHER's anger against those who crucified CHRIST; for CHRIST himself, by his cry on the cross, most fully proved the contrary. *My God! My God!* (said the Holy Sufferer), *why hast thou forsaken me!* But this part is abundantly plain, that CHRIST was now expiating sin by the sacrifice of himself. And as such, the whole weight of sin, and the punishment due to sin, fell upon him. And as the damned in hell have eternal darkness, unvisited by the light of GOD's countenance, the SON of GOD in our nature while sustaining the judgment due to his Church for sin, shall be in darkness and unvisited by that light whose absence he had never known before. He is now sustaining what is his Church's due. He shall therefore feel the effect. But wherefore not go into hell then to endure this? No, there was no necessity. It is not the *place*, but the *extremity*, which constitutes the fulness of misery. When therefore CHRIST was lifted up upon the cross, he was suspended between heaven and earth, as one unworthy of either. Indeed CHRIST might be said to be then in the territories of *Satan*, for he is called *the prince of the power of the air*, when *hanging on the tree, and according to the law cursed.* Ephes. ii. 2. Gal. iii. 13. And it is worthy remark, that CHRIST called his sufferings by this name. *The sorrows of death* (said JESUS) *compassed me; the pains of hell gat hold upon me.* Psm. cxvi. 3. And elsewhere by the same spirit of prophecy the LORD said, *All thy waves and billows have gone over me.* Psm. xlii. 7.

50 ¶ And, behold, *there was* a man named Joseph, a counsellor; *and he was* a good man, and a just:

51 (The same had not consented to the counsel and deed of them.) *He was* of Arimathea, a city of the Jews; who also himself waited for the kingdom of God.

52 This *man* went unto Pilate, and begged the body of Jesus.

53 And he took it down, and wrapped it in linen, and laid it in a sepulchre that was hewn in stone, wherein never man before was laid.

54 And that day was the preparation, and the sabbath drew on,

55 And the women also which came with him from Galilee followed after, and beheld the sepulchre, and how his body was laid.

56 And they returned, and prepared spices and ointments: and rested the sabbath day according to the commandment.

Concerning this *Joseph*, the HOLY GHOST hath made mention of him to his advantage, in calling him *an honorable counsellor;* and though of the *Sanhedrim*, he had not joined them in the horrible transactions concerning the death of JESUS. So far from it, that he determined to give CHRIST, though crucified at *Golgotha*, a decent interment. See, Reader! how, by seemingly unlooked for causes, the LORD overrules things to his own glory. The HOLY GHOST, ages before had said, that the *Messiah should make his grave with the rich in his death.* Isaiah liii. 9. A thing the most improbable, seeing that CHRIST was to die under the hands of both Jews and Gentiles, and as a common felon, and at *Golgotha*, a place where the bodies of the criminals executed there, lay, for the most part, unburied, and their skulls kicked about with contempt. Yet so it was. JESUS shall have an

honorable burial, partly that his death, which is the life of the
Church, may thereby be fully proved; and partly, that the identity
of his person, being put into a tomb wherein before never man lay,
may be the more perfectly known.   Reader! let you and I follow
in solemn meditation, the funeral of the Lord Jesus; and behold those
holy sacred remains, which the grave cannot detain, lodged there for
a few hours, until the time appointed for his resurrection!   Never did
the grave, though but for a short season, hold such a prisoner! But
let us not overlook the needs be for Christ's interment.   It proved
his death.   It proved the truth of the prophecies.   He must, as a
part of his Suretyship, be *brought into the dust of death.*   Psalm
xxii. 15.   The type of Christ implied this, and Jesus himself taught
it.   For, saith Christ, *as Jonas was three days and three nights in
the whale's belly, so shall the Son of Man be three days and three
nights in the heart of the earth.*   Matt. xii. 40.   And above all, as
Christ must be brought down to the dust of death, to fulfil the
whole of his abasement, so from the grave it became necessary to
prove the triumphs of his exaltation.   In the grave Christ destroyed
the power of the grave, and by his own death, the power of Sin,
Satan, and Death.   Read Hosea xiii. xiv. explained by 1 Cor. xv. 55,
56, 57.   Heb. ii. 14.   Here then it was, from this memorable sepulchre, the faithful in Christ Jesus were taught to look up, and behold
the compleat victory over death.   And here the everlasting mansions
of glory first clearly opened by Christ to his people.   Precious
Jesus! it is thou, by thy death, hast overcome death; and by thy
resurrection hast secured the final resurrection of thy members.

REFLECTIONS.

See, my soul! thy Lord taken from prison and from judgment.
And *who shall declare his generation?* Behold *Pilate, Herod,* the
Chief *Priests,* and *Scribes,* yea, the whole multitude, all engaged in
the foul act of Christ's crucifixion.   And was there none beside?
Think, my soul! how much thy sins, both in the original and actual
transgression of thine *Adam*-nature, added to the vast account.   Oh!
for grace, that in a conscious sense of my own sins, upon this solemn
occasion, I may look unto him *whom I have pierced, and mourn, as one
that mourneth for his only son; and be in bitterness, as one that is in
bitterness for his first born!*

Precious Jesus! enable me to connect with the solemn view of
thine unequalled sufferings, that thou hast made my peace by the
blood of thy cross, and by thy stripes I am healed.   And from the
cross enable me to behold thee proclaiming peace to all thy people,
and doing away the whole of sin by the sacrifice of thyself.   Yes!
thou Almighty Lord! truly, in the instance of the dying thief, thou
hast shewn the sovereign efficacy of thy finished salvation.   Here
may poor, despairing, self-condemned, and self-condemning sinners,
find the sweetest encouragement.   And, if Jesus in the days of his
flesh offered up strong crying and tears, and was heard in that he
feared, will he not have compassion on the ignorant, and on them that
are out of the way, since he himself was thus compassed with infirmity?

Lord! I would take my stand at the door of the sepulchre. Like Mary, I would wait in humble sorrow until my risen and triumphant Savior shall speak to me, as the Lord did to that poor woman. Oh! for grace, to have the first views of Jesus, the first love tokens as she had of Jesus, that I might hasten with the same tender commission, and tell the brethren of Jesus of the glorious tidings of the resurrection. Lord! give me the assured earnest, in a resurrection of grace, for that great day of my God, when all his redeemed will partake in a resurrection to glory!

C H A P. XXIV.

CONTENTS.

In folding up his Gospel, Luke relates in this Chapter, the necessary Witnesses to the Resurrection of Jesus. The Lord makes a Manifestation of himself upon a great Variety of Occasions; and having given his final Commission to his Disciples, he ascends in their Presence, visibly to Heaven.

NOW upon the first *day* of the week, very early in the morning, they came unto the sepulchre, bringing the spices which they had prepared, and certain *others* with them.

2 And they found the stone rolled away from the sepulchre.

3 And they entered in, and found not the body of the Lord Jesus.

4 And it came to pass, as they were much perplexed thereabout, behold, two men stood by them in shining garments:

5 And as they were afraid, and bowed down *their* faces to the earth, they said unto them, Why seek ye the living among the dead?

6 He is not here, but is risen; remember how he spake unto you when he was yet in Galilee,

7 Saying, The Son of man must be delivered into the hands of sinful men, and be crucified, and the third day rise again.

8 And they remembered his words,

9 And returned from the sepulchre, and told all these things unto the eleven, and to all the rest.

10 It was Mary Magdalene, and Joanna, and Mary *the mother* of James, and other *women that were* with them, which told these things unto the apostles.

11 And their words seemed to them as idle tales, and they believed them not.

12 Then arose Peter, and ran unto the sepulchre; and stooping down, he beheld the linen clothes laid by themselves, and departed, wondering in himself at that which was come to pass.

I detain the Reader, immediately at his entrance into this Chapter, to remind him, that the blessed doctrine contained in it, is the most momentous and interesting which can possibly engage his attention. For, as God the Holy Ghost taught the Church, by Paul: *If* Christ *be not risen, then is our preaching vain, and the faith* of God's people *is also vain: Yea, and we are found false witnesses of* God! 1 Cor. xv. 14. See, Reader! the infinite importance of the thing itself, and let that importance arrest your closest attention, to regard, with suitable thankfulness and affection, the vast chain of evidences the Lord the Spirit hath granted the Church of this most glorious event, in the certainty of which the sure resurrection of all the mystical body of Christ is included.

In those verses we have the account as related by *Luke.* There is a beautiful variety, and yet a uniform sameness, to the relation of the fact itself of our Lord's resurrection; as delivered by the several Evangelists: but this was evidently intended by the Holy Ghost, for the more full and satisfying testimony to the glorious truth, springing forth from so many quarters. And *Paul,* years after, was brought into a personal acquaintance with the Lord Jesus, when Christ called to him from heaven; and which became an additional proof in confirming this precious doctrine. *Last of all,* (saith Paul) after Christ had been seen *of above five hundred brethren at once, he was seen of me also, as of one born out of due time.* 1 Cor. xv. 6, 7, 8.

I do not think it necessary to notice to the Reader the consternation of those godly women; neither of the eleven Apostles, at the first account of Christ's resurrection. It is enough to observe from it, how little disposed their minds were to the faith of it, notwithstanding all the discourses of Jesus, which one might have supposed would have prepared them for the event. Reader! I pray you learn from it, that nothing short of God the Holy Ghost's influence in teaching, can bring home a feeling sense of his truths, to his people. The Lord must take away the stone out of the heart, as well as roll it from the mouth of the sepulchre, or we shall not enter into a joyful apprehension of the resurrection of Jesus.

13 ¶ And, behold, two of them went that same day to a village called Emmaus, which was from Jerusalem *about* threescore furlongs.

14 And they talked together of all these things which had happened.

15 And it came to pass, that while they communed *together*, and reasoned, Jesus himself drew near, and went with them.

16 But their eyes were holden, that they should not know him.

17 And he said unto them, What manner of communications *are* these that ye have one to another as ye walk, and are sad?

18 And one of them, whose name was Cleopas, answering, said unto him, Art thou only a stranger in Jerusalem, and hast not known the things which are come to pass there in these days?

19 And he said unto them, What things! and they said unto him, Concerning Jesus of Nazareth, which was a prophet mighty in deed and word before God and all the people:

20 And how the chief priests, and our rulers, delivered him to be condemned to death, and have crucified him.

21 But we trusted that it had been he which should have redeemed Israel. And beside all this, to-day is the third day since these things were done.

22 Yea, and certain women also of our company made us astonished, which were early at the sepulchre.

23 And when they found not his body, they came, saying, That they had also seen a vision of angels, which said that he was alive.

24 And certain of them which were with us, went to the sepulchre, and found *it* even so as the women had said : but him they saw not.

25 Then he said unto them, O fools, and slow of heart to believe all that the prophets have spoken!

26 Ought not Christ to have suffered these things, and to enter into his glory?

27 And beginning at Moses, and all the prophets, he expounded unto them in all the scriptures the things concerning himself.

28 And they drew nigh unto the village whither they went : and he made as though he would have gone further.

29 But they constrained him, saying, Abide with us; for it is toward evening, and the day is far spent. And he went in to tarry with them.

30 And it came to pass, as he sat at meat with them, he took bread, and blessed *it*, and brake, and gave to them.

31 And their eyes were opened, and they knew him; and he vanished out of their sight.

32 And they said one to another, Did not our heart burn within us, while he talked with us by the way, and while he opened to us the scriptures?

33 And they rose up the same hour, and returned to Jerusalem, and found the eleven gathered together, and them that were with them.

34 Saying, The Lord is risen indeed, and hath appeared to Simon.

35 And they told what things *were done* in the way, and how he was known of them in breaking of bread.

The relation of this interview between CHRIST and the two disciples, is given in so beautiful and interesting a manner, that I have always thought it receives an injury, rather than good, from all attempts by comment. Indeed it needs no illustration, for it explains itself. The demand of JESUS, when he said, *Ought not* CHRIST *to have suffered these things and to enter into his glory?* is a question which at once answers the demand; and doth in fact yet more strongly confirm the truth. I beg the Reader not to overlook in those words of our LORD, how blessedly he shews, what the Spirit of CHRIST, which was in the Prophets all along testified, on those two great branches of the LORD's Person and Ministry, namely, *Of the sufferings of* CHRIST; *and of the glory that should follow.* 1 Pet. i. 11. For these comprehended the whole. I have sometimes been led to wish, that this heart-warning discourse of JESUS, had been recorded. But I have as often found grace, to check the wish, as improper. Nay, I have learnt the blessedness intended from the concealment. For it prompts the soul under divine teaching, to search after CHRIST, in all those Scriptures from whence the LORD preached, to those two disciples. We read, that the LORD began at *Moses*, and all the *Prophets;* and not confining himself to these, he expounded unto them in *all the Scriptures,* the things concerning himself. Hence we are taught, as plain as words can make it, that the whole body of Scripture is concerning the LORD JESUS CHRIST. And shall not I look for the LORD JESUS in all? (I have said to myself, as often as I have thought upon this passage,) Is my LORD as one pearl of great price in this field of his divine word; and shall not I as a spiritual merchant-man seek diligently for him through all, till I find him? And am I not encouraged to hope, that as JESUS drew near to those disciples while in the way, and discoursing about their LORD; so will he draw near to me? And if JESUS made *their* hearts burn with holy fervor, will he not make mine? If Old Testament saints, and New Testament believers, were made partakers of such mercies then; why not the humble followers of JESUS now? Jerem. xx. 9. Malachi iii. 16.

36 ¶ And as they thus spake, Jesus himself stood in the midst of them, and saith unto them, Peace *be* unto you.

37 But they were terrified and affrighted, and supposed that they had seen a spirit.

38 And he said unto them, Why are ye troubled? and why do thoughts arise in your hearts?

39 Behold my hands and my feet, that it is I myself: handle me, and see; for a spirit hath not flesh and bones, as ye see me have.

40 And when he had thus spoken, he shewed them *his* hands and *his* feet.

41 And while they yet believed not for joy, and wondered, he said unto them, Have ye here any meat?

42 And they gave him a piece of a broiled fish, and of an honeycomb.

43 And he took *it*, and did eat before them.

How truly blessed is it to behold, the gracious attention of the LORD JESUS, in thus affording such repeated testimonies of the reality of his resurrection to his disciples, both when separate, and when collected together. And I think the Reader will, with me admire, the palpable evidence the LORD gave of his bodily presence, not only in submitting the pierced hands and feet, through which the nails had passed, when fastening his body to the cross; but also, in the proof the LORD gave of his human nature being alive, in eating of *the broiled fish and the honeycomb.* Reader! gather from this view of thy Lord's grace, some, at least, of the sweet instructions it brings. Remember that Jesus had now finished redemption-work: and yet there is no change of nature in him. Moreover, He is the same tender, the same all-loving, and lovely Lord Jesus as ever! And, observe the humble fare Jesus partook of, the part of *a broiled fish, and of the honeycomb.* Humble fare is, for the most part, the fare of the Lord's people; but Jesus partook of it then, and thus sweetly sanctified it for ever. But more particularly do I intreat the Reader not to forget, that the very wounds which Jesus shewed to his disciples, to convince them of his person, and of his triumph over death by his resurrection, are the same marks which he everlastingly presents to his Father for them, in pleading the merits of his soul-offering, and death, for their salvation. *Paul* was commissioned by the Holy Ghost to tell the Church, that Christ's return to heaven, was, *to appear in the presence of God for us.* Heb. ix. 24. And that his blood *speaketh* for them to God. Heb. xii. 24. And *John* was admitted into visions of heaven, purposely to behold Christ as *a lamb which had been slain.* Rev. v. 6. So, that the Church of God now enjoy, in full testimony of faith, what the Old Testament Saints had in figure represented to them; namely, the High Priest going in before the mercy seat, with the names of Israel to appear before God. Exod. xxviii. 29, 30. And this was what the Church so passionately longed for in the coming of Christ. Song viii. 6. Think, Reader! and may the Lord give me also grace never to lose sight of it; what a blessed encouragement it is, under all deadness in myself, and heart-straitenings in prayer, there is One whose pierced hands and side plead for me, when I have no power to plead for myself. We have, saith John, *an advocate with the* Father, *and He is the propitiation for our sins.* 1 John ii. 1, 2.

44 And he said unto them, These *are* the words which I spake unto you, while I was yet with you, that all things must be fulfilled which were written in the law of Moses, and *in* the prophets, and *in* the psalms, concerning me.

45 Then opened he their understanding, that they might understand the scriptures,

46 And said unto them, Thus it is written, and thus it behoved Christ to suffer, and to rise from the dead the third day:

47 And that repentance and remission of sins should be preached in his name, among all nations, beginning at Jerusalem.

48 And ye are witnesses of these things.

49 And, behold, I send the promise of my Father upon you: but tarry ye in the city of Je-

rusalem, until ye be endued with power from on high.

Though I venture not to enlarge on those very blessed words of the LORD JESUS CHRIST, for all comments must fail, in attempting to shew their full blessedness, yet I entreat the Reader to ponder deeply every sentence, and consider how the solemnity of the season, when CHRIST so addressed his disciples, rendered all he said peculiarly affecting. What a moment it must have been! What holy awe the disciples must have felt! How differently the words of JESUS must have operated upon their minds, to all his former discourses before his death; now they beheld him risen from the dead, and as coming from the other world to give them this endearing interview; and by opening their understanding, in giving them suitable apprehensions, both of the vast importance of his mission, and of his unceasing love towards them! And, as all the LORD JESUS then said had respect to his whole Church, as well as to them, the then representatives of his Church, I pray the Reader not to overlook the boundless grace and mercy of JESUS, when giving his parting commission to them, to go forth in his name, as soon as the FATHER's promise of the HOLY GHOST should descend upon them, and in particularly charging them *to begin at Jerusalem!* Observe, Reader! how the LORD manifested his watchful care over the still beloved city! JESUS had many whom the FATHER had given to him there. Those Jerusalem-sinners, whose hearts were to be called by sovereign grace on the then approaching day of *Pentecost*, were there; many of whom had joined the Scribes and Elders in his crucifixion, and were now triumphing in having shed his blood. Yet, to this *Jerusalem*, this slaughter-house of his Prophets, and himself also, JESUS will have the first proclamation of mercy in his death made! Oh! the riches of his grace! Oh! the boundless love of CHRIST, which passeth knowledge!

The Reader will, I hope, observe how JESUS hath expressed himself concerning the coming of the HOLY GHOST. He calls him the promise of my FATHER. Sweet consideration! GOD the HOLY GHOST, in one and the same moment is the promise of the FATHER, CHRIST's promise, and the sovereign agent, GOD the HOLY GHOST, in his own Almighty power, from his everlasting love, engaged in covenant offices. These things will appear more fully from the consultation of those numberless scriptures which refer to the subject. I beg the Reader to turn to a few in point. Isaiah xliv. 3, 4. Joel ii. 28, &c. Isaiah lix. 21. John vii. 37, 38, 39. and John xiv. xv. and xvi. chapters. Acts xiii. 2, 3, 4, &c.

50 ¶ And he led them out as far as to Bethany: and he lifted up his hands, and blessed them.

51 And it came to pass, while he blessed them, he was parted from them, and carried up into heaven.

52 And they worshipped him, and returned to Jerusalem with great joy;

53 And were continually in the temple, praising and blessing God. Amen.

The Evangelist hath made a long step, from this first day of CHRIST's resurrection, to the day of his ascension, which this paragraph relates. *Luke* himself, who was the writer of this Gospel, was the writer also of the Acts of the Apostles. And in the opening of the records there, he speaks of JESUS having shewed himself alive after his passion by many infallible proofs, *being seen of them forty days, and speaking of the things pertaining to the kingdom of* GOD. Acts i. 3. But the Evangelist takes no notice in his Gospel of any further appearance of CHRIST during those forty days after his resurrection, beside those we have gone through, but at once proceeds to record the particulars of his ascension.

He led them as far as *Bethany*. If the town of *Bethany*, where *Lazarus* and his sisters dwelt, be meant, that place was very memorable to JESUS; and numberless instances of past events were upon JESUS's mind. And if, as some have thought, there was a little mount so called close to the Mount of *Olives*, the garden of *Gethsemane* was at the foot of it, and still more interesting scenes then opened to the LORD. See Mark xi. 1. I do not venture to decide, but I merely direct the Reader to that memorable prophecy of Zechariah, Chap. xiv. 4. whether this prediction referred to this great event? I think it might. But I also think, there may be a day yet to be seen, when it will be more fully realized. Job xix. 25.

I have only in the close of *Luke's* Gospel, and in this most interesting scene of our LORD's ascension, to beg the Reader to observe the several sweet and precious things here recorded. The farewell of JESUS! How affectionate and how tender! He was now going to his Church above. The *Abrahams*, and the *Isaacs*, and the *Jacobs*, waited and longed for his coming. But amidst all this, JESUS's heart was still with his redeemed below. He said himself, *I will not leave you orphans, I will come to you.* John xiv. 18. Precious LORD! Sure I am from this proof, if there were no other, (and there are thousands,) thy Church on earth is as dear to thee as thy Church in heaven.

There is somewhat very gracious, that JESUS, while in the act of blessing his Church, should be parted from them, and carried up into heaven. Yes! this was not without significancy. The blessing of JESUS is continued. It is one great whole. There is no interruption. The Jewish High Priest typified CHRIST in the lifting up of his hands. *He*, however, *prayed* for it. JESUS *commanded* it. Our Great High Priest ascended therefore, while blessing, as if to say that his blessing is for ever. And, as in the instance of *Manoah*, CHRIST ascended in the fragrancy of his own incense. Judges xiii. 20.

The joy of the Apostles forms a blessed conclusion to this most precious Gospel of *Luke*. They worshipped him as GOD. They had now sweet and precious views, since JESUS opened their understanding, to the apprehension of the Person, Work, Offices, Character, and Relation of the LORD JESUS; and were now only waiting the Ordination of GOD the HOLY GHOST, as promised, to send them forth in the ministry. They waited therefore daily in the temple for this blessing, praising and adoring the LORD. And the Evangelist hath put an *Amen* to the whole, as one of the precious names of JESUS, in confirmation of the glorious record. Amen. Reader! can You and I, from a conscious interest in the saving truths, put to it our Amen, as our JESUS? Isa. lxv. 16. Rev. iii. 14.

REFLECTIONS.

READER! ponder well the blessed contents of this chapter. Never, surely, was there upon earth any record given to any one matter of fact, as plainly, as fully, and as circumstantially, to bear down with a full stream of evidences all opposition, as the testimony to the Resurrection of JESUS. But while the vast chain of testimonies surround the glorious citadel of truth, as an impregnable fortress, to the full doctrine of the Person and Salvation of the LORD JESUS CHRIST; what will the whole be found, where the heart is not renewed by grace? CHRIST is indeed risen from the dead? but are we risen with him? *Blessed and holy is he that hath part in the first resurrection. On such the second death hath no power!* Oh! for the earnest of the SPIRIT, by which the souls of the faithful are sealed unto the day of redemption!

Farewell *Luke!* Blessed be thy GOD, and my GOD, the Almighty SAVIOR of both, for the ministry of thy record of JESUS! Ere long, the whole Church will be called home, to enter upon the personal enjoyment of those glorious things which the LORD hath here commissioned thee to deliver to his people! And then will burst forth, from millions of the redeemed souls, the song of salvation to GOD and the Lamb. In the mean time, may my poor offering of praise be often awakened by grace, through this, and all the other blessed portions of the holy Scriptures of truth, to bless the united source of all covenant mercies, FATHER, SON, and HOLY GHOST, for all their love and purpose, counsel, will, and pleasure, in JESUS CHRIST. Amen.

THE GOSPEL ACCORDING TO

ST. JOHN.

GENERAL OBSERVATIONS ON THE GOSPEL ACCORDING TO ST. JOHN.

THE Gospel according to *St. John*, comes home endeared to the Church of GOD in such a fulness of blessings, as cannot fail, under divine teaching, to call forth from every heart of the redeemed, unceasing praises to the Almighty Author *of every good, and every perfect gift,* for so precious a treasure given to his people. Some of the antient Fathers, in their warmth of affection to this part of the inspired writings, was accustomed to call it a *spiritual Gospel.* And such it certainly is; for GOD the SPIRIT is the Author of it. But then it should at the same time be remembered, that such are all the Gospels. For the LORD JESUS saith, *The words that I speak unto you, they are spirit, and they are life,* John vi. 63. And these divine and spiritual words of the LORD JESUS, are in the writings of all the Evangelists. But, perhaps the beloved Apostle, (for such *John* was specially called,) was led by the HOLY GHOST to dwell more largely on the discourses of the LORD JESUS than the other inspired writers of the Gospel; and therefore as the early saints of GOD, under divine teaching, felt the blessedness of his spiritual and heavenly writings on these subjects, they were prompted thus to distinguish them.

We cannot sufficiently bless GOD the HOLY GHOST for the ministry of this man, in all his writings, and eminently on account of this most blessed portion of the word of GOD. Here we have not only more contained in it of our LORD's divine discourses than the other Evangelists were commissioned to deliver, but we have also, both in relation to CHRIST's sermons and miracles, many glorious truths which were not noticed by the other Evangelists. And what tends, if possible, yet more to endear the Gospel according to St. *John* to the Church, is, that by this man's ministry herein, we have preserved to us those most blessed discourses of CHRIST, concerning the Person, Work, Offices, and Character of GOD the HOLY GHOST, without whose soul-quickening, and life-giving operations, none can be brought forth into spiritual apprehensions of union with CHRIST; and *be made wise unto salvation, through the faith which is in* CHRIST JESUS. Every child of GOD, who is conscious of the great work of regeneration having passed upon him, and hath felt in his own soul the renewing influences of GOD the HOLY GHOST's sovereign and Almighty power, will clasp this blessed Gospel of the ever blessed GOD in his arms, and press it to his heart, crying out in words like those of the Apostles, *Thanks be unto* GOD *for his unspeakable gift!*

It were needless to tell the Reader what were the plain designs of GOD the SPIRIT, in commissioning his servant *John* to give those records of the LORD JESUS CHRIST to his Church. They are made manifest in every chapter. The Apostle opens with the fullest declaration to the GODHEAD of CHRIST; and then proceeds to make manifest, in equal terms of plainness, the *Manhood* of our LORD; and, from the most ample demonstrations of the union of *both,* he shews what all the Scriptures of GOD blessedly harmonize in to confirm, that CHRIST is *the power of* GOD, *and the wisdom of* GOD, *for salvation to every one that believeth.* These glorious truths the Reader will meet in every part of the Gospel according to St. *John*, if the LORD the HOLY GHOST be his teacher.

I shall not think it necessary to detain him any longer by way of Preface. *John* hath not related to us in this Gospel, any circumstances of his own history, but confined himself wholly to the one momentous subject for which he wrote, and which seems to have fully occupied his mind. The LORD JESUS, and Him alone, swallowed up the Apostle's sole attention. *John* hath not so much as dated the *time* of writing his Gospel; neither hath he made mention of the *place* from whence it was written. Various dates have been given to it by others. *Some* make it as early as about *thirty years* after our LORD's ascension. And some place it so late as *sixty years* from that glorious event. But the whole is conjecture. It is our happiness that this is of no moment. That the penman of it was *John*, the beloved Apostle, who lay in CHRIST's bosom; that he was inspired in the writing of it; that GOD the HOLY GHOST hath blessed it in all ages of the Church; that He. doth bless it, and will continue to bless it in the Church of GOD to the latest ages, while she remains in her present time-state, until the LORD JESUS, as her bridegroom, comes to take her home to glory; these are the grand points with which we are chiefly concerned, and these, blessed be our covenant-GOD in CHRIST, are abundantly confirmed and assured. May the LORD the HOLY GHOST grant to both Writer and Reader his blessed teachings in the perusal of this, and every other part of the word of GOD, that as *John* himself said, so we may find, *we have an unction from the* HOLY ONE, *and know all things.* 1 John ii. 20. Amen.

CHAPTER I.

CONTENTS.

. John *opens his Gospel in this Chapter, with declaring both to the* GODHEAD *and Manhood of the* LORD JESUS CHRIST. *The Testimony of* John the Baptist *is here given to the Person and Glory of* CHRIST. *The calling of* Andrew *and* Peter. *An Account of* Nathaniel.

I N the beginning was the Word, and the Word was with God, and the word was God.

Every word in this verse is big with importance. LORD! I would say on entering the sacred portal, vouchsafe to go before, guide, and direct every step to the right apprehension of those solemn truths, that both Writer and Reader may receive them, *not in the words which man's wisdom teacheth, but which the* HOLY GHOST *teacheth, comparing spiritual things with spiritual.* 1 Cor. ii. 13.

And here let the Reader observe, how blessedly *John* was taught to speak of the WORD: One of those Holy Three which bear record in heaven. Had we no other authority to this great truth, but what GOD the HOLY GHOST commissioned *John* to give the Church, this would be enough in confirmation, when he said, *For there are three that bear record in heaven, the* FATHER, *the* WORD, *and the* HOLY GHOST, *and these Three are One.* 1 John v. 7. So blessedly *John* opens his Gospel, in attestation to the Essential GODHEAD of the SON OF GOD, as GOD. This was in the beginning, before all time, before all worlds, before all things. He was with GOD, and was GOD, and is GOD! And elsewhere he calls him *Eternal Life.* 1 John i. 1, 2. I beseech the Reader to mark this down, or rather to beg of GOD the HOLY GHOST to mark it down for him in the fleshy tables of his heart, as the sure and unerring foundation of all the fundamental principles of faith. John xvi. 14. 2 Cor. iii. 3.

When this first and leading principle is fully established in the soul, we may from this opening of *John's* Gospel go on to enquire, and from the same divine teaching, whether, when the Apostle thus speaks of *the beginning,* in which this word was with GOD, and was GOD, is not meant, that in the beginning of JEHOVAH's purposes, and decrees, and will, and council, and pleasure concerning the Church, this Almighty One was set apart, as in the fulness of time, and (as soon after related by *John*) to become flesh, and dwell among his people? Is he not also called the Word, not only as in relation to his essence in the GODHEAD, but as He is himself the revealed word, and indeed the only revelation in himself of JEHOVAH to his people? The Reader will not forget, that on so sublime a subject I humbly propose the question, but do not decide upon it. But, according to my apprehension, the very word *beginning* so explains it. For what beginning? Not the beginning of eternity: the very phrase is not admissible. But the beginning of the manifestation of JEHOVAH's purposes, as relating to the Church. The *beginning* of this work to the Church of grace and *glory,* being a similar expression to what is used in the *beginning,* in reference to what is said in the opening of *Genesis,* when JEHOVAH went forth in his threefold character of person, in the works of *creation.* Gen. i. 1. And if this be the sense concerning the word, we are taught in this verse to consider the SON OF GOD in it, both as the Essential Word, and as the Revealed Word, standing forth in JEHOVAH's council, and set up as he is elsewhere revealed, as the Essential Wisdom, the Head of his Church from everlasting. See Prov. viii. 22—31.

2 The same was in the beginning with God.

3 All things were made by him; and without him was not any thing made that was made.

These words throw a further light upon the verse before, and considered in conjunction with it, very blessedly explain the whole, as far as a subject of such mystery is capable of being explained to our present unripe faculties. This WORD, this Logos, was not only in himself essentially GOD, but together with the other persons of the GODHEAD, was in all the council, will, and purpose of JEHOVAH. So that when JEHOVAH went forth in acts of creation, in his threefold character of person, he was engaged in the same Almighty agency. To this grand point the HOLY GHOST by the Apostle bears testimony, when he saith, GOD *created all things by* JESUS CHRIST. Ephes. iii. 9.

And in further confirmation of this unquestionable truth, we learn from the same authority, that, *by Him were all things created that are in heaven, and that are in earth, visible and invisible; whether they be thrones, or dominions, or principalities, or powers; all things were created by him, and for him, and he is before all things, and by him all things consist.* Coloss. i. 15—19. Here we have ascribed to the LORD JESUS the works of all creation, comprehending from the highest created being to the lowest. And not only created *by* him, but *for* him; and not only giving him the precedency of being *before* all things, but declaring that as he is the Creator, so he is the upholder and preserver of all things; for their consistency, or very being, is in him and by him. And that these things are spoken of the SON of GOD, not as GOD only, but as the WORD here described, subsisting in the SON of GOD, as GOD, in consequence of those antient decrees between the persons of the GODHEAD before all worlds, in relation to the Church, is evident from hence, that it is in this very character, as the Head of his Church, he is here considered, and who, hereafter, in the fulness of time, was openly to tabernacle in our nature. See Rev. v. 6—10. explained by Psm. ii. 7.

I must not detain the Reader. But I cannot dismiss the subject opened to us by those verses, before that I have first desired of him to consider what is said in the passage just quoted, of *the Image of the Invisible* GOD. Not surely an image, or resemblance, of what is invisible. For the Reader need not be told that GOD is invisible. 1 Tim. i. 17. and vi. 16. But the HOLY GHOST hath explained the sense of it in this very chapter, (verse 18.) *No man hath seen God,* (that is, hath seen him in his essence and glory as GOD; FATHER, SON, and HOLY GHOST,) *at any time, the only begotten* SON, *which is in the bosom of the* FATHER, *he hath declared him*; that is, the SON, in this begotten character, set up in the infinite mind of JEHOVAH as making manifest all the purposes of GOD concerning the Church, he hath laid open the mind of GOD, and as such is *the brightness of his* FATHER's *glory, and the express image of his person.* Heb. i. 1, 2, 3. See my further observations on this subject in the *Poor Man's Commentary,* on Coloss. i. 15. And is it not in this sense (I only ask, not determine the question,) we are to understand that Scripture at the creation, when the first earthly man was to be formed; *Let us make man in our image, after our likeness.* Gen. i. 26. Was not this likeness to be in reference to CHRIST, as CHRIST, subsisting in covenant engagements? How, otherwise, can it be said, that *in all things he might have the pre-eminence?* Coloss. i. 18. And is it not in the same sense, (I again ask the question, but do not decide,) that scripture hath respect, when it is said, *Behold! the man is become as one of us!* Gen. iii. 22. Who was thus become? Not *Adam,* surely! For, by transgression, he had lost all knowledge of GOD, and was spiritually dead in trespasses and sin. And the whole passage that follows with his expulsion from *Eden* proves it. But I must trespass no further.

4 In him was life ; and the life was the light of men.

What a beautiful account doth this verse give of CHRIST, when considered in connection with what went before. *In him*, that is, essentially, and in himself underived, and in common with the FATHER, and the HOLY GHOST, he is life, the origin, fountain, and source of all life, natural, spiritual, eternal. And as by virtue of his own eternal power and GODHEAD, he is the efficient cause of all life to all creatures, so in a special and personal manner he is the life, and the light of men ; natural life and light to them who are in a state of nature; and spiritual life and light to them to whom he communicates grace. Nothing can be more evident than this statement, and nothing can be more blessed.

5 And the light shineth in darkness; and the darkness comprehended it not.

Here is drawn the line of distinction between the character of those who from the natural blindness of a fallen state, unawakened by the HOLY GHOST, have no perception of the person and glory of CHRIST ; and those who from grace-union with him, are called out of darkness into his marvellous light. Pause, Reader ! and contemplate the vast privileges of the LORD's people.

6 There was a man sent from God, whose name *was* John:

7 The same came for a witness, to bear witness of the Light, that all *men* through him might believe.

8 He was not that Light, but *was sent* to bear witness of that Light.

I refer the Reader for some account of *John the Baptist* to Matt. iii. and Luke i. I shall have occasion to state somewhat more of the peculiar blessedness of this man's ministry before we close this Chapter.

9 *That* was the true Light, which lighteth every man that cometh into the world.

The sense of this verse, which in itself, under divine teaching, is as plain as any portion of the word of GOD, by the perversion or ignorance of men, is brought forward to strengthen the opinion of those who profess that all men are endued with an inward light, which, they say, is sufficient for all the purposes of religion. And this they advance in direct opposition to what the LORD JESUS himself hath said, that *the light which is in a man* may be altogether *darkness*. And in consequence hath left upon record this solemn precept, *Take heed therefore, that the light which is in thee be not darkness!* Matt. vi. 23. Luke xi. 35. But *John's* account of CHRIST in this verse is both plain and obvious. If we accept the words as referring to mere *natural* light, nothing can be more true than that CHRIST, as the Great Creator and Author of nature, *lighteth every man that cometh into the world* with all the understanding which in nature that man hath. And if we refer the expression to the light of *grace*, equally certain it is, that every man that cometh into the world who is enlightened by grace, must derive it wholly from CHRIST. So that CHRIST is the Author and Giver of both. And it is clearly in this sense the Apostle meant it. For it should be observed, that the Evangelist is here advancing the glory of CHRIST, and not of the glory of man.

10 He was in the world, and the world was made by him; and the world knew him not.

11 He came unto his own, and his own received him not.

12 But as many as received him, to them gave he power to become the sons of God, *even* to them that believe on his name:

13 Which were born, not of blood, nor of the will of the flesh, nor of the will of man, but of God:

This is a most beautiful passage, and serves to illustrate and explain the many glorious truths which the Evangelist had before been advancing concerning CHRIST. *He was in the world.* When? Yea! from all eternity. Not in his *human* nature, for he had not as then, openly tabernacled in flesh. And it is not said of his *divine* nature *only*, for in that sense it would have been a needless observation. But He was in the world when in his covenant character he was *set up from everlasting*, and when JEHOVAH *possessed him* (as he himself expresses it) under another of his Mediator-names, *Wisdom*; see Prov. viii. 22. with 1 Cor. i. 24. *And the world was made by him.* This hath been before shewn, see verses 2, 3. *And the world knew him not.* By the fall in the Adam-nature of sin, all men lost all apprehension of GOD, and became ignorant both of themselves and their Maker. Psm. xiv. 1, 2. Psm. x. 4. *He came unto his own.* What own? The world and all that is therein was his own by right of *creation.* But this is not what is meant by the phrase *his own.* Neither is it meant his own by right of *redemption*, when it is added, *that his own received him not.* For they did, and will all of them receive him. For so the promise in the charter of grace runs, *Thy people shall be willing in the day of thy power.* Psm. cx. 3. And the LORD JESUS himself confirms the same, when he saith, *All that the* FATHER *giveth me shall come to me.* John vi. 37. But the *own* of CHRIST here spoken of, means his own nation the Jews, to whom was committed *the law, and the service of* GOD *and the promises;* and they fulfilled their own scriptures in rejecting him. See Rom. ix. 4. with Acts xiii. 27. For a further account of CHRIST'S *own*, see John xiii. 1. Now, Reader! having taken notice of those who, though CHRIST'S *own*, as a nation received him *not;* I pray you to mark the very different character of those his own in right that *did.* And observe well for your own sake how they are known; and then see whether in experience you bear a correspondence to them. They are described as *not born of blood.* Nothing of the hereditary blood of *Adam* gives birth to this chosen seed ; neither the outward blood of circumcision by *Moses ;* not the old birth of nature contributing to the new birth of grace. *Nor of the will of the flesh.* Nothing derived by human generation from father to son; nothing arising out of the corrupt stock of a fallen race, can lead to a spiritual regeneration by the Lord. *Nor of the will of man, but of God.* No ungodly man can *will* an ungodly man into these high privileges. No! Neither can a godly father *will* the son he loves into them. The great father of the faithful *Abraham* wished it for *Ishmael,* but could not *will* it. Gen. xvii. 18. *It is not* (saith One that could not be mistaken,) *of him that willeth, nor of him that runneth, but of God that sheweth mercy.* Rom. ix. 16. Reader! what saith your own personal knowledge of these things? Oh! the preciousness of distinguishing mercy !

14 And the Word was made flesh, and dwelt among us, (and we beheld his glory, the glory as of the only begotten of the Father,) full of grace and truth.

If there be a single verse in the Bible marked with the special emphasis of God the Holy Ghost, surely this is one. Every word tells. Here is the glorious person so much and so highly spoken of before under the name of the Word, declared to be made *flesh.* And this distinct from the person of either the Father or the Holy Ghost. It is the Son of God *only.* He is made flesh. The original word translated *flesh,* is very strong. It is *Sarx.* The same word as is used Rom. iii. 20. where no flesh is said to be justified. And elsewhere Christ is said to be made in the likeness of *sinful* flesh. Rom. viii. 3. And it is a word of the same significancy with one in the Hebrew, used Gen. vi. 12. *corrupt* flesh. So that no word of stronger import can be found to denote the vast humiliation of the Son of God in the assuming of our nature. Had the verse expressed that the Word was made *Man,* though the same nature would have been implied, yet it would not have been so strong, as to the point of degradation. The word means our full nature, both of soul and body, compleat man. And it is so very fully expressed by the word *flesh,* that the assumption implies the most perfect union of the both natures, divine and human. Not by any change or alteration of the one by the taking the other; but by the junction forming and constituting one whole person, God and Man Mediator, the Lord Jesus Christ. As *Augustine* hath happily expressed it, when speaking of the word being made flesh ; "Not (said he) by changing what he was, but by taking what he was not." And what endears the whole, and renders it truly blessed to all his people who are *members of his body, of his flesh, and of his bones,* is, that this union of God and Man in one person, is indissoluble and for ever. Jesus Christ, *the same yesterday, and to-day, and for ever.* Heb. xiii. 8.

And how blessedly *John* speaks of his and his brethren's knowledge of Christ under this precious union. *He dwelt among us* (said *John,*) *tabernacled,* as the word is, alluding to the Tabernacle in the wilderness, which was (and no doubt considered as such by holy men of old,) a type of CHRIST's human nature, in which JEHOVAH dwelt, and from which manifestations were made. *We beheld his glory,* (said he,) observe, *his glory.* Yes! because in his divine nature, truly his own, underived as it was, it could be called no other. And this glory, like to that of GOD's own SON, *full of grace and truth.* Reader! think what a blessed testimony is here to the GODHEAD of CHRIST, to the Manhood of CHRIST, and to the union of both. And do not fail to observe, that all this was in the same time while CHRIST came to his own, and his own received him not; distinguishing grace taught *John* and his brethren thus to behold CHRIST's glory, and rejoice in it. Depend upon it, so is it now, so hath it been in all ages of the Church, and so will it be as long as the earth shall continue!

15 ¶ John bare witness of him, and cried, saying, This was he of whom I spake, He that cometh after me is preferred before me: for he was before me.

16 And of his fulness have all we received, and grace for grace.

17 For the law was given by Moses, *but* grace and truth came by Jesus Christ.

18 No man hath seen God at any time: the only begotten Son, which is in the bosom of the Father, he hath declared *him.*

19 And this is the record of John, when the Jews sent priests and Levites from Jerusalem to ask him, Who art thou?

20 And he confessed, and denied not; but confessed I am not the Christ.

21 And they asked him, What then? Art thou Elias? and he saith, I am not. Art thou that prophet? and he answered, No.

22 Then said they unto him, Who art thou? that we may give an answer to them that sent us. What sayest thou of thyself?

23 He said, I *am* the voice of one crying in the wilderness, Make straight the way of the Lord, as said the prophet Esaias.

24 And they which were sent were of the Pharisees:

25 And they asked him, and said unto him, Why baptizest thou then, if thou be not that Christ, nor Elias, neither that prophet?

26 John answered them, saying, I baptize with water: but there standeth one among you, whom ye know not;

27 He it is, who coming after me, is preferred before me, whose shoe's latchet I am not worthy to unloose.

28 These things were done in Bethabara, beyond Jordan, where John was baptizing.

29 The next day John seeth Jesus coming unto him, and saith, Behold, The Lamb of God, which taketh away the sin of the world!

Here we have the introduction of *John the Baptist*, the herald and harbinger of CHRIST. In addition to what hath been offered on the Person and Office of this man, Matt. iii. and xi. to which I refer, I would just remark what a dignity and glory *John* ascribes unto the LORD JESUS CHRIST, in testimony of his own nothingness, and the infinite greatness of JESUS. I pray the Reader to observe these things. He speaks of his water baptism, when compared to CHRIST's spiritual baptism, as nothing. And do not overlook how fully *John* preached the GODHEAD of the LORD JESUS, when declaring that he should baptize with the HOLY GHOST. Could any less than GOD baptize with the baptisms of the HOLY GHOST? Could any less than GOD bless with the blessing of GOD? And I beg the Reader to observe, yet further, with what equal strength *John* bare witness to the momentous doctrine of redemption by the blood of the Lamb, when he called upon the people to behold CHRIST, *the Lamb of* GOD, *which taketh away the sin of the world!* CHRIST is called *the Lamb slain from the foundation of the world.* Rev. xiii. 8. Indeed the scripture is full of this subject, in allusion to CHRIST. Exod. xii. throughout. Levit. ix. 3. Isaiah liii. 7. Rev. v. 6. And what is never to be lost sight of, CHRIST is the Lamb of GOD, one of GOD's own providing. Rom. iii. 25. And I must beg yet further to observe, from the very great preciousness of this man's testimony to both those grand points; namely, the GODHEAD of CHRIST, and redemption by his blood, that *John* was specially and personally ordained for this express purpose. He was predicted by the Prophets *Isaiah* and *Malachi*, to come as *a voice in the wilderness to prepare the way of the* LORD. And he was to come in the spirit and power of *Elias*, and cry aloud as the witness of the LORD. And to set forth the greatness of this man's character and office yet more, when the time arrived for his appearing, an angel was sent to speak of his birth, who declared that he should be great in the sight of the LORD, *and be filled with the* HOLY GHOST *even from his mother's womb.* Luke i. 11—15. Thus ordained, and thus consecrated, the whole purport of his ministry may be summed

up in those two grand evidences which he bore to the person of
CHRIST, and to the one great work of CHRIST. So that here is GOD
the HOLY GHOST raising up this man, this greatest of Prophets (as
our LORD declared him,) born among women, to bear testimony to
JESUS, and to make a public outcry of it through the Church. Reader!
what are *your* views of these things? Oh! how truly blessed to my
soul! Oh! how gracious in GOD the HOLY GHOST, to give such testimony in the present day of a CHRIST-despising generation!

30 This is he of whom I said, After me cometh
a man which is preferred before me : for he was
before me.

31 And I knew him not : but that he should be
made manifest to Israel, therefore am I come
baptizing with water.

32 And John bare record, saying, I saw the
Spirit descending from heaven like a dove, and it
abode upon him.

33 And I knew him not : but he that sent me to
baptize with water, the same said unto me, Upon
whom thou shalt see the Spirit descending, and remaining on him, the same is he which baptizeth
with the Holy Ghost.

34 And I saw, and bare record that this is the
Son of God.

There is somewhat very interesting from the simplicity and artless-
ness in which the *Baptist* relates the account of his knowledge of
JESUS. It appears very plain from what is here said, that CHRIST and
his servant *John* had never met until about the time of CHRIST's baptism. For we read that *John* was *in the deserts until the day of his*
shewing unto Israel. Luke i. 80. And JESUS is said to have lived at
Nazareth. Hence when CHRIST went to *Jordan* for baptism, *John* was
then preaching in the wilderness of *Judæa.* And John's account of
his discovery of CHRIST, by the marks wherewith he was told he
should know him, these were the only testimonies John received for
the knowledge of his LORD. *He that sent me to baptize,* (said *John*,)
the same said unto me, Upon whom thou shalt see the Spirit descend-
ing, and remaining upon him, the same is he which baptizeth with
the HOLY GHOST. *And I saw,* (saith *John*,) *and bare record that this*
is the SON OF GOD. Doth the Reader ask who sent *John?* Let him
once more read the 6th verse of this chapter, and probably he will be
inclined to think with me, that it was GOD the HOLY GHOST. *There*
was a man (saith the Evangelist) *sent from* GOD, *whose name was*
John. Reader! will you not feel increasing cause, as you pass on
from one evidence to another, to bless GOD the HOLY GHOST for the
testimony of this man? Think, I beseech you, how that Almighty

3 Z 2

LORD hath watched, and is watching over the interests of his Church and people, in affording such a cloud of witnesses wherewith we are encompassed? Again I say, Blessed be GOD the HOLY GHOST for the preciousness of such a testimony in the present day of a CHRIST-despising generation!

35 ¶ Again, the next day after, John stood, and two of his disciples:

36 And looking upon Jesus as he walked, he saith, Behold the Lamb of God!

37 And the two disciples heard him speak. And they followed Jesus.

38 Then Jesus turned and saw them following, and saith unto them, What seek ye? They said unto him, Rabbi, (which is to say, being interpreted, Master?) where dwellest thou?

39 He saith unto them, Come and see. They came and saw where he dwelt, and abode with him that day: for it was about the tenth hour.

40 One of the two which heard John *speak*, and followed him, was Andrew, Simon Peter's brother.

41 He first findeth his own brother Simon, and saith unto him, We have found the Messias, which is, being interpreted, the Christ.

42 And he brought him to Jesus. And when Jesus beheld him, he said, Thou art Simon, the son of Jona: thou shalt be called Cephas, which is, by interpretation, a stone.

I do not presume to speak decidedly upon the subject, but I confess that I am inclined to think that these words of *John*, and the earnest look which he cast on the LORD JESUS, as he said, *behold the Lamb of* GOD! were commissioned with peculiar power to the minds of these two disciples. It is supposed that *John*, the writer of this Gospel, was one of the two. But it is not said. However, we are told that they followed JESUS. Somewhat, it is certain, arrested their attention. The gracious invitation of CHRIST, the earnestness of *Andrew* to find his brother, and the great joy he expressed in having found the CHRIST: our LORD's first address to *Peter*, and all that followed, form very interesting matter for our meditation. But I must not trespass.

43 The day following, Jesus would go forth into Galilee, and findeth Philip, and saith unto him, Follow me.

44 Now Philip was of Bethsaida, the city of Andrew and Peter.

45 Philip findeth Nathanael, and saith unto him, We have found him of whom Moses in the law and the prophets did write, Jesus of Nazareth, the son of Joseph.

46 And Nathanael said unto him, Can there any good thing come out of Nazareth! Philip saith unto him, Come and see.

47 Jesus saw Nathanael coming to him, and saith of him, Behold an Israelite indeed, in whom is no guile!

48 Nathanael said unto him, Whence knowest thou me? Jesus answered and said unto him, Before that Philip called thee, when thou wast under the fig-tree, I saw thee.

49 Nathanael answered and saith unto him, Rabbi, thou art the Son of God: thou art the king of Israel.

50 Jesus answered and said unto him, Because I said unto thee, I saw thee under the fig-tree, believest thou? thou shalt see greater things than these.

51 And he saith unto him, Verily, verily, I say unto you, Hereafter ye shall see heaven open, and the angels of God ascending and descending upon the Son of man.

The call of *Philip* and *Nathaniel*, and the relation of CHRIST's conversation with them, is most sweet and instructing. But what I would chiefly beg the Reader to notice, in what remains in this chapter, is, the LORD's exercise of his divine knowledge to the conviction of *Nathaniel*, in that he said, he saw him under the fig-tree, and that *Philip* had called him. The fig-trees in *Judæa* were large and shady, and godly persons made them what is called *Proseuches*, or places for prayer. By JESUS telling him that he was there when *Philip* called him, the heart of *Nathaniel* was at once convinced he must be GOD, since no eye but the eye of GOD could have seen him there. Our LORD's kind approbation of his faith, and as gracious a promise of the greater manifestations he should receive, should be considered as not relating to *Nathaniel* only, but a general assurance of *Bethel*-visits, like the ladder of *Jacob*, to all his redeemed, both to their own private and personal enjoyments, and to the public and universal happiness of the Church at the last day. Perhaps I should have observed, concerning our Lord's testimony to *Nathaniel*, that Jesus meant not that this seed of *Abraham* was without guile. For this can be said of none but Christ himself. Neither, rightly considered, do our Lord's words go to such extent. By an *Israelite indeed*, I should conceive is meant, not simply one that is a real descendant after the flesh, from the stock of *Abraham; for all are not Israel which are of Israel.* Rom. ix. 6. but an Israelite indeed, means one of the *children of promise.* Gal. iv. 28. whom God the Father hath given to his dear Son. And in this sense, the guileless mind of *Nathaniel*, hath a respect to the man's state as he stood accepted in Christ, and not as to his own holiness before God, for in this sense, he had none, neither could have been without guile. The Reader, if he knows any thing of the plague of his own heart, and of the covenant righteousness in which the whole Church, both in heaven and earth, is considered before God as wholly in Christ, will enter into a full apprehension of the inestimable preciousness of this doctrine, which is after godliness, and gladly join issue with the Prophet when he said, *In the* Lord *shall all the seed of Israel be justified, and shall glory.* Isaiah xlv. 25. For the double *Verily*, used by our Lord, in the last verse of this chapter: See John x. 1.

REFLECTIONS.

Reader let you and I, in the review of this blessed Chapter, do as *Moses* and *Israel* did, at the borders of the Red Sea; stand still, and contemplate what is here revealed of the salvation of the Lord. Never surely was there ever a proclamation from heaven more full, conclusive, and satisfactory, in confirmation of the Godhead of Christ; the glories of his Person, the infinite preciousness of his work, and the greatness of his salvation! Oh! what a thought for the Church of God to cherish, and to feast upon, to all eternity; that *the* Word *was made flesh, and dwelt among us.* And Oh! for grace, like the chosen disciples of the Lord, to behold his glory, *the glory, as of the only begotten of the* Father, *full of grace and truth!*

Blessed for ever be the God, and Father of our Lord Jesus Christ, who hath so loved us as to give his only begotten Son! And blessed be God the Son, who hath so loved us as to give himself for us. And blessed be God the Holy Ghost, whose everlasting love prompted his infinite mind to give all the precious manifestations of the Lord in his scriptures. Oh! how inexpressibly sweet are all those views of Jesus, which God the Spirit hath here given of the Godhead, Person, Work, Glory, Grace, and Love, of the Lord Jesus.

And Lord! give thy whole Church upon earth grace to praise thee, for the wonderful witness of that wonderful man, *John the Baptist.* Lord, the Spirit! do thou graciously be pleased to give to every child of God, thy heavenly teachings, that we may enter into a full apprehension of the design of his ministry; and behold him as raised up on purpose, and filled with the Holy Ghost, even from the womb, to testify to those two great features of the Lord Jesus, contained in this Chapter; namely, his GODHEAD, and the efficacy of his one all-effectual sacrifice. For surely, the testimonies alone, which this herald of the LORD hath given, are in themselves enough to carry before them all the infidelity of the present CHRIST-despising generation. Oh! for a boldness in the faith, to say as *Paul* did upon a like occasion, to the infidels of his day; *behold ye despisers, and wonder and perish!* Dearest JESUS! may it be my portion, with all the *Andrews,* and *Peters,* and *Philips,* and *Nathaniels,* of this age of the Church, having found Him, of whom Moses in the law, and the Prophets did write; to testify to thy glorious name and character, and say, *Rabbi! thou art the* SON *of* God! *thou art the King of Israel!*

CHAP. II.

CONTENTS.

CHRIST *at a Marriage Feast, converteth Water into Wine. He departeth to* Capernaum. *He drives the Buyers and Sellers from the Temple.*

AND the third day there was a marriage in Cana of Galilee: and the mother of Jesus was there.

2 And both Jesus was called, and his disciples, to the marriage.

3 And when they wanted wine, the mother of Jesus saith unto him, They have no wine.

4 Jesus saith unto her, Woman, what have I to do with thee? mine hour is not yet come.

5 His mother saith unto the servants, Whatsoever he saith unto you, do *it*.

And there were set there six water-pots of stone, after the manner of the purifying of the Jews, containing two or three firkins apiece.

7 Jesus saith unto them, Fill the water-pots with water. And they filled them up to the brim.

8 And he saith unto them, Draw out now, and bear unto the governor of the feast. And they bare *it*.

9 When the ruler of the feast had tasted the water that was made wine, and knew not whence it was; but the servants which drew the water knew; the governor of the feast called the bridegroom,

10 And saith unto him, Every man at the beginning doth set forth good wine. And when men have well drunk, then that which is worse: *but* thou hast kept the good wine until now.

11 This beginning of miracles did Jesus in Cana of Galilee, and manifested forth his glory: and his disciples believed on him.

The circumstances of this marriage feast, and the miracle JESUS then wrought, are so beautifully expressed, in the plain and artless language of the Evangelist, as to need no comment. I only take occasion therefore to observe, how many sweet instructions the subject ministers to us, in the contemplation of JESUS, and his disciples.

We are told, that this was the beginning of miracles, and most probably the first the LORD JESUS wrought, upon his entrance on his public ministry. And certain it is, that it is the first, and among the highest miracles the SON of GOD ever wrought in his own marriage with our nature. Then JESUS indeed turned our water into wine, for every thing then became blessings in CHRIST. And certainly there was somewhat of significancy in this miracle. For it is remarkable, that *Moses*, commissioned by the LORD, turned the water of Egypt into blood. Our Almighty *Moses*, whom JEHOVAH hath sent into the Egypt of our world, hath turned both our common mercies and our gospel mercies into wine. Exod. vii. 19. The miracle of *Moses* the servant, was for destruction! The miracle of Moses's LORD was, and is for life everlasting. Sweetly the Church sings to this: Song i. 2. Isaiah xxvii. 2, 3.

I cannot dismiss the view of this marriage in *Cana* of *Galilee*, which the LORD and his disciples graced with their presence, without observing how much JESUS hath sanctioned the holy and honorable estate of marriage, by this act. Surely as the Apostle hath said, *Marriage is honorable in all, and the bed undefiled.* Heb. xiii. 4. And methinks, I would take occasion therefrom, to enforce the same plan the Jewish bridal feast set forth, of inviting JESUS and his disciples to every godly marriage union. If the holy order be founded in CHRIST, and each party becomes a true yoke-fellow in the LORD; what a pleasing prospect it affords of promoting, under his blessing, the truest happiness of the life that now is, and of that which is to come. And to the wants of this world, where JESUS dwells, every supply necessary may be hoped for. He that turned water into wine to answer the momentary feast, can soon convert every thing even of evil into good; and rather than that his redeemed shall want any thing needful, will bring resources from their enemies' table. *All things shall work together for good to them that love* GOD: *to them that are called according to his purpose.* Rom. viii. 28.

12 ¶ After this he went down to Capernaum, he, and his mother, and his brethren, and his disciples: and they continued there not many days.

13 ¶ And the Jews' passover was at hand, and Jesus went up to Jerusalem,

14 And found in the temple those that sold oxen, and sheep, and doves, and the changers of money sitting:

15 And when he had made a scourge of small cords, he drove them all out of the temple, and the sheep, and the oxen; and poured out the changers' money, and overthrew the tables;

16 And he said unto them that sold doves, Take these things hence; make not my Father's house an house of merchandize.

17 And his disciples remembered that it was written, The zeal of thine house hath eaten me up.

I pass by every lesser consideration contained in those verses, to attend to that one event here recorded, of our Lord's making a scourge of small cords, and driving the buyers and sellers out of the Temple. If the Reader coolly and deliberately turns over in his mind the wonderful event here recorded, perhaps when all the circumstances are taken together into one point of view, and duly pondered, he will be inclined to think, with me, that excepting that one miracle mentioned by this same Evangelist, John xviii. 6, of the armed soldiers falling to the ground at the mere word of Christ, in answer to their question; this is the greatest miracle Christ wrought in the days of his flesh. Let the Reader figure to himself the Lord Jesus, thus going into the Temple, carrying every thing before him; driving the herds of cattle; overturning the tables; and pouring out the changer's money: and not a creature daring to resist him! What invincible power must have shone forth in his countenance! how their minds must have been overawed? Such indeed was the consternation on their part, and such the majesty that shone in Christ, that it brought the passage of the Prophet to the Apostles' minds; and they then saw the accomplishment of it. Psm. lxix. 9. And to the same purport where the Lord again speaks: Psm. cxix. 139. And what I beg yet more particularly the Reader to notice in this miracle, is the words of Jesus, when he was driving all before him: *Make not my* Father's *house an house of merchandize!* No prophet ever used such language. None but Christ ever called God Father! Neither did ever God call any among all his prophets, Sons. It is Jesus only, which useth this name. And Christ only whom God so owns. Let the Reader, while he views, and reviews, this wonderful transaction, turn to the prophecy of *Malachi,* and read the *first five* verses of the *third* Chapter; and then ask himself, whether this was not the Lord of his Temple so acccurately described in the Portrait of Prophecy; and so completely answered by the original, when this event of purging the Temple took place? I must not close my observations on this transaction, without first remarking to the Reader, that I conceive our LORD made another visit of the same kind to the Temple just before his crucifixion. But if he compares the scripture where that second cleansing is related, with this; he will find, that there is between them a difference. Indeed it could hardly be one and the same, because this which *John* relates, was in the early part of CHRIST's ministry; whereas, the other was nearly at the close of it. See Matt. xxi. 12, 13.

18 Then answered the Jews, and said unto him, What sign shewest thou unto us, seeing that thou doest these things?

19 Jesus answered and said unto them, Destroy this temple, and in three days I will raise it up.

20 Then said the Jews, Forty and six years was this temple in building, and wilt thou rear it up in three days?

21 But he spake of the temple of his body.

22 When therefore he was risen from the dead, his disciples remembered that he had said this unto them: and they believed the scripture, and the word which Jesus had said.

It really should seem, by the conduct of those men, and their asking CHRIST to shew them some sign, for such an exercise of his authority; as if for the moment, they had been overawed, and more than half convinced, who CHRIST was. Had this not been the case, one should have expected to have seen them to a man reddened with anger, and seizing JESUS, to bring him to punishment. Whereas, they never attempted to oppose what the LORD did; neither to gainsay what the LORD said. JESUS called GOD his FATHER; and in confirmation purged the Temple, which they had profaned. To all which, the whole body of them made no resistance; but after a pause, they asked him for some further sign in proof of his mission:

Doth my Reader also wonder in beholding them thus panic struck? Surely not. He, I hope, can well explain the cause. Did not the countenance of the LORD JESUS, as well as his actions, manifest somewhat both of his Almighty Person, and Power? If the zeal of his FATHER's house had eaten him up; (as he himself expresses it;) did not his face bespeak it? Reader! think, I beseech you, if in the days of CHRIST's flesh such glory occasionally broke forth, as in this instance, to the confusion of all his enemies; (See also John xviii. 6.) and as in another, to the joy of his friends; (See Matt. xvii. 1—5.) what will be his appearance in that day, when *the ungodly shall be punished with everlasting destruction from the presence of the* LORD, *and from the glory of his power; and when he shall come to be glorified in his saints, and to be admired in all them that believe?* 2 Thess. i. 9, 10. Oh! the forbearance of our adorable LORD, when driving those buyers and sellers from the temple, that he drove them not into hell!

But I pray the Reader yet further to observe, the LORD's grace to his Church and people, in the sign he gave, to the demand of his foes. It is his redeemed, and not others, for whom this precious sign was meant; and to whom it ministers blessedness. When JESUS thus spake of the destruction of the temple, the HOLY GHOST would not leave the Church to make her own comment upon it; but by the mouth of the Apostles, taught his redeemed, that JESUS *spake of the temple of his body.* So that when JESUS arose from the dead, which was at the distance of *three years after* this conversation the LORD held with the Jews, they called to mind what had then passed, and felt as we now feel under the divine conviction, the blessed testimony to the whole; *they believed the scripture, and the word which he had spoken.*

I must not suffer the Reader to overlook the greatness and compleatness of this sign; which, while it acted to those blind Jews as *a stone of stumbling, and rock of offence;* to the enlightened believer, it becomes a blessed testimony to that *glorious Rock which* JEHOVAH *laid in Zion.* They made this sign of JESUS the great charge of blasphemy against CHRIST, when arraigned before *Pilate.* Matt. xxvi. 61. And, Reader! you and I, if taught of GOD, make it a most precious evidence of his eternal Power, and GODHEAD. *Destroy this temple,* (said the LORD,) this temple of my body; and *in three days I will raise it up!* The former was done, when (as *Peter* under the HOLY GHOST charged them) *with wicked hands,* JESUS was *taken by them and crucified and slain.* Acts ii. 23. And JESUS accomplished the *latter,* when by his own Almighty Power, he arose from the dead. Observe the expression which CHRIST made use of, *I will raise it up!* And if you ask the cause? the HOLY GHOST, by the mouth of *Peter* answers; *having loosed* (said he) *the pains of death, because it was not possible that He should be holden of it.* Acts ii. 24. But it would not only have been possible, but certain and sure, that the pains of death, which are the wages of sin, would have held any man and every man a prisoner, which died for sin; had not the divine nature of CHRIST, been in this solemn transaction. But in the Person of CHRIST, GOD and Man in One, it became impossible. The Prophets which foretold his death, foretold at the same time, that *his soul should not be left in hell; neither* GOD's *holy one to see corruption.* Psm. xvi. 10. Hence, as the HOLY GHOST by *Peter,* in another scripture, hath said; CHRIST was *put to death in the flesh, but quickened by the* SPIRIT. 1 Pet. iii. 18. Reader! what are now your apprehensions of this blessed sign?

23 Now when he was at Jerusalem at the passover, in the feast *day,* many believed in his name, when they saw the miracles which he did.

24 But Jesus did not commit himself unto them, because he knew all *men,*

25 And needed not that any should testify of man; for he knew what was in man.

Reader! I detain you no longer on those verses, than to ask you, what further proofs can be needed to the GODHEAD of your LORD, than what is here said. Who less than He that made man, can know the thoughts of man?

REFLECTIONS.

How is it possible to behold my LORD, honoring the bridal feast with his presence and miracles without having the mind led to the consideration of that yet more astonishing miracle, when the SON of GOD first betrothed his Church to himself, *in righteousness, in judgment, in loving kindness, and in mercies; and in faithfulness for ever!* Here I would say, as often as my soul reviews the vast mercy, here my LORD, my *Ishi*, my Husband, is indeed everlastingly blessing his Church with his presence; supplying every want, and turning all my water into wine. LORD! do thou daily manifest forth thy glory; and cause me by thy sweet influences, unceasingly to believe in thee.

Blessed LORD the SPIRIT! praised be thy name for this precious record of my LORD's zeal in purging his Temple. Do thou, LORD, so cleanse my heart; for thou hast said, the bodies of thy people are the temple of the HOLY GHOST, which dwelleth in them. And if my GOD will drive out all the vain thoughts which lodge there, which like the buyers and sellers in the Temple, so defile my poor heart; then, by my LORD's indwelling presence, shall I be enabled *to glorify* GOD, *in my body and in my spirit, which are his.*

And praised be my LORD for the very precious sign he gave the Jews; and for the very precious confirmation of it which followed. Yes! thou glorious LORD; while both the power of GOD the FATHER, and GOD the HOLY GHOST, were manifested in thy triumphs over death and the grave; thou wast most fully *declared to be the* SON *of* GOD *with power, according to the* SPIRIT *of holiness, by thy resurrection from the dead!* And is it not by this same blessed testimony, the whole Church rests in hope for the sure accomplishment of the same in all thy mystical members! Hail! thou that art the resurrection and the life! Sure I am, that because thou livest, thy redeemed shall live also!

C H A P.   III.

CONTENTS.

CHRIST *hath a conversation with* Nicodemus. *The* LORD *discourseth on the New-birth; and declares its absolute Necessity, for an Entrance into his Kingdom. Some further Account of* John the Baptist.

THERE was a man of the Pharisees, named Nicodemus, a ruler of the Jews:

2 The same came to Jesus by night, and said unto him, Rabbi, we know that thou art a teacher

come from God : for no man can do these miracles that thou doest, except God be with him.

3 Jesus answered and said unto him, Verily, verily, I say unto thee, Except a man be born again, he cannot see the kingdom of God.

4 Nicodemus saith unto him, How can a man be born when he is old ? can he enter the second time into his mother's womb, and be born ?

5 Jesus answered, Verily, verily, I say unto thee, Except a man be born of water, and *of* the Spirit, he cannot enter into the kingdom of God.

6 That which is born of the flesh is flesh ; and that which is born of the Spirit is spirit.

7 Marvel not that I said unto thee, Ye must be born again.

8 The wind bloweth where it listeth, and thou heareth the sound thereof, but canst not tell whence it cometh, and whither it goeth : so is every one that is born of the Spirit.

We can never be sufficiently thankful to our adorable LORD, for this blessed discourse of his, upon the important doctrine of regeneration, or the new birth; neither to the person and grace of GOD the HOLY GHOST, in causing it to be so circumstantially recorded. LORD ! give to thy people a clear apprehension of the precious truth itself, and of their personal interest in it.

I not only admire the very sweet and engaging manner in which the LORD hath explained the subject; but that he should make choice of a *Pharisee* to explain it, by way of conveying it to his Church. A *Pharisee,* had all the high notions of self-righteousness; and considering himself as a true descendant of *Abraham* after the flesh, he concluded, that this gave a legal right to all the promises of GOD. And in the case of *Nicodemus,* a ruler of the Jews, one of the *Sanhedrim,* and a master in Israel, no doubt he stood among the highest order of that leading class of people.

JESUS, hath so very plainly stated, both the principles of the new birth, and the effects which follow; that there can need, when taught of GOD, nothing more than an attention to our LORD's own words, to enter into a full apprehension of the subject. By the birth of nature, involved in the Adam-fall of sin and transgression, the Church of CHRIST, as well as the whole world at large, is born in a polluted, carnal, and ungodly state. So that there must be a new birth by grace, and which the glorious Covenant of Redemption hath secured for the whole seed of CHRIST, to bring forth into a new and spiritual life. Without this saving change passing upon the sinner, there can be no possibility of entering the kingdom of GOD.

From a grace-union with CHRIST, given by GOD the FATHER, before all worlds, to the Church, (Ephes. i. 4.) this interest in the adoption-character of children is secured; and by the act of regeneration, wrought by GOD the HOLY GHOST upon the soul, a meekness for grace here, and glory hereafter, is accomplished.

But plain as this statement is, to every truly regenerated child of GOD, who is himself an happy partaker of the unspeakable mercy; every carnal man, like this *Pharisee*, with whom our LORD conversed on the subject, will cry out, *how can these things be?* But so hath the HOLY GHOST taught us to expect. *The natural man receiveth not the things of the* SPIRIT *of* GOD, *for they are foolishness unto him; neither can he know them, because they are spiritually discerned. But he that is spiritual judgeth all things.* 1 Cor. ii. 14, 15. Reader! this is a blessed reality, to which the whole Church of GOD, in heaven and earth, can and do bear witness. There is not one now among *the spirits of just men made perfect* in heaven, but what was once in the Adam-nature of an unawakened, carnal state : and out of which he was brought, by this sovereign work of GOD the HOLY GHOST upon his soul. Neither is there one among the children of GOD in the Church upon earth, when regenerated, but what hath by the same distinguishing mercy, *passed from death to life;* and been *translated from the power of darkness, into the kingdom of* GOD's *dear* SON. John iii. 14. Coloss. i. 13.

I must request the Reader not to overlook the beautiful similitude which the LORD made use of, for illustrating this sovereign work of GOD the HOLY GHOST. The source of the air in nature, is altogether unknown. We see, and feel, the powerful effects of it; and that is all we know of it. The greatest philosopher, and the poorest peasant, are here upon a level. Neither of them can explain, how storms are gendered; where winds are first raised; what keep them up, and carry them on; where they retire when the blast is over; and what becomes of them when gone. Now (saith JESUS,) so is *every one that is born of the* SPIRIT. And the figure is beautiful also on another account, in respect to the free agency of the air : *The wind bloweth where it listeth.* So GOD the SPIRIT displays the sovereignty of his Almighty Power, in coming; *when,* and *where,* and *how;* as seemeth good to his holy will and pleasure. But how is every one who is made the happy partaker of such distinguishing mercy constrained to join the Apostle's hymn of praise, and say with him, *Thanks be unto* GOD *for his unspeakable gift.* 2 Cor. ix. 15. On the subject of Regeneration, see Titus iii. 4, 5.

If I detain the Reader one moment longer on this blessed discourse of the LORD JESUS, it shall be only to call his attention to what the LORD hath said, when declaring that, *Except a man be born of water and of the* SPIRIT, *he cannot enter into the kingdom of* GOD. But what water are we to suppose that our LORD meant? Not surely the common elementary water of the earth! Would JESUS have classed this upon a level with GOD the HOLY GHOST? Yea, have put the water in precedency before Him! One of the creatures of GOD before the Infinite Creator? Moreover, how can a man be said to be born of water? Born of the SPIRIT every new-born child of GOD is said to be : (John i. 12, 13.) but is there a possibility of what is *Spiritual,* being born of what is wholly *natural?* Can any man for a moment suppose, that such was our Lord's meaning?

Though in this, and all other questionable points, I beg to be understood as never speaking decidedly; yet I think, if the Reader will call to mind the record of *John,* when at the foot of the cross, he tells the Church, that he saw blood and water streaming from the body of Christ, when his sacred side was pierced by the soldier's spear; (see John xix. 34, 35.) and if to this view he will add the further testimony of *John* which he hath given in one of his Epistles, that Christ *came, by water and blood;* (1 John v. 6.) perhaps he will be inclined to think with me, that it is Christ himself, and not the elementary water of nature, which he hath joined together in his blessed scripture, of being *born of water, and of the* Spirit. Certain it is, that the blood of Christ is sometimes in scripture spoken of by the name of water; as in that memorable passage of Ezekiel xxxvi. 25. and that it is *blood,* and not *water,* which is intended by the expression, is evident; because, God promiseth to sprinkle it upon the people. Water is never said to be *sprinkled,* nor *put upon* the people: but Christ's blood in justification, is said to be sprinkled; and the Church is said to *be come to the blood of sprinkling.* Heb. xii. 24. But when water is at any time spoken of in allusion to God the Holy Ghost, it is as a spring, not *without* us but *within* us. Hence Christ, giving this promise, saith; *The water that I shall give him shall be in him a well of water, springing up to everlasting life.* John iv. 14.

Neither can the term, of being *born of water* and of the Spirit, be in the smallest degree connected with the idea of *water baptism.* That man must be very weak in understanding, or very strong in prejudice, who for a moment can suppose, that water baptism, either in children or in adults, hath any regenerating efficacy. Surely common sense must know, that the baptism of the Holy Ghost is wholly unconnected with any thing and every thing, of a material nature. When the Apostles were baptised with the Holy Ghost on the day of *Pentecost,* agreeably to our Lord's most sure promise, (See Acts i. 5.) we read of no water-baptism accompanying that divine out-pouring. And we no where before in the history of those men, trace the shadow of their being baptised after Jesus called them. If it be said, yes! it is probable that some of them were disciples of *John the Baptist* before that they followed Christ; and therefore might have been baptised by him. To which I answer: this would only tend to strengthen what I have said. For *Paul,* when taught of God the Holy Ghost, was instructed to inform the Church, that *John's* baptism never was intended to set forth more than *the doctrine of repentance.* It was designed, *Paul* saith, to lead them to Christ. For *John* saith, that *they should believe on him which should come after him, that is on* Christ Jesus. (See Acts xix. 1—6.) Hence it must undeniably follow, that *water-baptism* of every kind, could not be what Jesus insisted upon, for an entrance into the kingdom of God. And, indeed, the thing itself is fully proved. For baptism by water was altogether a novel service in the Church of God, until introduced by *John the Baptist.* And if this became so essentially necessary, that without it there could be no entrance into God's kingdom; what became of the whole body of Old Testament saints, which never heard of it?

Is it not (for I simply ask the question) to be apprehended by what we see in life, that *many*, whether men or children, may be baptized with water-baptism, and yet remain everlasting strangers to the gift of the HOLY GHOST. While on the other hand, *others*, who never knew, either of the infant or adult baptism by water; have enjoyed the blessing of regeneration, and been truly baptized with the HOLY GHOST? No one I presume will venture to doubt but that *the dying Thief* on the cross, was made a rich partaker of the HOLY GHOST, and had the baptisms of the SPIRIT: and yet no elementary water accompanied the blessing. But (awful to relate) *Simon Magus* was fully baptized in the due form of the Apostles' baptism, with water of the earth; and no saving work of GOD the SPIRIT was wrought in his heart: for he continued *in the gall of bitterness, and in the bond of iniquity*. Acts viii. 9—24. But I add no more. The LORD himself be the teacher, both of the Writer and Reader, to the right apprehension of those words of JESUS.

9 Nicodemus answered and said unto him, How can these things be?

10 Jesus answered and said unto him, Art thou a master of Israel, and knowest not these things?

11 Verily, verily, I say unto thee, We speak that we do know, and testify that we have seen; and ye receive not our witness.

12 If I have told you earthly things, and ye believe not, how shall ye believe if I tell you *of* heavenly things?

13 And no man hath ascended up to heaven, but he that came down from heaven, *even* the Son of man which is in heaven.

14 And as Moses lifted up the serpent in the wilderness, even so must the Son of man be lifted up:

15 That whosoever believeth in him should not perish, but have eternal life.

16 For God so loved the world, that he gave his only begotten Son, that whosoever believeth in him should not perish, but have everlasting life;

17 For God sent not his Son into the world, to condemn the world; but that the world through him might be saved.

18 He that believeth on him is not condemned: but he that believeth not is condemned already,

because he hath not believed in the name of the only begotten Son of God.

19 And this is the condemnation, that light is come into the world; and men loved darkness rather than light, because their deeds were evil.

20 For every one that doeth evil hateth the light, neither cometh to the light, lest his deeds should be reproved.

21 But he that doeth truth cometh to the light, that his deeds may be made manifest, that they are wrought in God.

I must not in a *Poor Man's Commentary* swell our pages, even though it be the words of JESUS that we are here attending to. What a lovely and sweet discourse is this of our LORD! Every verse is a sermon. But let me call the Reader's attention to those *two* most striking passages in the midst of it: I mean, first, of what JESUS hath said of his ascension, and descension, and everlasting presence in heaven; and, secondly, of what the LORD hath said in relation to the lifting up of the serpent in the wilderness.

The former of these passages will, I apprehend, appear very plain and obvious, if we consider the words as CHRIST delivered them, relating wholly to the SON *of Man;* that is, GOD-Man, CHRIST JESUS. *No man* but the GOD-Man, hath either ascended, or descended, in the character and office work of JEHOVAH's servant, to make known the Being, Perfections, and Love, of JEHOVAH, in his threefold character of Person, to the Church. It is He, and He only, which lay in the bosom of the FATHER, hath come forth to declare Him. For though *Enoch* and *Elijah* simply as men, had special tokens of divine favor, in being translated to heaven, different from the common mass of *the spirits of just men made perfect;* yet none but CHRIST could act in this high capacity, from being GOD and Man, in one Person, of making known JEHOVAH. The office was solely and properly his, and no other: Matt. xi. 27. And hence that question of CHRIST: John vi. 62.

And in respect to the everlasting presence of *the* SON *of Man,* as such in heaven; nothing can be plainer, than that it means, his everlasting representation in Covenant engagements there. He hath been so from the first, in the eternal counsel. The expression is similar to what is said, Proverbs viii. 22—31. CHRIST there, speaking in his wisdom character, saith; *The* LORD *possessed me from the beginning of his ways. I was set up from everlasting. And my delights were with the sons of men.* And this was said at a time, not only before the SON of GOD became incarnate, but before the foundations of the earth were laid. How was he then possessed; and how set up; and his delights with the sons of men? Evidently in the representation of all these grand events, planned and brought forward in the eternal counsel; and to be accomplished in the fulness of time. So that in fact, the things were as good as done, which in JEHOVAH's mind were determined upon. And in this sense CHRIST's presence as SON of MAN, was everlastingly in heaven. A similar passage we have, Coloss. i. 15, &c. See John i. 2, 3. and observations thereon. As also *Poor Man's Commentary* on Coloss. i. &c.—That the passage must be understood in this light, or somewhat like it, is evident from hence. For it cannot refer to the divine nature of the SON of GOD *only;* because, as GOD, he is every where present. The LORD filleth all space; and is no more present in heaven than on earth. Neither as man *only,* would it have been correct. For CHRIST in his human nature, was at that time conversing with *Nicodemus* upon the earth. But all difficulties are at once removed, if the expression be considered as speaking of CHRIST, in his high representing character, the SON of Man; the *Head of his body, the Church:* for here he evidently becomes that *fulness which filleth all in all.* Ephes. i. 22, 23.

In respect to the *latter* of these passages in our LORD's sermon, where JESUS speaks of the lifting up of the serpent in the wilderness; I beg the Reader to attend to the subject with that due regard so beautiful a representation of CHRIST in the type evidently sets forth. According to my view, it is one of the most blessed shadows of CHRIST in the Bible; and I have found cause, very often, to thank GOD the HOLY GHOST for it.

For the better apprehension of the subject, I beg the Reader to remark with me, that among the several office-characters of CHRIST; there were *two,* more immediately express, and striking. The *one* was, that He who knew no *sin,* should be made *sin* for his people: that they, who knew in themselves no righteousness, should be made the righteousness of GOD in him. 2 Cor. v. 21. The *other* was, that as the Church, by the Adam-fall, came justly under the sentence of GOD's *curse;* CHRIST, as the husband and surety of his people, should be made a *curse* for them; that they might be redeemed from it. Gal. iii. 13. 1 Heb. ii. 17. And both these the SON of GOD in our nature, in what is called the fulness of time, undertook to do: and hath done most completely and effectually. But before the accomplishment of CHRIST's undertaking, that Old Testament saints might not lose the just apprehension of New Testament blessings, the HOLY GHOST was pleased to appoint, that these things should be shadowed out, in lively type, and figure. Hence the *Scape-Goat* was appointed on the day of atonement, to set forth the *former,* and the *Brazen Serpent* to manifest the *latter:* and both directly pointing to the LORD JESUS CHRIST, and in Him alone, to have their accomplishment. And while the *Scape Goat* became so very direct and pointed, that no Israelite whose eyes were opened, could overlook CHRIST, as bearing the sins of his people, *the Brazen Serpent,* the only creature of GOD, declared cursed at the fall, was expressly suited to prefigure Him, who bore both the weight, and displeasure, due to the sins of his Church; in the curse of GOD's broken law, and the indignation which became justly due thereon. And thus the LORD JESUS explains it. As the type was lifted up, that the dying Israelite might look with an eye of hope to it, as GOD's own appointed way, and be healed: so now, the thing signified, even CHRIST himself, which is the sole method of redemption, and appointed by JEHOVAH, is lifted up, that the dying sinner might look to Him with an eye of faith, and be saved. Isaiah xlv. 22.

I hope that the Reader will be led by the HOLY GHOST, to enjoy with me the blessedness of this subject, explained as it is to the Church, by the LORD JESUS himself.

22 ¶ After these things came Jesus and his disciples into the land of Judea; and there he tarried with them, and baptized.

23 And John also was baptizing in Enon, near to Salem; because there was much water there: and they came, and were baptized.

24 For John was not yet cast into prison.

25 Then there arose a question between *some* of John's disciples and the Jews, about purifying.

26 And they came unto John, and said unto him, Rabbi, he that was with thee beyond Jordan, to whom thou bearest witness; behold, the same baptizeth, and all *men* come to him.

27 John answered and said, A man can receive nothing, except it be given him from heaven.

28 Ye yourselves bear me witness, that I said, I am not the Christ, but that I am sent before him.

29 He that hath the bride is the bridegroom: but the friend of the bridegroom, which standeth and heareth him, rejoiceth greatly because of the bridegroom's voice. This my joy therefore is fulfilled.

30 He must increase, but I *must* decrease.

31 He that cometh from above is above all: he that is of the earth is earthly, and speaketh of the earth: he that cometh from heaven is above all.

32 And what he hath seen and heard that he testifieth; and no man receiveth his testimony.

33 He that hath received his testimony, hath set to his seal that God is true.

34 For he whom God hath sent speaketh the words of God: for God giveth not the Spirit by measure *unto him*.

35 The Father loveth the Son, and hath given all things into his hand.

36 He that believeth on the Son hath everlasting life : and he that believeth not the Son, shall not see life; but the wrath of God abideth on him.

We have here a short, but sweet sermon, of John the Baptist. And I beg the Reader to remark with me, how blessedly he preacheth CHRIST. How beautifully he sets him forth, as the glorious Bridegroom of his Church! What a striking distinction he draws, between the LORD JESUS and all his servants! And how could he do this as effectually, as when stating the vast difference in the gifts of the HOLY GHOST. In all the servants of the LORD, the HOLY GHOST was in them as portions in a vessel. *To every one of us* (saith an Apostle) *is given grace according to the measure of the gift of* CHRIST. Ephes. iv. 7. In CHRIST, as a fountain, GOD *giveth not the* SPIRIT *by measure unto him.* And let not the Reader overlook what is further said. What CHRIST hath seen and heard in coming from above, he testifieth; yea, he speaketh the words of GOD, for he is GOD. And all things are given unto him, as Mediator; eternal life, with all its preliminaries. Reader! pause, and think! How sure is that soul of blessedness, who hath the SON? How sure the certain consequence of misery, to every one, which hath not the SON? For the wrath of GOD, not taken away by CHRIST, remaineth! Oh! for grace that while the LORD's people set to their seal that GOD is true, GOD the HOLY GHOST may set to his seal in our souls, *the seal of the promise!* Ephes. i. 13.

REFLECTIONS.

EVERLASTING praise to thee, my honored LORD, for the sweet and precious doctrine of the New-birth, so graciously taught thy Church, in this discourse with *Nicodemus.* Oh! for the distinguishing grace of GOD the SPIRIT upon my heart, that I may have all the blessed testimonies, in the assurance of it there; that I may not only know it, in the written word, but enjoy it in the engrafted word; to make me *wise unto salvation through the faith which is in* CHRIST JESUS.

Do thou, dearest LORD, accompany those thine heavenly discourses, with thine Almighty grace; that from the words of my LORD, and the commissioned discourse of his servant the Baptist, my soul may receive the truth, and the truth may make me free. JESUS hath all things in his Almighty hand. May I then LORD look to thee for all things, in grace, mercy, pardon, peace, and every New Covenant blessing here; and all the fulness of glory in JESUS, and from JESUS, to all eternity!

CHAP. IV.

CONTENTS.

CHRIST *discourseth with a Woman of* Samaria. *He visits the* Samaritans. *Many believe on him. He healeth a Nobleman's Son.*

WHEN therefore the Lord knew how the Pharisees had heard that Jesus made and baptized more disciples than John,

2 (Though Jesus himself baptized not, but his disciples,)

3 He left Judea, and departed again into Galilee.

I pause at these verses, just to remark what appears to me highly proper to be noticed. JESUS *himself baptized not.* Was it not, (I ask the question, but do not decide,) because that this was the peculiar office of GOD the HOLY GHOST? Had CHRIST baptized, surely it would not have been (as all his servants are confined to) water baptism only. The question is of moment. I leave it with the Reader.

4 And he must needs go through Samaria.

5 Then cometh he to a city of Samaria, which is called Sychar, near to the parcel of ground that Jacob gave to his son Joseph.

6 Now Jacob's well was there. Jesus therefore being wearied with *his* journey, sat thus on the well. And it was about the sixth hour.

7 There cometh a woman of Samaria to draw water. Jesus saith unto her, Give me to drink.

8 (For his disciples were gone away unto the city to buy meat.)

9 Then saith the woman of Samaria unto him, How is it that thou, being a Jew, askest drink of me which am a woman of Samaria? For the Jews have no dealings with the Samaritans.

10 Jesus answered and said unto her, If thou knewest the gift of God, and who it is that saith to thee, Give me to drink; thou wouldest have asked of him, and he would have given thee living water.

11 The woman saith unto him, Sir, thou hast nothing to draw with, and the well is deep: from whence then hast thou that living water?

12 Art thou greater than our father Jacob, which gave us the well, and drank thereof himself, and his children, and his cattle?

13 Jesus answered and said unto her, Whosoever drinketh of this water shall thirst again:

14 But whosoever drinketh of the water that I shall give him, shall never thirst; but the water that I shall give him shall be in him a well of water springing up into everlasting life.

15 The woman saith unto him, Sir, give me this water, that I thirst not, neither come hither to draw.

16 Jesus saith unto her, Go, call thy husband, and come hither.

17 The woman answered and said, I have no husband. Jesus said unto her, Thou hast well said, I have no husband:

18 For thou hast had five husbands, and he whom thou now hast is not thy husband: in that saidst thou truly.

19 The woman saith unto him, Sir, I perceive that thou art a prophet.

20 Our fathers worshipped in this mountain: and ye say that in Jerusalem is the place where men ought to worship.

21 Jesus saith unto her, Woman, believe me, the hour cometh when ye shall neither in this mountain, nor yet at Jerusalem, worship the Father.

22 Ye worship ye know not what: we know what we worship: for salvation is of the Jews.

23 But the hour cometh, and now is, when the true worshippers shall worship the Father in spirit and in truth: for the Father seeketh such to worship him.

24 God *is* a spirit: and they that worship him must worship *him* in spirit and in truth.

25 The woman saith unto him, I know that Messias cometh, which is called Christ: when he is come, he will tell us all things.

26 Jesus saith unto her, I that speak unto thee *am* he.

27 ¶ And upon this came his disciples, and marvelled that he talked with the woman; yet no man said, What seekest thou? or, Why talkest thou with her?

28 The woman then left her water-pot, and went her way into the city, and saith to the men,

29 Come, see a man which told me all things that ever I did; is not this the Christ?

30 Then they went out of the city, and came unto him.

31 ¶ In the mean while his disciples prayed him, saying, Master, eat.

32 But he said unto them, I have meat to eat that ye know not of.

33 Therefore said the disciples one to another, Hath any man brought him *ought* to eat?

34 Jesus saith unto them, My meat is to do the will of him that sent me, and to finish his work.

35 Say not ye, There are yet four months, and *then* cometh harvest? behold, I say unto you, Lift up your eyes, and look on the fields; for they are white already to harvest.

36 And he that reapeth receiveth wages, and gathereth fruit unto life eternal; that both he that soweth, and he that reapeth, may rejoice together.

37 And herein is that saying true, One soweth, and another reapeth.

38 I sent you to reap that whereon ye bestowed no labour: other men laboured, and ye are entered into their labours.

39 And many of the Samaritans of that city believed on him, for the saying of the woman, which testified, He told me all that ever I did.

40 So when the Samaritans were come unto him, they besought him that he would tarry with them. And he abode there two days.

41 And many more believed because of his own word;

42 And said unto the woman, Now we believe, not because of thy saying : for we have heard *him* ourselves, and know that this is indeed the Christ, the Saviour of the world.

Were I to enter into a full comment upon this interesting interview of CHRIST with this woman of *Samaria,* it would fill very many pages; and after all I should leave unnoticed, as all Commentators gone before have done, numberless precious things contained in it. I must therefore pass over the consideration of what is *generally* brought forward by our LORD, to the Reader's own observation; praying, and hoping, that GOD the HOLY GHOST will sweetly open the whole, and bring home our LORD's words to his heart, as he did to the woman of *Samaria,* and many of her countrymen; and render his own most blessed discourse profitable, by his own most gracious power. Some few of the more prominent features contained in this sermon of JESUS, I beg the Reader to remark with me; and may the LORD write them on our hearts. And, first: it is not the least subject of moment to observe, the *needs be,* which is said for JESUS going through *Samaria.* It is true indeed that if CHRIST was going into *Galilee,* (see verse 43,) as he now came out of *Judæa,* he could go no other way. But it doth not follow, that there was a necessity that he should go at that time into *Galilee.* But whatever other causes there might be to this constraint, the conversion of this woman to the faith of CHRIST, and certain of her countrymen also, became sufficient cause. This was the time, the place, the manner, the method, and the whole train of events, linked in the chain with it; which, from all eternity had been marked for CHRIST's calling to himself this woman, and other *Samaritans,* who were effectually wrought upon, to the knowledge and belief of JESUS. Reader! what a sweet thought is it, that all things are arranged with infinite wisdom, for all the purposes of CHRIST's Church and people, *in the determinate counsel and foreknowledge of* GOD. What the world calls chance, and accident; the believer cannot admit in his creed. Every thing, from the numbering of the hairs of our head, to the bringing home the Church to glory, is arranged, ordered, and appointed; and to a minuteness, which nothing can counteract, by the stratagem of men, or devils. Dan. iv. 35. Rom. xi. 36.

The conversation which took place at the well, between JESUS and this woman, I pray the Reader to observe, began with our LORD. Yes! all the overtures of grace come first *from* the LORD. 1 John iv. 19. But what wonderful discoveries the LORD made to her of herself. He unrips her very heart, and lays open to her, some of her most secret sins. He next reveals to her himself, and sweetly inclines her affection to feel her want of him, and to incline her heart to desire him. And so earnest was she when once these great things were done for her, that every poor sinner like herself should be made a partaker of such free rich mercy; that she forgot her errand at the well, left her water pot there, and ran to the city, with a pressing invitation to her countrymen to come and see JESUS! Reader! depend upon it, that such effects as this woman felt, will be, in the instance of every poor sinner, whom the LORD by his SPIRIT, hath convinced *of sin, of righteousness, and of judgment.* Those *two* grand points, are always joined together. In the same moment that GOD the HOLY GHOST humbles the soul for sin; he leads that soul to feel the need of a SAVIOR. So that self-abhorrence, and CHRIST exalted, will always go together. I must not enlarge: but before I quit this most important view of the subject, I entreat the Reader for his further conviction on this point, to read the certain truth of it, in the lives of holy men of old. What said *Job,* when he had seen GOD in CHRIST. *Behold I am vile,* (said he,) *what shall I answer thee: I will lay my hand upon my mouth!* Job xl. 4. See also xlii. 5, 6. What said *Isaiah,* after he had been admitted to a view of that glorious vision, of the glory of CHRIST: *Woe is me,* (said he,) *I am undone; for I am a man of unclean lips; mine eyes have seen the King, the* LORD *of hosts.* Isaiah vi. 1—.5, compared with John xii. 41. What said *David,* Psm. cxliii. 2. What said *Paul,* Romans vii. 23, 24. Reader! such will the best of men say, when once the HOLY GHOST hath opened to their view their own vileness, and the LORD's holiness!

And, Reader! do allow me to lead you into an enquiry, before you quit the subject; that you may ask your own heart, whether you have met the LORD GOD *of the Hebrews,* as this woman did, and he hath made similar discoveries to your conscience, as he did to hers. Have you seen sin, exceeding sinful? Have you seen CHRIST exceeding precious? Hath JESUS truly discoursed with you by his SPIRIT: and have you with Him by faith? If you have met with CHRIST in this most blessed saving way, then do you know him as he is: the CHRIST of GOD, the Sent of GOD, and One with GOD; so that you can truly say with holy men of old, *We believe, and are sure, that thou art* CHRIST *the* SON *of the living* GOD! John vi. 69. Nothing short of this knowledge of the LORD JESUS CHRIST, and this knowledge of yourself, can enable you to do as this woman did; believe on him for yourself, and commend him to others. Oh! for grace, in this CHRIST-despising day, and generation, so to know the LORD, and so to believe in him, for life and salvation, that like this woman, we may be able to invite others from heart-felt joy; and like the *Samaritans* under the same heart-felt conviction, to say: *Now we believe, not because of the saying of another, but from having heard him ourselves; and know that He is indeed the* CHRIST, *the* SAVIOR *of the world!*

43 ¶ Now after two days he departed thence, and went into Galilee.

44 For Jesus himself testified, that a prophet hath no honour in his own country.

45 Then when he was come into Galilee, the Galileans received him, having seen all the things that he did at Jerusalem at the feast; for they also went unto the feast.

46 So Jesus came again into Cana of Galilee, where he made the water wine. And there was a

certain nobleman, whose son was sick at Capernaum.

47 When he heard that Jesus was come out of Judea into Galilee, he went unto him, and besought him that he would come down and heal his son ; for he was at the point of death.

48 Then said Jesus unto him, Except ye see signs and wonders, ye will not believe.

49 The nobleman saith unto him, Sir, come down ere my child die.

50 Jesus saith unto him, Go thy way; thy son liveth. And the man believed the word that Jesus had spoken unto him, and he went his way.

51 And as he was now going down, his servants met him, and told *him*, saying, Thy son liveth.

52 Then enquired he of them the hour when he began to amend. And they said unto him, Yesterday at the seventh hour the fever left him.

53 So the father knew that *it was* at the same hour, in which Jesus said unto him, Thy son liveth. And himself believed, and his whole house.

54 This *is* again the second miracle *that* Jesus did when he was come out of Judea into Galilee.

The departure of Jesus into *Galilee*, it should seem, was not because of the little honor paid him; for the Lord was prepared for all this: Isaiah liii. 1, &c. but for the manifestation of this act of grace, in healing a son's bodily infirmity, and giving comfort to a father's mind. And who shall say, what effects beside were wrought in the family and neighbourhood, by such a manifestation of Christ's power? The distance from *Capernaum* to *Galilee*, could not have been less, at the nearest extremity of both towns, to each other, than fourteen or fifteen miles. For Jesus therefore to have wrought this cure of the sick child, and that the hour in which the Lord bid the father go his way, his child was then healed, should exactly correspond as the father afterwards found, on enquiry to the time the child's fever left him; was in his view, such a proof of Christ's Godhead, as under the Lord's grace, ended in a conviction to the faith of the Lord Jesus. Reader! if our inattentive hearts were but more alive to such events as pass and repass in the present hour, in proof of the same in Christ's words; we should be not unfrequently overwhelmed, with the continued evidences. Isaiah lxi. Luke iv. 18, 19.

REFLECTIONS.

READER! we have reason to believe, that the history of this woman of *Samaria*, handed down as it is, and hath been for ages past in the Church of GOD, hath been blessed to thousands. And what encouragement, indeed, doth such a record of grace hold forth, to poor sinners? Think how gracious the LORD dealt with this poor adulteress? How blessedly the view holds up CHRIST, to our love and adoration? Do not overlook what the LORD JESUS said to her as the sad cause CHRIST is so little regarded, and GOD's love in CHRIST so little known. Men do not know the gift of GOD. They have no apprehension that CHRIST is the remedy of GOD's own providing, for the wants of sinners. They neither know CHRIST in his Person, work, character, offices, and relationship to his Church; neither GOD's love in the free and full gift, he hath made of him, to the Church. But when GOD the HOLY GHOST, as in the case of this poor woman, opens to the sinner's view, who CHRIST is, both in himself, and in the gift of his FATHER; the heart and affections are won: and the soul's thirst for CHRIST is excited by the same power, and as blessedly assuaged, in the knowledge and love of him. *With the heart,* (saith the Apostle) *man believeth unto righteousness; and with the mouth, confession is made unto salvation!*

Methinks I could long for parents, and all that are interested in the temporal and everlasting interests of children, to do as this nobleman did; hasten to CHRIST, for their little ones. Behold! what a sweet miracle is here held forth, for the encouragement of all such. But how blessedly doth it preach to the believing parents of soul-sick children! Dearest LORD JESUS! did thy people but know thee more; how would thy courts be thronged, from day to day, in sending in petitions to the king! LORD, be it my portion, not to wait for signs and wonders; but faithfully to believe in thee, and all thy gracious promises, to the salvation of my soul!

CHAP. V.

CONTENTS.

JESUS *visits the pool of Bethesda. He healeth one there, after thirty and eight years disease. He preacheth most blessedly to the Jews.*

AFTER this there was a feast of the Jews; and Jesus went up to Jerusalem.

I beg the Reader at this verse to remark with me, that *John* is the only Evangelist, which hath noticed all the *Passovers* during our LORD's ministry; and he hath marked down every one. And it is by virtue of this record, how unimportant soever it might otherwise appear, that we are able to calculate the length of CHRIST's going in and out before the people, from his baptism to his cross: which was just *three years and half.* The *first* Passover is noted John ii. 13. This mentioned in this verse, was the *second.* The *third,* John vi. 4. And the *fourth* and last, John xviii. 28. The LORD JESUS attending them,

and what he said, particularly about the last, Luke xxii. 14, 15. will
serve to shew, how much he prized Ordinances. Psm. lxxxvii. 2.
And when he did away the Passover by his death, how graciously he
instituted the holy supper in its place; as if to say, he expected all
his family frequently to meet him there. 1 Cor. v. 7. and xi. 26.

2 Now there is at Jerusalem by the sheep-*market*, a pool, which is called in the Hebrew tongue, Bethesda, having five porches.

3 In these lay a great multitude of impotent folk, of blind, halt, withered, waiting for the moving of the water.

4 For an angel went down at a certain season into the pool, and troubled the water; whosoever then first after the troubling of the water stepped in was made whole of whatsoever disease he had.

5 And a certain man was there, which had an infirmity thirty and eight years.

6 When Jesus saw him lie, and knew that he had been a long time *in that case*, he saith unto him, Wilt thou be made whole?

7 The impotent man answered him, Sir, I have no man, when the water is troubled, to put me into the pool; but while I am coming another steppeth down before me.

8 Jesus saith unto him, Rise, take up thy bed and walk.

9 And immediately the man was made whole, and took up his bed and walked, and on the same day was the sabbath.

10 ¶ The Jews therefore said unto him that was cured, It is the sabbath-day: it is not lawful for thee to carry *thy* bed.

11 He answered them, He that made me whole, the same said unto me, Take up thy bed and walk.

12 Then asked they him, What man is that which said unto thee, Take up thy bed and walk.

13 And he that was healed wist not who it was: for Jesus had conveyed himself away, a multitude being in *that* place.

14 Afterward Jesus findeth him in the temple,
and said unto him, Behold, thou art made whole:
sin no more, lest a worse thing come unto thee.

Concerning this Pool, if we consult the Old Testament, we shall
find some light thrown upon it, as to its situation, near the field of
Kidron. John xviii. 1. *Nehemiah,* and *Jeremiah,* seem to have had
it in view. See Nehem. iii. 1. 32.—Jerem. xxxi. 38, 39. It was not
a *market* for sheep, but rather a sheep gate, or fold, near it; where, probably, the cattle were pent up for sacrifice. And the Pool, probably
formed from the waters of *Shiloah.* Isaiah viii. 6. But I would rather
call the attention of the Reader to some of the very interesting subjects, which are proposed to us, in our LORD's visit to the Pool,
and the miracle JESUS wrought there.

Is it not highly probable, (for I do not speak decidedly,) that as
this pool possessed this miraculous quality *John* describes, when excited by the ministry of the angel, that during the long dark night,
in which no open vision was made, from the time of *Malachi* to
Zacharias; the LORD was pleased to appoint this pool, as a standing monument in his Church; that the LORD was still watching over
them, and *had not cast away his people whom he foreknew?* Rom. xi.
1, 2. And was it not to keep alive in the minds of his chosen, by
the miracle itself, that He would come, who was *a fountain open for
sin and for uncleanness to the house of David, and to the inhabitants
of Jerusalem?* Zech. xiii. 1. Under those views, they certainly became no unapt representation of spiritual mercies, in the thing itself;
and much of the LORD JESUS, in his Person and offices, might have
been veiled under it.

The name of *Bethesda,* or House of Mercy, is near a-kin to *Bethel,*
or House of GOD. And as both are only mediums, or channels, for
conveying blessings from the LORD to his people; the house of GOD
and the house of Mercy, becomes one and the same. But as in this
pool of *Bethesda,* the descent of the angel was needful, to give
efficacy to the water; so the presence of the LORD in his house, is necessary, to make it blessed.

The pool of *Bethesda,* however, fell far short of the LORD's *Bethels.*
In this pool, it was but one at a season, which could be benefited.
But JESUS in his gospel ordinances, hath blessings for all, who through
the Spirit come to GOD by him. Those means of grace far exceed
the waters of the Prophet's vision. They not only extend in blessedness from *Engedi to En-eglaim;* but, when impregnated by the
descent of the HOLY GHOST, they reach from *sea to sea; and from the
river unto the ends of the earth.* Ezek. xlvii. 1—10. Psm. lxxii. 8.

I admire the very interesting account *John* hath given, of the many
diseased and miserable objects, which lay around the pool, in those
cloisters, waiting for the moment of healing. Blind, halt, withered;
all descriptive of the totally blind, halt, and helpless state of our
fallen nature: yea, dead in trespasses and sins. Reader! surely in
beholding this groupe of miserable objects, we discover the whole
race of Adam-nature. And though those *five porches* might contain
the whole of that neighbourhood, yet the globe itself is but as one great
hospital of human woe. But what a mercy, when JESUS the Angel of

the Covenant descends in the midst, under that endearing character, JEHOVAH ROPHE, to heal. Malachi iii. 1. Exod. xv. 26.

It were needless to run over the several particulars enumerated in the account of the *Bethesda* : neither of the one, the LORD singled out to manifest his mercy more particularly upon. No grace like distinguishing grace : neither are there any mercies which come home to the heart, with sweetness of so high a nature, as those which are personal and direct. How it must have struck every beholder, when the LORD JESUS singled out this man? And though he had been eight and thirty years in waiting for a cure; yet it was well worth waiting for, when the LORD JESUS thus came at length in person, to heal him; and chose him from among all the crippled, and sinew-shrank objects of misery around, to manifest his grace upon. And, Reader! if it be so, in natural things; what must it be in spiritual? If the blessing, from its distinguishing nature, be so valuable to the body; what must it be to the soul?

I will only detain the Reader, with a short observation on what the LORD JESUS said to this man, when he afterwards found him in the temple. *Sin no more*, (said CHRIST,) *lest a worse thing come unto thee.* Did this precept of JESUS refer to his *bodily* complaint, as if, (which is indeed the case,) both sickness and death are the effect of sin? In this sense, our LORD'S words will be, to avoid every thing which in its nature is sinful, and which hath a tendency, in the present state of things, to induce disease in the body. But, under an impression that this man was a child of GOD, of which there appears nothing to the contrary; and though not expressly said, (as in some other miracles JESUS wrought, is taken notice of: See Luke xiii. 16. and Luke xix. 9.) seems probable, I should rather be inclined to think, our LORD referred to the case of his soul. And then the subject becomes more abundantly interesting, to discover what was the express object of our LORD'S caution to him.

We cannot suppose that the LORD meant to say, that if he fell into a single transgression, he would lose thereby the LORD'S favor, and come under condemnation, not to be pardoned. For *James* saith, *in many things we offend all.* And *John* adds, that *if we say we have no sin, we deceive ourselves, and the truth is not in us.* James iii. 2. 1 John i. 8. Neither could the LORD mean, that such an after act of transgression, when a soul had been regenerated by the HOLY GHOST, would destroy that renewing of the SPIRIT, and subject the soul to everlasting death. For *there is not a just man* (that is, a truly justified soul in CHRIST,) *upon earth, that doeth good and sinneth not.* Eccles. vii. 20. And *a just man falleth seven times a day, and riseth up again.* Prov. xxiv. 16.

But though a child of GOD cannot forfeit, by any act of his, what was never bestowed upon him, for any deservings of his; but is the result of GOD'S grace, and not man's merit; yet he may have a much worse thing of soul befal him, than any calamity of the body. Though he cannot, when justified freely, lose GOD'S favor, yet he may be under great sorrow of heart, from the want of the light of GOD'S countenance. Holy men of old, groaned bitterly under such a state, in their seasons of soul exercise. *While I suffer thy terrors,* (said one of them,) *I am distracted.* Psm. lxxxviii. 15. And another cried out in anguish of spirit; *The terrors of* GOD *do set themselves in array against me.* Job. vi. 4. And who that reads *David's* groans under sin, will conceive, that any bodily pain could equal them. Psm. li. throughout. Reader! do not such views form the best comment to our LORD's advice to his patient in the Temple.

15 The man departed, and told the Jews that it was Jesus which had made him whole.

16 And therefore did the Jews persecute Jesus, and sought to slay him, because he had done these things on the sabbath-day.

17 But Jesus answered them, My Father worketh hitherto, and I work.

18 Therefore the Jews sought the more to kill him, because he not only had broken the sabbath, but said also, that God was his father, making himself equal with God.

19 Then answered Jesus, and said unto them, Verily, verily, I say unto you, The Son can do nothing of himself, but what he seeth the Father do: for what things soever he doeth, these also doeth the son likewise.

20 For the Father loveth the Son, and sheweth him all things that himself doeth: and he will shew him greater works than these, that ye may marvel.

21 For as the Father raiseth up the dead, and quickeneth *them;* even so the Son quickeneth whom he will.

22 For the Father judgeth no man; but hath committed all judgment unto the Son:

23 That all *men* should honour the Son, even as they honour the Father; he that honoureth not the Son, honoureth not the Father which hath sent him.

24 Verily, verily, I say unto you, He that heareth my word, and believeth on him that sent me, hath everlasting life, and shall not come into condemnation; but is passed from death unto life.

25 Verily, verily, I say unto you, The hour is coming, and now is, when the dead shall hear the voice of the Son of God: and they that hear shall live.

26 For as the Father hath life in himself, so hath he given to the Son to have life in himself;

27 And hath given him authority to execute judgement also, because he is the Son of man.

28 Marvel not at this: for the hour is coming in the which all that are in the graves shall hear his voice,

29 And shall come forth, they that have done good, unto the resurrection of life, and they that have done evil, unto the resurrection of damnation.

30 I can of mine own self do nothing: as I hear, I judge: and my judgement is just: because I seek not mine own will, but the will of the Father which hath sent me.

31 If I bear witness of myself, my witness is not true.

32 There is another that beareth witness of me, and I know that the witness which he witnesseth of me is true.

33 Ye sent unto John, and he bare witness unto the truth.

34 But I receive not testimony from man; but these things I say that ye might be saved.

35 He was a burning and a shining light: and ye were willing for a season to rejoice in his light.

36 But I have greater witness than *that* of John: for the works which the Father hath given me to finish, the same works that I do, bear witness of me that the Father hath sent me.

37 And the Father himself which hath sent me, hath borne witness of me, ye have neither heard his voice at any time, nor seen his shape.

38 And ye have not his word abiding in you: for whom he hath sent, him ye believe not.

39 Search the scriptures; for in them ye think ye have eternal life: and they are they which testify of me.

40 And ye 'will not come to me, that ye might have life.

41 I receive not honour from men.

42 But I know you, that ye 'have not the love of God in you.

43 I am come in my Father's name, and ye receive me not: if another shall come in his own name, him will ye receive.

44 How can ye believe, which receive honour one of another, and seek not the honour that *cometh* from God only?

45 Do not think that I will accuse you to the Father; there is *one* that accuseth you, *even* Moses, in whom ye trust.

46 For had ye believed Moses, ye would have believed me: for he wrote of me.

47 But if ye believe not his writings, how shall ye believe my words?

No doubt the poor man concluded, that the Jews would rejoice in the information that it was the LORD JESUS who had healed him? How little did he know of human nature! Very different is CHRIST's account. Verse 44, chap. xii. xxxix. xl. Very different also the testimony of the HOLY GHOST. 1 Cor. ii. 14.

This precious discourse of CHRIST is in itself so very plain, that it can need no comment. I shall therefore only detain the Reader with a few short observations upon it, which under the divine teaching, may be made helpful, both to the Writer and Reader, in attending to some of its beauties.

And, *first*, I beg the Reader to remark with me, how blessedly our LORD insists upon his own eternal Power and GODHEAD; and with what indignation the Jews received it. That the LORD JESUS preached this grand momentous truth himself: and that the Jews understood it as such; is as plain and palpable a fact, as any in the Bible. And when they charged him with blasphemy, for so doing; the LORD confirms what he had said, with a double Amen: that is, His own most blessed name as *the faithful and true witness.* Rev. iii. 14. Reader! what an awful thought is it, that while JESUS asserts it, proves it, and confirms it; and the Jews actually brought him to the cross for it: (John xix. 7.) many who call themselves by his sacred name, deny it. Oh! the delusion of every mind untaught of GOD. See John x. 30.

Secondly: In this divine discourse of Jesus, we discover no less, how blessedly the Lord speaks in his Office-character, as God-Man Mediator. Reader! I pray you not only in this place, but in every part of our Lord's discourses, when speaking in similar language to what he here useth, to note it down as a very sweet, precious, and incontrovertible truth; that Jesus is thus to be considered in his twofold nature: God and Man, in one Person, Mediator. Hence, he saith: *The Son can do nothing of himself, but what he seeth the Father do.* Hence Christ speaks of having life given to him in himself; as the Father hath life in himself. And hence he hath power and authority given to him to execute judgment, raise the dead, and to quicken whom he will. That all these things, and every other of a like nature, Christ thus exerciseth; are in his Office-character, as God-Man Mediator, is evident from hence: they could not be said of Him as God *only;* for as God, all were his own by right in common with the Father, and the Holy Ghost. Neither could they be said of Him as man *only:* for such powers as are said to be in the possession and exercise of Jesus as are here, and elsewhere described, are beyond all human excellency, unconnected with divine. But when considered, as Christ all along is, and must be considered, God, and man united, in One Person, every difficulty is removed.

Reader! pause over the sweet view. And though as our Lord told the Jews in this very Chapter, when speaking of his Father; as it may be said, and must be said, to every unregenerated sinner upon earth: *Ye have neither heard his voice at any time, nor seen his shape;* yet every child of God, in whose heart God that commanded the light at the old creation of nature to shine out of darkness, hath shined in the new creation of grace, hath given the light of the knowledge, both of God's voice, and shape, in the face of Jesus Christ. For the invisibility of Jehovah, in his threefold nature of Person, is made known, as far as any revelation can be made known, in time and to all eternity, in the Person of the God-Man Christ Jesus. For all the glory of Jehovah capable of being manifested, is manifested in Him. And it is in this high character of God-Man Mediator, making known Jehovah, which Christ is here speaking of, through all, and in all, the departments of nature, providence, grace, and glory.

One word more on this blessed discourse of the Lord Jesus. As Jesus is here chiefly speaking in his Mediator-character, and the several glorious offices in which he is said here to act; as the giver of life, the quickener of dead and living, and the sole judge to whom all judgment is committed, are every one of them His, by virtue of Covenant settlements: what an endearment of Christ's Person do they bring with them, to the hearts of all his people? Reader! do not fail to connect with those views of Christ, the interest which all his members have in them. As the head of his body the Church, *the fulness that filleth all in all;* he communicates all that is communicable of gifts, and graces, and royalties, and the whole members of his body, are made blessed in him and by him. As in this union of nature, he hath all power in heaven and earth; so is He at the head of all principality and power, both for the final destruction of his enemies, and the gathering together to himself his friends. Ephes. i. 10. It is his, to have life in himself, and to communicate life to others. His to save, and his to destroy. His to keep from going down to the pit of hell; and his to cast into it. And what makes both the Person and the Power of JESUS so exceedingly dear, under all these, and every other, in his office-character, is, that all authority is given him to execute judgment; *because he is the* SON *of Man.* Not because he is the SON of GOD; for had this been the case, as hath been before observed, it was impossible as GOD he could have had any of these *given* him. But it was, and is, in his Mediator-character, GOD and Man, in one Person. Reader! never dismiss the sweet thought! He that is to be the final judge of quick and dead, is now, and will be then, the Church's Brother, Head, Surety, and Husband! Oh! the preciousness of those scriptures! See John vi. 62.——I must no longer trespass. May He of whom I speak, unveil all and every other of his gracious characters, to the heart.

REFLECTIONS.

BLESSED Mediator! do thou still continue by thy HOLY SPIRIT, to visit the *Bethesdas* of Ordinances, among thy people; and as in the instance of this poor man, the longest and most inveterate diseases, induced by the Adam-nature of our fallen state, will be done away, when JESUS speaks the soul-quickening, the health-restoring word, to his people.

I desire to praise thee my honored LORD, for this sweet and blessed discourse of thine, thou hast caused to be left on record; for the joy and consolation of thy Church. What the infidel and unbelieving Jews of old, and all of modern times, which they say are Christians, and are not, call blasphemy, all the regenerated family of CHRIST embrace, as from the faithful and true witness in his own testimony, when he said, *I and my* FATHER *are One.* And must it not be then as GOD the FATHER hath appointed, that all should honor the SON, even as they honor the FATHER? Oh! for grace to honor JEHOVAH, FATHER, SON, and HOLY GHOST, in, and through, and by the GOD-Man CHRIST Jesus. And do thou, dearest LORD, unceasingly bless and refresh my soul in the view of all thy powers, that they are thine, and thine to execute, because thou art the SON of Man.

CHAP. VI.

CONTENTS.

JESUS feedeth a Multitude in the Wilderness. He retireth to a Mountain. At Night he walketh on the Sea. He preacheth to the People.

AFTER these things, Jesus went over the sea of Galilee, which is *the sea* of Tiberias:

2 And a great multitude followed him, because they saw his miracles, which he did on them that were diseased.

4 D 2

3 And Jesus went up into a mountain, and there he sat with his disciples.

4 And the passover, a feast of the Jews, was nigh.

5 When Jesus then lifted up *his* eyes, and saw a great company come unto him, he saith unto Philip, Whence shall we buy bread, that these may eat?

6 And this he said to prove him: for he himself knew what he would do.

7 Philip answered him, Two hundred pennyworth of bread is not sufficient for them, that every one of them may take a little.

8 One of his disciples, Andrew, Simon Peter's brother, saith unto him,

9 There is a lad here which hath five barley loaves, and two small fishes: but what are they among so many?

10 And Jesus said, Make the men sit down. Now there was much grass in the place. So the men sat down, in number about five thousand.

11 And Jesus took the loaves; and when he had given thanks, he distributed to the disciples, and the disciples to them that were set down; and likewise of the fishes as much as they would.

12 When they were filled, he said unto the disciples, Gather up the fragments that remain, that nothing be lost.

13 Therefore they gathered *them* together, and filled twelve baskets with the fragments of the five barley loaves, which remained over and above unto them that had eaten.

14 Then those men, when they had seen the miracle that Jesus did, said, This is of a truth that prophet that should come into the world.

If the Reader observes what is here said of the approach of the Passover, and compares it with the opening of the last Chapter, he will perceive, that there must have been very little less than a

whole year have passed between the one and the other. Here, therefore, we must bring in to our recollection what the other Evangelists
have recorded of that portion in the life and ministry of CHRIST.
The sea of *Galilee*, the same with what *Luke* calls *Gennesareth*, Luke
v. 1. was made memorable upon many occasions for the manifestation of our LORD's glory, Luke v. 1—11. particularly after he arose
from the dead. John xxi. 1. I do not swell the page with observations on this miracle of JESUS feeding the multitude. I sometimes
purposely use shortness, (and I beg the Reader to remember it,) in
order that he may be led to seek with more earnestness for the teachings of GOD the HOLY GHOST. Let me therefore upon the present
occasion, in addition to what hath been already said, Matt. xiv. 14.
Mark vi. 35. Luke ix. 12. only observe, that the compassion of
JESUS, manifested at those seasons, in working a miracle to supply the
pressing wants of the body, and for a multitude, which the LORD then
knew, and afterwards proved, were none of His, in the covenant of
redemption, (see verse 66.) should be a constant source of comfort,
both for the wants of body and soul, to his people, during the whole
of their time-state upon earth. My brother! I would say to every
child of GOD, let nothing tempt you to cast away your faith, or suffer
you to be cast down with fear; both your bread that perisheth with
using, and that which endureth to everlasting life, shall be given, and
your water sure. Isaiah xxxiii. 16. Remember CHRIST's own words,
Consider the ravens, for they neither sow nor reap, which neither have
store-house nor barn, and GOD *feedeth them! how much are ye better*
than the fowls? Read the whole passage, for it is very sweet. Luke
xii. 22—40.

15 ¶ When Jesus therefore perceived that they
would come and take him by force, to make him a
king, he departed again into a mountain himself
alone.

16 And when even was *now* come, his disciples
went down unto the sea,

17 And entered into a ship, and went over the
sea, toward Capernaum. And it was now dark,
and Jesus was not come to them.

18 And the sea arose, by reason of a great wind
that blew.

19 So when they had rowed about five and
twenty or thirty furlongs, they see Jesus walking
on the sea, and drawing nigh unto the ship: and
they were afraid.

20 But he saith unto them, It is I, be not
afraid.

21 Then they willingly received him into the

ship: and immediately the ship was at the land whither they went.

How little did the multitude know, that Jesus was indeed Jeho-vah's king in Zion, which from everlasting had been set up in the decrees of covenant engagements! How little was Christ known then, and how little even now, by many that follow him and profess themselves to be Christians, but are no more so than by name! I do not think it necessary to notice in this place again, what hath been observed in the relation of the same account by *Matthew*. See chap. xiv. 24. But I beg the Reader both then and now, not to lose sight of such a demonstration of Christ's Godhead, by two such mighty acts, as walking upon the sea, and causing the arrival of the ship the moment he entered it, to be at the destined place the disciples had embarked for. And doth not Jesus now in spirit walk over all the stormy dispensations of his people, to come to their relief? And doth he not after bring them home, long before their expectations, when through fire and water he brings them through into a wealthy place? Psm. lxvi. 12.

22 ¶ The day following, when the people which stood on the other side of the sea saw that there was none other boat there, save that one where-into his disciples were entered, and that Jesus went not with his disciples into the boat, but that his disciples were gone away alone;

23 Howbeit there came other boats from Tibe-rias, nigh unto the place where they did eat bread after that the Lord had given thanks:

24 When the people therefore saw that Jesus was not there, neither his disciples, they also took shipping, and came to Capernaum, seeking for Jesus.

25 And when they had found him on the other side of the sea, they said unto him, Rabbi, when camest thou hither?

26 Jesus answered them and said, Verily, verily, I say unto you, Ye seek me, not because ye saw the miracles, but because ye did eat of the loaves, and were filled.

27 Labour not for the meat which perisheth, but for that meat which endureth unto everlasting life, which the Son of man shall give unto you: for him hath God the Father sealed.

28 Then said they unto him, What shall we do, that we might work the works of God?

29 Jesus answered and said unto them, This is the work of God, that ye believe on him whom he hath sent.

30 They said therefore unto him, What sign shewest thou then, that we may see, and believe thee? What dost thou work?

31 Our fathers did eat manna in the desert: as it is written, He gave them bread from heaven to eat.

32 Then Jesus said unto them, Verily, verily, I say unto you, Moses gave you not that bread from heaven; but my Father giveth you the true bread from heaven.

33 For the bread of God is he which cometh down from heaven, and giveth life unto the world.

34 Then said they unto him, Lord, evermore give us this bread.

35 And Jesus said unto them, I am the bread of life, he that cometh to me shall never hunger; and he that believeth on me shall never thirst.

36 But I said unto you, That ye also have seen me, and believe not.

37 All that the Father giveth me shall come to me; and him that cometh to me I will in no wise cast out.

38 For I came down from heaven, not to do mine own will, but the will of him that sent me.

39 And this is the Father's will which hath sent me, that of all which he hath given me I should lose nothing, but should raise it up again at the last day.

40 And this is the will of him that sent me, That every one which seeth the Son, and believeth on him, may have everlasting life: and I will raise him up at the last day.

41 The Jews then murmured at him, because he said, I am the bread which came down from heaven.

42 And they said, Is not this Jesus, the son of Joseph, whose father and mother we know? how is it then that he saith, I came down from heaven?

43 Jesus therefore answered and said unto them, Murmur not among yourselves:

44 No man can come to me, except the Father which hath sent me draw him: and I will raise him up at the last day.

45 It is written in the prophets, And they shall be all taught of God. Every man therefore that hath heard, and hath learned of the Father cometh unto me.

46 Not that any man hath seen the Father, save he which is of God, he hath seen the Father.

47 Verily, verily, I say unto you, He that believeth on me hath everlasting life.

48 I am that bread of life.

49 Your fathers did eat manna in the wilderness, and are dead.

50 This is the bread which cometh down from heaven, that a man may eat thereof, and not die.

51 I am the living bread which came down from heaven. If any man eat of this bread, he shall live for ever; and the bread that I will give is my flesh, which I will give for the life of the world.

52 The Jews therefore strove among themselves, saying, How can this man give us *his* flesh to eat?

53 Then Jesus said unto them, Verily, verily, I say unto you, Except ye eat the flesh of the Son of man, and drink his blood, ye shall have no life in you.

54 Whoso eateth my flesh, and drinketh my

blood, hath eternal life : and I will raise him up at the last day.

55 For my flesh is meat indeed, and my blood is drink indeed.

56 He that eateth my flesh, and drinketh my blood, dwelleth in me, and I in him.

57 As the living Father hath sent me, and I live by the Father : so he that eateth me, even he shall live by me.

58 This is that bread which came down from heaven : not as your fathers did eat manna, and are dead. He that eateth of this bread shall live for ever.

59 These things said he in the synagogue, as he taught in Capernaum.

I have thought it right not to break the thread of our LORD's discourse, but to go through it, and then propose a few general observations at the close, which may the LORD graciously make profitable.

And, *first*, I pray the Reader to remark with me, the wonderful sublimity of our LORD's words. How evidently they manifested the greatness of his Almighty character. What Prophet, what Apostle, what servant of JEHOVAH ever made use of such language! *I am the bread of life, the living bread of God, which came down from heaven. He that eateth of this bread shall live for ever!* Carnal, unawakened men, may, as the Jews did, mistake the blessedness of our LORD's words, and cry out, *how can this man give us his flesh to eat?* But, every truly regenerated believer, will enter into the full apprehension of our LORD's meaning, and say with the Apostles, *Lord! evermore give us this bread!*

I detain the Reader to observe with me the beauty and aptness of the similitude. As the common bread is the staff of the body, so CHRIST, the heavenly bread, is the life of the soul. And, as the body cannot subsist without daily food, so neither can the soul without her spiritual support in CHRIST. Yea, the soul hath more need for CHRIST, in his person, fulness, and grace, than the body hath for the bread that perisheth. For, put the case to the worst, that by reason of a famine of bread, the body languisheth and dieth, it is but a death a little premature, and which would otherwise have died in due time. But the soul without CHRIST, the bread of life, must famish for ever, and though existing, lives only to eternal misery.

Reader! see, I beseech you, the vast and infinite importance of feeding spiritually on CHRIST. Oh! how sweet a life of faith, to be thus eyeing CHRIST, and knowing CHRIST to be the bread of life! To feel a daily longing for him, an hungring for him, as the keen appetite of an healthy laboring man doth for his daily food. It was thus holy men of old longed for CHRIST. They felt their need of him. They found their souls satisfied in him, and as one of them expressed it, so all of them enjoyed it, more panting for Christ than the hart for the water brooks. Reader, do not dismiss this part of our Lord's discourse, until that you have well pondered it over, and consulted those scriptures. Psm. xlii. and xliii. Ephes. iii. 17. Psm. lxxxix. 16. Hosea xiv. 8. Psm. lxiii.

I would beg the Reader next to notice that very precious part in this discourse of Jesus, where Christ speaks of his designation to the high office of Mediator. *For Him hath* God *the* Father *sealed.* Let it be observed, that within the compass of those *seven* words, is contained the office characters of the whole Godhead, in the appointment of the God-Man-Mediator. *Him,* that is, Christ, God *the* Father, that is, in his own peculiar personal character in the covenant. And sealing is the special act in the anointing of Christ by the Holy Ghost. How sweet, how very sweet, and richly consolatory to the soul of a believer, is it to behold the joint act of the Holy Three in One, in the mission of Christ Jesus? I pray the Reader to turn to a few scriptures in point, by way of confirmation. Isaiah xlii. 1—8. Psm. cx. 1—7. Heb. vii. 21—25. Acts x. 38. Isa. lxi. 1, &c. Luke iv. 18, 19. Heb. v. 1—5.

Let me lead the Reader by the hand, to a *third* improvement, which this most blessed discourse of Jesus teacheth. For when the Jews demanded what they should *do,* that they might *work the work of* God? Jesus made this remarkable answer, *This is the work of* God, (said Jesus,) that *ye believe on him whom he hath sent.* As if, and which in fact is truly the case, the whole work of God consists in a right belief and apprehension of God's dear Son. And small, as in some men's eyes these things may appear, it is the greatest work upon earth, and never wrought in any man's heart but by a miracle. It is indeed what Christ calls it, God's work, and not man's. It is inwrought by the Spirit of God in the heart. Oh! for grace, *to believe the record which* God *hath given of his Son!* 1 John v. 10, 11.

One word more, by way of improvement, from this divine discourse of Jesus. How truly blessed is it to learn from the lips of Christ himself, that the provision made for bringing home his whole redeemed, here in grace, and hereafter in glory, is so secure, that all whom the Father hath given him shall come to him; and him that cometh, Jesus will in no wise cast out. As Moses told Pharaoh, not an hoof should be left behind. Exod. x. 26. So here, the flocks must all again *pass under the hand of him that telleth them.* Jerem. xxxiii. 13. Nothing upon earth can be equal to the precious assurance of this most glorious truth. Neither can it fail, no, not in a single instance. The loss of one soul, for whom Christ died, and whom the Father gave to him, would tarnish the crown of the Lord Jesus Christ for ever. But the thing is impossible. It is founded in a covenant which is *ordered in all things and sure.* 2 Sam. xxiii. 5. The tenor of the covenant is everlasting, and of perpetual efficacy, and in which God himself undertakes, both for himself, and for his people, *I will not, and they shall not.* Jer. xxxii. 40. And the Lord Jesus refers, in further confirmation of the soul-reviving truth, that as a testimony of divine teaching the coming to him proves it. *All the children shall be taught of* God, saith Christ. Then, saith Jesus, here is the evidence, *Every one that hath heard, and hath learned of the* FATHER, *cometh unto me.* Reader! it will be a blessed fulfilment of CHRIST's words, if you and I, from being come to JESUS for life, and salvation, hereby prove no less, that *we are taught of* GOD ! Isaiah liv. 13. Jer. xxxi. 34. And this is to do what *John the Baptist* said, *to set to our seal that* GOD *is true.* John iii. 33.

I will only detain the Reader with one observation more, from this most blessed sermon of CHRIST, just to call his attention to what our LORD hath said, that *no man can come unto me,* (said JESUS,) *except the* FATHER, *which hath sent me, draw him !* There is somewhat very strong, both in the words of CHRIST, and the doctrine of CHRIST, as contained in this verse. *No man,* be his natural gifts whatsoever they may, or outward advantages of hearing GOD's word ever so many, *can,* in himself, find either a disposition or ability *to come to* JESUS, so as to believe in him, *except my* FATHER (that is, not to the exclusion of the quickenings of CHRIST, or the HOLY GHOST, for all the persons of the GODHEAD are included in the saving act,) *which hath sent me, draw him ;* that is, secretly and sweetly incline the heart to come to JESUS. Reader! pause over the words. They are very sweet to a child of GOD, and very solemn to the carnal! The child of GOD discovers in the everlasting love of GOD, the sure drawings of the FATHER. See Jer. xxxi. 3. and take comfort. And, Reader, if GOD the FATHER draws his people to CHRIST, who or what shall ever draw them away ? John x. 27—29.

60 Many therefore of his disciples, when they had heard *this*, said, This is an hard saying ; who can hear it ?

61 When Jesus knew in himself that his disciples murmured at it, he said unto them, Doth this offend you ?

62 *What*, and if ye shall see the Son of man ascend up where he was before ?

63 It is the spirit that quickeneth ; the flesh profiteth nothing : the words that I speak unto you, *they* are spirit, and *they* are life.

64 But there are some of you that believe not. For Jesus knew from the beginning who they were that believed not, and who should betray him.

65 And he said, Therefore said I unto you, That no man can come unto me, except it were given unto him of my Father.

What disciples were these which so expressed themselves? It could not be the Apostles. Neither was it any on whom a saving work of grace had been wrought in their heart. The word *disciple* is comprehensive of all that go after another. And, as our LORD told the great mass which followed him, that it was because they did eat

of the loaves, and were filled, for which they came to him, so
when they found that such carnal enjoyments were not likely any
longer to take place, they took offence, and called CHRIST's sayings
hard. But, Reader! I pray you, do not overlook the occasion JESUS
took from their murmuring to drop some most sweet and precious discourse concerning himself and his people. See John iii. 13. and
Commentary.

66 ¶ From that *time* many of his disciples went
back, and walked no more with him.

67 Then said Jesus unto the twelve, Will ye
also go away?

68 Then Simon Peter answered him, Lord, to
whom shall we go? thou hast the words of eternal
life.

69 And we believe, and are sure that thou art
that Christ, the Son of the living God.

70 Jesus answered them, Have not I chosen you
twelve, and one of you is a devil?

71 He spake of Judas Iscariot, *the son* of Simon:
for he it was that should betray him, being one of
the twelve.

I beg the Reader to mark well the character of those who are here
said to have gone back, and walked no more with JESUS. Not the
Apostles. Not a single one whom the FATHER had given to CHRIST,
and in whose hearts a saving work of GOD the HOLY GHOST had
been wrought. None of these are in the least hinted at. But the persons alluded to are the carnal and mere nominal disciples which followed JESUS, some, that they might eat of the loaves and fishes,
and some which had hoped that CHRIST would set himself up as a
king, to deliver the nation from the Roman yoke, under which they
had long groaned. While these objects were in view, all such were
ready to follow CHRIST. But when JESUS discountenanced all their
hopes of a temporal kingdom, and in the stead of this world's
opulence, spake of a cross, and self-denial to all which would follow him, their *Hosannahs* became soon changed into the cry of
Crucify him. Reader! Is it not to be feared, from what we see daily
in common life, that such instances are not singular? Is this heavenly
preacher in reality better loved, in the present day of much profession, when the exalting wholly of CHRIST, and levelling to the
dust all sinners, are made the sole subjects of his salvation? Do not
all modern *Pharisees* equally revolt at the doctrine of a spiritual life
in CHRIST, and a compleat self-loathing in the consciousness of their
own total depravity before GOD?

I have often paused to admire the very tender, sweet, and gracious
words of our LORD, to his few faithful followers, in the question, *will
ye also go away?* Not as if JESUS had the smallest apprehension

of the departure of any, who, from the *gift* of his FATHER, and the *grace-union in himself* before all worlds, were secured in the covenant, and made *willing in the day of his power.* Ephes. i. 4. John vi. 37—40. Psm. cx. 3. And, as another blessed Scripture saith, JESUS well knew *what was in man.* John ii. 25. and *who should betray him.* John xiii. 11. But the words were sweetly expressive of the love and tenderness of the heart of JESUS to his own. It is as if JESUS had said, the departure of all that are gone is just as it should be. They none of them ever had any grace-union with me. John xvii. 9. But ye are mine.

And I admire the fervent zeal, and love, and attachment of *Peter,* expressed in the few, but striking words, he uttered on this occasion. And he spake as the mouth of the rest, that is, all but the traitor *Judas.* For it is plain, that at this time, and for a considerable space after, not one of the faithful Apostles had the smallest suspicion of the infamy of this awful man. And how must they have been struck with the LORD's answer to *Peter : Have not I chosen you twelve ? And one of you is a devil!* Yes! chosen *twelve* to an outward office. But not the *whole* to inward grace. The whole twelve were indeed chosen to be Apostles. Luke vi. 13. But *Judas* obtained only *part,* as *Peter* afterward explained it, of this ministry. Acts i. 17. No part in the book of life. Never chosen in CHRIST by the FATHER, before the foundation of the world. Ephes. i. 4. The only part of a mere *office,* without union or communion in grace. Oh! the awfulness of such a state! [See Heb. vi. 4. and Commentary there.]

REFLECTIONS.

PRECIOUS LORD JESUS! while I behold thee, my GOD and SAVIOR, as set forth in this Chapter, feeding the multitudes with the bread which perisheth with using, and becoming in the same moment to all thy people the living bread, imparting solid, substantial, soul-feeding, soul-nourishing food, for time, and for eternity; LORD, I praise thee for the distinguishing mercy, and beg of my GOD to excite in my heart such a craving appetite to be fed and nourished in the divine life, as none but CHRIST himself can satisfy! LORD! *evermore give me this bread! Lift up the light of thy countenance upon my soul, and it shall put gladness in my heart, more than in the time when their corn and their wine are increased!*

And art thou, dearest LORD, the sealed of the FATHER? Doth GOD the HOLY GHOST prove to thy people his anointings, both of the glorious Head, and also of his members? Oh! for grace thus to receive thee, thus to come to thee, since such a rich provision is made for all the FATHER hath given thee, to come. Yea, methinks I would have every poor, awakened, and sensible sinner, to come. Hear, my brother, what JESUS saith. They shall all come which are of this description and character. And sure I am JESUS will accept all that so come, for he here saith, that *he will in no wise cast them out.* LORD! I would say for myself, and all thy redeemed family, behold! *we come unto thee, for thou art the LORD our GOD! Thou hast the words of eternal life.*

C H A P. VII.

CONTENTS.

*Jesus keepeth the Feast of Tabernacles. He teacheth in the Temple.
The Scribes and Pharisees are more and more enraged at him.*

AFTER these things Jesus walked in Galilee : for he would not walk in Jewry, because the Jews sought to kill him.

2 Now the Jews' feast of tabernacles was at hand.

3 His brethren therefore said unto him, Depart hence, and go into Judea, that thy disciples also may see the works that thou doest.

4 For *there is* no man *that* doeth any thing in secret, and he himself seeketh to be known openly. If thou do these things, shew thyself to the world.

5 For neither did his brethren believe in him.

6 Then Jesus said unto them, My time is not yet come; but your time is alway ready.

7 The world cannot hate you ; but me it hateth, because I testify of it, that the works thereof are evil.

8 Go ye up unto this feast : I go not up yet unto this feast ; for my time is not yet full come.

9 When he had said these words unto them, he abode *still* in Galilee.

The feast of tabernacles was one of the three great Jewish festivals in the Church. Levit. xxiii. 39. Deut. xvi. 16. The brethren of Jesus here spoken of, were not his brethren in grace, neither in nature, for *Joseph* was not the real, but the reputed father of Christ. Neither is it certain that *Mary* had any other child. See Matt. xii. 46. and Commentary. And those who are called brethren of Christ, were the sons of *Alpheus*, the brother of *Joseph*, and according to Jewish customs, from being brought up with Christ were called brethren, and these were all believers ; and *James*, and *Simon*, and *Judas*, were of the number of the Apostles. But I pass over the consideration of these things, as of lesser import, to attend to what is infinitely more interesting, the Person, and Work, and Offices of the Lord Jesus. This chapter is very highly interesting on this point.

10 ¶ But when his brethren were gone up, then went he also up unto the feast, not openly, but as it were in secret.

11 Then the Jews sought him at the feast, and said, Where is he ?

12 And there was much murmuring among the people concerning him. For some said, He is a good man : others said, Nay ; but he deceiveth the people.

13 Howbeit, no man spake openly of him for fear of the Jews.

14 ¶ Now, about the midst of the feast, Jesus went up into the temple and taught.

15 And the Jews marvelled, saying, How knoweth this man letters, having never learned ?

16 Jesus answered them, and said, My doctrine is not mine, but his that sent me.

17 If any man will do his will, he shall know of the doctrine, whether it be of God, or *whether* I speak of myself.

18 He that speaketh of himself seeketh his own glory : but he that seeketh his glory that sent him, the same is true, and no unrighteousness is in him.

19 Did not Moses give you the law, and *yet* none of you keepeth the law ? Why go ye about to kill me ?

20 The people answered and said, Thou hast a devil : who goeth about to kill thee ?

21 Jesus answered and said unto them, I have done one work, and ye all marvel.

22 Moses therefore gave unto you circumcision, (not because it is of Moses, but of the fathers,) and ye on the sabbath-day circumcise a man.

23 If a man on the sabbath-day receive circumcision, that the law of Moses should not be broken ; are ye angry at me, because I have made a man every whit whole on the sabbath day ?

24 Judge not according to the appearance, but judge righteous judgment.

25 Then said some of them of Jerusalem, Is not this he whom they seek to kill ?

26 But lo, he speaketh boldly, and they say nothing unto him, do the rulers know indeed that this is the very Christ?

27 Howbeit, we know this man whence he is: but when Christ cometh, no man knoweth whence he is.

28 Then cried Jesus in the temple as he taught, saying, Ye both know me, and ye know whence I am: and I am not come of myself, but he that sent me is true, whom ye know not,

29 But I know him: for I am from him, and he hath sent me.

30 Then they sought to take him: but no man laid hands on him, because his hour was not yet come.

31 And many of the people believed on him, and said, When Christ cometh, will he do more miracles than these which this *man* hath done?

32 The Pharisees heard that the people murmured such things concerning him; and the Pharisees and chief priests sent officers to take him.

33 Then said Jesus unto them, Yet a little while am I with you, and *then* I go unto him that sent me.

34 Ye shall seek me, and shall not find *me* : and where I am, *thither* ye cannot come.

35 Then said the Jews among themselves, Whither will he go, that we shall not find him; will he go unto the dispersed among the Gentiles, and teach the Gentiles?

36 What *manner of* saying is this that he said, Ye shall seek me, and shall not find *me* : and where I am, *thither* ye cannot come?

It is very blessed to behold CHRIST going up to keep this ordinance, in the fulfilling the whole law. And we have abundant reason to bless him that he did, for the Church would have lost this divine Sermon, which this chapter records, had he not gone there. Yea, indeed, as this was the last public preaching of JESUS, at the feast of tabernacles, it merits the attention of his people the more, as being decisive to the great points of his doctrine.

I need not go over the several features of it. The language of our LORD is designed, as it was delivered, for popular use; and, like the Prophet's vision, *he that runs may read it.* But I beg to make one observation upon it, which I hope may not be unprofitable. It is blessed to see that then, as now, though CHRIST himself was the preacher, the same effects always follow. To some it is *the savor of life unto life*; to others *of death unto death.* And JESUS himself hath assigned the cause. *My sheep* (saith he) *hear my voice, and I know them, and they follow me.* John x. 27. But to the ungodly, the LORD saith, *Ye therefore hear them not, because ye are not of* GOD. John viii. 47.

37 In the last day, that great *day* of the feast, Jesus stood and cried, saying, If any man thirst, let him come unto me, and drink.

38 He that believeth on me, as the scripture hath said, out of his belly shall flow rivers of living water.

39 (But this spake he of the Spirit, which they that believe on him should receive: for the Holy Ghost was not yet *given;* because that Jesus was not yet glorified.)

40 ¶ Many of the people therefore, when they heard this saying, said, Of a truth this is the Prophet.

41 Others said, This is the Christ, but some said, Shall Christ come out of Galilee?

42 Hath not the Scripture said, That Christ cometh of the seed of David, and out of the town of Bethlehem, where David was?

43 So there was a division among the people because of him.

44 And some of them would have taken him: but no man laid hands on him.

I would beg to pause over this short but powerful sermon of JESUS, on the last day of the feast. The LORD knew that all his public ministry was now closing. He stood therefore and cried. Reader! I pray you to turn to Prov. viii. 1 to the end. Isaiah lv. 1—4. Rev. iii. 20. And let it not be forgotten, that as CHRIST ended his public preaching with this cry, so did the HOLY GHOST close the sacred canon of scripture with words to the same effect. Rev. xxii. 16, 17.

I leave the Reader to form his own conclusions as to the result of such powerful preaching on the minds of the people. We read indeed of the different effects. Some were overawed, like the buyers and sellers in the temple, for the moment, and said, *of a truth this is the Prophet*. Others, hardened, still contended that it could not be. And some, more daring than the rest, would have seized CHRIST. Reader! pause and contemplate the awful state of Adam-nature by the fall. Though JESUS sweetly gave the gracious invitation to the thirsty soul, yet we read of none that thirsted.

The observation of the Evangelist, which is inclosed within a parenthesis at the 39th verse, is worthy our closest regard. How blessed is it to have our LORD's words so fully explained, in reference to the HOLY GHOST. And how doubly blessed when kindred souls are made sensible of that influence, in their own experience? I beg the Reader to observe in this verse the word *given,* that it is in Italics, meaning that it is not in the original. And I would desire, with all due respect to the labors of our most able translators, to substitute for it rather the word *come :* for the HOLY GHOST was not indeed yet come in all that plenitude of power, in which he was to come after CHRIST's return to glory; but GOD the SPIRIT had always been in his Church, and manifesting grace to his people in all ages. The spirit of CHRIST, saith *Peter*, was in the Prophets, when *testifying beforehand of the sufferings of* CHRIST, *and the glory which should follow.* 1 Peter i. 11. And every child of GOD, under the Old Testament dispensation, as well as under the New, are alike partakers in his quickening, regenerating, and renewing mercy. Nehem. ix. 20. But, when it is said that the HOLY GHOST was not yet given, or come, it is meant in respect to that more open display of his Almighty power, which was reserved for the latter day glory, when those promises were to be eminently fulfilled. Isaiah xliv. 3—5. Joel ii. 28. Acts ii. 1, &c. The kingdom of grace, in the ordination of the Apostles and first preachers of the Gospel, was to be introduced, with visible marks of the personality and GODHEAD of the HOLY GHOST, as the Almighty and Sovereign Minister in the Church of GOD. See John xiv. and Commentary.

45 ¶ Then came the officers to the chief priests and Pharisees; and they said unto them, Why have ye not brought him?

46 The officers answered, Never man spake like this man.

47 Then answered them the Pharisees, Are ye also deceived?

48 Have any of the rulers, or of the Pharisees, believed on him?

49 But this people who knoweth not the law are cursed.

50 Nicodemus saith unto them, (He that came to Jesus by night, being one of them,)

51 Doth our law judge *any* man before it hear him, and know what he doeth?

52 They answered and said unto him, Art thou also of Galilee? Search and look : for out of Galilee ariseth no prophet.

53 And every man went unto his own house.

Every word here is so plain as to need no comment. I only think it necessary to detain the Reader to enquire, whether he hath so heard the words of the LORD JESUS, as to say, as those men were compelled to say, *Never man spake like this man!* Every truly regenerated child of GOD feels constrained to say so. For, when a man is brought from the Adam-nature of sin and corruption, in which he, and every son of Adam was born, into a state of adoption and grace in CHRIST, he then knows *the joyful sound*, and is led to walk *in the light of* GOD's *countenance.* He will be the first to join in the same conviction, never man spake like the GOD-Man CHRIST JESUS. And he will enter into an heartfelt enjoyment of what the LORD hath said, for he knows the truth by his own personal experience, *the words that I speak unto you,* (saith Jesus,) *they are Spirit, and they are Life.* John vi. 63. Reader! the grand question, as it concerns yourself, is, are they so to *you?* Oh! the blessedness of knowing and enjoying the quickening, life-giving, soul-renewing, soul-strengthening grace of GOD the SPIRIT, in daily, hourly communications from the LORD JESUS, and living *to* JESUS, by a life of faith on the SON of GOD! Our need of CHRIST will become a sweet and sanctified mercy, constraining to go to CHRIST for the supply of all that we need, and giving continual cause for running on errands to the LORD, to his mercy seat and pardon office, that we may be unceasingly receiving out of *his fulness and grace for grace!*

REFLECTIONS.

READER! behold the glories of the LORD JESUS, as set forth in this chapter. Say! do not the accumulated testimonies to his eternal power and GODHEAD, shine like the rich constellation of the heavenly bodies, in one full cluster? And in his Mediator-character no less; behold, what rich and splendid proofs the LORD manifested, that his doctrine was of GOD! But yet we are told, that *even his brethren believed not on him!* How should they, who were no brethren in the grace-union of his body the Church, but only brethren in the Jewish nation and character, after the flesh? Ah! no. *All are not Israel, which are of Israel; neither because they are the seed of Abraham, are they all children.* What hath the *Ishmaels,* and the *Esaus,* to do with the covenant? Oh! the distinguishing grace of GOD! oh! the blessedness of the children of promise!

Dearest LORD JESUS! do thou condescend still to come to our feasts, by the sweet manifestations of thy SPIRIT. For without thy presence, the richest ordinances have no savor. All the stars in the firmament to our world, will not make one sun. And where JESUS, the Sun of Righteousness is not, it is in vain to look for light, or warmth, from all our services. But if my LORD come up to his banquetting house the Church, and cause his redeemed to sit under his shadow with great delight, then shall the whole Jerusalem of our GOD upon earth, like the Jerusalem of our GOD which is above, be feasted with the same love of JESUS. Then shall that scripture promise be fulfilled; we shall *suck and be satisfied with the breasts of her consolations, and milk out and be delighted with the abundance of her glory!*

Reader! let you and I be continually seeking grace from the LORD, that under this divine discourse of JESUS, brought home to our warmest affection by the gracious teachings of GOD the HOLY GHOST, we may each for ourselves be enabled to set our seals *that* GOD *is true.* And surely, my brother, if so be you have tasted that the LORD is gracious, however you behold JESUS as *a stumbling block, and a rock of offence* to those blind rulers in Israel, to you he will be more precious, *more glorious and excellent than the mountains of prey.* Every one who is made partaker of the grace in JESUS, will confess his graciousness, and know that *never man spake like this man!* Dearest Master! may it be my portion to derive all that is truly blessed and desirable in the present life from thee; for sure I am all that is truly glorious in another can only flow from thee. And be it, my honored LORD, my supreme happiness to live upon what JESUS is to me, and hath done for me, and not upon any supposed attainments of mine in following after thee. Indeed, indeed, thou Almighty SAVIOR, the sole joy of the Church, both above and below, can only be in thyself, as that sweet scripture most blessedly confirms, *In the* LORD *shall all the seed of Israel be justified and shall glory!*

C H A P.   VIII.

CONTENTS.

A woman taken in Adultery is brought to CHRIST *for Judgment. The* LORD *pardons her. He preacheth a divine Discourse. The Jews oppose him, and are about to stone him; but he passeth by, and escapeth their Hands.*

JESUS went unto the mount of Olives.
2 And early in the morning he came again into the temple, and all the people came unto him; and he sat down, and taught them.

I take occasion at the very mention of the Mount of Olives, to remind the Reader, what a memorable place this was. JESUS delighted in it. And doth the Reader ask wherefore? The Scriptures will answer the question. See Luke xxii. 39, &c. John xviii. 1, 2. Here it was, that David, a memorable type of CHRIST, ascended bare-footed in his sorrows. 2 Sam. xv. 23. And here it was, the LORD JESUS had to encounter the power of darkness, and sweat a bloody sweat. The LORD had all these things in view; and knew when, and where, his soul-travail would be. Hence JESUS loved the Garden of *Gethsemane!* and the Mount of *Olives.* These were his sacred haunts. Reader! you and I by faith should like to tread the hallowed ground, made sacred to the Redeemer's sufferings!

3 And the scribes and Pharisees brought unto him a woman taken in adultery: and when they they had set her in the midst,

4 They say unto him, Master, this woman was taken in adultery, in the very act.

5 Now Moses in the law commanded us, that such should be stoned: but what sayest thou?

6 This they said tempting him, that they might have to accuse him. But Jesus stooped down, and with *his* finger wrote on the ground, *as though he heard them not.*

7 So when they continued asking him, he lifted up himself, and said unto them, He that is without sin among you, let him first cast a stone at her.

8 And again he stooped down, and wrote on the ground.

9 And they which heard *it*, being convicted by *their own* conscience, went out one by one, beginning at the eldest, *even* unto the last: and Jesus was left alone, and the woman standing in the midst.

10 When Jesus had lifted up himself, and saw none but the woman, he said unto her, Woman, where are those thine accusers? hath no man condemned thee?

11 She said, no man, Lord. And Jesus said unto her, Neither do I condemn thee: go, and sin no more.

It is worthy remark, that these sworn foes of CHRIST did not bring the Adulterer as well as the Adulteress. Had their designs in coming to JESUS been purely from a regard to the sanctity of GOD's law, they would have been as anxious to punish the man, as the woman; for so the law enjoined. See Levit. xx. 10. But the object they had in view was not so much about the Adulteress, as to entangle the LORD JESUS in a snare. Had CHRIST commanded her to be stoned, they would have reproached him for acting contrary to the meekness of the Messiah; and thereby opposing his own doctrine in receiving Publicans and Harlots. And had he screened her from the law, they would have charged him with setting at nought the law of *Moses.*

Deut. xxii. 22, 23, 24.   Dearest LORD! what an everlasting *contra-diction of sinners didst thou endure against thyself.*   Heb. xii. 3. Matt. xxi. 31, 32.

There is somewhat uncommonly interesting in this relation of our LORD's conduct towards this Adulteress. What a lovely portrait is it of the SON of GOD in our nature? Look at JESUS in this sweet point of view, pardoning the sinner, while reproving the sin. There was for a little space some question as to the authenticity of the history; it not being in all the copies of the Testament. And it was confidently said by such, that it was in none of the editions of the *Syriac* version. But *Archbishop Usher*, at no small expence and labor, procured a copy of it in which it was found. It hath exercised also the curiosity of *some,* to know what it was JESUS wrote with his finger on the ground, while the Pharisees were accusing the woman. And it hath been said, that in an ancient Greek manuscript, it was found, that JESUS wrote some of the leading sins of the Scribes and Pharisees then present; which of course, as GOD, he knew. But this is mere conjecture. But as the HOLY GHOST is silent upon the subject, it becomes us to be the same. It is enough for the Church to be in possession of so very sweet a testimony, of the mercifulness of Him, who is the judge of quick and dead. And I venture to believe, that no child of GOD, who hath himself passed under the sentence of GOD's holy law, and, from self-condemnation, hath been led by the HOLY GHOST, to know the grace of JESUS; but must feel delight in so lovely a representation of JESUS, in the exercise of it.

I hope that I shall be forgiven, even if I err, when I venture to behold this woman as a lively emblem and figure of the Church, in the LORD's pardon of her. For surely there never was an Adulteress equally vile in baseness to the Church. Many have departed from their husbands, and dealt shamefully: But what adultery ever came up to the spiritual fornication of the Church? Read the Bible through, and hear the LORD's complaints. See particularly Jerem. ii. Hosea ii. and iii. And then observe how graciously the LORD hath dealt, and doth deal, with his people. Jerem. iii. John v. 14.

12 ¶ Then spake Jesus again unto them, saying, I am the light of the world : he that followeth me shall not walk in darkness, but shall have the light of life.

13 The Pharisees therefore said unto him, Thou bearest record of thyself, thy record is not true.

14 Jesus answered and said unto them, Though I bear record of myself, *yet* my record is true : for I know whence I came, and whither I go : but ye cannot tell whence I come, and whither I go.

15 Ye judge after the flesh ; I judge no man.

16 And yet, if I judge, my judgment is true :

for I am not alone, but I and the Father that sent me.

17 It is also written in your law, that the testimony of two men is true.

18 I am one that bear witness of myself, and the Father that sent me beareth witness of me.

19 Then said they unto him, Where is thy Father? Jesus answered, Ye neither know me, nor my Father: if ye had known me, ye should have known my Father also.

20 These words spake Jesus in the treasury, as he taught in the temple: and no man laid hands on him; for his hour was not yet come.

We enter here upon one of the most blessed discourses of JESUS. Who but the LORD JESUS ever called himself, or could call himself, *the light of the world?* Let the Reader gather into one view, some few only of those unequalled expressions of CHRIST, which he applied to himself; and then ask, whether any less than GOD could possibly assume such language? *I am the light of the world. I am the living bread which came down from heaven: if any man eat of this bread he shall live for ever.* John vi. 51. *I am the resurrection and the life: he that believeth in me, though he were dead, yet shall he live. And whomsoever liveth and believeth in me shall never die.* John xi. 25, 26. Reader! I charge you to pause over these words of CHRIST. What can we suppose, in CHRIST's assuming this language, if for the moment it could be thought that he was not GOD? And on the conclusion, which is the only conclusion on principles of common sense, that he is; what must be the awful situation of those men, who call themselves Christians, after Him, and yet indirectly charge him with blasphemy in denying his GODHEAD?

21 Then said Jesus again unto them, I go my way, and ye shall seek me, and shall die in your sins. Whither I go, ye cannot come.

22 Then said the Jews, Will he kill himself? because he saith, Whither I go, ye cannot come.

23 And he said unto them, Ye are from beneath, I am from above: ye are of this world; I am not of this world.

24 I said therefore unto you, That ye shall die in your sins: for if ye believe not that I am *he,* ye shall die in your sins.

25 Then said they unto him, Who art thou? and Jesus saith unto them, Even *the same* that I said unto you from the beginning.

26 I have many things to say and to judge of you: but he that sent me is true: and I speak to the world those things which I have heard of him.

27 They understood not that he spake to them of the Father.

28 Then said Jesus unto them, When ye have lifted up the Son of man, then shall ye know that I am *he,* and *that* I do nothing of myself; but as my Father hath taught me, I speak these things.

29 And he that sent me is with me : the Father hath not left me alone; for I do always those things that please him.

30 As he spake these words many believed on him.

If the Reader will take into account the different characters here described, he will be led to discover, (the LORD being his teacher,) wherefore it was, that from the same words and the same preacher, even CHRIST himself; some rejected the counsel of GOD, against their own souls: and some, *while he spake these words, believed on him.* It was so in the days of CHRIST, and under CHRIST; and it hath been the same in every age, and must remain so, until the consummation of all things. And the reason is given in the Scriptures. They who are born in the Adam-state of nature by the fall, and void of all grace-union in CHRIST; have no apprehension of the divine life. Our LORD describes them: *Ye are from beneath, I am from above: ye are of this world, I am not of this world.* And of such the LORD speaks: *If ye believe not that I am; ye shall die in your sins:* And as the LORD had said in the former Chapter; *whither I am ye cannot come.* John vii. 34. And on the other hand, they who were *given to* CHRIST *before the world began;* who are of *the first born whose names are written in heaven;* and by virtue thereof, have had a grace-union in CHRIST; and CHRIST hath betrothed them to himself for ever, in a covenant which cannot be broken: these are secured for recovery from the Adam-nature of a fallen state; in which they were also born, but from their oneness in CHRIST, are in the fulness of time called out of it and regenerated, and *made willing in the day of* GOD's *power.* See Ephes. i. 4. Luke x. 20. Hosea ii. 18, 19. Psm. cx. 3.

By making the true scriptural distinction between these very opposite characters; a light is thrown over this whole discourse, and others of the same nature, of our LORD's. Hence the everlasting opposition made, by the Scribes and Pharisees, to all the divine preaching of JESUS. And hence the light of grace which broke out in the minds of the LORD's people, under the very same discourses of JESUS, by which, while he spake these words, it is said, that *many believed on him.*

I beg the Reader to notice the particularity of the expression. *If ye believe not*, said JESUS, *that I am;* (the *he* subjoined is not in the original, neither ought it to be considered elliptical,) by which there is an evident allusion to Exodus iii. 14: and there can be no question, but that our LORD meant it in the same sense. *I am, that I am.* So he spake to *Moses,* at the bush. So again he spake here. And so once more, in the close of this same Chapter, verse 58. And I venture to believe, that our LORD meant the words not only in the eternity of his nature, as GOD; but also in his Mediator-character and office, as GOD-Man. And the change of words in this last verse, from *was* to *am, Before Abraham was I am;* most plainly and decidedly proves this most blessed and glorious truth. Reader! ponder it well. Carry it about with you wherever you are; with the credentials of your holy faith. All the blessedness, the marrow, and sweetness, of the Person, Headship, and Office-character of the LORD JESUS, are included in it.

31 Then said Jesus to those Jews which believed on him, If ye continue in my word, *then* are ye my disciples indeed:

32 And ye shall know the truth, and the truth shall make you free.

33 They answered him, We be Abraham's seed, and were never in bondage to any man: how sayest thou, Ye shall be made free?

34 Jesus answered them, Verily, verily, I say unto you, Whosoever committeth sin is the servant of sin.

35 And the servant abideth not in the house for ever: *but* the Son abideth ever.

36 If the Son therefore shall make you free, ye shall be free indeed.

37 I know that ye are Abraham's seed: but ye seek to kill me, because my word hath no place in you.

38 I speak that which I have seen with my Father: and ye do that which ye have seen with your Father.

39 They answered and said unto him, Abraham

is our father. Jesus saith unto them, If ye were
Abraham's children, ye would do the works of
Abraham.

40 But now ye seek to kill me, a man that hath
told you the truth which I have heard of God:
this did not Abraham.

41 Ye do the deeds of your Father. Then said
they to him, We be not born of fornication: we
have one Father *even* God.

42 Jesus said unto them, If God were your
Father, ye would love me; for I proceeded forth
and came from God: neither came I of myself,
but he sent me.

In this part of our LORD's discourse, we have a subject equally interesting with the former; but JESUS takes another form, by way of
discriminating his people from the world. He adopts a beautiful
figure, of an house, and family; in order to shew the striking difference. He represents the image of that fallen state of Adam, by
reason of sin, as a servant; and shews, that every one who committeth
sin, is the servant of sin. And the similitude is just. Every son and
daughter of *Adam*, by transgression hath forfeited all right of inheritance; and is in bondage to sin and Satan. The LORD calls his
people, *the lawful captives of the mighty; and the prey of the terrible.*
Isaiah xlix. 25. And the LORD represents the children of his kingdom
as his, by virtue of his adoption; and shews, that by his abiding in
his own house, as a SON for ever, he preserves them, and makes them
free. Whereas the servant, having no inheritance, is shortly turned
to the door.

This forms a beautiful illustration of the subject. As the whole
Adam-race, were all alike involved in the ruin of the fall; they all
come forth from the womb of nature in the same natural bondage of
sin; all alike serving divers lusts, and pleasures; all under the guilt
of sin, the curse of sin, the dominion of sin, the punishment due to
sin; the wrath of GOD, and the terrors of his justice. It is only such
as the SON of GOD makes free, that *are free indeed!* The carnal
Jews could not brook this pointed discourse of CHRIST. Priding
themselves on being lineally descended from *Abraham*, they thought
that they were entitled to all *Abraham's* privileges. But JESUS taught,
that freedom was only in himself. It was not *Abraham's* seed in
nature, which gave a right and title to *Abraham's* inheritance; but
Abraham's seed in grace. *He saith not and to seeds as of many, but
as of one; and to thy seed which is* CHRIST. Gal. iii. 16. Hence
all the natural children of *Abraham* only, (and he had many,) were
servants in the family, and no other; and had no part, nor lot, in
the promises. But the charter of grace ran in these words: *In Isaac
shall thy seed be called.* Rom. ix. 7.

I beseech the Reader to pause over our LORD's own illustration of this subject, as here set forth. Nothing can be more plain, nothing more evident, in proof of that everlasting and irreconcileable separation, between the Church and the world; between the seed of the woman, and the seed of the serpent. Both the one, and the other; the Israel after the flesh and the Israel after the Spirit, possess for a time, as servants and children in the same family, apparently the same privileges. In respect of ordinances, and means of grace, they sit down under the same. And like those Pharisees, who never believed in CHRIST, and those true disciples of JESUS who did; the same discourses were delivered before all. But by and by, when the LORD comes to take account, the *Ishmaels*, and the *Isaacs*, are found to be of very different stock; and an everlasting separation takes place. For what saith the scripture; *Cast out the bond woman and her son; for the son of the bond woman shall not be here with the son of the free woman.* Reader! learn to estimate the vast distinction. See whether you can enter into a relish of the Apostle's conclusion, when he saith: *So then brethren, we are not children of the bond woman, but of the free.* Gal. iv. 22. to the end.

43 Why do ye not understand my speech; *even* because ye cannot hear my word.

44 Ye are of *your* father the devil, and the lusts of your father ye will do. He was a murderer from the beginning, and abode not in the truth, because there is no truth in him. When he speaketh a lie, he speaketh of his own: for he is a liar, and the father of it.

45 And because I tell *you* the truth, ye believe me not.

46 Which of you convinceth me of sin? and if I say the truth, why do ye not believe me?

47 He that is of God heareth God's words: ye therefore hear *them* not, because ye are not of God.

48 Then answered the Jews, and said unto him, Say we not well that thou art a Samaritan, and hast a devil?

49 Jesus answered, I have not a devil; but I honour my Father, and ye do dishonour me.

50 And I seek not mine own glory: there is one that seeketh and judgeth.

51 Verily, verily, I say unto you; If a man keep my saying, he shall never see death.

52 Then said the Jews unto him, Now we know that thou hast a devil. Abraham is dead, and the prophets: and thou sayest, If a man keep my saying, he shall never taste of death.

53 Art thou greater than our father Abraham, which is dead? and the prophets are dead: whom makest thou thyself?

54 Jesus answered, If I honour myself, my honour is nothing: it is my Father that honoureth me; of whom ye say that he is your God:

55 Yet ye have not known him: but I know him. And if I should say, I know him not, I should be a liar like unto you: but I know him, and keep his saying.

56 Your father Abraham rejoiced to see my day; and he saw *it*, and was glad.

57 Then said the Jews unto him, Thou art not yet fifty years old: and hast thou seen Abraham?

58 Jesus said unto them, Verily, verily, I say unto you, Before Abraham was, I am.

59 Then took they up stones to cast at him: but Jesus hid himself, and went out of the temple, going through the midst of them, and so passed by.

We have the continuation of our LORD's Sermon, on much the same subject; only, that JESUS is rising higher, and making use of much stronger language in the doctrine, when separating the precious from the vile; the wheat from the chaff; the Church from the world. He here considers the Pharisees as totally incapable of receiving his word, because of their total inability of understanding it. And the LORD traces up the effect, to the cause; in decidedly declaring, and without the smallest reserve or limitation whatever, that *they were of their father the devil, and the works of their father they would do.* Here opens at once the whole matter, and becomes a decision to all the subjects of dispute, which, from age to age, have divided the opinions of men in the world. Wherefore some are everlastingly obdurate, whilst others relent. Some believe in CHRIST, to the salvation of their souls; whilst others are entrenched in invulnerable unbelief. JESUS, by assigning the cause of infidelity, in Satan, plainly shews the cause of faith, in the gift of GOD. I beg the Reader not to turn away from this solemn but just view of the subject, before that he hath first carefully looked over those scriptures, which very

fully explain it: Matt. xxiii. 15. 33. 1 John iii. 8—12. Matt. xiii.
38, 39. Acts xiii. 10. There can be no concord between CHRIST
and Belial; between the Church and the world: they differ, in
beginning and end; in cause, and effect. They never can coalesce.
Tares and wheat may grow together; but tares and wheat they must
everlastingly remain, as long as they remain. Hence CHRIST's final
sentence to the characters of the Serpentine brood; *ye shall die in
your sins: and whither I go ye cannot come.*

I will only detain the Reader with just observing, what a very
blessed, and decisive declaration, the LORD JESUS made of himself,
when, in the close of his sermon, he said, *Before Abraham was I am!*
In every sense how truly blessed! Considered as to his eternal nature, and essence. Considered as to his Mediator-character, as set
up the Head and Husband of his Church, from everlasting. Considered as to his Office-work before he openly tabernacled in substance
of our flesh, when in his goings forth at creation, and in the garden,
with our first Parents; with *Noah,* and before and after the flood!
And though it was subsequent to the days of *Abraham,* when the
LORD went before his people, in the wilderness; yet *Stephen,* under
the immediate influence of the HOLY GHOST declared, that he it was
who spake to *Moses,* in Mount *Sinai.* Acts vii. 35. And that the
Jews understood our LORD in this sense is very plain, for they took
up stones to cast at him for what they considered blasphemy.
Hence, that the LORD JESUS asserted his GODHEAD in this blessed
expression; *Before Abraham was I am*: and that the Jews took it in
this sense is as plain as words can make it. Neither do I think the
action of CHRIST which followed, less convincing than his *words* in
proof of Deity. For as he had done once before upon a like occasion, (See Luke iv. 28 to 30.) to escape their malice for that season;
so now he did the same, either by rendering himself for a time invisible, or blinding their apprehension of him: but in either case,
manifesting his GODHEAD so as to pass them by.

REFLECTIONS.

PRECIOUS LORD JESUS! may my soul gaze with rapture on every
feature of thy divine Person, while by faith I behold thee, as in this
Chapter, pardoning the poor Adulteress; and manifesting the mercy
of thine heart. Oh! thou dear LORD! well is it for thine Adulteress
Church, that thou art a GOD, pardoning iniquity, transgression, and
sin; or what would have become of all thy redeemed.

And LORD! I find new occasion to admire, to love, to adore,
my compassionate GOD, in that he brings his people from the Adam-
nature and servitude of sin, into the freedom and adoption of children,
in my LORD's family. Truly LORD *thou hast loosed my bands!* Thou
hast brought all thy redeemed from the dominion and guilt of sin, into
the glorious liberty of the children of GOD. And as it is GOD the
SON hath made his people free, they shall be free indeed. And although all thy children, thy blood-bought family, do still carry
about with them a body of sin and death, which harrass and afflict
the soul: though still the subjects of outward troubles, and inward
fears: though many a fiery dart Satan still hurls at them; and many

a wearisome path by his craft and cruelty, he causes them to tread in their pilgrimage: yet thou LORD hast brought them out of his servitude, where once they lived as his drudges; doing his work, and wearing his livery, and delighted with both: and art bringing them home, and wilt bring them all in, to thine heavenly kingdom! Blessed be my GOD and SAVIOR, for all his love and mercy.

Reader! let us both join in thanksgivings to the great I AM; both for his own eternal power and GODHEAD, and for thus drawing the line of everlasting distinction as this Chapter hath it, between those awful characters who by denying CHRIST die in their sins; and those who believe in him to the salvation of their souls. Blessed, for ever blessed, be our great I AM!

CHAP. IX.

CONTENTS.

JESUS *giveth Sight to a Man which was born blind. The Pharisees are enraged at it.* JESUS *preacheth a sweet Sermon on the Occasion.*

AND as *Jesus* passed by, he saw a man which was blind from *his* birth.

Such seems to have been the importance of this miracle of CHRIST, as it related to his own glory, and as it related to his Church, that the HOLY GHOST hath been pleased to cause the relation of it to occupy an whole Chapter, of more than forty verses. And excepting that memorable one, in respect to the resurrection of *Lazarus,* John xi. and which, for very obvious reasons, may be considered as demanding also the special attention of the Church, we do not find any of the LORD's miracles on the bodies of men, so largely dwelt upon. Under the apprehension therefore of its greater importance to our regard, than some of the more ordinary miracles of CHRIST, I hope the Reader will indulge me with calling his more immediate attention to it: and may both Writer and Reader seek of that *wisdom which is from above,* in the perusal of it, that we may enter into the design of GOD the SPIRIT, in the large relation he hath given; and the glories of GOD the SON in so distinguishing an act of grace as is here shewn; and to the praise of GOD the FATHER, whose name is glorified in his dear SON. John xvii. 1.

And here, according to my view of the subject, and among the other designs of GOD the HOLY GHOST, in the special, and large relation of this miracle; I humbly conceive, that beside the thing itself in so divine an act of CHRIST, in displaying the GODHEAD of his nature, and identifying his Person and Character, as GOD-MAN-Mediator; it was intended as a beautiful illustration of the recovery of every individual member of CHRIST's mystical body, from the blind estate in which they are all born in the Adam-nature of the fall: and out of which the LORD JESUS alone brings them, as the life and light of his people. If the thought be well founded, and is of GOD's teaching; and if both Writer and Reader be enabled to consider it through the whole in this point of view, and the LORD should be pleased to bless their attention to it with his grace, both will then find cause to say, as one of old did concerning JESUS and his works : *My meditation of Him shall be sweet.* Psm. civ. 34.

Let us enter on the Chapter. It is said, that *as* JESUS *passed by, he saw a man which was blind from his birth.* And who so blind as even GOD's dear children are to spiritual things, when first born in the Adam-nature of original sin, and transgression, sinners from the womb? Scripture saith, that *they are children of wrath even as others, and consequently, until called by grace, have their understanding darkened, being alienated from the life of* GOD *through the ignorance that is in them, because of the blindness of their hearts.* Ephes. iv. 18. They are, in the fullest and strictest sense of the word, blind to the knowledge of GOD the FATHER, and his everlasting love to the Church in CHRIST! Blind to the Person, work, grace, mercy, favor, and all the ten thousand beauties, and excellencies which are in GOD the SON, in his Mediator-character, as Head, and Husband of his Church, and people! Blind to every thing relating to the eternal Power and GODHEAD of the blessed SPIRIT, both in his own essence and glory; and in his grace and mercy to the Church: so that in point of knowledge, as to their own apprehension in spiritual understanding, they have never *so much as heard whether there be any* HOLY GHOST! Acts xix. 2. And of their own utterly lost, ruined, and undone estate, in the Adam-fall of nature, they are perfectly unconscious! Reader! Pause, and ask, whether there can be a blindness like this! And yet whether you are now conscious of it or not: this is the real state of every son and daughter of Adam by nature. None so near to us as GOD: and none so little known, or so little regarded!

2 And his disciples asked him, saying, Master, who did sin, this man, or his parents, that he was born blind?

By this question of the disciples, we cannot suppose that they meant in relation to original sin; as if they doubted the universal corruption of mankind in *Adam.* This could not be the sense of the disciples' words. They knew what the LORD had said by *Moses;* that *the iniquity of the Father is visited upon the children.* Exod. xx. 5. But the Reader should be told, that many years before the coming of CHRIST, a system of Philosophy had been introduced, by one called *Pythagoras,* who taught, that all mankind had existed in some other body before their appearance in the present form of human nature : and that the sins which had been committed by any of them during that former state, was punished in this. The disciples availed themselves perhaps of this opportunity, to know CHRIST's sentiments upon it, and put the question, whether the present blindness of this man was according to this system, the result of his father's sins, or his own. I should not have noted the folly and wickedness of such a doctrine, but with a view to call upon the Reader to remark with me, the awful blindness and ignorance of the world before the coming of CHRIST; when among the wisest of men, such childish and ridiculous notions prevailed. My brother! calculate, if you be able, the auspicious and blessed consequences which the SON of GOD brought with him, when he graciously visited our world!

3 Jesus answered, Neither hath this man sinned, nor his parents: but that the works of God should be made manifest in him.

When our LORD gave this answer to his disciples, that neither this man nor his parents had sinned in that he was born blind; JESUS could not be supposed to mean, that they were not sinners; for Scripture declares that *all have sinned, and come short of the glory of* GOD. Rom. iii. 23. But the plain and obvious meaning of CHRIST, is, that this man's blindness was not the immediate effect of any one particular sin, in a way of judgment, but rather to afford occasion for the greater display of the works and glory of GOD. And in this very instance, our LORD's doctrine in this particular is proved. For what greater glory could possibly be shewn, than by the blindness of this man, the LORD JESUS might manifest his divine nature and mercy, in giving him sight? How sweetly did it teach also the blindness of soul; and CHRIST's glory in such instances, in giving sight to the spiritually dark, and eyes to the blind in sin. And who shall say, how often the record of this man's history hath proved instrumental in raising trophies of glory to the LORD, through the many intermediate ages from that hour to the present, where sinners, made spiritually alive by grace, have read of the LORD's goodness to him, and felt the LORD's goodness to themselves, in having been brought *from darkness to light, and from the power of Satan unto* GOD. Acts xxvi. 18. Reader! think, I pray you, in how many cases in life such events are perpetually occurring? What numberless opportunities are afforded for the manifestations of the LORD's grace, which grow, out of all the exercises of the LORD's people? And if you know any thing of the LORD, I would desire you to say, how would the LORD JESUS prove his love to you, in seasons of sorrow, in hours of temptation, and in all times of trouble; if you had never known sorrow, never felt temptation, or knew what trouble meant?

4 I must work the works of him that sent me while it is day: the night cometh when no man can work.

5 As long as I am in the world, I am the light of the world.

I beg the Reader to pause over these verses, and mark *some* of the great things contained in them. *First,* observe, how sweetly JESUS speaks in his Mediator-character and office, of doing the works of Him that sent him. Mark the LORD's duty to his FATHER, and his love to his people, in this zeal of his heart. *Secondly,* mark no less, the FATHER's love to the Church, in thus giving, and sending, his dear SON, that the whole body might live, in, by, and through Him. And here before you go further, look at that sweet Scripture in further proof, 1 John iv. 10. *Thirdly,* connect what the LORD JESUS here saith, with what he elsewhere added, upon the subject of doing his FATHER's work. *I have* (said JESUS) *glorified thee on the earth: I have finished the work which thou gavest me to do.* John xvii. 4.

Reader! pause over these very very blessed words. There can be none more blessed upon earth; no, nor in heaven. Redemption-work is finished. The Church of CHRIST is saved. JEHOVAH is glorified. And none but CHRIST could ever assume such language. No angel of light; no, nor all the creation of GOD, can use such words. For though they all set forth GOD's glory, in being the works of his hands; yet no act of theirs, truly and strictly speaking, can add an atom to render GOD more glorious. Sooner might we increase the sun's brightness by the light of the candle, or swell the ocean by our tears; than we can bring in a greater revenue of glory to the LORD by any thing of ours. But the GOD-Man CHRIST JESUS hath added to that glory of JEHOVAH which alone is capable of being exalted, in the manifestation of all that is communicable, to his intellectual creation. Precious LORD JESUS! truly didst thou say in those blessed words: *As long as I am in the world, I am the light of the world.* And far better would it be that the sun of this lower world should be extinguished from the heavens, than that CHRIST the Sun of righteousness, should cease to be the light and life of his Church!

6 When he had thus spoken, he spat on the ground, and made clay of the spittle, and he anointed the eyes of the blind man with the clay.

7 And said unto him, Go, wash in the pool of Siloam, (which is, by interpretation, Sent.) He went his way therefore, and washed, and came seeing.

We now come to the part of this interesting miracle, in which JESUS entered upon the work, of giving sight to the man born blind. The clay, and the spittle, and the pool of *Siloam*, (which the Evangelist takes care to note, is by interpretation *Sent*,) were the means only, the LORD was pleased to make use of, in this marvellous work. But we must look higher than to means of any kind, to discover the first and great cause of the deed. If we consider the case of blindness in general, and especially in the instance before us, where the man was born blind, and where the loss of sight could not have been induced from any injury to the organs of vision; it is but a fair conclusion, as in a multitude of blind persons, it is not merely loss of sight, but a total loss of eyes. Hence, if it be only allowed, that a single one of the many blind to whom the LORD JESUS gave sight in the days of his flesh, had eyeless sockets; here was a compleat act of creation, and as manifest a display of divine power, as at the creation of the world. So that CHRIST hereby gave a full demonstration of his GODHEAD. The Reader will observe, that I do not presume to say that this was literally the case, in the instance of this man, or any other among the blind which JESUS healed. But no one can say that it was not so. And I venture to think, from what the man himself said, that the probability in favor of this opinion is greater than it is against it. *Since the world began*, (said he,) *was it not heard that any man opened the eyes of one that was born blind,* ver. 32. I leave the Reader to form his conclusions. Bnt I cannot help observing, that it would be well for every man who hath the least pause in his mind, whether CHRIST be GOD, or not; and infinitely more so, for every man who presumes to deny CHRIST's GODHEAD, to ascertain this point. For if this blind man, or any other to whom CHRIST gave sight, had eyeless sockets; (as is, I believe, in blindness more generally the case than otherwise;) here was, to all intents and purposes, a creation of the organs of vision. And I again repeat, this deed as fully, and as clearly defined the GODHEAD, as all the other parts of creation.

I only detain the Reader with a short observation more, before that we pass to the next verses in the history, just to remark, that such were the features of character, by which CHRIST was to be known. Ages before our LORD's incarnation, the Prophet was commissioned to tell the Church, when pointing to his Person, and Character: *behold!* (said he,) *your* GOD *will come and save you!* And how was he to be known? *Then the eyes of the blind shall be opened.* Isaiah xxxv. 4, 5.

8 The neighbours therefore, and they which before had seen him, that he was blind, said, Is not this he that sat and begged?

9 Some said, This is he. Others *said,* He is like him, *but* he said, I am *he.*

10 Therefore said they unto him, How were thine eyes opened?

11 He answered and said, A man that is called Jesus, made clay, and anointed mine eyes, and said unto me, Go to the pool of Siloam, and wash. And I went and washed, and I received sight.

12 Then said they unto him, Where is he? he said, 1 know not.

Let the Reader figure to himself, if he can, the wonderful effect which was wrought on the minds of the neighbors, and those who knew him, in beholding one, who from a child, like many we now meet with in life, was blind; having new eyes, and the organs of vision in full exercise! How must they have been astonished? And what a talk must it have made, in the circle of all his acquaintance? But, Reader! how much greater the astonishment to himself, when he saw clearly the objects with which he had long conversed; and daylight, and all the sweet prospects of nature, appearing to his view, every where around him! Pause a moment more. If such to a blind man in nature, were the wonders of sight; what must it be, yea what is it daily to a child of GOD in grace, when his spiritual eyes are opened *to see the wonderful things of* GOD's *law?*

13 ¶ They brought to the Pharisees him that aforetime was blind.

14 And it was the sabbath-day when Jesus made the clay, and opened his eyes.

15 Then again the Pharisees also asked him, how he had received his sight? he said unto them, He put clay upon mine eyes, and I washed, and do see.

16 Therefore said some of the Pharisees, This man is not of God, because he keepeth not the sabbath-day. Others said, How can a man that is a sinner do such miracles? And there was a division among them.

17 They say unto the blind man again, What sayest thou of him, that he hath opened thine eyes? He said, He is a prophet.

18 But the Jews did not believe concerning him, that he had been blind, and received his sight, until they called the parents of him that had received his sight.

19 And they asked them, saying, Is this your son, who ye say was born blind? How then doth he now see?

20 His parents answered them and said, We know that this is our son, and that he was born blind:

21 But by what means he now seeth, we know not; or who hath opened his eyes, we know not: he is of age; ask him: he shall speak for himself.

22 These *words* spake his parents, because they feared the Jews; for the Jews had agreed already, that if any man did confess that he was Christ, he should be put out of the synagogue.

23 Therefore said his parents, He is of age, ask him.

24 Then again called they the man that was blind, and said unto him, Give God the praise: we know that this man is a sinner.

25 He answered and said, Whether he be a

sinner, *or no*, I know not: one thing I know, that whereas I was blind, now I see.

26 Then said they to him again, What did he to thee? how opened he thine eyes?

27 He answered them, I have told you already, and ye did not hear: wherefore would ye hear *it* again? will ye also be his disciples?

28 Then they reviled him, and said, Thou art his disciple; but we are Moses' disciples.

29 We know that God spake unto Moses: *as for* this *fellow*, we know not from whence he is.

30 The man answered and said unto them, Why, herein is a marvellous thing, that ye know not from whence he is, and *yet* he hath opened mine eyes.

31 Now we know that God heareth not sinners: but if any man be a worshipper of God, and doeth his will, him he heareth.

32 Since the world began was it not heard, that any man opened the eyes of one that was born blind.

33 If this man were not of God, he could do nothing.

34 ¶ They answered and said unto him, Thou wast altogether born in sins, and dost thou teach us? and they cast him out.

If there be a part of this interesting narrative that we may pass over, as less demanding attention, one, than another, it is this. To behold the wretched delusion of those awful characters, the *Pharisees!* Their natural enmity to CHRIST. Their implacable malice to his doctrine. Their determined resolution to oppose, and deafen if possible, the voice of this Charmer, *charm he never so wisely!* Psm. lviii. 5. But, Reader! let you, and I, learn from hence the unspeakable mercy of distinguishing grace! *Who is it that maketh us to differ from another? And what have we*, or what are we, *that we did not receive?* 1 Cor. iv. 7.

Their bitterness in excommunicating the blind man, shews to what a desperate state they were arrived. Whether this was the milder act of excommunication, called *Niddui*, which extended but to thirty days separation; or whether the more severe, called *Cherem*, which was a total separation for ever from the congregation of Israel, is not said. But, Reader! how sweetly may we apply the words of the LORD, which he used upon another occasion, to this and all the other cruelties of men. *And I say unto you my friends*, (said JESUS,) *be not afraid of them that kill the body, and after that, have no more that they can do. But I will forewarn you whom ye shall fear. Fear him, which after he hath killed, hath power to cast into hell. Yea, I say unto you, fear him.* Luke xii. 4, 5.

But, Reader, it is high time to look at this miracle in another, and a far more endearing point of view, than the mercy shewn to the body; and see, what rich and blessed lessons there are taught in it, in relation to the soul. I remarked, at the opening of the Chapter, that according to my apprehension, while I behold GOD the HOLY GHOST appointing a whole Chapter to this record of a single miracle of CHRIST, I am inclined to think, that it was intended, among other things, to minister to this great end; that by so beautiful an illustration, might be shewn, the LORD JESUS spiritually giving sight to the blind in soul, and opening the mind born in trespasses and sins, to the knowledge of himself, in grace here, and to glory hereafter.

And I cannot begin my observations on this ground, without remarking, that if it was the gracious design of GOD the SPIRIT, from this miracle of JESUS, to instruct the Church in this precious truth, nothing can be more exactly suited from every circumstance of it. Though the Church of JESUS hath from everlasting a grace-union with her glorious Head; hath a being in him, and a well-being, which nothing in her time-state can finally destroy: yet born as in every individual instance the whole Church is, in the Adam-nature of a fallen, sinful, and corrupt state; all are blind to all knowledge of GOD, or themselves. So that like this poor man in nature, such is the Church as to grace, all blind from birth.

And as it was JESUS passing by and seeing him, which first led to the mercy he obtained, so is it in grace; there are no advances made by the blind sinner to the LORD, until the LORD hath *passed by and bid him live.* Ezek. xvi. 1—14. John was taught by the HOLY GHOST, thus to teach the Church: *If we love him, it is because he first loved us.* 1 John iv. 19.

Moreover, the case is the same, with respect to the divine glory, in both instances. This man's blindness of body, gave occasion for the works of GOD to be made manifest in him; so the blindness of soul, affords opportunity for GOD in CHRIST, to be magnified in the works of grace. The clay and the pool of *Siloam*, were merely instrumental, in the hand of CHRIST: so ordinances and means of grace are but mere channels of communication, from him to his people. And without him, as the clay would rather have contributed to obstruct sight than to give it; so ordinances unaccompanied with his blessing, tend more to increase spiritual blindness than remove it. *We are* (saith Paul,) *unto GOD a sweet savor of CHRIST in them that are saved, and in them that perish.* 2 Cor. ii. 15, 16. Rev. iii. 18.

The conduct of the neighbors upon this occasion, in the surprize they expressed, at beholding one, so long known to them as blind, now suddenly blessed with sight; is not unsimilar to that wonder and astonishment the carnal world not unfrequently shew, when at any time some ungodly sinner hath his eyes spiritually opened, to the light of the divine life. The work itself is so great and altogether so divine, that GOD the HOLY GHOST hath caused it to be celebrated

in one of his songs of praise. *When the* LORD *turned again the capti-*
vity of Zion; *then were we like to them that dream. Then was our*
mouth filled with laughter, and our tongue with singing. Then said
they among the heathen, the LORD *hath done great things for them.*
The LORD *hath done great things for us: whereof we are glad.*
Psm. cxxvi.

One word more in relation to the poor man who stands forth in
this scripture, and in the LORD's Church so precious a monument of
sovereign mercy.   He was not conscious at the first, who his great
benefactor was.   Neither could he tell, how the LORD had accomplished the wonderful cure.   He only knew, that he was once blind,
and now had sight.   Such is not unfrequently the case in respect
to spiritual mercies.   How little do we know of JESUS, when first he
manifests himself to us *otherwise than he doth to the world.*   And
even after renewed love tokens of his favor, how backward we are,
in apprehension.   All the objects we at first behold in spiritual dis-
cernment, are but indistinct, like the sight to him, who *saw men as*
trees walking.   Mark viii. 22—26.   But, Reader! it is blessed to be
able to give the same sweet testimony as this man.   Though you, or I,
or any other child of GOD cannot exactly tell how or when or where,
as to time place and method, the LORD was pleased to adopt to our
effectual calling; still *the day of small things is not to be despised,*
when we can truly say as he did: *One thing I know, that whereas I*
was blind, now I see.

35 ¶ Jesus heard that they had cast him out:
and when he had found him, he said unto him,
Dost thou believe on the Son of God?

36 He answered and said, Who is he, Lord,
that I might believe on him?

37 And Jesus said unto him, Thou hast both
seen him, and it is he that talketh with thee.

38 And he said, Lord, I believe.   And he worshipped him.

39 And Jesus said, For judgment I am come
into this world: that they which see not might
see, and that they which see might be made blind.

40 And *some* of the Pharisees which were with
him, heard these words, and said unto him, Are
we blind also?

41 Jesus said unto them, If ye were blind ye
should have no sin: but now ye say, We see;
therefore your sin remaineth.

What a most beautiful and interesting view do those few verses
give the Church, of the Person, grace, and benignity of her LORD?

aud what a wonderful work doth that grace and benignity of JESUS accomplish in a short time both upon the bodies and souls of men in every instance to his redeemed, when called forth in exercise. Here is a man born blind in nature, and·equally blind in grace. And by the sovereign act of JESUS, without one act of his own, immediately recovered to the blessed sight, both in body and soul. For' evidently by his worshipping CHRIST, he gave ample testimony that this miracle also the LORD had wrought upon him! And I pray the Reader not to overlook the very distinguishing manner, and extent of the mercy, manifested by JESUS to his poor patient. The SON of GOD, as GOD, had not at this time made so full and open a revelation of his Name, in the general exercise of his ministry. Excepting to the woman of *Samaria,* John iv. 26; and his disciples in the Mount of Transfiguration, and where he charged secrecy: the LORD had not been as communicative, as to the man born blind. See Matt. xvii. 5—9. But the Pharisees had cast him out. JESUS therefore in taking him in, will make a glorious discovery who he is, and in whom he hath to trust.

Neither doth the close of the Chapter minister less comfort to the Church, in the awful account the LORD JESUS hath given, of the double purpose of his mission. To root out of his kingdom all things that offend, is as needful a display of his sovereignty, as the gathering of his people to himself. *The day of vengeance is in his heart, when the year of his redeemed is come.* Isaiah lxiii. 4. Methinks these verses, of CHRIST's judgment on the Pharisees, stand as the cloud did in the camp of Israel, to make dark the Egyptians, while it gave light to Israel. Exod. xiv. 19, 20. Reader! no doubt, the contemplation is tremendously awful. But it is not more awful than sure. CHRIST is the Rock of ages; the sure foundation, which JEHOVAH hath laid in Zion. *He that believeth shall never be ashamed, nor confounded, world without end.* But he is in the same moment, a *stone of stumbling, and a rock of offence.* And on whomsoever he shall fall, *it will grind him to powder.* Deut. xxxii. 4. Isaiah xxviii. 16. 1 Pet. i. 6, 7, 8. Matt. xxi. 44.

REFLECTIONS.

My soul! contemplate in this man, thy state by nature; blind indeed, from thy birth, and in spiritual things, as ignorant as the very brute that perisheth. And how long didst thou remain, stumbling over the dark mountains of sin, and unbelief? Nay, wouldest thou not have remained so for ever, had not JESUS passed by, and created life and light to thy spiritual apprehension? It was indeed the sabbath day when JESUS did this; for He himself became the very sabbath of thy soul. And in this sovereign act of grace, how sweetly hath he proved to thee his own eternal power and GODHEAD! Surely thou canst say, with this fellow-partaker in the rich mercy: *Since the world began was it not heard, that any man opened the eyes of one that was born blind.*

Oh! ye blind Pharisees! How long will ye have to learn a right knowledge of the Person and righteousness of JESUS? An whole eternity ye will have to mourn over the darkness of blackness for ever!

How awfully verified, in that day which unfolds all, will be the words of Jesus! *When ye have lifted up the* Son *of Man; then shall ye know that I am.* Yes! know it, to your everlasting condemnation; but not to your joy, as the Lord's people!

Reader! Doth Jesus now put the question to you, and to me, which he put to the man born blind, when he had opened his eyes; *Dost thou believe on the* Son *of* God? Hath the Lord opened our eyes? Have we seen the king in his beauty? Seen ourselves in our deformity? Can we, from the heart, and from the soul, fall down and worship him? crying out, as one of old: *Rabbi, thou art the* Son *of* God! *Thou art the King of Israel!* Oh! the blessedness of being taught by him! Surely the Lord will say to us, as he did to the Apostle, on his confession: *Blessed art thou Simon Bar-jona; for flesh and blood hath not revealed it unto thee, but my* Father *which is in heaven.*

CHAP. X.

CONTENTS.

The Lord Jesus *opens this Chapter with describing himself under the Character of the Good Shepherd; and his Church as his Sheep. He sweetly discourseth, and causeth a Division of Opinion thereby among the Jews. Many are brought to believe on Him.*

VERILY, verily, I say unto you, He that entereth not by the door into the sheepfold, but climbeth up some other way, the same is a thief and a robber.

2 But he that entereth in by the door is the shepherd of the sheep.

3 To him the porter openeth; and the sheep hear his voice: and he calleth his own sheep by name, and leadeth them out.

4 And when he putteth forth his own sheep, he he goeth before them, and the sheep follow him: for they know his voice.

5 And a stranger will they not follow, but will flee from him: for they know not the voice of strangers.

6 This parable spake Jesus unto them: but they understood not what things they were which he spake unto them.

7 Then said Jesus unto them again, Verily, verily, I say unto you, I am the door of the sheep.

8 All that ever came before me are thieves and robbers : but the sheep did not hear them.

9 I am the door : by me if any man enter in he shall be saved, and shall go in and out, and find pasture.

10 The thief cometh not but for to steal, and to kill, and to destroy : I am come that they might have life, and that they might have *it* more abundantly.

11 I am the good shepherd : the good shepherd giveth his life for the sheep.

12 But he that is an hireling : and not the shepherd, whose own the sheep are not, seeth the wolf coming, and leaveth the sheep, and fleeth, and the wolf catcheth them, and scattereth the sheep.

13 The hireling fleeth, because he is an hireling, and careth not for the sheep.

14 I am the good shepherd, and know my *sheep*, and am known of mine.

15 As the Father knoweth me, even so know I the Father : and I lay down my life for the sheep.

16 And other sheep I have which are not of this fold : them also I must bring, and they shall hear my voice and there shall be one fold, *and* one shepherd.

I beg the Reader, at his entrance on this most blessed Chapter, that he will not overlook the double mention of one of Christ's precious names, as Jesus opened his discourse. *Verily, Verily;* or *Amen, Amen.* There is somewhat more in the word itself, than is generally supposed. Some have said, let us set *our* Amen to the Lord's words, if we hope Christ will set *his* to our salvation. But though it may be, and no doubt it is, highly proper to be able to set *to our seal that* God *is true;* and the general acceptation of *Amen* is not amiss, when *from the heart man believeth unto salvation :* yet it is equally proper, the truly spiritual Reader should have a yet higher apprehension of the *Verily,* or *Amen* of Christ. If he will consult what the Lord Jesus hath himself said on this point, when sending his solemn message, unto the angel of the Church of the *Laodiceans,* (Rev. iii. 14.) he will there discover, that the Lord introduced the whole of his awful threatenings with the authority of this great Name. *These things saith the Amen, the faithful and true witness.* And his servant the Prophet, commissioned by his authority, taught the,

Church, that whenever a child of God *blessed himself in the earth,* that is stood in need of blessings, and asked for them, they should be sought for *in the* God *of truth;* or, as the words may be rendered, shall bless himself in God, Amen; meaning CHRIST. Isaiah lxv. 16. John xiv. 6. 2 Cor. i. 20. Ephes i. 3. So that in the two Verilys, or *Amen* twice uttered, by CHRIST himself, at his entrance on this Chapter, *Verily, Verily, I say unto you!* it is as if this glorious Amen, this faithful and true witness, confirmed the whole of his discourse, both with his word, and with his oath. The Apostle, speaking of God the FATHER, in his Personal office in the Covenant, saith, *that because he could swear by no greater, he sware by himself.* Heb. vi. 13. In like manner, God the SON, in his Personal office GOD-Man-Mediator, doth the same in his doubled *Verily.* In the first *Amen,* JESUS takes his glorious name; *the Amen, the faithful witness.* And in the second *Amen,* it becomes as his word and oath, confirming, and making sure all he saith. I pray the Reader not to lose sight of this, in all the *Verilys* of CHRIST, which he meets with in the whole of his divine discourses. The LORD JESUS hath been pleased to use the word nearly *fifty times,* as we read in what the three former Evangelists have recorded of his ministry. And a double *Verily,* as in this Chapter, in more than *twenty* instances as recorded by *John.* Well therefore may it merit our close attention.

But let us now enter upon the LORD's discourse in this Chapter. The general scope of which is, under the similitude of a sheepfold, to describe his Church, which his FATHER had given to him, as his flock; and himself as the Shepherd, under all the endearing characters of such an office. The Reader should recollect, that the chief treasure of the East, at the time of our LORD's appearing, and for ages before, consisted chiefly in flocks, and herds, and vines, and fig-trees, and corn, and the like; and all the riches of agriculture. And as our LORD availed himself upon every occasion, to raise subjects for discourse from the objects around, and from such things as his hearers were most familiarly acquainted with: that of a sheepfold seems to have been the one chiefly used by him, and his servants. Indeed not only JESUS takes to himself this character, but God the FATHER called him by that name: Zech. xiii. 7. And the Church herself, catching the words from the LORD, invites the LORD JESUS to hear her as the Great Shepherd of Israel, from between the Cherubim. Psm. lxxx. 1. And if the Reader wishes to have a most compleat view of the LORD JESUS under this blessed office, he will find a whole Chapter, directed by the HOLY GHOST in the ministry of the Prophet *Ezekiel,* to this one subject. Ezek. xxxiv.

It should seem, by the manner in which CHRIST hath introduced his discourse, of a robbery, in an entrance into the sheepfold, in an improper way, that the LORD had in view the Scribes, which sat in Moses's seat, and assumed the office of teaching the people, unauthorized of God. Matt. xxiii. 2. Mark xii. 38. And it is of such the LORD again speaks in the 8th verse; of *all that ever came before him were thieves and robbers:* meaning all false shepherds and hirelings, *who feed themselves but not the flock!* Ezek. xxxiv. 2, 3, 4. But Reader, do not fail to observe, what JESUS saith concerning them. *But the sheep did not hear them:* that is, were not led away by their false leadings, into unwholsome pasture. Sweet thought to the true sheep of Christ! There hath indeed, in all ages of the Church, been such false Pastors. And tremendously awful must be their final doom. But Jesus the true Shepherd, hath watched over the whole of his flock, and not suffered one of them to be lost; neither shall one of them be found wanting, in the day he maketh them up. The Prophet was commissioned to tell the Church, that *the flocks must all pass again under the hands of Him that telleth them.* Jerem. xxxiii. 13.

I must not indulge myself as I could wish, in entering into the several most interesting particulars, which the Lord Jesus hath here set before us under this beautiful similitude, of a Shepherd and his flock; as descriptive of himself and his Church. I must content myself with only calling upon the Reader to a few of the more prominent features of character by which Jesus hath set it forth. The Father is blessedly shewn by Christ in his Covenant-character, as the giver of this fold. Jesus delights upon every occasion to keep this in view to the Church. *Thine they were,* (saith Christ,) *and thou gavest them me.* John xvii. 6. And in this Chapter, when speaking of the everlasting safety of his flock; he ascribes both the gift of his sheep, and their security in him to the Father. *My* Father *which gave them me is greater than all; and none is able to pluck them out of my* Father's *hand. I and my* Father *are One.* Christ declares himself to be the Great Shepherd of his sheep, both by speaking of himself, under this character, as entering in by the door; and twice in the course of his description of the office, calling himself the *good* Shepherd. Verses 11 and 14. See also Ezek. xxxiv. 23. Isaiah xl. 11. Heb. xiii. 20. 1 Pet. v. 4. And God the Holy Ghost is in my view very blessedly represented by the Lord Jesus, as opening the door of the sheep-fold to Christ, which he doth most effectually, when that gracious Lord opens the hearts of his people to receive Jesus, as it is here said, *he calleth his own sheep by name and leadeth them out.* And let it not be thought unsuitable or unbecoming to make application of the office of a *Porter* to God the Spirit, when using similitudes. Hosea xii. 10. For if Christ calls himself, as he doth in this Chapter, *the door,* (verse 9,) there can be nothing improper in considering God the Holy Ghost, in that precious office of his, in opening to Christ as the *Porter.* Reader! pause over the review of the subject, as far as we have already gone. Behold! each of the glorious Persons of the Godhead, in their Covenant-offices, as here blessedly set forth, in reference to the Sheep-fold of Christ. Here is God the Father, giving the whole to Christ. Here is the Lord Jesus Christ, calling his Sheep his own by virtue of taking them for his own, and as the gift of the Father, before all worlds. Ephes. i. 4. And here is God the Holy Ghost, in his sweet office-work, in the same everlasting Covenant, opening to Christ for his entrance into his fold; causing the sheep to hear his voice, and to follow Jesus, that they may go in, and out, and find pasture.

Let us now observe some of the more prominent features of character, in relation to the fold. Jesus not only owns them, and calls them all by name; but hath given several strong and leading marks, by which his sheep are known and distinguished from all the goats of the world, and from every false resemblance which might appear, of goats in sheeps' cloathing.

And *first*, they are said to be the Sheep of CHRIST, given to him before the foundation of the world, when as JESUS under one of his well known office-characters of wisdom, saith, *the* LORD *possessed me in the beginning of his way before his works of old, when I was set up from everlasting.* And in the same moment that the SON of GOD in his Wisdom-character was set up, the Head and Husband of his Church, and the Great Shepherd of his Sheep; then must have been set up with him, and from him, and for him, his Church, his Spouse, his Sheep. For in none of those relations could he have stood; neither have had ability to have acted in the office, without the relative characters to have exercised such relations and offices towards. And hence in the same scripture, where the SON of GOD speaks of being thus set up from the beginning, he no less saith, *that he was rejoicing in the habitable part of his earth, and his delights were with the sons of men.* And this at a time, (or rather before time,) when as yet JEHOVAH, in his threefold character of Persons *had not made the earth, nor the fields, nor the highest part of the dust of the world.* Prov. viii. 22—31. And I beg the Reader, before he proceeds further, to consult some at least, of those many blessed scriptures, which both confirm this precious truth, of the grace-union between CHRIST and his Church, before all worlds; and also of the going forth of all the Persons of the GODHEAD in the after acts of creation. Ephes. i. 4. Coloss. i. 15—18. Ephes. iii. 9, 10, 11. Gen. i. 26.

Secondly. When those great leading truths are fully impressed upon the Reader's mind, I beg him to go on to notice, in relation to this Sheep-fold of JESUS, that it is a gathered fold, out of Nature's wild wilderness, chosen, fenced in, made separate, and distinct; from the everlasting love of GOD the FATHER, the apprehending union of GOD the SON, and the blessed grace, and anointing influence of GOD the HOLY GHOST. For it is a point of infinite consequence to be observed, when giving to the HOLY THREE in ONE, the honor due to JEHOVAH's name; that as GOD the FATHER chose the Church in CHRIST before the foundation of the world, and GOD the SON betrothed the Church to himself from everlasting: Hosea ii. 19. So GOD the HOLY GHOST, in his gracious Covenant-office, respecting CHRIST and his Church, did equally manifest his everlasting love in the divine appointment, by anointing the head and members as one, revealing and making known to the Church the Messiah as GOD's anointed, many ages before CHRIST was born. And as CHRIST was thus anointed in this office and relation character to his Church; consequently GOD the HOLY GHOST had an eye to the Church in this gracious act, and foreviewed the Church, and loved the Church in CHRIST, with an everlasting love, as the Church of CHRIST, and with proportioned love of the body, as he loved the glorious Head. The oneness and union in the divine nature of the whole GODHEAD prove this. John xvii. 23.

Thirdly. It forms a most sweet, and precious part, in the contemplation of this subject of CHRIST and his Church, the Shepherd and his Sheep; that while distinguished as the fold is, by the electing love of GOD the FATHER, the redeeming love of GOD the SON, and the regenerating love of GOD the HOLY GHOST; the whole Sheepfold is but one, however divided into distinct branches, whether *Jew or Gentile, whether bond or free.* So the LORD speaks in this very Chapter; when he saith *there shall be one fold, and one Shepherd.* And so he blessedly speaks elsewhere, when comforting his Church. *My dove, my undefiled is but one; she is the only one of her mother: she is the choice one of her that bare her.* Song vi. 9. Reader! do not lose sight of this. CHRIST's Sheepfold can be but one. CHRIST, the Husband of his Church, hath but one Bride. None can be added to his Church. None taken from it. The world's goats can never pass under his hands for sheep. No! neither goats in sheep-cloathing escape his eye. Here, in this world's wilderness, they may, and too often do, break over the fence, and mingle in the pastures of CHRIST's sheep. Indeed too often worry the LORD's sheep, and make them, as the LORD calls his oppressed ones, *the flock of slaughter.* Zech. xi. 4—7. Rom. viii. 36. But ere long, these things will for ever cease. JESUS the Great Shepherd will come and cause an everlasting separation. Matt. xxv. 31 to the end. Pause over this lovely subject. CHRIST and his fold as one. JESUS calls them by every endearing name, in a way of distinction and delight. They are a *little* flock: but yet a numerous body, *a multitude which no man can number.* Compare Luke xii. 32. with Rev. vii. 9. They are black in their own esteem, but comely in the eyes of JESUS. Song i. 5. Ezek. xvi. 14. And elsewhere, the LORD calls them a *beautiful* flock. Jerem. xiii. 20. And what can the imagination form to itself more beautiful than the Church, made up of a vast multitude, as first presented to her Husband, in his eternal mind before all worlds; then recovered out of her fallen and polluted time state, in her *Adam*-nature, in being washed from her sins in CHRIST's blood, and clothed in his righteousness; and finally presented by JESUS *to himself, not having spot, or wrinkle, or any such thing, but holy and without blemish before him for ever.* Ephes. i. 4. Psm. xlv. 9—17. Ephes. v. 25 to the end.

I must not swell our observations on those verses any further. But otherwise, what a subject opens to our view in the contemplation of JESUS in the extensive office of a Shepherd? It is indeed endless. The personal knowledge CHRIST hath of every individual of his fold. How can it be otherwise, than that he must know them, when he hath received every one of them at his FATHER's hands; their names written in the book of life; they are every one of them married to his person, united to himself, yea, part of himself: He calleth them all by name. He hath died for them, shed his blood for them, become the Surety for them, cleansed them in his blood from all their sins, hath ascended for them to glory, is gone before them to take possession of his Mediator-kingdom in their name, is everlastingly appearing in the presence of his FATHER for them, and he hath promised to come again, and take them home to himself, that where he is, there they shall be also! Reader! under such precious views and assurances, can it be possible that JESUS can overlook, forget, and be regardless of each, and every individual of his fold, when his own glory is concerned in the event of their present and everlasting welfare? Yea, the very charge of his office, as Mediator and Shepherd, will not be fulfilled until he hath brought the whole home, and *not an hoof left behind* in that great day of GOD, when they *must all pass again under the hands of him that telleth them?* Reader, do not fail, in confirmation, to turn to the perusal of some of those sweet scriptures, such as John xvii. 2. Psm. cxxxix. 16. Isaiah iv. 3. Dan. xii. 1. Luke x. 20. 1 Cor. vi.

17. 2 Cor. v. 15. Heb. vi. 20. John xiv. 3. Exod. x. 26. Jerem. xxxiii. 13. Blessed and Almighty Shepherd of thy blood-bought flock! very sure I am of thy pastoral love and care. As the Great Shepherd and Bishop of our souls, thou wilt everlastingly be in thy diocese. Thou wilt feed thy flock like a shepherd. Thou wilt cause them *to lie down in wholesome pastures.* And, as thou hast said, *thou wilt search, and seek out thy flock in the day* (this time state of our wilderness dispensations,) *in which thou art among thy sheep, to bring again that which was driven away, and bind up that which was broken, and strengthen that which was sick.* Yea, LORD JESUS, thou wilt seek me, even me, *for I have gone astray like a sheep that is lost!* But JESUS hath said, *I must bring the other sheep which are not of this fold;* thousands, and tens of thousands, which were not in the Jewish fold of the Old Testament, but of the Gentile fold, under both the Old and New Testament dispensation. JESUS *must* bring them. Why must my LORD do so? Because they are part of himself, they are the body of CHRIST, the Church the FATHER gave him, and purchased by his blood, and regenerated by the HOLY GHOST. Hence JESUS must bring them all home, and they shall be *for a crown of glory in the hand of the* LORD, *and a royal diadem in the hand of my* GOD! Isaiah lxii. 3.

17 Therefore doth my Father love me, because I lay down my life that I might take it again.

18 No man taketh it from me, but I lay it down of myself, I have power to lay it down, and I have power to take it again. This commandment have I received of my Father.

Reader! make a long pause over these blessed verses, for they are most blessed. The love JESUS here speaks of cannot possibly mean the love of GOD the FATHER to GOD the SON, as GOD; for then, in this sense, no such reason as is here assigned, would be given. Neither did GOD the SON lay down his life as GOD. And, moreover, the observation of GOD the FATHER loving GOD the SON would have been unnecessary in CHRIST to have informed the disciples. For unless the Church had faculties suitable to the apprehension, (which is impossible,) we never could have the least conception what that infinite love is, which One of the divine Persons in the GODHEAD bears to another. But the love of the FATHER to CHRIST here spoken of by JESUS, is the love he hath to him as GOD-Man-Mediator. He loved him for his voluntary undertaking to become the Head and Husband of his body the Church. He loved him for all the offices connected with it, in rescuing his Spouse, his Bride, which the FATHER gave him before all worlds, from that dreadful state of sin and ruin into which, in the time-state of her Adam-nature, she had fallen. This, I venture to believe, was the love which the LORD JESUS here spake of, and which JESUS prized so highly. And well might all the persons of the GODHEAD delight in the GOD-Man love of JESUS to his Church. For the perfect unsinning obedience of the whole creation of GOD, yea, had the whole creation of GOD, added to that obedience, been offered up as one rich and full oblation, the whole would have been nothing in comparison to the holy life, and spotless death of CHRIST upon the cross, when doing away the whole penal effect of sin by the sacrifice of himself, and magnifying the law of GOD, and making it honorable. Reader! pause a moment longer, and then say, did GOD the FATHER thus love CHRIST on our account, think then how GOD the FATHER must love us. And if JESUS was so loved by the FATHER for us, how ought CHRIST to be loved by us?

I must not suffer the Reader to pass away from those sweet verses before that he hath also noticed, and with the due attention it merits, what JESUS hath said of his own sovereign power and GODHEAD. If no man had power to take his life from him, but as he elsewhere saith: *As the* FATHER *hath life in himself, so hath he given to the* SON *to have life in himself.* John v. 26. let the Reader receive from those precious words, the LORD'S assurance of his nature and office as GOD-Man-Mediator! Oh! how infinitely great must be his nature, how full of glory and dignity his person, who thus possessed such infinite power? And how unspeakably great his love, who so loved us, as *to give himself for us an offering, and a sacrifice to* GOD *for a sweet smelling savor?*

19 ¶ There was a division therefore again among the Jews for these sayings.

20 And many of them said, He hath a devil, and is mad; why hear ye him?

21 Others said, These are not the words of him that hath a devil. Can a devil open the eyes of the blind?

22 ¶ And it was at Jerusalem, the feast of the dedication, and it was winter.

23 And Jesus walked in the temple, in Solomon's porch.

24 Then came the Jews round about him, and said unto him, How long dost thou make us to doubt? If thou be the Christ, tell us plainly.

25 Jesus answered them, I told you, and ye believed not: the works that I do in my Father's name, they bear witness of me.

26 But ye believe not, because ye are not of my sheep, as I said unto you.

I beg the Reader to ponder what is here said. The observations made by the Jews concerning the person and office of CHRIST, is very striking. More than half convinced by reason and argument they frequently were, that JESUS was the CHRIST, but never brought into a belief of it by divine teaching. And so it is in the present hour.

The carnal and the ungodly are not unfrequently alarmed in their consciences, but their apprehension of GOD's truths is only head knowledge; no heart-influence. Devils have this knowledge. So they said, Luke iv. 41. But devils they remained, and will eternally remain. Reader! oh! see to it, that your knowledge of the LORD JESUS is of the LORD. It is GOD the FATHER makes known the SON. Matt. xi. 27. GOD the HOLY GHOST makes known the SON. 1 Cor. xii. 3. And the consequence of this divine teaching produceth those blessed effects which CHRIST describes, John vi. 45. And the reverse of this JESUS teacheth in this chapter, and elsewhere. See 26, 27, verses. See also John viii. 42, 43.

27 My sheep hear my voice, and I know them, and they follow me:

28 And I give unto them eternal life; and they shall never perish, neither shall any *man* pluck them out of my hand.

29 My Father which gave *them* me, is greater than all: and no *man* is able to pluck *them* out of my Father's hand.

30 I and *my* Father are one.

In addition to what hath been offered in the former part of this chapter, on the subject of CHRIST and his Church, as a shepherd and his sheep; I would only beg the Reader to observe here, how blessedly CHRIST dwells upon those grand features of character. His sheep *hear his voice*, they *know him*, they *follow him*. They hear the voice of JESUS in his word, in his promises, in his providences. They discern the truth, because JESUS himself is *the way, the truth, and the life*. They are enabled, through the SPIRIT, to discern CHRIST's voice from strangers, from hirelings, from false teachers, and false preachers. What doth not tend to humble the sinner, and exalt the SAVIOR, is not of CHRIST. And as JESUS knows them, calleth them all by their names, that is, speaketh in his word, and by his word, to their cases, wants, and circumstances; so they *know him* and *follow him* in the regeneration. And the eventful happy consequence of the whole is, that from their oneness with CHRIST, and interest in CHRIST, their present and everlasting welfare is secured, and both the FATHER and the SON are engaged in the ultimate glory of the whole. So sure, so certain, and so unalterable, are all the purposes of GOD in CHRIST. JEHOVAH saith himself, *My counsel shall stand, and I will do all my pleasure.* Isaiah xlvi. 10.

I detain the Reader at the last verse of this paragraph, for his distinct and separate attention. For, although the LORD JESUS adduceth this oneness between the FATHER and himself, by way of confirmation to what he had said before, and which to be sure becomes the most decisive testimony in proof, that ever can be given; for if CHRIST and the FATHER are One, in nature, essence, will, power, and design, nothing of creature strength, or creature policy, can counteract JEHOVAH's purpose; but I detain the Reader at this verse by way of requesting his closest attention to it on every other account, connected with a doctrine of so highly important a nature. And I do very earnestly beg that he will regard it with all due observation. *I, and my* FATHER, (saith CHRIST,) *are One.* And this oneness runs through all the various parts by which this union can be manifested. Distinct only in person, they are one in every thing beside. *First,* in relation to the essence and nature of the GODHEAD. In Being, Attributes, Property, Dignity, Glory, and Happiness. In proof, I refer to those blessed scriptures. Deut. vi. 4. 1 John v. 7. Zech. xiii. 7. Philip. ii. 6. Rom. ix. 5. Hence, is GOD the FATHER the mighty GOD? So is the SON, Isaiah ix. 6. Is GOD the FATHER omnipresent? So is the SON, Matt. xxviii. 20. Is GOD the FATHER omniscient? So is the SON, John xxi. 17. Is GOD the FATHER unchangeable? So is the SON. Heb. xiii. 8. And the whole tenor of the divine word, is, that *all men should honor the* SON, *even as they honor the* FATHER. John v. 23. *Secondly,* This oneness in design, plan, and execution of the whole purposes relating to the Church, marks all the persons of the GODHEAD. If the sacred Three in One have graciously entered into covenant engagements with each other, this is, to bring about and accomplish one and the same design. Though, as distinct persons, they have been pleased to undertake distinct offices, yet the whole are directed to manifest their unity, in the promotion of their sovereign will, all harmonizing to the divine glory, and the Church's happiness in CHRIST. So that when CHRIST saith, as in this blessed scripture; *I, and my* FATHER, *are One,* is included every thing of oneness, the distinction of persons only excepted. And, in proof of this distinction of persons, the words themselves are abundantly satisfactory and conclusive. The word *are* is plural to the two names, *I,* and my FATHER; which could not in common sense have been used without implying this plurality of persons. Reader! pray ponder well these things. They are always blessed to be particularly regarded, but infinitely more so in a CHRIST-despising generation like the present.

31 Then the Jews took up stones again to stone him.

32 Jesus answered them, Many good works have I shewed you from my Father: for which of those works do ye stone me?

33 The Jews answered him, saying, For a good work we stone thee not: but for blasphemy; and because that thou, being a man, makest thyself God.

34 Jesus answered them, Is it not written in your law, I said, Ye are gods?

35 If he called them gods, unto whom the word of God came, and the scripture cannot be broken;

36 Say ye of him whom the Father hath sanctified, and sent into the world, Thou blasphemest: because I said, I am the Son of God?

37 If I do not the works of my Father, believe me not.

38 But if I do, though ye believe not me, believe the works: that ye may know and believe that the Father *is* in me, and I in him.

39 Therefore they sought again to take him: but he escaped out of their hand;

40 And went away again beyond Jordan, into the place where John at first baptized: and there he abode.

41 And many resorted unto him, and said, John did no miracle: but all things that John spake of this man were true.

42 And many believed on him there.

I would appeal to the common sense of mankind, whether any unprejudiced person upon earth can be found, who would say, that the Jews did not consider what CHRIST had just said as claiming an equality with GOD? And, I would demand yet further, is it not as plain as words can make it, that upon these principles, and according to their laws, they took up stones to stone him for what they supposed to be blasphemy? And I appeal to the same common sense of mankind, whether any form of words could be used by CHRIST more firm, or decided, in proof of his claims to GODHEAD, than JESUS hath here adopted. And, under these impressions, what but the most hardened blindness, could hesitate to acknowledge him, what JEHOVAH had all along acknowledged him, *the Man that is my fellow, saith the* LORD *of hosts.* Zech. xiii. 7.

REFLECTIONS.

READER! you and I here plainly discover that CHRIST is the good Shepherd. Both his office, relation, and character, under this sweet figure, he is chosen into by GOD the FATHER, and all his sheep given by the FATHER to him as his own. They were his, in this appointment, from everlasting. And now in the time-state of a wilderness, where the LORD finds them wandering, he comes to seek and save that which was lost. Have you and I known CHRIST under this endeared character? Have we the features JESUS hath here described, by which we alone prove, that we are the sheep of his pasture. Nothing can be more plain than what JESUS hath here marked to discover his sheep from the world's goats. He saith, the sheep hear his voice, they know his call, they follow him. A stranger they will not follow, but will flee from him, for they know not the voice of strangers. Have we these undeniable tokens? Oh! for grace to be so distinguished! Blessed it is to lie down in his fold, to feed in his pastures, and to go in and out by those wholesome waters of comfort, beside which, *the Great Shepherd of Israel feeds his flock!* Reader! Jesus will do by all his fold as the Holy Ghost hath said. He will feed, protect, heal, strengthen, guide, and, in short, do all that pertains to the office of a shepherd; he will carry the lambs in his arms, and gently lead those that are with young. And, to crown all, he will most effectually preserve from all evil, and give them eternal life, so that *none shall perish, or any pluck them out of his and his* Father's *hands.* Hail! Almighty Shepherd of thy flock.

Reader! behold the triumphs of thy Lord over all the enemies of his Godhead, and against all the awful opposition made to his divine person and character. So was it then, so is it now, and so shall it be, until the Lord hath brought the whole under his footstool. Lord Jesus! establish thy people in their most holy faith, until that thou shalt bring them home unto *the fountains of living water, where, as a Lamb in the midst of the throne, thou art feeding them, and where thou hast wiped all tears from off all faces, and the rebuke of thy people thou hast taken away from off all the earth!*

CHAP. XI.

CONTENTS.

Jesus *raiseth Lazarus from the Dead. The Priests and Pharisees become more desperately enraged at* Jesus. *They gather a Council to deliberate on his Death.*

NOW a certain *man* was sick, *named* Lazarus, of Bethany, the town of Mary and her sister Martha.

2 (It was *that* Mary which anointed the Lord with ointment, and wiped his feet with her hair, whose brother Lazarus was sick.)

3 Therefore his sisters sent unto him, saying, Lord, Behold, he whom thou lovest is sick.

4 When Jesus heard *that*, he said, This sickness is not unto death, but for the glory of God, that the Son of God might be glorified thereby.

5 Now Jesus loved Martha, and her sister, and Lazarus.

6 When he had heard therefore that he was sick, he abode two days still in the same place where he was.

7 Then after that saith he to his disciples, Let us go into Judea again.

8 *His* disciples say unto him, Master, the Jews of late sought to stone thee; and goest thou thither again?

9 Jesus answered, Are there not twelve hours in the day? If any man walk in the day, he stumbleth not, because he seeth the light of this world.

10 But if a man walk in the night, he stumbleth, because there is no light in him.

11 These things said he: and after that he saith unto them, Our friend Lazarus sleepeth; but I go, that I may awake him out of sleep.

12 Then said his disciples, Lord, if he sleep, he shall do well.

13 Howbeit Jesus spake of his death: but they thought that he had spoken of taking of rest in sleep.

14 Then said Jesus unto them plainly, Lazarus is dead.

15 And I am glad for your sakes that I was not there, to the intent ye may believe; nevertheless let us go unto him.

16 Then said Thomas, which is called Didymus, unto his fellow disciples, Let us also go, that we may die with him.

Every incident in this wonderful relation ought to be regarded with peculiar notice, for the Evangelist hath been very particular in record ing it. And very sure it is, that GOD the HOLY GHOST meant it for a subject of great blessedness to the Church.

And here let us admire the emphasis with which it is said, LORD, *behold, he whom thou lovest is sick!* Reader! do not fail to remark, that JESUS hath those whom he loveth. And many such there are concerning whom the LORD might be told, and, I hope, is told, by faithful souls on occasion of the sickness and afflictions of themselves and brethren in CHRIST; LORD! such and such an one, whom thou lovest, is sick. And may we not very frequently hear CHRIST's answer by the ear of faith: *As many as I love, I rebuke and chasten.* Rev. iii. 19. Heb. xii. 5—11.

The abode of our LORD two days after he had received tidings of the sickness of *Lazarus*, appears to have been blessedly designed for the greater manifestation of the miracle he intended. And JESUS speaking first of his sleep, then of his death, and of his going to raise him out of this sleep of death, all these are so many heightenings, in preparing the minds of his disciples for the miracle, as should be particularly noticed by us. His knowledge of his death, and his declaration that he would raise him again, are all so many collateral proofs of his GODHEAD. The affection of *Thomas*, in accompanying CHRIST to *Bethany*, and his invitation to his fellow disciples to the same, are sweet tokens of attachment to the person of CHRIST, although in a more memorable hour *they all forsook him and fled.* Mark xiv. 50.

17 Then when Jesus came, he found that he had lain in the grave four days already.

18 Now Bethany was nigh unto Jerusalem, about fifteen furlongs off.

19 And many of the Jews came to Martha and Mary, to comfort them concerning their brother.

20 Then Martha, as soon as she heard that Jesus was coming, went and met him: but Mary sat *still* in the house.

21 Then said Martha unto Jesus, Lord, if thou hadst been here, my brother had not died.

22 But I know, that even now, whatsoever thou wilt ask of God, God will give *it* thee.

23 Jesus saith unto her, Thy brother shall rise again.

24 Martha saith unto him, I know that he shall rise again in the resurrection at the last day.

25 Jesus said unto her, I am the resurrection, and the life: he that believeth in me, though he were dead, yet shall he live:

26 And whosoever liveth and believeth in me shall never die. Believest thou this?

27 She saith unto him, Yea, Lord: I believe that thou art the Christ, the Son of God, which should come into the world.

As *Bethany* was somewhat less than two miles from *Jerusalem*, it is somewhat wonderful that no tidings had reached the city of the death of *Lazarus*. But we see how this was overruled for the greater display of the foreknowledge of JESUS, and for the greater manifestation of his power in the miracle which afterwards followed, in CHRIST's raising him from the dead.

I pass by very many incidents which the Evangelist hath related, all of which are full of sweet instruction, but cannot be brought for remarks upon within the compass of a *Poor Man's Commentary*, in order to attend to such as are more immediately demanding our regard. But the conversation the LORD held with *Martha* is too big with importance to be hastily passed over, and I beg the Reader's indulgence in attending to a short view of it.

The faith which this woman had in CHRIST, seems to have been a general belief only that JESUS was the *Messiah*; and therefore from the miracle he had wrought, she had no question but that he could have prevented the death of her brother. But, in relation to any other views, in which CHRIST would manifest that character, *Martha* at this time had but little consciousness. However, it is our mercy, that her dulness gave occasion to the LORD to deliver himself in the manner he did, on the great subject of the resurrection; that, by putting it on its own proper basis, the Church, under the HOLY GHOST's teaching, might have blessed scriptural proofs of the same. And by the miracle which followed CHRIST's discourse with *Martha*, in the LORD's giving such a palpable demonstration of its reality in the resurrection of *Lazarus*, there might be a foundation for faith to rest upon in the cordial belief of it.

And now let the Reader attend to the sublime words of the LORD JESUS CHRIST, which, as CHRIST, he uttered. And may GOD the HOLY GHOST, the Glorifier of JESUS, give them a deep impression, both upon the Reader's heart and mine. JESUS said, *I am the resurrection and the life. He that believeth in me, though he were dead, yet shall he live. And whosoever liveth and believeth in me shall never die.* What words are these? What a palpable proof they carry with them of the Almightiness of the Speaker? Who, but the living and true GOD in CHRIST, could ever use such language? Who but He, who is *one with the* FATHER, *over all* GOD, *blessed for ever*, could prove the truth of it?

And what I beg the Reader more especially also to mark with me, in those unequalled words of CHRIST, is, that JESUS spake them in his glorious character of Mediator. Not as GOD *only*, for in that case, though it would be without doubt no less than the sovereign act of Him that alone can give life, to re-animate, by renewing life, yet JESUS, though raising the dead, could not in this case be said to be *himself the Resurrection*. Neither as man *only*, would the act, which is truly divine, have been possible. But, in the union of both, as GOD-Man-Mediator, JESUS himself, personally, and peculiarly, becomes the resurrection and the life, for it could belong to no other. Hence the LORD JESUS had before said to the Jews, *Destroy this temple*, (meaning his body,) *and I* (meaning his divine nature,) *will raise it up*. John ii. 19. See the Commentary on that passage, from John ii. 18—22. And thus CHRIST becomes the Resurrection and the Life to his redeemed, both in the *spiritual* resurrection of grace, from the death of the soul by sin, in the Adam-nature of a fallen state; and at the last day, from the *natural* resurrection of the body, become dead through sin, and sleeping in JESUS unto the consummation of all things. In both, CHRIST is the resurrection and the life, being the life-giving source in himself to all his members both in body and soul, communicating life, both spiritual and eternal, from Himself to them, for grace here, and glory hereafter.

As this view of the subject is on every account very highly interesting, I would request the Reader's attention to it yet somewhat more particularly.

That CHRIST is *the Resurrection and the Life*, spiritually considered, in relation to the first awakening from the death of sin to a life of righteousness, I can hardly suppose the Reader to be altogether unconscious. Every one that reads his Bible, must have been led to see, that in the Adam-nature in which the Church, as well as all the world is born, all are, in consequence, *dead in trespasses and sins.* And hence the word of GOD, when speaking of the Church's recovery from this spiritual death, speaks of it as a resurrection from the death of sin to a life of righteousness. *And you* (saith the Apostle,) *hath he quickened, who were dead in trespasses and sins, wherein in time past ye walked, according to the course of this world, according to the prince of the power of the air, the spirit that now worketh in the children of disobedience: among whom we all had our conversation in times past, in the lusts of our flesh, fulfilling the desires of the flesh and of the mind; and were by nature children of wrath, even as others.* Ephes. ii. 2, 3. But that this spiritual life imparted to the Church, is the result of a grace-union with CHRIST, by virtue of a being in him, and with him, before all worlds; this is not so generally considered. And very certain it is, that *Martha*, the sister of *Lazarus*, with whom CHRIST was then conversing, had not at that time the smallest apprehension of it. But it is a great point for the Church of GOD to regard. For it is in consequence of this oneness between CHRIST and his people, before all worlds, that this recovery from the *Adam-fall* is accomplished in all his members. JESUS is to them, spiritually considered, the resurrection and the life. He is their head, and they are his body. Hence, he himself is the life-giving source of their renewed life in him, and from him, by which they are united to himself, and *because he lives, they live also.* It is by virtue of this membership in CHRIST, that they are awakened, regenerated, born again, arise from the death of sin to a life of righteousness, and are *translated from the kingdom of darkness into the kingdom of* GOD'S *dear* SON. Of such the LORD JESUS saith, with peculiar emphasis of expression, *I am the resurrection and the life.*

But we must not stop here. JESUS adds, *He that believeth in me, though he were dead, yet shall he live: and whosoever liveth and believeth in me, shall never die.* Redeemed souls in CHRIST are subject to temporal death, as well as the graceless. They are appointed to taste the *fruit* of Adam's sin, though, from their union with CHRIST, they are delivered from the *curse* of it. And, in respect to those that live and believe in CHRIST, they who are so found when CHRIST shall come *the second time, without sin unto salvation,* Heb. ix. 28. shall not die even in body, but *be caught up together in the clouds, to meet the* LORD *in the air.* 1 Thess. iv. 17. And those who die in body before, die *only* in body. Their spirits live with CHRIST to the great day. Luke xxiii. 43. Heb. xii. 23.

⸳ But, added to all these considerations, we must consider, according to scripture authority, the LORD JESUS as *the resurrection and the life,* to all the members of his mystical body, in a different point of view from that of the ungodly world, in the manner in which the bodies of his saints, which sleep in Jesus, will arise at the last day, from this communicating principle, as their resurrection and life. I beg the Reader for a few moments attention also under this particular.

It is a solemn scripture, but most sure and certain. *The hour is coming, in the which all that are in their graves shall hear the voice of the* Son *of* God, *and shall come forth. They that have done good unto the resurrection of life; and they that have done evil unto the resurrection of damnation.* John v. 28, 29. But here lies the essential difference in these characters. As the object and end for which they arise is totally different, so also will be the means and course of their resurrection. The sovereign voice of Almighty Jesus will rouse up dead sinners to the sentence of eternal judgment. At his command both earth and the sea shall give up their dead. But not so the dead in Christ will arise. They died *in* Jesus when they died. They were united *to* the Lord in death. And so shall they be in their resurrection. For so saith the scripture. *If the* Spirit *of Him that raised up* Jesus *from the dead dwell in you, He that raised up* Christ *from the dead shall also quicken your mortal bodies by his* Spirit *which dwelleth in you.* Rom. viii. 11. By virtue of their union with Him they arise. And hence, in this instance, as in the former, Christ is to them *the Resurrection and the Life.* I hope the Reader will at least enter into an apprehension of this subject; and if so, and the Lord be his teacher, he will have to enjoy numberless very sweet views of the Lord Jesus in this most blessed character, as he stands related to his people, *the Resurrection and the Life.*

28 And when she had so said, she went her way, and called Mary her sister secretly, saying, the Master is come, and calleth for thee.

29 As soon as she heard *that,* she arose quickly, and came unto him.

30 Now Jesus was not yet come into the town, but was in that place where Martha met him.

31 The Jews then which were with her in the house, and comforted her, when they saw Mary that she rose up hastily and went out, followed her, saying, She goeth unto the grave to weep there.

32 Then when Mary was come where Jesus was, and saw him, she fell down at his feet, saying unto him, Lord, if thou hadst been here, my brother had not died.

33 When Jesus therefore saw her weeping, and the Jews also weeping which came with her, he groaned in the spirit, and was troubled.

34 And said, Where have ye laid him? They said unto him, Lord, come and see.

35 Jesus wept.

36 Then said the Jews, Behold how he loved him!

37 And some of them said, Could not this man which opened the eyes of the blind, have caused that even this man should not have died?

Here are many interesting things said in these verses, which, had we room to enlarge upon, would afford ample subject for meditation. The call of *Mary;* the company of the Jews; their observations; and the affecting interview of CHRIST with the sisters, when *Mary* fell at his feet, with the reiterating what *Martha* had said before; these are all capable of calling forth much matter for improvement. But I pass the whole by, in order to direct the Reader to have his mind solely engaged in contemplating CHRIST. Every incident in this memorable event becomes tenfold interesting from its relation to JESUS. And it were to lose sight of the great object for which the HOLY GHOST caused it to be recorded, to be looking to any other.

The tears of JESUS open an endless subject for contemplation. I dare not, for sure I am I cannot, explain the wonderful circumstance in a thousandth part of it. Nevertheless, in a matter which interests the Church of GOD so highly, I must not be wholly silent. JESUS *wept.* Yes! Reader! it is our mercy that the LORD JESUS perfectly knew, and as truly felt the whole of what human nature is in all its parts, *yet without sin.* Had it been otherwise, he would have been man in appearance, and not in reality. Whereas, the HOLY GHOST expressly saith, that *in all things it behoved him to be made like unto his brethren; that he might be a merciful and faithful High Priest, in things pertaining to* GOD, *to make reconciliation for the sins of the people. For in that he himself hath suffered, being tempted, he is able to succor them that are tempted.* Heb. ii. 17, 18.

Let us only attend for a few moments to the necessity of the measure, according to what the HOLY GHOST here saith. *It behoved him to be so.* The original marriage and union between CHRIST and his Church made it so. For had the SON of GOD taken upon him the nature of angels, what union would our nature have had with him? But it is expressly said, that *he took not on him the nature of angels, but he took on him the seed of Abraham.* Heb. ii. 16. It was essentially necessary also, that the SON of GOD should become man, not only to marry, and to take into union with himself his spouse the Church as one nature, but also for the purpose of redeeming that nature from the Adam-transgression into which that nature fell. The right of redemption was by the law belonging to the next of kin. Levit. xxv. 25. It could be redeemed by no other. Hence it behoved the SON of GOD, under both these grand and indispensible obligations, to take upon him our nature, and to be united to it. And this union was to be *in all points.* He was to be very and truly man, as he was very and truly GOD. All the sinless infirmities of our nature to know, and feel, in order that he might not only know them as God, but feel them as man. And it was by this very process alone, that he became fitted for our High Priest and Mediator. Most blessedly God the Holy Ghost bears testimony to this, when by his servant the Apostle, he saith, *For every High Priest taken from among men, is ordained for men in things pertaining to* God, *that he may offer both gifts and sacrifices for sins; who can have compassion on the ignorant, and on them that are out of the way, for that he himself also is compassed with infirmity.* Heb. v. 1, 2.

Reader! pause over this blessed view of Jesus, for it is indeed most blessed. Thy God, thy Husband, thy Jesus, felt in his human nature, yet without sin, all that thou feels. He wept, groaned in spirit, knew sorrow, temptation, soul-agonies, hunger, thirst, weariness, affliction, persecution, and the long train of human evils which frail flesh is subject to, in this time-state of the Church. Before that holy portion of our nature which he took into union with the Godhead, should put on that glory which is the ultimate design for which he took it, it behoved him to be cloathed with all the sinless infirmities with which his Church is cloathed. And, oh! the unspeakable blessedness of thus viewing Christ, thus knowing him, and going to him, under all our exercises! When upon earth, behold how he entered into the feelings of his people; and how their sorrows called forth the groans of his heart! And now in heaven, the sweetest of all thoughts is, that his nature is not changed, but his feeling is the same. All the affections of tenderness in Jesus, in his human nature, however highly glorified that nature is, are as truly so now as when below. He that wept upon earth at the sorrows of his redeemed, hath the everlasting continuance of the same tender feelings for them now he is in heaven. Reader! let you and I never lose sight of it, but always seek for grace to keep in remembrance those sweet views of Jesus, as often as we read, Jesus wept!

38 Jesus therefore again groaning in himself, cometh to the grave. It was a cave, and a stone lay upon it.

39 Jesus said, Take ye away the stone. Martha, the sister of him that was dead, saith unto him, Lord, by this time he stinketh: for he hath been *dead* four days.

40 Jesus saith unto her, Said I not unto thee, that, if thou wouldest believe, thou shouldest see the glory of God?

41 Then they took away the stone *from the place* where the dead was laid, and Jesus lifted up *his* eyes, and said, Father, I thank thee that thou hast heard me.

42 And I knew that thou hearest me always:

but because of the people which stand by I said *it,* that they may believe that thou hast sent me.

43 And when he had thus spoken, he cried with a loud voice, Lazarus, come forth.

44 And he that was dead came forth, bound hand and foot with grave clothes : and his face was bound about with a napkin. Jesus saith unto them, Loose him, and let him go.

Reader! let you and I, by faith, take our stand also at the mouth of the cave. Never, surely, excepting in the instance of the triumphs of Jesus himself over death, at his own resurrection, was there such a marvellous work ever wrought upon earth! Oh! what an unanswerable testimony did it carry with it of Christ's power! And, oh! what a precious pledge it afforded of the great purpose of Christ's mission, in thus bringing life and immortality to light by his sovereignty and grace. And I beg the Reader to have a special regard to what Jesus said, when addressing his Father. Not to seek aid, for the Lord thanks his Father for having, in what was past, heard him. And every little in this miracle proved it to be solely his own. But it was wrought as God-Man; as *the Resurrection and the Life.* And it became a full confirmation of what the Lord Jesus had before said, that *as the* Father *had life in himself, so had he given to the* Son *to have life in himself; and had given him authority to execute judgment also, because he is the* Son *of Man.* John v. 26, 27. See the Commentary on those verses.

45 Then many of the Jews which came to Mary, and had seen the things which Jesus did, believed on him.

46 But some of them went their ways to the Pharisees, and told them what things Jesus had done.

Reader! be not in the least astonished at the different effects the sight of *Lazarus* coming forth from the grave wrought on the lookers-on. It must have been so then. It is so now. It will be at the great day of the universal resurrection of all men. The *many* which are here said to have believed, are like those in all ages of the Church which belong to Christ, concerning whom the Lord said, *My sheep hear my voice, and I know them, and they follow me.* John x. 27. The *some* which went their way to the *Pharisees,* to seek accusation against Jesus, are the representatives of all those in every age of the Church, which belong not to Jesus, but of whom he saith, *Ye believe not, because ye are not of my sheep, as I said unto you!* John x. 26. And what will it be at the last day but the same? When the Infidel of every description and character shall see with open eye, and be then awfully convinced; it will be a conviction not to believe and be saved, but the forced conviction of believing and be lost.   For so the Lord' speaks, John xvii. 21—23.   Rev. i. 7.

47 ¶ Then gathered the chief priests and the Pharisees a council, and said, What do we? for this man doeth many miracles.

48 If we let him thus alone, all *men* will believe on him: and the Romans shall come and take away both our place and nation.

49 And one of them, *named* Caiaphas, being the high priest that same year, said unto them, Ye know nothing at all,

50 Nor consider, that it is expedient for us, that one man should die for the people, and that the whole nation perish not.

51 And this spake he not of himself: but being high priest that year, he prophesied that Jesus should die for that nation:

52 And not for that nation only, but that also he should gather together in one, the children of God that were scattered abroad.

53 Then from that day forth they took counsel together for to put him to death.

54 Jesus therefore walked no more openly among the Jews; but went thence unto a country near to the wilderness, into a city called Ephraim, and there continued with his disciples.

55 And the Jews' passover was nigh at hand: and many went out of the country up to Jerusalem before the passover, to purify themselves.

56 Then sought they for Jesus, and spake among themselves as they stood in the temple, What think ye, that he will not come to the feast?

57 Now both the chief priests and the Pharisees had given a commandment, that if any man knew where he were, he should shew *it*, that they might take him.

Every thing here is very interesting, but I have already exceeded my limits, and therefore shall only detain the Reader with requesting his attention to what the Evangelist hath recorded, of the memorable prophecy of *Caiaphas.*

It is worthy thè closest attention of the Reader, that the dying Patriarch *Jacob* should have left so memorable a prophecy, concerning the gathering of the people to *Shiloh.* Gen. xlix. 10. And that here again, as if to remind the Church of GOD of it, after so many ages had run out, GOD the HOLY GHOST, who taught the faithful *Jacob* to utter such a prophecy; should have put the fellow of it in the mouth of this infidel *Caiaphas* to the same amount. But what cannot the LORD accomplish? By friend, or foe, the LORD will bring about his holy will, as best suits his sovereign purpose. *Even the Wrath of man shall praise him.* Psm. lxxvi. 10. Reader! do not overlook the sweet feature in both prophecies. *To Him* (the *Shiloh,* said *Jacob,) shall the gathering of the people be!* *H*e shall gather together in one, (the Evangelist explains was the burden of *Caiaphas'* prophecy) *the children of* GOD *that were scattered abroad.* Yes! this is the first, and ultimate design of the whole Covenant of grace. CHRIST hath a people, his children; yea, the children of GOD, for GOD hath from all eternity given them to him. In this time-state, they were lost, were scattered abroad. *My Sheep* (saith the LORD by the spirit of prophecy,) *wandered through all the mountains, and upon every high hill; yea my flock was scattered upon all the face of the earth, and none did search or seek after them:* Ezek. xxxiv. 6. But to Him, they must all be gathered. *Not an hoof shall be left behind.* Exod. x. 26. *In that day that the great trumpet shall be blown, they shall come which were ready to perish.* Isaiah xxvii. 13. John vi. 37.

But what a wonderful subject, that GOD the HOLY GHOST should make use of such a monster of iniquity, to utter so blessed a prophecy. True indeed the man meant what he said, in a very different sense. Yes! But there is the blessedness of the LORD's working by contrary means; and rendering that, which he meant for evil, to be productive of the greatest good. And Scripture abounds with unconscious instances to the same amount. The sons of *Jacob* selling *Joseph,* Gen. xlv. 7, 8. *Haman,* for the destruction of *Mordecai.* Esther vii. 10. And infinitely more, and above all, the *Jews* crucifying the LORD of life and glory! Acts ii. 23.

REFLECTIONS.

WHAT a blessed thing it is, when at any time, upon the sickness of our friends or ourselves, we are enabled to tell JESUS, as those sorrowful sisters did: LORD! *behold he whom thou lovest is sick!* Oh! the privilege of knowing the LORD, and knowing that we are beloved by him! Reader! do you know the sweetness of thus daily, yea, sometimes hourly, going to the court of this gracious heavenly King, and receiving a look, a love-token, from JESUS himself, amidst the crouds which attend his Levee? And my soul observe: Reader do you also observe, how graciously the LORD proposed to visit the sorrowful family of *Lazarus,* under their bereaving providence. And although *two days* elapsed before he went, yet this delay was all in greater mercy, as the sequel of the history proved. Learn then from hence, how to interpret silence in the LORD. It is for the greater glory of the LORD, and the greater good of his people.

Reader! look, and look again, to the LORD, as he approached the grave of him whom he loved. Oh! that I had the power of persuasion, methinks I would call all whom JESUS loves, and who love JESUS, to take their stand there, and by faith, and behold the SON of GOD in our nature, shedding tears and groaning in spirit, over the sad consequence of sin, in our death. And didst thou, dearest LORD, mingle thy tears with ours, at such a sight. Didst thou indeed give such a proof, that *because the children were partakers of flesh and blood, thou thyself hast taken part of the same?* Oh! for grace to have it always in remembrance. JESUS *wept.* JESUS knows, and hath felt, what human sorrows are. Never, never my soul be thou afraid to go to him, in all thy afflictions. He that wept at the grave of *Lazarus,* and took part in the weepings of the sorrowful sisters, will take part in thine. *He knoweth thy frame, and remembereth that thou art dust.*

Hail! thou that *livest and wast dead; and behold thou art alive for evermore.* Still by the ear of faith, I hear thy soul-reviving, body-quickening words: *I am the resurrection and the life!* LORD JESUS! give me that sweet earnest and pledge of the first resurrection in grace, here below; and sure I am that in thee, and from thee, I shall have part in the resurrection to glory hereafter. And dearest LORD! while my soul rejoiceth in hope of the glory of GOD; in the awful character of this High Priest *Caiaphas,* and in all the awful characters beside in every generation, which like those who went their way to the *Pharisees,* unconvinced at the resurrection of *Lazarus*; most fully deciding that grace alone makes all the difference; teach me to whom to look, and to whom to ascribe the source of all my mercies. *Though one arose from the dead,* such will not believe. And wherein LORD do I differ from them, but what grace hath made? Oh! prepare me, by living wholly *upon* thee, deriving all *from* thee, and ascribing all *to* thee; for the great and awful day of my GOD, when the dead shall hear thy voice, and come forth; *some to everlasting life, and some to everlasting shame and contempt.* In that all-decisive hour, be thou to me *the resurrection and the life, and my portion for ever.*

CHAP. XII.

CONTENTS.

The LORD JESUS *is at a Supper.* Mary *anointeth his Feet. He entereth Jerusalem, as foretold by the Prophet. He maketh a very blessed Discourse; and is answered by a Voice from Heaven.*

THEN Jesus, six days before the passover, came to Bethany, where Lazarus was which had been dead, whom he raised from the dead.

2 There they made him a supper; and Martha served: but Lazarus was one of them that sat at the table with him.

3 Then took Mary a pound of ointment of spike-

nard, very costly, and anointed the feet of Jesus, and wiped his feet with her hair : and the house was filled with the odour of the ointment.

4 Then saith one of his disciples, Judas Iscariot, Simon's son, which should betray him,

5 Why was not this ointment sold for three hundred pence, and given to the poor?

6 This he said, not that he cared for the poor; but because he was a thief, and had the bag, and bare what was put therein.

7 Then said Jesus, Let her alone: against the day of my burying hath she kept this.

8 For the poor always ye have with you; but me ye have not always.

9 Much people of the Jews therefore knew that he was there: and they came not for Jesus' sake only, but that they might see Lazarus also, whom he had raised from the dead.

10 But the chief priests consulted that they might put Lazarus also to death;

11 Because that by reason of him many of the Jews went away, and believed on Jesus.

The Passover here mentioned, was the *fourth* during our LORD's ministry. JESUS was looking forward to it with peculiar satisfaction; and he very earnestly wished to eat it with his disciples before his death. Luke xxii. 15. With the celebration of this Passover, the ordinance of it was to cease for ever. CHRIST, the substance, being come, to which it all along ministered; the shadow died away. Heb. ix: 26. 1 Cor. v. 7, 8. Coloss. ii. 17.

I hope the Reader will pause with me to remark, with what earnestness those lovers of JESUS sought after his company. Here were two Suppers made for CHRIST, in one week; and both in *Bethany*. This, here spoken of, at the house of *Lazarus* and his sisters; which was *six* days before the Passover. And that, at the house of *Simon* the Leper, which was but two days preceding it. Compare Matt. xxvi. 2—6, with what is here said. The Reader, if he be a lover of JESUS, will not be surprized, that the company of the LORD should be so sought after. See how the Church longed for it! Song i. 7. 13. See how the faithful individual in the Church desired it. Psm. ci. 2. See how JESUS hath all along promised it to his people. Rev. iii. 20. Song v. 2.

There is somewhat beautifully interesting, in the account given of *Mary*, anointing the feet of CHRIST. I feel a certain undescribable pleasure, while I read it. What a wonderful condescension in CHRIST,, when it be considered who CHRIST is! What a privilege to the woman, when considered who she was! There are in it, many things which interest our feelings, as we read the relation. And very sure I am, had it not been in itself important, never would it have been recorded, and handed down as it is, through all ages by the HOLY GHOST, for the mediation of the Church of GOD. JESUS himself took notice of that instance of it, which took place in the house of *Simon* the leper; and declared that it should be as memorable as his Gospel. See Matt. xxvi. 7—13. And the LORD appears to have taken equal pleasure, in the instance of the poor woman, which anointed his feet in the house of *Simon* the *Pharisee.* See Luke vii. 37.

It may not be amiss to remark, that though some, through mistake, have confounded those acts of the *Maries,* as if they were one and the same; yet very certain it is, that they were different persons, and the acts themselves were at different times, and places, and upon different occasions. *Mary* the sister of *Lazarus,* as this scripture relates, anointed CHRIST's feet. The other woman, (if her name was *Mary,* for it is not said,) which anointed CHRIST, in the house of *Simon* the *leper,* poured the costly ointment on his *head.* And both these again, differed from the instance recorded Luke vii. 37. For that was in the house of *Simon* the *Pharisee.* And both the former were in *Bethany:* this latter in *Galilee.* Perhaps the mistake arose from the name of *Simon.* For JESUS was anointed twice in the house of *Simon.* But then it was not the same house, nor the same person. The one was *Simon the Pharisee,* and the other *Simon the Leper.* So that it is most clear and evident there were *three* of those anointings of the LORD JESUS, while upon earth.

But while I thought it right to put this matter in a clear light; I think it yet more to our purpose, to consider, as far as we have ability to do so, under divine teaching, what may be supposed as veiled under it. JESUS hath informed the Church, in relation to one of those acts, that it was an anointing for his burial. Matt. xxvi. 12, 13. Probably, *Mary* herself had no consciousness of this, when she found her mind prompted to the deed. And how often are the LORD's people under such influences, in administering to the mystical body of CHRIST; and they themselves not in the least apprehensive of it? One thing is certain. JESUS hath noticed such love tokens in his people. And blessedly the Church speaks of her enjoyments, when in those hallowed seasons, she found her soul going forth in the exercises of faith and love, upon the Person of CHRIST; and when her Spikenard sent forth the smell of those graces the LORD had given her, while *the king himself sat at the table!* Song iii. 12. There is much in the expression; the house filled with the odour of the ointment. CHRIST's house, the Church, both in heaven and on earth, is filled with the odour of his Person. Song i. 3.

12 ¶ On the next day, much people that were come to the feast, when they heard that Jesus was coming to Jerusalem,

13 Took branches of palm-trees, and went forth

to meet him, and cried, Hosanna: Blessed *is* the King of Israel, that cometh in the name of the Lord!

14 And Jesus, when he had found a young ass, sat thereon; as it is written,

15 Fear not, daughter of Sion: behold, thy King cometh sitting on an ass's colt.

16 These things understood not his disciples at the first: but when Jesus was glorified, then remembered they that these things were written of him, and *that* they had done these things unto him.

17 The people therefore that was with him when he called Lazarus out of his grave, and raised him from the dead, bare record.

18 For this cause the people also met him, for that they heard that he had done this miracle.

In addition to what was offered by way of observation, on the similar passage to this, on our LORD's entrance into Jerusalem, Matt. xxi, to which I refer: I would beg to remark, (and to remark it with suitable emphasis) that the *Hosannas*, which were offered to JESUS, could be offered to him in no other light, but as the CHRIST of GOD. The words were applicable to none but CHRIST. For the Psalmist, under the spirit of prophecy, a thousand years before, so expressed himself. Psm. viii. with Heb. ii. 6—9. Psm. cxviii. 25, 26. with Acts iv. 11, 12. And the recollection, which the disciples are said to have had of those things in the after day of the Church, when their understanding had been opened by the coming of the HOLY GHOST; very decidedly proves, that the sole application of those words, and the scriptures referring to them, could be to no other than the LORD JESUS. Reader! I entreat you to be very cheery of those things; their testimony is precious! John vii. 39. John xiv. 26. Acts i. 8.

19 The Pharisees therefore said among themselves, Perceive ye how ye prevail nothing? behold, the world is gone after him.

20 ¶ And there were certain Greeks among them that came up to worship at the feast:

21 The same came therefore to Philip, which was of Bethsaida of Galilee, and desired him, saying, Sir, we would see Jesus.

22 Philip cometh and telleth Andrew : and again Andrew and Philip tell Jesus.

The Reader, if his views are at all in correspondence with mine, will not be offended that I so often call him, to remark the awful character of those *Pharisees*. It is not surely without design, that GOD the HOLY GHOST hath interspersed so much of their history, worthless as it is, with that of CHRIST, which is so infinitely endearing; but with an eye to the Church's improvement. The LORD knew, that such characters from generation to generation would arise, like weeds, in the garden of the Church; and scatter their baleful seed in every direction. The LORD therefore hath marked their prominent appearances, that they may be everlastingly distinguished from plants of the LORD's right hand planting, and separated from what is pure. *Ye shall know them by their fruits.* They profess great sanctity of character, great zeal for promoting their own tenets, they long to proselyte the world; they abound, or would have the world suppose they abound, in good deeds, alms-giving, and unbounded charity. But in the same moment, they burn with the bitterest rancour of heart against that faith in CHRIST, as their forefathers, the *Pharisees* in CHRIST's days, did before them; which hangs the whole of salvation upon the Person, Blood, and Righteousness of the LORD JESUS CHRIST only. They desire it may be considered, that they profess CHRIST, and hope to be saved by CHRIST: but they consider their good works, as partly recommendations. To rob them of these, would be like *Micah's* gods taken from him, having nothing left. Judges xviii. 24. They have never known, neither felt, the plague of their own hearts; and therefore are more in enmity against the faith once delivered to the saints, than the openly profane. May the LORD the SPIRIT, who hath so graciously watched over his Church, in holding forth so frequently the awful history of such men, keep his people from being tainted with their doctrine. Luke xii. 1.

23 And Jesus answered them, saying, The hour is come, that the Son of man should be glorified.

24 Verily, verily, I say unto you, Except a corn of wheat fall into the ground and die, it abideth alone : but if it die, it bringeth forth much fruit.

25 He that loveth his life shall lose it; and he that hateth his life in this world shall keep it unto life eternal.

26 If any man serve me, let him follow me; and where I am, there shall also my servant be: if any man serve me, him will *my* Father honour.

What a blessed discourse we have of our LORD's in those few, but striking verses! All the great events approaching, no doubt arose to the view of his divine mind. And never surely did the glory of Jesus break forth with equal lustre during the whole of his ministry upon earth, than in the garden and on the cross. The triumphs of the Son of God incarnate, in those seasons, far exceeded all the miracles of his former ministry. It was by death, Jesus conquered death. He was indeed crucified in weakness; but in that weakness, sin, death, hell, and the grave, were overcome. The Lord entered their territories, and destroyed their empire for ever. Then was that glorious prophecy fulfilled, which ages before, the Lord had spoken by the Prophet: *I will remove the iniquity of that land in one day.* Zech. iii. 9.

If I trespass a little longer on the Reader's time, in meditating on these sweet verses of our Lord; it shall only be to observe, the beauty of that similitude which the Lord Jesus was pleased to make use of, in allusion to his own death; when describing it, under the figure of a corn of wheat falling into the ground and dying, thereby to bring forth much fruit. And if it be true, as it is said, that corn is nearly the only grain, if not the only, which must die before it can take root: the image is yet more beautiful and express. And if it be further true, as it is said, that pure corn falling into a moist and favourable soil, begins to put on the appearance of a change the *third day* from the time sown, the figure increaseth in its similarity, considered as to the third day, Christ arose from the dead. But passing by these things, I beg the Reader to attend to such points in the similitude, as are most obvious and unquestionable.

When our Lord saith, that except a corn of wheat *fall* into the ground, Jesus did not mean that wheat falls by accident and without design, into the earth. For corn is too highly prized, and in itself too highly valuable, to be thus dealt with. The Husbandman, who is said *to wait for the precious fruit of the earth;* is also supposed to observe *seed time and harvest. For his* God (saith the Prophet,) *doth instruct him to discretion.* See James v. 7. Gen. viii. 22. Isaiah xxviii. 24—29. And Christ, that one, single, pure, and invaluable grain of Corn, did not fall into the ground of our nature, nor die to bring forth fruit to his Church, without design; for the whole of his mission was *by the determinate counsel and foreknowledge of* God. *My* Father (saith Jesus,) *is the Husbandman.* Acts ii. 23. John xv, 1.

And as corn wheat is the most precious of all grain, so our nature in the Person of Christ, is the most precious of all seed. *He is holy, harmless, undefiled, separate from sinners, and made higher than the heavens.* Heb. vii. 26. And as the bread which perisheth with using, is necessary to support our bodies, and therefore called *the staff of life:* so Christ *the living bread which came down from heaven,* is essential to give life to our souls: and therefore called the bread of life. Jesus saith, *he that eateth of it shall live for ever.* And, to add no more; as the corn of the earth must be bruised, in order to be worked up into food for our natural life; so *it pleased the* Father *to bruise* Christ, *and put him to grief,* that he might become the true sustenance for our spiritual life, that we might eat and live for ever. Isaiah liii. 10. Yea, so very necessary is it that all his mystical body should eat of this bread, that Jesus himself saith: *Except ye eat of the flesh of the* Son *of man, and drink his blood, ye have no life in you.* John vi. 48. &c.

But the striking feature of similitude in this verse remains yet to be considered, in that of the corn falling into the ground and dying, without which it remaineth alone; but by dying, bringeth forth much fruit. Here Christ is eminently set forth. For had not Jesus fallen into the ground of this our world, had he remained alone, without taking our nature into union with the divine: yea, even if taking that holy portion of our nature into union with the Godhead, yet had he not died to redeem his Church from the Adam-transgression into which she had fallen; still he would in that case have been like pure corn not earthed, and consequently without fruit. He might indeed have derived all that personal glory, which belongs to him as God-Man: neither would he in that sense, have been said to be alone, because he would still have been in his divine nature One with the Father, and the Holy Ghost, in the essence of the Godhead over all God blessed for ever; and in this sense he might have said, as upon another occasion he did say: *I am not alone because the* Father *is with me.* John xvi. 32. But in relation to his body the Church: she must have remained without the possibility of recovery, in the awful state of the *dead in trespasses and sins,* in which the whole nature was involved by the means of Adam's transgression; and so must have continued unawakened, unregenerated, unrenewed, and without hope, and without God for ever. Reader! pause over the subject. Behold the love of God in Christ which passeth all understanding. God the Father will not suffer those whom he hath given to his dear Son thus to perish. God the Son will not leave his spouse the Church, notwithstanding all her adulteries, so to be everlastingly ruined. God the Holy Ghost will regenerate the Church, whom he hath loved in Christ before all worlds. Jesus, therefore, the pure, the single grain of corn, falls into the ground, and by dying, brings forth fruit; yea a full compleat harvest, of every individual seed, which were his seed from all eternity: and finally gathers the whole into the garner of heaven. *Oh! the depths of the riches both of the wisdom and knowledge of* God! *how unsearchable are his judgments; and his ways past finding out.* Rom. xi. 33. Psm. cxxvi. 5, 6. Isaiah lix. 21. Matt. xiii. 24—52.

27 Now is my soul troubled; and what shall I say? Father, save me from this hour, but for this cause came I unto this hour.

28 Father, glorify thy name. Then came there a voice from heaven, *saying,* I have both glorified *it,* and will glorify *it* again.

29 The people therefore, that stood by, and heard *it,* said that *it* thundered: others said, An angel spake to him.

30 Jesus answered and said, This voice came not because of me, but for your sakes.

In reading the first of these verses, in consequence of the words of the LORD JESUS being improperly marked in the stops, the sense is apt to be overlooked. The LORD speaks of his soul being troubled. And, as the words are in our Bibles, it seems to convey an idea, as if the LORD was at a loss what to say. *And what shall I say?* But this could not be the case. He, *in whom are hid all the treasures of wisdom and knowledge,* could never pause, by way of considering what to say. Neither do our LORD's words convey any such meaning, when the words themselves are placed as they ought to have been. *Now is my soul troubled. And what. Shall I say* FATHER *save me from this hour?* As if the LORD had said. *Now is my soul troubled.* And what if it be so. Shall I call upon the FATHER to save me from this hour? Oh! no. This were to defeat the very purpose for which I came. *But for this cause came I unto this hour.* I will therefore say, FATHER *glorify thy Name.* By reading the verse in this manner, we have the whole rendered perfectly clear and intelligible. And what a blessed view, the words give us of the LORD JESUS, at this solemn season. He had in full prospect before him, those tremendous exercises both of body and soul, which as the Head and Surety of his people, he had to go through. He felt, all that human nature could feel, upon the occasion. (See Heb. v. 7, 8. 9.) But in the midst of all, nothing of personal sorrow would he allow to stand in the way to obstruct the divine glory. Yea, the LORD intimated by his expressions, that in those humiliations, the divine glory should be the more manifested.

And the answer from heaven became the most blessed confirmation of what CHRIST had said. *I have both glorified it, and will glorify it again.* This was the *third* time, during our LORD's ministry upon earth, in which GOD the FATHER had publicly proclaimed his perfect approbation to the Person, and Office-work, as Mediator, of his dear SON. Once, at CHRIST's entrance upon it at his baptism, Matt. iii. 16, 17. Once again at *Mount Tabor,* at the transfiguration. Matt. xvii. 5. And now just before the close of his ministry, in the garden, and at the cross. I beg the Reader to ponder the subject well, for it is most blessed. All the words of the LORD are precious words, when at any time he speaks in love and mercy to his Church. But those are eminently so, in which GOD the FATHER, or GOD the HOLY GHOST, speak to CHRIST as Mediator. For they confirm CHRIST's authority, and prove that he was called of GOD, to be the servant and High Priest of JEHOVAH, as was *Aaron.* Heb. v. 4, 5. The perfection of CHRIST's person, and the perfection of his office, as our surety, are blessed things. But it forms a most essential part to our assurance in pleading both before GOD, when we can and do tell him, that the LORD himself both ordained the plan of mercy, and consecrated CHRIST his dear SON into the office of performing it. For when CHRIST took both the names and the nature of his people, to bear their sins, and to become their righteousness; the whole was in consequence of covenant-agreement between the persons of the GODHEAD. Hence the Church is represented as pleading this in prayer, and in which every child of GOD, truly taught of GOD, finds joy and comfort to join. *Behold, O GOD! our shield! and look upon the face of thine anointed!* Psalm lxxxiv. 9.

In relation to the soul-troubles of CHRIST, and GOD's glorifying his

name in CHRIST; these are subjects in which our most earnest enquiries go but a little way. Who indeed can be competent to the apprehension of the soul agonies of the Redeemer, when the frowns and
rebukes of his FATHER, as the Sinner's Surety, went so near, as he
saith himself, *to break his heart.* Psm. lxix. 20. And we must be
possessed of somewhat more than human, or even angelic intellect,
before we' can enter into an apprehension of the full extent of the
glory of JEHOVAH's name, in the great events connected with the
person and offices of CHRIST. It may not be improper, however, to
attend to the scriptural account of this wonderful subject, in order to
gather some few glimpses of the LORD's manifested glory, when in answer to CHRIST's prayer for the glorifying of his name, the LORD said,
I have both glorified it, and will glorify it again.

That JEHOVAH in his three-fold character of person can receive no
possible addition to his *essential* glory, by any act of his creatures,
is a truth which both Scripture and reason loudly confirm. The
everlasting obedience of the whole creation of GOD, had it been so
without interruption, could not have added to GOD's glory. Yea, the
obedience and death of CHRIST did not. For the being and glory of
JEHOVAH is incapable of accession or increase. And hence CHRIST
himself, under the spirit of prophecy, saith, *My goodness extendeth
not to thee, but to the saints that are in the earth, and to the excellent,
in whom is all my delight.* Psm. xvi. 2, 3. But, there is a glory
which the LORD hath been pleased to manifest of himself, in his threefold character of person, in covenant engagements towards the
Church, whereby his name is glorified in every display of it, when at
any time the LORD is pleased to make it known in any of the departments of nature, providence, and grace. And it is in this sense we
are to consider the words of the LORD, when in answer to CHRIST's
prayer, GOD the FATHER said, *I have both glorified it, and will glorify
it again.*

And hath not the LORD done so, in all the revelations he hath been
pleased to make of himself, in his three-fold character of person, when
in CHRIST, GOD-Man united, he hath communicated all that is capable
of communication, in relation to his love to the Church from all
eternity? Hath he not glorified himself to our apprehension, in the
personal glory put upon CHRIST, as GOD-Man, when before a single
revelation was made of him to the Church, yea, before the Church
had been called into being, in this time-state of her existence, CHRIST
was set up from everlasting, the wonder of heaven, the adoration of
angels, and the present, future, and eternal *praise of all his saints?*
Prov. viii. 22, 23. Isa. ix. 6. Heb. i. 6. Psm. cxlviii. 14.

And, to come down to the time-state of the Church, when we behold with what a vast apparatus JEHOVAH introduced CHRIST into the
world, commanding all the angels to worship him, and the Church to
love and adore him, what greater demonstrations could be given of
JEHOVAH's glorifying his name, than in such decided tokens of glory?
In short, what is the Bible itself, from beginning to end, but one continued manifestation of JEHOVAH's glory, set forth and magnified in all
the riches of it, in the Person, Work, Offices, Relations, and Characters
of the LORD JESUS CHRIST? And what but JEHOVAH's glory is the
ultimate object of the innumerable instances of love shewn to the

Church in the FATHER's favor, the Redeemer's grace, and the communion and fellowship of the HOLY GHOST? Rev. iv. 11.

And, as in every manifestation JEHOVAH hath glorified his name in all that is past, so will he glorify it again in all that is to come. Particularly in reference (as this scripture might be supposed to have in view) to what remained, in the personal work and offices of CHRIST. GOD's glory had been displayed in the whole of CHRIST's ministry to the present hour, and GOD the FATHER engaged that it should be to the end. And when did ever the glory of GOD shine with more lustre than in the day of CHRIST on the cross, when he made his soul an offering for sin. Reader! let you and I attend to those gracious words of our GOD and FATHER to his dear SON, as they relate to the divine glory in JESUS CHRIST; and then, under the HOLY GHOST's teaching, we shall have a more sure word to take heed to, than all our own reasonings, or all those men here spoken of debated upon, whether it thundered, or whether it was an angel which spake to Jesus.

31 Now is the judgment of this world: now shall the prince of this world be cast out.

32 And I, if I be lifted up from the earth, will draw all *men* unto me.

33 This he said, signifying what death he should die.

I only pause over those verses to remark, what a beautiful correspondence there is between what the LORD JESUS here saith of divine drawing, and the uniform language of scripture on this point. The gracious act belongs to the whole persons of the GODHEAD, and every poor sinner drawn to CHRIST hath the witness in himself that it is so. Read these scriptures in proof. Jer. xxxi. 3. John vi. 44. John vi. 63. 1 John v. 7.

34 The people answered him, We have heard out of the law that Christ abideth for ever: and how sayest thou, The Son of man must be lifted up? who is this Son of man?

35 Then Jesus said unto them, Yet a little while is the light with you. Walk while ye have the light, lest darkness come upon you; for he that walketh in darkness knoweth not whither he goeth.

36 While ye have light, believe in the light, that ye may be the children of light. These things spake Jesus, and departed, and did hide himself from them.

37 But though he had done so many miracles before them, yet they believed not on him:

38 That the saying of Esaias the prophet might be fulfilled, which he spake, Lord, who hath believed our report? and to whom hath the arm of the Lord been revealed?

39 Therefore they could not believe, because that Esaias said again,

40 He hath blinded their eyes, and hardened their heart; that they should not see *with* their eyes, nor understand with *their* heart, and be converted, and I should heal them.

41 These things said Esaias, when he saw his glory, and spake of him.

42 Nevertheless among the chief rulers also many believed on him; but because of the Pharisees they did not confess *him*, lest they should be put out of the synagogue:

43 For they loved the praise of men more than the praise of God.

44 Jesus cried and said, He that believeth on me, believeth not on me, but on him that sent me.

45 And he that seeth me, seeth him that sent me.

46 I am come a light into the world, that whosoever believeth on me should not abide in darkness.

47 And if any man hear my words, and believe not, I judge him not: for I came not to judge the world, but to save the world.

48 He that rejecteth me, and receiveth not my words, hath one that judgeth him: the word that I have spoken, the same shall judge him in the last day.

49 For I have not spoken of myself; but the Father which sent me, he gave me a commandment, what I should say, and what I should speak.

50 And I know that his commandment is life everlasting : whatsoever I speak therefore, even as the Father said unto me, so I speak.

I have only to lament that the limits of a Poor Man's Commentary will not grant me the indulgence to enlarge as I could wish on this very blessed discourse of CHRIST. Every verse, more or less, is full of divine instructions. But I will only detain the Reader on that part of it which respects the vision of *Esaias*, which is here most decidedly declared to be the glory of CHRIST which he saw. And the Reader will observe, that the observation is not the Evangelist's, but GOD the HOLY GHOST's. In proof, I beg of him first to read the Prophet's own account of it, Isaiah vi. Then I wish him to consult Acts xxviii. 26, 27. And when he hath done both these things, let the Reader himself determine what less than the glory of GOD could have been set forth in the presence of CHRIST, in that vision which the Prophet saw. The train of the LORD, which filled the temple, was a beautiful representation of GOD in his divine nature filling the temple of CHRIST's body, agreeably to what the HOLY GHOST hath said, that *in him dwelleth all the fulness of the* GODHEAD *bodily.* Coloss. ii. 9. GOD the HOLY GHOST be praised and adored; *first,* for explaining to the Church the Prophet's vision; and, *secondly,* in causing it to be recorded for the everlasting instruction and comfort of the Church in all ages.

REFLECTIONS.

PONDER well, my soul, the many blessed things contained in this chapter concerning thy GOD and SAVIOR. And while thou beholdest the gracious condescension of JESUS in the days of his flesh, granting his sweet presence and divine discourses, in supping with his people, as in the house of *Lazarus,* and *Simon* the *Leper;* do not for a moment question, but that now, in the day of his power, he will come, as he hath said, and sup with his people, and cause them by faith to sup with him. And what though thou hast no costly ointment, as *Mary* had, to anoint thy LORD's feet, yet, when JESUS comes, he will bring every thing that is blessed with him. Remember, that thy LORD comes not to receive, but to give, not that He may be made more blessed, for that is impossible, but that thou mayest be made more happy. It is enough when through his grace enabling them, his people lay low at his feet, and *while the king sitteth at the table* of his own providing, he will cause the spikenard of his own graces, called forth into exercise from thine heart by his HOLY SPIRIT, *to send forth the smell thereof.*

Blessed LORD JESUS! may I never forget that soul trouble of thine which is here spoken of! Give me grace to meditate on the wondrous subject. Oh! for a solemnity of soul always suited to the contemplation. The very recollection is enough to damp all unsuited and unbecoming lightness of mind at all times. Did JESUS feel soul-heaviness on the account of his redeemed, and shall they be light minded? Did JESUS groan, and shall I be unconcerned? Blessed be my GOD and FATHER, who so graciously answered his dear SON by a

voice from heaven. And blessed be the LORD for his mercy to all his
redeemed by the act, since it came for their sakes. And oh! for
grace, to rejoice with a joy unspeakable, and full of glory, in what
GOD the FATHER then declared to his dear SON, concerning his Media-
tor-office and character, that the LORD had glorified his name, and
will glorify it again, yea, for ever! And blessed be GOD for that precious assurance, more precious than the gold of Ophir, it was the glory
of CHRIST, which *Esaias* saw when he spake of Him. It is, and
everlastingly must be the glory of CHRIST, which is the joy of all
his people. Oh! thou dear LORD! write these blessed words of thine
in my heart, to lift up my soul with joy for ever: *I am come* (saith my
LORD,) *a light into the world, that whosoever believeth on me shall not
abide in darkness.*

CHAP. XIII.

CONTENTS.

The LORD *washeth his Disciples' Feet. He intimates to the Twelve,
that One of them is a Traitor. The Sorrow of the Eleven at the Account.* Peter *is admonished of his Denial.*

NOW before the feast of the passover, when
Jesus knew that his hour was come that he
should depart out of this world unto the Father,
having loved his own which were in the world, he
loved them unto the end.

Of the Passover much hath been already noticed in this Commentary on Matt. xxvi. 1, 2. and Mark xiv. 1, 2. to which I refer. I
beg the Reader to remark with me, what is here said of the unalterable
love of JESUS to *his own*. And I beg the Reader to attend to the sense
of the words, *his own*. The words differ very widely from the same
words, *his own*. John i. 11. For though they appear to an *English*
Reader as one and the same, yet they are not so in the original.
By *his own*, as it is rendered, John i. 11. is meant *his own* nation, the
Jews. But here in this place, by *his own* is meant, his own Church,
his own people, his own children, whom his FATHER gave to him *before the foundation of the world.* Ephes. i. 4. And the original
words in the two passages make all this difference. The *former*
means such as we are used to say of a person in relation to his own
place of birth, it is his own country, his own town or people there
dwelling. But the *latter* carries with it an idea of relationship and
property, such as we should say of a man's wife or children, yea, his
own flesh. So that the *one* implies no more, than that CHRIST and the
nation to which he came, were countrymen. The *other* bespeaks his
own house and family, his spouse the Church. Reader! do not fail to
mark the vast difference, wherever you meet it. And never forget
also, that CHRIST's love to his own is an everlasting love, or as the
words themselves express, *to the end;* which end is eternity, unchangeable like CHRIST himself, *the same yesterday, and to day, and
for ever.* Heb. xiii. 8. Isaiah liv. 10.

2 And supper being ended, the devil having now put into the heart of Judas Iscariot, Simon's *son*, to betray him;

3 Jesus knowing that the Father had given all things into his hands, and that he was come from God, and went to God :

4 He riseth from supper, and laid aside his garments; and took a towel, and girded himself.

5 After that he poureth water into a bason, and began to wash the disciples' feet, and to wipe *them* with the towel wherewith he was girded.

6 Then cometh he to Simon Peter : and Peter said unto him, Lord, dost thou wash my feet?

7 Jesus answered and said unto him, What I do thou knowest not now; but thou shalt know hereafter.

8 Peter saith unto him, Thou shalt never wash my feet. Jesus answered him, If I wash thee not, thou hast no part with me.

9 Simon Peter saith unto him, Lord, not my feet only, but also *my* hands and *my* head.

10 Jesus saith to him, He that is washed needeth not save to wash *his* feet, but is clean every whit: and ye are clean, but not all.

11 For he knew who should betray him; therefore said he, Ye are not all clean.

12 So after he had washed their feet, and had taken his garments, and was set down again, he said unto them, Know ye what I have done to you?

13 Ye call me Master and Lord: and ye say well; for *so* I am.

14 If I then, *your* Lord and Master, have washed your feet: ye also ought to wash one another's feet.

15 For I have given you an example, that ye should do as I have done to you.

4 N 2

16 Verily, verily, I say unto you, The servant
is not greater than his lord; neither he that is sent
greater than he that sent him.

17 If ye know these things, happy are ye if ye
do them.

The supper here spoken of could not be what we call the LORD's
Supper, which JESUS instituted in the place of the Passover; for this
supper is said to have been before the feast of the Passover (ver. 1).
See Luke xxii. 14—22. And moreover this was an ordinary supper.:
most probably the same as we read of Matt. xxvi. 2, 6, which
Simon the Leper made for JESUS. Whereas the LORD's Supper was
after the Passover. Matt. xxvi. 20—26. See Luke xxii. 7—13.

But I would more particularly beg the Reader's notice to what is
related in this Chapter, of our LORD's washing his disciples' feet.
And I desire his attention the rather, because *John* is the only one of
the *four* Evangelists, whom the HOLY GHOST was pleased to appoint,
to make this record. The circumstances indeed in it are so very
singular, and the humbleness of our LORD in the act so striking: a
service which was never performed by any but the very lowest of the
servants in a family; that I confess I am inclined to think, there was
somewhat of no small importance veiled under it. I am far from supposing, that I can throw any new light upon the subject: nevertheless, in a work of this kind, it would be wrong to pass it by unnoticed. May GOD the HOLY GHOST be our Teacher!

And here let us *first* observe how the subject is introduced. JESUS,
knowing that *all things were given into his hands.* So that in the
very moment when he knew himself, as GOD-MAN-MEDIATOR, to be
the LORD, Proprietor, and Governor of heaven and earth; JESUS did
that which the lowest of the sons of men, and such as are slaves, only
perform. Let the impression which such a view of CHRIST's unbounded condescension ought to have upon the mind, be first considered by us; and then let us go on to another observation, which
ariseth out of what the Evangelist hath said.

Secondly. It is added, that JESUS knew he was *come from* GOD, *and
went to* GOD. With these thoughts before him, the LORD performs an
act of service upon each of his disciples present; as if under the
conviction, that now only could such an outward demonstration of
his regard for them be given, because he was about to return to his
FATHER, and for a while, *they would see him no more.* John xvi. 10.

Thirdly. The act itself of washing his disciples' feet, hath somewhat
very striking in it. The manner in which the LORD set about it.
The deliberate and personal way in which he did it to all: and
the confinement of the thing itself to their feet only: these are certainly special, and particular characters, in which there is much signification. Some have supposed, that in this act of humiliation, of
the LORD JESUS laying aside his garments, and putting on the towel of
the menial servant; may be viewed, a beautiful representation of the
SON of GOD laying aside his glory which he had with the FATHER
before all worlds, and taking upon him the form of a servant, when
he came to wash his people from their sins in his blood. And some

have thought, that the washing of his disciples' feet, and not their hands, was in reference to the Apostles as preachers of the Gospel; and that in this sense, the ceremony had an allusion to that scripture of the Prophet, when he saith: *how beautiful upon the mountains are the feet of him that bringeth good tidings.* Isaiah lii. 7. But I confess, that in my apprehension, whatever the act itself of washing the feet implied, (for I do not presume to decide,) it was not intended by our LORD to be limited to his Apostles, as preachers of the word; but the whole Church, of which they were then the representatives, were included in it. For the LORD's answer to *Peter*, who modestly declined this service of CHRIST's, plainly proved, that it was of general importance to the whole Church: *If I wash thee not, thou hast no part with me.*

Fourthly. Another remarkable circumstance in this transaction, and which is highly in proof of its importance, is, that the LORD insisted upon it, as hath been just observed in answer to *Peter's* objection; while we are expressly told by the same Evangelist, that in respect to baptism, JESUS *himself baptized not, but his disciples.* John iv. 2. So that the LORD laid no stress upon his own baptizing of his disciples, yea, that he baptized none, and yet here the LORD layeth the greatest importance upon the washing himself his disciples feet, declaring that *if he washed them not, they had no part with him.* And which words of CHRIST, and probably spoken in a firm and decided manner, carried such conviction with them to the heart of *Peter*, that he cried out in great earnestness of desire for the LORD to do it; LORD! (saith he) *not my feet only, but also my hands, and my head.*

And, *lastly*, to mention no more. What can be more marvellous and astonishing, than to observe in this transaction, that *Judas*, as is most evidently the case, partook in this washing by CHRIST, in common with the other Apostles. This is as striking a particularity as either of the former. I have said that this was most evidently the case, for had *Judas* being passed over, and not washed, no sooner had JESUS finished the service, and had sat down again, when we are told, that he immediately declared that one of them should betray him. Now had Judas not been washed with the rest, it would have been known by this omission which it was that would do this deed. Whereas we find the declaration of JESUS threw the whole into a consternation, and called forth the anxious question, one by one, LORD! *is it I?*

Let no child of GOD, however, be hurt, that *Judas* partook in this common act of washing the feet. For whatever grand points were intended from it by our LORD, the thing itself, like ordinances of all kinds, had no saving efficacy in it. The ministration of it most probably had some very blessed design in view, in reference to the LORD's own people. But to others it had none, but like the rain or dew of heaven, which falls upon the rocks and sands, and produceth nothing. There could be no more efficacy in the LORD's washing *Judas's* feet, than in his administering to him the LORD's Supper; and all the other ordinances he had in common with the Apostles. These are all *outward* things; and however sweet and refreshing they are made to the LORD's people, from the LORD's blessing upon them, it is that blessing which becomes the sole cause of usefulness, in their being accompanied with an *inward* grace. What the Apostle saith of the ministration of the Gospel, may be said in relation to every thing connected with the Gospel. *We are* (saith he) *unto* GOD *a sweet savor of* CHRIST, *in them that are saved, and in them that perish. To the one, we are the savor of death unto death; and to the other, the savor of life unto life. And who is sufficient for these things?* 2 Cor. ii. 15, 16.

And I take occasion from hence (and with such an awful character in view as *Judas,* who partook of those means of grace, but to his greater condemnation,) to remark, that it should seem our dear LORD intended from it to teach his people how to draw improvements to their comfort, rather than at any time to be discouraged at the unavoidable minglings with the ungodly, whether in ordinances, or elsewhere in the present world. JESUS knew that *Judas* was a devil, when he chose him to be an Apostle. John vi. 70. Notwithstanding this, the LORD permitted him to excrcise all the *outward* acts of the Apostleship, until *the measure of his iniquity was full,* in betraying his master. But to shew his Church that this man, and every other man in like circumstances with him, had no part nor lot in the matter of salvation; JESUS declared, as soon as he had finished the washing, that though *they* (meaning his faithful ones) *were clean, yet not all,* said JESUS. For, added the Evangelist, *he knew who should betray him, therefore said he, ye are not all clean.* And, surely, from hence the Church is taught, never to feel concern when at any time the christless and despisers of the pure truths of GOD, mingle with the LORD's people at his house, or his table. For as the presence of *Judas* had no effect to injure the Apostles in those hallowed seasons with their LORD, so neither can devils, or bad men, hinder the blessed manifestations which the LORD makes to his own, when handing to them their portions in secret, and causing them to eat of the *hidden manna.* Rev. ii. 17. Yea, more than this. Such things sometimes are made to act, under the LORD's grace, as instruments in his hand, the better to form our views of distinguishing mercy. Many a child of GOD, when beholding the scoffers and ungodly around them, have been constrained to say with the Apostle, LORD! *how is it that thou shouldest manifest thyself unto me, and not unto the world?* And that sweet question hath been found to arise in the soul in all its gracious influence, *Who made thee to differ from another?* See John xiv. 22. 1 Cor. iv. 7. And it is blessed, yea, very blessed, both in ordinances and providences, to call to mind that the LORD JESUS himself purposely chose one among twelve men only, which attended his person, that was a devil, to be of the number, when the LORD's tried ones are compelled *to sojourn in Mesech, and to dwell in the tents of Kedar.* Psalm cxx. 5. Job i. 6.

I have largely trespassed in entering into those several particulars as they struck my mind, respecting this wonderful act of CHRIST's washing his disciples feet. I again repeat that I do not speak decidedly upon what might or might not be the LORD's design in an act so very gracious. But there are two very sweet improvements, which, according to my apprehension of the subject, arise from it; and before we close our review of it, I would beg the Reader's indulgence to bring before him.

The *first* is, What a most endearing portrait hath GOD the HOLY GHOST given to the Church, by the pencil of the Evangelist, of the person of our LORD JESUS CHRIST? Can the imagination conceive any thing equally lovely, as in thus beholding the SON of GOD in our nature, washing the feet of poor fishermen? And what tends to give yet more the highest coloring of grace and mercy to the picture, it is drawn at that moment of all others, when Jesus *knew that the* FATHER *had given all things into his hands!* Reader! ponder it well. What a lesson is here taught to mortify the pride of human nature! While the great ones of the earth carry themselves so proudly, and will hardly condescend to behold the poor of the people, the King of heaven stoops to the lowest humiliation, and washeth his disciples' feet. Now I pray the Reader never to lose sight of this unequalled condescension of CHRIST. Shall you, or shall I, or shall any poor sinner, in the view of such clemency, evermore draw conclusions, as if it was beneath the dignity of the SON of GOD to regard his people, when we behold such a palpable proof of that regard, in an act so humbling? Did JESUS wash their feet, and will he not wash my soul? Did JESUS unasked, yea, when *Peter* refused him, persist to do such an act of grace, and will he turn a deaf ear to your or my earnest petitions? Can any child of GOD, in the contemplation of such love in the LORD, say, I am too low, too abject, too unworthy for JESUS to notice? Speak, ye humble souls! ye, who like those faithful Apostles, have tasted that the LORD is gracious, do you say, for you can tell, whether CHRIST's exaltation and glory do not become the very grounds of your hope, that because he is exalted he will condescend, and because he is all glorious, he will be all merciful? Yea, say, doth not the LORD appear in your view the more blessed, when he appears the more condescending, and the more he stoops to look on you, doth he not appear the higher to your eyes. Precious LORD, in humbleness, as well as greatness, thou must have the pre-eminence! Coloss. i. 18.

The *other* improvement suggested to us from this blessed Scripture, is, in my view, equally endearing with the *former*, namely, how JESUS, by this act of washing his disciples' feet before his departure, intended to convince them, that the tendencies of his love to them would be the same after that he was gone. He knew (the Evangelist saith,) that *he was come from* GOD, *and went to* GOD; and under these impressions, he taketh the towel, and the water, and immediately begins to wash his disciples' feet. So that with his mind full of the glory to which he was then going, returning to his FATHER, and to all his redeemed gone before, yet he doth this to leave a palpable testimony behind him, that neither time nor place could alter his regard for them. But his last act upon earth, when in familiarity he was sitting down with them, should not be more expressive of affection than he would carry with him in all his remembrance of them in heaven. And as he could not do such an act then, when returned to glory, he did it now, as his last upon earth, that they might always have it in remembrance concerning him when he was gone, until he came again to take them home to himself, that where he was they should be also. John xiv. 3. Dearest LORD JESUS! may my soul have these things always in remembrance! And it will not be long before that He who washed his disciples feet will bring home his whole Church washed from all her sins in his blood, and become *a glorious Church, sanctified and cleansed, and made holy, and without blemish before him, in love!* Ephes. v. 25, 26.

18 I speak not of you all: I know whom I have chosen: but that the scripture may be fulfilled. He that eateth bread with me hath lifted up his heel against me.

19 Now I tell you before it come, that, when it is come to pass, ye may believe that I am *he*.

20 Verily, verily, I say unto you, He that receiveth whomsoever I send, receiveth me; and he that receiveth me, receiveth him that sent me.

21 When Jesus had thus said, he was troubled in spirit, and testified, and said, Verily, verily, I say unto you, that one of you shall betray me.

22 Then the disciples looked one on another, doubting of whom he spake.

23 Now there was leaning on Jesus' bosom one of his disciples, whom Jesus loved.

24 Simon Peter therefore beckoned to him, that he should ask who it should be of whom he spake.

25 He then lying on Jesus' breast saith unto him, Lord, who is it?

26 Jesus answered, He it is, to whom I shall give a sop, when I have dipped *it*. And when he had dipped the sop, he gave *it* to Judas Iscariot, *the son* of Simon.

27 And after the sop Satan entered into him. Then said Jesus unto him, That thou doest, do quickly.

28 Now no man at the table knew for what intent he spake this unto him.

29 For some *of them* thought, because Judas had the bag, that Jesus had said unto him, Buy *those things* that we have need of against the feast; or, that he should give something to the poor.

30 He then having received the sop went immediately out: and it was night.

I would wish in this place to call the Reader's attention to the scriptural account of the character of *Judas*, the traitor; having passed over the history of this man in the preceding Evangelists, purposely to gather into one point of view the several particulars relating to him.

And, first, it will be proper to look at what is said of him in respect to the many great advantages he possessed, in being brought by the LORD himself to attend his person.   He had the privilege of being always in the society of JESUS, and this not transiently, but for nearly three years and half.   He had seen CHRIST's miracles, heard his divine discourses, and was in the daily habit of conversing with Him, *who spake as never man spake*.   Add to these, he was sent forth to the service of the ministry, and beheld (at least the outward tokens of it,) what mighty events followed CHRIST's power.   Matt. x. 1—8.

Let us next consider some of the many aggravated circumstances which attended the perfidy of his conduct.   Without going over the ground in the numberless opportunities he had found of CHRIST's kindness to him in common with the other Apostles, we need have reference no further than to what is related in this Chapter.   The LORD JESUS washed his feet.   And when he had re-assumed his seat at the table, the gentle intimation JESUS made, that there was one present which would betray him, was enough in any breast less obdurate than *Judas*, to have stung him to the quick.   Could any arrow of conviction have reached his heart, surely the one drawn and levelled by CHRIST would have penetrated.   But there he sat, unmoved and hardened, up to all the possibilities of determined guilt. And while all the other Apostles were tremblingly alive at the bare suspicion only, that one of them could do such a thing as betray their Master; *Judas* sat, like another *Ætna*, with all the fire of hellish malice burning within, until the LORD had given to him the fatal sop, intended to identify the traitor, and then, and not before, he withdrew.

Nay, after all this, as if it was not enough to shew the desperately wicked state of his hardened heart, when he left the table, he must have gone away immediately to *Jerusalem*, which was two miles from *Bethany*, though it was now night, in order to concert schemes with the chief priests, the better to deliver CHRIST into their hands.   For here we find him, as *Matthew* hath related, soon after, Matt. xxvi. 14, 15, 16.   And during the whole of this solitary walk by night, from *Bethany* to the city, we read of no one compunction that he felt; neither during the *two days* which intervened between this evening and the Passover, is there the smallest intimation of any softenings or relentings in his mind.   Yea, so much to the contrary, that we next hear of him as taking his place with the other Apostles at the Passover, and actually receiving at the LORD's hands the sacramental Supper, as if a faithful disciple.

And as all tenderness was lost upon the wretch, so the alarms of judgment had no effect also.   For when he daringly headed the band of men and officers which went to apprehend CHRIST, and they all fell to the ground, when the LORD JESUS, to the question *whom seek ye?* answered, *I am he; Judas* must have fell with them.   See John xviii. 2—6.   But neither this miracle, nor every former; neither judgments nor mercies could affect *Judas*.   Satan had taken the compleat possession of him, and *the last state of that man was worse than the first.*   Luke xi. 26.

Reader! here let us pause, as we behold the awful history of one of whom the LORD JESUS said, *good were it for that man if he had never been born.*   Mark xiv. 21.   Let us look into the cause, and, under divine teaching, we shall soon be led to discover it. The scriptures of GOD, in tracing effects to their source, have drawn the line of everlasting distinction between the precious and the vile, between the righteous and the wicked, between *him that serveth* GOD, *and him that serveth him not*, Malachi iii. 18. One of the Apostles in a single chapter hath done this business to our hand. He contemplates the Adam-apostacy of our whole nature, the Church, as well as the Christless, all alike involved in the ruin of a fallen state, and then marks the different features of character which distinguish the Church in her grace-union with CHRIST, from the seed of the serpent, which are for ever precluded from any possibility of salvation. Of the *former*, he describes them as *sanctified by* GOD *the* FATHER, *preserved in* JESUS CHRIST, *and called*. Of the *latter*, he declares, that *they were of old ordained to this condemnation*. And hence, as the lineal descendants of *Cain*, they have ran, and do run greedily after the error of *Balaam*, and must perish in the gainsaying of *Core*. Jude i. 4—11. And what further testimony doth GOD the HOLY GHOST give of all such, but such as the LORD JESUS himself gave of *Judas*. *Ye are of your father the devil*, (said CHRIST to some of this race,) *and the lusts of your father ye will do*. John viii. 44. And *John* follows up the same doctrine as his Master. For, speaking of *Cain*, he expressly saith, that *he was of that wicked one*. Not simply under the temptations of the devil, but *of him*. For he is speaking at the time, how *the children of* GOD *are manifest, and the children of the devil*. 1 John iii. 8—12. And *Judas* is not merely said to have been *tempted* of the devil, but that he *was* a devil, and *Satan entered into him*, took an entire possession of him. John vi. 70. Hence the enemy calls the heart of such *his house*. Luke xi. 24. Reader! ponder well the whole, for the doctrine is truly awful. But, remember the awfulness of it doth by no means lessen the truth of it. See, in confirmation, Psm. cix. 6, 7, 8. compared with Acts i. 16—20. and hence that Psalm is called the *Iscariotic* Psalm. See John xviii. 2.

31 Therefore, when he was gone out, Jesus said, Now is the Son of man glorified, and God is glorified in him.

32 If God be glorified in him, God shall also glorify him in himself, and shall straightway glorify him.

33 Little children, yet a little while I am with you. Ye shall seek me: and as I said unto the Jews, Whither I go, ye cannot come; so now I say to you.

34 A new commandment I give unto you, That ye love one another; as I have loved you, that ye also love one another.

35 By this shall all *men* know that ye are my disciples, if ye have love one to another

Doth not the Reader feel a certain somewhat like relief in his mind, from this blessed and divine discourse of JESUS, after going over the awful subject of the traitor's character? No sooner was *Judas* gone out, than JESUS said, *Now is the* SON *of Man glorified, and* GOD *is glorified in him.* Yes! when the traitor was departed, there remained none with CHRIST but his family, his children, his mystical body. In these the LORD was glorified, and *they* made everlastingly happy in him. Yea, all the persons of the GODHEAD were glorified in the same. And I pray the Reader not to overlook in this contemplation of CHRIST, and his Church, that the whole Church is to be considered in this. For the eleven Apostles were at that time the representatives of CHRIST's whole body the Church. And as such, when *Judas* was gone out, who represented the devil and his whole family, JESUS and his family were left alone, and hence CHRIST's glory. Reader! so will it be in that great day, when sin, and Satan, and all the seed of the serpent in the *Judas* of every generation, shall be gone out for ever! How do the faithful now enjoy themselves in the LORD, when at times two or three are met together in his name, and JESUS in the midst of them, and for a while they are uninterrupted by the ungodly? And what a glorious day of GOD will that be, when *the Zion of* GOD, as one of the Psalms blessedly sings of it, shall be brought home, and *the rod of the wicked* shall no longer fall, much less *rest upon the lot of the righteous. As for such,* saith that sweet Psalm, *as turn aside unto their crooked ways, the* LORD *shall lead them forth with the workers of iniquity : but peace shall be upon Israel.* Psm. cxxv.

36 ¶ Simon Peter said unto him, Lord, whither goest thou? Jesus answered him, Whither I go, thou canst not follow me now; but thou shalt follow me afterwards.

37 Peter said unto him, Lord, why cannot I follow thee now? I will lay down my life for thy sake.

38 Jesus answered him, Wilt thou lay down thy life for my sake? Verily, verily, I say unto thee, The cock shall not crow, till thou hast denied me thrice.

For the observations on the fall of *Peter,* and the LORD's recovery of him by his grace. See Luke xxii. 31. and the Commentary.

REFLECTIONS.

READER! do not close your view of this most blessed Chapter, which unfolds so sweetly the heart of CHRIST to his people, and shews them that his whole heart towards them is love, before that you have begged also of GOD the HOLY GHOST, who hath given the

Church such a view of that love, that the LORD will cause all the gracious streams of it to flow from CHRIST's heart into ours. Can the imagination form to itself any thing more lovely, than thus to behold CHRIST encircled with his family, and forgetting his own personal concerns in the tremendous exercises both of soul and body the LORD had then to go through, and now opening before him, but yet in the midst of all, washing his disciples feet? Was there ever an instance of the kind heard of among the histories of the world for a Master to act thus towards his Servants? And here it was the LORD of heaven and earth performing the service to poor sinners? *Wonder, O heavens, and be astonished, O earth, for the* LORD *hath done it!*

But, dearest JESUS! wilt thou not in some measure, (as far as our poor short-sighted capacities can have any suitable apprehension of thy gracious design,) wilt thou not shew us of thy meaning? Was it as a parting act to say, when I am gone, as no opportunity can then occur of demonstrating by any such an *outward* act towards you, of what my *inward* affections are; I hereby shew you that I think no condescension too great to serve and bless my people? If I have washed your feet upon earth, fear not but that I will wash your souls from sin when I am in heaven. And though I am now going to my FATHER, and for a while ye will see me no more, let this shew you, that though my state is changed, yet not my nature. There, as well as here, I am the same JESUS. And though I am going to my FATHER, and to my redeemed gone before, nothing will lessen or remove my affection for my redeemed below. As oft as my Church calls to remembrance this act of mine, in washing my poor disciples' feet, let such a love-token become, as among other designs which I have had in view in the doing it. I intended a palpable proof, that *having loved my own which are in the world, I love them to the end!* Precious LORD JESUS! may not thy redeemed venture to form such conclusions from this gracious act of thine, as if JESUS thus opened to us his heart. Think often of this, I pray the Reader, yea, the whole Church of God. May my poor soul think of nothing beside! And, oh! that GOD the HOLY GHOST, the sweet Remembrancer of JESUS, may keep the thought warm in my heart, until the cold clay hand of death come upon me, and my soul escape from the prison of the body to enjoy the fruition of it for ever.

And, oh! my honored LORD! let even the awful view of the traitor *Judas,* make my mercies infinitely more and more precious, from learning therefrom how distinguishing they are. LORD! it is all thy grace, it is all thy rich, free, sovereign mercy. Be it my daily delight to receive the whole, and every part of thy Church's peace and safety, and happiness, to covenant love; and to ascribe the whole to the united grace of FATHER, SON, and HOLY GHOST, for ever. Amen.

CHAP. XIV.

CONTENTS.

The LORD *is here comforting his Disciples, to prepare their Minds against the Time of his Departure. He describes the Person, Work, and Grace, of the* HOLY GHOST.

L ET not your heart be troubled : ye believe in God, believe also in me.

2 In my Father's house are many mansions : if *it were* not *so*, I would have told you. I go to prepare a place for you.

3 And if I go and prepare a place for you, I will come again, and receive you unto myself; that where I am, *there* ye may be also.

4 And whither I go ye know, and the way ye know.

5 Thomas saith unto him, Lord, we know not whither thou goest : and how can we know the way?

6 ¶ Jesus saith unto him, I am the way, and the truth, and the life. No man cometh unto the Father but by me.

7 If ye had known me, ye should have known my Father also : and from henceforth ye know him, and have seen him.

It hath been a matter of question, and indeed it cannot be determined with such certainty as to leave the matter without question, at what time or place the LORD JESUS delivered this precious discourse. I do not presume to speak on this, or indeed any other point with decision, but I venture to believe that the whole of our LORD's discourse in this and the two following Chapters, was delivered after or partly at the time of his instituting his holy Supper. This chapter, perhaps at the table, and at the close of this chapter, JESUS said, *Arise, let us go hence,* it is probable that then they all arose from the table, and went toward the garden of *Gethsemane.* And as they went, the LORD still continuing his discourse, as contained in the two following chapters. And as his custom was to avail himself of any surrounding circumstances to raise improvement from, and beholding the luxuriancy of the vines, which in warm countries like *Judæa* run over the hedges, and along the ground; the LORD took occasion to compare himself to a vine, and his people to the branches, as the opening of the next chapter begins with. See Chapter XV. But I conceive that both the following chapters, and the prayer which follows in the XVIIth chapter, were all delivered before the LORD and his disciples arrived at the garden of *Gethsemane.* For the Reader may notice that the XVIIIth. Chapter begins in this manner : *When JESUS had spoken these words, he went forth with his disciples over the brook Cedron, where was a garden, into which he entered with his disciples.* John XVIII. 1. Whether the hymn which is said to have been sung by them, was before or after this Chapter, I presume not to say ; but it appears to me, that this was the order of the LORD's discourse in

those Chapters, and his divine prayer which followed, but I do not
determine upon it.   Matt. xxvi. 30.

To enter into the subject of this discourse of the LORD JESUS,
would require many volumes, and after all numberless beauties would
still remain unnoticed.   I shall rather therefore recommend it both
to myself and Reader to look to GOD the HOLY GHOST for his sweet
teaching, through the several parts of it, to unfold and explain the
whole to our hearts while we sit at the feet of JESUS, and hear those
gracious words which proceeded from his mouth.   John vi. 63.

If the Reader will have in remembrance the season when JESUS
delivered this discourse as he goes through it, the recollection will
tend to endear yet more every portion of it to his heart.   The LORD
was now in the moment of departure.   This was the last quiet and uninterrupted meeting he knew that he should ever enjoy with his few
faithful disciples before his sufferings and death.   And if I am right
in my conjectures, that this discourse and prayer which followed was
after the institution of his Supper, the traitor was then gone out.
As a dying father therefore in the midst of his family, and standing
now upon the threshold of the eternal world, with his mind full of
those glories opening before him, he addresses his disciples in those
soul-comforting words, *Let not your heart be troubled!*   And as an
everlasting support that they should not be troubled, he begins his
discourse, and takes it as a text for his whole sermon ; the eternal nature of his GODHEAD in his oneness and equality with GOD ; and
reminds them that he is with the FATHER, and the HOLY GHOST,
the equal object of faith; and therefore enjoins their belief in GOD
and in Him, as the grand and sure security for comfort against all
the sorrows and temptations of life.   *Ye believe in* GOD, that is, in his
threefold character of persons, FATHER, SON, and HOLY GHOST, as
GOD in covenant; *believe also in me,* that is, as GOD-Man-Mediator.
Which interpretation of the passage, I humbly conceive to be in
exact agreement with our LORD's prayer, which immediately followed
this sermon, when he said, *And this is life eternal, that they might
know thee the only true* GOD, *and* JESUS CHRIST, *whom thou hast
sent.*   John xvii. 3.

And, Reader! do not fail to observe with what tenderness the LORD
speaks to his disciples concerning those sure mansions of glory which
he was going to take possession of in their name.   He had, and
not long before, washed their feet, to convince them both of his condescending love, and that by such an act while he was with them,
they might be convinced that there was nothing but what he would
do for them when he was gone from them into heaven, and incapable
of shewing by such outward tokens how much he loved them.
And now he repeats in the tenderest form of words every assurance
of his unalterable affection.   I pray the Reader, before he goes further, to gather into one point of view the several very endearing expressions of the LORD JESUS on this one point, as they are interspersed here and there in this our LORD's discourse.

First, He assures them of his unceasing love for them, and pro-
poseth himself in common with GOD, to be the great object of their
faith and love after his departure. Verse 1.   *Secondly,* He gives them
the most absolute assurance of his unalterable regard for them.   Yea,
to convince them of this, he declares that their very life is bound up

in his, and *because he lives, they shall live also*, ver. 19. *Thirdly*, He tells them that it is for them, and for their everlasting welfare, for which he goes away. Their interest, as well as his glory, was concerned in his departure. *Nevertheless, I tell you the truth; it is expedient for you that I go away. I go to prepare a place for you. If I go not away the Comforter will not come unto you; but if I depart, I will send him unto you.* John xvi. 7. The Reader will observe, that I do but just glance at those precious things in the LORD's discourse. To enlarge on them, as I pray the LORD the HOLY GHOST to do, in his opening them both to the Reader's mind and my own, would far exceed the limits of any Commentary but GOD the SPIRIT's. *Fourthly*. The LORD declares, that when he had dispatched the great concerns on their account, for which he was about to leave them, and return to glory, and had sent the HOLY GHOST to them, and prepared all things for their reception, *he would come again and receive them unto himself, that where he was, there they should be also.* Reader! pause here. Would it not have been enough in our LORD, and as a proof of his love, had he said, I am going away on your account, and when I have prepared and made every thing ready for you, I will send my angels to fetch you, and bring you home to me? No! Our dear LORD, by what he hath here said, hath declared that this would not have been enough in his esteem. I will come myself, said the blessed Redeemer. *I will receive you unto myself, that where I am, there you may be also.* Oh! matchless love of a glorious lover! The Reader should be told, in order that he may enter yet further into the heartfelt enjoyment of those precious words of JESUS, that it was the custom with the Jews in their marriages, when all things were prepared and made ready for the reception of the bride, the husband goes himself to his bride's house to fetch her home to his own, and trusts not this embassy to any other person. JESUS, therefore, our bridegroom, will not be out-done in acts of love to his spouse, but in the marriage his FATHER hath made for his SON with his Church, will himself come and bring her home to *the marriage supper of the lamb.* Rev. xix. 6, 9. *Fifthly*. The LORD assures them yet further, that though absent in body, he will be present with them in spirit. *I will not leave you comfortless*, (or as the margin of the Bible renders the word, *orphans*. John xvi. 18.) *I will come to you.* Yea, he added, that the FATHER also would come, *and we* (said JESUS,) *will make our abode with you.* And *the* HOLY GHOST *shall abide with you for ever.* Verses 23, 26. So that, however to outward appearance the LORD was gone from them into heaven, yet in reality he was *always with them, even unto the end of the world.* Matt. xxviii. 20. Isaiah xxvii. 3. *Sixthly*. And JESUS, as if to endear himself yet more to them, and to convince them that his whole heart and soul was their's, (Jer. xxxii. 41.) desires them to be continually sending to him their wishes and prayers, that he might present them to his and their FATHER. And he assures them, that *whatsoever they should ask the* FATHER *in his name he would do it for them, that the* FATHER *might be glorified in the* SON, verse 13. Yea, the LORD seems to be gently reproving them of a backwardness in those applications in times past; and therefore now bids them be the more bold, as He will be with the FATHER, when their petitions come before the throne. *Hitherto have ye asked nothing in my name*, (that is, in comparison to what you might, and as you shall, when GOD the HOLY GHOST is come upon you to teach you how to pray, and what to pray for,) *ask, and ye shall receive, that your joy may be full.* John xvi. 24. *Seventhly.* JESUS not only promiseth to send the HOLY GHOST to them immediately on his departure, and which he assured them was one great cause wherefore he went away, but he gives them to understand, that in having Him, the SPIRIT, they would in fact have CHRIST, for his great office would be to glorify CHRIST. And so much of union and design there was in all that belonged to the HOLY GHOST, in teaching of JESUS that that blessed SPIRIT was in one and the same moment an Almighty LORD in his own eternal power and GODHEAD, the promise of the FATHER, and the effect of CHRIST's ascension, so that every one hath the mind of CHRIST that was under the influences of the HOLY GHOST. 1 Cor. xii. 11. Luke xxiv. 49. 1 Cor. ii. 16. And *Eighthly* and *Lastly,* to mention no more. The LORD JESUS assured them that GOD the HOLY GHOST would not do as He was now about to do from the necessity of the measure, leave them when once he came, and which would be soon after CHRIST was gone from them, for he would soon come, but he would abide with them for ever, and never for a moment depart from them, until JESUS himself came in person to take them home, where they should then dwell with him, and part no more. These, and many more sweet assurances to the same purport, the LORD JESUS delivered to them in this parting discourse, to convince them of his unalterable affection. And, in confirmation of the whole, in their hearing, and before he went into the garden of *Gethsemane,* as soon as he had finished his discourse he followed the subject up with prayer, and solemnly committed them into the FATHER's hands with his whole Church and people. See John xvii.

After so long a page of contents (for they are but contents,) as I have given, in reciting *some* of the many interesting heads of our LORD's discourse, I shall not trespass further in dwelling on our LORD's answer to *Thomas,* than just to observe, that CHRIST is not only the way, as pointing to it, teaching of it, and going before in it, but is Himself the *way,* in being the whole of it in his person, works, offices, characters, and relations. His obedience and death constitute the way, for there is no other. He is the *truth,* for he is truth itself, in whom JEHOVAH centers the whole of all grace and all glory; *the Amen, the faithful and true witness.* Isa. lxv. 16. Rev. iii. 14. Ephes. i. 10. And He is the life and light of the whole creation of GOD, in all the departments of life, natural, spiritual, and eternal. John i. 4. Ephes. i. 3. John iii. 36. 1 John i. 1, 2.

8 Philip saith unto him, Lord, shew us the Father, and it sufficeth us.

9 Jesus saith unto him, Have I been so long time with you, and yet hast thou not known me, Philip? he that hath seen me, hath seen the Father; and how sayest thou *then,* Shew us the Father?

10 Believest thou not that I am in the Father, and the Father in me? the words that I speak unto you, I speak not of myself: but the Father, that dwelleth in me, he doeth the works.

11 Believe me, that I *am* in the Father, and the Father in me: or else believe me, for the very works' sake.

12 Verily, verily, I say unto you, He that believeth on me, the works that I do shall he do also: and greater *works* than these shall he do: because I go unto my Father.

13 And whatsoever ye shall ask in my name, that will I do, that the Father may be glorified in the Son.

14 If ye shall ask any thing in my name, I will do *it*.

15 If ye love me, keep my commandments.

The Church hath great reason to bless the LORD for so sweetly answering *Philip's* question, and thereby removing all doubts on the great subject of CHRIST's oneness with the FATHER. Oh! what a flood of light hath the LORD in this one verse, and by this one declaration, thrown upon it, when JESUS said, *he that hath seen me, hath seen the* FATHER. Blessed oneness indeed! Not only one with the FATHER, and the HOLY GHOST, in the essence of the GODHEAD, but one in the nature, purpose, and design of all the grand causes for which the SON of GOD took into union with himself the holy portion of manhood, and became GOD-Man-Mediator. So that in seeing CHRIST, as CHRIST, the believer sees GOD in all his perfections, attributes, graces, love, and the purposes of his will and pleasure, in every thing relating to the Church before the foundation of the world, in the whole time-state of existence, and the eternity to follow. CHRIST is seen, when properly seen by the enlightened eye of the renewed mind, as the wisdom of GOD, and the power of GOD, 1 Cor. i. 24. yea, the manifold wisdom of GOD. Ephes. iii. 9, 10. Coloss. ii. 3. the holiness of GOD, and the justice of GOD, Rom. iii. 25. the love of GOD, and the faithfulness of GOD, 1 John iv. 9, 10. Deut. vii. 9. 1 John i. 9. In short, all that is communicable of GOD and his glory, can only be seen, and is seen in the face of JESUS CHRIST. 2 Cor. iv. 6.

Reader! do not pass away from this most interesting of all subjects, before that you have first enquired at your own heart, whether you yourself have so seen CHRIST? Every child of GOD, truly regenerated, can have no other views of CHRIST. *Paul*, for himself, saith, that *when it pleased* GOD, *who separated him from his mother's womb to call him by his grace, he revealed his* SON (said Paul) *in me*. Gal. i 15, 16. And it must be the same in a greater or less degree in all.

16 And I will pray the Father, and he shall give you another Comforter, that he may abide with you for ever;

17 *Even* the spirit of truth: whom the world cannot receive, because it seeth him not, neither knoweth him: but ye know him; for he dwelleth with you, and shall be in you.

18 I will not leave you comfortless: I will come to you.

19 Yet a little while, and the world seeth me no more; but ye see me: because I live, ye shall live also,

20 At that day ye shall know that I *am* in my Father, and ye in me, and I in you.

21 He that hath my commandments, and keepeth them, he it is that loveth me: and he that loveth me shall be loved of my Father, and I will love him, and will manifest myself to him.

22 Judas saith unto him, not Iscariot, Lord, how is it that thou wilt manifest thyself unto us, and not unto the world?

23 Jesus answered and said unto him, If a man love me, he will keep my words: and my Father will love him, and we will come unto him, and make our abode with him.

24 He that loveth me not keepeth not my sayings; and the word which ye hear is not mine, but the Father's which sent me.

25 These things have I spoken unto you, being *yet* present with you.

26 But the Comforter, *which is* the Holy Ghost, whom the Father will send in my name, he shall teach you all things, and bring all things to your remembrance, whatsoever I have said unto you.

27 Peace I leave with you, my peace I give unto you: not as the world giveth, give I unto you, let not your heart be troubled, neither let it be afraid.

We here enter upon the great subject of our Lord's Sermon, in what Jesus hath been pleased to teach his Church in relation to the person and glory of God the Holy Ghost. And as the whole efficient government and blessings of the Church are in the hands of this Almighty Lord, we never can be too thankful to our dear Lord, for having dwelt so largely as he hath done, in this and the two following Chapters, (which are but a continuation of the same Sermon,) in instructing the Church concerning his person and ministry. The Reader will perceive by what the Lord Jesus hath said of his coming, and the Father's coming, and the Holy Ghost's coming, and abiding for ever with his people, within the compass of those few verses, (see 16—21.) how needful it must be to have a proper apprehension of God the Holy Ghost, in his person and character. And I hope that he will not complain of my dwelling too particularly on the subject, while I aim to bring before him scriptural testimonies in proof.

That God the Holy Ghost is a person in the Godhead, is a truth to which the whole body of Scripture bears evidence. Indeed it were hardly necessary to go further than to what those words of Jesus afford in confirmation. Christ calls him *another* Comforter; consequently a distinct person from Jesus. And as he was to be sent by the Father, consequently also a distinct person from the Father, verse 26. In both Testaments of Scripture, the personality of God the Holy Ghost is fully proved. He was *seen* in a bodily shape, like a dove, at the baptism of Christ. Luke iii. 22. And there was a visible representation of Him also on the day of Pentecost, when, according to Jesus's promise of Him, he baptized Christ's disciples. Acts i. 5. compared with Acts ii. 3. Many times under both dispensations of Scripture, the Old Testament, and the New, the Lord the Holy Ghost was heard to *speak*. Compare Isaiah vi. 8, 9, 10. with Acts xxviii. 25, 26, 27. Probably the voice which *Daniel* heard on the banks of *Ulai* might be God the Holy Ghost. Dan. viii. 16. But whether in this instance or not, we are expressly told, that it was the Spirit in the Prophets, when they spake *of the sufferings of Christ, and of the glory which should follow.* 1 Pet. i. 10, 11. And *the prophecy came not in old time by the will of man; but holy men of God spake as they were moved by the* Holy Ghost. 2 Pet. i. 21. And we are further told, that when *Philip* was sent into the desert to preach to the Æthiopian; the Spirit spake to him, and said, *Go near and join thyself to this chariot.* Acts viii. 29. So again the Spirit spake to *Peter: behold three men seek thee.* Acts x. 19. So again, while the Church at *Antioch* were waiting upon the Lord, the Holy Ghost said; *Separate me Barnabas and Saul, for the work whereunto I have called them.* Acts xiii. 2. Surely these are all personal acts, and which as clearly and fully prove Personal Identity, as the existence and actions of a man demonstrate the reality of the being and nature of a man.

Indeed in addition to those testimonies, by which the certainty of Person is definable; in relation to God the Holy Ghost on this point, it should be further observed, that the *qualities* ascribed to him, and the *affections* he is spoken of as exercising; come in proof, to put the matter beyond all doubt. Both *actively*, and *passively*, such things are said of him as could never be said but on the certain ground of his being a Person. He is said to *create and give life, to uphold, and to destroy.* Job xxxiii. 4. Psm. civ. 29, 30. He is promised by JESUS, to act as a *teacher*; as a *witness, and to testify of Him.* John xiv. 26. Rom. ix. 1. John xv. 26. And all the affections of joy and grief, of mind, and will, and power; such as being *tempted, resisted,* having *despite done unto him,* and being *blasphemed*; these are all expressly spoken of in reference to the Person of the HOLY GHOST, and what higher proofs can be desired in confirmation of his Personality? Ephes. iv. 30. Rom. viii. 27. 1 Cor. xii. 11. Rom. xv. 13. Acts v. 9. vii. 51. Heb. x. 29. Mark iii. 29. If the Reader considers the subject in the important point of view in which it ought to be considered, he will think with me, that too great a stress, and especially in an age like the present, cannot be laid upon this momentous article of the faith, of every true believer. The Person of GOD the HOLY GHOST is with many scarcely ever considered; and with many more, denied. And yet nothing is more plain in Scripture, than that the LORD the SPIRIT is a Person, equal in every point of view, with the FATHER and the SON, in glory, in dignity, and in every divine perfection: and no less equal in acts of love, and grace, towards the Church. Reader! is it not then our highest concern to give the LORD the honor due unto his name; and daily, hourly to hear what *the* SPIRIT *who speaketh expressly, saith unto the Churches?* 1 Tim. iv. 1. Rev. ii. 29.

From the clear conviction of the Personality of GOD the HOLY GHOST, our next enquiry must be in relation to his *eternal power and* GODHEAD. Having fully shewn, that He is a Being, defined by personal properties; it must follow, that he is GOD: One with the FATHER and the SON in the essence of GODHEAD, over all, GOD blessed for ever. A few of the more prominent Scriptures on this point, will abundantly explain and confirm this doctrine. The several *names* by which the HOLY GHOST is distinguished in Scripture, and which he possesseth in common with the FATHER and the SON, are very high proofs. He is called the *Eternal* SPIRIT; in express reference to himself. Heb. ix. 14. And the name of GOD, is not only his, as One of the Persons in the GODHEAD, Isaiah xl. 28. John iv. 24; but with special regard to the HOLY GHOST, he that is called the HOLY GHOST in one verse, is in the following declared to be GOD. Acts v. 3, 4. *Moses* declared that it was JEHOVAH alone, which led Israel in the wilderness. Deut. xxxii. 12. *Isaiah* confirms the same truth, and saith, that it was *the* HOLY SPIRIT *which led the people with his glorious arm.* Isaiah lxiii. 10. The people are said to have tempted the LORD at the waters of *Meribah.* But the Apostle explains this in reference to the HOLY GHOST. Compare Exod. xvii. 2. with Heb. iii. 7, 8, 9. JEHOVAH declared concerning prophecy, that *if there was a prophet among the people, I, the* LORD, (said JEHOVAH) *will make myself known unto him in a vision.* But an Apostle explains this, and refers the whole gifts of prophecy into the immediate agency of GOD the HOLY GHOST. Compare Numb xii. 6. with 2 Pet. i. 21. Are not these decisive evidences in proof?

To the *names* by which the HOLY GHOST is declared to be GOD, must be added, the *attributes* and *perfections* which confirm the same: every one of which is discoverable as being His, in common with the FATHER and the SON. The *Power* of JEHOVAH is manifested in all the departments of nature, providence, grace, and glory. And hence while we are told, that *it is* GOD *which worketh in his people, both to will and to do of his good pleasure,* we are as expressly told, that it is *the* SPIRIT *which worketh in them, and divideth to every man severally as he will.* Compare Philip. ii. 13. with 1 Cor. xii. 6. 11. The same holds good in the exercise of every other attribute. The LORD's unceasing and everlasting *Presence.* Psm. cxxxix. 1, 2. *Wisdom.* Jude 25. Isaiah xi. 2. Ephes. i. 17. Life-giving, Soul-renewing, *Strength.* Job xxxiii. 14. John vi. 63. Ephes. ii. 1. Rom. viii. 11. In short, there is not one perfection of JEHOVAH definable of GOD-HEAD, but what we find in Scripture, ascribed to the HOLY GHOST.

And what tends yet further to the confirmation of the doctrine, and must, if properly considered, for ever silence every doubt, is this, that the HOLY GHOST is spoken of as possessing and exercising those Almighty Perfections in the same acts as the FATHER and the SON. The FATHER is said *to have life in himself.* John v. 26. The SON is said to be *the life and light of men.* John i. 4. And the HOLY GHOST is said *to give life.* 2 Cor. iii. 6. Psm. civ. 29, 30. And, as in time, so in eternity; for while eternal life is said *to be the gift of* GOD *the* FATHER, Rom. vi. 23. eternal life is said *to be in the* SON, 1 John v. 11. and another scripture saith, that it is *of the* SPIRIT, believers in CHRIST *shall reap life everlasting.* Gal. vi. 8. And what is the natural and unavoidable result of these and the like testimonies, but what the same holy scripture hath elsewhere declared, that *there are Three that bear record in heaven, the* FATHER, *the* WORD, *and the* HOLY GHOST, *and these Three are One.* 1 John v. 7. Hence all the blessed consequences which follow. The Church is *baptized* into the joint name of the HOLY THREE in One. Matt. xxviii. 19. The Church is blessed in their joint name. 2 Cor. xiii. 14. *Redemption* equally ascribed. 2 Cor. v. 19. Ephes. i. 7. Heb. ix. 14. Ephes. v. 30. *Justified.* Rom. viii. 33. Rom. iv. 25. 1 Cor. vi. 11. *Sanctified.* Jude 1. Heb. xiii. 12. 2 Thess. ii. 13. And the *glory* to which the Church will be ultimately brought, the result of the whole: Ephes. i. 4. 2 Cor. viii. 23. 2 Pet. i. 1—4.

From all these undeniable testimonies in confirmation of the *person* and GODHEAD of the HOLY GHOST, may be added the special and personal office of His, in *the everlasting covenant,* which tends to endear him to the Church, in equal degrees of affection, in common with the FATHER and the SON, as well as to entitle Him to an equal degree of adoration, love, obedience, and praise, to all eternity. I need not in this place dwell upon those several *covenant offices* which peculiarly mark the character of GOD the HOLY GHOST, some of which JESUS hath noted in this Sermon, and will meet us in their proper place. I am now simply endeavouring to establish, from scriptural proofs, the certainty of his person and GODHEAD. And therefore I shall only for the present observe, that the Personal act of the HOLY GHOST, in the great work of the regeneration of the Church, becomes an equal demonstration of love, and power, with those of the FATHER's choice of the Church, in giving the Church to his dear SON: and the SON's taking into union with himself his Church, redeeming her, when in the time-state of her being, she had fallen into sin, and became justly exposed to divine wrath. Until this act of regeneration is wrought, the child of GOD is unconscious of his high birth, and character. He knows nothing of the FATHER's love, or the SON's grace, respecting the purposes of JEHOVAH towards the Church from all eternity. And although that everlasting love of GOD, like the river spoken of Psalm xlvi. 3, had been always running; and in the Person of CHRIST had passed through his very heart, in love to his people: yet the whole was hidden from every individual of the Church, until by regeneration, the sinner *dead in trespasses and sins* had his eyes opened, to behold *the fountain opened to the house of David and to the inhabitants of Jerusalem, for sin and for unclean-ness.* Then, and not before, *the streams of that river* are discovered, *which make glad the city of* GOD. Ephes. i. 4. 2 Tim. i. 9. Titus i. 2. Jude 1. Titus iii. 4, 5. Zech xiii. 1.

The several sweet and blessed office characters of the HOLY GHOST, which JESUS hath noticed in this Chapter, I postpone the considera-tion of, to the succeeding Chapters. Enough, I hope, hath been ad-vanced in this, and from scriptural authority, to establish the certainty of His Person, GODHEAD, and the part he hath in the everlasting Covenant. Here for the present I rest, to attend to a few other points contained in this Chapter, which must not be wholly passed by. See Chapters xv. xxvi. xxvii.

I beg the Reader to notice, what the LORD JESUS hath here said, in respect to his coming to them again, after his departure. He pro-mised that he would not leave them comfortless, or as *Orphans.* And though the HOLY GHOST would come, and abide with them for ever, yet this should not supersede his visits. Reader! do not lose sight of this, for it is very blessed. See Song ii. 10, &c. Rev. iii. 20.

And I beg the Reader to notice no less, what a sweet promise fol-lows, in what JESUS hath said, that while men of the world who on his departure would see him no more, his people his redeemed should have a spiritual apprehension of his everlasting presence. *Because I live ye shall live also.* Not only in his eternal nature and GODHEAD doth the SON of GOD live, but as GOD-MAN-Mediator, and as such is the life of his people: for they, as members of his body, live *in* him, and live *from* him, and live *upon* him, and live *to* him. All the springs of spi-ritual life are in Him. All the springs of eternal life are in Him also. Yea, said JESUS, as if to intimate somewhat more; *At that day,* meaning that day when the HOLY GHOST should come upon them and open to their minds the clearer apprehension of these things; *ye shall know, that I am in my* FATHER, *and ye in me, and I in you.* What words are here! Who shall undertake to explain the full extent of the oneness and union which they express? Those unions between the FATHER and the SON, and between CHRIST as CHRIST (that is, GOD and Man in one Person) and his people, had been from everlasting. But in that day, (saith CHRIST,) when the HOLY GHOST shall more fully open to your view my Person and Glory; ye shall know it. Reader! ponder well the subject. Oh! that the LORD the HOLY GHOST may unfold the blessedness of it, more and more, to my heart.

I beg the Reader not to overlook with what tenderness GOD the HOLY GHOST hath mentioned the name of his faithful servant *Judas,* (or *Jude*), that he might not for a moment be mistaken for the traitor. *Not Iscariot!* It is in my esteem a very great mark of the love and regard of the HOLY GHOST to his people.

28 Ye have heard how I said unto you, I go away, and come *again* unto you. If ye loved me, ye would rejoice, because I said, I go unto the Father: for my Father is greater than I.

29 And now I have told you before it come to pass, that when it is come to pass ye might believe.

30 Hereafter I will not talk much with you: for the prince of this world cometh, and hath nothing in me.

31 But that the world may know that I love the Father; and as the Father gave me commandment, even so I do. Arise, let us go hence.

I should not think it necessary to pause over what our LORD hath said in relation to himself and the FATHER, had it not been sometimes perverted, and applied in a way, in which CHRIST never intended the expression. When JESUS saith, *My* FATHER *is greater than I;* he could not mean in respect to his *divine* nature: for the One glorious Essence of JEHOVAH is possessed in common with the whole Persons of the GODHEAD; FATHER, SON, and HOLY GHOST: and the whole are equally great and glorious. Neither in the Personal nature of the GODHEAD could the words be meant. For both the FATHER and the SON are here also equal. And although the FATHER be called by the Church, and by way of distinction from the SON and the HOLY GHOST, the *first* in point of order; yet this is never understood, neither is it ever meant, by way of precedency. GOD the FATHER had not being before the SON and HOLY GHOST: neither though called FATHER in a way of distinction, is it meant to intimate as if he was the cause of the SON's being; both being in their nature and essence eternal. Equal in the eternity of Being, in dignity, power, and glory: and the whole Three Persons possessing in common every attribute which constitutes the GODHEAD. So that under these distinctions of Person and character in relation to the GODHEAD, JESUS could not have reference when speaking of the superiority of his FATHER. But in respect to his Covenant Office, as GOD-Man-Mediator; no question for a moment can be entertained, but what the SON of GOD hath condescended to act in a subordinate character. Hence he is called JEHOVAH's servant: and the Surety of his Church and People. And in all the departments of those offices, every thing manifested that his FATHER was greater than he. For while CHRIST was subjected to all the indignities and sorrows of his Mediator nature and character, GOD the FATHER lost nothing of his original honor and felicity. The comparison therefore, is not made in relation to the *nature* of both in the GODHEAD, for that must be unalterable and impossible to admit of increase or lessening. But the whole refers to the *office-character* which each Person entered into, and engaged for, in the Covenant. And here JESUS might truly say, as he did in this verse; *My* FATHER *is greater than I!*

REFLECTIONS.

ALMIGHTY Preacher!. give me grace to set at thy feet and hear by faith thy sweet and all-powerful voice in this unequalled sermon of thine, causing all the gracious truths of it to sink deep in my heart. Yes! thou dearest LORD! thou art indeed *the way, and the truth, and the life.* None can have access to GOD but by thee. GOD hath set thee up in thy Mediator-character. And in thee, and by thee, as the life and the light of thy people, thy whole Church hath access by one SPIRIT to the FATHER.

Welcome HOLY and Eternal GOD the SPIRIT, to thy Church! Thou art indeed the very Comforter: for LORD thy great work is consolation. Oh! give me to know thee in thy sweet manifestations, in comforting my poor soul under all discouragements, with the suitableness of CHRIST. Yea, LORD, in all thy gifts and graces, make known to me the glory, the grace, the love, the infinite tenderness, and compassion, of my GOD and SAVIOR, in taking of the things of CHRIST, and shewing them to me. Be it my unceasing happiness, to be brought daily, hourly, under thy quickening, refreshing, soul-reviving influences, that I may be filled with that *joy which is unspeakable and full of glory, receiving the end of my faith, even the salvation of my soul.*

FATHER of mercies, and GOD of all grace! blessed, for ever blessed, be that everlasting love, which hath followed up the manifestation of GOD's dear SON, in the manifestation of GOD's holy SPIRIT. *Thanks be unto GOD for his unspeakable gift!*

CHAP. XV.

CONTENTS.

The LORD *continues his Discourse through the whole of this Chapter. Under the Similitude of a Vine and the Branches,* JESUS *describes his Union with his Church. In the close of the Chapter,* JESUS *again speaks of the coming of the* HOLY GHOST.

I AM the true vine, and my Father is the husbandman.

2 Every branch in me that beareth not fruit he taketh away : and every *branch* that beareth fruit, he purgeth it, that it may bring forth more fruit.

3 Now ye are clean through the word which I have spoken unto you.

4 Abide in me, and I in you, as the branch cannot bear fruit of itself, except it abide in the vine ; no more can ye, except ye abide in me.

5 I am the vine, ye *are* the branches, he that abideth in me, and I in him, the same bringeth

forth much fruit: for without me ye can do nothing.

6 If a man abide not in me, he is cast forth as a branch, and is withered: and men gather them, and cast *them* into the fire, and they are burned.

7 If ye abide in me, and my words abide in you, ye shall ask what ye will, and it shall be done unto you.

8 Herein is my Father glorified, that ye bear much fruit; so shall ye be my disciples.

Nothing can be more beautiful in the illustration of that sweet and precious doctrine, of the oneness and union of CHRIST with his Church, than the figure of the Vine and its Branches, which the LORD JESUS hath here been pleased to explain it by. He is indeed the One true Vine, and as the Prophet calls him, the *Branch;* to which the Evangelist, under the same authority, gives testimony when saying: the *Branch* (for so it should have been rendered, and so it is indeed in the margin of our old Bibles,) *from on high hath visited us.* Luke i. 78. See Isaiah xi. 1. Jerem. xxiii. 5. Zech. iii. 8.—vi. 12. And it is a very blessed part in this figure, wherein JESUS speaks of his FATHER, under the character of the Husbandman. For all CHRIST is, as CHRIST, is of JEHOVAH. Hence the Prophet, speaking of the *sufferings* of CHRIST, under this similitude, saith; *And the Branch that thou madest so strong for thyself, it is burnt with fire and cut down.* Psm. lxxx. 15, 16. And another servant of the LORD, when speaking under the same spirit of prophecy, in relation to the *glories* of CHRIST, saith: *In that day the Branch of the* LORD *shall be beautiful and glorious.* Isaiah iv. 2. It hath been supposed, that in the memorable prophecy of the dying Patriarch *Jacob,* the *Vine* unto which the foal he said should be bound; referred to the same. And when it be considered what went before in the Patriarch's prophecy of the *Shiloh,* to whom the gathering of the people should be, there seems a great connection with the whole. Gen. xlix. 10, 11. Matt. xxi. 2, 7. I do not think it necessary to dwell upon the several characters of a Vine and its branches, by way of illustrating the doctrine, concerning the union and communion between CHRIST and his people. Every way by which the dependance of the Church is shewn to be wholly on CHRIST; a branch on a Vine strikingly displays. It springs from the Vine, derives all its life, sap, moisture, fruitfulness, wholly from the Vine. And JESUS is all this, and infinitely more, to his people. In his *divine nature,* deep rooted in his own self-existence, in common with the FATHER, and the HOLY GHOST. In his *human nature,* the Branch of growth arising from the root of Jesse. And in *both,* the source of all fruitfulness, to the Church, in time, and to all eternity. Hail! thou LORD of *Joseph, the fruitful bough, whose branches run over the wall!* Gen. xlix. 22.

I detain the Reader to remark to him, that the *second* verse should be read, as the original will truly allow; *Every branch that beareth not fruit in me.* For there can be no Branch, really, and truly in CHRIST, but what must bear fruit. But there may be many, that appear as branches in the LORD's garden the Church; and yet have no union with him. So that what fruit soever they bear, it is not in CHRIST, neither from CHRIST; and therefore their root is in themselves, and shall be, as *rottenness, and their blossom go up as the dust.* Isaiah v. 24. Deut. xxxii. 32. Whereas the true branches, in the true Vine, derive all *from* the Vine. Every portion of life, and fruitfulness, come from CHRIST. *From me* (the LORD saith,) *is thy fruit found.* Hosea xiv. 8. Reader! be very jealous over your own heart, on these grand points. See to it, that not only in the first grafting upon CHRIST, when taken from the old olive tree, which is wild by nature, thou art grafted contrary to nature, (being wholly an act of free sovereign grace in GOD, and nothing of man concurring with it,) into this true Olive Tree, CHRIST JESUS; but in all the after actings of life, see to it that it is all upon CHRIST, and all from CHRIST. Grace is no self acting principle. All our fresh springs are in Him. *Of his fulness do we all receive, and grace for grace;* meaning, that we need daily, yea momently, grace from JESUS, to act upon and keep alive, the grace we have before had from JESUS. CHRIST is all. Rom. xi. 24. Psm. lxxxvii. 7. John i. 16.

I detain the Reader one moment longer to remark, respecting what our LORD saith; *Abide in me, and I in you.* I humbly apprehend, that this is not a mere precept of CHRIST, but rather a promise. JESUS meant by the expression to say, that by his HOLY SPIRIT, which he was going from them purposely to send, they should be enabled to abide in him. The words, according to my view, are similar to that sweet scripture of CHRIST, when JESUS *breathed on them, and said unto them, Receive ye the* HOLY GHOST. John xx. 22. This was no precept: commanding them to receive what they had no power to take hold of, without the LORD making them receivers, of what he communicated. In like manner here. *Abide in me.* JESUS undertakes for them, that they shall abide in him. *And I in you.* How, but from his own sole grace, could they receive this abiding of CHRIST in them? But if the LORD JESUS with the precept, wills them into the apprehension of the blessing; and while he thus speaks, communicates the power to receive, and enjoy: how very blessed are our LORD's words read in this sense? Ye *shall* abide in me; and I *will* abide in you. And all this is in perfect conformity to our LORD's own everlasting Covenant with his people; in which he hath undertaken, both for himself, and for them. *And I will make an everlasting Covenant with them; that I will not turn away from them to do them good: but I will put my fear in their hearts, that they shall not depart from me.* Jerem. xxxii. 40. Here we behold the security. The LORD engageth (and well it is that he doth) for both. I *will* not, saith the LORD, and they *shall* not. I leave the Reader to his own conclusions, under GOD the HOLY GHOST's teaching, on this subject. But I venture to observe, that there are numberless portions in the word of GOD, which in their first view, however they may seemingly appear as precepts; yet, explained upon Gospel principles, will be found more in the sweet language of promises, and such as tend to refresh, rather than alarm the soul, in a conscious inability of performance. See Matt. v. 48. 1 Pet. i. 15.

9 As the Father hath loved me, so have I loved you: continue ye in my love.

10 If ye keep my commandments, ye shall abide in my love; even as I have kept my Father's commandments, and abide in his love.

11 These things have I spoken unto you, that my joy might remain in you, and *that* your joy might be full.

12 This is my commandment, that ye love one another, as I have loved you.

13 Greater love hath no man than this, that a man lay down his life for his friends.

14 Ye are my friends, if ye do whatsoever I command you.

15 Henceforth I call you not servants; for the servant knoweth not what his lord doeth; but I have called you friends: for all things that I have heard of my Father I have made known unto you.

16 Ye have not chosen me, but I have chosen you, and ordained you, that ye should go and bring forth fruit, and *that* your fruit should remain: that whatsoever ye shall ask of the Father in my name, he may give it you.

17 These things I command you, that ye love one another.

18 If the world hate you, ye know that it hated me before *it hated* you.

19 If ye were of the world, the world would love his own, but because ye are not of the world, but I have chosen you out of the world, therefore the world hateth you.

20 Remember the word that I said unto you, The servant is not greater than his lord: if they have persecuted me, they will also persecute you: if they have kept my saying, they will keep your's also.

21 But all these things will they do unto you for my name's sake, because they know not him that sent me.

22 If I had not come and spoken unto them, they had not had sin: but now they have no cloke for their sin.

23 He that hateth me hateth my Father also.

24 If I had not done among them the works which none other man did, they had not had sin: but now they have both seen and hated both me and my Father.

25 But *this cometh to pass,* that the word might be fulfilled that is written in their law, They hated me without a cause.

Some of the many blessed things here spoken of by our LORD, are so sweet and plain, as to need no comment: indeed their beautiful simplicity, would suffer by one. I shall only therefore venture to offer an observation or two, which may not at first view appear so obvious as others.

When our LORD saith, in the opening of this passage, that as the FATHER hath loved him, so hath CHRIST loved his Church: it is very proper that we should consider, in what sense JESUS meant it. The love here spoken of in relation to the FATHER's affection towards JESUS, cannot be supposed to be the love he bears to the SON, as GOD. For in this sense, none but GOD himself, can apprehend the nature or extent of it. We must be blessed with infinite capacities, before that we can have the smallest conceptions, concerning any one thing, that is in its nature infinite. This, therefore, is not the love to which JESUS refers. Neither is it to be supposed, that the FATHER's love of CHRIST, in the Personal glory of GOD-Man-Mediator, as CHRIST, is the love here meant. This must far exceed CHRIST's love of the Church. But the sense seems to be, that the love JESUS here speaks of, in relation to his Church, is of *the same nature and kind,* though not in equal degree. Under these limitations, and with an eye to CHRIST, as the predisposing cause, in whom, and for whose sake, GOD the FATHER loved the Church before all worlds, and chose the Church in CHRIST before all worlds; there is nothing upon earth can be more blessed, than the assurance JESUS hath here given: both of his FATHER's love of Him, and his love of the Church in Him. It is blessed, yea very blessed, to ponder the subject in this point of view! JESUS desires the Church to keep always in remembrance, that as the FATHER loveth Him, in this precious view, as the Head of his body the Church, and as such CHRIST hath been from everlasting infinitely delightful in his sight: so, saith JESUS, is my Church dear to me, as my FATHER's gift, and as the several members of my mystical body. Reader! fold up in your bosom those precious words of JESUS, for your unceasing meditation and delight!

I beg the Reader next to notice, what Jesus hath said, in respect
to *the keeping his commandments, by way of abiding in his love.* Not,
as if the love of Jesus was suspended on any act of his people: for
this would be to subvert the whole plan of the Gospel; and to make
the grace of God to depend upon the free will of man. In this case,
human merit, and not divine favor, would become the standard of
acceptance. Reader! I hope that you have not so learned Christ!
Christ's love, is the sole cause of ours. And as we never obtained
that love, because we kept his commandments: so our continuing in
that love doth not rest, or depend upon, our present or future deservings, more than our past or original merit. The word *If,* in the beginning of the verse, *if ye keep my commandments,* seem to be used
by Christ in a similar way and manner to the words of his servant
the Apostle Paul, in his Epistle to the Hebrews: not as forming a
cause, or *condition,* but rather as the *consequence.* For speaking of
Christ and his house, he saith, *whose house are we,* if *we hold fast the
confidence.* Heb. iii. 6. So again, verse 14, *We are made partakers
of* Christ (saith he) *if we hold the beginning of our confidence stedfast
unto the end.* In both those instances, it is our mercy, that neither our
being of the house of Christ, built on Him the foundation, nor our
being made partakers of Christ as part of himself; depend upon the
least act of ours. These things were all settled before the foundation
of the world; being chosen in Him, that we should be holy, and without blame, before God and our Father in love. Ephes. i. 4. But
the Apostle in both places is speaking of the *result* of things, and not
the *cause,* or *condition* of them; but as of a thing actually enjoyed.
It is, as if he had said, we manifestly prove that we are Christ's,
because we remain on the foundation: and we shew to all the world,
that we are made partakers of Christ, because the sweet fruits of his
grace, and love, are manifested in our lives, and conversation. In
like manner, the keeping Christ's commandments are not meant
as the cause, of abiding in his love; but his love is the cause, how
his people are enabled to keep his commandments, and abide in him:
and these become so many proofs and evidences that they are
His, and who continue in his love.

I hope the Reader can, and doth, enter with me, into a suitable
apprehension of the sweet character, Jesus makes use of, as a friend.
Jesus is indeed *the friend that loveth at all times, and one that sticketh
closer than a brother.* Prov. xvii. 17.—xviii. 24. And who that
considers, how from everlasting, Jesus engaged for his Church, as a
surety; how he died for us; paid all our debts for us; bought us out
of the hands of infinite justice; married our nature; is gone to
heaven, to take possession of it in our name; will come again to
receive us to himself, that where he is, we may be also: and in the
mean time, supplies all our wants, answers all our necessities; and
in every circumstance of life, is a constant friend, a faithful friend,
an unchanging friend, an everlasting friend: who that thinks of these
things, but must enter into a proper apprehension of what the Lord
Jesus saith, when he calleth his children friends? Dearest Jesus!
how shall I enumerate the thousandth part of the acts of the most dis-
interested friendship, which thou hast manifested to my soul? What
a Friend was the Son of God to our nature, when he passed by that
of angels, and took on him the seed of Abraham? What friendship

was that, when JESUS became poor, that we through his poverty might
be made rich? What love, so unequalled, to die, the just for the unjust, to bring us to GOD! And what love like thine; when though all
forsake us, JESUS will never leave nor forsake his redeemed? Yea,
LORD! though we so often believe not, yet thou abidest faithful:
JESUS cannot, will not, deny himself. Shall I not say then as the
wise man; *Thine own friend and thy Father's friend forsake not!*
Prov. xxvii. 10. Yes! blessed LORD, every where, and in all things,
I will speak of thee, with the Church of old, and say, *This is
my beloved, and this is my friend, O daughters of Jerusalem!*
Song v. 16.

26 But when the Comforter is come, whom I
will send unto you from the Father, *even* the spirit
of truth, which proceedeth from the Father, he
shall testify of me.

27 And ye also shall bear witness, because ye
have been with me from the beginning.

If the Reader recollects what was observed, in the preceding
Chapter, on the one, chief, and great subject, of this Sermon of our
LORD's, namely, concerning the Person, GODHEAD, Work, and Ministry of the HOLY GHOST; he will remember, that it was reserved
to the subsequent parts of CHRIST's discourse, to notice the several
offices of GOD the SPIRIT, as they were mentioned. Now here, in
those verses, the LORD JESUS takes observation of *two* of them,
namely, as the *Comforter*, and as the SPIRIT *of truth.* I therefore beg
the Reader to remark with me, some few particulars relating to those
blessed offices of GOD the HOLY GHOST.

First, as the Comforter. Now it is the special work of GOD the
SPIRIT, to bring comfort into the conscience of the LORD's people, in
taking of the things of CHRIST and shewing to them; whereby he
fills their hearts with joy and peace in believing, while he makes
them to abound in hope through his own sovereign power. His very
employment is consolation. And hence nothing can be more suited
to him as a name, than the HOLY GHOST the Comforter! And, if a
child of GOD at any time feels refreshed with the consolations of JESUS,
or the contemplation of the love of GOD the FATHER; these precious
things are of His working. And hence we are taught to pray for
the quickenings of the SPIRIT; because the LORD the HOLY GHOST
by those sweet influences, opens a communion between CHRIST and
out souls. He manifests the love of the FATHER and the Son to the
heart; and thus by holding up to our view their love, he awakens his
own graces in our hearts, and leads forth the actings of faith and
love in them, upon the Persons of the GODHEAD. Oh! the blessedness of the HOLY GHOST, when acting as the Comforter of the
Church! What are all the promises and encouragements in the
Word, until they are opened and applied by the LORD the SPIRIT?
Blessed GOD! do thou prove thyself to my soul's joy, as the HOLY
GHOST the Comforter, in all thy sevenfold gifts; that by opening
and keeping open, a continual communion between CHRIST and my
soul, I may hourly rejoice in hope of the glory of GOD.

Secondly. The Lord Jesus speaks of him as *the* Spirit *of truth,* to lead into all truth. And what a gracious, compassionate, and wise office, is this? How would the poor, dark ,ignorant, and senseless children of men, under the Adam-nature of a fallen sinful state, ever have the least apprehension of divine things, but from his divine teaching? Oh! thou Matchless Instructor! hadst thou not shewn me the utterly lost estate of my poor nature by the fall, how should I have ever known my ruin and misery? And hadst thou not opened mine eyes to see the glory and suitableness of the Lord Jesus, what should I ever have apprehended of his glory, and my need of him? Yea! gracious God the Spirit! hadst thou not warmed my soul with his love, as well as informed my understanding by thy grace, thousands of errors would have remained; and though I had obtained an head knowledge, yet no heart influence would have followed, but from thy sovereign saving power. But now, dearest Lord, whilst thou art mercifully pleased to be to me a Spirit of truth, leading to the right apprehension of all truth, and a Spirit of grace, leading to the right performance of all prayer; then the whole comes home warmed and endeared to my heart. I hear the voice behind me, and I feel a power within me, when at any time exercised with doubts or misgivings, saying, *This is the way,* (even Christ the way,) *walk ye in it, when ye turn to the right hand, and when ye turn to the left.* Isaiah xxx. 21. See chap. xvi. 8.

REFLECTIONS.

Reader! do not fail to observe the intimate oneness and union between Christ and his Church. The vine and its branches are not more closely formed in one, than Jesus and his people. Indeed, there are no figures, no images, either in nature or art, which can fully come up to the resemblance. All figures must fall short of the reality. But while we observe the closeness of union, let you and I be still more anxious to know whether we are the happy partakers of it. Are we indeed One with Christ, and Christ with us? *He that is joined to the* Lord *is one* Spirit. One principle actuates both. What Jesus loves, we love; what Jesus hates, we hate. We look to Jesus for all things, and desire to eye Jesus in all things. Moreover, if one Spirit be in both, we shall undertake nothing but in his strength, and seek nothing but his glory. And as the branch wholly hangs upon, and is kept alive by the vine, so all our graces are kept alive by life *in* Jesus, and communications *from* Jesus. Oh! for grace to know these things in a lively, active, spiritual enjoyment of them, that we may be increasing in desires after him, and loosening from every thing that is not in him, till we come to see him as he is, and dwell with him for ever.

Blessed Holy Comforter of the Lord's people! Gracious Spirit of truth to lead into all truth! Oh! grant to me the knowledge of my Lord under all his sweet and precious offices! Send out Lord! thy light and thy truth to guide my poor soul continually! And, oh! for the daily, hourly renewing of the Holy Ghost, to be shed abundantly upon the churches and people, through Jesus Christ our Savior. Amen.

CHAP. XVI.

CONTENTS.

The LORD's *Sermon is continued through this Chapter, and here it is ended.* JESUS *comforts his Disciples with many sweet and precious Promises, and again dwells upon the gracious consolations which they should receive from the* HOLY GHOST.

THESE things have I spoken unto you, that ye should not be offended.

2 They shall put you out of the synagogues: yea, the time cometh, that whosoever killeth you will think that he doeth God service.

3 And these things will they do unto you, be-·cause they have not known the Father, nor me.

4 But these things have I told you, that when the time shall come, ye may remember that I told you of them: and these things I said unto you at the beginning, because I was with you.

5 But now I go my way to him that sent me; and none of you asketh me, Whither goest thou?

6 But because I have said these things unto you, sorrow hath filled your heart.

7 Nevertheless, I tell you the truth; it is expe-dient for you that I go away: for if I go not away, the Comforter will not come unto you: but if I depart, I will send him unto you.

I pray the Reader to remark how JESUS dwells upon the expediency of his departure, on the Church's account. *It is expedient for you that I go away.* So that the LORD doth not at all mention the joy that was before him, in returning to his FATHER, neither of the felicity to which he was going, in being received by the faithful gone before, who would come forth to congratulate the King on his taking possession of his kingdom. We hear of none of those things in the LORD's farewell, but all that JESUS is discoursing upon is, concerning his dear children which he was about to leave behind. As if the whole heart of JESUS he would leave behind him. Precious LORD! Oh! for grace to have it always in remembrance.

8 And when he is come, he will reprove the world of sin, and of righteousness, and of judge-ment;

9 Of sin, because they believe not on me;

10 Of righteousness, because I go to my Father, and ye see me no more :

11 Of judgement, because the prince of this world is judged.

12 I have yet many things to say unto you, but ye cannot bear them now.

13 Howbeit, when he, the Spirit of truth, is come, he will guide you into all truth: for he shall not speak of himself; but whatsoever he shall hear, *that* shall he speak ; and he will shew you things to come.

14 He shall glorify me : for he shall receive of mine, and shall shew *it* unto you.

Reader! It must have been a matter of great importance, that the Lord Jesus in this farewell sermon, dwelt so much upon the Person and Offices of God the Holy Ghost. Never would Christ have described him so particularly, had it not been, that his Church might be taught every thing concerning Him, in whose teachings and consolations they were so highly concerned. I pray the Reader to indulge me in my endeavors to follow the footsteps of the Lord Jesus, in marking some at least, of the several features of character, by which God the Spirit, according to the Lord's representation of him, was to be known.

The *regeneration*, which God the Holy Ghost, in his covenant office-character, engaged to perform on the whole Church of Christ, no doubt comprehended, (as the greater includes the less,) all his blessed work. And this sovereign act, as hath been already observed, (see note on John xiv. 16—27.) is no doubt in point of importance, equal to the electing love of God the Father, or the betrothing and redeeming love of God the Son. But in the Almighty act of *regeneration*, is included every other office of God the Spirit. For as an Apostle under his authority hath said, in all the manifestations of the divine life, in which the Church *is changed into the same image from glory to glory; it is, even as by the* Spirit *of the* Lord. 2 Cor. iii. 18.

It will not be improper, neither I hope unprofitable, to take a brief view of some of those office-characters of God the Holy Ghost, which have not been already noticed, and which the Lord Jesus hath specially marked in this sermon. They will serve in some degree to manifest the love of the Spirit to the Church.

I pass over, (because not spoken of in this place by Jesus,) the consideration of the work of God the Holy Ghost on the Person of Christ. This forms a separate subject, but yet highly worthy of the first attention when speaking of the office-characters of God the Spirit, in relation to the everlasting covenant. He it was who formed the human nature of the Son of God in the womb. Matt. i. 18, 20. Luke i. 35. He it was who consecrated Christ to the Messiahship.

Isaiah xi. 1, 2. Acts x. 38. He it was who anointed Christ to all his offices, and so Jesus himself declared. Isaiah lxi. 1. with Luke iv. 18. He it was who wrought with Jesus in all his miracles. Matt. xii. 28. Acts x. 38. who wrought with Christ and the Father in his resurrection. Rom. i. 4. viii. 11. And He it is who now proclaims Christ in the hearts of his redeemed, when, like Christ in his resurrection from the dead, they are quickened from the death of sin by the Holy Ghost. Ephes. ii. 1. For none can say, *that* Jesus *is the* Lord, *but by the* Holy Ghost. 1 Cor. xii. 3. All these, and others of a like nature mentioned in scripture, are in proof of the work of God the Holy Ghost upon the Person of Jesus; and in a subject, where at any time the Sacred Writers are speaking of his office-characters in the covenant, these things ought not to be overlooked or forgotten. But the Lord Jesus in this sermon, mentions only his gracious acts towards, and over the Church; and therefore it is to such only I would call more particularly the Reader's attention.

The Lord Jesus begins the subject here in speaking of the office-work of the Holy Ghost, with observing how he will work conviction in the heart on account of *sin;* how he will proclaim *righteousness,* even the personal righteousness of Jesus, as all-effectual and compleat in the great work of redemption; and of *judgment* in the fullest establishment of the Lord Jesus, as Judge of quick and dead, which the Jews had attempted to call in question and deny.

Reader! it is a blessed confirmation of the truths of God, when the outward ministry of God's word, is inwrought in the heart by the inward effect. Will you allow me to ask, whether God the Spirit hath so glorified Christ in your heart by such testimonies of his office-work as these, in receiving of Christ's and shewing unto you? The question finds an answer as luminous as though written with a sun beam, when God the Holy Ghost hath truly wrought these operations in the heart and conscience. He proves to a man's own feelings, the filth and guilt, and the loathsome nature of sin. He holds up Jesus in such views of his glory, greatness, fulness, suitableness, and all-sufficiency, as determine the soul to behold in him, every thing suited to the want and misery of the sinner. He shews not only the ability, but the readiness of Jesus to receive, and bless the sinner in his low estate. And at length so overrules all the arguments, which sin, unbelief, the world, or the powers of darkness raise up in the way, that the heart is constrained to come to Him; and the soul, that in the first awakenings, under the conviction of sin, trembled with apprehensions to approach; at length finds the Holy Ghost witnessing to the gracious estate of an interest in Christ, from the gift of God the Father, *before the foundation of the world.* Gal. iv. 6. Rom. viii. 14—17.

I pray the Reader to notice another of the blessed employments of the Holy Ghost in his office-work, namely, in *glorifying* Christ Jesus. And how is this done? Surely in the most blessed way and manner that the imagination can conceive. God the Spirit holds up the Lord Jesus as a most compleat Savior. And while he shews us the sinfulness of our nature, he shews the holiness of Jesus; and with these different views, he so graciously works in the soul by his persuasive power and grace, that he inclines the heart of the true Israel of God to receive Christ, and to barter sin for righteousness, and joy for sorrow; that while Jesus is glorified, the sinner is made happy; and thus this office of the Holy Ghost is most compleatly answered.

I have known, however, some precious souls at a loss to apprehend what is meant by the Holy Ghost's receiving of Christ, and shewing to them. They have been fearful that the application hath not been made. But, if they were to attend to the scripture words and not their own, and as Jesus hath stated this office-work of God the Spirit, the difficulty would vanish. The Lord does not say, that the Holy Ghost shall glorify him by receiving of his, and *applying* to his people; but shewing them. And what is it to shew the people? Certainly it is simply this, and no more. The Holy Ghost shews the sinner his own wants, and Christ's suitableness to supply those wants, and readiness in supplying them. And thus having shewn that a rich Savior is suited for a poor sinner, and a poor sinner for a rich Savior; sweetly and powerfully the blessed Spirit inclines the heart of the needy sinner to receive, and belief to the salvation of his soul. Hence Christ is glorified, and the sinner is made happy. This is to believe *the record* God *hath given of his* Son!

15 All things that the Father hath are mine: therefore said I, that he shall take of mine, and shew *it* unto you.

16 A little while, and ye shall not see me: and again, a little while, and ye shall see me, because I go to the Father.

17 Then said *some* of his disciples among themselves, What is this that he saith unto us? A little while, and ye shall not see me: and again, a little while, and ye shall see me: and, Because I go to the Father?

18 They said therefore, What is this that he saith, A little while? we cannot tell what he saith.

19 Now Jesus knew that they were desirous to ask him, and said unto them, Do ye enquire among yourselves of that I said, A little while, and ye shall not see me: and again, a little while, and ye shall see me?

20 Verily, verily, I say unto you, That ye shall weep and lament, but the world shall rejoice; and ye shall be sorrowful, but your sorrow shall be turned into joy.

21 A woman, when she is in travail hath sorrow,

because her hour is come: but as soon as she is delivered of the child, she remembereth no more the anguish, for joy that a man is born into the world.

22 And ye now therefore have sorrow: but I will see you again, and your heart shall rejoice, and your joy no man taketh from you. '

23 And in that day ye shall ask me nothing. Verily, verily, I say unto you, Whatsoever ye shall ask the Father in my name, he will give *it* you.

24 Hitherto have ye asked nothing in my name: ask, and ye shall receive, that your joy may be full.

25 These things have I spoken unto you in proverbs: but the time cometh when I shall no more speak unto you in proverbs, but I shall shew you plainly of the Father.

26 At that day ye shall ask in my name: and I say unto you, that I will pray the Father for you:

27 For the Father himself loveth you, because ye have loved me, and have believed that I came out from God.

28 I came forth from the Father, and am come into the world: again, I leave the world, and go to the Father.

In what a full and comprehensive manner the LORD JESUS here speaks, at the opening of this paragraph, in relation to the common interest and property the FATHER and himself possessed *in all things;* and which included in it, all the persons of his Church and people. And, Reader! what a sweet thought is it for you, for me, for the whole Church, to keep in everlasting remembrance; that both the persons and the things which CHRIST takes such interest in, for his Church's present and eternal welfare, are as much the FATHER's, and in which He takes equal regard with that of his SON; Oh! for grace to know this, and to live in the constant enjoyment of it!

I beg the Reader particularly to notice, what the LORD JESUS hath here said concerning prayer. He first observes, that *at that day, ye shall ask me nothing.* Not that he meant to discourage their coming to him in prayer, but rather on the contrary, for he soon after adds: *Ask, and ye shall receive, that your joy may be full.* But according to my view, it forms a beautiful and an affectionate method of JESUS,

to invite them to be very often making their requests known unto
him.　He had just before said, that he was going away from them;
that *they should weep and lament, while the world would rejoice.*
Well! how will the Lord keep up their spirits during these exercises?　This shall be the way.　At that day you shall ask me nothing, but what I have already outrun your expectations in giving;
agreeably to that sweet promise, Isaiah lxv. 24.　It is as if Jesus
had said, I shall be so much with you in spirit by the Holy Ghost,
whom I am going away to send to you, and he will endite all your
petitions for you, in teaching you what your wants are, and my fulness to supply; that I shall be daily expecting to hear from you,
and in comparison to what I expect to hear from you, hitherto you
have asked nothing in my name; *Ask, therefore, and ye shall receive,
that your joy may be full.*

And I pray the Reader to observe yet further, in confirmation, that
this was Christ's meaning; that they should be frequent and clamorous at the mercy seat; *I say not unto you that I will pray for you,*
(said Christ,) *for the* Father *himself loveth you, because ye have
loved me, and have believed that I came out from* God.　What a tender,
blessed method, was here of Jesus, in shewing them how his whole
heart was with them, and that he took part in all that concerned
them.　Jesus did not mean to say, that his office of Intercessor would
cease when he got to heaven.　So far from it, that it was one of the
great purposes for which he was going there.　Jesus would bear them
unceasingly upon his breast, and upon his heart, as the Jewish high
priest bore the names of the twelve tribes, when he went in before the
mercy-seat.　But saith Jesus, my Father takes such an interest, as
well as myself, in all that concerns you, that all your causes and interests must be eternally safe and secure.　Reader! put the whole
of those words of Jesus together, and look at them in one united view.
I say not unto you, that I will pray the Father *for you.*　I need not
say it.　You know it.　You know my whole heart is with you.　Nay,
if I leave you, it is on this very account, to carry up every thing that
concerns you before my Father, and to see the whole of my grand
designs for which I came on earth, accomplished for you.　And
moreover, though I shall unceasingly be thus engaged for you in
heaven, in my office of an unchanging priesthood; yet such is my
Father's love to you, because ye have loved me, that whatsoever ye
shall ask the Father in my Name, he will give it you.　So that your
persons and your concerns are everlastingly secured, both in my Father's love and mine.　And I will send the Holy Ghost, who shall
not only act in my place and room, and shew you all your wants
and my glory, with my infinite readiness to supply; but He shall
endite all the letters and petitions you send me, and such a blessed in-
tercourse shall be kept up between me and you, by reason of these
things, that what He teacheth you to pray for upon earth, shall be in
exact correspondence to my intercession for you in heaven.　Reader!
what saith your heart's joy to this view of the subject?　*Have you so
learned* Christ, *and heard him, and been taught of Him, as the
truth is in* Jesus?　Ephes. iv. 20, 21.

29 His disciples said unto him, Lo, now speakest thou plainly, and speakest no proverb.

30 Now are we sure that thou knowest all things, and needest not that any man should ask thee: by this we believe that thou camest forth from God.

31 Jesus answered them, Do ye now believe?

32 Behold, the hour cometh, yea, is now come, that ye shall be scattered every man to his own, and shall leave me alone: and yet I am not alone, because the Father is with me.

33 These things I have spoken unto you, that in me ye might have peace, in the world ye shall have tribulation: but be of good cheer; I have overcome the world.

It should seem by those acknowledgements of the Apostles, that now they understood plainly all that Jesus meant, and his sweet words were no longer proverbs; as Jesus just before had said they were, (verse 25.) but plain, and suited to their apprehension. And hence I venture to suppose, (but by no means to speak positively,) that the Lord was pleased as he drew near the close of his sermon to enlarge their minds, that they might have more clear and extended views of this great subject, on which he had been speaking to them. And, Reader! it will be our mercy in like manner, on this glorious view Jesus hath here given of the Person, Work, and Offices of God the Holy Ghost; if you and I can join issue with the Apostles, and say, *Now speaketh our* Lord *plainly, and speaketh no parable. Now are we sure that* Jesus *knoweth all things, and needeth not that any man should ask him. By this we believe that He came forth from* God!

It will form I hope no unprofitable conclusion in our Commentary upon this blessed sermon of Christ, if we briefly gather into one point of view, some of the precious things which Jesus hath left in it to his Church, concerning the Person and love-offices of God the Holy Ghost. Sure I am, the review of the whole will be profitable, if so be, (and which I humbly beg both for myself and Reader,) that the Almighty Spirit of whom I write, shall graciously condescend to be our teacher.

We have beheld in these chapters, with what a world of tenderness the Lord Jesus hath introduced the subject of the coming of the Holy Ghost, and how Jesus before his departure brought them into an acquaintance with his person, and nature, and offices. We have seen how minutely the Lord Jesus hath dwelt upon the many distinguishing testimonies of character, by which the Holy Ghost should be known. And we have discovered at the close of our Lord's discourse on this most interesting subject, that so much grace from the Lord accompanied his divine instruction on the same, that the Apostles entered into a perfect apprehension both of the person and coming of the Holy Ghost. Here then I would beg the Reader to pause, and before we pass away from our review of the same sermon of CHRIST, which was made so blessed to them; I would very affectionately ask the Reader, as I desire to put the same question to my own heart, with what sentiments do we close the LORD's discourse, concerning the same momentous truths of GOD, in our apprehensions of GOD the HOLY GHOST?

Behold him in the eternity of his nature, and essence, and GOD-HEAD. One of the HOLY undivided Three, which bear record in heaven. 1 John v. 7. Contemplate Him in the numberless, undeniable testimonies, which have been brought before you of his Person, through both volumes of Scripture. Mark well his special *offices*, in his covenant character as relating to the Church. And here most eminently, and indeed as comprehending every other, in the great work of *regeneration;* which sovereign and Almighty act becomes so essential to every child of GOD to partake in, that not a single spiritual mercy can we lay claim to, until this is wrought, and when done, CHRIST with all his blessings and benefits are ours. For so it is written in the scripture. *To them,* (saith the Apostle,) *that have obtained like precious faith with us through the righteousness of* GOD *and our* SAVIOR JESUS CHRIST: *Grace and peace be multiplied; according as His divine power hath given unto us all things that pertain unto life and godliness, through the knowledge of Him that hath called us to glory and virtue; being made partakers of the divine nature.* 2 Pet. i. 1, 2, 3, 4.

And when this gracious act is wrought in the soul of him, who is the highly favoured object of JEHOVAH's love, in his Threefold character of Person; all the after manifestations of the HOLY GHOST, as might be expected, are made to maintain and carry on that divine nature, of which, as the HOLY GHOST by the Apostle hath said, the regenerated are made partakers. From this commencement of the renewed life, when quickened by the SPIRIT in the souls of those who were before dead in trespasses and sins, Ephes. ii. 1. the whole is dated in every subsequent act of grace. The HOLY GHOST, as JESUS hath described him, becomes to all on whom his regenerating mercy hath passed, the *Comforter;* to give joy and peace in believing, and the abounding in hope, through his sovereign power. He becomes the SPIRIT *of truth,* when errors creep into the mind, *to guide into all truth.* The *Glorifier of* JESUS, in holding him up in all his glory to his people, and secretly and sweetly inclining their hearts to believe in his name. The *Remembrancer* of JESUS, in bringing again to the forgetful minds of his people, some past manifestations of JESUS, and supporting them in the recollection with abiding hopes of future love-tokens from the LORD, in the review of former. In short, as a teacher, a *spirit of grace and supplication;* of *holiness* and *sanctification;* an *helper in the infirmities of his people;* and an *earnest* and *seal* of the promised inheritance; and in the numberless, nameless ways, by which His Almighty Ministry is carried on, from the first moment of regeneration until grace is finished in glory; the whole efficient work of the Church, in her ministers, ordinances, and people; all is GOD's the SPIRIT. *He it is that worketh in us both to will and to do of his good pleasure!* Philip. ii. 13.

Reader! what saith your experience to these things! Are the Apostles conclusions our conclusions? their views of the HOLY GHOST our views of the HOLY GHOST? Or, after all, the LORD JESUS hath said in this most blessed Chapter concerning Him, do we say of JESUS, as they did of the Prophet's Sermon, *Ah,* LORD GOD! *doth he not speak parables?* Ezek. xx. 49.

REFLECTIONS.

HAIL! HOLY, HOLY, HOLY LORD GOD Almighty, which is, and which was, and which is to come! Blessed for ever be GOD the FATHER, for his everlasting love, in having chosen the Church in CHRIST, before the foundation of the world. And blessed be GOD the SON, for having betrothed the Church from everlasting, and having redeemed her from all the ruins of the fall, in this time state of existence. And blessed be GOD the HOLY GHOST for his everlasting love, and accomplishing the regeneration of the Church, when *dead in trespasses and sins!*

Oh! for grace, to be often contemplating the office acts and manifestations of love, as shewn towards the Church in the communications of all that is communicable in grace, from each glorious person of the GODHEAD. Do thou, blessed SPIRIT, daily make a sweet revelation of the whole to, and in the souls of the redeemed, that the glory of the FATHER's provision for the Church, in the person and blood of CHRIST, and the full mercy of the everlasting covenant, may, through thy sovereign power, be brought home, and confirmed in the heart. Oh! for grace to know GOD the HOLY GHOST, in every sweet office-act in which JESUS hath here so blessedly represented him. Thou knowest, Almighty *Comforter,* that my poor soul can find no comfort but from thy gracious operations. I can have no access, can find no freedom at the throne, nay, can have no disposition to go there, unless thy sweet leadings influence and guide me thither. Oh! then do thou, Almighty *Quickener* of the LORD's people, *direct my heart into the love of* GOD, *and into the patient waiting for* CHRIST. Do thou become to my poor soul, the SPIRIT *of truth;* and sure I am, amidst all the heresies of the day, I shall be guided into all truth. Do thou *glorify* to my view the LORD JESUS, and then no Infidel amidst a CHRIST-despising generation, will for a moment raise a mist to obscure my clear apprehension of His GODHEAD. Precious, precious *Teacher,* in the Church of JESUS! do thou but mercifully fulfil all thy sweet office-characters, in and to my poor soul, and more will be accomplished to the settlement of that peace of mind, and peace of GOD, which passeth all understanding in my heart, than can be wrought in ten thousand years of human endeavors without thee. Yes! thou Almighty SPIRIT of *Sanctification* and *Holiness,* if thou wilt condescend to communicate of thy divine unction, thou wilt bring my LORD JESUS, in all his fulness and suitability, so immediately home in union with my redeemed soul, that I shall know him as *the* LORD *my righteousness,* and live upon him, and live to him, as being made *the righteousness of* GOD *in Him.*

CHAP. XVII.

CONTENTS.

The LORD JESUS *having finished in the foregoing Chapter his Sermon,
here follows it up with Prayer. He first makes the Subject of it Personal, in Relation to Himself and the* FATHER. *He next offers up
Prayer for his Apostles. And, lastly, for his whole Church.*

THESE words spake Jesus, and lifted up his
eyes to heaven, and said, Father, the hour is
come; glorify thy Son, that thy Son also may
glorify thee:

2 As thou hast given him power over all flesh,
that he should give eternal life to as many as thou
hast given him.

3 And this is life eternal, that they might know
thee the only true God, and Jesus Christ whom
thou hast sent.

4 I have glorified thee on the earth: I have
finished the work which thou gavest me to do.

5 And now, O Father, glorify thou me with
thine ownself, with the glory which I had with
thee before the world was.

I desire to enter upon this Chapter with all humility of soul, looking
up for continual grace to go before me, and follow me, as I tread
over every part of the sacred ground in the contents of it. And I
request the Reader to remember, that in every observation which I
venture to propose, I propose it but as an humble offering rather of
enquiry than of decision. May GOD the HOLY GHOST be my teacher!

And, first, let us contemplate the glorious Speaker, and the manner
in which he opened this wonderful prayer. He had been unfolding
his very heart in all the fulness which lay there of his love to his
people. He now opens his very heart to his FATHER. And, as our
Great High Priest, he lifted up his eyes to heaven, as intimating the
heaven of his mind, and said, FATHER! *the hour is come!* What
hour? Nay, that hour for which the numbering of hours became
important, and to which every preceding hour from the fall, in the
time-state of the Church ministered. It was that hour to which heaven
and earth had respect, in the death of CHRIST, as the one grand and
momentous event of all time, and to the accomplishment of which
the LORD of hosts referred, when he said, *And I will remove the iniquity of that land in one day.* Zech. iii. 9.

Glorify thy Son, that thy SON *may also glorify thee.* I pray the
Reader not to overlook in this request of JESUS, the mutual interest
which is expressed in the object desired. It hath been before observed,
that the glory of the LORD JESUS, as GOD-Man-Mediator, never was

more highly manifested than when it brake through the dark cloud
which covered the face of the earth at CHRIST's crucifixion. And
what transcendent dignity and glory did JEHOVAH put upon CHRIST,
when he committed to him the great work of redemption. Yea, in
the very hour, as CHRIST called it, (though it was *six* full hours he
hung upon the cross,) when CHRIST bore in *his* own person the sins
of all his Church, and the wrath of GOD due to sin; yet such was the
victory he then obtained over death, hell, and the grave, and such
the everlasting happiness he procured by it for his members, and such
the rich revenue of everlasting glory and honor to himself by this one
offering of himself, that it may be truly said, never did JEHOVAH
more fully glorify his dear SON, through the whole of his ministry,
than on that solemn, but most auspicious day. And on the other
hand, never was JEHOVAH more glorified, than by the obedience and
blood shedding of his dear SON in our nature. For although, strictly
and properly speaking, GOD in his essence and perfections is incapable
of receiving accessions to his glory by any acts offered unto him, no,
not even by CHRIST himself, for so JESUS by the Spirit of prophecy
ages before had said ; (see Psm. xvi. 2, 3.) yet in the manifested glory
of the LORD, as sin had attempted to tarnish it, JESUS, by his great
undertaking, had done more than restored it. For what could more
display the glory of JEHOVAH, than One in his own nature fulfilling all
his commands, when taking into himself an union with our's, and thus
giving a perfection to his obedience, as the obedience of the GOD-
Man CHRIST JESUS? Here was glory indeed manifested to the LORD,
such as the everlasting and unsinning obedience of men and angels,
yea, the whole creation of GOD to all eternity could not have
wrought. This then JESUS did, when having by his righteousness
brought in an everlasting righteousness, and by his death having
overcome death ; *he finished transgression, made an end of sin, made
reconciliation for iniquity,* destroyed Satan's empire, procured salvation for his whole body the Church, and *restored perfect order among
all the works of* GOD. Full of these grand ideas, and infinitely more
than our highest conceptions can possibly enter into, we may suppose the mind of the Great Redeemer of his Church to have been
occupied, when with his eyes lifted to heaven, he said, FATHER! *the
hour is come, glorify thy* SON, *that thy* SON *may also glorify thee!*

Our LORD proceeds. *As thou hast given him power over all flesh.*
Here let us pause, and ponder well those words of CHRIST, which he
speaks as CHRIST-GOD-Man. Not as GOD only, for as such he could
have nothing given him. All was his, in common with the FATHER,
and the HOLY GHOST. But JESUS here speaks in his *office-character,*
in the covenant. It is of the highest importance to have a proper apprehension of these things. The everlasting covenant between the
persons of the GODHEAD, for making manifest all that is communicable of JEHOVAH's glory to his creatures, consists in certain office-
characters, by which each glorious person in the GODHEAD is known.
Both the eternal and original appointment of the Church before all
worlds, and the recovery and salvation of the Church during her
time-state of being, are the result of everlasting love, equally flowing
from the HOLY THREE in One ; and by which the whole become the
equal and united object of love, obedience, and praise to all eternity.
In these *office-characters,* the Scriptures inform us, how each glorious

person co-operated in the accomplishment of the great design. And, as on the part of the FATHER, he is said to have *sent* the SON to be the SAVIOR of the world, 1 John iv. 14. and the LORD JESUS is said to have all things *given* to him by the FATHER, John iii. 35. so here CHRIST speaks of it under this view, and in his office-character, as GOD-Man-Mediator. It is in this sense the LORD JESUS thus expressed himself in those words.

And it may not be improper to remark, that this power is said by CHRIST to be given to him *over all flesh.* Not simply in relation to his Church, but as universal and eternal LORD of heaven and earth. *Paul* saith, that by CHRIST were *all things created that are in heaven, and that are in earth.* And not only created *by* him, but *for* him; and that *by him* all things consist. So that he is not only the head of his body the Church, but *the fulness which filleth all in all.* I pray the Reader to consult those scriptures. Coloss. i. 15—20. Ephes. i. 15, to the end. We begin at the middle of the subject in relation to CHRIST as GOD-Man-Mediator, when we begin at his work of redemption. The SON of GOD, as the Wisdom of GOD, was set up from everlasting. Prov. viii. 22—31. And the Church had a being in CHRIST, as CHRIST, before the foundation of the world. Ephes. i. 4. Ephes. iii. 9, 10, 11. And who shall say what other objects were designed in the infinite mind of JEHOVAH, FATHER, SON, and HOLY GHOST, in One of those sacred Persons taking into union with himself that holy portion of human nature, by which the SON of GOD became man? Who shall determine what other glory, beside that of JEHOVAH's glory in the Church, hath been and shall everlastingly be manifested by it? Nay, who shall draw the limits to what that glory shall extend, in the wonderful discovery made of JEHOVAH in the person of CHRIST, without whom, as it should seem from scripture, no manifestation could have been made for ever? John i. 18.—But I can venture no further.

We see then by our LORD's words, that CHRIST hath power given him over all flesh. And JESUS adds, *that he should give eternal life to as many as the* FATHER *had given him.* Pause over these precious words. And, first, observe what an unanswerable proof they carry with them of the GODHEAD of CHRIST. For who less than the Eternal GOD, can give Eternal life? The very possession of the property implies the eternal nature of the possessor. Reader! never lose sight of this! Next observe what JESUS speaks of those to whom he is to give eternal life. It is to *as many as the* FATHER *hath given him.* If there were no other passage in Scripture, this would be sufficient in proof that CHRIST hath a Church, for whom this blessing of eternal life, with all its preliminaries, is intended. But the word of GOD is full in point to the same purport. John vi. 37. John x. 27—30. 1 John v. 11, 12. Jude 1. Reader! what a sweet thought ariseth out of this view, short as it is, concerning CHRIST's power, and concerning CHRIST's office-character. JESUS hath eternal life, yea, is himself eternal life. And JESUS hath it to impart to as many as the FATHER hath given him; yea, is himself their life, and their portion for ever. John xiv. 19, 20.

Our blessed LORD next proceeds to shew, as far as our present unripe faculties can comprehend the subject, in what this eternal life consists. JESUS saith, *And this is life eternal, that they might know thee the only true* GOD, *and* JESUS CHRIST, *whom thou hast sent.* Our apprehensions go but a little way in this subject. Life, in every sense of the word, is a mystery. Our *natural* life is involved in endless difficulties to explain. That we live, and that we perform the several actions of life, we know. And the word of the LORD informs us, that it is *in Him that we live, and move, and have our being.* Acts xvii. 28. But further our greatest discoveries do not extend. *Spiritual* life becomes yet more remote from our knowledge, more than of the fact itself. And *eternal* life JESUS here declares to consist in the knowledge of *the only true* GOD, *and* JESUS CHRIST, *whom he hath sent.* Here then we have authority to conclude, that in the proper apprehension of the only true GOD, in his three-fold character of persons, and of the person, and offices, and relations of JESUS CHRIST, as the GOD-Man-Mediator the glorious Head and Husband of his Church, *this is life eternal.* Our LORD doth not say that it leads to it, but that it is. Not that this knowledge shall hereafter bring the happy possessors of it to life eternal, but that it is now already in possession. *He that believeth on the* SON *hath everlasting life.* John iii. 36. GOD *hath given to us eternal life; and this life is in his* SON. *He that hath the* SON *hath life.* 1 John v. 11, 12. So that this eternal life, be it what it may, is not to be the possession only of the world to come; but in the present state. For being in CHRIST, in the possession of Him; his people possess eternal life in him.

I do not think it necessary, to detain the Reader, with endeavouring to explain, what all the Bible in every part is explaining, in relation to the knowledge of GOD, and of CHRIST. I shall only beg to observe, that it is not concerning the nature and Being of JEHOVAH, and the mode of his existence, that is proposed to us in those words of CHRIST, or any other part of Scripture, to know. These subjects must ever be, both in time, and to all eternity, beyond the grasp of our faculties. JEHOVAH would no longer be incomprehensible, if any of his creatures could attain that knowledge. But the knowledge our LORD speaks of, is in relation to those discoveries, which he hath been pleased to make of himself, in his threefold character of Persons, in the departments of nature, providence, grace, and glory; and which have a special regard to his Church and people. Reader! I humbly conceive, that this is life eternal, to know GOD the FATHER in his office-character! his everlasting love to the Church in CHRIST before the foundation of the world: to know GOD the SON in his office-character, his oneness and union with the FATHER in his divine nature; and his oneness and union with his Church in his human nature: And to know GOD the HOLY GHOST, as distinct in Person from both, yet in essence and in glory One with the FATHER and the SON; and in relation to his office-character to the Church, loving the Church with the same everlasting love, and as engaged in all Covenant offices, for her being, and well being in CHRIST, to all eternity.

This I humbly conceive to form the outlines of what the LORD JESUS CHRIST hath here said, of life eternal: *to know the only true* GOD *and* JESUS CHRIST *whom he hath sent.* Isaiah xlviii. 16.

Our LORD proceeds. *I have glorified thee on the earth: I have finished the work which thou gavest me to do.* Reader! let you and I seek grace to bless GOD, for what JESUS hath here said. None but JESUS could thus speak. No angel of light; no, nor the whole crea-

tion of God, could ever adopt such language. For although Jehovah's glory is seen *in* them, and *by* them; and in this sense the
Psalmist speaks, when he saith, *The heavens declare the glory of
God, &c.* Psm. xix. 1. Yet nothing can add to Jehovah's glory, neither can any take from it. But in the Person of the God-Man
Christ Jesus, Jehovah is glorified, and hath been glorified, when in
the dignity of his Person and work, the glory of Jehovah is made
manifest, to the whole intellectual creation of God. And what endears
this view of Christ still more, is the part which his Church bears
in it; because in the great work, the Lord Jesus stood forth and
acted as the Head, and Representative of his people. Reader! do
not fail to connect this view of the subject, with Christ's finished
work. The Church of Christ, in every individual member, hath *all
sinned and come short of the glory of* God. Jesus, our Head and Husband, hath fulfilled all righteousness; and hath done the whole for his
people. Yea, in consequence of the perfection of his Person, and the
perfection of his work, being the obedience and merits of God-Man
Mediator; he hath done more in honoring God's law, than we have
done by sin to dishonor God: and infinite in value, and in efficiency,
is the finished work of Christ. Oh! for grace, while we thus contemplate our Great High Priest and Representative, in the close of his
ministry, thus speaking to the Father, in giving in before him the
blessed accomplishment of his mission; all his Church and people may
by faith come under the Censer of his Incense, and behold our compleat justification in Him!

　And now, (saith Jesus,) *O* Father, *glorify thou me with thine ownself, with the glory which I had with thee before the world was.* The
work finished, Christ looks to the consequences, as by Covenant
settlements agreed upon. Hence the Apostle saith, when speaking of
Christ; *who for the joy that was set before him endured the cross,
despising the shame, and is set down at the right hand of the throne of
God.* Heb. xii. 2.

　The great question here is, what glory doth Jesus here allude to!
I speak with all possible reverence when I say, I humbly apprehend,
it could not be that essential underived glory, which equally belongs
to the whole, and to each Person of the Godhead, as Jehovah. For
the Son of God, as God, could never ask, or receive this; being
from all eternity his own. But the glory here spoken of by Christ,
seems very plainly to refer to that glory which belonged to Him as
God-Man Mediator, when from everlasting he stood up, the Head,
and Husband of his Church. There was a *Personal* glory as God-
Man, which he had with the Father before the world was, before that
he became incarnate; in the time-state of the Church, and consequently before that Jesus had acquired any *office*-glory, in finishing
the work the Father gave him to do. Yea, the Son of God had
this glory, as God-Man, from the union of nature of God and Man
in one Person, though he had never in the time-state of the Church
purchased the glory of redemption, in bringing his Church out of the
ruins of the fall. But while I say thus much, I beg it may be understood, that I do not presume to say which of those glories it was to
which Christ referred: whether of *Person* or of *Office,* or of both,
when he thus addressed the Father.

　Thus much, however, we may, under divine teaching, safely say :

CHRIST had a glory with the FATHER *before the world was.* In the time-state of the Church during his ministry, this glory was in a great measure obscured. For, although he manifested forth his glory by miracles; and occasionally as in the Mount of Transfiguration, there was given certain burstings forth, in proof, that *in Him dwelleth all the fulness of the* GODHEAD *bodily.* Coloss. ii. 9. Yet it may be truly said, that while upon earth, he for the most part appeared, as *the man of sorrows and acquainted with grief.* But though I presume not to speak concerning the nature of that glory which the LORD JESUS had in view in those words: yet I detain the Reader to observe, that we learn from them those very sweet and precious instructions. *First,* That CHRIST, as CHRIST, that is, the SON of GOD in our nature, had glory in this Personal Character with the FATHER before all worlds: *Secondly,* That the glory JESUS here speaks of, was a glory which he had with the FATHER; though the distinction of the Persons at the same time is hereby plainly proved. And *thirdly.* As the LORD JESUS prays to be glorified by the FATHER, *with thine ownself:* (as JESUS wordeth it,) the unity and design of the whole GODHEAD, in all the purposes and pleasure of JEHOVAH, concerning the Church, is fully manifested and confirmed. *My* FATHER *worketh hitherto,* (saith CHRIST,) *and I work.* John v. 17.

Thus far, this prayer of our LORD, had special respect to himself and his FATHER. In which the Reader will perceive, how much our dear LORD dwells upon those great points; the glory which he had manifested of his FATHER, in his finished work in time: and the glory to which JESUS looked, both in what was opening before him, in the hour now come; and in the future enjoyment of the same glory, which he had with the FATHER, before all worlds. Precious JESUS! may all thy Church know thee in all thy glory; and *every knee bow before thee, and every tongue confess that* JESUS CHRIST *is* LORD *to the glory of* GOD *the* FATHER.

6 I have manifested thy name unto the men which thou gavest me out of the world: thine they were, and thou gavest them me; and they have kept thy word.

7 Now they have known that all things whatsoever thou hast given me are of thee.

8 For I have given unto them the words which thou gavest me; and they have received *them,* and have known surely that I came out from thee, and they have believed that thou didst send me.

9 I pray for them: I pray not for the world, but for them which thou hast given me; for they are thine.

10 And all mine are thine, and thine are mine; and I am glorified in them.

11 And now I am no more in the world, but these are in the world, and I come to thee. Holy Father, keep through thine own name those whom thou hast given me, that they may be one, as we *are*.

12 While I was with them in the world, I kept them in thy name: those that thou gavest me I have kept, and none of them is lost, but the son of perdition; that the scripture might be fulfilled.

13 And now come I to thee; and these things I speak in the world, that they might have my joy fulfilled in themselves.

14 I have given them thy word; and the world hath hated them, because they are not of the world, even as I am not of the world.

15 I pray not that thou shouldest take them out of the world, but that thou shouldest keep them from the evil.

16 They are not of the world, even as I am not of the world.

17 Sanctify them through thy truth: thy word is truth.

18 As thou hast sent me into the world, even so have I also sent them into the world.

19 And for their sakes I sanctify myself, that they also might be sanctified through the truth.

In this part of our LORD's prayer, JESUS hath a special eye to his Apostles; not indeed to the exclusion of any of his Church, which no doubt were all alike equally dear to him; but probably, as the first Preachers, Ministers of his Gospel, and in an age when peculiarly difficulties would arise to oppose their persons and their labors; the LORD had them more immediately in view. And before we enter upon the several parts of our LORD's prayer, concerning them, I cannot but notice with particular attention, and entreat the Reader to regard it with me also, how very gracious it was in JESUS to say what he hath said, in the strong recommendation which he makes of them to his FATHER, in their hearing; that they might perceive, how deep they lay in his heart. Neither was it less attentive in GOD the HOLY GHOST, to cause it to be recorded, that the Church in all ages might see, how much CHRIST loved his people; what interest and property the FATHER had in them: and with what care and love, the HOLY

GHOST watched over them, in preserving such sweet testimonies of the Redeemer's affection, in everlasting remembrance.

I must not indulge myself as I could wish, to go over, verse by verse, the many blessed things which are contained in them. It would far exceed the limits of *a Poor Man's Commentary*. I shall therefore content myself, (and I hope the Reader will be contented also,) in just sketching some of the more prominent parts of this most unequalled prayer of our LORD. May the LORD bless it.

And here, *first*, I beg the Reader to notice, the ground, upon which JESUS lays the principal stress of confidence, in the recommendation of his people to his FATHER. He speaks of them, as the men whom the FATHER *gave him out of the world :* that they were the FATHER's, before he gave them to CHRIST ; his property, and consequently his care. Yea, JESUS intimates by the earnestness of his recommendation of them, that he prized them the more highly, on the FATHER's account. And the LORD JESUS found the greater confidence from this consideration, that his FATHER would preserve them, and keep them, and watch over them, for good, and at length bring them home, to behold that glory, which the FATHER had given him and be with him for ever. Reader! do not fail to observe, these sweet things in CHRIST's prayer. Neither overlook, how much JESUS dwells upon that one consideration, of the FATHER's property in his Church and people. He repeats it again, and again : *thine they were, and thou gavest them me. All mine are thine ; and thine are mine : and I am glorified in them.* Think how dear that Church must be in GOD the FATHER's view, who in proof of it, gave that Church to his dear SON ? And think how dear to CHRIST, in that he hath redeemed it with his blood ? And how dear to GOD the HOLY GHOST, who notwithstanding that He is *of purer eyes than to behold iniquity ;* yet condescends to make the bodies of those poor sinners his temple ? 1 Cor. vi. 19, 20.

The next thing to be noticed, in this most blessed prayer of CHRIST, is his own personal love for his Church, and particularly manifested to the Apostles, as representatives of the Church, in thus taking such concern for them, before his departure. Nothing can more fully express the love of the blessed JESUS, than in the very earnest pleadings he here makes use of, with the FATHER, in their behalf. He knew their nature, their weakness, their corruptions. He knew the enemies which they would have to encounter ; and the sharp exercises of persecutions, to which they would be exposed, after he had left them. And hence the earnestness and vehemency of his recommendation of them to the FATHER. HOLY FATHER! *keep* (said he) *through thine own name those whom thou hast given me.* Reader! do not forget, that in this vast interest JESUS took in the concerns of his disciples *then,* that he equally takes concern in all the interests of his people *now. He knoweth our frame, and remembereth that we are but dust.* And if the Apostles needed such attention, surely JESUS will not be less regardful of us. Never fail to connect such regard of JESUS for the Church, in every age of her warfare, while beholding the LORD's tenderness over the Apostles. His love is the same : and his attention the same. *Having loved his own which are in the world, he loveth them unto the end.* John xiii. 1.

nd as another token of CHRIST's love to his Church in this beautiful prayer, I pray the Reader to observe, with what tenderness and affection JESUS speaks of them : *They have kept thy word. They have received the words which I have given them. They have believed that thou didst send me.* Every thing by which the LORD JESUS could recommend them, he graciously takes notice of, by way of endearment. Not a word but in their favor. No complaint of their dulness, and unbelief, which they had frequently manifested, during his going in and out before them. But all is tender and affectionate in JESUS, in presenting them to his FATHER. Reader! remember, such is JESUS now. Though he knows what subjects we are of sin, and temptation; and what *fools and slow of heart to believe all that the Prophets have spoken:* yet doth he still take up our cause, plead for all our mercies, and never ceaseth, nor will cease, his intercession, until he hath brought home his whole Church to glory.

Neither should we overlook, in this prayer of JESUS, the striking contrast he makes, between his Church and the ungodly. The LORD draws in it a line of the most marked discrimination. *I pray for them,* (saith CHRIST,) *I pray not for the world. The world hath hated them, because they are not of the world; even as I am not of the world.* Reader! If there be a single truth of GOD more pointed and express than another, surely it is that, in which CHRIST's union and personal relationship with his people is insisted upon. The LORD seems to delight in it. He dwells upon it. His FATHER's interest in his people. His own interest, and the HOLY GHOST's interest. His people's distinction from the world; the world's hatred on this account: and their union with him, the cause of the whole. Upon this subject I would just add, If JESUS delighted to make this discrimination between his people and the world, ought not his people to do the same? Did JESUS mark it in his prayer, and shall not we in praise? Was the LORD pleased to behold his people with this marked distinction, and to speak of it with complacency and delight; and shall not his people, the highly favored objects of discriminating grace, notice it in like manner.

One observation more in this sweet prayer of JESUS. He saith, that, *those whom thou gavest me I have kept, and none of them is lost but the son of perdition, that the Scripture might be fulfilled.* What a subject is opened and answered in those few words, in confirmation of discriminating grace? And how very fully do they prove, what indeed all the other parts of Scripture concur in, to the same point: that the Church of CHRIST is chosen in CHRIST, all the members preserved and kept in CHRIST, have their being and well being in CHRIST; and being one with CHRIST, He is their sole life of grace here, in the time-state of the Church, and will be their life of glory in the eternal world for ever. While on the other hand, where there is no grace-union with CHRIST, in the original and eternal purpose of JEHOVAH: FATHER, SON, and HOLY GHOST; in the FATHER's gift, the SON's betrothing, and the HOLY GHOST's unction; the fall in the Adam-nature must remain, and from having no relation *to* CHRIST, neither interest *in* CHRIST, the Scripture must be fulfilled; that while all that are given to CHRIST are kept, the son of perdition cannot but be lost. And in relation to *Judas,* to whom CHRIST here refers; though given, and chosen as an Apostle, yet not as a member of CHRIST's mystical body. He had indeed obtained part of the ministry, but not the

least part of grace. JESUS knew him for a devil, at the time he chose
him for an Apostle. And the subsequent acts of his life, were the
effects of that diabolical influence. (See John xiii. 2—17. and Commentary). And the preservation of the eleven Apostles, was not from
works of righteousness which they had done, for *they were men of like
passions with ourselves;* but for their safety, and security in CHRIST.
JESUS saith: *those whom thou gavest me I have kept.* Their being
chosen in CHRIST, and accepted in the beloved, the HOLY GHOST
declares, by *Paul,* to have been prior acts to those of redemption
through CHRIST's blood, and the forgiveness of sins. I pray the
Reader to notice these grand and momentous truths, with the attention
they so highly merit, as they are stated: Ephes. i. 3—7. And may
the LORD the HOLY GHOST be praised, for the very great sweetness
and preciousness of that Scripture. In relation to the awfulness of
this doctrine, in our LORD's prayer, it would be the wisdom of the
LORD's people, to ponder well their high privileges, and *rejoice
with trembling.* And some of those many sweet scriptures, which are
in confirmation of the truths of GOD, will always bring relief to the
mind, under every distressing thought, which may at times arise, concerning the reprobate. Strictly, and properly speaking, the Church
hath no more to do with the fall of man, in the graceless and irre-
claimable; than we have to do with the fall of angels. And those
soul reviving words of the LORD JESUS, will act on the mind, when
graciously applied by the HOLY GHOST, in any dark and tempting
hour, as an anchor to the soul, both sure and stedfast, which like an
anchor to the ship on an enemy's coast, enables the mariners to weather
out the storm. *I thank thee, O FATHER,* (said the LORD JESUS,)
LORD *of heaven and earth, because thou hast hid these things from
the wise and prudent, and hast revealed them unto babes. Even
so FATHER, for so it seemed good in thy sight.* Matt. xi. 25, 26.

Allow me to call the Reader's attention to one feature more in this
part of our LORD's prayer as more immediately relating to his
Apostles; and I will trespass no longer. JESUS prays for *their sanctification;* and declares, that *for their sakes he sanctifies himself.*

That CHRIST is the sanctification of his Church, and the compleat
holiness of his people, is a truth, to which the whole tenor of the
Gospel bears record. Hence, all the Persons of the GODHEAD are
said to have concurred in this gracious act. Jude i. Ephes. v. 25, 26,
27. 2 Thess. ii. 13. 1 Cor. i. 30. Heb. x. 10. And sanctification is
as compleat a work as justification. Grace in the knowledge of the
LORD, is indeed progressive: for the Church is said to *grow in
grace and in the knowledge of our* LORD *and* SAVIOR JESUS CHRIST.
2 Pet. iii. 18. But we no where read of a progressive sanctification.
Indeed the very principle itself implies perfection. A soul regenerated is brought into a spiritual life: made partaker of the divine
nature, for that *divine power is said to have given all things that pertain to life and godliness.* See 2 Pet. i. 1—4. And this regeneration is equal in all, whom the HOLY GHOST quickens. All the after
acts of the SPIRIT, are acts upon this new life, drawn forth into exercise, upon the Person and work of CHRIST, in the actings of faith and
love. But the life of sanctification in CHRIST, once imparted, can be
no more than life: neither capable of increase or diminution.

In relation to the persons of the Apostles, in the LORD's prayer for them, that they might be sanctified through the truth; I venture to believe, it had respect to their personal ministry, and character: that being sanctified through the truth, they might have more and more enlarged views of truth, in the great purposes of the everlasting Covenant: and from being taught themselves in a more extensive manner, when the Holy Ghost should come upon them, in an open display of his power, they might be made the medium and channel, of informing others. And, Reader! the same holds equally good, with every child of God, when regenerated by the Holy Ghost. That blessed and gracious Covenant work of the Spirit, is as compleat an act, *as the offering of the body of* Jesus Christ *once for all.* God the Holy Ghost will indeed call forth the soul he hath regenerated, and brought forth, from the death of sin unto a life of righteousness in Christ; in daily actings of faith and grace, as from a soul alive to God, in, and through, Jesus Christ our Lord: but the quickening, from death to life, and sanctifying the renewed nature of the new man, *which after* God *is created in righteousness and true holiness* is wrought but once, and that all effectual. So that as *Paul* saith; *but ye are washed, but ye are sanctified, but ye are justified in the name of the* Lord Jesus, *and by the* Spirit *of our* God. 1 Cor. vi. 11.

And in relation to what Jesus saith, *For their sakes I sanctify myself.* Never surely can it be supposed, that Christ meant to say, that he made himself more holy, for that was and is impossible; but that he set himself apart for their sakes, in his Office-Character of Redeemer. Not for the Apostles only, but his whole Church: *All* (as he elsewhere saith,) *whom the* Father *hath given him.* John vi. 37. And that all might be sanctified in Him, and through Him, the truth. And from this most precious Scripture, every child of God, when regenerated and made alive in Christ, may gather the richest assurance of faith; that in the perfection of Christ, and his dedication of himself for his people, they may know their sanctification, *by the offering of the body of* Jesus Christ *once for all.* They feel the efficacy of it in their hearts, and consciences. And they are enabled through faith *in* Christ, and strength *from* Christ, through the blessed influences of the Spirit, to live and *rejoice in hope of the glory of* God. For such believing views become the full desire of the soul, in that Covenant *that is ordered in all things and sure,* and founded in Christ *before the world began.* Titus i. 2. 2 Sam. xxiii. 5.

So much for the second part, of this most blessed prayer of our Lord; which, beside the *general* respect, it hath, here and there to the whole Church, hath some more immediate and special regard to the Apostles; and all taken together, serve to lay open the heart of Christ to his people, and to shew, that every thing of love, and grace, and mercy, is there flowing, in endless streams, towards his chosen.

20 Neither pray I for these alone, but for them also which shall believe on me through their word;

21 That they all may be one; as thou, Father,

art in me, and I in thee, that they also may be one in us: that the world may believe that thou hast sent me.

22 And the glory which thou gavest me I have given them ; that they may be one, even as we are one :

23 I in them, and thou in me, that they may be made perfect in one; and that the world may know that thou hast sent me, and hast loved them, as thou hast loved me.

24 Father, I will that they also, whom thou hast given me be with me where I am; that they may behold my glory which thou hast given me ; for thou lovedst me before the foundation of the world.

25 O righteous Father, the world hath not known thee: but I have known thee, and these have known that thou hast sent me.

26 And I have declared unto them thy name, and will declare *it :* that the love wherewith thou hast loved me may be in them, and I in them.

In this part of the LORD's prayer, his whole Church is included, yea, expressly prayed for. And I have often found cause to bless the LORD JESUS, for the very sweet and gracious manner of expression which he was pleased to use, in the introduction of it, when he said, by way of distinction, from what he had before said for the Apostles: *Neither pray I for these alone, but for them also which shall believe on me, through their word.* It is in my view, as if the LORD JESUS had said : The blessings I am procuring for those my redeemed, which are now around me, and within the hearing of what I say, I mean not to limit to them, but that the whole may be extended to all my Church; in the thousands, and ten thousands of my children, which are yet unborn. And while I desire some more special effects of my great salvation may be communicated to those my Apostles, to qualify them for the ministry of the word; my will is, that the whole body of the Church may partake together, in all the blessed consequences of my mission. That oneness and union, that perfection and glory *in* me, and that everlasting presence *with* me, to which the whole Church shall finally be brought; may be the privilege and blessed-hess of all. I humbly conceive, that our LORD's words, in the opening of this concluding clause of his prayer, may, without violence to the several expressions contained in it, be supposed as conveying those things. And I beg the Reader to remark with me, the manner in which the LORD JESUS enforceth the several blessings he enumerates.

FATHER! *I will.* Here is no petition, nor request; but what JESUS saith, is expressed in the nature of a right, or demand. And the reason is obvious. In the several transactions of the HOLY THREE in ONE, the glorious Almighty Covenanters have mutually engaged to each other. They are all alike equal in GODHEAD. And they are alike equal in Covenant Offices. They have therefore guaranteed to each other. So that in the Intercession of CHRIST; though by virtue of his human nature, this office leads to the exercise of prayer: yet not by a way of petition, but of right. JESUS demands the fulfilment of Covenant stipulations; and as such saith, for all he pleads: FATHER! *I will!*

I must not indulge here again, no more than upon the former occasion, to enlarge on the several subjects, which are contained in those concluding verses of our LORD's prayer: But I crave the favor of the Reader, that I may be permitted to glance at one or two or the more prominent points, JESUS hath so sweetly dwelt upon.

And *first:* that union and oneness which JESUS here insists upon; and which, the LORD speaks of so frequently, in this Chapter. We shall do well to notice it at least, though to enter into the full apprehension of it is impossible. That JESUS himself took much delight in it is very certain, for he makes mention of it continually in his prayer. And if it was dear to CHRIST, how very dear ought it to be to his people? Indeed it forms the basis of all communicable grace and glory. For without union, there can be no communion. Unless married to CHRIST, we have no claim to maintenance or dower? Unless grafted into this holy Vine, how shall we derive sap or fruitfulness from the Vine? It is by virtue of this oneness with CHRIST, in the eternal purpose of JEHOVAH, being chosen in CHRIST before the foundation of the world, that the Church derives all her blessedness from CHRIST. This union is the foundation of all the after blessings, which arise out of it. All the blessings and mercies we derive from CHRIST, in this time-state of the Church, are the result of the Church's being considered as one with CHRIST, from all eternity. So that our redemption by CHRIST, is among the blessed *effects* of this union: and our union with CHRIST is the *cause.* CHRIST came to redeem his Church, from the ruins of the Adam-fall. But this was, because JESUS hath betrothed himself to this Church, before the foundation of the world. Ephes. i. 4. Hosea ii. 18.

But while we esteem so very highly this union, on account of the blessings flowing from it: (and never can it be too highly prized, or too often meditated upon,) I would desire the Reader to observe, that the union itself is as far superior, as any *cause* is to the *effect.* An union with CHRIST, makes a child of GOD one with CHRIST. It forms a personal union: for the whole Person of CHRIST, GOD-Man is one with his Church, in every individual member of it: body, soul, and spirit. *He that is joined to the* LORD *is One* SPIRIT. 1 Cor. vi. 17. Hence CHRIST is precious: not only for his gifts, or for his graces, or for his benefits; but for himself. He is not only the source of happiness, but is himself our happiness. Not only gives his people life, but is himself their life, and their portion for ever. So sweet and precious therefore, is this conscious union with CHRIST.

Secondly, JESUS saith, that *the glory which thou gavest me I have given them.* Here also we discover a blessedness, which merits our

highest regard, and our unceasing thankfulness.   There is a glory of
the Lord Jesus Christ in his divine nature as God, one with the
Father over all blessed for ever.   But then this is not communicable,
neither was it ever *given to him.*   And there is a glory, even a Personal glory, as God-Man, which is his, and incapable also of
communication.   And there is a glory of dignity and merit, as God-
Man, which he hath acquired by virtue of his sufferings, and death.
Philip. ii. 6—11.   Neither is this capable of being communicated.
But his glory as Head of his body the Church, as the head of influence,
and the head of communication; this glory, given to him by Jehovah,
is purposely given, to be communicated to all the members of his
mystical body; and Jesus here saith, he hath given it to his people.
And it is most blessed to observe, how the Lord is for ever doing it,
here in grace, and above in glory!   And the oneness of the Church
of Christ with Christ, is such, that while the Church is made everlastingly blessed and happy in her Head and Husband, Jesus is made
glorious in his Church, and becomes as the Prophet described her,
a crown of glory in the hand of the Lord, *and a royal diadem in the
hand of her* God.   Isaiah lxii. 3.

  Thirdly, It is not the smallest part of Christ's regard, which he
hath shewn to his Church in this prayer, in the striking discrimination which he hath made, between his Church and the world; and
the knowledge his people have of him, compared to the world.   *O
righteous* Father, (said Jesus) *the world hath not known thee: but I
have known thee : and these have known that thou hast sent me.*   There
is somewhat very particular and striking, in Christ calling the
Father, in this place, and upon this account, *O righteous* Father!
Was it not (for I only ask the question, without deciding upon it,) to
shew the righteousness and strict equity of God, in leaving the world
shut up in the unbelief of their own minds by the fall, and revealing
himself in Christ, to all the Church; chosen in Christ, and called?
Rom. xi. 7, 8.   Reader! do not fail to mark this as you pass over the
several parts, of this most precious Chapter.   And while you mark it,
look to God the Spirit, to cause the sweet savor of it, to rest with
suitable affection, to call forth praise and love in the mind.

  I will only detain the Reader just to observe, with what tenderness and love the Lord closeth the whole of his prayer, with an intimation of continuing to declare unto his people the Name of his Father; that the love of God to Christ, as God-Man Mediator: and
the love of God to the Church in Christ, might be unceasingly
known and enjoyed, by his whole household.   It is impossible that
any thing could be said more expressive, in token of the Lord's love.
He was now in the moment of separation from them.   When he had
finished his prayer, he was going into the garden of *Gethsemane.*
Jesus knew what would then follow.   This was the last, the farewell
interview, of Christ and his eleven Apostles alone.   And what were
his last words in this sweet season.   That *the* Father's *love wherewith
he had loved him, might be in them; and I* (said Jesus) *in them.*   Here
was an assurance then, of the everlasting love of Jesus, and the
sameness of love in Jesus to his Church, to the end of the world.
That love could not increase, neither could it diminish.   Jesus leaves
his heart with them therefore, and not only them, but all the Church,
of which they were then the representatives.   That his love shall be

with them; and constant, fresh manifestations, and discoveries of it, shall be for ever. So the LORD JESUS declared. And so his people in the present hour of the Church, can bear witness; and *set to their seal in having received this testimony, that* GOD *is true.* John iii. 33. Amen.

REFLECTIONS.

My soul! do thou, with uplifted eyes, and thankful heart, behold thy GOD and SAVIOR, in this most blessed representation the HOLY GHOST hath made of him, in this Chapter, here entering upon His High Priestly Office; and through faith, come under the golden Censer of his Offering! Oh! what a sample hath he here given, of his all powerful, all prevailing, and unchanging Priesthood. Yes! thou blessed LORD! let my poor soul, I pray thee, never lose sight of *the Pillar and ground of the truth*, on which thy Church, in all her members, both Apostles and people, stand everlastingly firm and secure; the perfection of thy finished work, and the faithfulness of JEHOVAH's word and oath, in the Covenant, *ordered in all things and sure.* It is indeed eternal life, and it is thy office-character, to give it, to know JEHOVAH, the only true GOD ; FATHER, SON, and HOLY GHOST; and JESUS CHRIST, whom JEHOVAH hath sent.

Oh, ye Apostles of CHRIST ! what unspeakable mercies did JESUS, in this sweet prayer, confer on you! And ye no less, whom in all the after ages of the Church, GOD the SPIRIT hath called to the ministry ; how are ye all, from age to age, included, in this rich priestly blessing of my GOD! Oh! for an holy jealousy, over the fold of CHRIST, in all the under pastors of the Church; to see and know that their commission is of GOD. JESUS! in mercy to thy Church, grant that none may run unsent; but that all may bear with them, the same sweet testimony as JESUS in this address to his FATHER gave, concerning his Apostles: *As thou hast sent me into the world; even so have I also sent them into the world.* Oh! the blessedness for all of this description and character, to have a consciousness of being interested in CHRIST's prayer; from being sent forth to the ministry from CHRIST's ordination: HOLY FATHER! *keep through thine own Name, those whom thou hast given me, that they may be one as we are!*

And no less ye whole Church of CHRIST! Never, never, lose sight of those most precious words of JESUS, when he said; *Neither pray I for these alone, but for them also which shall believe on me through their word.* Yes! thou dearest LORD! though thou hast given *some Apostles, and some Prophets, and some Evangelists; and some Pastors and Teachers:* yet the whole is for *the perfecting of the saints, for the work of the ministry; for the edifying of the body of* CHRIST. Thy little ones dearest LORD, are as dear to thee, as the greatest and the best; for all is derived from thee, and none hath ought, but what he hath received from thee. Precious LORD JESUS ! the hour is hastening, when that will of thine will be fully accomplished; and from an everlasting Oneness of thy Church and People with thyself, the whole Church will appear as thou hast said : FATHER *I will that they also whom thou hast given me be with me where I am, that they may behold my glory which thou hast given me !* Amen.

CHAP. XVIII.

CONTENTS.

JESUS *is here in the Garden of Gethsemane.* Judas, *with the Band of Soldiers, apprehend* CHRIST. *He is arraigned before* Pilate.

WHEN Jesus had spoken these words, he went forth with his disciples over the brook Cedron, where was a garden, into the which he entered, and his disciples.

I detain the Reader at the very entrance on this Chapter, in order to beg his attention to what the Sacred Writer hath said of this brook *Cedron,* or *Kidron.* It is evidently the same as that mentioned, 2 Sam. xv. 23. And as *David,* in passing over this brook in his distresses, was clearly a type of CHRIST, it merits our attention the more. Some have thought that the name of *Cedron,* or *Kidron,* which signified *black,* was given to it because it lay in a dark valley. And others conclude, that its name was taken from the black and foul waters which ran into it from the temple sacrifices. In either sense, the gloominess of it, and the filth of it, rendered it loathsome. And if, as is supposed, the prophetic Psalm concerning CHRIST had an eye to this brook when it is said, that *he should drink of the brook in the way,* Psm. cx. 7. it may serve to lead the mind to some very solemn and interesting reflections. Here it was that the good king *Josiah* caused the polluted vessels of the temple to be burnt. 2 Kings xxiii. 4. And all the uncleanness found in the house of the LORD in *Hezekiah's* reign, was carried here. 2 Chron. xxix. 16. JESUS passing over it, and drinking of the brook in his way, may not unaptly be supposed to represent the filth and blackness of sin, in which CHRIST as our representative appeared. And his drinking of it might be supposed to refer to the cup of trembling, which, as the Church's Surety he drank to the very dregs, that his people might drink the cup of salvation, and call upon the name of the LORD. Isa. li. 22. Psalm cxvi. 13.

2 And Judas also, which betrayed him, knew the place : for Jesus oft-times resorted thither with his disciples.

3 Judas then, having received a band *of men* and officers from the chief priests and Pharisees, cometh thither with lanterns, and torches, and weapons.

It is sweetly said, that JESUS oft-times resorted thither with his disciples. Yes! no doubt the LORD had enjoyed many blessed hours in communion with his FATHER in this hallowed spot. And no doubt had oft refreshed his faithful Apostles in it with his divine discourses. Here then, where CHRIST in his human nature had received the richest consolations, shall he now sustain the bitterest conflicts.

And as in a garden his Church in her Adam-nature fell under the temptation of the devil, so in a garden will JESUS begin his triumph over hell, to take his Church out of the hands of Satan. *Judas*, it is said, knew the place. No doubt had often heard, in common with the other Apostles, the LORD's heavenly discourses there. But what discourses of heaven, and heavenly things, can affect the minds of them *who are earthly, sensual, devilish?* Reader! depend upon it, if all the damned in hell were liberated from their chains, no other mind would they have, but what would be still hellish. And if the devils were permitted to change their place, there would be no change accomplished by this of their nature: devils they would still be. Nothing but a sovereign act of grace could alter their mind. And this we are told will never be accomplished. They are reserved, scripture saith, *in everlasting chains under darkness, unto the judgment of the great day.* Jude 6.

Of this awful character *Judas*, I have said so much already (John xiii.) as to render it unnecessary to enlarge in this place in adding to the account. But I cannot forbear observing, in this miserable man's history, to what a desperate degree of hardness the mind of man, under hellish influence, is capable of arriving. It is very evident, from the relation which follows in this Chapter, that when the band of soldiers fell to the ground at the voice of CHRIST, *Judas* must have fallen with them, for the Evangelist is express in noting, that *Judas also, which betrayed him, stood with them.* Reader! pause over the trembling account. Here were chief priests and Pharisees, Roman soldiers and officers, and *Judas* the traitor, all standing together in conspiracy against the person of CHRIST. Now, I humbly ask, were not these the different heads and representatives of all the enemies of GOD, and of his CHRIST? The chief priests and Pharisees were the representatives of the Jewish church. The Roman soldiers of the Gentiles. And both were prophesied to join hand in hand to the death of CHRIST. See Psm. ii. And what was *Judas?* Was he not the awful representative of all the reprobate? Jude 4.

I must not pass away from these verses, without first noticing the circumstance of this band of armed men coming to apprehend CHRIST, *with lanterns, and torches, and weapons.* What was this for? In all probability it was moon-light, being full moon according to the season of the Passover; yet, as if to make sure of their object, they bring lights with them, as well as weapons. *Judas*, their leader, no doubt had told them of some of CHRIST's miracles, and therefore they used every precaution. But, if the Reader will attend to what is related in the following verses, he will discover how the LORD rendered all these circumstances, (as he did indeed every other) to minister to his own glory, the joy of his Church, and the confusion of his enemies. Luke iv. 28—31. John vi. 15.

4 Jesus, therefore, knowing all things that should come upon him, went forth, and said unto them, Whom seek ye?

5 They answered him, Jesus of Nazareth.

Jesus saith unto them, I am *he*. And Judas also, which betrayed him, stood with them.

6 As soon then as he had said unto them, I am *he*, they went backward, and fell to the ground.

7 Then asked he them again, Whom seek ye? and they said, Jesus of Nazareth.

8 Jesus answered, I have told you that I am *he*, if therefore ye seek me, let these go their way:

9 That the saying might be fulfilled which he spake, Of them which thou gavest me have I lost none.

10 Then Simon Peter, having a sword, drew it, and smote the high priest's servant, and cut off his right ear. The servant's name was Malchus.

11 Then said Jesus unto Peter, Put up thy sword into the sheath: the cup which my Father hath given me, shall I not drink it?

12 Then the band, and the captain and officers of the Jews took Jesus, and bound him,

It is not wonderful that the *Roman* soldiers should have been ignorant of Christ's person, for they little regarded the Great Redeemer of mankind, unconscious of their need of one. But that the chief priests and Pharisees, and especially *Judas*, should not instantly have recognized Christ, is astonishing. Some have thought that the Lord for the moment struck the whole party with blindness, as the angels at Lot's house struck the *sodomites*, before that the Lord struck them to the ground. Gen. xix. 11. But be this as it may, certain it is that somewhat overawed the whole company, and probably it was a large one, if, as some suppose that the *Chiliarch* (who in verse 12 is so called) commanded not less than five hundred men.

But I pass over this, and indeed every other consideration, to call the Reader's attention to two grand points here presented to our contemplation. *First*, the promptness of Jesus to meet his enemies, in going to them unasked. And, *Secondly*, the miracle which he wrought in smiting them to the ground. Of the *first*, I shall have occasion to speak more particularly in the succeeding verses. And of the *second*, I will only beg to observe, that, according to my apprehension of things, this was the greatest miracle that we have upon record, produced by apparently the slightest exertion of Christ's power. Reader! figure to yourself an army of soldiers, with weapons, falling backward to the earth only at the simple words of Jesus, *I am!* And then ask your own heart, Who but God could have wrought such a miracle! How was that prophecy of the Psalmist concerning Christ fulfilled, *When the wicked, even mine enemies and my foes*

came upon me to eat up my flesh, they stumbled and fell. Psm.
xxvii. 2. And how blessedly also was that prophecy of *Isaiah* accomplished, which he spake concerning this *stem of Jesse, and the
Branch which should grow out of his roots,* when it was said of him,
that *he should smite the earth with the rod of his mouth, and with the
breath of his lips he should slay the wicked.* Isaiah xi. 1—4. Oh!
how easily might the same breath which cast them to the ground, have
cast them into hell! And, Reader! do not overlook how graciously
the same words of JESUS which minister comfort to his people, prove
destructive to his enemies. See Isaiah lviii. 9. Matt. xiv. 25—33.
For when at any time the LORD speaks graciously to his own, it is
for the most part in making himself known unto them. *I, even I,
am he that comforteth you. Then thou shalt call, and the* LORD *shall
answer: thou shalt cry, and He shall say, here I am. It is I, be not
afraid.* See Isaiah li. 12. Isaiah lviii. 9. Mark vi. 49, 50. So that
the very presence of the LORD, and the manifestation of that presence,
which confounds the LORD's enemies, comforts his friends; yea,
the very same words, according to the manner in which the LORD
speaks them, give life, or destroy.

When the Reader hath duly pondered these things, I would beg
to call his attention to what I before glanced at in these words and
actions of CHRIST, in the promptness of JESUS, in going forth to
meet his enemies, and voluntarily surrendering himself into their
hands. JESUS *knowing all things that should come upon him, went
forth and said unto them, whom seek ye?* Now the voluntary surrender of himself as a sacrifice for the redemption of his Church and
people, is among the grand events of the whole business, and therefore I more earnestly request the Reader's attention to it.

And for the proper apprehension of it, we must look back, according to the scriptural account of these transactions, to the everlasting
covenant, *ordered in all things and sure,* in which the Almighty Covenanters engaged before the foundation of the world. We are too
apt to begin the subject of CHRIST and his Church, at that part of it
which concerns the redemption of the Church; whereas, in truth,
this is but the consequence of things, and not the first chapter in this
wonderful volume of GOD! CHRIST, and his Church, were set up
from everlasting. And for the time-state of the Church, the LORD
JESUS, as the Head and Husband of his Church, volunteered from all
eternity to come and deliver her from the ruin of the fall, which in
the Adam-nature, in which she was to be born, in common with the
whole Adam-race, it was foreseen she would be involved. And hence
we hear CHRIST, by the Spirit of prophecy, ages before his incarnation, saying, *Sacrifice and offering thou didst not desire: mine ears
hast thou opened: burnt offering and sin offering hast thou not required; then said I, Lo! I come! In the volume of the book it is
written of me. I delight to do thy will, O my* GOD; *yea, thy law is
within my heart.* Psm. xl. 6, 7, 8. Now the freewill offering of
CHRIST as a sacrifice, constituted the principal feature in the merit of
it. So that we find, no sooner doth scripture open to the Church the
subject of redemption, and proclaim the LORD JESUS CHRIST as the
High Priest, the Altar, and the Sacrifice, but we discover also, in
the same Scriptures, the voluntary will and freeness of the LORD
JESUS, in giving himself a sacrifice.

I must not, in a work of this kind, amplify pages in bringing a selection of scriptures to this point, in proof at large. But I earnestly request the Reader to consult those I refer to. They may be classed under their several heads. *First,* what the Scriptures relate of these things, in CHRIST's willingness to offer himself a sacrifice for his Church, before the foundation of the world. See, in confirmation, Psm. lxxxix. 19—29. Prov. viii. 22 to the end. Rom. xvi. 25, 26. *Secondly.* The further relation of those things from the first dawn of revelation, and before CHRIST openly tabernacled in substance of our flesh. Every service under the law ministered to this one end, and every type and shadow had no other object but in allusion to *the one offering of the body of* JESUS CHRIST, *once for all.* Heb. x. 10. In proof of this the whole Jewish dispensation might be brought forward, and the whole code of prophecy also. See Psm. xxii. and Psm. lxix. Isaiah liii. Zech. ix. 11. *Thirdly.* When the Son of GOD appeared, and came to accomplish the full purposes of the covenant, every act of CHRIST, before the time arrived for his sufferings and death, most fully proved that his entire consent was in it. *My meat is to do the will of him that sent me,* said JESUS, *and to finish his work.* John iv. 34. *Wist ye not that I must be about my* FATHER's *business.* Luke ii. 49. Yea, *the zeal of the* LORD's *house* is said *to have eaten him up.* John ii. 17. So that every thing indicated how exceedingly his heart was engaged in this work. Jer. xxx. 21. And perhaps as striking an instance in proof, as ever could be given, was the reproof he gave to *Peter,* who, from his love to JESUS, when the LORD was foretelling his disciples of his sufferings, cried out, LORD, *be it far from thee! Get thee behind me, Satan,* (said JESUS,) *thou art an offence unto me; for thou savorest not the things which be of* GOD, *but those that be of men!* Matt. xvi. 21—23. See the Commentary there. From all which appears the earnestness with which the LORD looked forward to this great event of his sacrifice and death, as the delight of his heart. He engaged in it from all eternity. And in time, no sooner had his Almighty hands, in common with the FATHER and the HOLY GHOST, created the world, than he began to shew forth, in types and sacrifices, his redemption of the world; yea, he is said to have been *the Lamb slain from the foundation of the world,* because every offering shadowed forth the offering of his body once for all. Rev. xiii. 8. Heb. x. 10. And, *lastly,* to mention no more: the freeness and willingness with which CHRIST here came forward from the garden, to give himself up to the band of men and officers, becomes a full confirmation of the whole. He who struck to the ground the whole band, could have delivered himself from them for ever; but, as he himself said, *how then would the Scriptures have been fulfilled, that thus it must be.* See Matt. xxvi. 50—54. If the Reader wishes to consult more scriptures in proof of the voluntary offering of CHRIST, and the LORD's delight in the prospect of his death, he may turn to Luke ix. 18—22. and 51. Matt. xx. 20—28. Luke xii. 49, 50. John ix. 4. John x. 17. John xiii. 27, 31, 32.

I beg the Reader's particular notice to the wonderful authority of CHRIST, expressed in these words, in the very moment of surrendering himself: *If, therefore, ye seek me, let these* (meaning his disciples) *go their way.* I humbly conceive, that JESUS spake not as a matter of request, as though he begged it as a favor for his disciples to be at freedom to depart; but a command, they shall go their way. *Touch not mine anointed, and do my Prophets no harm.* Psm. cv. 15. And, surely, if his overruling power had such sway in the safety of others, how much more, had it pleased the LORD, might he have exercised it for himself. I mention this as an additional testimony of the free-will offering of CHRIST, in which, beyond all doubt, consisted the infinite value of his sacrifice. And what a very sweet and comfortable thought ariseth out of this view of JESUS, thus giving his disciples a safe deliverance through the midst of their enemies. Surely he standeth round about his people now, as much as then. *The* LORD *knoweth how to deliver the godly out of temptation.* 2 Pet. ii. 9. When the Prophet's servant in the Mount, found himself surrounded with the horses and chariots, even a very great host, sent by the king of *Syria* to take prisoners, the Prophet and his servant, the poor distressed follower of *Elisha,* cried out, *Alas! my master, how shall we do?* But how different did he view things, when, at the Prophet's prayer, the LORD opened his eyes, he saw a mountain full of horses of fire, and chariots of fire, encircling them both around for protection? 2 Kings vi. 14, &c. So was it with the disciples of JESUS, in the hour here described. The presence of JESUS was a wall of fire round about. Zech. ii. 5. So is it now, and ever hath been, and will be in all ages of the Church. There is a suited grace, a suited strength in CHRIST, for every occasion. And when faith is in lively exercise, a child of GOD finds himself enabled to fetch all *from* CHRIST, and to live wholly *upon* CHRIST. *I can do all things,* said Paul, (and so may every child of GOD say the same, when the LORD the HOLY GHOST quickens to the act of faith,) *through* CHRIST *which strengtheneth* me. Philip. iv. 13. 2 Cor. xii. 9, 10.

If I detain the Reader one moment longer on this very interesting passage, it shall be only to remark to him the very great preciousness in the accomplishment of our LORD's prayer, respecting the safety of his people. The LORD JESUS had just before declared to his FATHER in that prayer, (see John xvii. 12.) that he had lost none of all that the FATHER had given him. And here the Evangelist records a blessed instance of it, so immediately upon accomplishment. Surely so sweet a proof, and so graciously handed down to the Church by GOD the HOLY GHOST, ought to be had in everlasting remembrance. For what is here said of the Apostles, holds equally good to all the Church of CHRIST. Not one of them whom the FATHER hath given to the SON can be lost, either in time or eternity, either body or soul, for both are equally the FATHER's gift, and equally united to CHRIST, and equally beloved by GOD the HOLY GHOST. And it would be well if every child of GOD, from so remarkable an instance as this before us, would take comfort from it against all the exercises he may meet with in his own life. And though *Peter* seemed for the moment to have made it doubtful by cutting off the ear of one of the party, yet even this act of violence on the Apostle's side called forth no resentment from them on their's. A plain proof of the restraint JESUS had over the minds of all that came against him, and, by the way, no small proof also of his divine nature in the act. So that the whole forms a very blessed instruction, and of comfort to all the children of GOD, in all ages of the Church, and I venture to hope that my Reader will not lose sight of it. John vi. 39. Heb. ii. 13.

Of the binding of CHRIST, which as a sacrifice became highly proper, I have already dwelt upon, Matt. xxvi. 57. But, in addition to what was there offered, I would request the Reader to connect with it the wonderful coincidence of circumstances, which arise from the view of CHRIST, as a free-will offering. To bind Him, who by the breath of his mouth cast to the ground the whole party of soldiers, and who could have commanded a legion of angels to attend his divine person, how mysterious it appears! And yet, so it must be. His divine nature is proved from the omnipotency he manifested; and the binding him, as another *Isaac*, as fully demonstrated that *he was crucified through weakness*, 2 Cor. xiii. 4. and both together confirm the wonders of his person; CHRIST *crucified, to the Jews a stumbling block, and to the Greeks foolishness; but unto them that are called both Jews and Greeks,* CHRIST *the power of* GOD, *and the wisdom of* GOD. 1 Cor. i. 23, 24.

13 And led him away to Annas first; for he was father-in-law to Caiaphas, which was the high priest that same year.

14 Now Caiaphas was he which gave counsel to the Jews, that it was expedient that one man should die for the people.

15 ¶ And Simon Peter followed Jesus, and *so did* another disciple; that disciple was known unto the high priest, and went in with Jesus into the palace of the high priest.

16 But Peter stood at the door without. Then went out that other disciple, which was known unto the high priest, and spake unto her that kept the door, and brought in Peter.

17 Then saith the damsel that kept the door unto Peter, Art not thou also *one* of this man's disciples? he saith, I am not.

18 And the servants and officers stood there, who had made a fire of coals, for it was cold: and they warmed themselves: and Peter stood with them and warmed himself.

I have before noticed in the former Evangelists, some of the leading circumstances concerning the wearisome and painful walks of JESUS, from the Garden to *Annas,* and from *Annas* to *Caiaphas,* to Pilate, and to Herod, to which I refer. But there are several very weighty things connected with this view of the LORD JESUS, when led as a lamb to the slaughter, that merit our closest attention, and which, in this place, I would beg to propose to the Reader's notice.

It was according to the law of sacrifices, that the Children of Israel should present them first to the Priest, at the door of the tabernacle of the congregation. And probably this with a view, to see, that the thing offered had no blemish. I beg the Reader to turn to Levit. xvii. 1—9. in proof. Now though *Annas*, and *Caiaphas*, were both silent as to the spotlessness of CHRIST, yet the HOLY GHOST so ordered, that JESUS should not be led away, without this testimony : and therefore *Pilate*, in passing sentence, shall declare the LORD's innocency. See Matt. xxvii. 24, 25. What a very blessed proof this is, of CHRIST, the great Sacrifice. Heb. vii. 26. 1 Pet. i. 17, 18.

And while we are taking this transient view of the LORD JESUS, in the presentation before the High Priest, as a spotless sacrifice, it may not be amiss to connect with it another; namely, that when led away to slaughter, and bound with the sins of his people; so here again there was a correspondence, in being led without the camp, and suffering without the gate, Heb. xiii. 12. *He was taken from prison and from judgment*, the Prophet said, when *the* LORD JEHOVAH *had laid on him the iniquity of us all.* Isaiah liii. 6. 8. Surely the wonderful correspondence of those things with the types of old, could not have had such an exact fulfilment, but from GOD the HOLY GHOST, watching over his Church, and arranging the whole to the LORD's glory, and to the joy of his people.

In relation to the following of CHRIST, by *Peter*, and another disciple; I do not think it necessary to enlarge. Whether this other disciple was *John*, as has been generally supposed, or not, cannot be a point of great consequence to seek to know, since the HOLY GHOST is silent upon it. I confess I should rather think that it was not *John*, or either of the Apostles; but rather one of those many private disciples we read of, John xii. 42. For *John* was of *Galilee*, as well as *Peter*, and therefore his speech would have betrayed *John*, as well as *Peter*. Neither is it likely that *John*, a poor fisherman of *Galilee*, should have had much acquaintance at the High Priest's palace. But be this as it may, it cannot be important to determine ; since the HOLY GHOST hath not explained.

But in relation to *Peter*, it was among the overruling providences of the LORD, that he should follow CHRIST at this memorable hall, because here was to take place that event, of his denial of CHRIST, and that grace of JESUS towards him, in his recovery from so awful a fall, as hath proved in the Church of CHRIST, and will prove until the whole Church is brought to heaven, a subject of the deepest teaching of man's nothingness, and CHRIST's all-sufficiency. See Luke xxii. 31.

I pray the Reader to remark what is said in this scripture of the fire in the hall, kindled to warm the servants, and of the coldness of the night, which made it necessary. And yet this was the selfsame night, and but a few hours before, when JESUS sweat the bloody sweat, under the burning heat of his agony in the garden. Reader! what must the sufferings of the GOD-MAN have been, when in the open air, in a garden, and in a night of extreme cold, the LORD was thus exercised, when within a hall, full of company, as it should seem, a fire was kindled to give warmth to the people!

19 The high priest then asked Jesus of his disciples, and of his doctrine ?

20 Jesus answered him, I spake openly to the world; I ever taught in the synagogue, and in the temple, whither the Jews always resort; and in secret have I said nothing.

21 Why askest thou me? ask them which heard me what I have said unto them: behold, they know what I said.

22 And when he had thus spoken, one of the officers which stood by, struck Jesus with the palm of his hand, saying, Answerest thou the high priest so?

23 Jesus answered him, If I have spoken evil, bear witness of the evil: but if well, why smitest thou me?

24 Now Annas had sent him bound unto Caiaphas, the high priest.

25 And Simon Peter stood and warmed himself. They said therefore unto him, Art not thou also *one* of his disciples? he denied *it*, and said, I am not.

26 One of the servants of the high priest, being *his* kinsman whose ear Peter cut off, saith, Did I not see thee in the garden with him?

27 Peter then denied again: and immediately the cock crew.

John is the only Evangelist which hath recorded this examination of Christ. And the drift of it was, if possible, to discover somewhat more particularly concerning what they deemed blasphemy. See Deut. xiii. But though they wished to make this in some measure a cover with the people, yet, as they desired above all things to bring Christ under the *Roman* power, in order that he might be crucified, and not stoned, as was the punishment for blasphemy, they only designed this examination as preparatory to the bringing him before Pilate. Hence we find, according to the account given by *Luke,* (chap. xxiii. 1, 2.) that their charge against Christ before Pilate was, that *they had found him perverting the nation, and forbidding to give tribute to Cæsar, saying, that he himself was* Christ, *a King.* There is nothing said of blasphemy; this charge would have thrown back Christ upon them, to be judged at their tribunal, which of all things they studied to avoid. Christ must, according to their wishes, be turned over to the civil power, and in this case, crucifixion must be the punishment.

And here I just detain the Reader to remark how the LORD over-ruled their minds to confess the very reverse of what they intended. First, by declaring that it was not lawful for them to put any man to death, according to the Roman custom, for sedition, whereby they confessed that the prediction of the Patriarch *Jacob*, when he lay a dying, was fulfilled, *the sceptre was departed from Judah, and the lawgiver from between his feet,* and consequently *the Shiloh was come.* Gen. xlix. 10. *We have no king* (said they) *but Cæsar!* John xix. 15. Reader! do not fail to ponder well these things!

28 ¶ Then led they Jesus from Caiaphas unto the hall of judgement : and it was early, and they themselves went not into the judgement hall, lest they should be defiled; but that they might eat the passover.

29 Pilate then went out unto them, and said, What accusation bring ye against this man?

30 They answered and said unto him, If he were not a malefactor, we would not have de-livered him up unto thee.

31 Then said Pilate unto them, Take ye him, and judge him according to your law. The Jews therefore said unto him, It is not lawful for us to put any man to death :

32 That the saying of Jesus might be fulfilled, which he spake, signifying what death he should die.

33 Then Pilate entered into the judgement hall again, and called Jesus, and said unto him, Art thou the King of the Jews?

34 Jesus answered him, Sayest thou this thing of thyself, or did others tell it thee of me?

35 Pilate answered, Am I a Jew? Thine own nation, and the chief priests, have delivered thee unto me : what hast thou done?

36 Jesus answered, My kingdom is not of this world : if my kingdom were of this world, then would my servants fight, that I should not be de-livered to the Jews: but now is my kingdom not from hence.

37 Pilate therefore said unto him, Art thou a king then? Jesus answered, Thou sayest that I am a king. To this end was I born, and for this cause came I into the world, that I should bear witness unto the truth. Every one that is of the truth heareth my voice.

38 Pilate saith unto him, What is truth? and when he had said this, he went out again unto the Jews, and saith unto them, I find in him no fault *at all.*

39 But ye have a custom, that I should release unto you one at the passover: will ye therefore that I release unto you the King of the Jews?

40 Then cried they all again, saying, Not this man, but Barabbas. Now Barabbas was a robber.

It appears from the earliness which is here spoken of in hurrying away JESUS to the hall of *Pilate,* that the *Sanhedrim* must have sat up all night. Oh! with what blood-thirstiness did those men hunt after the death of JESUS? Reader! do not fail to observe, amidst the misgivings, fears, and alarms of those wretched characters, both Jews and Gentiles, how sweet the testimony JESUS gave to his person and character. *Art thou a King?* saith Pilate to him. *Thou sayest that;* (said CHRIST,) *I am a King.* But not *of* this world, though *in* this world; here in grace, hereafter in glory. Oh! sweet and blessed assurance from the lips of truth. And, as the LORD here said, he bears witness to the truth, for he himself is truth. John xi. 6.

And, Reader, do not overlook the spiritual instruction which ariseth out of the Jews' preference of a robber to JESUS. You and I have robbed GOD of his glory, and our souls of happiness: and yet how are we released at the Passover, when CHRIST, our Passover, hath been sacrificed for us, while CHRIST is by wicked hands crucified and slain? Oh! thou Lamb of GOD! truly thou hast borne our sins, and carried our sorrows! And how often have thy people preferred sin and vanity, as those Jews did *Barabbas* of old, before thee, the LORD of life and glory.

REFLECTIONS.

Oh! Gethsemane! sacred, hallowed spot! Did JESUS oft-times resort thither with his disciples? And wilt thou now, O LORD, by thy sweet Spirit, aid my meditations, that I may take the wing of faith, and often traverse over the solemn ground? It was a garden in which the first *Adam* began to break through the fence of GOD's holy plantation. And in a garden the second *Adam,* so called, shall begin the soul-travail of sorrow, to do away the effects of it. And, oh! what humiliation, what agonies, what conflicts in the arduous

work? Oh! how vast the glory, when smiting to the earth his enemies, the LORD JESUS proved his GODHEAD by the breath of his
mouth! Sweetly do I see thee, LORD, by faith, going forth a willing
sacrifice. Lo! I come! said JESUS. So come, LORD, now, by
grace!

Hail, thou King of Zion, for thou hast here most blessedly borne
testimony to this glorious truth. Then as a King do thou reign and
rule over thy Church, thy people, both in heaven and earth. And
let my soul continually discover *the goings of my* GOD *and King, in
his sanctuary.* Surely, dear LORD, it is thine, both by nature, providence, grace, and glory, to maintain and order, to regulate and
appoint, to establish and confirm thy royal laws, and the government
of thy kingdom, in the hearts and minds of all thy people, whom
thou hast made willing in the day of thy power! Reign thou, and
rule in me, the LORD of life and glory! Amen.

CHAP. XIX.

CONTENTS.

The LORD JESUS *is here scourged, crowned with thorns, and mocked,
He is crucified. He giveth up the ghost. His burial.*

THEN Pilate therefore took Jesus, and scourged *him.*

2 And the soldiers platted a crown of thorns,
and put *it* on his head, and they put on him a
purple robe,

3 And said, Hail, King of the Jews! and they
smote him with their hands.

4 Pilate therefore went forth again, and saith
unto them, Behold, I bring him forth to you, that
ye may know that I find no fault in him.

Every thing in relation to the LORD JESUS CHRIST is interesting,
and merits our closest regard. To a child of GOD, whose eyes are
opened to behold in some measure or degree, the wonderous things
of GOD's law, here is a subject, which at every step we take, shews
us yet more and more, how the LORD was carrying on his own
design, and they who were the actors of it, the most unconscious
creatures what they were doing. What could *Pilate* mean by
scourging JESUS? Some say it was with a view to soften the minds
of those savages, who pushed him on to exercise an unjust sentence
against CHRIST, at which his own conscience revolted. I cannot
say that I think so. He was a mere instrument in my view to do
that, which all along had been determined by JEHOVAH to be done,
to fulfil that scripture in relation to his Church; *By his stripes we are
healed.* Isaiah liii. 5. And the soldiers, what did they do? Certainly, they had no consciousness what they were about, when they

4 X 2

put the thorny crown upon his divine head, and clothed him with the purple robe. But here they literally fulfilled what God had said in the curse: *Thorns and thistles* the earth was to bring forth to the man. And here Christ the God-man, as if to shew his pre-eminency in suffering as in glory, shall be crowned with them. Gen. iii. 18. Coloss. i. 18. And they bow the knee in mockery as they meant, but in reality fulfilling the prophecy; for Jehovah had said ages before, though the kings of the earth, like *Pilate* and *Herod,* and the rulers, like the Chief Priests, and Scribes, and Pharisees, are all agreed against the Lord, and against his Christ; yet in the very moment of their most violent outrage, the Lord then sets his King upon his holy hill of Zion. For never was the kingly office of Christ more blessedly shewn than in that day, when those soldiers said, *Hail, King of the Jews!* and *Pilate,* the unjust judge was compelled to declare, that in Him he could find no fault. Sweet and precious testimony from the mouth of an enemy, to the holiness of Christ! Psm. ii. 1—6.

5 Then came Jesus forth, wearing the crown of thorns, and the purple robe. And *Pilate* saith unto them, Behold the man!

6 When the chief priests therefore and officers saw him, they cried out, saying, Crucify *him,* crucify *him.* Pilate saith unto them, Take ye him, and crucify *him:* for I find no fault in him.

7 The Jews answered him, We have a law, and by our law he ought to die, because he made himself the Son of God.

8 When Pilate therefore heard that saying, he was the more afraid;

9 And went again into the judgement hall, and saith unto Jesus, Whence art thou? But Jesus gave him no answer.

10 Then saith Pilate unto him, Speakest thou not unto me? knowest thou not that I have power to crucify thee, and have power to release thee?

11 Jesus answered, Thou couldest have no power *at all* against me, except it were given thee from above: therefore he that delivered me unto thee hath the greater sin.

12 And from thenceforth Pilate sought to release him: but the Jews cried out, saying, If thou let this man go, thou art not Cæsar's friend: who-

soever maketh himself a king speaketh against Cesar.

13 When Pilate therefore heard that saying, he brought Jesus forth, and sat down in the judgement seat, in a place that is called the Pavement, but in the Hebrew, Gabbatha.

14 And it was the preparation of the passover, and about the sixth hour: and he saith unto the Jews, Behold your King?

15 But they cried out, Away with *him*, away with *him*; crucify him. Pilate saith unto them, Shall I crucify your King? The chief priests answered, We have no king but Cesar.

16 Then delivered he him therefore unto them to be crucified. And they took Jesus and led *him* away.

17 And he bearing his cross went forth into a place called *the place* of a skull, which is called in the Hebrew, Golgotha:

18 Where they crucified him, and two other with him, on either side one, and Jesus in the midst.

I beg the Reader to notice with particular regard, his Redeemer coming forth with his thorny crown and purple robe, his sacred body lacerated with stripes, and the blood streaming in every direction, and ponder well the cause. Isaiah, ages before, proclaimed the cause, and here the history confirms it; *He was wounded for our transgressions, he was bruised for our iniquities.* Isaiah liii. 5. Without an eye to this, as the surety of his people, how impossible would it be to reconcile the wonderful appearance on any principles of common justice. But, beheld as the Sponsor of his Church, and what a ray of light shines at once upon the whole, to explain the cause, and to endear such love to every heart.

If the Reader will read with attention the first verse in this paragraph, he will perceive, that in our translation it is said, when JESUS thus came forth, *Pilate saith, behold the man!* But if he observes, the name of *Pilate* is in Italics, by which is meant that the word is not in the original. And though I do not mean to speak decidedly upon the subject, I venture to think that it ought not to be there. For if it be supposed, that it is JESUS himself that saith, *behold the man!* it would be in conformity to the analogy of scripture. In the Old Testament CHRIST is intr..duced as calling upon his Church in like manner; *Behold me! Behold me!* Isa. lxv. 1. *Look unto me, and be ye saved.* Isaiah xlv. 22. And GOD the FATHER proclaims him to the Church in like manner, and bids the people to behold him. Isaiah xlii. 1. with Matt. xii. 18. And so doth GOD the HOLY GHOST. John i. 29, 36. Hence, therefore, when the LORD JESUS came forth before the high priests and rulers, having *given his back to the smiters, and his cheeks to them that plucked off the hair,* as the Prophet described him, CHRIST calls upon them *to behold the man!* And their cry at the sight of CHRIST to crucify him, becomes a yet further confirmation of this prophecy, which said, that he would be *despised and rejected of men.* Isaiah liii. 3. LORD! grant to me grace to eye thee with that melting look described by the prophet, until the whole heart goeth out in desires after thee, and every affection is awakened into love to thee. Zech. xii. 10.

I stay not to make long remarks upon the conduct of *Pilate.* It would keep us from higher subjects. But, it is interesting in some measure to observe, what different passions of fear and guilt, and the contending conflicts of this man's conscience, operated upon his mind. But I more particularly request the Reader to keep in view that most precious answer of the LORD JESUS, when after long silence, he reproved the unjust judge for his insolent assumption of power, which he said he had, either to crucify CHRIST or to release him. *Thou couldest have no power,* said JESUS, *at all against me, except it were given thee from above.* JESUS looked over the heads of all his foes, to eye the hand of JEHOVAH in this appointment. And, Reader! it would be always well for you and for me, and for all the LORD's people to do the same, in all the lesser considerations we meet with in life. See Gen. xlv. 7, 8. Acts ii. 23.

On the subject of CHRIST bearing his cross, I have already taken notice in the former Evangelists, to which therefore I refer.

19 And Pilate wrote a title, and put *it* on the cross, and the writing was, JESUS OF NAZARETH, THE KING OF THE JEWS.

20 This title then read many of the Jews: for the place where Jesus was crucified was nigh to the city : and it was written in Hebrew, *and* Greek, *and* Latin.

21 Then said the chief priests of the Jews to Pilate, Write not, The King of the Jews; but that he said, I am King of the Jews.

22 Pilate answered, What I have written, I have written.

There is somewhat very striking and well worthy of our regard, in the title which *Pilate* wrote and put on the cross of CHRIST. I will beg to detain the Reader while I propose an observation or two upon it.

It appears from history, that it was the custom of the *Romans,* when at any time inflicting capital punishment, first to proclaim the name and crimes of the person going to suffer. Sometimes this was done by an herald going before the culprit to the place of execution, and sometimes by publishing his name and crimes over his head, that all passing by might read. And in all those cases, it was done with a view to justify the sentence, and to make known the equity of the *Roman* nation and character.

In this instance of our dear LORD, there are *two* points which are more particularly deserving our notice. The first is, that the Inscription on CHRIST's cross was the very reverse of what they intended, for it confirmed both CHRIST's innocency, and proved by their own confession what JESUS had claimed; *This is the King of the Jews.* And the other is, that *Pilate* himself who had passed sentence of death upon JESUS for the claim, now confirmed it with his own hand. And no sooner was the thing done, than some of the more knowing ones perceived the oversight, and begged *Pilate to alter it.* But the LORD who compelled *Pilate's* hand thus to honor CHRIST, and write his own *mittimus* of condemnation, restrained his heart from allowing any change. *What I have written,* (said he,) *I have written.* And this positiveness in such a character as *Pilate* is the more wonderful, who had before shewn such a changeable, fearful, and irresolute mind. Reader! think of it, and behold how the LORD thus overruled the whole to vindicate CHRIST's innocency, to proclaim his royalties, and to have his name published in the three great languages of the chief part of the then governing world. The Hebrew tongue being the language of the Jews, the Greek of the Gentiles among the greater parts of the earth, and the Latin the ordinary dialect of the *Romans.* What but the predisposing power of the LORD could have induced all these things? And who but must see the divine hand in the whole?

23 Then the soldiers, when they had crucified Jesus, took his garments, and made four parts, to every soldier a part; and also *his* coat; now the coat was without seam, woven from the top throughout.

24 They said therefore among themselves, Let us not rend it, but cast lots for it, whose it shall be: that the scripture might be fulfilled, which saith, They parted my raiment among them, and for my vesture they did cast lots. These things therefore the soldiers did.

We cannot but be led to make similar observations of the overruling power of GOD, in respect to the soldiers casting lots for one of CHRIST's garments, and dividing the other into four parts, for each soldier a part. How should such an exact fulfilment of prophecy have taken place, and which was delivered at least a thousand years before, had not the LORD who gave the prediction, watched over the accomplishment, and predisposed and gave a direction to every thing leading to the end of it? The very words were minutely fulfilled; *They parted my raiment among them, and for my vesture they cast lots.* These things therefore the soldiers did!

Just let me add, that there seemeth somewhat very emblematical in these garments of JESUS. Infidels, like these soldiers, may, and will take a part of CHRIST, some that are infidels respecting his divine nature, and some that call in question his atonement. They are willing to call him a Prophet and a teacher of morality, and one who died as a martyr to confirm these characters. But they desire but a part in CHRIST, and therefore rend the scriptures to this purpose. Truth, however, like the seamless coat of JESUS, in the lot of every one where CHRIST is given, is a compleat whole. It admits nothing to be taken from it, neither admits any thing to be added to it. A whole sinner needs a whole SAVIOR. CHRIST must be all, or nothing. And blessed are they who thus have the LORD for their GOD. So sung the Church, and such will be the song of every individual of CHRIST's body. Isaiah lxi. 10.

25 Now there stood by the cross of Jesus, his mother, and his mother's sister, Mary, the *wife* of Cleophas, and Mary Magdalene.

26 When Jesus therefore saw his mother, and the disciple standing by, whom he loved, he saith unto his mother, Woman, behold thy son!

27 Then saith he to the disciple, Behold thy mother! and from that hour that disciple took her unto his own *home.*

28 ¶ After this, Jesus knowing that all things were now accomplished, that the scripture might be fulfilled, saith, I thirst.

29 Now there was set a vessel full of vinegar: and they filled a spunge with vinegar, and put *it* upon hyssop, and put *it* to his mouth.

30 When Jesus therefore had received the vinegar, he said, It is finished. And he bowed his head, and gave up the ghost.

We have within these verses, as recorded by this Evangelist, only *Three* of the last words of CHRIST on the cross. But, from the corresponding history of the crucifixion, as related by the other Evangelists, there were *Four* others, and all particularly striking and important. It is a very usual thing among men to treasure up the last words of dying friends, as being more than ordinarily ponderous and meriting regard. Those of the LORD JESUS must surely be eminently so. I would beg in this place, as *John* is the last of the Evangelists, and who closeth the history, to gather them into one point

of view, and as far as we can well form our judgment with correctness, to look at them one by one, in the order in which we may
suppose the LORD delivered them.

It is worthy our observation, that *three* of those last sayings of
CHRIST on the cross, were addressed to the FATHER, and *four* to those
around him. But, like his farewell prayer in the midst of his Apostles,
the greater part had respect to his Church, and not to himself. See
John xvii. The first in point of order, seems to have been that in
which JESUS said, FATHER *forgive them, for they know not what they
do.* Luke xxiii. 34. Was not this, (I ask the question,) as in the
LORD's High Priestly Office, now entering upon it, as on the great
day of atonement? The Cross his altar, himself both sacrifice and
sacrificer, his blood streaming over his sacred body, his wounds as
the incense of his censer, and his dying sweat ascending as the burnt-
offering before GOD? And in this manner, his arms extended, as the
High Priest his type in the temple was stretched forth to bless the
people; so JESUS when he cried out, FATHER! *forgive them, for they
know not what they do!* Reader! were you and I included in this
prayer? It is a grand enquiry. Let us pause over it, and ponder
it well.

The *second* voice of JESUS heard on the cross, was this, which is
recorded by *John* in this place. These words of CHRIST in their first
meaning, should seem to have had an especial regard to the disposing of *Mary* after the LORD's death, but I humbly conceive somewhat of higher moment was intended by JESUS, and in relation to his
whole Church and people. For, surely, the temporary care of this
woman might have been provided for in a less public way. It would
hardly have been left to this hour. Neither would the HOLY GHOST,
one might be led to suppose, have thought it necessary to have made
such a special record of it among the last weighty sayings of the
dying JESUS. But, as I have often in the course of this humble work
observed before, so here again I desire to say, that I do not presume
to speak decidedly. I venture to think that the LORD had higher
motives in view, than merely recommending *Mary* to the care of
John. And might it not be, (I ask the question,) to remind *Mary*,
and in her his whole Church, when he said, *Woman, behold thy Son!*
what the angel had announced to her before the incarnation of his
name and glory, as JESUS a Redeemer, and when in consequence she
called CHRIST her SAVIOR? See Luke i. 26—47. And when the
LORD said to *John, behold thy mother!* was not this intended no less to
correct, and reprove, all those honors which the LORD knew the
idolatry of the future ages of the world would produce, in ascribing
to *Mary*, whom CHRIST always called Woman, unsuitable and improper names?

The LORD's answer to the cry of the penitent thief on the cross, we
may, I think, without the danger of misplacing in point of order,
consider as the *third* voice of JESUS in those solemn hours. And, oh!
what a number of the richest contemplations arise out of those gracious words of CHRIST. LORD! *remember me*, said the dying malefactor, *when thou comest into thy kingdom! And* JESUS *said unto
him, Verily I say unto thee, to day shalt thou be with me in paradise,*
Luke xxiii. 42, 43. I must not allow myself to enter into the sweet
and almost endless subject those words lead to. But just let me re-

mark, what rich, free, unmerited, unlooked for, boundless grace, was
here shewn by Christ, to a poor perishing sinner? What wonders
hath Jesus here at once opened of the invisible world; and the instant possession of paradise, and Jesus with it, by every spirit when
departing the body, in the faith and enjoyment of Christ's blood and
righteousness? And what a most effectual silence doth it give to the
ungracious and unbecoming pretensions of all self-righteous Pharisees? How sweetly were the Apostle's words proved in this instance,
and how suitably to be applied to every other; *Not by works of
righteousness which we have done, but according to his mercy he saved
us by the washing of regeneration and renewing of the* Holy Ghost,
which he shed on us abundantly through Jesus Christ *our* Savior,
Titus iii. 5, 6.

The *fourth* words of Jesus on the cross, were remarkable indeed,
and full of the highest import. The Lord of life and glory had
hung upon the cross full three hours, when he uttered this dolorous
cry: *Eli, Eli,* (or as Mark renders it, *Eloi, Eloi,* for both are the
same, Mark xv. 34.) *lama sabachthani, which is, being interpreted,
My* God! *my* God! *why hast thou forsaken me?* Matt. xxvii. 46, 47.
The first three of these words are Hebrew, and the latter *Chaldee* or
Syriac. We have the same word in the Chaldee paraphrase of the
Psm. xxii. 1. So that Christ here fulfilled that prophecy, and the
application of it was plainly seen to be to Him, and to Him only.

It is impossible with our scanty faculties, to fathom the depth of
this wonderful cry of Christ. One thing, however, is very plain.
The forsaking which the Lord speaks of, could not mean that that
union of God and man in One Person was in the smallest degree lessened, for death itself could not accomplish this. In Christ dwelleth
for ever and uninterruptedly, *the fulness of the* Godhead *bodily.*
Col. ii. 9. Neither had he lost the favor and love of Jehovah, for
that also was, and is, impossible. But, if one may venture to offer a
conjecture on a subject of such a deepness in mystery, probably it
might be for the time, the Lord's having lost an enjoying sense of
that favor, which all along before he had possessed. And as Jesus
was now sustaining the whole weight and burden of the sins of his
people, he felt what those sins merited; and was therefore for a space,
as one deprived of the refreshing presence of Jehovah, that his
people might not be deprived of it for ever. Reader! think, if the
beloved Son of God was thus exercised, and sent forth such an heart
piercing cry at the apprehension of divine withdrawings; what must
be the shrieks of the eternally miserable who have lost the gracious
presence of God for ever?

The *fifth* voice we hear from our Lord on the cross, seems most
probably to have been that which *John* hath noticed, (verse 28.)
when he said, *I thirst.* I say most probably this might be according to the order in which the Lord spake, for I am not able to
determine. Neither is it I should suppose material. But what I think
of more importance is what *John* hath said concerning it, that Jesus
*knowing that all things were now accomplished, that the scripture
might be fulfilled, saith, I thirst.* The fulfilling of the scripture,
was in reference to that prophecy of Christ, Psm. xxii. 15. where
the Lord is described as brought into the dust of death; and where,
according to another prophecy, vinegar is said to be given to him.

Psm. lxix. 21. The soldiers who gave CHRIST the offered vinegar were unconscious what they did; but how precious are such things to a child of GOD? And what was implied in this thirst of JESUS? Not merely a thirst of body, but of soul. An holy thirst to see all the whole purposes of his soul-travail, and sufferings, and death, accomplished in the salvation of his people. Reader! JESUS thirsted for his chosen. And shall not you and I thirst after Him? Oh! for a vehement thirst as one of old expressed, when he cried out, *As the hart thirsteth for the water-brooks, so longeth my soul after thee O* GOD! Psm. xlii. 1. Song viii. 6.

The two last cries of CHRIST upon the cross, are those related by *John* and *Luke.* Perhaps the former was that which *John* hath recorded, for he saith, *when* JESUS, *therefore, had received the vinegar, he said, it is finished.* And *Luke* adds, *when* JESUS *had cried with a loud voice, he said,* FATHER! *into thy hands I commend my spirit; and having said thus, he gave up the ghost,* Luke xxiii. 46. It should seem, therefore, that it was in this order the LORD thus spake. But I presume not to determine. However, the words themselves are the same, in whatever manner they were delivered; and they are full of the highest import and richest consolation. Redemption-work was finished; and all the purposes for which CHRIST made his soul an offering for sin, were fully answered. The SON of GOD, therefore, in our nature, as a mighty conqueror retiring from the field of battle, having gotten himself the victory, cried out with a loud voice; not as one whose strength was consumed, but as One who laid down his life, as he had said, that he might take it again, and no man taking it from him, (John x. 17.) it is finished. And now committed himself into his FATHER's hands; as if to teach all his redeemed how to die in faith, and to whom *to commit their souls* in a dying hour, *as unto a faithful Creator.* 1 Pet. iv. 19. Psm. xxxi. 5. Acts vii. 55, to end.

31 The Jews therefore, because it was the preparation, that the bodies should not remain upon the cross on the sabbath-day, (for that sabbath-day was an high day,) besought Pilate that their legs might be broken, and *that* they might be taken away.

32 Then came the soldiers, and brake the legs of the first, and of the other which was crucified with him.

33 But when they came to Jesus, and saw that he was dead already, they brake not his legs:

34 But one of the soldiers with a spear pierced his side, and forthwith came thereout blood and water.

35 And he that saw *it* bare record, and his re-

cord is true : and he knoweth that he saith true, that ye might believe.

36 For these things were done, that the scripture should be fulfilled, A bone of him shall not be broken.

37 And again another scripture saith, They shall look on him whom they pierced.

The preparation here spoken of, was, I apprehend, that which was usual for the sabbath, see Mark xv. 42. and this was still more highly esteemed, being a sabbath in the passover season; and added to these, it was the sabbath in which all the people presented themselves before the LORD. Levit. xxiii. 10, &c. And the law allowed none to hang on a tree until the night. Deut. xxi. 22, 23. But what is most worthy our observation, and indeed the HOLY GHOST hath put his divine emphasis upon what is here recorded, in the preservation of the bones of CHRIST unbroken, (as his mystical body forms a compleat whole, and never to be broken,) and the side of JESUS pierced ; thereby fulfilling at once two memorable prophecies. See Exod. xii. 46. Numb. ix. 12. Psm. xxxiv. 10. Zech. xii. 10. Rev. i. 7. See also John iii. 5. and the commentary upon it. And I beg to detain the Reader with a short observation more on the words of *John*, in quoting the passage from Zech. xii. 10. If the Reader will compare what *John* here saith with the words of the Prophet, he will find, that in the prophecy, JEHOVAH is speaking of himself; and therefore saith, that when he hath poured upon the house of David and the inhabitants of Jerusalem, the spirit of grace and of supplications; the consequence, saith the LORD, shall be, that they shall look upon *me*. Whereas *John* records the fact, and is, therefore, only the historian to prove the correspondence. But, Reader! do not overlook that *He* who predicted and promised these things was JEHOVAH; (indeed who less than JEHOVAH could so foresee and so promise,) and that JEHOVAH is JESUS. Nothing can be more plain and palpable. And how was the whole yet further accomplished, when at the day of Pentecost, as JESUS promised his disciples, he sent the HOLY GHOST with these tokens? Luke xxiv. 49. John xv. 26, 27. Acts ii. 33—41.

38 ¶ And after this, Joseph of Arimathea, being a disciple of Jesus, but secretly for fear of the Jews, besought Pilate that he might take away the body of Jesus: and Pilate gave *him* leave. He came therefore, and took the body of Jesus.

39 And there came also Nicodemus, which at the first came to Jesus by night, and brought a mixture of myrrh and aloes, about an hundred pound *weight*.

40 Then took they the body of Jesus, and wound it in linen clothes with the spices, as the manner of the Jews is to bury.

41 Now in the place where he was crucified there was a garden; and in the garden a new sepulchre, wherein was never man yet laid.

42 There laid they Jesus therefore, because of the Jews' preparation *day;* for the sepulchre was nigh at hand.

I do not think it necessary to enlarge on the circumstances relating to these honorable men. But in addition to what hath been offered by way of note in the history of it, as recorded by *Mark* and *Luke;* I would just observe, that the interment of the body of CHRIST became a most important service, both as it proved the reality of his death, and as it confirmed the types and prophecies concerning him. Isaiah xxvi. 19. Psm. xvi. 9, 10. Matt. xii. 38—40. And as the life of the Church in her recovery from the Adam-nature fall, ariseth out of the assurance, that CHRIST by his death had destroyed death; so the reality and certainty of it became a momentous article of the faith in CHRIST. It was necessary CHRIST should die, to do away sin and death by the sacrifice of himself. It was as necessary that he should be *buried,* that his humblings might be compleat. The LORD had said by the spirit of prophecy a thousand years before; *thou hast brought me into the dust of death.* Psm. xxii. 15. And it was necessary, that though he died as one under the hands of justice, he should have an honorable *funeral,* and therefore, though his body was forfeited; yet to fulfil the seemingly contradictory prophecies, in which it was said, *he is taken from prison and from judgment, and cut off out of the land of the living;* yet, contrary to all human probabilities, *he should make his grave with the wicked, and with the rich in his death;* Isaiah liii. 8, 9. these godly men, *Joseph of Arimathea,* an honorable counsellor, and *Nicodemus,* a ruler of the Jews, should arise to perform this office. And, as all these things were done by his death, his burial, and the honorable nature of it to fulfil those grand purposes; so his resurrection which followed, arose out of all those circumstances. JESUS must conquer death by his own death. He must go into the grave to subdue the power of the grave. And he must arise from the dead, in proof that he hath triumphed over both death and the grave in their own territories, and shewed the way to all his followers, how they are by virtue of their union with him, and communion in all that belongs to him, secured in all the blessings of his resurrection. So interesting an article of our holy faith, becomes therefore the certainty of CHRIST's burial; and blessed be GOD, who hath made such ample provision in the scriptures to ascertain its reality.

REFLECTIONS.

My soul! never give over thy meditations of this unequalled subject! Follow the footsteps of thy LORD from place to place, the hall of Pilate, the hill of Calvary, from Gabbatha to Golgotha, and through all the painful process of the wonderful sights exhibited on that memorable day, and hear the voice of thy LORD at every one; *Behold! and see! if there be any sorrow like unto my sorrow, which is done unto me, wherewith the LORD hath afflicted me in the day of his fierce anger!*

But do not barely contemplate the astonishing scene, but meditate the cause. Read the inscription on the cross. *He was wounded for our trangressions, he was bruised for our iniquities, the chastisement of our peace was upon him, and with his stripes we are healed!* Matchless love! The SON of GOD becomes man that man might become a son of GOD. JESUS the HOLY, harmless, undefiled JESUS, is made sin who knew no sin, that his people might be made the righteousness of GOD in him.

From the cross let my soul in holy meditation follow the LORD to the tomb. And why not hear the same voice as the holy women did, which said, *Come, see the place where the LORD lay.* Never, surely, did the grave receive such a Prisoner, though but for a short space! Never had death and the grave their full triumphs, when in the same hour their empire received a full overthrow. Precious JESUS! thou hast the keys of death, hell, and the grave. Oh! for grace frequently by faith to visit the garden and the tomb where the body of JESUS hath lain. Here let my soul meditate the wonderous subject, until He who hath the key of David, opens my little spot and grave to receive my body. Even now I hear the voice of consolation, *blessed are the dead which die in the* LORD!

CHAP. XX.

CONTENTS.

The LORD *appeareth to* Mary Magdalene. *Afterwards to his Disciples.* Thomas *doubteth the Resurrection of* JESUS, *is convinced of the Truth of it, and expresseth his Joy.*

THE first *day* of the week cometh Mary Magdalene early, when it was yet dark unto the sepulchre, and seeth the stone taken away from the sepulchre.

2 Then she runneth, and cometh to Simon Peter, and to the other disciple whom Jesus loved, and saith unto them, They have taken away the Lord out of the sepulchre, and we know not where they have laid him.

3 Peter therefore went forth, and that other disciple, and came to the sepulchre.

4 So they ran both together; and the other dis-

ciple did outrun Peter, and came first to the sepulchre.

5 And he stooping down, *and looking in*, saw the linen clothes lying; yet went he not in.

6 Then cometh Simon Peter following him, and went into the sepulchre, and seeth the linen clothes lie,

7 And the napkin that was about his head, not lying with the linen clothes, but wrapped together in a place by itself.

8 Then went in also that other disciple, which came first to the sepulchre, and he saw and believed.

9 For as yet they knew not the scripture, that he must rise again from the dead.

10 Then the disciples went away again unto their own home.

Part of three days, agreeably to scripture prediction, the LORD lay in the grave. On the third day he arose, and the events induced by it in the minds of his people, are first recorded. The sepulchres among the Jews were roomy places, so as to admit of the entrance of several at a time, being as some are described, four cubits by six. This explains what is said by *Mark*, that they entered into it, Mark xvi. 5. But what is most to our purpose, is to consider the very great backwardness in the whole of our LORD's company of disciples, both men and women, to the belief of CHRIST's resurrection. Nothing can be more certain, than that they had no apprehension what the resurrection from the dead should mean. *They knew not the scripture* it is said, that is, they had never considered the subject. And although the Old Testament scriptures had in a great variety of places spoken of it, both by prophecy and by figure, and JESUS himself had more than once taught it, yet their only views of CHRIST had respect to a kingdom of this world, and not the smallest apprehension of another. So that the surprize of *Mary Magdalene*, and *Peter*, and *John*, going to the sepulchre at her wonderful account was evident, yet we find it excited consternation for the present only, and all except *Mary* soon returned again unto their own home. See Hosea vi. 2. James ii. 17. Matt. xii. 40. xvi. 21. and xxii. 23—32.

11 ¶ But Mary stood without at the sepulchre weeping: and as she wept, she stooped down, *and looked* into the sepulchre,

12 And seeth two angels in white sitting, the

one at the head, and the other at the feet, where
the body of Jesus had lain.

13 And they say unto her, Woman, why weepest thou? she saith unto them, Because they have
taken away my Lord, and I know not where they
have laid him.

14 And when she had thus said, she turned herself back, and saw Jesus standing, and knew not
that it was Jesus.

There is somewhat particularly interesting in this short account
of *Mary* still waiting at the sepulchre. So attached was she to the
Person of JESUS, that, though she had no hopes of ever seeing him
again, and convinced that he was not there, yet still she waits in
silence, weeping with great sorrow, and still looking in, not knowing
how to leave the sacred spot. And is it not so with waiting souls now
when they miss JESUS where before they have found him; and
though ordinances, and hearing the word preached, or reading it
themselves in dark seasons, do not bring such sweet views of CHRIST
as in times past; yet can they not go away from the means, but will
be sending forth the anxious enquiry like the spouse of old; *Saw ye
Him whom my soul loveth?* Song iii. 3.

It doth not appear that *Mary* felt any fear at the surprizing sight
of those angels in white, which she saw in looking in again to the sepulchre. One might have been led to suppose, that though her grief
was great, yet such a supernatural appearance would have alarmed
her. Neither did their address, as it should seem, affect her with any
concern, for she answered their questions as though they had been
men. And when she turned herself about, perhaps at hearing the
footsteps of JESUS, and beheld JESUS without knowing him, we do
not read of any of that alarm, which at such a place, and upon such
an occasion, might have been reasonably expected. No doubt, agreeably to that sweet promise, *as thy days, so shall thy strength be;* the
LORD who was so near her, strengthened her mind with suitable
firmness. And so we may conclude the LORD doth by all his people.
Many sweet instructions arise out of this short scripture. You see the
LORD may be, and, as in this instance, certainly is, very near his redeemed, when they like *Mary* are very unconscious of his presence.
And you observe, that the first discovery of JESUS, as here, must
begin on the LORD's side; for otherwise, like her, our eyes will be
holden, we shall not know him. And I pray the Reader to observe
yet further, that however earnest we are at any time in seeking
JESUS, the LORD is still before-hand in seeking us. For it is not only
one of the most precious truths of our charter in grace, *if we love
him, it is because he hath first loved us;* but it is a blessed promise
of the same divine covenant, that before his people at any time call,
he answers. 1 John iv. 19. Isaiah lxv. 24.

15 Jesus saith unto her, Woman, why weepest
thou? whom seekest thou? she, supposing him to

be the gardener, saith unto him, Sir, if thou have borne him hence, tell me where thou hast laid him, and I will take him away.

16 Jesus saith unto her, Mary. She turned herself, and saith unto him, Rabboni; which is to say, Master.

17 Jesus saith unto her, Touch me not: for I am not yet ascended to my Father: but go to my brethren, and say unto them, I ascend unto my Father and your Father: and *to* my God and your God.

This is a most interesting account of the first interview of the LORD JESUS with his redeemed, after he arose from the dead. *Mark* seems so struck with the gracious act, that JESUS should make choice of this woman to have the first sight of his person, when coming forth out of the other world, that he hath made a special record of it. *He appeared first,* (said he,) *to Mary Magdalene, out of whom he had cast seven devils,* Mark xvi. 9. As if to say, mark the astonishing grace of JESUS! All his redeemed shall know him; but that precious child of his whom Satan hath most worried, shall have the first love token of JESUS.

I pass over the relation, beautiful as it is, to read of *Mary's* supposing JESUS to have been the gardener, and her request to JESUS under the then unconscious state of her mind; I pass over these things to call the Reader's attention to matters yet of higher moment, in our LORD's gracious condescension to this woman. And I pray the Reader not to forget in the whole of what is here said to connect with it, that the humblest and poorest of JESUS's little ones, are as much interested in the account as *Mary* was herself. Surely JESUS made choice of this woman purposely to impress this upon his Church. Who could be apparently further from the LORD, than one in whom seven devils had raged and reigned? And yet who could be dearer to the LORD, when this woman is chosen before the whole college of Apostles, to have the first sight and conversation with a risen and triumphant JESUS? Reader! do not forget this.

How JESUS manifested himself to *Mary* when calling her by name, and what a look or gesture, or special token of his Person accompanied that call, may be supposed, but is not capable of being described. How doth that dear LORD now in numberless instances, though not in a visible form, manifest himself to his people otherwise than he doth to the world? But what must have been the first feelings of *Mary's* heart, when she discovered that it was JESUS. The name by which she addressed CHRIST is very striking, *Rabboni.* And if, as some say, that it is never made use of but when speaking of GOD, it is indeed very precious. We know that *Rab,* though a name of great dignity, was always in use among the Jews after their return from *Chaldea,* for it is a *Syriac* word. And our LORD's direction to his disciples concerning it, may serve to throw some light upon the subject. Matt. xxiii. 7—10. *Rabboni* is the plural also of *Rab*, and as such must certainly be considered very different from the common acceptation of the word when used in the singular. And as it is allowed by all to be of higher import than *Rab*, or *Rabbi*, I confess that I am inclined to accept it in this place, (and which is the only place we find it used in the whole Bible,) as the full confession of *Mary* to the GODHEAD of CHRIST. Struck by such a palpable testimony of his eternal nature, in his resurrection from the dead, she hailed him *Rabboni!*

The LORD's answer to her comes now to be considered. JESUS *saith unto her, touch me not.* By which we are to understand, not that the LORD would have objected to this token of her affection, for we find that soon after the LORD made *Thomas* put his hand into his side, (verse 25.) But this was not the moment for *Mary* to be so employed. The LORD had a message to send her upon to his disciples. It was time that they, as well as herself, should receive the joyful tidings of his resurrection, and therefore he would first send her to them. *I am not yet ascended to my* FATHER. As if he had said, there will be time enough before my return to glory, to grant both to you, and to them, many an opportunity of indulging all in those desires; but for the present, hasten *to my brethren, and say unto them, I ascend to my* FATHER, *and your* FATHER, *and to my* GOD, *and your* GOD. See Mark xvi. 7. There is somewhat uncommonly precious and blessed in those words of the LORD JESUS. GOD was CHRIST's GOD and FATHER, in a way perfectly distinct from every other, as CHRIST, that is, God and Man in One Person. For, when the SON of GOD took into union with himself that holy portion of human nature, and became the Head and Husband of his Church, he put himself, as Mediator, into those relations, as Servant of JEHOVAH, and Surety of his Church. So that in this view, GOD, that is, FATHER, SON, and HOLY GHOST, is both the GOD and FATHER of CHRIST, as such; and the GOD, and the FATHER of the Church in CHRIST, by adoption and grace. All which differs from the eternal relationship which subsist between the persons of the GODHEAD, and in which there is a perfect equality, by whatever names the persons in the GODHEAD are distinguished, in nature, and in essence, and in all divine perfections and glory.

In addition to the observations already offered on this first appearance of CHRIST, after he arose from the dead, and the message sent to his disciples, see Mark xvi. Luke xxiv. I would in this place only beg to remark, that those immediate manifestations the LORD JESUS so graciously made of himself at his resurrection, were evidently intended, (and it will be the highest wisdom of the Church so to accept them,) as the most decided proofs of his unalterable love to his people. Death had made no change, either in his nature, or in his affection. He was the same JESUS after his resurrection as before. For although by that death he had for ever put off all the weaknesses of nature, in the bodily wants of hunger, and the infirmities of weariness, and the like; and in his resurrection, which became the first act to glory, he arose suited for the everlasting enjoyment of heaven, yet, both in nature, and in relations to his people, there was not the smallest change.

And, in confirmation of this, the message the LORD sent by *Mary*, as well as the one his servant the angel sent in his name to his disciples, Matt. xxviii. 7. become an high proof. Surely, if there had been a moment in the life of CHRIST, when we might have been tempted to think the LORD would resent the perfidy of his disciples, who all forsook him and fled, it would have been then. Whereas the very first act of JESUS, after he arose from the dead, and before he entered into glory, was to appear to *Mary,* and suffer her not to pause over the mercy before that she had communicated the blissful tidings to his disciples. *Go, tell my brethren! He is not ashamed to call them brethren,* said one of the sacred writers, Heb. ii. 11. though they had all been ashamed of Him! Oh! matchless love, unequalled grace!

18 Mary Magdalene came and told the disciples that she had seen the Lord, and *that* he had spoken these things unto her.

19 ¶ Then the same day at evening, being the first *day* of the week, when the doors were shut where the disciples were assembled for fear of the Jews, came Jesus, and stood in the midst, and saith unto them, Peace *be* unto you.

20 And ‚when he had so said, he shewed unto them *his* hands and his side. Then were the disciples glad when they saw the Lord.

21 Then said Jesus to them again, Peace *be* unto you: as *my* Father hath sent me, even so send I you.

22 And when he had said this, he breathed on *them,* and saith unto them, Receive ye the Holy Ghost:

23 Whose soever sins ye remit, they are remitted unto them: *and* whose soever *sins* ye retain, they are, retained.

It should seem, that the message of the LORD to his disciples by *Mary,* was to prepare them for this most gracious visit of their risen SAVIOR. And what a refreshing and soul-satisfying visit must it have been! We hear no upbraidings for their late desertions: nothing of reproach, but all love. Moreover, in the shewing them his hands and his side, these were not merely by way of proving the reality of his resurrection, and the identifying his person, but of shewing them also those tokens of redemption which he was going with to heaven, that would everlastingly plead for them there. The LORD had said in his message by *Mary,* that she should say to his brethren, *I ascend unto my* FATHER, *and your* FATHER, *to my* GOD, *and your* GOD. So, that in my ascension, those marks will openly appear for you. And all the petitions you send after me, I will put into my pierced hands and side, to ensure the acceptance both of your persons and your prayers. Reader! if the disciples were then glad when they saw the Lord, are not all his disciples made joyful now, with every spiritual view which the Lord manifests to them of himself, in their public or private assemblies?

The peace which the Lord Jesus pronounced over them, was a confirmation of what he had said at his farewell discourse. See John xiv. 27. And the breathing on them, evidently intended as a communication of suited grace and strength for their spiritual necessities. (See John xv. 4. and Commentary upon it.) It could not mean the work of *regeneration,* neither the *ordination* of them to the ministry. For the *former,* no doubt, had been accomplished before; and the *latter* was to be the especial work of God the Holy Ghost at Pentecost. Luke xxiv. 49.

It is truly lamentable to behold the abuse which some have made of what the Lord Jesus at this time said, in relation to the remission of sins. And it is yet more awful what errors designing men have caused to spring from it. The Apostles wrought miracles, as they were appointed, in confirmation both of the Gospel, and their authority as Ministers of it; but we never read of either of them exercising power to forgive sins. Indeed, they knew better. It is God alone (as the Scribes and Pharisees justly in that instance, reasoned,) who can forgive sins; and Christ, as God, exercised it. (See Mark ii. 2—12. and Commentary.) But in whatever sense the Lord intended the words, either in the remission of sins, or the retaining of them, it should seem to be very clear, that no such power as hath been supposed was ever given. Certain it is, that when by the preaching of a full, free, and finished Gospel, under the Holy Ghost's influence, sinners are awakened, regenerated, and made new creatures in Christ; their sins are forgiven. And, as *faith cometh by hearing,* Christ's ministers, in this sense, may be said to remit sins. Romans x. 17. And on the contrary, where that Gospel is thus proclaimed, and not mixed with faith in them that hear it, there the sins are retained. Hence *Paul's* observation, of being *a sweet savor,* both *in them that are saved, and in them that perish.* Heb. iv. 2. 2 Cor. ii. 15, 16.

24 ¶ But Thomas, one of the twelve, called Didymus, was not with them when Jesus came.

25 The other disciples therefore said unto him, We have seen the Lord. But he said unto them, Except I shall see in his hands the print of the nails, and put my finger into the print of the nails, and thrust my hand into his side, I will not believe.

26 ¶ And after eight days again, his disciples were within, and Thomas with them. *Then* came

Jesus, the doors being shut, and stood in the midst, and said, Peace *be* unto you.

27 Then saith he to Thomas, Reach hither thy finger, and behold my hands; and reach hither thy hand, and thrust *it* into my side: and be not faithless, but believing.

28 And Thomas answered and said unto him, My Lord and my God.

29 Jesus saith unto him, Thomas, because thou hast seen me, thou hast believed : blessed *are* they that have not seen, and *yet* have believed.

30 And many other signs truly did Jesus in the presence of his disciples, which are not written in this book.

31 But these are written, that ye might believe that Jesus is the Christ, the Son of God, and that believing ye might have life through his name.

We are not told the cause for which *Thomas* was absent at the first interview of JESUS with his Apostles, after he arose from the dead. But whatever cause it was, had not CHRIST'S grace been greater than *Thomas's* deservings, never could he have been recovered from the daring unbelief, into which through temptation he had fallen. How rash his declaration in determining not to believe, except he had such evidences, as, humanly speaking, there seemed no probability to obtain! How gracious an act in JESUS to grant it! But how came *Thomas* to know that there were nails driven into the hands of JESUS, or that his side had been pierced? He was not present at the crucifixion; for he, in common with the rest, forsook JESUS and fled. And sometimes bodies were fastened with cords instead of nails, on the cross. But the truth was, that *Thomas* was for the time given up to unbelief, that the Church might thereby receive the more ample testimony, in his otherwise unaccountable obstinacy to the conviction of the truth of the resurrection of JESUS. Reader! do not overlook the precious instruction which this view of *Thomas's* incredulity gives to the whole Church of CHRIST. *Thomas* had been present at the resurrection of *Lazarus*. And such a demonstration of the power of CHRIST might have taught the Apostle that CHRIST was able to raise himself. But here *Thomas* lost all confidence. And what is any man unless supported by the power of GOD! Oh! what cause have we every day to cry out with the Apostles, LORD! *increase our faith !* Luke xvii. 5. But what a glorious confession did *Thomas* give, when JESUS in his boundless compassion had granted him his demand? Reader! do you not pray for grace to have the same, and not only to know CHRIST, both LORD and GOD, but to know him, and say as *Thomas* did, *My* LORD, *and my* GOD! Acts ii. 36.

It doth not appear that Jesus manifested himself to any but his disciples after he arose from the dead. Neither to them, but now and then, during the forty days in which he remained on earth. But what a gracious account the Evangelist gives, when he saith, that both his appearing, and the record of those appearances, were purposely for the confirmation of the faithful, that, *in believing, his whole Church might have life through his name.*

REFLECTIONS.

READER! you behold the privileges of God's people. JESUS will reward the humble waiting of his redeemed who seek him. They who went early to the sepulchre, and *Mary,* who remained there, at length had their full portion of the sight of Jesus. And now, what is it but the same? They that wait upon the LORD shall renew their strength.

And what a very precious encouragement is the first appearing of CHRIST to *Mary Magdalene!* She had the first view of JESUS. As if to comfort every poor sinner, that *where sin hath abounded, grace shall much more abound.* That soul in CHRIST's family shall have the first glimpse of JESUS, the first kiss of CHRIST, who most needs him. Precious LORD! let all thy Magdalenes, where Satan hath most cruelly wounded, be first healed!

Oh! dearest LORD JESUS! deal by the *Thomas's* of thine in the present hour, as thou didst by the Apostle of old. Thou knowest of the sin which doth so easily beset us, and thou knowest the cause. Oh! thou great and Almighty Author and Finisher of faith! keep thy redeemed from the sin of unbelief. LORD! *give us to believe, and help thou our unbelief!* Amen.

CHAP. XXI.

CONTENTS.

The LORD JESUS *renews his Appearance to his Disciples at the Sea of* Tiberias. *He feeds his Disciples: gives a particular Charge to* Peter. John *ends his Gospel.*

AFTER these things, Jesus shewed himself again to the disciples at the sea of Tiberias; and on this wise shewed he *himself.*

It seemed by the close of the foregoing Chapter, as if the Evangelist had then ended his Gospel, the last verses having all the appearance of a conclusion. But it is our mercy that GOD the HOLY GHOST directed the mind of the beloved Apostle to go on, and add this sweet Chapter, for it is indeed a sweet one. It is not said what an interval there was between the former manifestations the LORD JESUS made of himself, and this here recorded; but we are told in a subsequent verse, that this was the third time the LORD had been so gracious. See verse 14.

2 There were together, Simon Peter, and Thomas, called Didymus, and Nathanael, of Cana, in Galilee, and the *sons* of Zebedee, and two other of his disciples.

If the Reader counts over the number here said to be together, he will find it to be *seven*. No doubt, all upon the look out for the re- newed visits of the Lord Jesus. And as those here spoken of, were now at the borders of the sea of *Galilee*, which is the sea of *Tiberias*, see John vi. 1. it is evident that they were come here from Jeru- salem in obedience to Christ's commands, and as the Lord had pro- mised, to see him. Matt. xxviii. 10, 16.

3 Simon Peter saith unto them, I go a fishing. They say unto him, We also go with thee. They went forth, and entered into a ship immediately; and that night they caught nothing.

4 But when the morning was now come, Jesus stood on the shore: but the disciples knew not that it was Jesus.

There is somewhat very interesting in this account. And the plain and artless representation of the history is much more beautiful, than had the account been dressed up in all the pomp of language. The want of success in those fishers, and the Lord Jesus early in the morning standing on the shore, formed a blessed occasion for the ma- nifestation of his person and grace, which were to follow. When the Lord is about to reveal himself to his people, how graciously he some- times prepares the way for the greater display of his love!

5 Then Jesus saith unto them, Children, have ye any meat? they answered him, No.

6 And he said unto them, Cast the net on the right side of the ship, and ye shall find. They cast therefore, and now they were not able to draw it for the multitude of fishes.

7 Therefore that disciple whom Jesus loved, saith unto Peter, It is the Lord. Now when Simon Peter heard that it was the Lord, he girt *his* fisher's coat *unto him*, (for he was naked,) and did cast himself into the sea.

8 And the other disciples came in a little ship, (for they were not far from land, but as it were two hundred cubits,) dragging the net with fishes.

It is rather surprizing, that when JESUS called to them by so tender a name, and which was the very same words, *little children*, as he had used before, (see John xiii. 33.) that they had not immediately discovered who it was. But this was reserved for the miracle which he added, and which produced the effect. I pray the Reader to notice, from all these tender incidents of the LORD JESUS, how near his heart his people are. He saith now as much as then, *Children, have ye any meat? Cast on the right side, and ye shall find.* If we are backward to seek our spiritual sustenance from him, JESUS will be found of them that seek him not. And how often doth JESUS make himself known by his gracious acts, as here to *John*, when outward revelations do not always effect it. Is not the LORD known by his providence, and by his grace, in numberless instances where we least expected him?

9 As soon then as they were come to land, they saw a fire of coals there, and fish laid thereon, and bread.

10 Jesus saith unto them, Bring of the fish which ye have now caught.

11 Simon Peter went up, and drew the net to land full of great fishes, an hundred and fifty and three. And for all there were so many, yet was not the net broken.

12 Jesus saith unto them, Come *and* dine. And none of his disciples durst ask him, Who art thou? knowing that it was the Lord.

13 Jesus then cometh, and taketh bread, and giveth them, and fish likewise.

14 This is now the third time that Jesus shewed himself to his disciples, after that he was risen from the dead.

The first manifestation the LORD made of himself, in proof who he was, he shewed in calling them by the tender name in which he had so lately spoken to them, and following this with causing them to enclose a multitude of fishes. And now, as soon as they step on shore, they find immediate provision made for them in the same miraculous manner. Both instances could not fail to bring to their recollection, how JESUS, near the same spot, had fed the multitude in the wilderness, and gave them success also on the water. John vi. 1—14. Luke v. 1—11. Some have thought, and probably it might be so, that beside the supply those mercies gave to their present necessities, these things had respect to the Apostles' future ministry. And as those fishermen had caught nothing before they met with JESUS, so all labors in the word and doctrine are unprofitable without Him. John xv. 5. And as at CHRIST's command their capture was so abundant, so is it with all faithful ministers of salvation, when, at the direction of JESUS, and the presence of JESUS, they cast the net of the Gospel on the right side.

There is somewhat very sweet and gracious in the invitation of the LORD to come and dine. Though they knew him, and though JESUS had sufficiently shewn by such attention to them, that there was no alteration in his love towards them, yet, since the LORD was now come forth out of the invisible world, there was, no doubt, a certain somewhat in his aspect, which induced an holy solemnity in the Apostles. It must have been a solemn interview, though so highly gracious. The LORD's presence cannot but fill the mind with awe. A child of GOD will have the most lively sense of his own creature-ship and unworthiness, in those seasons when JESUS is giving out most largely of his love.

And was there not somewhat sacramental in this repast? JESUS took bread it is said, as well as gave to them. Precious LORD! how doth every view of thy tender words and actions, minister to the endearment of thy Person and Character?

The Evangelist saith, that this was the *third time* of JESUS shewing himself to his disciples after his resurrection. But he meant the third time in a public manner to the disciples in a body. For the LORD had shewn himself *five times*, before this. *First*, to *Mary* Magdalene. Mark xvi. 9. *Secondly*, to the other Women who went early to the Sepulchre, who at the command of the Angel, while running to tell the disciples of CHRIST's resurrection, were met by JESUS, saying, *All hail!* Matt. xxviii. 9. *Thirdly*, by the two disciples, in their walk to *Emmaus.* Luke xxiv. 13, &c. *Fourthly*, to the Eleven, as they sat at meat. Luke xxiv. 36, &c. And *fifthly*, the same day week after, when the LORD spoke particularly to *Thomas.* John xx. 26. But the Evangelist, by the *third time* meant the third visit to the disciples as a body. But *Paul* seems to intimate, as if *Peter* had been blessed with a visit and manifestation of JESUS alone, beside those which the LORD had granted him in common, with the other Apostles. For Paul, when speaking of CHRIST's resurrection saith, that *He was seen of Cephas, then of the twelve.* And I pray the Reader to observe, with what an air of triumph the Apostle adds, *after that he was seen of above five hundred brethren at once; of whom* (saith Paul) *the greater part remain unto this present.* As much as to say, if any of you doubt the fact itself of the resurrection of JESUS, you may enquire for yourselves; for they are alive and will inform you. *For this thing* (as Paul said on another occasion,) *was not done in a corner.* Acts xxvi. 26. 1 Cor. xv. 3—8. See Commentary also on that Chapter. And see for a testimony of the resurrection of CHRIST, by the HOLY GHOST's teaching. Acts xxv. 19.

15 ¶ So when they had dined, Jesus saith to Simon Peter, Simon, *son* of Jonas, lovest thou me more than these? he saith unto him, Yea, Lord: thou knowest that I love thee. He saith unto him, Feed my lambs.

16 He saith to him again the second time,
Simon, *son* of Jonas, lovest thou me? he saith
unto him, Yea, Lord: thou knowest that I love
thee. He saith unto him, Feed my sheep.

17 He saith unto him the third time, Simon, *son*
of Jonas, lovest thou me? Peter was grieved, because he said unto him the third time, Lovest thou
me? And he said unto him, Lord, thou knowest
all things; thou knowest that I love thee. Jesus
saith unto him, Feed my sheep.

18 Verily, verily, I say unto thee, When thou
wast young, thou girdedst thyself, and walkedst
whither thou wouldest; but when thou shalt be
old, thou shalt stretch forth thy hands, and another
shalt gird thee, and carry *thee* whither thou
wouldest not.

19 This spake he, signifying by what death he
should glorify God. And when he had spoken
this, he saith unto him, Follow me.

20 ¶ Then Peter turning about, seeth the disciple whom Jesus loved following, which also
leaned on his breast at supper, and said, Lord,
which is he that betrayeth thee?

21 Peter seeing him, saith to Jesus, Lord, and
what *shall* this man *do?*

22 Jesus saith unto him, If I will that he tarry
till I come, what *is that* to thee? Follow thou
me.

23 Then went this saying abroad among the
brethren, that that disciple should not die; yet
Jesus said not unto him, He shall not die; but if
I will that he tarry till I come, what *is that* to
thee?

24 This is the disciple which testifieth of these
things, and wrote these things: and we know that
his testimony is true.

25 And there are also many other things which

Jesus did, the which, if they should be written every one, I suppose that even the world itself could not contain the books that should be written. Amen.

What a beautiful and interesting discourse immediately took place, as soon as the LORD and his disciples had finished their repast at this holy table. Oh! that the LORD's people had it frequently in remembrance. How truly blessed would it be if the tables of the LORD's faithful ones were thus closed: and when the imperious demands of the body had been satisfied; the soul was not suffered to go lean. Deut. vi. 67. Malachi iii. 16, 17.

I pray the Reader not to overlook, in this most interesting conversation of the LORD JESUS with *Peter*, the chief test JESUS put to him in proof of his sincerity, was love. The LORD doth not say; hast thou honored me or obeyed me, or what proofs canst thou bring of thy duties towards me; but simply, dost thou love me? And although the LORD repeated the question three times, which *Peter's* conscious heart, in his threefold denial, interpreted to have been the cause; yet it is not said, no neither is it at all intimated by the LORD JESUS, as if this was the cause, for which the LORD asked him thrice the question. Indeed I rather think, from the well known and long proved love and grace of JESUS to his people, that the LORD rather intended to give *Peter* the opportunity of thrice repeating the assurances of his love, to do away the impression of his thrice denial. The LORD knew from what cause *Peter* had fallen. And the LORD knew that his whole Church must have fallen from the same cause, did not his all powerful grace keep up, and preserve. It appears, therefore, in my view, one more of those numberless instances we have upon record, of the tenderness of JESUS to his people, that in those circumstances where they have shewn greater weakness, his grace may be the more manifested, in enabling them to shew greater love!

There is somewhat very blessed also in the LORD's giving the Apostle such firmness of faith; not only to assert his love, but to appeal to Him, who could, as GOD, read his heart, and knew that love to be there. Though *Peter* felt grieved, as it is said, at the *third* demand of JESUS, *lovest thou me?* yet I venture to think, it was but the grief of the moment. Yea, I am inclined to believe, that the Apostle afterwards rejoiced at it; when from being led into the mind of JESUS, he discovered the LORD's grace, and intention in it. This was the *third*, if not the *fourth time*, Peter had seen his LORD, after he arose from the dead: and not a word (as far as we know from the Gospel,) had passed between the LORD and his servant, on the subject of *Peter's* denial. No doubt the Apostle longed for an interview to tell JESUS of his shame, and to receive his pardon from the mouth of JESUS. And what then could be more satisfactory to *Peter*, than thus for JESUS to ask of him concerning his love; and in proof that the LORD knew the extent of that love, had committed to him the care of his Lambs and his Sheep.

I need not in this place enlarge on the subject of JESUS's charge to *Peter*. CHRIST himself is the great Pastor, and Shepherd of his flock.

And it is his province to feed them. For He is both the life and sustenance of all his fold; being the bread of life, and the water of life: and *his flesh is meat indeed, and his blood is drink indeed.* But the Lord doth condescend to appoint under pastors, to feed his people with understanding and knowledge. And they are supposed as in this charge to *Peter*, to have respect to the different ages of his flock; to lead the sheep of the fold, and to regard the tender state of the lambs. But one great character Jesus points out, in his demands of *Peter*, as the first quality of a pastor, is, the love of Jesus. For whatever abilities of head knowledge they possess, the whole is nothing without this love of the heart.

In what follows of the Lord's foretelling *Peter* by what death he should glorify God, and the Apostle's curiosity to know what was to become of *John;* it were unnecessary to dwell. *John's* testimony to the truth of the Gospel, which bears his name, is more interesting to regard. And while he knew, that his testimony was true, and the Church then in being, knew the same; it will be blessed both to the Writer and Reader of this *Poor Man's Commentary*, if from the witness of God the Holy Ghost in each of our hearts, we can bear a like testimony. 1 John v. 20. And while we bless God for this precious portion of his holy word, which is able to make us wise unto salvation, through faith in Christ Jesus; we may truly say with *John*, that the world, yea, the whole creation of God, is not large enough in its bosom to contain all that might be said, if all were said of Jesus, since his riches and wisdom are unsearchable, and of Himself, as the sacred Writer hath expressed it, *there is no end of his greatness.* Psm. cxlv. 3.

REFLECTIONS.

Blessed Lord Jesus! what praise, what thanks, what love, doth thy Church owe thee, dearest Lord, for the many repeated manifestations which thou didst so kindly shew to thy poor despised disciples, after thy resurrection from the dead. Miracles upon miracles: and grace for grace. Oh! let it teach my poor soul, and the souls of all thy redeemed, from such striking testimonies as are here recorded, how very nigh Jesus is to his people, when they are unconscious of it. Yea, Lord! how much thou art watching over all their concerns, and providing, both for their bodily and spiritual sustenance, when they can provide for neither. Oh! for the grace shewn *Peter*, to comfort all the exercised members of Christ's mystical body. Oh! for faith, and love, to be able to appeal, as *Peter* did to Jesus, saying, Lord *thou knowest all things: thou knowest that I love thee!*

Praised be the Father, Son, and Spirit, for all the revelations which Jehovah hath graciously made to the Church of God's dear Son. Lord! grant that all thy redeemed under the Holy Ghost's teaching, may, with the disciple, *which hath testified of these things, and wrote these things*, be able to add, from their own assurance, and say, as the Church then did: *we know that his testimony is true.*

Farewell! for the present, thou beloved Apostle *John!* We hope to meet thy further records of thy dear Lord, and our dear Lord, when we come to those precious writings of thine, under the inspiration of GOD the HOLY GHOST, which are in the same sacred volume. But here we thank thee, for thy labors in this Gospel, and for all the precious relations thou hast given, of CHRIST our LORD.   And blessed, for ever blessed be He, that called thee to this service, in his Church. Shortly the whole Church of GOD will be called to see Him, in whose bosom the beloved Apostle lay, who wrote these things of his divine LORD.   And then, all the redeemed with *John* will surround the throne, and sound their united praises, in one full hymn of thanksgiving, to GOD and the Lamb, for evermore.   Amen.

THE END OF VOLUME I. OF THE NEW TESTAMENT.

W. Stratford, Printer, Crown-Court, Temple-Bar.

ERRATA:

Amidst several Errata of a less Nature in the Orthography, the Reader is requested to pardon and correct the following, which escaped the Printer's Observation.

Page   **8,** in the Preface, line 13, *flows* should be *flow.*

        29, Note, line 5, *into one mass.*

        48, Note, line 15, dele—*upon them.*

        66, line 27, for *acceptable,* read *accessible.*

     107, line 11, read *whose we are,* for *where.*

     139, line 3, for *light,* read *life.*

     142, line 19, for *have,* read *had.*

     190, line 20, it should be, *before by Jeremiah.*

     223, line last, leave out the word *is.*

     252, line 8, from the bottom, for *all,* read *for not all.*

     268, line 5, from the bottom, for *grow,* read *gnaw.*

     447, line 1, for *never,* read *ever.*

     546, line 4, for *meekness,* read *meetness.*

     604, Verse 4, *he,* is twice.

     623, in the first note, line 11, for *little,* read *tittle.*

     628, line 7, for *mediation,* read *meditation.*

     701, line 3, leave out the word *First.*

     702, line 11, in the note, *John xi.* should be *John xiv.*

Other Related Titles

In addition to *The Poor Man's New Testament* in three volumes that you now possess, Solid Ground Christian Books is delighted to announce our intention to publish the following by summer 2004:

Hawker's Poor Man's Old Testament Commentary in six wonderful volumes. This set contains more than 4,200 pages of exposition and reflection by the man who loved Christ and delighted to make Him known to others. The volumes are as follows:

> Volume One: Genesis - Numbers
> Volume Two: Deuteronomy - 2 Samuel
> Volume Three: 1st Kings - Esther
> Volume Four: Job - Psalms
> Volume Five: Proverbs - Lamentations
> Volume Six: Ezekiel - Malachi

Hawker's Poor Man's Morning and Evening Portions which is a daily devotional work of more than 900 pages. In the words of Pastor Don Fortner:

> *"Robert Hawker's* **Poor Man's Daily Portions** *is, in my opinion, the very best book of daily devotional readings I have yet read. My wife and I have used it for many years, always with great profit to our souls. Why is it such a blessing? It is full of Christ and full of grace. Every reading leaves the reader looking to, resting in, and rejoicing in our all-glorious Savior.*

Hawker's Concordance and Dictionary to the Sacred Scriptures both of the Old and New Testament is a large one volume work that was written to assist the people of God in searching the Word of God for themselves. This volume has been long unavailable.

Solid Ground Christian Books
2090 Columbiana Rd, Suite 2000
Birmingham AL 35266
(205) 443-0311
sgcb@charter.net
http://solid-ground-books.com